Learn Java™
GUI Applications

A JFC Swing NetBeans Tutorial

11th Edition

By
Philip Conrod & Lou Tylee

KIDWARE SOFTWARE, LLC

PO Box 701
Maple Valley, WA 98038
www.kidwaresoftware.com

Published by:
Kidware Software, LLC
PO Box 701
Maple Valley, Washington 98038
1.425.413.1185
www.kidwaresoftware.com

Printed in the United States of America

ISBN-13 978-1-937161-90-3 (Print Edition)
ISBN-13 978-1-937161-91-0 (Electronic Edition)

Cover Illustration by Kevin Brockschmidt
Copy Editors: Stephanie Conrod & Jessica Conrod
Compositor: Michael Rogers

This guide was developed for the course, "Learn Java GUI Applications," produced by Kidware Software LLC, Maple Valley, Washington. It is not intended to be a complete reference to the Java language. Please consult the Oracle website for detailed reference information. This guide refers to several software and hardware products by their trade names. These references are for informational purposes only and all trademarks are the property of their respective companies and owners. Oracle and Java are registered trademarks of Oracle Corporation and/or its affiliates.   JCreator is a trademark product of XINOX Software. Microsoft Word, Excel, and Windows are all trademark products of the Microsoft Corporation. All other trademarks are the property of their respective owners, and Kidware Software makes no claim of ownership by the mention of products that contain these marks. Kidware Software is not associated with any products or vendors mentioned in this book. Kidware Software cannot guarantee the accuracy of this information.

The example companies, organizations, products, domain names, e-mail addresses, logos, people, places, and events depicted are fictitious. No association with any real company, organization, product, domain name, e-mail address, logo, person, place, or event is intended or should be inferred.

This book expresses the author's views and opinions. The information in this book is distributed on an "as is" basis, without and expresses, statutory, or implied warranties. Neither the author(s) nor Kidware Software LLC shall have any liability to any person or entity with respect to any loss nor damage caused or alleged to be caused directly or indirectly by the information contained in this book.

About The Authors

Philip Conrod has authored, co-authored and edited over two dozen computer programming books over the past thirty years. Philip holds a bachelor's degree in Computer Information Systems and a Master's certificate in the Essentials of Business Development from Regis University. Philip has served in various Information Technology leadership roles in companies like Sundstrand Aerospace, Safeco Insurance, FamilyLife, Kenworth Truck Company, and PACCAR. Philip last served as the Chief Information Officer (CIO) at Darigold for over a decade before returning to teaching and writing full-time. Today, Philip serves as the President & Publisher of Kidware Software LLC which is based in Maple Valley, Washington.

Lou Tylee holds BS and MS degrees in Mechanical Engineering and a PhD in Electrical Engineering. Lou has been programming computers since 1969 when he took his first Fortran course in college. He has written software to control suspensions for high speed ground vehicles, monitor nuclear power plants, lower noise levels in commercial jetliners, compute takeoff speeds for jetliners, locate and identify air and ground traffic and to let kids count bunnies, learn how to spell and do math problems. He has written several on-line texts teaching Visual Basic, Visual C# and Java to thousands of people. He taught computer programming courses for over 15 years at the University of Washington and currently teaches math and engineering courses at the Oregon Institute of Technology. Lou also works as a research engineer at a major Seattle aerospace firm. He is the proud father of five children, has six grandchildren and is married to an amazing woman. Lou and his family live in Seattle, Washington.

Acknowledgements

I want to thank my three wonderful daughters - Stephanie, Jessica and Chloe, who helped with various aspects of the book publishing process including software testing, book editing, creative design and many other more tedious tasks like finding all our typos. I could not have accomplished this without all your hard work, love and support. I also want to thank by best friend Jesus who is always stands by my side.

Last but definitely not least, I want to thank my multi-talented co-author, Lou Tylee, for doing all the real hard work necessary to develop, test, debug, and keep current all the 'kid-friendly' applications, games and base tutorial text found in this book. Lou has tirelessly poured his heart and soul into so many previous versions of this tutorial and there are so many beginners who have benefited from his work over the years. Lou is by far one of the best application developers and tutorial writers I have ever worked with.   Thanks Lou for collaborating with me on this book project.

Table of Contents

Course Description xiii

Course Prerequisites xiv

System Requirements xiv

Installing and Using the Downloadable Solution Files xv

Installing Learn Java xvi

How To Take the Course xvi

Forward by Alan Payne, A Computer Science Teacher xvii

1. Introduction to Java

Preview 1-1

Course Objectives 1-2

What is Java? 1-3

What is a GUI Application? 1-4

A Brief Look at Object-Oriented Programming (OOP) 1-6

Downloading and Installing Java and NetBeans 1-7

Testing the Installation 1-8

Getting Help with a Java Program 1-14

Structure of a Java Program 1-15

Structure of a Java GUI Application 1-16

Swing Controls 1-18

Creating a Java Project with Netbeans 1-21

Create a Frame 1-29

Saving Java Projects with Netbeans 1-32

Netbeans and Java Files 1-33

Create the User Interface 1-34

Example 1-1: Stopwatch Application - Adding Controls 1-38

Adding Event Methods 1-45

Variables 1-49

Java Data Types 1-50

Variable Declaration 1-52

Arrays 1-53

Constants 1-54

Variable Initialization 1-55

Example 1-2: Stopwatch Application - Writing Code 1-56

Class Review 1-64

Practice Problems 1 1-65

Problem 1-1. Beep Problem
Problem 1-2. Caption Problem
Problem 1-3. Enabled Problem
Problem 1-4. Date Problem
Exercise 1: Calendar/Time Display 1-66

2. The Java Language

Review and Preview... 2-1
A Brief History of Java.. 2-2
Rules of Java Programming 2-3
Java Statements and Expressions 2-4
Type Casting 2-6
Java Arithmetic Operators 2-7
Comparison and Logical Operators 2-9
Concatenation Operators.. 2-11
Strings to Numbers to Strings... 2-12
Java String Methods 2-14
Dates and Times 2-20
Random Number Generator 2-25
Math Functions... 2-26
Example 2-1: Savings Account 2-28
Focus Traversal 2-39
Example 2-2: Savings Accounts – Setting Focus 2-40
Improving a Java Application 2-41
Java Decisions - if Statements.. 2-42
Switch Statement - Another Way to Branch 2-46
Control Focus 2-49
Input Validation 2-51
Example 2-3: Savings Account – Input Validation....................... 2-53
Java Looping 2-63
Java Counting 2-66
Example 2-4: Savings Account - Decisions 2-68
Class Review... 2-85
Practice Problems 2... 2-86
    Problem 2-1. Random Number Problem
    Problem 2-2. Price Problem
    Problem 2-3. Odd Integers Problem
    Problem 2-4. Pennies Problem
    Problem 2-5. Code Problem
Exercise 2-1: Computing a Mean and Standard Deviation 2-87
Exercise 2-2: Flash Card Addition Problems 2-88

3. Java Swing Controls

Review and Preview.. 3-1
Function Overloading 3-2
Confirm Dialog (JOptionPane) 3-3
Font Object 3-8
Color Object.. 3-10
JFrame Object 3-13
Frame Layout and Centering 3-17
JButton Control... 3-23
JLabel Control 3-25
JTextField Control 3-28
JTextArea Control 3-31
Example 3-1: Password Validation 3-33
JCheckBox Control 3-45
JRadioButton Control 3-47
JPanel Control 3-50
Handling Multiple Events in a Single Procedure 3-52
Control Arrays... 3-54
Example 3-2: Pizza Order 3-56
JList Control.. 3-81
JScrollPane Control 3-86
JComboBox Control 3-89
Example 3-3: Flight Planner 3-93
Class Review.. 3-109
Practice Problems 3... 3-110
   Problem 3-1. Message Box Problem
   Problem 3-2. Tray Problem
   Problem 3-3. List Box Problem
   Problem 3-4. Combo Box Problem
Exercise 3: Customer Database Input Screen 3-111

4. More Java Swing Controls

Review and Preview.. 4-1

JSpinner Control.. 4-2

Example 4-1: Date Input Device... 4-7

JScrollBar Control 4-16

JSlider Control 4-21

Example 4-2: Temperature Conversion 4-24

JLabel Control (Revisited) 4-36

Example 4-3: "Find the Burger" Game...................................... 4-41

JFileChooser Control (Open Files) 4-51

Example 4-4: Image Viewer... 4-59

Class Review... 4-66

Practice Problems 4... 4-67

    Problem 4-1. Number Guess Problem

    Problem 4-2. RGB Color Problem

    Problem 4-3. Tic-Tac-Toe Problem

    Problem 4-4. File Times Problem

Exercise 4: Student Database Input Screen 4-68

5. Java GUI Application Design and Distribution

Review and Preview... 5-1
Application Design Considerations 5-2
JTabbedPane Control 5-3
Example 5-1: Shopping Cart 5-6
Using General Methods in Applications...................................... 5-30
Example 5-2: Average Value 5-33
Returning Multiple Values from General Methods 5-49
Example 5-3: Circle Geometry 5-51
Adding Menus to Java Applications 5-65
Example 5-4: Note Editor 5-80
Distribution of a Java GUI Application 5-95
Executable (jar) Files... 5-96
Creating a Manifest File in NetBeans... 5-96
Creating a jar File in Netbeans... 5-97
Application Icons 5-99
Using IconEdit... 5-101
Running a Project on Another Computer 5-105
Class Review.. 5-109
Practice Problems 5... 5-110
    Problem 5-1 Tabbed Pane Problem
    Problem 5-2 Note Editor About Box Problem
    Problem 5-3 Normal Numbers Problem
Exercise 5: US/World Capitals Quiz.. 5-111

6. Exception Handling, Debugging and Sequential Files

Review and Preview.. 6-1
Program Errors 6-2
Exception Handling... 6-4
Debugging Java Programs 6-8
Simple Debugging.. 6-9
Example 6-1: Debugging Example..................................... 6-10
Using the Java Debugger 6-18
Using the Debugging Tools 6-19
Debugging Strategies.. 6-24
Sequential Files... 6-25
Sequential File Output (Variables).................................... 6-27
Example 6-2: Writing Variables to Sequential Files 6-31
Sequential File Input (Variables)..................................... 6-34
Example 6-3: Reading Variables from Sequential Files 6-37
Parsing Data Lines 6-40
Example 6-4. Parsing Data Lines 6-42
Reading Tokenized Lines 6-47
Example 6-5. Reading Tokenized Data Lines 6-48
Building Data Lines 6-50
Example 6-6: Building Data Lines 6-53
Configuration Files 6-66
Example 6-7: Configuration Files 6-68
Writing and Reading Text Using Sequential Files 6-74
JFileChooser Control (Save Files) 6-77
Example 6-8: Note Editor - Reading and Saving Text Files............ 6-82
Class Review... 6-97
Practice Problems 6.. 6-98
    Problem 6-1. Debugging Problem
    Problem 6-2. Option Saving Problem
    Problem 6-3. Text File Problem
    Problem 6-4. Data File Problem
Exercise 6-1: Information Tracking 6-100
Exercise 6-2: 'Recent Files' Menu Option.............................6-101

7. Graphics Techniques with Java

Review and Preview... 7-1
Simple Animation.. 7-2
Example 7-1: Simple Animation 7-4
Timer Object... 7-11
Example 7-2: Timer Example 7-14
Basic Animation... 7-18
Example 7-3: Basic Animation 7-20
Random Numbers (Revisited) and Games... 7-30
Randomly Sorting Integers 7-32
Example 7-4: Random Integers 7-34
Java 2D Graphics 7-44
Graphics2D Object 7-45
Stroke and Paint Objects 7-46
Shapes and Drawing Methods 7-47
Line2D Shape.. 7-49
Graphics Demonstration 7-51
Persistent Graphics 7-56
Example 7-5: Drawing Lines 7-62
Rectangle2D Shape 7-73
RoundRectangle2D Shape 7-76
Example 7-6: Drawing Rectangles... 7-78
Ellipse2D Shape 7-92
Example 7-7: Drawing Ellipses... 7-95
Arc2D Shape 7-103
Example 7-8: Drawing Pie Segments.. 7-106
Pie Charts.. 7-119
Line Charts and Bar Charts... 7-123
Coordinate Conversions 7-127
Example 7-9: Line, Bar and Pie Charts... 7-138
Class Review.. 7-156
Practice Problems 7... 7-157
    Problem 7-1. Dice Rolling Problem
    Problem 7-2. Shape Guessing Problem
    Problem 7-3. Pie Chart Problem
    Problem 7-4. Plotting Problem
Exercise 7: Information Tracking Plotting 7-158

8. More Graphics Techniques, Multimedia Effects

Review and Preview... 8-1
Mouse Events... 8-2
Example 8-1: Blackboard... 8-7
Persistent Graphics, Revisited (Vector Class)............................... 8-28
Example 8-2: Blackboard (Revisited).. 8-32
More Graphics Methods... 8-42
Point2D Object.. 8-43
GeneralPath Object.. 8-44
Drawing Polygons.. 8-46
Example 8-3: Drawing Polygons.. 8-49
Drawing Curves.. 8-63
Example 8-4: Drawing Curves.. 8-70
Example 8-5: Animated Curves... 8-78
GradientPaint Object.. 8-85
Example 8-6: Gradient Paint.. 8-87
TexturePaint Object..8-102
Example 8-7: Texture Paint...8-108
drawString Method..8-116
Multimedia Effects...8-120
Animation with drawImage Method..8-121
Example 8-8: Bouncing Ball...8-124
Scrolling Backgrounds..8-135
Example 8-9: Horizontally Scrolling Background.............................8-138
Sprite Animation...8-148
Keyboard Methods...8-151
Example 8-10: Sprite Animation...8-155
Collision Detection..8-162
Example 8-11: Collision Detection..8-163
Sounds in Java...8-171
Example 8-12: Playing Sounds...8-174
Example 8-13: Bouncing Ball with Sound!....................................8-180
Class Review...8-185
Practice Problems 8..8-186
    Problem 8-1. Blackboard Problem
    Problem 8-2. Rubber Band Problem
    Problem 8-3. Plot Labels Problem
    Problem 8-4. Bouncing Balls Problem
    Problem 8-5. Moon Problem
Exercise 8: The Original Video Game - Pong!................................8-187

9. Other Java Topics

Review and Preview... 9-1
Other Controls 9-2
JTextPane Control.. 9-3
Example 9-1: Note Editor (Revisited) 9-7
JToolBar Control... 9-17
Example 9-2: Note Editor Toolbar 9-21
More Swing Controls 9-33
Even More Controls... 9-40
Calendar Control 9-46
Example 9-3: Date Selection.. 9-50
Printing with Java 9-57
Printing Pages of a Document 9-60
Printing Text 9-62
Printing Lines and Rectangles 9-64
Printing Swing Components 9-66
pageDialog Method 9-69
printDialog Method 9-70
Example 9-4: Printing... 9-72
Class Review.. 9-88
Course Summary 9-89
Practice Problems 9... 9-90
    Problem 9-1. Loan Printing Problem
    Problem 9-2. Plot Printing Problem
Exercise 9-1: Phone Directory 9-91
Exercise 9-2: The Ultimate Application 9-92

Contents

Appendix I. General Purpose Methods and Classes..................AI-1

   average AI-2

   BarChartPanel..AI-3

   blankLine AI-6

   circleGeometry AI-7

   degFTodegC AI-8

   GraphicsPanel..AI-9

   LineChartPanel AI-10

   loanPayment AI-12

   midLine AI-13

   PieChartPanel.. AI-14

   PrintUtilities AI-16

   randomNormalNumber... AI-18

   rectangleInfo.. AI-19

   sortIntegers... AI-20

   soundEx AI-21

   standardDeviation AI-22

   Transparency... AI-23

   validateDecimalNumber AI-24

   validateIntegerNumber AI-26

   xPhysicalToxUser AI-27

   yPhysicalToyUser AI-28

Appendix II. Brief Primer on Classes and Objects AII-1

Introduction AII-1
Objects in Java AII-3
Adding a Class to a Java Project AII-4
Declaring and Constructing an Object AII-6
Adding Properties to a Class AII-7
Another Way to Add Properties to a Class AII-9
Validating Class Properties.. AII-13
Adding Constructors to a Class AII-16
Adding Methods to a Class AII-19
Inheritance AII-24
Example II-1. Savings Account... AII-30
Inheriting from Java Controls... AII-47
Building a Custom Control AII-48
Adding New Properties to a Control AII-53
Adding Control Methods AII-55
Example II-2. Savings Account (Revisited) AII-62
Class Review... AII-68

The following solutions are included in the digital download file available from the Publisher's website after book registration:

Practice Problems Solutions (Part 1: Classes 1 to 5) P1-1
Practice Problems Solutions (Part 2: Classes 6 to 9) P2-1

Exercise Solutions (Part 1: Classes 1 to 5) E1-1
Exercise Solutions (Part 2: Classes 6 to 9) E2-1

Appendix III.   Installing Java and NetBeans for Windows Linux or MAC OS X

Course Description

Learn Java GUI Applications is a self-paced overview of the Java programming language, with specific attention to graphic user interface (GUI) applications. Upon completion of the course, you will:

1. Understand the benefits of using Java as a GUI application development tool.
2. Understand the Java event-driven programming concepts, terminology, and available Swing controls.
3. Learn the fundamentals of designing, implementing, and distributing a wide variety of Java GUI applications.

Learn Java GUI Applications is presented using a combination of course notes (written in Microsoft Word format) over 1100 pages of Java examples and applications.

Course Prerequisites

To grasp the concepts presented in **Learn Java GUI Applications**, you should possess a working knowledge of your particular operating system (Windows, Linux, MacOS). You should know how to locate, copy, move and delete files. You should be familiar with the simple tasks of using menus, toolbars, resizing windows, and moving windows around.

You should have had some exposure to the Java programming language. You should understand enough Java to build simple console applications. We offer a companion course, **Beginning Java** (or **Java for Kids**, if you're a kid), which will provide this background.

You will also need the ability to view and print documents saved in Microsoft Word format. This can be accomplished in one of two ways. The first, and easiest, is that you already have Microsoft Word on your computer. The second way, and a bit more difficult, is that you can download the Microsoft Word Viewer. This is a free Microsoft product that allows viewing Word documents.

Finally, and most obvious, you need to have Java. This is a FREE product that can be downloaded from the Java website. The website is:

https://www.oracle.com/technetwork/java/javase/downloads/jdk11-downloads-5066655.html

This site contains complete downloading and installation instructions for the latest version of Java. You can also download all Java documentation from this same site. Look for the Standard Edition (**Java SE**). You need to download the corresponding Java Development Kit (**JDK**). The current version is **JDK 11**.

Our tutorials use **NetBeans** as the IDE (Integrated Development Environment) for building and testing Java applications. This is also a free product available for download at:

https://netbeans.apache.org/download/nb110/nb110.html

This site contains downloading and installation instructions for **Netbeans**.   The notes and code use Version 11. Detailed downloading instructions can be found in the Appendix located at the end of this tutorial.

System Requirements

You will need the following software to complete the exercises in this book:

- Oracle Java Standard Edition JDK11
- NetBeans 11.0

Installing and Using the Downloadable Solution Files

If you purchased this directly from our website you received an email with a special and individualized internet download link where you could download the compressed Program Solution Files.   If you purchased this book through a 3rd Party Book Store like Amazon.com, the solutions files for this tutorial are included in a compressed ZIP file that is available for download directly from our website at:

http://www.kidwaresoftware.com/learnjava11-registration.htm

Complete the online web form at this webpage above with your name, shipping address, email address, the exact title of this book, date of purchase, online or physical store name, and your order confirmation number from that store. We also ask you to include the last 4 digits of your credit card so we can match it to the credit card that was used to purchase this tutorial.   After we receive all this information we will email you a download link for the Source Code Solution Files associated with this book.

Warning: If you purchased this book "used" or "second hand" you are not licensed or entitled to download the Program Solution Files. However, you can purchase the Digital Download Version of this book at a highly discounted price which allows you access to the digital source code solutions files required for completing this tutorial.

Using Learn Java GUI Applications

The course notes and code for **Learn Java GUI Applications** are included in one or more ZIP file(s). Use your favorite 'unzipping' application to write all files to your computer. (If you've received the course on CD-ROM, the files are not zipped and no unzipping is needed.) The course is included in the folder entitled **LearnJava**. This folder contains two other folders: **LJ Notes** and **LJ Code**. The **LJ Code** folder includes all the Java applications developed during the course. The applications are further divided into **Class** folders. Each class folder contains the Java project folders.

How To Take the Course

Learn Java GUI Applications is a self-paced course. The suggested approach is to do one class a week for nine weeks. Each week's class should require about 4 to 10 hours of your time to grasp the concepts completely. Prior to doing a particular week's work, open the class notes file for that week and print it out. Then, work through the notes at your own pace. Try to do each example as they are encountered in the notes. If you need any help, all solved examples are included in the **LJ Code** folder.

After completing each week's notes, practice problems and homework exercise (sometimes, two) is given; covering many of the topics taught that in that class. Like the examples, try to work through the practice problems and homework exercise, or some variation thereof, on your own. Refer to the completed exercise in the **LJ Code** folder, if necessary. This is where you will learn to be a Java programmer. You only learn how to build applications and write code by doing lots of it. The problems and exercises give you that opportunity. And, you learn coding by seeing lots of code. Programmers learn to program by seeing how other people do things. Feel free to 'borrow' code from the examples that you can adapt to your needs. I think you see my philosophy here. I don't think you can teach programming. I do, however, think you can teach people how to become programmers. This course includes numerous examples, problems, and exercises to help you toward that goal. We show you how to do lots of different things in the code examples. You will learn from the examples!

Forward By Alan Payne, Computer Science Teacher

What is "Learn Java GUI Applications" ... and how it works.

The lessons are a highly organized and well-indexed set of tutorials meant for high school students and young adults. Netbeans, a specific IDE (Integrated Development Environment) is used to create GUI (Graphical User Interface applications) by employing the Swing Controls of Java Development Kit Version 11.

The tutorials provide the benefit of completed age-appropriate applications for high school students - fully documented projects from the teacher's point of view. That is, while full solutions are provided for the adult's benefit, the projects are presented in an easy-to-follow set of lessons explaining object-oriented programming concepts, Java Swing controls, the rational for the form layout, coding design and conventions, and specific code related to the problem. High school learners may follow tutorials at their own pace. Every bit of the lesson is remembered as it contributes to the final solution. The finished product is the reward, but the student is fully engaged and enriched by the process. This kind of learning is often the focus of teacher training. Every computer science teacher knows what a great deal of preparation is required for projects to work for senior students. With these tutorials, the research behind the projects is done by an author who understands the classroom experience. That is extremely rare!

Graduated Lessons for Every Project ... Lessons, examples, problems and projects. Graduated learning. Increasing and appropriate difficulty... Great results.

With these projects, there are lessons providing a comprehensive, student-friendly background on the programming topics to be covered. Object-oriented concepts are stressed. Once understood, concepts are easily applicable to a variety of applications.

The "Learn Java GUI Applications" tutorials are organized by presenting relevant programming concepts first, fully drawn out examples second, followed by short problems where the student must recall the required programming concept with correct language syntax. Finally, exercises in the form of summative projects are presented at the end of the lesson. This graduated approach to problems leads to a high level of retention.

By presenting lessons in this graduated manner, students are fully engaged and appropriately challenged to become independent thinkers who can come up with their own project ideas and design their own GUIs and do their own coding. Once the process is learned, then student engagement is unlimited! I have seen literacy improve dramatically because students cannot get enough of what is being presented.

Indeed, lessons encourage *accelerated* learning - in the sense that they provide an enriched environment to learn computer science, but they also encourage *accelerating* learning because students cannot put the lessons away once they start! Computer science provides this unique opportunity to challenge students, and it is a great testament to the authors that they are successful in achieving such levels of engagement with consistency.

My History with Kidware Software products.

I have used Kidware's Programming Tutorials for over a decade to keep up my own learning. By using these lessons, I am able to spend time on things which will pay off in the classroom. I do not waste valuable time ensconced in language reference libraries for programming environments – help screens which can never be fully remembered! These projects are examples of how student projects should be as final products - thus, the pathway to learning is clear and immediate in every project.

If I want to use or expand upon some of the projects for student use, then I take advantage of site-license options. I have found it very straight forward to emphasize the fundamental computer science topics that form the basis of these projects when using them in the classroom. I can list some computer science topics which everyone will recognize, regardless of where they teach – topics which are covered expertly by these tutorials:

- Data Types and Ranges

- Scope of Variables

- Naming Conventions

- Decision Making

- Looping

- Language Functions – String, Date, Numerical

- Arrays

- Writing Your own Methods (subroutines)

- Writing Your Own Classes (stressing object-oriented concepts)

- Understanding the Swing Controls in the Java Software Development Kit Version 8, for Java for GUI applications, and more... it's all integrated into the tutorials.

In many States or Provinces, the above-listed topics would certainly be formally introduced in High School computer science, and *would* form the basis of most projects undertaken by students. With these tutorials, you as the teacher or parent may choose where to put the emphasis, to be sure to cover the curricular expectations of your curriculum documents.

Any further High School computer programming topics derive directly from those listed above. Nothing is forgotten. All can be integrated with the lessons provided.

Quick learning curve for teachers! How teachers can use the product:

Having projects completed ahead of time can allow the teacher to present the design aspect of the project FIRST, and then have students do all of their learning in the context of what is required in the finished product. This is a much faster learning curve than if students designed all of their own projects from scratch. Streamlined lessons focusing on a unified outcome engages students, as they complete more projects within a short period of time and there is a context for everything that is learned.

With the *Learn Java GUI Applications* tutorials, sound advice regarding generally accepted coding strategies ("build and test your code in stages", "learn input, output, formatting and data storage strategies for different data types", build graphical components from Java's Swing Control class libraries, etc..) encourage independent thought processes among learners. After mastery, then it is much more likely that students can create their own problems and solutions from scratch. Students are ready to create their own summative projects for your computer science course – or just for fun, and they may think of projects for their other courses as well!

Meets State and Provincial Curriculum Expectations and More

Different states and provinces have their own curriculum requirements for computer science. With the Kidware Software products, you have at your disposal a series of projects which will allow you to pick and choose from among those which best suit your curriculum needs. Students focus upon design stages and sound problem-solving techniques from a computer-science, problem-solving perspective. Students become independent problem-solvers, and will exceed the curricular requirements of their computer science curriculum in all jurisdictions.

Useable projects - Out of the box!

The specific projects covered in the *Learn Java GUI Applications* tutorials are suitable for students in grades 11 to 12. Specific senior student-friendly tutorials and projects are found in the Contents document, and include

Stop Watch Application
Calendar/Time Display
Savings Calculator
Computing a Mean and Standard Deviation
Flash Card Addition Problems
Password Validation Program
Pizza Ordering Program
Flight Planner
Customer Database Input Screen
Temperature Conversion Application
Image Viewer
Student Database Input Screen
Debugging Strategies
Reading and Writing Variables using Sequential Access Files
Reading and Writing Text using Sequential Access Files
Information Tracking
Recent Files Menu Option
Timers
Basic Animation
Graphics Applications such as Dice Rolling, Shapes, Pie Charts, Blackjack, Plotting
Multimedia Application in The Original Video Game of Pong
And more Swing controls in these applications:
Biorhythms, Loan Printing, Plot Printing, Note Editor, Phone Directory

As you can see, there is a high degree of care taken so that projects are age-appropriate, and completely appropriate for high school computer science.

You as a parent or teacher can begin teaching the projects on the first day. It's easy for the adult to have done their own learning by starting with the solution files. Then, they will see how all of the parts of the lesson fall into place. Even a novice could make use of the accompanying lessons.

How to teach students to use the materials.

In a school situation, teachers might be tempted to spend considerable amounts of time at the projector or computer screen going over the tutorial – but the best strategy is to present the finished product first! That way, provided that the teacher has covered the basic concepts listed in the table of contents, then students will quickly grasp how to use the written lessons on their own. Lessons will be fun, and the pay-off for younger students is that there is always a finished product which is fun to use!

Highly organized reference materials for student self-study!

Materials already condense what is available from the Java SDK help files *(which tends to be written for adults)* and in a context and age-appropriate manner, so that students remember what they learn.

The time savings for parents, teachers and students is enormous as they need not sift through pages and pages of on-line help to find what they need.

How to mark the projects.

In a classroom environment, it is possible for teachers to mark student progress by asking questions during the various problem design and coding stages. It is possible for teachers can make their own oral, pictorial review or written pop quizzes easily from the reference material provided as a review strategy from day to day. I have found the requirement of completing projects (mastery) sufficient for gathering information about student progress - especially in the later grades.

Lessons encourage your own programming extensions.

Once concepts are learned, it is difficult to NOT know what to do for your own projects. This is true especially at the High School level – where applications can be made in as short as 10 minutes (a high-low guessing game, or a temperature conversion program, for example), or 1 period in length – if one wished to expand upon any of the projects using the "Other Things to Try" suggestions.

Having used Kidware Software tutorials for the past decade, I have to say that I could not have achieved the level of success which is now applied in the variety of many programming environments which are currently of considerable interest to kids! I thank Kidware Software and its authors for continuing to stand for what is right in the teaching methodologies which work with kids - even today's kids where competition for their attention is now so much an issue.

Regards,
Alan Payne
TA Blakelock High School
Oakville, Ontario
http://chatt.hdsb.ca/~paynea

1

Introduction to Java

Preview

In this first class, we will do an overview of how to build a GUI (graphic user interface) application using Java. You'll learn a new vocabulary, a new approach to programming, and how to use a development environment. Once finished, you will have written your first Java GUI program.

Course Objectives

- Understand the benefits of using Java as a GUI (graphic user interface) application tool
- Understand Java event-driven programming concepts and object-oriented programming terminology
- Learn the fundamentals of designing, implementing, and distributing a Java GUI application
- Learn to use Java Swing controls and the Abstract Windowing Toolkit (AWT)
- Learn to modify control properties and use of control event methods
- Use menu and toolbar design tools
- Learn how to read and write sequential files
- Understand proper debugging and error-handling procedures
- Gain an understanding of graphic methods and simple animations
- Learn how to print text and graphics from a Java application
- Gain skills to develop and implement an application help system

What is Java ?

If you're taking this course, you should already know the answer to this question. We answer it here to give you an idea of how we feel about **Java**. So how much Java do you need to know? You should have a basic understanding of the Java language and its syntax, understand the structure of a Java application, how to write and use Java methods and how to run a Java console application. We review each of these topics in the course, but it is a cursory review. If you haven't used Java before, we suggest you try one of our two beginning Java tutorials: **Java for Kids** or **Beginning Java**. See our website for details. Now, on to our answer to the question ...

Java is a computer **programming language** developed by Sun Microsystems (now owned by Oracle). Java is a relatively new language, being created in 1995, and has been very successful for many reasons.

The first reason for Java's popularity is its cost - absolutely FREE!! A second reason for the popularity of Java is that a Java program can run on almost any computer - it is **platform-independent**.

Java can be used to develop many types of applications. There are simple text-based programs called **console applications**. These programs just support text input and output to your computer screen. You can also build **graphic user interface** (GUI, pronounced 'gooey') **applications**. These are applications with menus, toolbars, buttons, scroll bars, and other controls which depend on the computer mouse for input. A last application that can be built with Java are **applets**. In this class, we concentrate on GUI applications.

Another popular feature of Java is that it is **object-oriented**. What this means to you, the Java programmer, is that you can build and change large programs without a lot of additional complication. As you work through this course, you will hear the word **object** many, many times.

A last advantage of Java is that it is a simple language. Compared to other languages, there is less to learn. This simplicity is necessary to help insure the platform-independence (ability to run on any computer) of Java applications. But, just because it is a simple language doesn't mean it lacks capabilities. You can do anything with Java that you can with any of the more complicated languages.

What is a GUI Application?

As mentioned, this course will emphasize graphic user interface (GUI) applications. In such applications, users interact with a set of visual **controls** (buttons, labels, text boxes, tool bars, menu items) to make an application do its required tasks. The applications have a familiar appearance to the user. As you develop as a Java programmer, you will begin to look at applications in a different light. You will recognize and understand how various elements of programs like Word, Excel, Access and other applications work. You will develop a new vocabulary to describe the elements of GUI applications.

Java GUI applications are **event-driven**, meaning nothing happens until an application is called upon to respond to some event (button pressing, menu selection, ...). GUI applications are governed by **event listeners** – they "listen" for events to occur. Nothing happens until an event is detected. Once an event is detected, a corresponding **event method** is located and the instructions provided by that method are executed. Those instructions are the actual code written by the programmer - code written using the Java language. Once an event method is completed, program control is returned to the event listener:

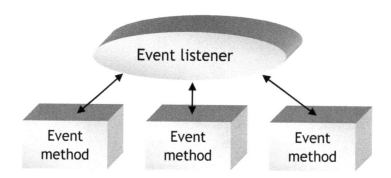

All GUI applications are event-driven. For example, nothing happens in a word processor until you click on a button, select a menu option, or type some text. Each of these actions is an event.

The event-driven nature of GUI applications developed with Java makes it very easy to work with. As you develop a Java application, event methods can be built and tested individually, saving development time. And, often event methods are similar in their coding, allowing re-use (and lots of copy and paste).

Here's an example of a simple Java GUI application, a computer stopwatch:

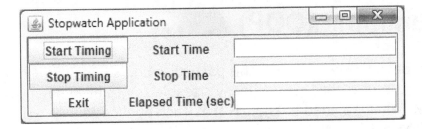

This **frame** hosts, or contains, several different **controls**. There are buttons to click, labels displaying information, and empty text areas. When a user clicks the button that says **Start Timing**, an event is generated. The application processes the method associated with that event and starts a timer, displaying the start time in the corresponding text area. Similarly, when **Stop Timing** is clicked, the event method associated with this button control's click event is processed. In this method, the timing is stopped, the stop time is displayed, the elapsed time is computed and displayed. An **Exit** button is used to stop the application. Here's a finished run of this GUI application:

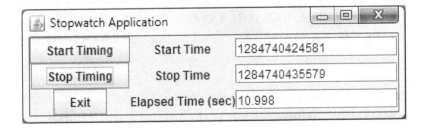

You will see that GUI applications offer flexibility, ease of use, familiarity (every user has used a GUI application before), and they're nice to look at. You'll see this stopwatch example again, very soon. You will build it before this first class is over.

The fundamental elements need to create a Java GUI application will come from two packages: the Abstract Windowing Toolkit (**AWT**) and **Swing**. These packages will be imported into every application we build.

AWT was the first attempt by Java to create tools for GUI applications. The Swing package provides updated GUI components using what is known as Java Foundation Classes (JFC). Swing still depends on AWT, so we need both. In this class, the controls we use will be Swing components.

A Brief Look at Object-Oriented Programming (OOP)

Java is fully **object-oriented**. For this particular course, we don't have to worry much about just what that means (many sizeable tomes have been written about OOP). What we need to know is that each application we write will be made up of **objects**. Just what is an object? It can be many things: a variable, a font, a graphics region, a rectangle, a printed document. Controls in a GUI frame are objects. The key thing to remember is that these objects represent reusable entities that are used to develop an application. This 'reusability' makes our job much easier as a programmer. The Java language has many objects we can use to build our applications.

In Java, there are two terms we need to be familiar with in working with object-oriented programming: **Class** and **Object**. **Objects** are what are used to build our application. We will learn about many objects throughout this course. Objects are derived from **classes**. Think of classes as general descriptions of objects, which are then specific implementations of a class. For example, a class could be a general description of a car, where an object from that class would be a specific car, say a red 1965 Ford Mustang convertible (a nice object!).

For this course, if you remember **class** and **object**, you have sufficient OOP knowledge to build applications. Once you complete this course, you can further delve into the world of OOP. Then, you'll be able to throw around terms like inheritance, polymorphism, overloading, encapsulation, and overriding. Appendix II presents a brief primer on classes and objects in Java.

Downloading and Installing Java and NetBeans

To write and run programs using Java, you need the **Java Development Kit** (JDK) and the **NetBeans Integrated Development Environment** (IDE). These are free products that you can download from the Internet. Complete download and installation instructions are provided in the Appendix (**Installing Java and NetBeans**) included with these notes.

Testing the Installation

We'll use **NetBeans** to load a Java project and to run a project. This will give us some assurance we have everything installed correctly. This will let us begin our study of the Java programming language.

Once installed, to start **NetBeans** , double-click the icon on your desktop. The NetBeans program should start. Several windows will appear on the screen.

Upon starting (after clearing the **Start Page**), my screen shows:

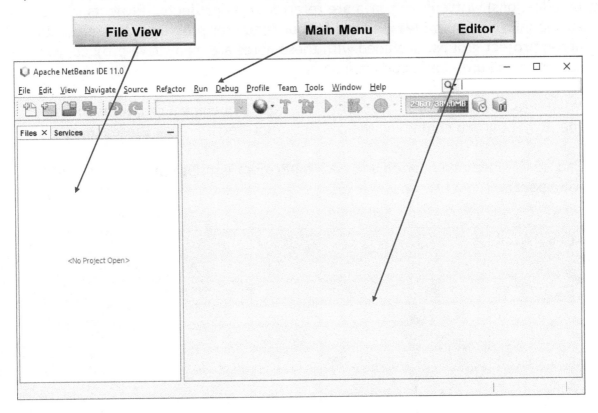

This screen displays the **NetBeans Integrated Development Environment (IDE)**. We're going to use it to test our Java installation and see if we can get a program up and running. Note the location of the **file view** area, **editor** area and the **main menu**. The file view tells you what Java programs are available, the editor area is used to view the actual code and the main menu is used to control file access and file editing functions. It is also used to run the program.

What we want to do right now is **open a project**. Computer programs (applications) written using Java are referred to as **projects**. Projects include all the information in **files** we need for our computer program. Java projects are in **project groups**. Included with these notes are many Java projects you can open and use. Let's open one now.

Make sure **NetBeans** is running. The first step to opening a project is to **open the project group** containing the project of interest. Follow these steps:

Choose the **File** menu option and click on **Project Groups** option. This window will appear:

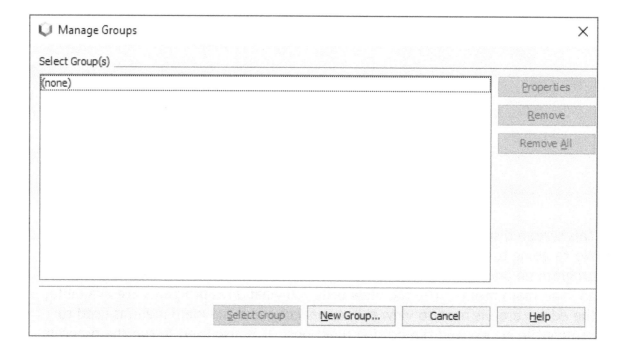

All projects in these notes are saved in a folder named **\LearnJava\LJ Code**. Projects are further divided by classes – the projects for this first class are in the project group **Class 1**. Click **New Group**, select **Folder of Projects**, **Browse** to that folder as shown. Click **Create Group**.

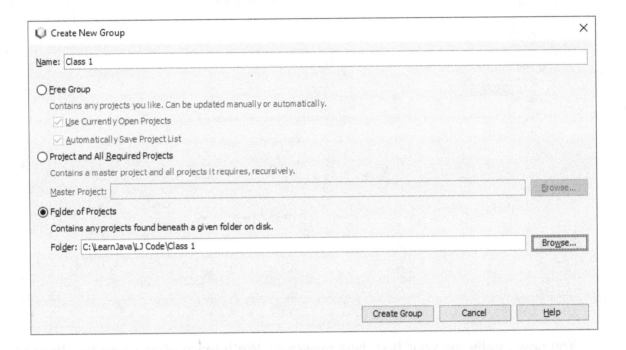

There will be several projects listed in the file view area in NetBeans. Find the project named **Welcome**. Expand the Welcome project node by clicking the plus sign. Open **Source Packages**, then **welcome**. Note there is one file named **Welcome.java**. If the file contents do not appear in the editor view area, double-click that file to open it.

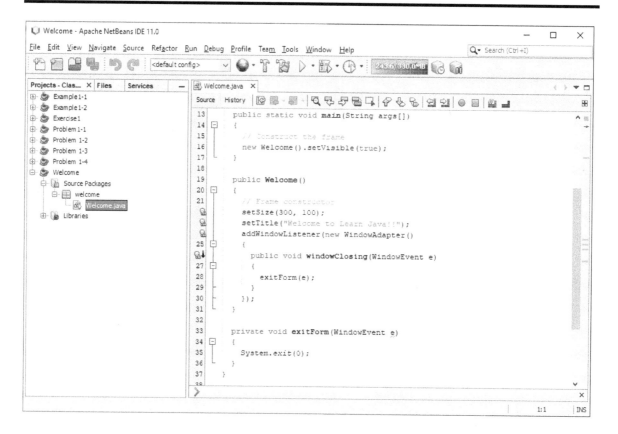

You now finally see your first Java program: We'll learn what these few lines of code do in the next class. Right now, we just want to see if we can get this program running.

Are you ready to finally run your first project? To do this, choose **Run** from the menu and select **Run Project (Welcome)** (or alternately press **<F6>** on your keyboard or click the green **Run** arrow on the toolbar). An **Output** window should open and you should see the following Welcome message:

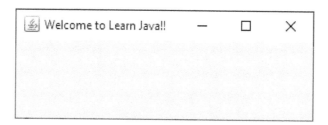

If you've gotten this far, everything has been installed correctly. If you don't see the Welcome message, something has not been installed correctly. You should probably go back and review all the steps involved with installing Java and NetBeans and make sure all steps were followed properly.

To stop this project, you click the boxed X in the upper right corner of the window. To stop NetBeans (don't do this right now, though):

> ➤ Select **File** in the main menu.
> ➤ Select **Exit** (at the end of the File menu).

NetBeans will close all open windows and you will be returned to the Windows desktop. Like with stopping a project, an alternate way to stop NetBeans is to click on the close button in the upper right hand corner of the main window.

Getting Help With a Java Program

As you build Java programs, there will be times when you get stuck. You will not know how to do a certain task using Java or you will receive error messages while compiling or running your program that you do not understand. What do you do in these cases? There are several options for getting help.

A highly recommended help method is to ask someone else if they know how to help you. Other Java programmers love to share their skills with people just learning the language. A second option is to look at one of the many Java books out there (you are reading one of them). If you have questions about these notes, just e-mail us (support@kidwaresoftware.com) and we'll try to help.

The **Java website** (http://www.oracle.com/technetwork/java/index.html) has a wealth of information that could possibly help. The problem with the website is that there is so much information, it can be overwhelming. There are tutorials, example, forums, ... The Java **API** (application programming interface) documentation (on-line at the Sun website) is a great place to get help if you can wade through the difficult format. The Java website does offer search facilities. I often type in a few keywords and find topics that help in my pursuit of answers.

There are also hundreds of other Java websites out in WWW-land. Many websites offer forums where you can ask other Java programmers questions and get quick answers. A good way to find them is to use a search utility like **Google** or **Yahoo**. Again, type in a few keywords and many times you'll find the answer you are looking for.

As you progress as a Java programmer, you will develop your own methods of solving problems you encounter. One day, you'll be the person other programmers come to for their answers.

Structure of a Java Program

Java, like any language (computer or spoken), has a terminology all its own. Let's look at the structure of a Java program and learn some of this new terminology. A Java program (or project) is made up of a number of files. These files are called **classes**. Each of these files has Java code that performs some specific task(s). Each class file is saved with the file extension **.java**. The filename used to save a class must match the class name. One class in each project will contain something called the **main method**. Whenever you run a Java program, your computer will search for the **main** method to get things started. Hence, to run a program, you refer directly to the class containing this **main** method.

Let's see how this relates to **Welcome** project. This particular project has a single file named **Welcome.java**. Notice, as required, the name **Welcome** matches the class name seen in the code (public class **Welcome**). If no code is seen, simply double-click on the filename **Welcome.java**. If the project had other classes, they would be listed under the **Welcome** project folder. Notice too in the code area the word **main**. This is the **main** method we need in one of the project's classes.

That's really all we need to know about the structure of a Java program. Just remember a **program** (or project, we'll use both terms) is made up of files called **classes** that contain actual Java code. One class is the **main** class where everything starts. And, one more thing to remember is that projects are in **project groups**.

NetBeans uses a very specific directory structure for saving all of the files for a particular application. When you start a new project, it is placed in a specific folder in a specific project group. That folder will be used to store all files needed by the project. We'll take another look at the NetBeans file structure when we create our first project. You can stop NetBeans now, if you'd like.

Structure of a Java GUI Application

We want to get started building our first Java GUI application. To do this, though, requires covering lots of new material. And, to build a Java application, you need to know the Java code that does the building. We're kind of putting the "cart before the horse" here. We'll just give you the Java code to do the necessary steps. You have to trust us right now – as you learn more Java, you will be able to write such code yourself. You should see, however, that the code is not really that hard to understand.

Let's look at the structure of a Java GUI application. In these notes, we tend to use the terms application, program and project synonymously. A GUI application consists of a **frame**, with associated **controls** and **code**. Pictorially, this is:

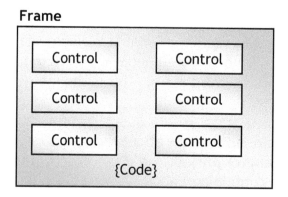

Application (Project) is made up of:

> **Frame** - window that you create for user interface (also referred to as a **form**)
> **Controls** - Graphical features positioned on frame to allow user interaction (text boxes, labels, scroll bars, buttons, etc.) (frames and controls are **objects**.) Controls are briefly discussed next.
> **Properties** - Every characteristic of a frame or control is specified by a property. Example properties include names, captions, size, color, position, and contents. Java applies default properties. You can change properties when designing the application or even when an application is executing.
> **Methods** - Built-in procedures that can be invoked to impart some action to or change or determine a property of a particular object.

> **Event Methods - Code** related to some object or control. This is the code that is executed when a certain event occurs. In our applications, this code will be written in the Java language (covered in detail in Chapter 2 of these notes).
> **General Methods - Code** not related to objects. This code must be invoked or called in the application.

The application displayed above has a single form, or frame. As we progress in this course, we will build applications with multiple forms. The code for each form will usually be stored in its own file with a **.java** extension.

We will follow three steps in building a Java GUI application:

1. Create the **frame**.
2. Create the user **interface** by placing controls on the frame.
3. **Write code** for control event methods (and perhaps write other methods).

These same steps are followed whether you are building a very simple application or one involving many controls and many lines of code. Recall, the GUI applications we build will use the Java **Swing** and **AWT** (Abstract Windows Toolkit) components.

Each of these steps require us to write Java code, and sometimes lots of code. The event-driven nature of Java applications allows you to build your application in stages and test it at each stage. You can build one method, or part of a method, at a time and try it until it works as desired. This minimizes errors and gives you, the programmer, confidence as your application takes shape.

As you progress in your programming skills, always remember to take this sequential approach to building a Java application. Build a little, test a little, modify a little and test again. You'll quickly have a completed application. This ability to quickly build something and try it makes working with Java fun – not a quality found in some programming environments!

Swing Controls

The controls we use in GUI applications will be **Swing** components. These components are defined in the **javax.swing** package and all have names beginning with **J**. Here, we briefly look at several controls to give you an idea of what they are, what they look like and what they do. In the first two classes, we will use four controls: a **frame (JFrame)**, a **button (JButton)**, a **label (JLabel)** and a **text field (JTextField)**. We will code them in our applications without a lot of discussion on how to use them (and, as mentioned earlier, you should see the code is easy to follow). The properties of and events associated with the different controls will be covered in detail in Class 3 and 4.

JFrame control:

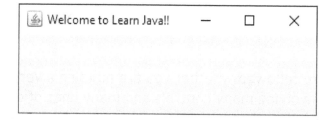

The frame control is the basic 'container' for other controls. It is the framework for a Java project. The **title** property establishes the caption information. Every application we build will start by building a **class** that **extends** the JFrame control.

JButton control:

The button control is used to start some action. The **text** property is used to establish the caption.

JLabel control:

The label control allows placement of formatted text information on a frame (**text** property).

JTextField control:

The text field control accepts a single line of typed information from the user (**text** property).

JTextArea control:

The text area control accepts multiple lines of scrollable typed information (**text** property).

JCheckBox control:

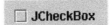

The check box control is used to provide a yes or no answer to a question.

JRadioButton control:

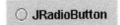

The radio button control is used to select from a mutually exclusive group of options. You always work with a group of radio buttons.

JComboBox control:

Combo box controls are very common in GUI applications. Users can choose an item from a drop down list (states, countries, product).

JList control:

A list control is like a combo box with the list portion always visible. Multiple selections can be made with a list control.

JScroll control:

A scroll bar control is used to select from a range of values. The scroll bar is always "buddied" with another control related to the scroll bar selection.

Now, we'll start NetBeans and look at each step in the application development process, including using Swing controls

Creating a Java Project with NetBeans

We will now start building our first Java GUI application (a computer stopwatch). It might seem like a slow, long process. But, it has to be in order to cover all the necessary material. The more projects you build, the simpler this process will become. We begin by creating a new project and creating a frame. We will store all created projects in a separate project group named **LJProjects**. Create that folder now. If using Windows, you can use **Windows Explorer** or **My Computer** to that task.

If it's not already running, start **NetBeans**. The project group containing the **Welcome** project should still be there. We are going to replace this project group with a new one. (You should only use the **LJ Code** project group when you want to refer to the code included with the class notes. For all your projects, you will use your own project group).

Now, create your project group – select **LJProjects**. Choose **File** from the main menu and select **Project Group** The **Manage Groups** window appears – choose **New Group** to see

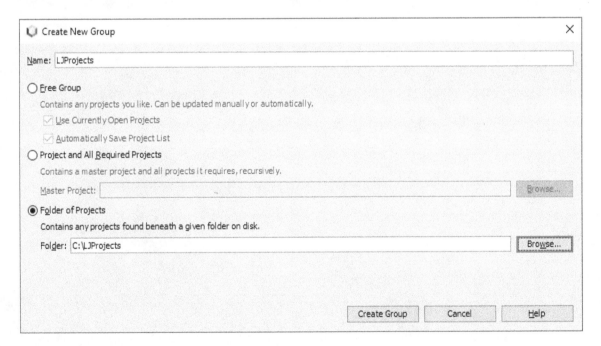

As shown, click **Folder of Projects**, then **Browse** to your **LJProjects** folder. Click **Create Group**. The project group is displayed in the file view area (it is empty).

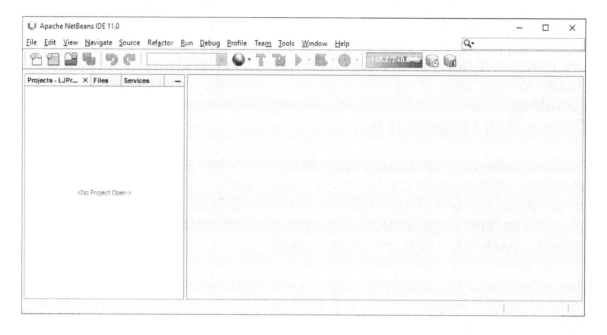

Now, we want to add a project to the project group. Pay close attention to these steps because you will repeat them every time you need to create a new Java project. Right-click the project group area in the file view and choose **New Project** to see:

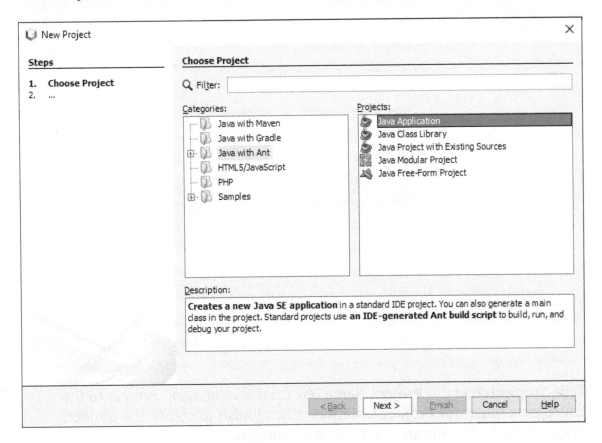

Select **Java with Ant** in **Categories** and **Java Application** in **Projects.** Click **Next.**

This window appears:

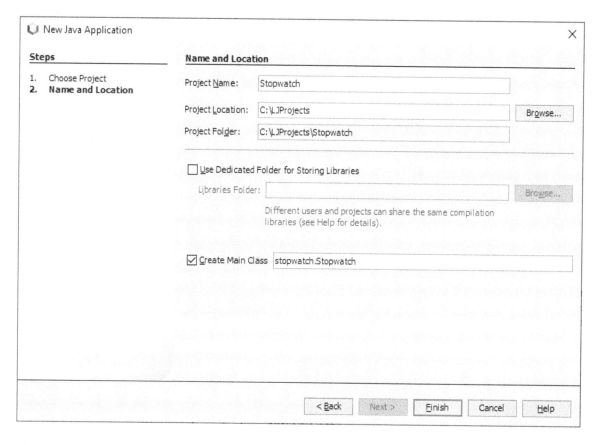

Type **Stopwatch** in the **Project Name** box (as shown above). Browse to the **LJProjects** folder for **Project Location**. Click **Finish** to create the project. Once created, click **Finish** in the resulting window.

The project group view window should now show a project (**Stopwatch**) in the project group (I've expanded all the folders):

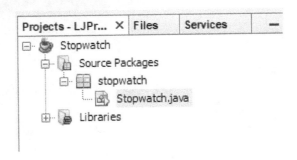

NetBeans uses a particular structure for each project you create. Under the Project main folder is a folder (**Source Packages**) with a **package** it names (in this case, **stopwatch**). In that package folder are the class files (**java** files) needed for your project. It creates a default class file (the one with your project name, **Stopwatch.java** in this case). You do not have to accept the default name (or default package name) – you can change it when creating the project, if desired. Just make sure there is a main class with the matching filename.

Double-click on the **Stopwatch.java** file to see a framework for the file in the editor view area:

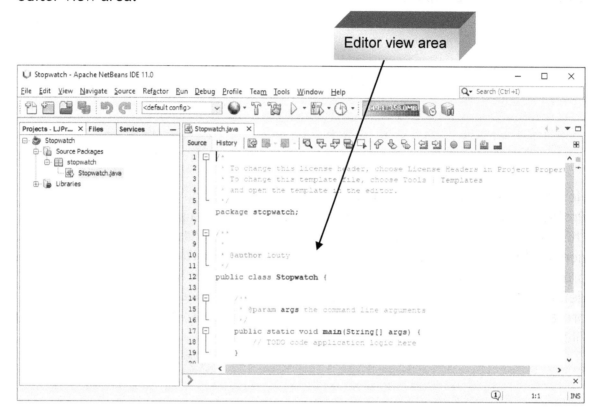

The default code created by NetBeans is:

```java
/*
 * To change this license header, choose License Headers in
Project Properties.
 * To change this template file, choose Tools | Templates
 * and open the template in the editor.
 */

package stopwatch;

/**
 *
 * @author tyleel
 */
public class Stopwatch
{

  /**
   * @param args the command line arguments
   */
  public static void main(String[] args)
  {
    // TODO code application logic here
  }

}
```

We will always replace this default code with our own code (or you can modify it if you want to avoid a little typing). Delete the default code.

As mentioned earlier, we will just be giving you code to type here. What all this code means will become more apparent as you work through the course. There are a few rules to pay attention to as you type Java code (we will go over these rules again in the next class):

> ➤ Java code requires perfection. All words must be spelled correctly.
> ➤ Java is case-sensitive, meaning upper and lower case letters are considered to be different characters. When typing code, make sure you use upper and lower case letters properly
> ➤ Java ignores any **"white space"** such as blanks. We will often use white space to make our code more readable.
> ➤ Curly **braces** are used for grouping. They mark the beginning and end of programming sections. Make sure your Java programs have an equal number of left and right braces. We call the section of code between matching braces a **block.**
> ➤ It is good coding practice to **indent** code within a block. This makes code easier to follow. NetBeans automatically indents code in blocks for you.
> ➤ Every Java statement will end with a semicolon. A **statement** is a program expression that generates some result. Note that not all Java expressions are statements (for example, the line defining the **main** method has no semicolon).

Create a Frame

The first step in building a Java GUI application is creating a frame. At the same time we create the frame, we establish the basic framework for the entire program. The code (**Stopwatch.java**) that creates a frame within this basic framework is defined by a Java **class** of the same name:

```java
/*
 * Stopwatch
 */
package stopwatch;
import javax.swing.*;
import java.awt.*;
import java.awt.event.*;
public class Stopwatch extends JFrame
{

  public static void main(String args[])
  {
    // Construct the frame
    new Stopwatch().setVisible(true);
  }

  public Stopwatch()
  {
    // Frame constructor
    setTitle("Stopwatch Application");
    setSize(300, 100);
  }
}
```

Type one line at a time, paying close attention that you type everything as shown (use the rules).

As you type, notice after you type each left brace ({), the NetBeans editor adds a corresponding right brace (}) and automatically indents the next line. This follows the rule of indenting each code block. Like the braces, when you type a left parenthesis, a matching right parenthesis is added. Also, another thing to notice is that the editor uses different colors for different things in the code. Green text represents comments. Code is in black and keywords are in blue. This coloring sometimes helps you identify mistakes you may have made in typing.

When done typing, you should see:

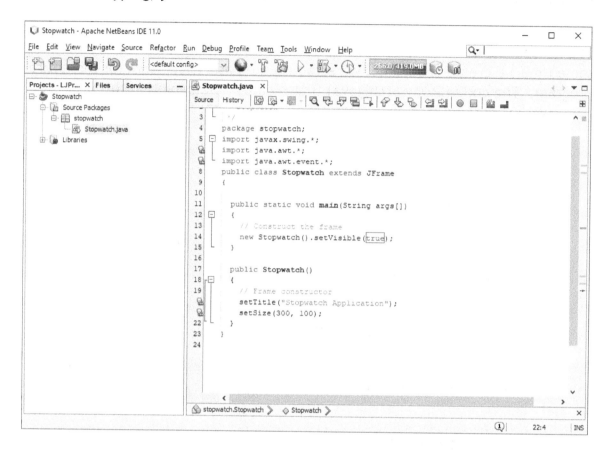

This code creates the frame by **extending** the Swing **JFrame** object, meaning it takes on all characteristics of such a frame. The code has a **constructor** for the **Stopwatch** object. You should see it executes two methods: one to set the title (**setTitle**) and one to set the size (**setSize**). The constructor is called in the **main method** to create the frame. We will use this same basic structure in <u>every</u> project built in this course. A constructor for the frame and all associated controls and control events will be built. The frame will be created in the **main** method.

Run the project (press <**F6**>, click the **Run** arrow in the toolbar or choose **Run**, then **Run Project** in the menu). You will see your first frame:

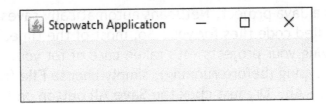

To stop choose **Run**, then **Stop Build/Run.**

Saving Java Projects with NetBeans

Whenever you run a Java project, NetBeans automatically saves both the source files and the compiled code files for you. So, most of the time, you don't need to worry about saving your projects - it's taken care of for you. If you want to save code you are typing (before running), simply choose **File** from the main menu and click **Save All**. Or, just click the **Save All** button on the toolbar:

You do need to save the project group anytime you make a change, for example, if you add/delete files from a project or add/delete projects. This is also done using the **Save All** option.   If you try to exit NetBeans and have not saved projects, NetBeans will pop up dialog boxes to inform you of such and give you an opportunity to save files before exiting.

NetBeans and Java Files

So, how does all this information about program structure, files, compiling and running fit in with NetBeans, our development environment. We have seen that Java projects are grouped in project groups. And projects are made up of different folders and files.

Using My Computer or Windows Explorer (if using Windows), go to the folder containing the **Stopwatch** project you just built. There are many folders and files. In the **src/stopwatch** folder, you will see

Stopwatch.java

This is the source code that appears in the editor view area of NetBeans. In the **build/classes/stopwatch** folder is **Stopwatch.class**. This the compiled version of Stopwatch.java (this is the file needed by the Java virtual machine). Most of the other files are used by NetBeans used to keep track of what files make up the project.

Be aware that the only true Java files here are the ones with **.java** and **.class** extensions. The other files are created and modified by our particular development environment, NetBeans. If you want to share your Java program with a friend or move your Java program to another development environment, the only files you really need to transfer are the **.java** files. These files can be used by any Java programmer or programming environment to create a running program.

Create the User Interface

Having created a frame, we now create the user interface by "placing" controls in the frame. This placement simply involves several lines of logical Java code per control desired.

An object called a **layout manager** determines how controls are arranged in a frame. Some of the layout managers and their characteristics are:

FlowLayout	Places controls in successive rows, fitting as many as possible in a given row.
BorderLayout	Places controls against any of the four frame borders.
CardLayout	Places controls on top of each other like a deck of cards.
GridLayout	Places controls within a specified rectangular grid.
GridBagLayout	Places controls with a specified very flexible rectangular grid.
BoxLayout	Arranges controls either in a row or column.
SpringLayout	Arranges controls with positions defined by sprints and struts.

In this class, we will use the **GridBagLayout**. In our opinion, it offers the nicest interface appearance. As we work through the course, you will learn more and more capabilities of this manager. Study the other layout managers if you'd like.

A frame is actually made up of several different **panes**. Controls are placed in the **content pane** of the frame. The **GridBagLayout** manager divides the content pane into a grid of rows and columns:

	Column 0	Column 1	Column 2	Column 3	Column 4	Column 5
Row 0						
Row 1						
Row 2						
Row 3						
Row 4						
Row 5						

The top row is Row 0 and row number increases as you go down the grid. The left column is Column 0 and column number increases as you move to the right in the grid.

The **GridBagConstraints** object is used for control placement and positioning within the various grid elements. Controls are placed in this grid by referring to a particular column (**gridx** location) and row (**gridy** location). Rows and columns both start at zero (0). The grid does not have to be (but can be) sized. It automatically grows as controls are added. We will see that the **GridBagLayout** manager is very flexible. Controls can span more than one column/row and can be spaced (using **insets**) anywhere within a grid element.

A single line of code in our frame constructor is needed to specify we are using the **GridBagLayout** in the frame content pane:

```
getContentPane().setLayout(new GridBagLayout());
```

To place a control in the **GridBagLayout** grid, we follow these steps:

> **Declare** the control.
> **Create** the control.
> Establish desired control **properties**.
> **Add** the control to the layout content pane at the desired position.

In the projects we build, all controls will be declared with **class level scope**, meaning the controls and associated properties and methods will be available to any method in the class. Hence, all controls will be declared following the left opening brace of the class, before the first method.

We will also give **meaningful names** to controls. Accepted practice is to give the control a name beginning with some description of its purpose, then concatenating the type of control at the end of the name. Such a naming convention makes reading and writing your Java code much easier. Examples of names for button, label and text field controls (the ones we use with our stopwatch example):

```
startButton
stopButton
elapsedLabel
startTextField
```

To declare a control, you type the statement:

```
ControlType controlName;
```

In the Swing library, a button control is of type **JButton**. Hence, to declare our **startButton**, we use:

```
JButton startButton;
```

To create a previously declared control, use:

```
controlName = new ControlType();
```

For our start timing button, the Java code is:

```
startButton = new JButton();
```

The process of **declaring** and **creating** a control can be combined into a single line of code. We will always do this. For our example, the control declaration would be:

```
JButton startButton = new JButton();
```

The next step is to set any desired control properties. The format for such code is:

```
controlName.setPropertyName(PropertyValue);
```

where **setPropertyName** is a method to set a desired property. When we discuss controls in detail, we will cover many of these methods. For now, we will just give them to you. As an example, to set the text appearing on the start timing button to **"Start Timing,"** you would use:

```
startButton.setText("Start Timing");
```

The next step (yes, I know there are lots of steps) is to position the control in the **GridBagLayout** grid. First, we need to declare an object of type **GridBagConstraints** to allow positioning. Assuming this object is named **gridConstraints**, the declaration is:

```
GridBagConstraints gridConstraints = new
GridBagConstraints();
```

This statement is placed near the top of the frame constructor code.

Now, we use a three-step process to place each control in the grid. Decide on an x location (**desiredColumn**) and a y location (**desiredRow**). Then, use this code for a sample control named **controlName**):

```
gridConstraints.gridx = desiredColumn;
gridConstraints.gridy = desiredRow;
getContentPane().add(controlName, gridConstraints);
```

We will place the start timing button in the upper left corner of the grid, so we use:

```
gridConstraints.gridx = 0;
gridConstraints.gridy = 0;
getContentPane().add(startButton, gridConstraints);
```

To finalize placement of controls in the frame, execute a pack method:

```
pack();
```

This "packs" the grid layout onto the frame and makes the controls visible.

In summary, decide what controls you want to place in a frame. For each control, you need:

> ➢ a **declaration** and **creation** statement (class level)
> ➢ three lines of code for **placement** (in constructor method)

Once all controls are in the frame, you must execute a **pack** method to finalize placement. We'll clear this up (hopefully) with an example.

Example 1-1

Stopwatch Application – Adding Controls

Continue with the Stopwatch example where we created a frame. We want to build this frame:

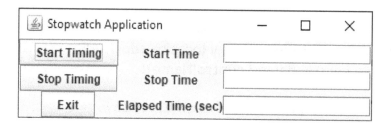

1. We will place nine controls in the frame: three buttons (**JButton** class), three labels (**JLabel** class) and three text fields (**JTextField** class). The buttons will start and stop the timing. The labels and text fields will be used to display the timing results: We will place these controls in a 3 x 3 array:

	gridx = 0	gridx = 1	gridx = 2
gridy = 0	**startButton**	**startLabel**	**startTextField**
gridy = 1	**stopButton**	**stopLabel**	**stopTextField**
gridy = 2	**exitButton**	**elapsedLabel**	**elapsedTextField**

Properties we will set in code:

startButton:

text	Start Timing
gridx	0
gridy	0

stopButton:

text	Stop Timing
gridx	0
gridy	1

exitButton:

text	Exit
gridx	0
gridy	2

startLabel:

text	Start Time
gridx	1
gridy	0

stopLabel:

text	End Time
gridx	1
gridy	1

elapsedLabel:

text	Elapsed Time (sec)
gridx	1
gridy	2

startTextField:

text	[Blank]
columns	15
gridx	2
gridy	0

stopTextField:

text	[Blank]
columns	15
gridx	2
gridy	1

elapsedTextField:

text	[Blank]
columns	15
gridx	2
gridy	2

2. First, type the code to declare the nine controls (recall these lines go after the opening left brace for the class definition:

```
JButton startButton = new JButton();
JButton stopButton = new JButton();
JButton exitButton = new JButton();
JLabel startLabel = new JLabel();
JLabel stopLabel = new JLabel();
JLabel elapsedLabel = new JLabel();;
JTextField startTextField = new JTextField();
JTextField stopTextField = new JTextField();
JTextField elapsedTextField = new JTextField();
```

3. Replace the **setSize** line with the line establishing the grid layout:

```
getContentPane().setLayout(new GridBagLayout());
```

4. The code to set properties of and place each of the nine controls:

```
GridBagConstraints gridConstraints = new
GridBagConstraints();
startButton.setText("Start Timing");
gridConstraints.gridx = 0;
gridConstraints.gridy = 0;
getContentPane().add(startButton, gridConstraints);

stopButton.setText("Stop Timing");
gridConstraints.gridx = 0;
gridConstraints.gridy = 1;
getContentPane().add(stopButton, gridConstraints);

exitButton.setText("Exit");
gridConstraints.gridx = 0;
gridConstraints.gridy = 2;
getContentPane().add(exitButton, gridConstraints);

startLabel.setText("Start Time");
gridConstraints.gridx = 1;
gridConstraints.gridy = 0;
getContentPane().add(startLabel, gridConstraints);

stopLabel.setText("Stop Time");
gridConstraints.gridx = 1;
gridConstraints.gridy = 1;
getContentPane().add(stopLabel, gridConstraints);
```

```
elapsedLabel.setText("Elapsed Time (sec)");
gridConstraints.gridx = 1;
gridConstraints.gridy = 2;
getContentPane().add(elapsedLabel, gridConstraints);

startTextField.setText("");
startTextField.setColumns(15);
gridConstraints.gridx = 2;
gridConstraints.gridy = 0;
getContentPane().add(startTextField, gridConstraints);

stopTextField.setText("");
stopTextField.setColumns(15);
gridConstraints.gridx = 2;
gridConstraints.gridy = 1;
getContentPane().add(stopTextField, gridConstraints);

elapsedTextField.setText("");
elapsedTextField.setColumns(15);
gridConstraints.gridx = 2;
gridConstraints.gridy = 2;
getContentPane().add(elapsedTextField, gridConstraints);

pack();
```

Notice how each control is located within the grid. Notice, too, how we set the number of columns for the text field controls. If we didn't do this, you wouldn't see the controls. I know there's lots of code here (and there will always be lots of code for GUI interfaces). You can choose to type the code or copy and paste from these notes into NetBeans. If you choose to type the code, notice much of the code is similar, so copy and paste operations come in very handy.

For reference, here is the complete **Stopwatch.java** code at this point (newly added code is shaded – the line setting the frame size has been deleted):

```
/*
 * Stopwatch.java
 */
package stopwatch;
import javax.swing.*;
import java.awt.*;
import java.awt.event.*;
public class Stopwatch extends JFrame
{
    // declare controls used
    JButton startButton = new JButton();
    JButton stopButton = new JButton();
    JButton exitButton = new JButton();
    JLabel startLabel = new JLabel();
    JLabel stopLabel = new JLabel();
    JLabel elapsedLabel = new JLabel();;
    JTextField startTextField = new JTextField();
    JTextField stopTextField = new JTextField();
    JTextField elapsedTextField = new JTextField();
    public static void main(String args[])
    {
        // Construct frame
        new Stopwatch().setVisible(true);
    }
    public Stopwatch()
    {
        // Frame constructor
        setTitle("Stopwatch Application");
        getContentPane().setLayout(new GridBagLayout());
        // add controls
        GridBagConstraints gridConstraints = new
GridBagConstraints();

        startButton.setText("Start Timing");
        gridConstraints.gridx = 0;
        gridConstraints.gridy = 0;
        getContentPane().add(startButton, gridConstraints);

        stopButton.setText("Stop Timing");
        gridConstraints.gridx = 0;
        gridConstraints.gridy = 1;
        getContentPane().add(stopButton, gridConstraints);

        exitButton.setText("Exit");
```

```
        gridConstraints.gridx = 0;
        gridConstraints.gridy = 2;
        getContentPane().add(exitButton, gridConstraints);

        startLabel.setText("Start Time");
        gridConstraints.gridx = 1;
        gridConstraints.gridy = 0;
        getContentPane().add(startLabel, new
GridBagConstraints());

        stopLabel.setText("Stop Time");
        gridConstraints.gridx = 1;
        gridConstraints.gridy = 1;
        getContentPane().add(stopLabel, gridConstraints);

        elapsedLabel.setText("Elapsed Time (sec)");
        gridConstraints.gridx = 1;
        gridConstraints.gridy = 2;
        getContentPane().add(elapsedLabel, gridConstraints);

        startTextField.setText("");
        startTextField.setColumns(15);
        gridConstraints.gridx = 2;
        gridConstraints.gridy = 0;
        getContentPane().add(startTextField, gridConstraints);

        stopTextField.setText("");
        stopTextField.setColumns(15);
        gridConstraints.gridx = 2;
        gridConstraints.gridy = 1;
        getContentPane().add(stopTextField, gridConstraints);

        elapsedTextField.setText("");
        elapsedTextField.setColumns(15);
        gridConstraints.gridx = 2;
        gridConstraints.gridy = 2;
        getContentPane().add(elapsedTextField, gridConstraints);

        pack();
    }
}
```

Run the project. The interface should look like this:

Notice how each control is located and sized in the layout of the frame. Save this project (saved as **Example1-1** project in **\LearnJava\LJ Code\Class1** project group). We have no code to stop this project. To do this, select **Run** in the NetBeans menu and choose **Stop Build/Run**.

Adding Event Methods

At this point, our interface has a finished look. What is missing is the code behind the control events. The next step in building a Java GUI application is to add this code. But, to add the code, we need a place to put it. We need to add event methods and their corresponding **listeners** to our application. There are two ways to add listeners, one for **AWT** objects and one for **Swing** objects. Listeners are added in the frame constructor code.

Java **event listeners** for AWT objects (primarily those for mouse and keyboard inputs) are implemented using something called **adapters** (also available from the AWT). The best way to see how to add such a listener is by example. In every project we build, we need to "listen" for the event when the user closes the window. The adapter that implements events for the frame (window) is called the **WindowAdapter** and it works with the **WindowListener**. There are certain window events that can be "listened for." In our case, we want to listen for the **windowClosing** event. The code that adds this event method to our application is:

```
addWindowListener(new WindowAdapter()
{
  public void windowClosing(WindowEvent e)
  {
        [Java code for window closing]
  }
});
```

This is actually one very long Java statement over several lines. It calls the **addWindowListener** method and, as an argument (all in parentheses), includes a **new** instance of a **WindowAdapter** event method (the **windowClosing** event). It's really not that hard to understand when you look at it, just very long!!

In the **windowClosing** method, we would write the code to execute when the window is closing. The **windowClosing** method must have a single argument (**WindowEvent e**). We can use this argument to determine just what event has occurred. In the stopwatch example, we assume a window closing event.

For Swing components, like the button, label and text field used here, event methods (**actionPerformed**) are added using the **ActionListener**. If the component is named **controlName**, the method is added using:

```
controlName.addActionListener(new ActionListener()
{
  public void actionPerformed(ActionEvent e)
  {
        [Java code to execute]
  }
});
```

Again, note this is just one long line of Java code. The method has a single argument (**ActionEvent e**), which tells us what particular event occurred (each control can respond to a number of events). For our stopwatch example, we will assume click events for the three button controls.

Note when we add a listener, we also need to add code for the event method. We could type the code at the same time we add the listener, but we take a different approach. When a method is added, the method code will be a single line of code invoking an "external" method where the actual code will reside. This separates the coding of method events from the code building the frame and makes for a "cleaner" code. For Swing components, we will name these external methods using a specific convention – the **control name** and **method name** will be concatenated into a new method name. Similar conventions are followed for AWT events. For our example above, the code adding such a method would be:

```
controlName.addActionListener(new ActionListener()
{
  public void actionPerformed(ActionEvent e)
  {
     controlNameActionPerformed(e);
  }
});
```

Once the method is added, the actual code is written in a method defined elsewhere in the program. The form for this method must be:

```
private void controlNameActionPerformed(ActionEvent e)
{
    [Java code to execute]
}
```

By separating the event method code from the code constructing the frame, editing, modifying and testing a Java GUI application is much easier. And, the naming convention selected makes it easier to find the event method associated with a particular control. The control event methods are usually placed after the constructor method.

Let's summarize the many steps to place a control (named **controlName** of type **controlType**) in a frame and add an event method:

> Declare and create the control (class level scope):

```
ControlType controlName = new ControlType();
```

> Position the control:

```
gridConstraints.gridx = desiredColumn;
gridConstraints.gridy = desiredRow;
getContentPane().add(controlName, gridConstraints);
```

(assumes a **gridConstraints** object has been created).

> Add the control listener:

```
controlName.addActionListener(new ActionListener()
{
  public void actionPerformed(ActionEvent e)
  {
      controlNameActionPerformed(e);
  }
});
```

➢ Write the control event method:

```
private void controlNameActionPerformed(ActionEvent e)
{
    [Java code to execute]
}
```

The first few times you add controls, this will seem to be a tedious process. As you develop more and more GUI applications, such additions will become second nature (and, you'll get very good at using the copy and paste features of NetBeans).

Variables

We're now ready to write code for our application. We can now add any event methods (for events we want our application to respond to). We then simply add code to these methods. But before we do this, we need to discuss **variables**.

Variables are used by Java to hold information needed by an application. Variables must be properly named. Rules used in naming variables:

> ➢ They may include letters, numbers, and underscore (_), though the underscore is rarely used
> ➢ The first character must be a letter
> ➢ You cannot use a reserved word (keywords used by Java)

Use meaningful variable names that help you (or other programmers) understand the purpose of the information stored by the variable. By convention, Java variable names begin with a lower case letter. If a variable name consists of more than one word, the words are joined together, and each word after the first begins with an uppercase letter.

Examples of acceptable variable names:

```
startingTime      interestValue      letter05
johnsAge          numberOfDays       timeOfDay
```

Java Data Types

Each variable is used to store information of a particular **type**. Java has a wide range of data types. You must always know the type of information stored in a particular variable.

boolean variables can have one of two different values: **true** or **false** (reserved words in Java). **boolean** variables are helpful in making decisions.

If a variable stores a whole number (no decimal), there are three data types available: **short**, **int** or **long**. Which type you select depends on the range of the value stored by the variable:

Data Type	Range
short	-32,678 to 32,767
int	-2,147,483,648 to 2,147,483,647
long	-9,223,372,036,854,775,808 to 9,223,372,036,854,775,807

We will almost always use the **int** type in our work when working with whole numbers.

If a variable stores a decimal number, there are two data types: **float** or **double**. The double uses twice as much storage as float, providing more precision and a wider range. Examples:

Data Type	Value
float	3.14
double	3.14159265359

We will usually use the **double** type to represent decimal numbers.

Java is a popular language for performing string manipulations. These manipulations are performed on variables of type **String**. A string variable is just that - a string (list) of various characters. In Java, string variable values are enclosed in quotes. Examples of string variables:

```
"Java is fun!"     "012345"     "Title     Author"
```

Single character string variables have a special type, type **char**, for character type. **Char** types are enclosed in single quotes. Examples of character variables:

`'a'`   `'1'`   `'V'`   `'*'`

A last data type is type **Object**. That is, we can actually define a variable to represent any Java object, like a button or frame. We will see the utility of the **Object** type as we progress in the course.

Variable Declaration

Once we have decided on a variable name and the type of variable, we must tell our Java application what that name and type are. We say, we must **explicitly declare** the variable.

To **explicitly** declare a variable, you must first determine its **scope**. Scope identifies how widely disseminated we want the variable value to be. We will use three levels of scope:

> ➢ Loop level
> ➢ Method level
> ➢ Class level

The values of **loop** level variables are only available within a computation loop. The use of such variables will be discussed in more detail in Class 2.

The values of **method** level variables are only available within a method. Such variables are declared within a method using the variable type as a 'declarer':

```
int myInt;
double myDouble;
String myString, yourString;
```

Class level variables retain their value and are available to all methods within that class. If any method changes a class level variable's value, that change is seen throughout the class. Class level variables are declared immediately following the opening left brace of the class definition, outside of all methods. Examples:

```
int myInt;
Date myDate;
long bigInteger;
```

Arrays

Java has powerful facilities for handling arrays, which provide a way to store a large number of variables under the same name. Each variable, called an element, in an array must have the same data type, and they are distinguished from each other by an array index (contained within square brackets). In this course, we work with one-dimensional arrays, although multi-dimensional arrays are possible.

We usually declare and create arrays in the same line of code. For example, to declare an integer array named '**item**', with dimension **9**, at the method level, we use:

```
int[] item = new int[9];
```

At the **class** level:

```
int[] item = new int[9];
```

The index on an array variable begins at 0 and ends at the dimensioned value minus 1. Hence, the **item** array in the above examples has **nine** elements, ranging from **item[0]** to **item[8]**. You use array variables just like any other variable - just remember to include its name and its index.

To refer to the last element in this example array, you write:

```
item[8] = newValue;
```

To sum the first three elements, use:

```
sum = item[0] + item[1] + item[2];
```

It is also possible to have arrays of controls. For example, to have 20 button types available use:

```
Button[] myButtons = new Button[20];
```

The utility of such a declaration will become apparent in later classes.

The length of an array is found using the length property:

```
myArray.length
```

Constants

You can also define constants for use in Java. The format for defining a constant named **numberOfUses** with a value **200** is:

```
final int numberOfUses = 200;
```

The scope of user-defined constants is established the same way a variables' scope is. That is, if defined within a method, they are local to the method. If defined in the top region of a class definition, they are 'global' to the class.

If you attempt to change the value of a defined constant, your program will stop with an error message.

Variable Initialization

Any declared numeric variables are initialized at whatever value happens to be in the assigned memory location. If desired, Java lets you initialize variables (and sometimes insists you do) at the same time you declare them. Just insure that the type of initial value matches the variable type (i.e. don't assign a string value to an integer variable).

Examples of variable initialization:

```
int myInt = 23;
String myString = "Java is fun!";
double myDouble = 7.28474746464;
char myChar = '#';
```

You can even initialize arrays with this technique. You must, however, delete the explicit dimension (number of elements) and let Java figure it out by counting the number of elements used to initialize the array. An example is:

```
int[] item = {0, 1, 2, 3, 4, 5, 6, 7, 8, 9};
```

Java will know this array has 10 elements (a dimension of 10).

Example 1-2

Stopwatch Application - Writing Code

All that's left to do is write code for the application. We write code for every event a response is needed for. In this application, there are three such events: clicking on each of the buttons.

1. Under the lines declaring the frame controls, declare three class level variables:

    ```
    long startTime;
    long stopTime;
    double elapsedTime;
    ```

    This establishes **startTime**, **endTime**, and **elapsedTime** as variables with class level scope.

2. In the frame constructor, add the **windowClosing** event method (every GUI project will need this code - place it after line establishing frame title):

    ```
    addWindowListener(new WindowAdapter()
    {
      public void windowClosing(WindowEvent e)
      {
        exitForm(e);
      }
    });
    ```

    And, add the corresponding event method code:

    ```
    private void exitForm(WindowEvent e)
    {
      System.exit(0);
    }
    ```

This method is placed before the final right closing brace of the **Stopwatch** class (the normal place for methods). This one line of code tells the application to stop.

3. Let's create an **actionPerformed** event for the **startButton**. Add the listener (I place this after the code placing the control on the frame):

```
startButton.addActionListener(new ActionListener()
{
  public void actionPerformed(ActionEvent e)
  {
    startButtonActionPerformed(e);
  }
});
```

Then, add the event method after the constructor method:

```
private void startButtonActionPerformed(ActionEvent e)
{
  // click of start timing button
  startTime = System.currentTimeMillis();
  startTextField.setText(String.valueOf(startTime));
  stopTextField.setText("");
  elapsedTextField.setText("");
}
```

In this procedure, once the **Start Timing** button is clicked, we read the current time using a system function (in milliseconds, by the way) and put it in a text field using the **setText** method. We also blank out the other text fields. In the code above (and in all code in these notes), any line beginning with two slashes (//) is a comment. You decide whether you want to type these lines or not. They are not needed for proper application operation.

4. Now, add a listener for the **actionPerformed** event method for the **stopButton**:

```
stopButton.addActionListener(new ActionListener()
{
  public void actionPerformed(ActionEvent e)
  {
    stopButtonActionPerformed(e);
  }
});
```

Then, add this event method after the **startButtonActionPerformed** method:

```
private void stopButtonActionPerformed(ActionEvent e)
{
  // click of stop timing button
  stopTime = System.currentTimeMillis();
  stopTextField.setText(String.valueOf(stopTime));
  elapsedTime = (stopTime - startTime) / 1000.0;
  elapsedTextField.setText(String.valueOf(elapsedTime));
}
```

Here, when the **Stop Timing** button is clicked, we read the current time (**stopTime**), compute the elapsed time (in seconds), and put both values in their corresponding text field controls.

5. Finally, we need code in the **actionPerformed** method for the **exitButton** control. Add the listener:

```
exitButton.addActionListener(new ActionListener()
{
  public void actionPerformed(ActionEvent e)
  {
    exitButtonActionPerformed(e);
  }
});
```

Now, add the method:

```
private void exitButtonActionPerformed(ActionEvent e)
{
  System.exit(0);
}
```

This routine simply closes the frame once the **Exit** button is clicked.

For reference, the complete, final **Stopwatch.java** code is (newly added code is shaded):

```java
/*
 * Stopwatch.java
 */
package stopwatch;
import javax.swing.*;
import java.awt.*;
import java.awt.event.*;

public class Stopwatch extends JFrame
{

  // declare controls used
  JButton startButton = new JButton();
  JButton stopButton = new JButton();
  JButton exitButton = new JButton();
  JLabel startLabel = new JLabel();
  JLabel stopLabel = new JLabel();
  JLabel elapsedLabel = new JLabel();;
  JTextField startTextField = new JTextField();
  JTextField stopTextField = new JTextField();
  JTextField elapsedTextField = new JTextField();

  // declare class level variables
  long startTime;
  long stopTime;
  double elapsedTime;

  public static void main(String args[])
  {
    new Stopwatch().setVisible(true);
  }

  public Stopwatch()
  {
    // frame constructor
    setTitle("Stopwatch Application");
    addWindowListener(new WindowAdapter()
    {
      public void windowClosing(WindowEvent e)
      {
        exitForm(e);
      }
    });
    getContentPane().setLayout(new GridBagLayout());
```

```
    // add controls
    GridBagConstraints gridConstraints = new
GridBagConstraints();
    startButton.setText("Start Timing");
    gridConstraints.gridx = 0;
    gridConstraints.gridy = 0;
    getContentPane().add(startButton, gridConstraints);
    startButton.addActionListener(new ActionListener()
    {
      public void actionPerformed(ActionEvent e)
      {
        startButtonActionPerformed(e);
      }
    });

    stopButton.setText("Stop Timing");
    gridConstraints.gridx = 0;
    gridConstraints.gridy = 1;
    getContentPane().add(stopButton, gridConstraints);
    stopButton.addActionListener(new ActionListener()
    {
      public void actionPerformed(ActionEvent e)
      {
        stopButtonActionPerformed(e);
      }
    });

    exitButton.setText("Exit");
    gridConstraints.gridx = 0;
    gridConstraints.gridy = 2;
    getContentPane().add(exitButton, gridConstraints);
    exitButton.addActionListener(new ActionListener()
    {
      public void actionPerformed(ActionEvent e)
      {
        exitButtonActionPerformed(e);
      }
    });

    startLabel.setText("Start Time");
    gridConstraints.gridx = 1;
    gridConstraints.gridy = 0;
    getContentPane().add(startLabel, new
GridBagConstraints());

    stopLabel.setText("Stop Time");
```

```
    gridConstraints.gridx = 1;
    gridConstraints.gridy = 1;
    getContentPane().add(stopLabel, gridConstraints);

    elapsedLabel.setText("Elapsed Time (sec)");
    gridConstraints.gridx = 1;
    gridConstraints.gridy = 2;
    getContentPane().add(elapsedLabel, gridConstraints);

    startTextField.setText("");
    startTextField.setColumns(15);
    gridConstraints.gridx = 2;
    gridConstraints.gridy = 0;
    getContentPane().add(startTextField, new
GridBagConstraints());

    stopTextField.setText("");
    stopTextField.setColumns(15);
    gridConstraints.gridx = 2;
    gridConstraints.gridy = 1;
    getContentPane().add(stopTextField, gridConstraints);

    elapsedTextField.setText("");
    elapsedTextField.setColumns(15);
    gridConstraints.gridx = 2;
    gridConstraints.gridy = 2;
    getContentPane().add(elapsedTextField, gridConstraints);
    pack();
  }
```

```
  private void startButtonActionPerformed(ActionEvent e)
  {
    // click of start timing button
    startTime = System.currentTimeMillis();
    startTextField.setText(String.valueOf(startTime));
    stopTextField.setText("");
    elapsedTextField.setText("");
  }
```

```
  private void stopButtonActionPerformed(ActionEvent e)
  {
     // click of stop timing button
    stopTime = System.currentTimeMillis();
    stopTextField.setText(String.valueOf(stopTime));
    elapsedTime = (stopTime - startTime) / 1000.0;
    elapsedTextField.setText(String.valueOf(elapsedTime));
  }
```

```
  private void exitButtonActionPerformed(ActionEvent e)
  {
    System.exit(0);
  }

  private void exitForm(WindowEvent e)
  {
    System.exit(0);
  }

}
```

Study this code to see where all the methods go.

Now, run the application (press **<F6>**). Try it out. If your application doesn't run, recheck to make sure the code is typed properly. Save your application. This is saved in the **Example1-2** project in **\LearnJava\LJ Code\Class 1** project group. Here's what I got when I tried:

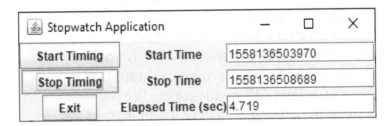

If you have the time, here are some other things you may try with the **Stopwatch Application**. To make these changes will require research on your part (use web sites, other books, other programmers) to find answers. This is an important skill to have – how to improve existing applications by discovering new things. The solutions to the problems and exercises at the end of this class' notes can also shed some light on these challenges:

A. Try changing the frame background color.

B. Notice you can press the '**Stop Timing**' button before the '**Start Timing**' button. This shouldn't be so. Change the application so you can't do this. And make it such that you can't press the '**Start Timing**' until '**Stop Timing**' has been pressed. Hint: Look at the button **enabled** property.

C. Can you think of how you can continuously display the '**End Time**' and '**Elapsed Time**'? This is a little tricky because of the event-driven nature of Java. Look at the **Timer** class (do a little Java research). By setting the **delay** property of this class to **1000**, it will generate its own events every one second. Put code similar to that in the event method for the **stopButton** in the **Timer** class' **actionPerformed** method and see what happens. Also, see the exercise at the end of the class for help on this one.

Class Review

After completing this class, you should understand:

> ➢ What a Java GUI application is
> ➢ The concept of an event-driven application
> ➢ What object-oriented programming (OOP) is about
> ➢ How to use NetBeans to build and run an application
> ➢ The structure of a Java GUI application
> ➢ The three steps in building a Java GUI application
> ➢ How to create a frame
> ➢ How to place a control on the frame using the GridBagLayout
> ➢ Proper control naming convention
> ➢ How to add event listeners and event methods
> ➢ Proper variable naming and typing procedures
> ➢ The concept of variable scope
> ➢ How to properly declare a variable
> ➢ How to declare an array
> ➢ How to define a constant
> ➢ How to add code to event methods

Practice Problems 1*

Problem 1-1. Beep Problem. Build an application with a single button. When the button is clicked, make the computer beep (use the **Toolkit.getDefaultToolkit().beep()** method).

Problem 1-2. Text Problem. Build an application with a single button. When the button is clicked, change the button's **text** property. This allows a button to be used for multiple purposes. If you want to change the button caption back when you click again, you'll need an **if** statement. We'll discuss this statement in the next class, but, if you're adventurous, give it a try.

Problem 1-3. Enabled Problem. Build an application with two buttons. When you click one button, make it disabled (**enabled = false**) and make the other button enabled (**enabled = true**).

Problem 1-4. Date Problem. Build an application with a button. When the button is clicked, have the computer display the current date in a text field control. You'll need to study the **Date** class.

---

*Note: Practice Problems are given after each class to give you practice in writing code for your Java applications. These are meant to be quick and, hopefully, short exercises. The NetBeans environment makes it easy to build and test quick applications - in fact, programmers develop such examples all the time to test some idea they might have. Use your imagination in working the problems - modify them in any way you want. You learn programming by doing programming! The more you program, the better programmer you will become. Our solutions to the **Practice Problems** are provided as an addenda to these notes.

Exercise 1*

Calendar/Time Display

Design a window that displays the current month, day, and year. Also, display the current time, updating it every second (look into the **Date** and **Timer** classes). Make the window look something like a calendar page.

---

*Note: After completing each class' notes, a homework exercise (and, sometimes, more) is given, covering many of the topics taught. Try to work through the homework exercise on your own. This is how programming is learned – solving a particular problem. For reference, solutions to all **Exercises** are provided as an addenda to these notes. In our solutions, you may occasionally see something you don't recognize. When this happens, use the usual help avenues (websites, other programmers, other texts) to learn what's going on. This is another helpful skill – understanding other people's applications and code.

2

The Java Language

Review and Preview

In the first class, we found there were three primary steps involved in developing a GUI application using Java: 1) Create the frame. 2) Create the user interface by placing controls in the frame. 3) Write code for control event methods.

In this class, we are primarily concerned with Step 3, writing code. We will become more familiar with event methods and review some of the elements of the Java language.

A Brief History of Java

It's interesting to see just where the Java language fits in the history of some other computer languages. You will see just how new Java is!

In the early 1950's most computers were used for scientific and engineering calculations. The programming language of choice in those days was called **FORTRAN**. FORTRAN was the first modern language and is still in use to this day (after going through several updates). In the late 1950's, bankers and other business people got into the computer business using a language called **COBOL**. Within a few years after its development, COBOL became the most widely used data processing language. And, like FORTRAN, it is still being used today.

In the 1960's, two professors at Dartmouth College decided that "everyday" people needed to have a language they could use to learn programming. They developed **BASIC** (**B**eginner's **A**ll-Purpose **S**ymbolic **I**nstruction **C**ode). BASIC (and its successors, GW-Basic, Visual Basic, Visual Basic .NET, Small Basic) is probably the most widely used programming language. Many dismiss it as a "toy language," but BASIC was the first product developed by a company you may have heard of – Microsoft! And, BASIC has been used to develop thousands of commercial applications.

Java had its beginnings in 1972, when AT&T Bell Labs developed the **C** programming language. It was the first, new scientific type language since FORTRAN. If you've every seen a C program, you will notice many similarities between Java and C. Then, with object-oriented capabilities added, came **C++** in 1986 (also from Bell Labs). This was a big step.

On May 23, 1995, Sun Microsystems released the first version of the **Java** programming language. It represented a streamlined version of C and C++ with capabilities for web and desktop applications on <u>any</u> kind of computer. No language before it had such capabilities. Since this introduction, just a few years ago, millions of programmers have added Java capabilities to their programming skills. Improvements are constantly being made to Java and there is a wealth of support to all programmers, even beginners like yourself, from the vast Java community

Rules of Java Programming

Before starting our review of the Java language, let's review some of the rules of Java programming seen in the first class:

➤ Java code requires perfection. All words must be spelled correctly.

➤ Java is case-sensitive, meaning upper and lower case letters are considered to be different characters. When typing code, make sure you use upper and lower case letters properly.

➤ Java ignores any **"white space"** such as blanks. We will often use white space to make our code more readable.

➤ Curly **braces** are used for grouping. They mark the beginning and end of programming sections. Make sure your Java programs have an equal number of left and right braces. We call the section of code between matching braces a **block**.

➤ It is good coding practice to **indent** code within a block. This makes code easier to follow. NetBeans automatically indents code in blocks for you.

➤ Every Java statement will end with a semicolon. A **statement** is a program expression that generates some. Note that not all Java expressions are statements (for example, the line defining the **main** method has no semicolon).

Java Statements and Expressions

The simplest (and most common) statement in Java is the **assignment** statement. It consists of a variable name, followed by the assignment operator (=), followed by some sort of **expression**, followed by a semicolon (;). The expression on the right hand side is evaluated, then the variable on the left hand side of the assignment operator is **replaced** by that value of the expression.

Examples:

```
startTime = now;
explorer = "Captain Spaulding";
bitCount = byteCount * 8;
energy = mass * LIGHTSPEED * LIGHTSPEED;
netWorth = assets - liabilities;
```

The assignment statement stores information.

Statements normally take up a single line. Since Java ignores white space, statements can be **stacked** using a semicolon (;) to separate them. Example:

```
startTime = now; endTime = startTime + 10;
```

The above code is the same as if the second statement followed the first statement. The only place we tend to use stacking is for quick initialization of like variables.

If a statement is very long, it may be continued to the next line without any kind of continuation character. Again, this is because Java ignores white space. It keeps processing a statement until it finally sees a semicolon. Example:

```
months = Math.log(final * intRate / deposit + 1)
/ Math.log(1 + intRate);
```

This statement, though on two lines, will be recognized as a single line. We usually write each statement on a single line. Be aware that long lines of code in the notes many times wrap around to the next line (due to page margins).

Comment statements begin with the two slashes (//). For example:

```
// This is a comment
x = 2 * y // another way to write a comment
```

You, as a programmer, should decide how much to comment your code.
Consider such factors as reuse, your audience, and the legacy of your code. In
our notes and examples, we try to insert comment statements when necessary
to explain some detail. You can also have a multiple line comment. Begin the
comment with /* and end it with */. Example:

```
/*
  This is a very long
  comment over
  a few lines
*/
```

Type Casting

In each assignment statement, it is important that the type of data on both sides of the operator (=) is the same. That is, if the variable on the left side of the operator is an **int**, the result of the expression on the right side should be **int**.

Java (by default) will try to do any conversions for you. When it can't, an error message will be printed. In those cases, you need to explicitly **cast** the result. This means convert the right side to the same side as the left side. Assuming the desired type is **type**, the casting statement is:

   leftSide = (type) rightSide;

You can cast from any basic type (decimal and integer numbers) to any other basic type. Be careful when casting from higher precision numbers to lower precision numbers. Problems arise when you are outside the range of numbers.

Java Arithmetic Operators

Operators modify values of variables. The simplest **operators** carry out **arithmetic** operations. There are five **arithmetic operators** in Java.

Addition is done using the plus (+) sign and **subtraction** is done using the minus (-) sign. Simple examples are:

Operation	Example	Result
Addition	7 + 2	9
Addition	3.4 + 8.1	11.5
Subtraction	6 - 4	2
Subtraction	11.1 - 7.6	3.5

Multiplication is done using the asterisk (*) and **division** is done using the slash (/). Simple examples are:

Operation	Example	Result
Multiplication	8 * 4	32
Multiplication	2.3 * 12.2	28.06
Division	12 / 2	6
Division	45.26 / 6.2	7.3

The last operator is the **remainder** operator represented by a percent symbol (%). This operator divides the whole number on its left side by the whole number on its right side, ignores the main part of the answer, and just gives you the remainder. It may not be obvious now, but the remainder operator is used a lot in computer programming. Examples are:

Operation	Example	Division Result	Operation Result
Remainder	7 % 4	1 Remainder 3	3
Remainder	14 % 3	4 Remainder 2	2
Remainder	25 % 5	5 Remainder 0	0

The mathematical operators have the following **precedence** indicating the order they are evaluated without specific groupings:

Multiplication (*) and division (/)
Remainder (%)
Addition (+) and subtraction (-)

If multiplications and divisions or additions and subtractions are in the same expression, they are performed in left-to-right order. **Parentheses** around expressions are used to force some desired precedence.

Comparison and Logical Operators

There are six **comparison** operators in Java used to compare the value of two expressions (the expressions must be of the same data type). These are the basis for making decisions:

Operator	Comparison
>	Greater than
<	Less than
>=	Greater than or equal to
<=	Less than or equal to
==	Equal to
!=	Not equal to

It should be obvious that the result of a comparison operation is a **boolean** value (**true** or **false**). **Examples:**

a = 9.6, b = 8.1, a > b returns true
a = 14, b = 14, a < b returns false
a = 14, b = 14, a >= b returns true
a = 7, b = 11, a <= b returns true
a = 7, b = 7, a == b returns true
a = 7, b = 7, a != b returns false

Logical operators operate on **boolean** data types, providing a **boolean** result. They are also used in decision making. We will use three **logical** operators

Operator	Operation
!	Logical Not
&&	Logical And
||	Logical Or

The Not (!) operator simply negates a **boolean** value. It is very useful for 'toggling' **boolean** variables. Examples:

If a = true, then !a = false
If a = false, then !a = true

The And (**&&**) operator checks to see if two different **boolean** data types are both true. If both are true, the operator returns a true. Otherwise, it returns a false value. Examples:

   a = true, b = true, then a **&&** b = true
   a = true, b = false, then a **&&** b = false
   a = false, b = true, then a **&&** b = false
   a = false, b = false, then a **&&** b = false

The Or (**||**) operator (typed as two "pipe" symbols) checks to see if either of two **boolean** data types is true. If either is true, the operator returns a true. Otherwise, it returns a false value. Examples:

   a = true, b = true, then a **||** b = true
   a = true, b = false, then a **||** b = true
   a = false, b = true, then a **||** b = true
   a = false, b = false, then a **||** b = false

Logical operators follow arithmetic operators in precedence. Use of these operators will become obvious as we delve further into coding.

Concatenation Operators

To **concatentate** two string data types (tie them together), use the + symbol, the string concatenation operator:

```
currentTime = "The current time is " + "9:30";
textSample = "Hook this " + "to this";
```

Java offers other concatenation operators that perform an operation on a variable and assign the resulting value back to the variable. Hence, the operation

```
a = a + 2;
```

Can be written using the addition concatenation operator (+=) as:

```
a += 2;
```

This says a is incremented by 2.

Other concatenation operators and their symbols are:

Operator Name	Operator Symbol	Operator Task
String	a += b;	a = a + b;
Addition	a += b;	a = a + b;
Subtraction	a -= b;	a = a - b;
Multiplication	a *= b;	a = a * b;
Division	a /= b;	a = a / b;

We often increment and decrement by one. There are operators for this also. The increment operator:

```
a++;      is equivalent to:   a = a + 1;
```

Similarly, the decrement operator:

```
a--;      is equivalent to:   a = a - 1;
```

Strings to Numbers to Strings

In Java GUI applications, string variables are used often. The **text** displayed in the label control and the text field control are string types. You will find you are constantly converting string types to numeric data types to do some math and then converting back to strings to display the information. Let's look at each of these operations. First, from **string to number** – the process is:

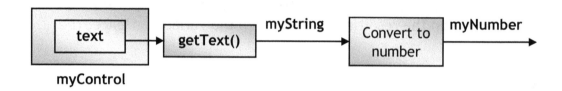

To retrieve the text value in a control, use the **getText** method. In this example,

```
myString = myControl.getText();
```

To convert a string type to a numeric value, use the **valueOf** function. We will look at two examples. To convert a string (**myString**) to an **int** (**myInt**), use:

```
myInt = Integer.valueOf(myString).intValue();
```

To convert a string (**myString**) to a **double** type (**myDouble**), use:

```
myDouble = Double.valueOf(myString).doubleValue();
```

You need to be careful with these methods – if the string is empty or contains unrecognizable characters, an error will occur.

Now, the conversion process from **number to string** is:

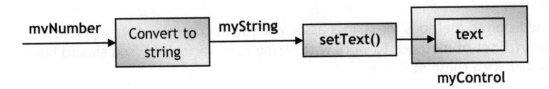

There are two ways to convert a numeric variable to a string. The **valueOf** function does the conversion with no regard for how the result is displayed. This bit of code can be used to convert the numeric variable **myNumber** to a string (**myString**):

```
myNumber = 3.1415926;
myString = String.valueOf(MyNumber);
```

In this case, **myString** will be "**3.1415926**" - if you need to control the number of decimal points, the **format** function is used. As an example, to display **myNumber** with no more than two decimal points, use:

```
myNumber = 3.1415926;
myString = new DecimalFormat("0.00").format(MyNumber);
```

In the display string ("0.00"), the pound signs represent place holders. **myString** is now "**3.14**" Using this format function requires that the **java.text.*** package be imported into your application.

To set the text value displayed in a control, use the **setText** method. If you want to display **myString** in **myControl**, use:

```
myControl.setText(myString);
```

Java String Methods

In addition to methods for strings associated with controls, Java offers a powerful set of methods to work with string type variables. You should become familiar with these methods.

To compare two strings for equality, you can't use the "equals to" operator (==). A common error is forgetting this. The reason we can't use this operator is in how Java stores strings. Say we have two **String** type variables, **aString** and **bString**. Writing:

```
aString == bString
```

checks to see if each of these strings is stored in the same memory location in memory. That's not what we want to do.

To properly compare two strings for equality, we use the **String** class **equals** method. This method does just what we want - compares two strings to see if they have the same characters in them. The code that does this comparison for our example strings is:

```
aString.equals(bString)
```

This method returns the **boolean** result of true if the **aString** and **bString** are the same length, that is have the same number of characters, and each character in one string is identical to the corresponding character in the other. And, the comparison is case-sensitive. To ignore case in the comparison, use:

```
aString.equalsIgnoreCase(bString)
```

We can also see if one string is "less than" or "greater than" another string to allow sorting. This requires the **compareTo** method. With our example strings, the syntax is:

```
aString.compareTo(bString)
```

This method will return one of three integer values:

Returned value	Meaning
-1	**aString** is less than **bString** in alphabetical order
0	**aString** is equal to **bString** (same as equals method)
1	**aString** is greater than **bString** in alphabetical order

To determine the number of characters in (or length of) a string variable, we use the **length** method. Using **myString** as example:

```
myString = "Read Learn Java!";
lenString = myString.length();
```

lenString will have a value of **16**. The location of characters in the string is zero-based. That is, the individual characters for this string start at character 0 and end at character 15.

Many times, you need to extract single characters from string variables. The **charAt** method does this. You specify the string and the desired character position. Recall, characters in a string start at character 0 and extend to the length of the string minus 1. To determine the character (**myChar**) at position **n** in a string **myString**, use:

```
myChar = myString.charAt(n);
```

For example:

```
myString = "Read Learn Java!";
myChar = myString.charAt(5);
```

will return the character 'L' in the variable **myChar**.

You can also extract substrings of characters. The **substring** method is used for this task. You specify the string, the starting position and one beyond the last character in the substring. This example starts at character 2 and extracts the characters "up to" character 8:

```
myString = "Read Learn Java!";
midString = myString.substring(2, 8);
```

The **midString** variable is equal to **"ad Lea"**

Perhaps, you just want a far left portion of a string. Use the **substring** method with a starting position of 0. This example extracts the 3 left-most characters from a string:

```
myString = "Read Learn Java!";
leftString = myString.substring(0, 3);
```

The **leftString** variable is equal to **"Rea"**

Getting the far right portion of a string with the **substring** method is easy. Simply specify the character you wish to start at and the function will return all characters from that point on. To get the 6 characters at the end of our example, you would use:

```
myString = "Read Learn Java!"
rightString = myString.substring(10);
```

The **rightString** variable is equal to **" Java!"** If general, if you want the N "rightmost" characters in a string variable (**myString**), you use:

```
rightString = myString.substring(myString.length() - N);
```

To locate a substring within a string variable, use the **indexOf** method. Three pieces of information are needed: **string1** (the variable), **string2** (the substring to find), and a starting position in **string1** (optional). The method will work left-to-right and return the location of the first character of the substring (it will return -1 if the substring is not found). For our example:

```
myString = "Read Learn Java!";
location = myString.indexOf("ea", 3);
```

This says find the substring **"ea"** in **myString**, starting at character **3**. The returned **location** will have a value of **6**. If the starting location argument is omitted, 0 is assumed, so if:

```
myString = "Read Learn Java!";
location = myString.indexOf("ea");
```

location will have value of **1**.

Related to the **indexOf** method is the **lastIndexOf** method. This method also identifies substrings using identical arguments, but works right-to-left, or in reverse. So, with our example string:

```
myString = "Read Learn Java!";
location = myString.lastIndexOf("ea");
```

This says find the substring **"ea"** in **myString**, starting at the right and working left. The returned **location** will have a value of **6**. Note when we used **indexOf** (without a starting location), the returned **location** was **2**.

Many times, you want to convert letters to upper case or vice versa. Java provides two methods for this purpose: **toUpperCase** and **toLowerCase**. The **toUpperCase** method will convert all letters in a string variable to upper case, while the **toLowerCase** function will convert all letters to lower case. Any non-alphabetic characters are ignored in the conversion. And, if a letter is already in the desired case, it is left unmodified. For our example (modified a bit):

```
myString = "Read Learn Java in 2010!";
a = myString.toUpperCase();
b = myString.toLowerCase();
```

The first conversion using **toUpperCase** will result in:

```
A = "READ LEARN JAVA IN 2010!"
```

And the second conversion using **toLowerCase** will yield:

```
B = "read learn java in 2010!"
```

There are a couple of ways to modify an existing string. If you want to replace a certain character within a string, use the **replace** method. You specify the character you wish to replace and the replacing character. An example:

```
myString = "Read Learn Java!";
myString = myString.replace(' ', '*');
```

This will replace every space in myString with an asterisk. **myString** will become "**Read*Learn*Java!**". To remove leading and trailing spaces from a string, use the **trim** method. Its use is obvious:

```
myString = "   Read Learn Java!       ";
myString = myString.trim();
```

After this, **myString = "Read Learn Java!"** – the spaces are removed.

You can convert a string variable to an array of **char** type variables using the **toCharArray** method. Here's an example:

```
myString = "Learn Java";
char[] myArray = myString.toCharArray();
```

After this, the array **myArray** will have 10 elements, **myArray[0]** = 'L', **myArray[1]** = 'e', and so on. You only need declare **myArray**, you do not need to create (size) it.

You can also convert an array of **char** types to a single string variable. The **copyValueOf** method does this. An example:

```
char[] myArray = {'H', 'o', 'w', ' ', 'a', 'r', 'e', ' ',
'y', 'o', 'u', '?'};
myString = String.copyValueOf(myArray);
```

After this, **myString** = "How are you?".

Every 'typeable' character has a numeric representation called a Unicode value. To determine the Unicode (**myCode**) value for a **char** type variable (named **myChar**), you simply cast the character to an **int** type:

```
myCode = (int) myChar;
```

For example:

```
myCode = (int) 'A';
```

returns the Unicode value (**myCode**) for the upper case A (65, by the way). To convert a Unicode value (**myValue**) to the corresponding character, cast the value to a **char** type::

```
myChar = (char) myCode;
```

For example:

```
myChar = (char) 49;
```

returns the character (**myChar**) represented by a Unicode value of 49 (a "1"). Unicode values are related to ASCII (pronounced "askey") codes you may have seen in other languages. I think you see that there's lots to learn about using string variables in Java.

Dates and Times

Working with dates and times in computer applications is a common task. In Class 1, we used the **Date** data type and the **currentTimeMillis** method without much discussion. We use these to specify and determine dates, times and the difference between dates and times. The information covered here requires two imported files:

```
import java.util.Date;
import java.text.DateFormat;
```

These statements are placed with other import statements in your code.

The **Date** data type is used to hold a date <u>and</u> a time. And, even though that's the case, you're usually only interested in the date <u>or</u> the time. To initialize a **Date** variable (**myDate**) to a specific date, use:

```
Date myDate = new Date(year, month, day);
```

where **year** is the desired year (less 1900, that is, a value of 0 represents the year 1900) (**int** type), **month** the desired month (**int** type), and **day** the desired day (**int** type). The month 'numbers' run from 0 (January) to 11 (December), not 1 to 12. As an example, if you use:

```
myDate = new Date(50, 6, 19);
```

then, display the result (after converting it to a string) in some control using:

```
String.valueOf(myDate)
```

you would get:

```
Wed Jul 19 00:00:00 GMT-08:00 1950
```

This is my birthday (July 19, 1950), by the way. The time is set to a default value since only a date was specified.

The **DateFormat** class is used to display the date in other formats. To format the object (**myDate**) just created, use:

```
DateFormat.getDateInstance(DateFormatValue).format(myDate)
)
```

The **DateFormatValue** can take on one of four different values. Those values and examples of the results are:

Value	Displayed Date
DateFormat.FULL	Wednesday, July 19, 1950
DateFormat.LONG	July 19, 1950
DateFormat.MEDIUM	Jul 19, 1950
DateFormat.SHORT	7/19/50

Individual parts of a **Date** object can be retrieved. Examples include:

```
myDate.getMonth()    // returns 6
myDate.getDate()     // returns 19
myDate.getDay()      // returns 3
```

Notice the **getDay** method yields a value from 0 (Sunday) to 6 (Saturday), so the 3 above represents a Wednesday.

Java also allows you to retrieve the current date and time using the **Date** data type. To place the current date in a variable use the 'default' constructor:

```
Date myToday = new Date();
```

The variable **myToday** will hold today's date with the current time. Doing this as I originally wrote this, I get:

```
String.valueOf(myToday)   // returns Mon Feb 28 20:13:18
GMT-08:00 2005
```

To represent dates in Java, a common and convenient method is to use string variables in a format similar to the **SHORT** format above. For example, we could have a string representation of **myDate**:

```
myDate = "4/7/03";
```

To use such a string representation of a date with dates represented by the **Date** class (for example, to subtract two dates or display the string version of the date in another format), we need to convert the string to a **Date** type. In Java terms, we want to **parse** the string representation of a **SHORT** date to a **Date** object. To do this requires another type of Java structure, the **Try/Catch** structure. This is used to "catch" errors that might occur in a Java program. We won't worry much about it here, other than recognizing the parsing must be within such a structure (a requirement of Java).

The code to convert the string **myDate** to a **Date** class **display** is:

```
// convert string date to Date class for display
try
{
  display =
DateFormat.getDateInstance(DateFormat.SHORT).parse(myDate)
;
}
catch(java.text.ParseException e)
{
  System.out.println("Error parsing date" + e);
}
```

After this code is executed, **display** is a **Date** object containing the date. We can display this object using any format and we can do "date math" discussed next.

A common task is to subtract two dates to determine the number of days between the dates. We can use this to find out how old someone is, see how old a loan is and to see how many days remain in a current year. To subtract two date objects, we first convert the dates to a time value using:

```
myDate.getTime()
```

This yields a millisecond representation (**long** type variable) of the date. You would use a similar statement to get a millisecond representation of a second date. Then to subtract the dates and obtain the result in days, you subtract the millisecond representations and divide the result by the number of milliseconds in a day (60 * 60 * 24 * 1000). This value comes from the fact there are 60 seconds in a minute, 60 minutes in an hour, 24 hours in a day and 1000 milliseconds in a second. As an example, to subtract **myDate** from **today**, use:

```
(today.getTime() - myDate.getTime()) / (60 * 60 * 24 *
1000)
```

Notice that by changing the denominator in this formula, you could also find out the number of seconds, minutes or hours between two dates.

As an example, let's use today's date (**myToday**) and the example date (**myDate**, my birthday) to see how long I've been alive.:

```
(today.getTime() - myDate.getTime()) / (60 * 60 * 24 *
1000) // returns 19948 days
(today.getTime() - myDate.getTime()) / (60 * 60 * 1000) //
returns 478772 hours
```

The tells me I've been alive 19,948 days or 478,772 hours. Looks like I should be getting ready to celebrate my 20,000 days birthday!!

In Class 1, we saw another way to find the difference between two times, the **currentTimeMillis** method. It is a system method and is referenced using:

```
System.currentTimeMillis()
```

This method returns the current time in milliseconds. The returned value is a **long** integer. To use this method, first declare a variable to store the returned value:

```
long myTime;
```

Then, the time (in milliseconds) is given by:

```
myTime = System.currentTimeMillis();
```

By obtaining a value at a later time and subtracting the two values, you will obtain an elapsed time in milliseconds, which could be converted to any units desired. Note this approach can be used without a need to use the **Date** data type. It is usually used for fairly short time periods.

We have introduced the **Date** data type and **currentTimeMillis** method. You will find these very useful as you progress in your programming studies. Do some research on your own to determine how best to use dates and times in applications you build.

Random Number Generator

In writing games and learning software, we use a random number generator to introduce unpredictability. This insures different results each time you try a program. Java has several methods for generating random numbers. We will use just one of them – a random generator of integers. The generator uses the Java **Random** object. This object is part of the **java.util.Random** package.

To use the **Random** object, it is first created using the object **constructor**:

```
Random myRandom = new Random();
```

This statement is placed with the variable declaration statements.

Once created, when you need a random integer value, use the **nextInt** method of this **Random** object:

```
myRandom.nextInt(limit)
```

This statement generates a random integer value that is greater than or equal to 0 and less than **limit**. Note it is less than limit, not equal to. For example, the method:

```
myRandom.nextInt(5)
```

will generate random integers from 0 to 4. The possible values will be 0, 1, 2, 3 and 4.

As other examples, to roll a six-sided die, the number of spots would be computed using:

```
numberSpots = myRandom.nextInt(6) + 1;
```

To randomly choose a number between 100 and 200, use:

```
number = myRandom.nextInt(101) + 100;
```

Math Functions

A last set of functions we need are mathematical functions (yes, programming involves math!) Java provides a set of functions that perform tasks such as square roots, trigonometric relationships, and exponential functions.

Each of the Java math functions comes from the Java **Math** class. This means is that each function name must be preceded by **Math.** (say Math-dot) to work properly. Some of these functions and the returned values are:

Math Function	Value Returned
`Math.abs`	Returns the absolute value of a specified number
`Math.acos`	Returns a double value containing the angle whose cosine is the specified number
`Math.asin`	Returns a double value containing the angle whose sine is the specified number
`Math.atan`	Returns a double value containing the angle whose tangent is the specified number
`Math.cos`	Returns a double value containing the cosine of the specified angle
`Math.E`	A constant, the natural logarithm base
`Math.exp`	Returns a double value containing e (the base of natural logarithms) raised to the specified power
`Math.log`	Returns a double value containing the natural logarithm of a specified number
`Math.max`	Returns the larger of two numbers
`Math.min`	Returns the smaller of two numbers
`Math.PI`	A constant that specifies the ratio of the circumference of a circle to its diameter
`Math.pow`	Returns the result of raising the first argument to the power of the second argument – an exponentiation.
`Math.round`	Returns the number nearest the specified value
`Math.sign`	Returns an Integer value indicating the sign of a number
`Math.sin`	Returns a double value containing the sine of the specified angle
`Math.sqrt`	Returns a double value specifying the square root of a number
`Math.tan`	Returns a double value containing the tangent of an angle

Examples:

`Math.abs(-5.4)` returns the absolute value of -5.4 (returns 5.4)

`Math.cos(2.3)` returns the cosine of an angle of 2.3 radians

`Math.max(7, 10)` returns the larger of the two numbers (returns 10)

`Math.pow(4, 3)` returns 4 raised to the 3rd power

`Math.sign(-3)` returns the sign on -3 (returns a -1)

`Math.sqrt(4.5)` returns the square root of 4.5

Example 2-1

Savings Account

Start a new project in **NetBeans**. Name the project **Savings**. Delete default code in **Savings.java** file. The idea of this project is to determine how much you save by making monthly deposits into a savings account. For those interested, the mathematical formula used is:

$$F = D [(1 + I)^M - 1] / I$$

where

    F - Final amount
    D - Monthly deposit amount
    I - Monthly interest rate
    M - Number of months

The finished frame will look like this:

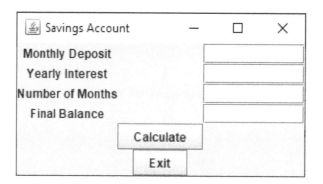

1. We will place 4 labels, 4 text fields, and 2 buttons on the frame. The arrangement in the **GridBagLayout** will be.

	gridx = 0	gridx = 1	gridx = 2
gridy = 0	depositLabel		depositTextField
gridy = 1	interestLabel		interestTextField
gridy = 2	monthsLabel		monthsTextField
gridy = 3	finalLabel		finalTextField
gridy = 4		calculateButton	
gridy = 5		exitButton	

Properties set in code:

Savings Frame:

title	Savings Account

depositLabel:

text	Monthly Deposit
gridx	0
gridy	0

interestLabel:

text	Yearly Interest
gridx	0
gridy	1

monthsLabel:

text	Number of Months
gridx	0
gridy	2

finalLabel:

text	Final Balance
gridx	0
gridy	3

depositTextField:

text	[Blank]
columns	10
gridx	2
gridy	0

interestTextField:

text	[Blank]
columns	10
gridx	2
gridy	1

monthsTextField:

text	[Blank]
columns	10
gridx	2
gridy	2

finalTextField:

text	[Blank]
Columns	10
gridx	2
gridy	3

calculateButton:

text	Calculate
gridx	1
gridy	4

exitButton:

text	Exit
gridx	1
gridy	5

2. We will build the project in three stages – frame, controls, code. Type this basic framework code to establish the frame and its **windowClosing** event:

```
/*
 * Savings.java
 */
package savings;
import javax.swing.*;
import java.awt.*;
import java.awt.event.*;

public class Savings extends JFrame
{
  public static void main(String args[])
  {
    //construct frame
    new Savings().setVisible(true);
  }
  public Savings()
  {
    // code to build the form
    setTitle("Savings Account");
    addWindowListener(new WindowAdapter()
    {
      public void windowClosing(WindowEvent e)
      {
        exitForm(e);
      }
    });
```

```
    getContentPane().setLayout(new GridBagLayout());
  }
  private void exitForm(WindowEvent e)
  {
    System.exit(0);
  }
}
```

Run the code to insure the frame appears (it will be very small and empty – I resized it so I could see the title):

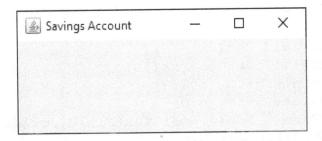

3. Now, we add the controls and empty event methods. Declare and create the 10 controls as class level objects (these lines go after the opening brace at the top of the **Savings** class):

```
JLabel depositLabel = new JLabel();
JLabel interestLabel = new JLabel();
JLabel monthsLabel = new JLabel();
JLabel finalLabel = new JLabel();
JTextField depositTextField = new JTextField();
JTextField interestTextField = new JTextField();
JTextField monthsTextField = new JTextField();
JTextField finalTextField = new JTextField();
JButton calculateButton = new JButton();
JButton exitButton = new JButton();
```

Position and add each control. Add methods for controls we need events for (**calculateButton** and **exitButton** in this case). This code goes at the bottom of the **Savings** constructor method:

```
// position controls (establish event methods)
GridBagConstraints gridConstraints = new
GridBagConstraints();
depositLabel.setText("Monthly Deposit");
gridConstraints.gridx = 0;
gridConstraints.gridy = 0;
getContentPane().add(depositLabel, gridConstraints);
```

```
interestLabel.setText("Yearly Interest");
gridConstraints.gridx = 0;
gridConstraints.gridy = 1;
getContentPane().add(interestLabel, gridConstraints);
monthsLabel.setText("Number of Months");
gridConstraints.gridx = 0;
gridConstraints.gridy = 2;
getContentPane().add(monthsLabel, gridConstraints);
finalLabel.setText("Final Balance");
gridConstraints.gridx = 0;
gridConstraints.gridy = 3;
getContentPane().add(finalLabel, gridConstraints);

depositTextField.setText("");
depositTextField.setColumns(10);
gridConstraints.gridx = 2;
gridConstraints.gridy = 0;
getContentPane().add(depositTextField, gridConstraints);
interestTextField.setText("");
interestTextField.setColumns(10);
gridConstraints.gridx = 2;
gridConstraints.gridy = 1;
getContentPane().add(interestTextField, gridConstraints);
monthsTextField.setText("");
monthsTextField.setColumns(10);
gridConstraints.gridx = 2;
gridConstraints.gridy = 2;
getContentPane().add(monthsTextField, gridConstraints);
finalTextField.setText("");
finalTextField.setColumns(10);
gridConstraints.gridx = 2;
gridConstraints.gridy = 3;
getContentPane().add(finalTextField, gridConstraints);

calculateButton.setText("Calculate");
gridConstraints.gridx = 1;
gridConstraints.gridy = 4;
getContentPane().add(calculateButton, gridConstraints);
calculateButton.addActionListener(new ActionListener()
{
  public void actionPerformed(ActionEvent e)
  {
calculateButtonActionPerformed(e);
  }
});
```

```
exitButton.setText("Exit");
gridConstraints.gridx = 1;
gridConstraints.gridy = 5;
getContentPane().add(exitButton, gridConstraints);
exitButton.addActionListener(new ActionListener()
{
   public void actionPerformed(ActionEvent e)
   {
exitButtonActionPerformed(e);
   }
});
pack();
```

Lastly, add the two methods (empty for now) needed (place after the frame constructor):

```
private void calculateButtonActionPerformed(ActionEvent e)
{
}

private void exitButtonActionPerformed(ActionEvent e)
{
}
```

Run to see the finished control placement:

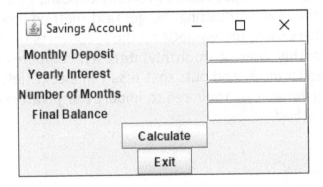

4. Finally, we write code for the two event methods. First, the
   calculateButtonActionPerformed method.

```
private void calculateButtonActionPerformed(ActionEvent e)
{
  double deposit;
  double interest;
  double months;
  double finalBalance;
  double monthlyInterest;
  // read values from text fields
  deposit =
Double.valueOf(depositTextField.getText()).doubleValue();
  interest =
Double.valueOf(interestTextField.getText()).doubleValue();
  monthlyInterest = interest / 1200;
  months =
Double.valueOf(monthsTextField.getText()).doubleValue();
  // compute final value and put in text field;
  finalBalance = deposit * (Math.pow((1 +
monthlyInterest), months) - 1) / monthlyInterest;
  finalTextField.setText(new
DecimalFormat("0.00").format(finalBalance));
}
```

This code reads the three input values (monthly deposit, interest rate, number
of months) from the text fields using the **getText** method, converts those string
variables to numbers using the **valueOf** method, converts the yearly interest
percentage to monthly interest (**monthlyInterest**), computes the final balance
using the provided formula, and puts that result in a text field (after converting
it back to a string variable). You need to import the **java.text.*** components to
use the format method.

5. Now, write code for the **exitButtonActionPerformed** event.

```
private void exitButtonActionPerformed(ActionEvent e)
{
   System.exit(0);
}
```

You're done. For reference, here is the complete **Savings.java** code listing (code added to basic frame code is shaded):

```
/*
 * Savings.java
 */
package savings;
import javax.swing.*;
import java.awt.*;
import java.awt.event.*;
import java.text.*;

public class Savings extends JFrame
{

  JLabel depositLabel = new JLabel();
  JLabel interestLabel = new JLabel();
  JLabel monthsLabel = new JLabel();
  JLabel finalLabel = new JLabel();
  JTextField depositTextField = new JTextField();
  JTextField interestTextField = new JTextField();
  JTextField monthsTextField = new JTextField();
  JTextField finalTextField = new JTextField();
  JButton calculateButton = new JButton();
  JButton exitButton = new JButton();

  public static void main(String args[])
  {
    //construct frame
    new Savings().setVisible(true);
  }

  public Savings()
  {
    // code to build the form
    setTitle("Savings Account");
    addWindowListener(new WindowAdapter()
    {
```

```
    public void windowClosing(WindowEvent e)
    {
      exitForm(e);
    }
  });
  getContentPane().setLayout(new GridBagLayout());

  // position controls (establish event methods)
  GridBagConstraints gridConstraints = new
GridBagConstraints();
  depositLabel.setText("Monthly Deposit");
  gridConstraints.gridx = 0;
  gridConstraints.gridy = 0;
  getContentPane().add(depositLabel, gridConstraints);
  interestLabel.setText("Yearly Interest");
  gridConstraints.gridx = 0;
  gridConstraints.gridy = 1;
  getContentPane().add(interestLabel, gridConstraints);
  monthsLabel.setText("Number of Months");
  gridConstraints.gridx = 0;
  gridConstraints.gridy = 2;
  getContentPane().add(monthsLabel, gridConstraints);
  finalLabel.setText("Final Balance");
  gridConstraints.gridx = 0;
  gridConstraints.gridy = 3;
  getContentPane().add(finalLabel, gridConstraints);

  depositTextField.setText("");
  depositTextField.setColumns(10);
  gridConstraints.gridx = 2;
  gridConstraints.gridy = 0;
  getContentPane().add(depositTextField, gridConstraints);
  interestTextField.setText("");
  interestTextField.setColumns(10);
  gridConstraints.gridx = 2;
  gridConstraints.gridy = 1;
  getContentPane().add(interestTextField, gridConstraints);
  monthsTextField.setText("");
  monthsTextField.setColumns(10);
  gridConstraints.gridx = 2;
  gridConstraints.gridy = 2;
  getContentPane().add(monthsTextField, gridConstraints);
  finalTextField.setText("");
  finalTextField.setColumns(10);
  gridConstraints.gridx = 2;
  gridConstraints.gridy = 3;
  getContentPane().add(finalTextField, gridConstraints);
```

```java
    calculateButton.setText("Calculate");
    gridConstraints.gridx = 1;
    gridConstraints.gridy = 4;
    getContentPane().add(calculateButton, gridConstraints);
    calculateButton.addActionListener(new ActionListener()
    {
      public void actionPerformed(ActionEvent e)
      {
        calculateButtonActionPerformed(e);
      }
    });
    exitButton.setText("Exit");
    gridConstraints.gridx = 1;
    gridConstraints.gridy = 5;
    getContentPane().add(exitButton, gridConstraints);
    exitButton.addActionListener(new ActionListener()
    {
      public void actionPerformed(ActionEvent e)
      {
        exitButtonActionPerformed(e);
      }
    });
    pack();
  }
```

```java
  private void calculateButtonActionPerformed(ActionEvent e)
  {
    double deposit;
    double interest;
    double months;
    double finalBalance;
    double monthlyInterest;
    // read values from text fields
    deposit =
Double.valueOf(depositTextField.getText()).doubleValue();
    interest =
Double.valueOf(interestTextField.getText()).doubleValue();
    monthlyInterest = interest / 1200;
    months =
Double.valueOf(monthsTextField.getText()).doubleValue();
    // compute final value and put in text field;
    finalBalance = deposit * (Math.pow((1 + monthlyInterest),
months) - 1) / monthlyInterest;
    finalTextField.setText(new
DecimalFormat("0.00").format(finalBalance));
  }
```

```
private void exitButtonActionPerformed(ActionEvent e)
{
  System.exit(0);
}

private void exitForm(WindowEvent e)
{
  System.exit(0);
}

}
```

Run the program. Make sure it works properly. Here's a run I tried – see if you get the same numbers:

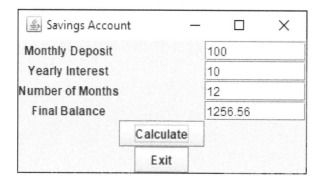

Save the project (**Example2-1** project in the **\LearnJava\LJ Code\Class 2** project group).

Focus Traversal

When you run Example 2-1, notice the cursor appears in the top text field where you enter the Monthly Deposit. Then, upon successive presses of the <Tab> key, you move from one control to the next.

When interacting with a Java GUI application, we can work with a single control at a time. That is, we can click on a single button or type in a single text field. We can't be doing two things at once. The control we are working with is known as the **active** control or we say the control has **focus**. In our **Savings Account** example, when the cursor is in a particular text field, we say that text field has focus. In a properly designed application, focus is shifted from one control to another (in a predictable, orderly fashion) using the <**Tab**> key. Focus can only be given to controls that allow user interaction – buttons and text fields in our example, but not labels.

Java does a good job of defining an orderly tab sequence using something called the **FocusTransversalPolicy**. Essentially, the tab sequence starts in the upper left corner of the **GridBagLayout** and works its way across a row. It then moves down to the next row and continues until it reaches the last column of the last row. At that point, the sequence begins again. The process can be reversed using <**Tab**>in combination with the <**Shift**> key.

There are times you would like to remove a control from the tab sequence (transversal policy). For example, in the savings account, there is no need for the focus to go to the **finalTextField** control, since it is not editable. And we wouldn't want control to go to the **Exit** button to avoid inadvertent stopping of the program. To remove a control (named **myControl**) from the sequence, use:

```
myControl.setFocusable(false);
```

It is also possible to reorder the tab sequence, but that is beyond the scope of this course.

Example 2-2

Savings Account - Setting Focus

This will be a quick modification to our **Savings Account** example to remove the **finalTextField** and **exitButton** controls from the tab sequencing.

1. Modify the code segment adding the **finalTextField** to the form so it is now (new line is shaded):

```
finalTextField.setText("");
finalTextField.setFocusable(false);
finalTextField.setColumns(10);
gridConstraints.gridx = 2;
gridConstraints.gridy = 3;
getContentPane().add(finalTextField, gridConstraints);
```

2. Modify the code segment adding the **exitButton** to the form so it reads (new line is shaded):

```
exitButton.setText("Exit");
exitButton.setFocusable(false);
gridConstraints.gridx = 1;
gridConstraints.gridy = 5;
getContentPane().add(exitButton, gridConstraints);
```

Rerun the project. Notice how the two controls now longer receive focus. When the **Calculate** button has focus, you can press the space bar to '**click**' the button. This is saved as **Example2-2** project in the **\LearnJava\LJ Code\Class 2** project group.

Improving a Java Application

In the previous section, we noted a weakness in the savings application (undesirable tab sequencing) and fixed the problem, improving the performance of our application. This is something you, as a programmer, will do a lot of. You will build an application and while running it and testing it, will uncover weaknesses that need to be eliminated. These weaknesses could be actual errors in the application or just things that, if eliminated, make your application easier to use.

You will find, as you progress as a programmer, that you will spend much of your time improving your applications. You will always find ways to add features to an application and to make it more appealing to your user base. You should never be satisfied with your first solution to a problem. There will always be room for improvement. And Java provides a perfect platform for adding improvements to an application. You can easily add features and test them to see if the desired performance enhancements are attained.

If you run the savings application a few more times, you can identify further weaknesses:

> For example, what happens if you input a zero interest? The program will stop with an error message because the formula that computes the final balance will not work with zero interest.
> As a convenience, it would be nice if when you hit the <**Enter**> key after typing a number, the focus would move to the next control.
> Notice you can type any characters you want in the text fields when you should just be limited to numbers and a single decimal point – any other characters will cause the program to stop with an error message because the string cannot be converted to numbers.

We can (and will) address each of these points as we improve the savings application. But, to do so, requires learning more Java coding. We'll address the zero interest problem first. To solve this problem, we need to be able to make a decision. If the interest is zero, we'll do one computation. If it's not zero, we'll use another. One mechanism for making decisions with Java is the **if** statement.

Java Decisions - if Statements

The concept of an **if** statement for making a decision is very simple. We check to see if a particular **boolean** condition is true. If so, we take a certain action. If not, we do something else. **if** statements are also called **branching** statements. **Branching** statements are used to cause certain actions within a program if a certain condition is met.

The simplest form for the Java **if** statement is:

```
if (condition)
{
    [process this code]
}
```

Here, if **condition** is **true**, the code bounded by the two braces is executed. If **condition** is false, nothing happens and code execution continues after the closing right brace.

Example:

```
if (balance - check < 0)
{
  trouble = true;
  sendLettertoAccount();
}
```

In this case, if **balance - check** is less than zero, two lines of information are processed: **trouble** is set to true and a method sending a letter to the account holder (**sendLettertoAccount**) is executed. Notice the indentation of the code between the two braces. NetBeans (and most IDE's) will automatically do this indentation. It makes understanding (and debugging) your code much easier. You can adjust the amount of indentation NetBeans uses if you like.

What if you want to do one thing if **condition** is true and another if it is false?
Use an **if/else** block:

```
if (condition)
{
    [process this code]
}
else
{
    [process this code]
}
```

In this block, if **condition** is true, the code between the first two braces is
executed. If **condition** is false, the code between the second set of braces is
processed.

Example:

```
if (balance - check < 0)
{
  trouble = true;
  sendLettertoAccount();
}
else
{
  trouble = false;
}
```

Here, the same two lines are executed if you are overdrawn (**balance - check <
0**), but if you are not overdrawn (**else**), the **trouble** flag is turned off.

Lastly, we can test multiple conditions by adding the **else if** statement:

```
if (condition1)
{
    [process this code]
}
else if (condition2)
{
    [process this code]
}
else if (condition3)
{
    [process this code]
}
else
{
    [process this code]
}
```

In this block, if **condition1** is true, the code between the **if** and first **else if** line is executed. If **condition1** is false, **condition2** is checked. If **condition2** is true, the indicated code is executed. If **condition2** is not true, **condition3** is checked. Each subsequent condition in the structure is checked until a true condition is found, an **else** statement is reached or the last closing brace is reached.

Example:

```
if (balance - check < 0)
{
  trouble = true;
  sendLettertoAccount();
}
else if (balance - check == 0)
{
  trouble = false;
  sendWarningLetter();
}
else
{
  trouble = false;
}
```

Now, one more condition is added. If your balance equals the check amount **[else if (balance - check == 0)]**, you're still not in trouble, but a warning is mailed.

In using branching statements, make sure you consider all viable possibilities in the **if/else if** structure. Also, be aware that each **if** and **else if** in a block is tested sequentially. The first time an **if** test is met, the code block associated with that condition is executed and the **if** block is exited. If a later condition is also true, it will never be considered.

Switch Statement - Another Way to Branch

In addition to **if/else if/else** type statements, the **switch** format can be used when there are multiple selection possibilities. **switch** is used to make decisions based on the value of a single variable. The structure is:

```
switch (variable)
{
  case [variable has this value]:
    [process this code]
    break;
  case [variable has this value]:
    [process this code]
    break;
  case [variable has this value]:
    [process this code]
    break;
  default:
    [process this code]
    break;
}
```

The way this works is that the value of **variable** is examined. Each **case** statement is then sequentially examined until the value matches one of the specified cases. Once found, the corresponding code is executed. If no case match is found, the code in the default segment (if there) is executed. The **break** statements transfer program execution to the line following the closing right brace. These statements are optional, but will almost always be there. If a **break** is not executed, all code following the case processed will also be processed (until a **break** is seen or the end of the structure is reached). This is different behavior than **if** statements where only one 'case' could be executed.

As an example, say we've written this code using the **if** statement:

```java
if (age == 5)
{
  category = "Kindergarten";
}
else if (age == 6)
{
  category = "First Grade";
}
else if (age == 7)
{
  category = "Second Grade";
}
else if (age == 8)
{
  category = "Third Grade";
}
else if (age == 9)
{
  category = "Fourth Grade";
}
else
{
  category = "Older Child";
}
```

This will work, but it is ugly code and difficult to maintain.

The corresponding code with **switch** is 'cleaner':

```
switch (age)
{
  case 5:
    category = "Kindergarten";
    break;
  case 6:
    category = "First Grade";
    break;
  case 7:
    category = "Second Grade";
    break;
  case 8:
    category = "Third Grade";
    break;
  case 9:
    category = "Fourth Grade";
    break;
  default:
    category = "Older Child";
    break;
}
```

Control Focus

Earlier we saw that, in a running application, only one control can have user interaction at any one time. We say that control has **focus**. A text field with the cursor has focus - if the user begins typing, the typed characters go in that text box. If a button control has focus, that button can be 'clicked' by simply pressing the space bar.

We also saw that the **<Tab>** key could be used to move from control to control, shifting the focus. Many times, you might like to move focus from one control to another in code, or programmatically. For example, in our savings example, once the user types in a **Deposit Amount**, it would be nice if focus would be moved to the **Interest** text field if the user presses **<Enter>**.

To programmatically give focus to a control (**myControl**), use the **requestFocus** method:

```
myControl.requestFocus();
```

To move from the current control to the next control in the tab sequence, use **transferFocus**:

```
myControl.transferFocus();
```

To move from the current control to the previous control in the tab sequence, use **transerFocusBackward**:

```
myControl.transferFocusBackward();
```

So, where does this code go in our example? When a text field has focus and
<**Enter**> is pressed, the **actionPerformed** method is invoked. Hence, for each
text field where we want to move focus based on keyboard input, we add an
event method and place the needed code there. Adding event methods for a
text field is identical to adding methods for other Swing components. For a text
field named **myTextField**, use:

```
MyField.addActionListener(new ActionListener ()
{
  public void actionPerformed(ActionEvent e)
  {
    myFieldActionPerformed(e);
  }
});
```

and the corresponding event method code to move focus would be:

```
private void myTextFieldActionPerformed(ActionEvent e)
{
  myTextField.transferFocus();
}
```

Input Validation

Recall in the savings example, there is nothing to prevent the user from typing in meaningless characters (for example, letters) into the text fields expecting numerical data. We want to keep this from happening – if the input is not a valid number, it cannot be converted from a string to a number. Whenever getting input from a user using a text field control, we need to **validate** the typed information before using it. Validation rules differ depending on what information you want from the user.

In this example, we will perform **input validation** in a Java method (named **validateDecimalNumber**) we write. The method will examine the text property of a text field, trimming off leading and trailing spaces and checking that the field contains only numbers and a single decimal point. It will return a **boolean** value indicating if a valid number is found. If the number is valid, the method will return a **true** value. If not valid, the method will return a **false** value. It will also blank out the text field and give that control focus, indicating the user needs to retype his/her input.

Here's the method that accomplishes that task (this uses some of the string functions we have seen):

```java
public boolean validateDecimalNumber(JTextField tf)
{
  // checks to see if text field contains
  // valid decimal number with only digits and a single
decimal point
  String s = tf.getText().trim();
  boolean hasDecimal = false;
  boolean valid = true;
  if (s.length() == 0)
  {
    valid = false;
  }
  else
  {
    for (int i = 0; i < s.length(); i++)
    {
      char c = s.charAt(i);
      if (c >= '0' && c <= '9')
      {
        continue;
      }
      else if (c == '.' && !hasDecimal)
```

```
      {
        hasDecimal = true;
      }
      else
      {
        // invalid character found
        valid = false;
      }
    }
  }
  if (valid)
  {
    tf.setText(s);
  }
  else
  {
    tf.setText("");
    tf.requestFocus();
  }
  return (valid);
}
```

You should be able to see how this works. The text field (**tf**) text property is stored in the string **s** (after trimming off leading and trailing spaces). Each character in this string is evaluated to see if it contains only allows number and a single decimal point. If only numbers and a decimal are found, **valid** is **true** and things proceed. If **valid** is **false**, indicating invalid characters or an empty string, the text field is blanked and given focus to allow reentry of the input value.

To use the method on a sample text field **myTextField**, the code is:

```
boolean isOK = validateDecimalNumber(myTextField);
```

If **isOk** is true, no action is taken - calculations can proceed. If **isOk** is false, the user needs to try again.

To make this a more general validation routine, you might also allow the **negative sign** (if, of course, your application uses negative numbers). To do this, you need to check that, if there is such a sign, it only appears in the first position in the input, or else it is also an invalid character.

You'll see how all this (control focus, input validation) works as we continue working with the saving account example.

Example 2-3

Savings Account – Input Validation

We modify the **Savings Account** example to handle a zero interest value. We also add code so if <**Enter**> is pressed, focus is passed to the next control. And, we validate the input values to only allow numbers and a decimal point.

1. Add a listener for the **actionPerformed** event for the **depositTextField** (to allow focus to move). Place this code after the lines placing the control in the frame:

```
depositTextField.addActionListener(new ActionListener()
{
  public void actionPerformed(ActionEvent e)
  {
    depositTextFieldActionPerformed(e);
  }
});
```

And, add the corresponding event method that transfers focus:

```
private void depositTextFieldActionPerformed(ActionEvent
e)
{
  depositTextField.transferFocus();
}
```

2. Add a listener for the **actionPerformed** event for the **interestTextField**. Place this code after the lines placing the control in the frame:

```
interestTextField.addActionListener(new ActionListener()
{
  public void actionPerformed(ActionEvent e)
  {
    interestTextFieldActionPerformed(e);
  }
});
```

And, add the corresponding event method that transfers focus:

```
private void interestTextFieldActionPerformed(ActionEvent
e)
{
  interestTextField.transferFocus();
}
```

3. Add a listener for the **actionPerformed** event for the **monthsTextField**.
    Place this code after the lines placing the control in the frame:

```
monthsTextField.addActionListener(new ActionListener()
{
  public void actionPerformed(ActionEvent e)
  {
    monthsTextFieldActionPerformed(e);
  }
});
```

And, add the corresponding event method that transfers focus:

```
private void monthsTextFieldActionPerformed(ActionEvent e)
{
  monthsTextField.transferFocus();
}
```

4. Modify the **calculateButtonActionPerformed** event code to accommodate a
    zero interest input. Also, add code to validate the values typed in the text
    fields (we use the **validateDecimalNumber** method). The modified routine is
    (new code shaded):

```
private void calculateButtonActionPerformed(ActionEvent e)
{
  double deposit;
  double interest;
  double months;
  double finalBalance;
  double monthlyInterest;
  // make sure each is a valid number
  if (!validateDecimalNumber(monthsTextField) ||
!validateDecimalNumber(interestTextField) ||
!validateDecimalNumber(depositTextField))
  {
    // if one or more fields not valid number, then exit
method
```

```
    return;
  }
  // read values from text fields
  deposit =
Double.valueOf(depositTextField.getText()).doubleValue();
  interest =
Double.valueOf(interestTextField.getText()).doubleValue();
  monthlyInterest = interest / 1200;
  months =
Double.valueOf(monthsTextField.getText()).doubleValue();
  // compute final value and put in text field;
  if (interest == 0)
  {
    finalBalance = deposit * months;
  }
  else
  {
    finalBalance = deposit * (Math.pow((1 +
monthlyInterest), months) - 1) / monthlyInterest;
  }
  finalTextField.setText(new
DecimalFormat("0.00").format(finalBalance));
}
```

In this code, notice each typed value is checked for proper format. Any text fields with improper values are cleared and given focus to allow the user to try again. Calculations do not proceed until all inputs are valid. Also, notice if interest is zero, the final balance is just the deposited amount times the number of months.

5. Add the **validateDecimalNumber** method for input validation (type it after the other methods):

```
public boolean validateDecimalNumber(JTextField tf)
{
  // checks to see if text field contains
  // valid decimal number with only digits and a single
decimal point
  String s = tf.getText().trim();
  boolean hasDecimal = false;
  boolean valid = true;
  if (s.length() == 0)
  {
    valid = false;
  }
  else
```

```
    {
      for (int i = 0; i < s.length(); i++)
      {
        char c = s.charAt(i);
        if (c >= '0' && c <= '9')
        {
          continue;
        }
        else if (c == '.' && !hasDecimal)
        {
          hasDecimal = true;
        }
        else
        {
          // invalid character found
          valid = false;
        }
      }
    }
    if (valid)
    {
      tf.setText(s);
    }
    else
    {
      tf.setText("");
      tf.requestFocus();
    }
    return (valid);
  }
```

The modified **Savings.java** code listing (newly added code is shaded):

```java
/*
 * Savings.java
 */
package savings;
import javax.swing.*;
import java.awt.*;
import java.awt.event.*;
import java.text.*;

public class Savings extends JFrame
{

  JLabel depositLabel = new JLabel();
  JLabel interestLabel = new JLabel();
  JLabel monthsLabel = new JLabel();
  JLabel finalLabel = new JLabel();
  JTextField depositTextField = new JTextField();
  JTextField interestTextField = new JTextField();
  JTextField monthsTextField = new JTextField();
  JTextField finalTextField = new JTextField();
  JButton calculateButton = new JButton();
  JButton exitButton = new JButton();

  public static void main(String args[])
  {
    //construct frame
    new Savings().setVisible(true);
  }

  public Savings()
  {
    // code to build the form
    setTitle("Savings Account");
    addWindowListener(new WindowAdapter()
    {
      public void windowClosing(WindowEvent e)
      {
        exitForm(e);
      }
    });
    getContentPane().setLayout(new GridBagLayout());

    // position controls (establish event methods)
    GridBagConstraints gridConstraints = new
GridBagConstraints();
```

Learn Java GUI Applications

```
depositLabel.setText("Monthly Deposit");
gridConstraints.gridx = 0;
gridConstraints.gridy = 0;
getContentPane().add(depositLabel, gridConstraints);
interestLabel.setText("Yearly Interest");
gridConstraints.gridx = 0;
gridConstraints.gridy = 1;
getContentPane().add(interestLabel, gridConstraints);
monthsLabel.setText("Number of Months");
gridConstraints.gridx = 0;
gridConstraints.gridy = 2;
getContentPane().add(monthsLabel, gridConstraints);
finalLabel.setText("Final Balance");
gridConstraints.gridx = 0;
gridConstraints.gridy = 3;
getContentPane().add(finalLabel, gridConstraints);

depositTextField.setText("");
depositTextField.setColumns(10);
gridConstraints.gridx = 2;
gridConstraints.gridy = 0;
getContentPane().add(depositTextField, gridConstraints);
depositTextField.addActionListener(new ActionListener()
{
  public void actionPerformed(ActionEvent e)
  {
    depositTextFieldActionPerformed(e);
  }
});

interestTextField.setText("");
interestTextField.setColumns(10);
gridConstraints.gridx = 2;
gridConstraints.gridy = 1;
getContentPane().add(interestTextField, gridConstraints);
interestTextField.addActionListener(new ActionListener()
{
  public void actionPerformed(ActionEvent e)
  {
    interestTextFieldActionPerformed(e);
  }
});

monthsTextField.setText("");
monthsTextField.setColumns(10);
gridConstraints.gridx = 2;
gridConstraints.gridy = 2;
```

```java
      getContentPane().add(monthsTextField, gridConstraints);
      monthsTextField.addActionListener(new ActionListener()
      {
        public void actionPerformed(ActionEvent e)
        {
          monthsTextFieldActionPerformed(e);
        }
      });

      finalTextField.setText("");
      finalTextField.setFocusable(false);
      finalTextField.setColumns(10);
      gridConstraints.gridx = 2;
      gridConstraints.gridy = 3;
      getContentPane().add(finalTextField, gridConstraints);

      calculateButton.setText("Calculate");
      gridConstraints.gridx = 1;
      gridConstraints.gridy = 4;
      getContentPane().add(calculateButton, gridConstraints);
      calculateButton.addActionListener(new ActionListener()
      {
        public void actionPerformed(ActionEvent e)
        {
          calculateButtonActionPerformed(e);
        }
      });
      exitButton.setText("Exit");
      exitButton.setFocusable(false);
      gridConstraints.gridx = 1;
      gridConstraints.gridy = 5;
      getContentPane().add(exitButton, gridConstraints);
      exitButton.addActionListener(new ActionListener()
      {
        public void actionPerformed(ActionEvent e)
        {
          exitButtonActionPerformed(e);
        }
      });
      pack();
    }

private void depositTextFieldActionPerformed(ActionEvent e)
{
  depositTextField.transferFocus();
}
```

```
  private void interestTextFieldActionPerformed(ActionEvent
e)
  {
    interestTextField.transferFocus();
  }


  private void monthsTextFieldActionPerformed(ActionEvent e)
  {
    monthsTextField.transferFocus();
  }


  private void calculateButtonActionPerformed(ActionEvent e)
  {
    double deposit;
    double interest;
    double months;
    double finalBalance;
    double monthlyInterest;
    // make sure each is a valid number
    if (!validateDecimalNumber(monthsTextField) ||
!validateDecimalNumber(interestTextField) ||
!validateDecimalNumber(depositTextField))
    {
      // if one or more fields not valid number, then exit
method
      return;
    }
    // read values from text fields
    deposit =
Double.valueOf(depositTextField.getText()).doubleValue();
    interest =
Double.valueOf(interestTextField.getText()).doubleValue();
    monthlyInterest = interest / 1200;
    months =
Double.valueOf(monthsTextField.getText()).doubleValue();
    // compute final value and put in text field;
    if (interest == 0)
    {
      finalBalance = deposit * months;
    }
    else
    {
      finalBalance = deposit * (Math.pow((1 +
monthlyInterest), months) - 1) / monthlyInterest;
    }
    finalTextField.setText(new
DecimalFormat("0.00").format(finalBalance));
```

```
}


private void exitButtonActionPerformed(ActionEvent e)
{
  System.exit(0);
}

private void exitForm(WindowEvent e)
{
  System.exit(0);
}
```

```
public boolean validateDecimalNumber(JTextField tf)
{
  // checks to see if text field contains
  // valid decimal number with only digits and a single
decimal point
  String s = tf.getText().trim();
  boolean hasDecimal = false;
  boolean valid = true;
  if (s.length() == 0)
  {
    valid = false;
  }
  else
  {
    for (int i = 0; i < s.length(); i++)
    {
      char c = s.charAt(i);
      if (c >= '0' && c <= '9')
      {
        continue;
      }
      else if (c == '.' && !hasDecimal)
      {
        hasDecimal = true;
      }
      else
      {
        // invalid character found
        valid = false;
      }
    }
  }
  if (valid)
  {
```

```
      tf.setText(s);
  }
  else
  {
    tf.setText("");
    tf.requestFocus();
  }
  return (valid);
}
}
```

Rerun the application and test the input validation performance. If you type anything other than numbers and a single decimal point, upon clicking **Calculate**, the improper input box should be pointed out to you. Watch how focus moves from control to control upon pressing <**Enter**>. Make sure you get a correct answer with zero interest. Save the application (**Example2-3** project in the **\LearnJava\LJ Code\Class 2** project group).

Java Looping

Many applications require repetition of certain code segments. For example, you may want to roll a die (simulated die of course) until it shows a six. Or, you might generate financial results until a certain sum of returns has been achieved. This idea of repeating code is called iteration or **looping**.

In Java, looping is done with one of two formats. The first is the **while** loop:

```
while (condition)
{
    [process this code]
}
```

In this structure, the code block in braces is repeated 'as long as' the **boolean** expression **condition** is true. Note a **while** loop structure will not execute even once if the **while** condition is false the first time through. If we do enter the loop, it is assumed at some point **condition** will become false to allow exiting. Notice <u>there is no semicolon</u> after the **while** statement.

This brings up a very important point – if you use a loop, make sure you can get out of the loop!! It is especially important in the event-driven environment of Java GUI applications. As long as your code is operating in some loop, no events can be processed. You can also exit a loop using the **break** statement. This will get you out of a loop and transfer program control to the statement following the loop's closing brace. Of course, you need logic in a loop to decide when a break is appropriate.

You can also use a **continue** statement within a loop. When a continue is encountered, all further steps in the loop are skipped and program operation is transferred to the top of the loop.

Example:

```
counter = 1;
while (counter <= 1000)
{
    counter += 1;
}
```

This loop repeats as long as (**while**) the variable **counter** is less than or equal to 1000.

Another example:

```
rolls = 0;
counter = 0;
while (counter < 10)
{
  // Roll a simulated die
  roll += 1;
  if (myRandom.nextInt(6) + 1 == 6)
  {
    counter += 1;
  }
}
```

This loop repeats **while** the **counter** variable is less than10. The **counter** variable is incremented each time a simulated die rolls a 6. The **roll** variable tells you how many rolls of the die were needed to reach 10 sixes.

A **do/while** structure:

```
do
{
    [process this code]
}
while (condition);
```

This loop repeats 'as long as' the **boolean** expression **condition** is true. The loop is always executed at least once. Somewhere in the loop, **condition** must be changed to false to allow exiting. Notice <u>there is a semicolon</u> after the while statement.

Examples:

```
sum = 0;
do
{
   sum += 3;
}
while (sum <= 50);
```

In this example, we increment a **sum** by 3 until that **sum** exceeds 50 (or **while** the **sum** is less than or equal to 50).

Another example:

```
sum = 0;
counter = 0;
do
{
   // Roll a simulated die
   sum += myRandom.nextInt(6) + 1;
   counter += 1;
}
while (sum <= 30);
```

This loop rolls a simulated die **while** the **sum** of the rolls does not exceed 30. It also keeps track of the number of rolls (**counter**) needed to achieve this **sum**.

Again, make sure you can always get out of a loop! Infinite loops are never nice. Sometimes the only way out is rebooting your machine!

Java Counting

With **while** and **do/while** structures, we usually didn't know, ahead of time, how many times we execute a loop or iterate. If you know how many times you need to iterate on some code, you want to use Java **counting**. Counting is useful for adding items to a list or perhaps summing a known number of values to find an average.

Java counting is accomplished using the **for** loop:

```
for (initialization; expression; update)
{
    [process this code]
}
```

The **initialization** step is executed <u>once</u> and is used to initialize a counter variable. The **expression** step is executed <u>before</u> each repetition of the loop. If **expression** is true, the code is executed; if false, the loop is exited. The **update** step is executed <u>after</u> each loop iteration. It is used to update the counter variable.

Example:

```
for (degrees = 0; degrees <= 360; degrees += 10)
{
  // convert to radians
  r = degrees * Math.PI / 180;
  a = Math.Sin(r);
  b = Math.Cos(r);
  c = Math.Tan(r);
}
```

In this example, we compute trigonometric functions for angles from 0 to 360 **degrees** in increments of 10 degrees. It is assumed that all variables have been properly declared.

Another Example:

```
for (countdown = 10; countdown <= 0; countdown--)
{
   timeTextField.setText(String.valueOf(countdown));
}
```

NASA called and asked us to format a text field control to count down from 10 to 0. The loop above accomplishes the task. Note the use of the **decrement** operator.

And, Another Example:

```
double[] myValues = new double[100];
sum = 0;
for (int i = 0; i < 100; i++)
{
   sum += myValues[i];
}
average = sum / 100;
```

This code finds the average value of 100 numbers stored in the array **myValues**. It first sums each of the values in a **for** loop. That **sum** is then divided by the number of terms (100) to yield the average. Note the use of the **increment** operator. Also, notice the counter variable **i** is declared in the initialization step. This is a common declaration in a loop. Such **loop level variables** lose their values once the loop is completed.

You may exit a **for** loop early using a **break** statement. This will transfer program control to the statement following the closing brace. Use of a **continue** statement will skip all statements remaining in the loop and return program control to the **for** statement.

Example 2-4

Savings Account - Decisions

As built, our **Savings Account** application is useful, but we can add more capability. For example, what if we know how much money we need in a number of months and the interest our deposits can earn. It would be nice if the program could calculate the needed month deposit. Or, what if we want to know how long it will take us to reach a goal, knowing how much we can deposit each month and the related interest. Here, we modify the **Savings Account** project to allow entering any three values and computing the fourth.

1. First, add a third button control that will clear all of the text fields. Assign the following properties:

clearButton:

text	Clear
focusable	false
gridx	2
gridy	4

Add the code to declare and create this button. The code to position it on the form and add a listener is:

```
clearButton.setText("Clear");
clearButton.setFocusable(false);
gridConstraints.gridx = 2;
gridConstraints.gridy = 4;
getContentPane().add(clearButton, gridConstraints);
clearButton.addActionListener(new ActionListener()
{
  public void actionPerformed(ActionEvent e)
  {
    clearButtonActionPerformed(e);
  }
});
```

and the method that clears the text fields is:

```
private void clearButtonActionPerformed(ActionEvent e)
{
  // clear text fields
  depositTextField.setText("");
  interestTextField.setText("");
  monthsTextField.setText("");
  finalTextField.setText("");
  depositTextField.requestFocus();
}
```

This code simply blanks out the four text boxes when the **Clear** button is clicked. It then redirects focus to the **depositTextField** control.

2. We will now (sometimes) type information into the **Final Balance** text field. Related to this, change the **focusable** property to **true**. We also need a **actionPerformed** event method for the **finalTextField** control. Add the listener:

```
finalTextField.addActionListener(new ActionListener()
{
  public void actionPerformed(ActionEvent e)
  {
    finalTextFieldActionPerformed(e);
  }
});
```

and the method moving focus is:

```
private void finalTextFieldActionPerformed(ActionEvent e)
{
  finalTextField.transferFocus();
}
```

Recall, we need this code because we can now enter information into the **Final Balance** text field. It is very similar to the other methods. This code moves focus to the **calculateButton** control if <Enter> is hit.

3. We need to modify the **actionPerformed** method of the **calculateButton** to compute the information in the "empty" text field. We also need to validate the **finalTextField** input. The modified code is (new code is shaded):

```java
private void calculateButtonActionPerformed(ActionEvent e)
{
    double deposit;
    double interest;
    double months;
    double finalBalance;
    double monthlyInterest;
    double finalCompute, intChange;
    int intDirection;
    // make sure each is a valid number
    // Determine which box is blank
    // Compute that missing value and put in text box
    if (depositTextField.getText().trim().equals(""))
    {
        // deposit missing
        // read other values from text fields
        // make sure valid before computing
        if (!validateDecimalNumber(monthsTextField) ||
!validateDecimalNumber(interestTextField) ||
!validateDecimalNumber(finalTextField))
        {
            // if one or more fields not valid number, then exit
method
            return;
        }
        interest =
Double.valueOf(interestTextField.getText()).doubleValue();
        monthlyInterest = interest / 1200;
        months =
Double.valueOf(monthsTextField.getText()).doubleValue();
        finalBalance =
Double.valueOf(finalTextField.getText()).doubleValue();
        if (interest == 0)
        {
            deposit = finalBalance / months;
        }
        else
        {
            deposit = finalBalance / ((Math.pow((1 +
monthlyInterest), months) - 1) / monthlyInterest);
        }
```

```
      depositTextField.setText(new
DecimalFormat("0.00").format(deposit));
  }
  else if (interestTextField.getText().trim().equals(""))
  {
    // interest missing - requires iterative solution
    // intChange is how much we change interest each step
    // intDirection is direction (+ or -) we change
interest
    // read other values from text fields
    // make sure valid before computing
    if (!validateDecimalNumber(monthsTextField) ||
!validateDecimalNumber(depositTextField) ||
!validateDecimalNumber(finalTextField))
    {
      // if one or more fields not valid number, then exit
method
      return;
    }
    deposit =
Double.valueOf(depositTextField.getText()).doubleValue();
    months =
Double.valueOf(monthsTextField.getText()).doubleValue();
    finalBalance =
Double.valueOf(finalTextField.getText()).doubleValue();
    interest = 0;
    intChange = 1;
    intDirection = 1;
    do
    {
      interest += intDirection * intChange;
      monthlyInterest = interest / 1200;
      finalCompute = deposit * (Math.pow((1 +
monthlyInterest), months) - 1) / monthlyInterest;
      if (intDirection == 1)
      {
        if (finalCompute > finalBalance)
        {
          intDirection = -1;
          intChange /= 10;
        }
      }
      else
      {
        if (finalCompute < finalBalance)
        {
          intDirection = 1;
```

```
                intChange /= 10;
            }
        }
    }
    while (Math.abs(finalCompute - finalBalance) >=
0.005);
    interestTextField.setText(new
DecimalFormat("0.00").format(interest));
  }
  else if (monthsTextField.getText().trim().equals(""))
  {
    // months missing
    // read other values from text fields
    // make sure valid before computing
    if (!validateDecimalNumber(depositTextField) ||
!validateDecimalNumber(interestTextField) ||
!validateDecimalNumber(finalTextField))
    {
      // if one or more fields not valid number, then exit
method
      return;
    }
    deposit =
Double.valueOf(depositTextField.getText()).doubleValue();
    interest =
Double.valueOf(interestTextField.getText()).doubleValue();
    monthlyInterest = interest / 1200;
    finalBalance =
Double.valueOf(finalTextField.getText()).doubleValue();
    if (interest == 0)
    {
      months = finalBalance / deposit;
    }
    else
    {
      months = Math.log(finalBalance * monthlyInterest /
deposit + 1) / Math.log(1 + monthlyInterest);
    }
    monthsTextField.setText(new
DecimalFormat("0.00").format(months));
  }
  else if (finalTextField.getText().trim().equals(""))
  {
    // Final value missing
    // compute final value and put in text field;
    // read other values from text fields
    // make sure valid before computing
```

```
    if (!validateDecimalNumber(monthsTextField) ||
!validateDecimalNumber(interestTextField) ||
!validateDecimalNumber(depositTextField))
    {
        // if one or more fields not valid number, then exit
method
        return;
    }
    deposit =
Double.valueOf(depositTextField.getText()).doubleValue();
    interest =
Double.valueOf(interestTextField.getText()).doubleValue();
    monthlyInterest = interest / 1200;
    months =
Double.valueOf(monthsTextField.getText()).doubleValue();
    if (interest == 0)
    {
      finalBalance = deposit * months;
    }
    else
    {
      finalBalance = deposit * (Math.pow((1 +
monthlyInterest), months) - 1) / monthlyInterest;
    }
    finalTextField.setText(new
DecimalFormat("0.00").format(finalBalance));
  }
}
```

In this code, first, we validate the input information. Then, we reread the text information from all four text boxes and based on which one is blank (the **trim** method strips off leading and trailing blanks), compute the missing information and display it in the corresponding text box.

Let's look at the math involved in solving for missing information. Recall the equation given in Example 2-1:

$$F = D \, [\, (1 + I)^M - 1] \, / \, I$$

where F is the final amount, D the deposit, I the monthly interest, and M the number of months. This is the equation we've been using to solve for **finalBalance** and we still use it here if the **finalBalance** field is empty, unless the **interest** is zero. For zero interest, we use:

$$F = DM, \text{ if } \textbf{interest} \text{ is zero}$$

See if you can find these equations in the code.

If the **deposit** field is empty, we can solve the equation for D (the needed quantity):

$$D = F/ \, \{[\, (1 + I)^M - 1] \, / \, I\}$$

If the **interest** is zero, this equation will not work. In that case, we use:

$$D = F/M, \text{ if } \textbf{interest} \text{ is zero}$$

You should be able to find these equations in the code above.

Solving for missing **months** information requires knowledge of logarithms. I'll just give you the equation:

$$M = \log (FI \, / \, D + 1) \, / \, \log (1 + I)$$

In this Java, the logarithm (**log**) function is one of the math functions, **Math.log**. Like the other cases, we need a separate equation for zero **interest**:

$$M = F/D, \text{ if } \textbf{interest} \text{ is zero}$$

Again, see if you can find these equations in the code.

If the **interest** value is missing, we need to resort to a widely used method for solving equations – we'll guess! But, we'll use a structured guessing method. Here's what we'll do. We'll start with a zero interest and increase it by one percent until the computed final amount is larger than the displayed final amount. At that point, we know the interest is too high so, we decrease the interest by a smaller amount (0.1 percent) until the computed final amount is less than the displayed final amount, meaning the interest is too low. We start increasing the interest again (this time by 0.01 percent). We'll repeat this process until the computed final amount is within 1/2 cent of the displayed amount. This kind of process is called **iteration** and is used often in computer programs. You should be able to see each step in the code – a good example of a **do** loop.

Don't be intimidated by the code in this example. I'll admit there's a lot of it! Upon study, though, you should see that it is just a straightforward list of instructions for the computer to follow based on input from the user.

For reference, the final **Savings.java** code listing (newly added code is shaded) is:

```java
/*
 * Savings.java
 */
package savings;
import javax.swing.*;
import java.awt.*;
import java.awt.event.*;
import java.text.*;
public class Savings extends JFrame
{
    JLabel depositLabel = new JLabel();
    JLabel interestLabel = new JLabel();
    JLabel monthsLabel = new JLabel();
    JLabel finalLabel = new JLabel();
    JTextField depositTextField = new JTextField();
    JTextField interestTextField = new JTextField();
    JTextField monthsTextField = new JTextField();
    JTextField finalTextField = new JTextField();
    JButton calculateButton = new JButton();
    JButton exitButton = new JButton();
    JButton clearButton = new JButton();
    public static void main(String args[])
    {
        //construct frame
        new Savings().setVisible(true);
```

```java
  }
  public Savings()
  {
    // code to build the form
    setTitle("Savings Account");
    addWindowListener(new WindowAdapter()
    {
      public void windowClosing(WindowEvent e)
      {
        exitForm(e);
      }
    });
    getContentPane().setLayout(new GridBagLayout());
    // position controls (establish event methods)
    GridBagConstraints gridConstraints = new
GridBagConstraints();
    depositLabel.setText("Monthly Deposit");
    gridConstraints.gridx = 0;
    gridConstraints.gridy = 0;
    getContentPane().add(depositLabel, gridConstraints);
    interestLabel.setText("Yearly Interest");
    gridConstraints.gridx = 0;
    gridConstraints.gridy = 1;
    getContentPane().add(interestLabel, gridConstraints);
    monthsLabel.setText("Number of Months");
    gridConstraints.gridx = 0;
    gridConstraints.gridy = 2;
    getContentPane().add(monthsLabel, gridConstraints);
    finalLabel.setText("Final Balance");
    gridConstraints.gridx = 0;
    gridConstraints.gridy = 3;
    getContentPane().add(finalLabel, gridConstraints);

    depositTextField.setText("");
    depositTextField.setColumns(10);
    gridConstraints.gridx = 2;
    gridConstraints.gridy = 0;
    getContentPane().add(depositTextField, gridConstraints);
    depositTextField.addActionListener(new ActionListener()
    {
      public void actionPerformed(ActionEvent e)
      {
        depositTextFieldActionPerformed(e);
      }
    });

    interestTextField.setText("");
```

```java
interestTextField.setColumns(10);
gridConstraints.gridx = 2;
gridConstraints.gridy = 1;
getContentPane().add(interestTextField, gridConstraints);
interestTextField.addActionListener(new ActionListener()
{
  public void actionPerformed(ActionEvent e)
  {
    interestTextFieldActionPerformed(e);
  }
});

monthsTextField.setText("");
monthsTextField.setColumns(10);
gridConstraints.gridx = 2;
gridConstraints.gridy = 2;
getContentPane().add(monthsTextField, gridConstraints);
monthsTextField.addActionListener(new ActionListener()
{
  public void actionPerformed(ActionEvent e)
  {
    monthsTextFieldActionPerformed(e);
  }
});

finalTextField.setText("");
finalTextField.setFocusable(true);
finalTextField.setColumns(10);
gridConstraints.gridx = 2;
gridConstraints.gridy = 3;
getContentPane().add(finalTextField, gridConstraints);
finalTextField.addActionListener(new ActionListener()
{
  public void actionPerformed(ActionEvent e)
  {
    finalTextFieldActionPerformed(e);
  }
});

calculateButton.setText("Calculate");
gridConstraints.gridx = 1;
gridConstraints.gridy = 4;
getContentPane().add(calculateButton, gridConstraints);
calculateButton.addActionListener(new ActionListener()
{
  public void actionPerformed(ActionEvent e)
  {
```

```
          calculateButtonActionPerformed(e);
      }
  });
  exitButton.setText("Exit");
  exitButton.setFocusable(false);
  gridConstraints.gridx = 1;
  gridConstraints.gridy = 5;
  getContentPane().add(exitButton, gridConstraints);
  exitButton.addActionListener(new ActionListener()
  {
    public void actionPerformed(ActionEvent e)
    {
      exitButtonActionPerformed(e);
    }
  });
  clearButton.setText("Clear");
  clearButton.setFocusable(false);
  gridConstraints.gridx = 2;
  gridConstraints.gridy = 4;
  getContentPane().add(clearButton, gridConstraints);
  clearButton.addActionListener(new ActionListener()
  {
    public void actionPerformed(ActionEvent e)
    {
      clearButtonActionPerformed(e);
    }
  });
  pack();
}
private void depositTextFieldActionPerformed(ActionEvent e)
{
  depositTextField.transferFocus();
}
private void interestTextFieldActionPerformed(ActionEvent
e)
{
  interestTextField.transferFocus();
}
private void monthsTextFieldActionPerformed(ActionEvent e)
{
  monthsTextField.transferFocus();
}
private void finalTextFieldActionPerformed(ActionEvent e)
{
  finalTextField.transferFocus();
}
private void calculateButtonActionPerformed(ActionEvent e)
```

```
{
  double deposit;
  double interest;
  double months;
  double finalBalance;
  double monthlyInterest;
  double finalCompute, intChange;
  int intDirection;
  // make sure each is a valid number
  // Determine which box is blank
  // Compute that missing value and put in text box
  if (depositTextField.getText().trim().equals(""))
  {
    // deposit missing
    // read other values from text fields
    // make sure valid before computing
    if (!validateDecimalNumber(monthsTextField) ||
!validateDecimalNumber(interestTextField) ||
!validateDecimalNumber(finalTextField))
    {
      // if one or more fields not valid number, then exit
method
      return;
    }
    interest =
Double.valueOf(interestTextField.getText()).doubleValue();
    monthlyInterest = interest / 1200;
    months =
Double.valueOf(monthsTextField.getText()).doubleValue();
    finalBalance =
Double.valueOf(finalTextField.getText()).doubleValue();
    if (interest == 0)
    {
      deposit = finalBalance / months;
    }
    else
    {
      deposit = finalBalance / ((Math.pow((1 +
monthlyInterest), months) - 1) / monthlyInterest);
    }
    depositTextField.setText(new
DecimalFormat("0.00").format(deposit));
  }
  else if (interestTextField.getText().trim().equals(""))
  {
    // interest missing - requires iterative solution
    // intChange is how much we change interest each step
```

```
       // intDirection is direction (+ or -) we change
interest
       // read other values from text fields
       // make sure valid before computing
       if (!validateDecimalNumber(monthsTextField) ||
!validateDecimalNumber(depositTextField) ||
!validateDecimalNumber(finalTextField))
       {
          // if one or more fields not valid number, then exit
method
          return;
       }
       deposit =
Double.valueOf(depositTextField.getText()).doubleValue();
       months =
Double.valueOf(monthsTextField.getText()).doubleValue();
       finalBalance =
Double.valueOf(finalTextField.getText()).doubleValue();
       interest = 0;
       intChange = 1;
       intDirection = 1;
       do
       {
          interest += intDirection * intChange;
          monthlyInterest = interest / 1200;
          finalCompute = deposit * (Math.pow((1 +
monthlyInterest), months) - 1) / monthlyInterest;
          if (intDirection == 1)
          {
            if (finalCompute > finalBalance)
            {
              intDirection = -1;
              intChange /= 10;
            }
          }
          else
          {
            if (finalCompute < finalBalance)
            {
              intDirection = 1;
              intChange /= 10;
            }
          }
       }
       while (Math.abs(finalCompute - finalBalance) >= 0.005);
       interestTextField.setText(new
DecimalFormat("0.00").format(interest));
```

```
    }
    else if (monthsTextField.getText().trim().equals(""))
    {
      // months missing
      // read other values from text fields
      // make sure valid before computing
      if (!validateDecimalNumber(depositTextField) ||
!validateDecimalNumber(interestTextField) ||
!validateDecimalNumber(finalTextField))
      {
        // if one or more fields not valid number, then exit
method
        return;
      }
      deposit =
Double.valueOf(depositTextField.getText()).doubleValue();
      interest =
Double.valueOf(interestTextField.getText()).doubleValue();
      monthlyInterest = interest / 1200;
      finalBalance =
Double.valueOf(finalTextField.getText()).doubleValue();
      if (interest == 0)
      {
        months = finalBalance / deposit;
      }
      else
      {
        months = Math.log(finalBalance * monthlyInterest /
deposit + 1) / Math.log(1 + monthlyInterest);
      }
      monthsTextField.setText(new
DecimalFormat("0.00").format(months));
    }
    else if (finalTextField.getText().trim().equals(""))
    {
      // Final value missing
      // compute final value and put in text field;
      // read other values from text fields
      // make sure valid before computing
      if (!validateDecimalNumber(monthsTextField) ||
!validateDecimalNumber(interestTextField) ||
!validateDecimalNumber(depositTextField))
      {
        // if one or more fields not valid number, then exit
method
        return;
      }
```

```
      deposit =
Double.valueOf(depositTextField.getText()).doubleValue();
      interest =
Double.valueOf(interestTextField.getText()).doubleValue();
      monthlyInterest = interest / 1200;
      months =
Double.valueOf(monthsTextField.getText()).doubleValue();
      if (interest == 0)
      {
        finalBalance = deposit * months;
      }
      else
      {
        finalBalance = deposit * (Math.pow((1 +
monthlyInterest), months) - 1) / monthlyInterest;
      }
      finalTextField.setText(new
DecimalFormat("0.00").format(finalBalance));
    }
  }
  private void exitButtonActionPerformed(ActionEvent e)
  {
    System.exit(0);
  }
  private void clearButtonActionPerformed(ActionEvent e)
  {
    // clear text fields
    depositTextField.setText("");
    interestTextField.setText("");
    monthsTextField.setText("");
    finalTextField.setText("");
    depositTextField.requestFocus();
  }
  private void exitForm(WindowEvent e)
  {
    System.exit(0);
  }
  public boolean validateDecimalNumber(JTextField tf)
  {
    // checks to see if text field contains
    // valid decimal number with only digits and a single
decimal point
    String s = tf.getText().trim();
    boolean hasDecimal = false;
    boolean valid = true;
    if (s.length() == 0)
    {
```

```java
        valid = false;
    }
    else
    {
      for (int i = 0; i < s.length(); i++)
      {
        char c = s.charAt(i);
        if (c >= '0' && c <= '9')
        {
          continue;
        }
        else if (c == '.' && !hasDecimal)
        {
          hasDecimal = true;
        }
        else
        {
          // invalid character found
          valid = false;
        }
      }
    }
    if (valid)
    {
      tf.setText(s);
    }
    else
    {
      tf.setText("");
      tf.requestFocus();
    }
    return (valid);
  }
}
```

Run the application. Try successively providing three pieces of information and seeing how the program computes the missing value. Here's a run I made (note the new **Clear** button):

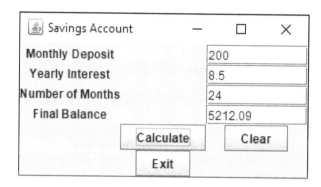

When done testing, save your application (**Example2-4** project in the **\LearnJava\LJ Code\Class 2** project group). Now, relax!.

Class Review

After completing this class, you should understand:

> ➤ Java statements and their use
> ➤ The Java assignment operator, mathematics operators, comparison and logic operators and concatenation operators
> ➤ The wide variety of built-in Java methods, especially string methods, the random number generator, and mathematics methods
> ➤ How to manage the tab transversal policy
> ➤ The **if** structure used for branching and decisions
> ➤ The **switch** decision structure
> ➤ How to validate input from text field controls
> ➤ The concept of control focus and how to assign focus in code
> ➤ How the **do** structure is used in conjunction with the **while** statements
> ➤ How the **for** loop is used for counting

Practice Problems 2

Problem 2-1. Random Number Problem. Build an application where each time a button is clicked, a random number from 1 to 100 is displayed.

Problem 2-2. Price Problem. The neighborhood children built a lemonade stand. The hotter it is, the more they can charge. Build an application that produces the selling price, based on temperature:

Temperature	Price
<50	Don't bother
50 – 60	20 Cents
61 – 70	25 Cents
71 – 80	30 Cents
81 – 85	40 Cents
86 – 90	50 Cents
91 – 95	55 Cents
96 – 100	65 Cents
>100	75 Cents

Problem 2-3. Odd Integers Problem. Build an application that adds consecutive odd integers (starting with one) until the sum exceeds a target value. Display the sum and how many integers were added.

Problem 2-4. Pennies Problem. Here's an old problem. Today, I'll give you a penny. Tomorrow, I'll give you two pennies. I'll keep doubling the amount I'll give you for 30 days. How much will you have at the end of the month (better use a **long** integer type to keep track)?

Problem 2-5. Code Problem. Build an application with a text field and two buttons. Type a word or words in the text field. Click one of the buttons. Subtract one from the Unicode value for each character in the typed word(s), then redisplay it. This is a simple encoding technique. When you click the other button, reverse the process to decode the word.

Exercise 2-1

Computing a Mean and Standard Deviation

Develop an application that allows the user to input a sequence of numbers. When done inputting the numbers, the program should compute the mean of that sequence and the standard deviation. If N numbers are input, with the ith number represented by x_i, the formula for the mean ($\bar{x}$) is:

$$\bar{x} = (\sum_{i=1}^{N} x_i)/ N$$

and to compute the standard deviation (s), take the square root of this equation:

$$s^2 = [N\sum_{i=1}^{N} x_i^2 - (\sum_{i=1}^{N} x_i)^2]/[N(N-1)]$$

The Greek sigmas in the above equations simply indicate that you add up all the corresponding elements next to the sigma. If the standard deviation equation scares you, just write code to find the average value – you should have no trouble with that one.

Exercise 2-2

Flash Card Addition Problems

Write an application that generates random addition problems. Provide some kind of feedback and scoring system as the problems are answered.

3

Java Swing Controls

Review and Preview

We have now learned and practiced the three steps in developing a Java GUI application (frame, controls, code) and have reviewed the Java language. In this class, we begin to look (in detail) at controls available from the Java Swing library.

We will revisit some controls we already know and learn a lot of new controls. Examples of how to use each control will be presented.

Function Overloading

As we delve further into Java, we will begin to use many of its built-in methods for dialog boxes, drawing graphics, and other tasks. Before using these methods (we will use the method to display an **confirm dialog** soon), you need be aware of an object-oriented concept known as **overloading**.

Overloading lets a method vary its behavior based on its input arguments. Java will have multiple methods with the same name, but with different argument lists. The different argument lists may have different numbers of arguments and different types of arguments.

What are the implications of overloading? What this means to us is that when using a Java method, there will be several different ways to use that method. In these notes, we will show you a few ways, but not all. You are encouraged to investigate all ways to use a method.

Overloading is a powerful feature of Java. You will quickly become accustomed to using multiple definitions of methods.

Confirm Dialog (JOptionPane)

An often used dialog box in Java GUI applications is a **confirm dialog** (also known as a **message box**). This dialog lets you display messages to your user and receive feedback for further information. It can be used to display error messages, describe potential problems or just to show the result of some computation. A confirm dialog is implemented with the Java Swing **JOptionPane** class. The confirm dialog is versatile, with the ability to display any message, an optional icon, and a selected set of buttons. The user responds by clicking a button in the confirm dialog box.

You've seen confirm dialog boxes if you've ever used a Windows (or other OS) application. Think of all the examples you've seen. For example, confirm dialogs are used to ask you if you wish to save a file before exiting and to warn you if a disk drive is not ready. For example, if while writing these notes in Microsoft Word, I attempt to exit, I see this confirm dialog:

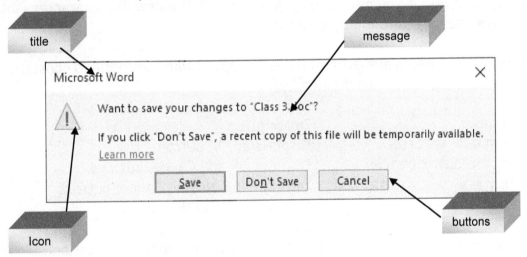

In this confirm dialog box, the different parts that you control have been labeled. You will see how you can format a confirm dialog box any way you desire.

To use the **confirm dialog** method, you decide what the **message** should be, what **title** you desire, and what **icon** and **buttons** are appropriate. To display the confirm dialog box in code, you use the **showConfirmDialog** method.

The showConfirmDialog method is **overloaded** with several ways to implement the dialog box. Some of the more common ways are:

```
JOptionPane.showConfirmDialog(null, message);
JOptionPane.showConfirmDialog(null, message, title,
buttons);
JOptionPane.showConfirmDialog(null, message, title,
buttons, icon);
```

In these implementations, if **icon** is omitted, a question mark is displayed. If **buttons** is omitted, **Yes**, **No**, **Cancel** buttons are displayed. And, if **title** is omitted, a title of **"Select an Option"** is displayed. The first argument (**null**) must be there - it indicates the confirm dialog box is associated with the current frame.

As mentioned, you decide what you want for the confirm dialog **message** and **title** information (string data types). Be aware there is no limit to how long the message can be. If you have a long message, use the new line character (**\n**) to break the message into multiple lines.

The other arguments are defined by Java **JOptionPane** predefined constants. The **buttons** constants are defined by:

Member	Description
DEFAULT_OPTION	Displays an OK button
OK_CANCEL_OPTION	Displays OK and Cancel buttons
YES_NO_CANCEL_OPTION	Displays Yes, No and Cancel buttons
YES_NO_OPTION	Displays Yes and No buttons

The syntax for specifying a choice of buttons is the usual dot-notation:

```
JOptionPane.Member
```

So, to display an **OK** and **Cancel** button, the constant is:

```
JOptionPane.OK_CANCEL_OPTION
```

The displayed icon is established by another set of constants:

Member	Description
PLAIN_MESSAGE	Display no icon
INFORMATION_MESSAGE	Displays an information icon
ERROR_MESSAGE	Displays an error icon
WARNING_MESSAGE	Displays an exclamation point icon
QUESTION_MESSAGE	Displays a question mark icon

To specify an icon, the syntax is:

```
JOptionPane.Member
```

To display an error icon, use:

```
JOptionPane.ERROR_MESSAGE
```

When you invoke the **showOptionDialog** method, the method returns a **JOptionPane** constant (an **int** type) indicating the user response. The available members are:

Member	Description
CLOSED_OPTION	Window closed without pressing button
OK_OPTION	The OK button was selected
YES_OPTION	The Yes button was selected
NO_OPTION	The No button was selected
CANCEL_OPTION	The Cancel button was selected

Confirm Dialog Example:

This little code snippet (the second line is very long):

```
int response;
response = JOptionPane.showConfirmDialog(null, "This is an
example of an confirm dialog box.", "Example",
JOptionPane.YES_NO_OPTION,
JOptionPane.INFORMATION_MESSAGE);
if (response == JOptionPane.YES_OPTION)
{
// Pressed Yes
}
else if (response == JOptionPane.NO_OPTION)
{
// Pressed No
}
else
{
// Closed window without pressing button
}
```

displays this message box:

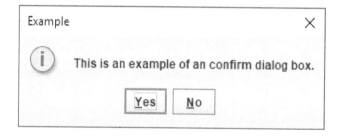

Of course, you would need to add code for the different tasks depending on whether **Yes** or **No** is clicked by the user (or the window is simply closed).

Another **Confirm Dialog Example:**

Many times, you just want to display a quick message to the user with no need for feedback (just an **OK** button). This code does the job:

```
JOptionPane.showConfirmDialog(null, "Quick message for
you.", "Hey you!!", JOptionPane.DEFAULT_OPTION,
JOptionPane.PLAIN_MESSAGE);
```

The resulting message box:

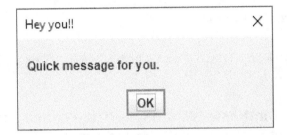

Notice there is no icon and the **OK** button is shown. Also, notice in the code, there is no need to read the returned value – we know what it is! You will find a lot of uses for this simple form of the message box (with perhaps some kind of icon) as you progress in Java.

We almost ready to start our study of the Java Swing controls, looking at important properties, methods and events for many controls. But, before starting, let's look at two concepts that help us "dress up" our GUI applications – font and color objects.

Font Object

In all of the GUI applications we have built so far, we have used the default font associated with the Swing controls (buttons, labels and text fields). Using the default font is limiting – and boring. Let's see how to modify the font used by a control to display information.

To change the default font assigned to a control, we introduce the idea of the **Font object**. The font object is the structure used by Java to define all characteristics of a particular font (name, style, size). To change the font associated with a control named **myControl**, use the **setFont** method:

```
myControl.setFont(new Font(fontName, fontStyle,
fontSize));
```

In this line of code, **fontName** is a string variable defining the name of the font and **fontSize** is an integer value defining the font size in points.

The **fontStyle** argument is a **Font** constant defining the style of the font. It has three possible values:

Value	Description
PLAIN	Regular text
BOLD	Bold text
ITALIC	Italic text

The basic (no effects) font is defined by **Font.PLAIN**. To add any effects, use the corresponding constant. If the font has more than one effect, combine them using a plus sign (+). For example, if you want an italicized, bold font, the **fontStyle** argument in the **Font** constructor would be:

```
Font.ITALIC + Font.BOLD
```

Let's look at a couple of examples. To change a button control (**myButton**) font to **Arial**, **Bold**, Size **24**, use:

```
myButton.setFont(new Font("Arial", Font.BOLD, 24));
```

or, to change the font in a text field (**myTextField**) to **Courier New**, **Italic**, **Bold**, Size **12**, use:

```
myTextField.setFont(new Font("Courier New", Font.ITALIC +
FontStyle.BOLD, 12));
```

You can also define a variable to be of type **Font**. Declare the variable according to the usual scope considerations:

```
Font myFont;
```

Then, assign a font to that variable for use in other controls:

```
myFont = new Font("Courier New", Font.PLAIN, 12);
thisControl.setFont(myFont);
thatControl.setFont(myFont);
```

The above can be shortened by defining the font at the same time it is declared:

```
Font myFont = new Font("Courier New", Font.PLAIN, 12);
```

Color Object

Colors play a big part in Java GUI applications. The background color of the frame and other controls can be set to a particular color. The text color in these controls is set by the foreground color. Later, when we study graphics methods, we will see that lines, rectangles, ovals can all be drawn and filled in various colors. These colors must be defined in Java code. How do we do this? There are two approaches we will take: (1) use built-in colors and (2) create a color.

The colors built into Java are specified by the **Color object**. Such a color is specified using:

```
Color.colorName
```

where **colorName** is a reserved color name. There are thirteen standard color names:

Darker colors: Lighter colors:

If for some reason, the selections built into the **Color** object do not fit your needs, you can create your own color using one of over 16 million different combinations. The code to create an **RGB** color named **myColor** is:

```
Color myColor = new Color(redValue, greenValue,
   blueValue);
```

where **redValue**, **greenValue**, and **blueValue** are integer measures of intensity of the corresponding primary colors. These measures can range from 0 (least intensity) to 255 (greatest intensity). For example, **new Color(255, 255, 0)** will produce yellow.

It is easy to specify colors using the **Color** object. Any time you need a color, just use one of the built-in colors or create your own using different red, green, and blue values. These techniques can be used anywhere Java requires a color. For example, to change a frame's (**myFrame**) background color, we use:

```
myFrame.getContentPane().setBackground(Color.colorName);
```

We color the **content pane** since this is the pane controls are placed on. So, you get a yellow background with:

```
myFrame.getContentPane().setBackground(Color.YELLOW);
```

Or knowing some red, green and blue combination:

```
myFrame.getContentPane().setBackground(new Color(redValue,
greenValue, blueValue));
```

You can also change the background and foreground colors of controls. To get white writing on a blue button control (**myButton**), you would use:

```
myButton.setBackground(Color.BLUE);
myButton.setForeground(Color.WHITE);
```

Some controls are transparent by default, meaning any background color assigned will not appear. To change this, we need to set such a control's **opaque** property to true. For example, to set the background color of a label , named **myLabel**, to white, you need two lines of code:

```
myLabel.setOpaque(true);
myLabel.setBackground(Color.WHITE);
```

We'll start using colors in our examples to show you further uses of color.

You can also define variables that take on color values. Say we want to define a variable named **myRed** to represent the color red. First, declare your variable to be of type **Color**:

```
Color myRed;
```

Then, define your color in code using:

```
myRed = Color.RED;
```

From this point on, you can use **myRed** anywhere the red color is desired. You can declare and define colors in the same line of code, if you like. For the above example, you would write:

```
Color myRed = Color.RED;
```

Now, let's start looking at the Swing controls. First, we study the most important 'control,' the frame.

JFrame Object

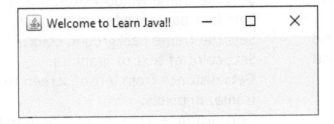

The **frame** is the object where the user interface is built. Every application we build **extends** the **JFrame** object, meaning our applications acquire all the characteristics of a frame. It is central to the development of Java GUI applications. The frame is a **container** object, since it 'holds' other controls. One feature of a container object is that if its **visible** property is set to false, all controls will become invisible.

Here, we present some of the more widely used **Properties**, **Methods** and **Events** for the frame. Recall **properties** describe the appearance and value of a control, **methods** are actions you can impose on controls and **events** occur when something is done to the control (usually by a user). This is not an exhaustive list – consult other Java resources for such a list. You may not recognize all of these terms now. They will be clearer as you progress in the course. The same is true for the remaining controls presented in this chapter.

Frame Properties:

title	Frame window title.
font	Font name, style, size.
background	Frame background color.
foreground	Color of text or graphics.
x	Distance from left of screen to left edge of frame, in pixels.
y	Distance from top of screen to top edge of frame, in pixels.
width	Width of frame in pixels.
height	Height of frame in pixels.
resizable	Boolean value indicating if frame is fixed size or resizable.
visible	If false, hides the frame (and all its controls).

Frame Methods:

setTitle	Sets the frame window title.
setFont	Sets font name, style, size.
setBackground	Sets the frame background color.
setForeground	Sets color of text or graphics.
getX	Gets distance from left of screen to left edge of frame, in pixels.
getY	Gets distance from top of screen to top edge of frame, in pixels.
getWidth	Gets width of frame in pixels.
getHeight	Gets height of frame in pixels.
setBounds	Used to position frame on screen.
setResizable	Sets boolean value indicating if frame is fixed size or resizable.
setVisible	Sets boolean value to indicate if frame is visible or not.

Frame Event:

windowClosing	Occurs (**WindowEvent**) when the form is closing. Added with **WindowListener** using **WindowAdapter**.

The listener for the **windowClosing** event is added in the frame constructor method using:

```
addWindowListener(new WindowAdapter()
{
public void windowClosing(WindowEvent e)
{
    exitForm(e);
}
});
```

And, the usual **exitForm** method is:

```
private void exitForm(WindowEvent e)
{
System.exit(0);
}
```

Typical use of **frame** object (for each control in this, and following chapters, we will provide information for how that control or object is typically used):

> ➢ Create frame object, employing the usual frame constructor method.
> ➢ Set the **title** property.
> ➢ Center the frame in the middle of the screen (we'll talk about how to do this next).
> ➢ Set **resizable** property to **false**. You can have resizable forms in Java GUI applications, but we will not use resizable forms in this course.
> ➢ Add listener for **windowClosing** event.
> ➢ Attach **GridBagLayout** manager. Place controls in the grid layout manager and execute a **pack** method.

A general framework of Java code to perform these steps for a frame named **MyFrame** (file must be saved in a package folder **myframe** as **MyFrame.java**) is:

```
/*
 * MyFrame.java
 */
package myframe;
import javax.swing.*;
import java.awt.*;
import java.awt.event.*;

public class MyFrame extends JFrame
{
  public static void main(String args[])
  {
    //construct frame
    new MyFrame().setVisible(true);
  }

  public MyFrame()
  {
    // code to build the form
    setTitle("My Frame");
    setResizable(false);
    addWindowListener(new WindowAdapter()
    {
      public void windowClosing(WindowEvent e)
      {
        exitForm(e);
      }
    });
```

```
    getContentPane().setLayout(new GridBagLayout());
    // code to position controls follows
      .
      .
      .

    pack();
  }
  private void exitForm(WindowEvent e)
  {
    System.exit(0);
  }
}
```

Frame Layout and Centering

Have you noticed how, in every application we've built so far, that the frame always starts out in the upper left corner of your screen? It would be nice if the frame were centered in the screen when the application begins. Here, we show you how to do that and more. First, let's see how the frame size is established by the **GridBagLayout** manager.

We use the **GridBagLayout** manager to set up our GUI applications (you can, of course, choose to use any layout manager you want). Recall, with this manager, a grid is used to place controls:

	gridx = 0	gridx = 1	gridx = 2	gridx = 3	gridx = 4
gridy = 0					
gridy = 1					
gridy = 2					
gridy = 3					
gridy = 4					
gridy = 5					

The **GridBagConstraints** object is used for control placement and positioning within the various grid elements. Controls are placed in this grid by referring to a particular column (**gridx** location) and row (**gridy** location). We have seen that the grid (and frame) automatically grows as controls are added. Column widths are set by the "widest" control in a particular column. And, row heights are set by the "tallest" control in a particular row.

There are other variables associated with **GridBagConstraints** that can be used to adjust control size and, hence, associated column, row, and frame size. A control can occupy more than one column or row. The number of columns spanned by a control is set with the **gridwidth** variable; the number of rows spanned is set with the **gridheight** variable. By default, a control fills one row and one column. If we have a **GridBagConstraints** object named **gridConstraints**, a control will occupy two rows and three columns, starting in the second column (**gridx = 1**) and fourth row (**gridy = 3**), with this code:

```
gridConstraints.gridx = 1;
gridConstraints.gridy = 3;
gridConstraints.gridheight = 2;
gridConstraints.gridwidth = 3;
```

In our example grid, this control would be placed like this:

	gridx = 0	gridx = 1	gridx = 2	gridx = 3	gridx = 4
gridy = 0					
gridy = 1					
gridy = 2					
gridy = 3		**Control goes here**			
gridy = 4					
gridy = 5					

A particular control may completely fill its region or may not. If the control is smaller than its allocated region, its dimensions may be adjusted to fill the region – use the **fill** variable. There are four values:

`GridBagConstraints.NONE`	Control is not resized (default value)
`GridBagConstraints.HORIZONTAL`	Control width fills display area.
`GridBagConstraints.VERTICAL`	Control height fills display area.
`GridBagConstraints.BOTH`	Control fills entire display area.

With our example **gridConstraints** object, a control will grow to fill the region width using:

```
gridConstraints.fill = GridBagConstraints.HORIZONTAL;
```

This control would look like this in its grid region:

Smaller changes in control size can be made using the **ipadx** and **ipady** variables. These determine how much a control size is to be increased beyond its minimum size (in each direction). To add five pixels to the width and height of a control using our **gridConstraints** example:

```
gridConstraints.ipadx = 5;
gridConstraints.ipady = 5;
```

If you choose not to expand a control to fill its area, its position within its allocated area is set with the **anchor** variable. There are nine possible values:

`GridBagConstraints.NORTH`	Control is centered at top
`GridBagConstraints.NORTHEAST`	Control is in upper right corner
`GridBagConstraints.EAST`	Control is at right, centered
vertically	
`GridBagConstraints.SOUTHEAST`	Control is in lower right corner
`GridBagConstraints.SOUTH`	Control is centered at bottom
`GridBagConstraints.SOUTHWEST`	Control is in lower left corner
`GridBagConstraints.WEST`	Control is at left, centered vertically
`GridBagConstraints.NORTHWEST`	Control is in upper left corner
`GridBagConstraints.CENTER`	Control is centered horizontally and
vertically	

To center a control (in both directions) in its display area, use:

```
gridConstraints.anchor = GridBagConstraints.CENTER;
```

This control would look like this in its grid region:

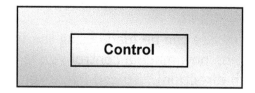

If a control completely fills its allocated display area, a border region (free space) can be established around the control using the **Insets** object. Four values are used to define the top, left, bottom and right side margins from the side of the display area. The default is **Insets(0, 0, 0, 0)**. With our example, if we want 10 pixels of space at the top and bottom, 20 on the left and 30 on the right, we would use:

```
gridConstraints.insets = new Insets(10, 20, 10, 30);
```

This control would look something like this in its grid region:

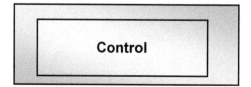

Once the **gridConstraints** are established for a control, it is added to the frame's content pane using the **add** method. If the control is **myControl**, the code syntax is:

```
getContentPane().add(myControl, gridConstraints);
```

I think you are starting to see the flexibility available with the **GridBagLayout** manager. Remember to establish all grid constraint values before adding a control to the grid. We will start using some of these new concepts in building our example applications. You, too, are encouraged to learn these ideas and use them to "beautify" your GUI interfaces.

Building an interface is an "art," not a science. You will see the process involves lots of trial and error and adjustments. And sometimes, you get results you would never expect – components may not appear as you wish or may not appear at all! The bottom line is – once all adjustments are made, your final frame size is established and we can finally learn how to do the task we started out with – centering the frame in the screen.

First, to place a frame (**width** by **height** in size) at a horizontal position **left** and vertical position **top**, we use the **setBounds** method:

```
setBounds(left, top, width, height);
```

All the dimensions are **int** types and measured in pixels. To center a frame in the computer screen, we need to know find **left** and **top**.

To find the centering position, we need two things: the dimensions of the frame (use **getWidth** and **getHeight** methods) and the dimensions of the screen. The dimensions of the screen are held in the frame's **'toolkit'**. A **Dimension** object holds the information we need. To retrieve this object, use:

```
Dimension screenSize =
Toolkit.getDefaultToolkit().getScreenSize();
```

With this, **screenSize.width** holds the screen width and **screenSize.height** holds the screen height. So, the code to center the frame using **setBounds** is:

```
setBounds((int) (0.5 * (screenSize.width - getWidth())),
(int) (0.5 * (screenSize.height - getHeight())),
getWidth(), getHeight());
```

This code needs to be after the **pack** method in the code establishing the frame, so that proper frame size is used. We'll use this centering code in every application built in the remainder of this course. Any initializations for a project will be placed after this line in the frame constructor.

JButton Control

We've seen the **button** control before. It is probably the most widely used Java GUI control. It is used to begin, interrupt, or end a particular process. Here, we provide some of the more widely used properties, methods and events for the button control.

Button Properties:

text	String displayed on button.
font	Font name, style, size.
background	Button background color.
foreground	Color of text.
icon	Picture displayed on button
enabled	If false, button is visible, but cannot accept clicks.
visible	If false, hides the button.

Button Methods:

setText	Sets the button text.
setFont	Sets font name, style, size.
setBackground	Sets the button background color.
setForeground	Sets color of text.
setEnabled	Sets boolean value to indicate if button is clickable or not.
setVisible	Sets boolean value to indicate if button is visible or not.
doClick	Generates a click event for a button.

Button Event:

actionPerformed	Event (**ActionEvent**) triggered when button is selected either by clicking on it or by pressing the space bar. Added with **ActionListener**.

To add a listener for the **actionPerformed** event for a button control named **myButton**, use:

```
myButton.addActionListener(new ActionListener()
{
  public void actionPerformed(ActionEvent e)
  {
    myButtonActionPerformed(e);
  }
});
```

And, the corresponding event code would be placed in a **myButtonActionPerformed** method:

```
private void myButtonActionPerformed(ActionEvent e)
{
    [method code]
}
```

Typical use of **button** control:

Declare and create button, assigning an identifiable **name**. For **myButton**, the statement is:

```
JButton myButton = new JButton();
```

> Set **text** property.
> Place control within layout manager.
> Add listener for and write code in the button's **actionPerformed** event.
> You may also want to change the **font**, **background** and **foreground** properties.

JLabel Control

JLabel

A **label** control is used to display text that a user can't edit directly. The text of a label control can be changed in response to events.

Label Properties:

text	String displayed in label.
font	Font name, style, size.
background	Label background color.
foreground	Color of text.
opaque	Determines whether the control is opaque or not.
horizontalAlignment	Horizontal position of text
verticalAlignment	Vertical position of text
border	Type of border used (if any)

Label Methods:

setText	Sets the label text.
setFont	Sets font name, style, size.
setBackground	Sets the label background color.
setForeground	Sets color of text.
setOpaque	If true, background colors can be applied.
setHorizontalAlignment	Sets horizontal position of text
setVerticalAlignment	Sets vertical position of text
setBorder	Used to establish border (if any) around label (see **BorderFactory** class)

Label Event:

mouseClicked	Event (**MouseEvent**) triggered when label is clicked by mouse (useful for selecting among label choices). Added with **MouseListener** using **MouseAdapter**.

The code to add the **mouseClicked** event for a label named **myLabel** is:

```
myLabel.addMouseListener(new MouseAdapter()
{
  public void mouseClicked(MouseEvent e)
  {
    myLabelMouseClicked(e);
  }
});
```

And, the **myLabelMouseClicked** method is:

```
private void myLabelMouseClicked(MouseEvent e)
{
   [Method code]
}
```

There are three possible values for the label text **horizontalAlignment**:

```
SwingConstants.LEFT        Text left justified
SwingConstants.CENTER      Text center justified
SwingConstants.RIGHT       Text right justified
```

and there are three values for **verticalAlignment**:

```
SwingConstants.TOP         Text is 'top' justified
SwingConstants.CENTER      Text is center justified vertically
SwingConstants.BOTTOM      Text is 'bottom' justified
```

So, you can see there are nine possible alignments.

A border is sometimes added to a label control "mimic" the beveled appearance of the text field. To add such a border to a label named **myLabel**, use:

```
myLabel.setBorder(BorderFactory.createLoweredBevelBorder()
);
```

There are many other possible borders. Consult the usual references for help on the **BorderFactory**.

Typical use of **label** control for static, unchanging display:

> ➤ Declare and create label, assigning an identifiable **name**. For **myLabel**, the statement is:

```
JLabel myLabel = new JLabel();
```

> ➤ Set the **text** property when frame is created.
> ➤ Place control within layout manager.
> ➤ You may also want to change the **font**, **background** and **foreground** properties.

Typical use of **label** control for changing display:

> ➤ Declare and create label, assigning an identifiable **name**. For **myLabel**, the statement is:

```
JLabel myLabel = new JLabel();
```

> ➤ Initialize **text** to desired string.
> ➤ Set **text** property (**String** type) in code where needed.
> ➤ Place control within layout manager.
> ➤ You may also want to change the **font**, **background** and **foreground** properties.

JTextField Control

JTextField

A **text field** control is used to display a single line of information initialized when the frame is created, entered by a user at run-time, or assigned within code. The displayed text may be edited.

Text Field Properties:

text	String displayed in text field.
font	Font name, style, size.
background	Text field background color.
foreground	Color of text.
columns	Displayed width of text field.
horizontalAlignment	Horizontal position of text
editable	Indicates whether text in the text field is read-only.

Text Field Methods:

setText	Sets the text field text.
getText	Retrieves the text field text.
setFont	Sets font name, style, size.
setBackground	Sets the text field background color.
setForeground	Sets color of text.
setColumns	Sets the number of columns.
setHorizontalAlignment	Sets the horizontal alignment.
setEditable	If set to false, text field cannot be edited.

Text Field Event:

actionPerformed	Occurs (**ActionEvent**) when the user presses <**Enter**>. Added with **ActionListener**.

To add a listener for the **actionPerformed** event for a button control named **myTextField**, use:

```
myTextField.addActionListener(new ActionListener()
{
  public void actionPerformed(ActionEvent e)
  {
    myTextFieldActionPerformed(e);
  }
});
```

And, the corresponding event code would be placed in a **myTextFieldActionPerformed** method:

```
private void myTextFieldActionPerformed(ActionEvent e)
{
    [method code]
}
```

There are three possible values for **horizontalAlignment**:

`SwingConstants.LEFT`	Text left justified
`SwingConstants.CENTER`	Text center justified
`SwingConstants.RIGHT`	Text right justified

Typical use of **text field** control as display control:

> Declare and create text field, assigning an identifiable **name**. Assign a **columns** value. For **myTextField**, the statement is:

```
JTextField myTextField = new JTextField();
```

> Initialize **text** property to desired string.
> Set **editable** property to **false**.
> Set **text** property in code where needed.
> Place control within layout manager.
> You may also want to change the **font**, **background** and **foreground** properties.

Typical use of **text field** control as input device:

> ➤ Declare and create text field, assigning an identifiable **name**. Assign a **columns** value. For **myTextField**, the statement is:

```
JTextField myTextField = new JTextField();
```

> ➤ Initialize **text** property to desired string.
> ➤ Place control within layout manager.
> ➤ Add listener for **actionPerformed** event.
> ➤ In code, give **focus** (use **requestFocus** method) to control when needed. Read **text** property when **actionPerformed** event occurs.
> ➤ You may also want to change the **font**, **background** and **foreground** properties.

Use of the text field control (and any control where the user types something) should be minimized if possible. Whenever you give a user the option to type something, it makes your job as a programmer more difficult. You need to validate the information they type to make sure it will work with your code (recall the **Savings Account** example in the last class, where we needed to make sure valid decimal numbers were being entered). There are many controls in Java that are 'point and click,' that is, the user can make a choice simply by clicking with the mouse. We'll look at such controls through the course. Whenever these 'point and click' controls can be used to replace a text field, do it!

JTextArea Control

The text field control (**JTextField**) can only display a single line of information. A related control which allows multiple lines of text (in a single font) is the **text area** control. Like the text field, this control can be used to display information initialized when the frame is created, entered by a user at run-time, or assigned within code. The displayed text may be edited.

Text Area Properties:

text	String displayed in text area.
font	Font name, style, size.
background	Text area background color.
foreground	Color of text.
columns	Displayed width of text area.
rows	Displayed height of text area.
lineCount	Number of lines of text.
lineWrap	Boolean variable indicating if text should be "word wrapped" – default is false.
wrapStyleWord	If true (and lineWrap is true), words are wrapped at word boundaries.
editable	Indicates whether text in the text area is read-only.

Text Area Methods:

setText	Sets the text area text.
getText	Retrieves the text area text.
setFont	Sets font name, style, size.
setBackground	Sets the text area background color.
setForeground	Sets color of text.
setColumns	Sets the number of columns.
setRows	Sets the number of rows.
setLineWrap	Turns line wrap on and off.
setWrapStyleWord	Turns wrap style on and off.
setEditable	If set to false, text area cannot be edited.

Typical use of **text area** control as display control:

> ➢ Declare and create text area, assigning an identifiable **name**. Assign **columns** and **rows** values. For **myTextArea**, the statement is:

```
JTextArea myTextArea = new JTextArea();
```

> ➢ Set **lineWrap** and **wrapStyleWord** to true.
> ➢ Initialize **text** property to desired string.
> ➢ Set **editable** property to **false**.
> ➢ Set **text** property in code where needed.
> ➢ Place control within layout manager.
> ➢ You may also want to change the **font**, **background** and **foreground** properties.

Typical use of **text area** control as input device:

> ➢ Declare and create text area, assigning an identifiable **name**.   Assign **columns** and **rows** values. For **myTextArea**, the statement is:

```
JTextArea myTextArea = new JTextArea();
```

> ➢ Set **lineWrap** and **wrapStyleWord** to true.
> ➢ Initialize **text** property to desired string.
> ➢ Place control within layout manager.
> ➢ In code, give **focus** (use **requestFocus** method) to control when needed. Read **text** property when **actionPerformed** event occurs.
> ➢ You may also want to change the **font**, **background** and **foreground** properties.

When you begin to use the text area control, you will notice there is no scrolling available. Fortunately, it is easy to embed a **JTextArea** control into another Swing component, the **JScrollPane** (discussed later in this class) to implement both horizontal and vertical scroll bars.

Example 3-1

Password Validation

Start a new project in **NetBeans**. Name the project **Password**. Delete default code in Java file named **Password**. The idea of this project is to ask the user to input a password. If correct, a confirm dialog box appears to validate the user. If incorrect, other options are provided. This example will use another control, **JPasswordField** to input the password. This control is nearly identical to the **JTextField** control with one major difference. When a user types in the password field an **echoChar** is seen, masking the typed entry. The default **echoChar** is an asterisk (*). The finished frame will be:

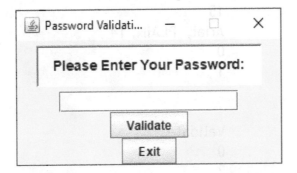

1. We place two buttons, a label control, and a password field on the frame. The **GridBagLayout** arrangement is:

	gridx = 0
gridy = 0	passwordLabel
gridy = 1	inputPasswordField
gridy = 2	validButton
gridy = 3	exitButton

Properties set in code:

Password Frame:

title	Password Validation
resizable	false
background	YELLOW

passwordLabel:

text	Please Enter Your Password:
opaque	true
background	WHITE
border	Lower beveled
font	Arial, BOLD, 14
setHorizontalAlignment	CENTER
insets	(5, 20, 5, 20)
ipadx	30
ipady	20
gridx	0
gridy	0

inputPasswordField:

text	[blank]
columns	15
font	Arial, PLAIN, 14
gridx	0
gridy	1

validButton:

text	Validate
gridx	0
gridy	2

exitButton:

text	Exit
gridx	0
gridy	3

2. We will build the project in the usual three stages – frame, controls, code. Type this basic framework code to build and center the frame:

```java
/*
 * Password.java
 */
package password;
import javax.swing.*;
import java.awt.*;
import java.awt.event.*;

public class Password extends JFrame
{
```

```java
  public static void main(String args[])
  {
    //construct frame
    new Password().setVisible(true);
  }

  public Password()
  {
    // code to build the form
    setTitle("Password Validation");
    getContentPane().setBackground(Color.YELLOW);
    setResizable(false);
    addWindowListener(new WindowAdapter()
    {
      public void windowClosing(WindowEvent e)
      {
        exitForm(e);
      }
    });
    getContentPane().setLayout(new GridBagLayout());
    pack();
    Dimension screenSize =
Toolkit.getDefaultToolkit().getScreenSize();
    setBounds((int) (0.5 * (screenSize.width -
getWidth())), (int) (0.5 * (screenSize.height -
getHeight())), getWidth(), getHeight());
  }

  private void exitForm(WindowEvent e)
  {
    System.exit(0);
  }

}
```

Run the code to make sure the frame (at least, what there is of it at this point) appears and is centered in the screen (it is also fixed size – the 'expand' button in the title area is grayed out):

Note (in the code) we set the background color of the content pane to yellow. This can't be seen. It will be more apparent when the controls are added.

3. Now, we can add the controls and empty event methods. Declare and create the four controls as class level objects:

```
JLabel passwordLabel = new JLabel();
JPasswordField inputPasswordField = new JPasswordField();
JButton validButton = new JButton();
JButton exitButton = new JButton();
```

Position and add each control. Add methods for controls we need events for (**inputPasswordField, validButton, exitButton**). Note a new **gridConstraints** is created for each control – this makes sure no values from previous controls "leak over" to the next control (this code immediately precedes the **pack()** statement):

```
// position controls
GridBagConstraints gridConstraints;
passwordLabel.setText("Please Enter Your Password:");
passwordLabel.setOpaque(true);
passwordLabel.setBackground(Color.white);
passwordLabel.setFont(new Font("Arial", Font.BOLD, 14));
passwordLabel.setBorder(BorderFactory.createLoweredBevelBo
rder());
passwordLabel.setHorizontalAlignment(SwingConstants.CENTER
);
gridConstraints = new GridBagConstraints();
gridConstraints.ipadx = 30;
gridConstraints.ipady = 20;
gridConstraints.gridx = 0;
gridConstraints.gridy = 0;
gridConstraints.insets = new Insets(5, 20, 5, 20);
getContentPane().add(passwordLabel, gridConstraints);

inputPasswordField.setText("");
inputPasswordField.setFont(new Font("Arial", Font.PLAIN,
14));
inputPasswordField.setColumns(15);
gridConstraints = new GridBagConstraints();
gridConstraints.gridx = 0;
gridConstraints.gridy = 1;
getContentPane().add(inputPasswordField, gridConstraints);
inputPasswordField.addActionListener(new ActionListener()
{
  public void actionPerformed(ActionEvent e)
  {
    inputPasswordFieldActionPerformed(e);
  }
```

```
});

validButton.setText("Validate");
gridConstraints = new GridBagConstraints();
gridConstraints.gridx = 0;
gridConstraints.gridy = 2;
getContentPane().add(validButton, gridConstraints);
validButton.addActionListener(new ActionListener()
{
  public void actionPerformed(ActionEvent e)
  {
    validButtonActionPerformed(e);
  }
});

exitButton.setText("Exit");
gridConstraints = new GridBagConstraints();
gridConstraints.gridx = 0;
gridConstraints.gridy = 3;
getContentPane().add(exitButton, gridConstraints);
exitButton.addActionListener(new ActionListener()
{
  public void actionPerformed(ActionEvent e)
  {
    exitButtonActionPerformed(e);
  }
});
```

Lastly, add the three empty methods:

```
private void inputPasswordFieldActionPerformed(ActionEvent
e)
{
}

private void validButtonActionPerformed(ActionEvent e)
{
}

private void exitButtonActionPerformed(ActionEvent e)
{
}
```

Run the project to see the finished control arrangement:

4. Now, we write code for the events. First, the
    inputPasswordFieldActionPerformed method:

```
private void inputPasswordFieldActionPerformed(ActionEvent
e)
{
  validButton.doClick();
}
```

When **<Enter>** is pressed, the **Validate** button is clicked.

5. Now, the code for the **validButtonActionPerformed** method:

```
private void validButtonActionPerformed(ActionEvent e)
{
  final String THEPASSWORD = "LetMeIn";
  //This procedure checks the input password
  int response;
  if (inputPasswordField.getText().equals(THEPASSWORD))
  {
    // If correct, display message box
    JOptionPane.showConfirmDialog(null, "You've passed
security!", "Access Granted", JOptionPane.DEFAULT_OPTION,
JOptionPane.WARNING_MESSAGE);
  }
  else
  {
    // If incorrect, give option to try again
    response = JOptionPane.showConfirmDialog(null,
"Incorrect password - Try Again?", "Access Denied",
JOptionPane.YES_NO_OPTION, JOptionPane.ERROR_MESSAGE);
    if (response == JOptionPane.YES_OPTION)
    {
      inputPasswordField.setText("");
      inputPasswordField.requestFocus();
    }
    else
    {
      exitButton.doClick();
    }
  }
}
```

This code checks the input password to see if it matches the stored value (set as a constant **THEPASSWORD** = "LetMeIn"- change if if you want). If correct, it prints an acceptance message. If incorrect, it displays a confirm dialog box to that effect and asks the user if they want to try again. If **Yes**, another try is granted. If **No**, the program is ended.

6. Use the following code in the **exitButtonActionPerformed** method:

```
private void exitButtonActionPerformed(ActionEvent e)
{
   System.exit(0);
}
```

For reference, here is the complete **Password.java** code listing (code added to basic frame code is shaded):

```
/*
 * Password.java
 */
package password;
import javax.swing.*;
import java.awt.*;
import java.awt.event.*;

public class Password extends JFrame
{
   JLabel passwordLabel = new JLabel();
   JPasswordField inputPasswordField = new JPasswordField();
   JButton validButton = new JButton();
   JButton exitButton = new JButton();

   public static void main(String args[])
   {
      //construct frame
      new Password().setVisible(true);
   }

   public Password()
   {
      // code to build the form
      setTitle("Password Validation");
      setResizable(false);
      getContentPane().setBackground(Color.yellow);
      addWindowListener(new WindowAdapter()
      {
         public void windowClosing(WindowEvent e)
         {
            exitForm(e);
         }
      });
      getContentPane().setLayout(new GridBagLayout());
```

```java
    // position controls
    GridBagConstraints gridConstraints;
    passwordLabel.setText("Please Enter Your Password:");
    passwordLabel.setOpaque(true);
    passwordLabel.setBackground(Color.white);
    passwordLabel.setFont(new Font("Arial", Font.BOLD, 14));

passwordLabel.setBorder(BorderFactory.createLoweredBevelBorde
r());

passwordLabel.setHorizontalAlignment(SwingConstants.CENTER);
    gridConstraints = new GridBagConstraints();
    gridConstraints.ipadx = 30;
    gridConstraints.ipady = 20;
    gridConstraints.gridx = 0;
    gridConstraints.gridy = 0;
    gridConstraints.insets = new Insets(5, 20, 5, 20);
    getContentPane().add(passwordLabel, gridConstraints);

    inputPasswordField.setText("");
    inputPasswordField.setFont(new Font("Arial", Font.PLAIN,
14));
    inputPasswordField.setColumns(15);
    gridConstraints = new GridBagConstraints();
    gridConstraints.gridx = 0;
    gridConstraints.gridy = 1;
    getContentPane().add(inputPasswordField,
gridConstraints);
    inputPasswordField.addActionListener(new ActionListener()
    {
      public void actionPerformed(ActionEvent e)
      {
        inputPasswordFieldActionPerformed(e);
      }
    });
    validButton.setText("Validate");
    gridConstraints = new GridBagConstraints();
    gridConstraints.gridx = 0;
    gridConstraints.gridy = 2;
    getContentPane().add(validButton, gridConstraints);
    validButton.addActionListener(new ActionListener()
    {
      public void actionPerformed(ActionEvent e)
      {
        validButtonActionPerformed(e);
      }
```

```
    });
    exitButton.setText("Exit");
    gridConstraints = new GridBagConstraints();
    gridConstraints.gridx = 0;
    gridConstraints.gridy = 3;
    getContentPane().add(exitButton, gridConstraints);
    exitButton.addActionListener(new ActionListener()
    {
      public void actionPerformed(ActionEvent e)
      {
        exitButtonActionPerformed(e);
      }
    });
    pack();
    Dimension screenSize =
Toolkit.getDefaultToolkit().getScreenSize();
    setBounds((int) (0.5 * (screenSize.width - getWidth())),
(int) (0.5 * (screenSize.height - getHeight())), getWidth(),
getHeight());
  }
  private void inputPasswordFieldActionPerformed(ActionEvent
e)
  {
    validButton.doClick();
  }
  private void validButtonActionPerformed(ActionEvent e)
  {
    final String THEPASSWORD = "LetMeIn";

    //This procedure checks the input password
    int response;
    if (inputPasswordField.getText().equals(THEPASSWORD))
    {
      // If correct, display message box
      JOptionPane.showConfirmDialog(null, "You've passed
security!", "Access Granted", JOptionPane.DEFAULT_OPTION,
JOptionPane.WARNING_MESSAGE);
    }
    else
    {
      // If incorrect, give option to try again
      response = JOptionPane.showConfirmDialog(null,
"Incorrect password - Try Again?", "Access Denied",
JOptionPane.YES_NO_OPTION, JOptionPane.ERROR_MESSAGE);
      if (response == JOptionPane.YES_OPTION)
      {
        inputPasswordField.setText("");
```

```
            inputPasswordField.requestFocus();
        }
        else
        {
          exitButton.doClick();
        }
    }
}

private void exitButtonActionPerformed(ActionEvent e)
{
    System.exit(0);
}
private void exitForm(WindowEvent e)
{
    System.exit(0);
}
}
```

Run the program. You may receive a warning that "Password.java uses or overrides a deprecated API." If so, that's okay, just ignore it (we'll tell you why we get this message in a bit). Run the program. Here's a run I made:

Notice the echo characters (*) when I typed a password.

Try both options: input correct password (note it is case sensitive) – you should see this:

and input incorrect password to see:

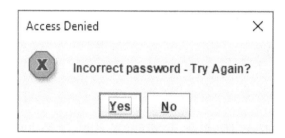

Save your project (saved as **Example3-1** project in the **\LearnJava\LJ Code\Class 3** project group).

If you have time, define a constant, **tryMax = 3**, and modify the code to allow the user to have just **tryMax** attempts to get the correct password. After the final try, inform the user you are logging him/her off. You'll also need a variable that counts the number of tries (make it a class level variable).

Remember that "deprecated error?" The reason we got this is because we used the **getText** method to retrieve the typed password. This method is not the preferred way to do this retrieval, hence the deprecated (not recommended) message. The password field control offers a preferred method for retrieving the password - the **getPassword** method. This returns a **char** array with the password. From this array, you can reconstruct the typed password. The advantage to this method is you can destroy the password (character by character) once it is entered. You can't change a string variable – we say such variables are **immutable**. Try modifying the code to use **getPassword** instead of **getText**.

JCheckBox Control

☐ **JCheckBox**

As mentioned earlier, Java features many 'point and click' controls that let the user make a choice simply by clicking with the mouse. These controls are attractive, familiar and minimize the possibility of errors in your application. We will see many such controls. The first, the **check box** control, is examined here.

The **check box** control provides a way to make choices from a list of potential candidates. Some, all, or none of the choices in a group may be selected. Check boxes are used in almost all GUI applications. Examples of their use would be to turn options on and off in an application or to select from a 'shopping' list.

Check Box Properties:

text	String displayed next to check box.
font	Font name, style, size.
background	Check box background color.
foreground	Color of text.
selected	Indicates if box is selected or not.

Check Box Methods:

setText	Sets the check box text.
setFont	Sets font name, style, size.
setBackground	Sets the check box background color.
setForeground	Sets color of text.
setOpaque	If true, background colors can be applied.
setSelected	Sets whether box is selected or not.
isSelected	If true, check box is selected.
doClick	Generates a click event for a check box.

Check Box Event:

actionPerformed	Occurs (**ActionEvent**) when check box is clicked. Added with **ActionListener**.

To add a listener for the **actionPerformed** event for a check box control named **myCheckBox**, use:

```
myCheckBox.addActionListener(new ActionListener()
{
  public void actionPerformed(ActionEvent e)
  {
    myCheckBoxActionPerformed(e);
  }
});
```

And, the corresponding event code would be placed in a **myCheckBoxActionPerformed** method:

```
private void myCheckBoxActionPerformed(ActionEvent e)
{
   [method code]
}
```

When a check box is clicked, if there is no check mark there (**isSelected = false**), Java will place a check there and change the **selected** property to true. If clicked and a check mark is there (**isSelected = true**), then the check mark will disappear and the **selected** property will be changed to false.

Typical use of **check box** control:

Declare and create check box, assigning an identifiable **name**. For **myCheckBox**, the statement is:

```
JCheckBox myCheckBox = new JCheckBox();
```

➢ Set the **text** property. Initialize the **selected** property to desired value.
➢ Place control within layout manager.
➢ Add listener for and monitor **actionPerformed** event to determine when check box is clicked. At any time, read **selected** property (use **isSelected** method) to determine check box state.
➢ You may also want to change the **font**, **background** and **foreground** properties.

JRadioButton Control

○ JRadioButton

Radio button controls provide the capability to make a "mutually exclusive" choice among a group of potential candidate choices. This simply means, radio buttons work as a group, only one of which can be selected. Radio buttons are seen in many GUI applications. They are called radio buttons because they work like a tuner on a car radio - you can only listen to one station at a time! Examples for radio button groups would be twelve buttons for selection of a month in a year, a group of buttons to let you select a color or buttons to select the difficulty in a game.

Radio Button Properties:

text	String displayed next to radio button.
font	Font name, style, size.
background	Radio button background color.
foreground	Color of text.
selected	Indicates if button is selected or not.

Radio Button Methods:

setText	Sets the radio button text.
setFont	Sets font name, style, size.
setBackground	Sets the button background color.
setForeground	Sets color of text.
setOpaque	If true, background colors can be applied.
setSelected	Sets whether button is selected or not.
isSelected	If true, radio button is selected.
doClick	Generates a click event for a radio button.

Radio Button Event:

actionPerformed	Occurs (**ActionEvent**) when radio button is clicked. Added with **ActionListener**.

To add a listener for the **actionPerformed** event for a radio button control named **myRadioButton**, use:

```
myRadioButton.addActionListener(new ActionListener()
{
  public void actionPerformed(ActionEvent e)
  {
    myRadioButtonActionPerformed(e);
  }
});
```

And, the corresponding event code would be placed in a **myRadioButtonActionPerformed** method:

```
private void myRadioButtonActionPerformed(ActionEvent e)
{
   [method code]
}
```

Notice radio buttons always work as a **group**, guaranteeing that no more than one button from that group can be selected at a time. How do you define a 'group' of radio buttons? Groups of radio buttons are defined using the **ButtonGroup** class. A group is created and buttons are added to that group using the **ButtonGroup add** method. As an example, say we have three radio buttons: **firstRadioButton**, **secondRadioButton**, **thirdRadioButton**, and we want them to be part of **myGroup**. The code that accomplishes this is:

```
ButtonGroup myGroup = new ButtonGroup();
myGroup.add(firstRadioButton);
myGroup.add(secondRadioButton);
myGroup.add(thirdRadioButton);
```

When a radio button is clicked, it's **selected** property is automatically set to true, filling the circle next to the selected button. And, all other radio buttons in that button's group will have a **selected** property of false.

Typical use of **radio button** controls:

> ➤ Declare and create a group of radio buttons. For **myGroup**, the statement is:

```
ButtonGroup myGroup = new ButtonGroup();
```

> ➤ For each button in the group, declare and create the button, assigning an identifiable **name** (give each button a similar name to identify them with the group). For **myRadioButton**, the statement is:

```
JRadioButton myRadioButton = new JRadioButton();
```

> ➤ Set the **text** property. You may also want to change the **font**, **background** and **foreground** properties.
> ➤ Initialize the **selected** property on one button to **true**.
> ➤ Add control to layout manager.
> ➤ Add listener for and monitor **actionPerformed** event of each button to determine when button is clicked. The 'last clicked' button in the group will always have a **selected** property of **true**.

JPanel Control

We've seen that radio buttons (and, many times, check boxes) work as a group. Often in GUI applications, there are logical groupings of controls. For example, you may have a scroll device setting the value of a displayed number. The **panel** control provides a convenient way of grouping related controls in a Java GUI application.

Panel Properties:

enabled	Indicates whether the panel is enabled. If false, all controls in the panel are disabled.
visible	If false, hides the panel (and all its controls).

Panel Methods:

setBorder	Establishes the panel's border (if any).
setOpaque	If true, background colors can be applied.
setEnabled	Sets whether panel is enabled.
setVisible	Sets whether panel is visible.

The panel control is a **container** control like the frame. Hence, the process of placing controls in a panel control is identical to the process used to place controls in a frame. Each panel control has its <u>own</u> layout manager (we will still use the **GridBagLayout**). So, controls are placed on the panel using its layout manager. Panels are placed on the frame using the frame's layout manager. Let's look at a simple example of placing one control (**myControl**) on a panel (**myPanel**) that is in **myFrame**. We'll assume **myControl** and **myFrame** have been declared and created. So, we need to declare and create the panel:

```
JPanel myPanel = new JPanel();
```

Then, assign a layout manager (**GridBagLayout** here):

```
myPanel.setLayout(new GridBagLayout());
```

Place the control on the panel (after setting desired **gridConstraints**):

```
myPanel.add(myControl, gridConstraints);
```

Add any other controls to panel, then add panel to frame using the frame's set of constraints:

```
getContentPane().add(myPanel, gridConstraints);
```

A titled border is often added to a panel control. The code to add such a border with the title "**My Panel**" to our sample panel is:

```
myPanel.setBorder(BorderFactory.createTitledBorder("My
Panel"));
```

The titled panel will look something like this:

Other (overloaded) versions of the **createTitledBorder** method allow you to set the title font and color.

Typical use of **panel** control:

> ➤ Declare and create the panel, assigning an identifiable **name**. For **myPanel**, the code is:

```
JPanel myPanel = new JPanel();
```

> ➤ Add a border if desired.
> ➤ Place desired controls in panel. Monitor events of controls in panel using usual techniques.
> ➤ Add panel to frame layout manager.

Handling Multiple Events in a Single Event Method

In the few applications we've built in this course, each event method handles a single event for a single control. Now that we are grouping controls like check boxes and radio buttons, it would be nice if a single procedure could handle multiple events. For example, if we have 4 radio buttons in a group, when one button is clicked, it would be preferable to have a single method where we decide which button was clicked, as opposed to having to monitor 4 separate event methods. Let's see how to do this.

We use the radio button example to illustrate. Assume we have four radio buttons (**radioButton1**, **radioButton2**, **radioButton3**, **radioButton4**). Assigning each button to the same event method is simple. In the code adding event listeners for each button, just make sure each button refers to the same **actionPerformed** event. The code for the first example button would be:

```
radioButton1.addActionListener(new ActionListener()
{
  public void actionPerformed(ActionEvent e)
  {
    radioButtonActionPerformed(e);
  }
});
```

Use similar code for the other three buttons, making sure each refers to the method named **radioButtonActionPerformed**. Hence, if any of the four radio buttons are clicked, this method will be invoked.

If we have a single method responding to events from multiple controls, how do we determine which particular event from which particular control invoked the method? In our example with a single method handling the **actionPerformed** event for 4 radio buttons, how do we know which of the 4 buttons was clicked to enter the method? The **e** argument of the event procedure provides the answer. Examining the **string** value returned by the **e.getActionCommand()** method tells us the **text** property of the selected button.

For our radio button example, we could use code like this in the **radioButtonActionPerformed** method:

```
private void radioButtonActionPerformed(ActionEvent e)
{
    String choice = e.getActionCommand();
}
```

In this code, we define a string variable (**choice**) to receive the value returned by **e.getActionCommand().** This variable will have the **text** shown on the selected button. With this information, we now know which particular button was clicked and we can process any code associated with clicking on this radio button.

Control Arrays

When using controls that work in groups, like check boxes and radio buttons, it is sometimes desirable to have some way to quickly process every control in that group. A concept of use in this case is that of a **control array**.

We have seen variable arrays – variables referred by name and index to allow quick processing of large amounts of data. The same idea applies here. We can define an array of controls, using the same statements used to declare a variable array. For example, to declare an array of 20 buttons, use:

```
JButton[] myButton = new JButton[20];
```

Recall indices will start at 0 and go to 19. This array declaration is placed according to desired scope, just like variables. For class level scope, it is outside all other methods. For method level scope, place it in the respective method. Once the array has been declared, each element of the 'control array' can be referred to by its name (**myButton**) and index. An example will clarify the advantage of such an approach.

Say we have 10 check boxes (**chkBox0**, **chkBox1**, **chkBox2**, **chkBox3**, **chkBox4**, **chkBox5**, **chkBox6**, **chkBox7**, **chkBox8**, **chkBox9**) on a frame and we need to examine each check box's **selected** property. If that property is true, we need to process 30 lines of additional code. For one check box, that code would be:

```
if (chkBox0.isSelected())
{
   [do these 30 lines of code]
}
```

We would need to repeat this 9 more times (for the nine remaining check boxes), yielding a total of 32 x 10 = 320 lines of code. And, if we needed to add a few lines to the code being processed, we would need to add these lines in 10 different places – a real maintenance headache. Let's try using an array of check boxes to minimize this headache.

Here's the solution. Define an array of 10 check box controls and assign the array values to existing controls:

```
JCheckBox[] myCheck = new JCheckBox[10];
myCheck[0] = chkBox0;
myCheck[1] = chkBox1;
myCheck[2] = chkBox2;
myCheck[3] = chkBox3;
myCheck[4] = chkBox4;
myCheck[5] = chkBox5;
myCheck[6] = chkBox6;
myCheck[7] = chkBox7;
myCheck[8] = chkBox8;
myCheck[9] = chkBox9;
```

Again, make sure the declaration statement is properly located for proper scope. Having made these assignments, the code for examining the selected property of each has been reduced to these few lines:

```
for (int i = 0; i < 10; i++)
{
  if (myCheck[I].isSelected())
  {
        [do these 30 lines of code]
  }
}
```

The 320 lines of code have been reduced to about 45 (including all the declarations) and code maintenance is now much easier.

Obviously, it is not necessary to use control arrays, but they do have their advantages. You will start to see such arrays in the course examples and problems, so you should understand their use.

Example 3-2

Pizza Order

Start a new project in **NetBeans**. Name the project **Pizza**. Delete default code in Java file named **Pizza**. We'll build a frame where a pizza order can be entered by simply clicking on check boxes and radio buttons. The finished frame will look like this:

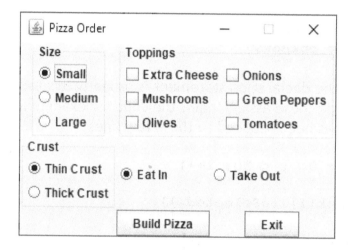

1. Begin by adding three panel controls, two radio buttons and two buttons on a frame. The **GridBagLayout** arrangement for these controls is:

	gridx = 0	gridx = 1	gridx = 2
gridy = 0	sizePanel	toppingsPanel	
gridy = 1	crustPanel	eatInRadioButton	takeOutRadioButton
gridy = 2		buildButton	exitButton

Set the properties of the frame and each control.

Pizza Frame:
    title   Pizza Order
    resizable   false

sizePanel:
    title   Size
    gridx   0
    gridy   0

crustPanel:

title	Crust Type
gridx	0
gridy	1

toppingsPanel:

title	Toppings
gridx	1
gridy	0
gridwidth	2

eatInRadioButton:

text	Eat In
group	whereButtonGroup
selected	true
gridx	1
gridy	1

takeOutRadioButton:

text	Take Out
group	whereButtonGroup
gridx	2
gridy	1

buildButton:

text	Build Pizza
gridx	1
gridy	2

exitButton:

text	Exit
gridx	2
gridy	1

The layout of the **sizePanel**:

	gridx = 0
gridy = 0	**smallRadioButton**
gridy = 1	**mediumRadioButton**
gridy = 2	**largeRadioButton**

smallRadioButton:

text	Small
group	sizeButtonGroup
selected	true
gridx	0
gridy	0
anchor	WEST

mediumRadioButton:

text	Medium
group	sizeButtonGroup
gridx	0
gridy	1
anchor	WEST

largeRadioButton:

text	Large
group	sizeButtonGroup
gridx	0
gridy	2
anchor	WEST

The layout of the **crustPanel**:

	gridx = 0
gridy = 0	**thinRadioButton**
gridy = 1	**thickRadioButton**

thinRadioButton:

text	Thin Crust
group	crustButtonGroup
selected	true
gridx	0
gridy	0
anchor	WEST

thickRadioButton:

text	Thick Crust
group	crustButtonGroup
gridx	0
gridy	1
anchor	WEST

The layout of the **toppingsPanel**:

	gridx = 0	gridx = 1
gridy = 0	**cheeseCheckBox**	**onionsCheckBox**
gridy = 1	**mushroomsCheckBox**	**peppersCheckBox**
gridy = 2	**olivesCheckBox**	**tomatoesCheckBox**

cheeseCheckBox:
text	Extra Cheese
gridx	0
gridy	0
anchor	WEST

mushroomsCheckBox:
text	Mushrooms
gridx	0
gridy	1
anchor	WEST

olivesCheckBox:
text	Black Olives
gridx	0
gridy	2
anchor	WEST

onionsCheckBox:
text	Onions
gridx	1
gridy	0
anchor	WEST

peppersCheckBox:
text	Green Peppers
gridx	1
gridy	1
anchor	WEST

tomatoesCheckBox:

text	Tomatoes
gridx	1
gridy	2
anchor	WEST

2.　Build the basic framework first:

```
/*
 * Pizza.java
 */
package pizza;
import javax.swing.*;
import java.awt.*;
import java.awt.event.*;

public class Pizza extends javax.swing.JFrame
{

  public static void main(String args[])
  {
    // construct frame
    new Pizza().setVisible(true);
  }

  public Pizza()
  {
    setTitle("Pizza Order");
    setResizable(false);
    addWindowListener(new WindowAdapter()
    {
      public void windowClosing(WindowEvent e)
      {
        exitForm(e);
      }
    });
    getContentPane().setLayout(new GridBagLayout());
    pack();
    Dimension screenSize =
Toolkit.getDefaultToolkit().getScreenSize();
    setBounds((int) (0.5 * (screenSize.width -
getWidth())), (int) (0.5 * (screenSize.height -
getHeight())), getWidth(), getHeight());

  }
```

```
    private void exitForm(WindowEvent e)
    {
      System.exit(0);
    }
  }
```

Run to make sure the frame appears.

3. Let's build each panel separately. First, we'll build the **Size** panel. Add these as class level declarations:

```
JPanel sizePanel = new JPanel();
ButtonGroup sizeButtonGroup = new ButtonGroup();
JRadioButton smallRadioButton = new JRadioButton();
JRadioButton mediumRadioButton = new JRadioButton();
JRadioButton largeRadioButton = new JRadioButton();
```

Position and add each control, adding needed events (goes immediately before the **pack()** statement:

```
// position controls
GridBagConstraints gridConstraints;
sizePanel.setLayout(new GridBagLayout());
sizePanel.setBorder(BorderFactory.createTitledBorder("Size
"));

smallRadioButton.setText("Small");
smallRadioButton.setSelected(true);
sizeButtonGroup.add(smallRadioButton);
gridConstraints = new GridBagConstraints();
gridConstraints.gridx = 0;
gridConstraints.gridy = 0;
gridConstraints.anchor = GridBagConstraints.WEST;
sizePanel.add(smallRadioButton, gridConstraints);
smallRadioButton.addActionListener(new ActionListener()
{
  public void actionPerformed(ActionEvent e)
  {
    sizeRadioButtonActionPerformed(e);
  }
});
mediumRadioButton.setText("Medium");
sizeButtonGroup.add(mediumRadioButton);
gridConstraints = new GridBagConstraints();
gridConstraints.gridx = 0;
gridConstraints.gridy = 1;
```

```
gridConstraints.anchor = GridBagConstraints.WEST;
sizePanel.add(mediumRadioButton, gridConstraints);
mediumRadioButton.addActionListener(new ActionListener()
{
  public void actionPerformed(ActionEvent e)
  {
    sizeRadioButtonActionPerformed(e);
  }
});
largeRadioButton.setText("Large");
largeRadioButton.setSelected(true);
sizeButtonGroup.add(largeRadioButton);
gridConstraints = new GridBagConstraints();
gridConstraints.gridx = 0;
gridConstraints.gridy = 2;
gridConstraints.anchor = GridBagConstraints.WEST;
sizePanel.add(largeRadioButton, gridConstraints);
largeRadioButton.addActionListener(new ActionListener()
{
  public void actionPerformed(ActionEvent e)
  {
    sizeRadioButtonActionPerformed(e);
  }
});
gridConstraints = new GridBagConstraints();
gridConstraints.gridx = 0;
gridConstraints.gridy = 0;
getContentPane().add(sizePanel, gridConstraints);
```

Add an empty **sizeRadioButtonActionPerformed** method:

```
private void sizeRadioButtonActionPerformed(ActionEvent e)
{
}
```

Save, run the project. You should see the first panel:

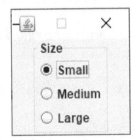

4. Now, we'll build the **Crust** panel. Add these as class level declarations:

```
JPanel crustPanel = new JPanel();
ButtonGroup crustButtonGroup = new ButtonGroup();
JRadioButton thinRadioButton = new JRadioButton();
JRadioButton thickRadioButton = new JRadioButton();
```

Position and add each control, adding needed events:

```
crustPanel.setLayout(new GridBagLayout());
crustPanel.setBorder(BorderFactory.createTitledBorder("Cru
st"));
thinRadioButton.setText("Thin Crust");
thinRadioButton.setSelected(true);
crustButtonGroup.add(thinRadioButton);
gridConstraints = new GridBagConstraints();
gridConstraints.gridx = 0;
gridConstraints.gridy = 0;
gridConstraints.anchor = GridBagConstraints.WEST;
crustPanel.add(thinRadioButton, gridConstraints);
thinRadioButton.addActionListener(new ActionListener()
{
  public void actionPerformed(ActionEvent e)
  {
    crustRadioButtonActionPerformed(e);
  }
});
thickRadioButton.setText("Thick Crust");
crustButtonGroup.add(thickRadioButton);
gridConstraints = new GridBagConstraints();
gridConstraints.gridx = 0;
gridConstraints.gridy = 1;
gridConstraints.anchor = GridBagConstraints.WEST;
crustPanel.add(thickRadioButton, gridConstraints);
thickRadioButton.addActionListener(new ActionListener()
{
  public void actionPerformed(ActionEvent e)
  {
    crustRadioButtonActionPerformed(e);
  }
});
gridConstraints = new GridBagConstraints();
gridConstraints.gridx = 0;
gridConstraints.gridy = 1;
getContentPane().add(crustPanel, gridConstraints);
```

Add an empty **crustRadioButtonActionPerformed** method:

```
private void crustRadioButtonActionPerformed(ActionEvent
e)
{
}
```

Save, run the project. You should see the added panel:

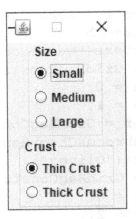

5. Next, we'll build the **Toppings** panel. Add these as class level declarations:

```
JPanel toppingsPanel = new JPanel();
JCheckBox cheeseCheckBox = new JCheckBox();
JCheckBox mushroomsCheckBox = new JCheckBox();
JCheckBox olivesCheckBox = new JCheckBox();
JCheckBox onionsCheckBox = new JCheckBox();
JCheckBox peppersCheckBox = new JCheckBox();
JCheckBox tomatoesCheckBox = new JCheckBox();
```

Position and add each control (there are no methods for the check boxes):

```
toppingsPanel.setLayout(new GridBagLayout());
toppingsPanel.setBorder(BorderFactory.createTitledBorder("
Toppings"));
cheeseCheckBox.setText("Extra Cheese");
gridConstraints = new GridBagConstraints();
gridConstraints.gridx = 0;
gridConstraints.gridy = 0;
gridConstraints.anchor = GridBagConstraints.WEST;
toppingsPanel.add(cheeseCheckBox, gridConstraints);
mushroomsCheckBox.setText("Mushrooms");
gridConstraints = new GridBagConstraints();
gridConstraints.gridx = 0;
gridConstraints.gridy = 1;
gridConstraints.anchor = GridBagConstraints.WEST;
toppingsPanel.add(mushroomsCheckBox, gridConstraints);
olivesCheckBox.setText("Olives");
gridConstraints = new GridBagConstraints();
gridConstraints.gridx = 0;
gridConstraints.gridy = 2;
gridConstraints.anchor = GridBagConstraints.WEST;
toppingsPanel.add(olivesCheckBox, gridConstraints);
onionsCheckBox.setText("Onions");
gridConstraints = new GridBagConstraints();
gridConstraints.gridx = 1;
gridConstraints.gridy = 0;
gridConstraints.anchor = GridBagConstraints.WEST;
toppingsPanel.add(onionsCheckBox, gridConstraints);
peppersCheckBox.setText("Green Peppers");
gridConstraints = new GridBagConstraints();
gridConstraints.gridx = 1;
gridConstraints.gridy = 1;
gridConstraints.anchor = GridBagConstraints.WEST;
toppingsPanel.add(peppersCheckBox, gridConstraints);
tomatoesCheckBox.setText("Tomatoes");
gridConstraints = new GridBagConstraints();
gridConstraints.gridx = 1;
gridConstraints.gridy = 2;
gridConstraints.anchor = GridBagConstraints.WEST;
toppingsPanel.add(tomatoesCheckBox, gridConstraints);
gridConstraints = new GridBagConstraints();
gridConstraints.gridx = 1;
gridConstraints.gridy = 0;
gridConstraints.gridwidth = 2;
getContentPane().add(toppingsPanel, gridConstraints);
```

Save, run the project. You should see the newly added panel:

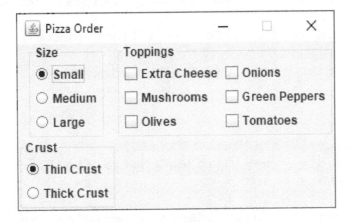

6. Finally, we add the four controls not in panels, two more radio buttons and two buttons. Declare the controls:

```
ButtonGroup whereButtonGroup = new ButtonGroup();
JRadioButton eatInRadioButton = new JRadioButton();
JRadioButton takeOutRadioButton = new JRadioButton();
JButton buildButton = new JButton();
JButton exitButton = new JButton();
```

Position and add each control and their methods:

```
eatInRadioButton.setText("Eat In");
eatInRadioButton.setSelected(true);
whereButtonGroup.add(eatInRadioButton);
gridConstraints = new GridBagConstraints();
gridConstraints.gridx = 1;
gridConstraints.gridy = 1;
gridConstraints.anchor = GridBagConstraints.WEST;
getContentPane().add(eatInRadioButton, gridConstraints);
eatInRadioButton.addActionListener(new ActionListener()
{
  public void actionPerformed(ActionEvent e)
  {
    whereRadioButtonActionPerformed(e);
  }
});
takeOutRadioButton.setText("Take Out");
whereButtonGroup.add(takeOutRadioButton);
gridConstraints = new GridBagConstraints();
gridConstraints.gridx = 2;
gridConstraints.gridy = 1;
gridConstraints.anchor = GridBagConstraints.WEST;
```

```
getContentPane().add(takeOutRadioButton, gridConstraints);
takeOutRadioButton.addActionListener(new ActionListener()
{
  public void actionPerformed(ActionEvent e)
  {
    whereRadioButtonActionPerformed(e);
  }
});

buildButton.setText("Build Pizza");
gridConstraints = new GridBagConstraints();
gridConstraints.gridx = 1;
gridConstraints.gridy = 2;
getContentPane().add(buildButton, gridConstraints);
takeOutRadioButton.addActionListener(new ActionListener()
{
  public void actionPerformed(ActionEvent e)
  {
    buildButtonActionPerformed(e);
  }
});
exitButton.setText("Exit");
gridConstraints = new GridBagConstraints();
gridConstraints.gridx = 2;
gridConstraints.gridy = 2;
getContentPane().add(exitButton, gridConstraints);
takeOutRadioButton.addActionListener(new ActionListener()
{
  public void actionPerformed(ActionEvent e)
  {
    exitButtonActionPerformed(e);
  }
});
```

Add the thee empty methods:

```
private void whereRadioButtonActionPerformed(ActionEvent
e)
{
}

private void buildButtonActionPerformed(ActionEvent e)
{
}

private void exitButtonActionPerformed(ActionEvent e)
{
}
```

Save, run the project. You will see the finished control arrangement. Try out the radio buttons to see how they work as groups:

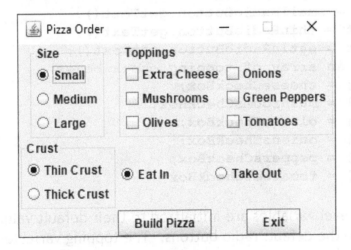

7. Now, we add code for the event methods. Declare four variables with class level scope:

```
String pizzaSize;
String pizzaCrust;
String pizzaWhere;
JCheckBox[] topping = new JCheckBox[6];
```

This makes the size, crust, and location variables global to the class. The array of check box controls will help us determine which toppings are selected. As mentioned in the notes, it is common to use 'control arrays' when working with check boxes and radio buttons.

8. Add this code at the end of the frame constructor. This initializes the pizza size, crust, eating location and topping controls.

```
// Initialize parameters
pizzaSize = smallRadioButton.getText();
pizzaCrust = thinRadioButton.getText();
pizzaWhere = eatInRadioButton.getText();
// Define an array of topping check boxes
topping[0] = cheeseCheckBox;
topping[1] = mushroomsCheckBox;
topping[2] = olivesCheckBox;
topping[3] = onionsCheckBox;
topping[4] = peppersCheckBox;
topping[5] = tomatoesCheckBox;
```

Here, the form level variables are initialized to their default values, corresponding to the default radio buttons. The topping variables are set to their values.

9. Use this code in the methods for each of the three groups of radio buttons:

```
private void sizeRadioButtonActionPerformed(ActionEvent e)
{
  pizzaSize = e.getActionCommand();
}

private void crustRadioButtonActionPerformed(ActionEvent
e)
{
  pizzaCrust = e.getActionCommand();
}

private void whereRadioButtonActionPerformed(ActionEvent
e)
{
  pizzaWhere = e.getActionCommand();
}
```

In each of these routines, when an radio button is clicked (changing the selected property), the value of the corresponding button's text is loaded into the respective variable.

10. Use this code in the **buildButtonActionPerformed** method.

```
private void buildButtonActionPerformed(ActionEvent e)
{
  // This procedure builds a confirm dialog box that
displays your pizza type
  String message;
  message = pizzaWhere + "\n";
  message += pizzaSize + " Pizza" + "\n";
  message += pizzaCrust + "\n";
  // Check each topping using the array we set up
  for (int i = 0; i < 6; i++)
  {
    if (topping[i].isSelected())
    {
      message += topping[i].getText() + "\n";
    }
  }
    JOptionPane.showConfirmDialog(null, message, "Your
Pizza", JOptionPane.DEFAULT_OPTION,
JOptionPane.INFORMATION_MESSAGE);
  }
```

This code forms the first part of a message for a message box by concatenating the pizza size, crust type, and eating location (recall \n is a character sequence representing a 'new line' that puts each piece of ordering information on a separate line). Next, the code cycles through the six topping check boxes (defined by our **topping** array) and adds any checked information to the message. The code then displays the pizza order in a confirm message box.

11. Use this code in the **exitButtonActionPerformed** event.

```
private void exitButtonActionPerformed(ActionEvent e)
{
  System.exit(0);
}
```

For reference, here is the final **Pizza.java** code listing (code added to basic frame is shaded):

```java
/*
 * Pizza.java
 */
package pizza;
import javax.swing.*;
import java.awt.*;
import java.awt.event.*;
public class Pizza extends javax.swing.JFrame
{
    JPanel sizePanel = new JPanel();
    ButtonGroup sizeButtonGroup = new ButtonGroup();
    JRadioButton smallRadioButton = new JRadioButton();
    JRadioButton mediumRadioButton = new JRadioButton();
    JRadioButton largeRadioButton = new JRadioButton();
    JPanel crustPanel = new JPanel();
    ButtonGroup crustButtonGroup = new ButtonGroup();
    JRadioButton thinRadioButton = new JRadioButton();
    JRadioButton thickRadioButton = new JRadioButton();
    JPanel toppingsPanel = new JPanel();
    JCheckBox cheeseCheckBox = new JCheckBox();
    JCheckBox mushroomsCheckBox = new JCheckBox();
    JCheckBox olivesCheckBox = new JCheckBox();
    JCheckBox onionsCheckBox = new JCheckBox();
    JCheckBox peppersCheckBox = new JCheckBox();
    JCheckBox tomatoesCheckBox = new JCheckBox();
    ButtonGroup whereButtonGroup = new ButtonGroup();
    JRadioButton eatInRadioButton = new JRadioButton();
    JRadioButton takeOutRadioButton = new JRadioButton();
    JButton buildButton = new JButton();
    JButton exitButton = new JButton();

    String pizzaSize;
    String pizzaCrust;
    String pizzaWhere;
    JCheckBox[] topping = new JCheckBox[6];

    public static void main(String args[])
    {
        // construct frame
        new Pizza().setVisible(true);
    }
    public Pizza()
    {
        setTitle("Pizza Order");
```

```
    setResizable(false);
    addWindowListener(new WindowAdapter()
    {
      public void windowClosing(WindowEvent e)
      {
        exitForm(e);
      }
    });
    getContentPane().setLayout(new GridBagLayout());

    // position controls
    GridBagConstraints gridConstraints;
    sizePanel.setLayout(new GridBagLayout());

sizePanel.setBorder(BorderFactory.createTitledBorder("Size"))
;

    smallRadioButton.setText("Small");
    smallRadioButton.setSelected(true);
    sizeButtonGroup.add(smallRadioButton);
    gridConstraints = new GridBagConstraints();
    gridConstraints.gridx = 0;
    gridConstraints.gridy = 0;
    gridConstraints.anchor = GridBagConstraints.WEST;
    sizePanel.add(smallRadioButton, gridConstraints);
    smallRadioButton.addActionListener(new ActionListener()
    {
      public void actionPerformed(ActionEvent e)
      {
        sizeRadioButtonActionPerformed(e);
      }
    });
    mediumRadioButton.setText("Medium");
    sizeButtonGroup.add(mediumRadioButton);
    gridConstraints = new GridBagConstraints();
    gridConstraints.gridx = 0;
    gridConstraints.gridy = 1;
    gridConstraints.anchor = GridBagConstraints.WEST;
    sizePanel.add(mediumRadioButton, gridConstraints);
    mediumRadioButton.addActionListener(new ActionListener()
    {
      public void actionPerformed(ActionEvent e)
      {
        sizeRadioButtonActionPerformed(e);
      }
    });
    largeRadioButton.setText("Large");
```

```java
      largeRadioButton.setSelected(true);
      sizeButtonGroup.add(largeRadioButton);
      gridConstraints = new GridBagConstraints();
      gridConstraints.gridx = 0;
      gridConstraints.gridy = 2;
      gridConstraints.anchor = GridBagConstraints.WEST;
      sizePanel.add(largeRadioButton, gridConstraints);
      largeRadioButton.addActionListener(new ActionListener()
      {
        public void actionPerformed(ActionEvent e)
        {
          sizeRadioButtonActionPerformed(e);
        }
      });
      gridConstraints = new GridBagConstraints();
      gridConstraints.gridx = 0;
      gridConstraints.gridy = 0;
      getContentPane().add(sizePanel, gridConstraints);

      crustPanel.setLayout(new GridBagLayout());

crustPanel.setBorder(BorderFactory.createTitledBorder("Crust"
));
      thinRadioButton.setText("Thin Crust");
      thinRadioButton.setSelected(true);
      crustButtonGroup.add(thinRadioButton);
      gridConstraints = new GridBagConstraints();
      gridConstraints.gridx = 0;
      gridConstraints.gridy = 0;
      gridConstraints.anchor = GridBagConstraints.WEST;
      crustPanel.add(thinRadioButton, gridConstraints);
      thinRadioButton.addActionListener(new ActionListener()
      {
        public void actionPerformed(ActionEvent e)
        {
          crustRadioButtonActionPerformed(e);
        }
      });
      thickRadioButton.setText("Thick Crust");
      crustButtonGroup.add(thickRadioButton);
      gridConstraints = new GridBagConstraints();
      gridConstraints.gridx = 0;
      gridConstraints.gridy = 1;
      gridConstraints.anchor = GridBagConstraints.WEST;
      crustPanel.add(thickRadioButton, gridConstraints);
      thickRadioButton.addActionListener(new ActionListener()
      {
```

```
      public void actionPerformed(ActionEvent e)
      {
        crustRadioButtonActionPerformed(e);
      }
    });
    gridConstraints = new GridBagConstraints();
    gridConstraints.gridx = 0;
    gridConstraints.gridy = 1;
    getContentPane().add(crustPanel, gridConstraints);

    toppingsPanel.setLayout(new GridBagLayout());

toppingsPanel.setBorder(BorderFactory.createTitledBorder("Top
pings"));
    cheeseCheckBox.setText("Extra Cheese");
    gridConstraints = new GridBagConstraints();
    gridConstraints.gridx = 0;
    gridConstraints.gridy = 0;
    gridConstraints.anchor = GridBagConstraints.WEST;
    toppingsPanel.add(cheeseCheckBox, gridConstraints);
    mushroomsCheckBox.setText("Mushrooms");
    gridConstraints = new GridBagConstraints();
    gridConstraints.gridx = 0;
    gridConstraints.gridy = 1;
    gridConstraints.anchor = GridBagConstraints.WEST;
    toppingsPanel.add(mushroomsCheckBox, gridConstraints);
    olivesCheckBox.setText("Olives");
    gridConstraints = new GridBagConstraints();
    gridConstraints.gridx = 0;
    gridConstraints.gridy = 2;
    gridConstraints.anchor = GridBagConstraints.WEST;
    toppingsPanel.add(olivesCheckBox, gridConstraints);
    onionsCheckBox.setText("Onions");
    gridConstraints = new GridBagConstraints();
    gridConstraints.gridx = 1;
    gridConstraints.gridy = 0;
    gridConstraints.anchor = GridBagConstraints.WEST;
    toppingsPanel.add(onionsCheckBox, gridConstraints);
    peppersCheckBox.setText("Green Peppers");
    gridConstraints = new GridBagConstraints();
    gridConstraints.gridx = 1;
    gridConstraints.gridy = 1;
    gridConstraints.anchor = GridBagConstraints.WEST;
    toppingsPanel.add(peppersCheckBox, gridConstraints);
    tomatoesCheckBox.setText("Tomatoes");
    gridConstraints = new GridBagConstraints();
    gridConstraints.gridx = 1;
```

```
    gridConstraints.gridy = 2;
    gridConstraints.anchor = GridBagConstraints.WEST;
    toppingsPanel.add(tomatoesCheckBox, gridConstraints);
    gridConstraints = new GridBagConstraints();
    gridConstraints.gridx = 1;
    gridConstraints.gridy = 0;
    gridConstraints.gridwidth = 2;
    getContentPane().add(toppingsPanel, gridConstraints);

    eatInRadioButton.setText("Eat In");
    eatInRadioButton.setSelected(true);
    whereButtonGroup.add(eatInRadioButton);
    gridConstraints = new GridBagConstraints();
    gridConstraints.gridx = 1;
    gridConstraints.gridy = 1;
    gridConstraints.anchor = GridBagConstraints.WEST;
    getContentPane().add(eatInRadioButton, gridConstraints);
    eatInRadioButton.addActionListener(new ActionListener()
    {
      public void actionPerformed(ActionEvent e)
      {
        whereRadioButtonActionPerformed(e);
      }
    });
    takeOutRadioButton.setText("Take Out");
    whereButtonGroup.add(takeOutRadioButton);
    gridConstraints = new GridBagConstraints();
    gridConstraints.gridx = 2;
    gridConstraints.gridy = 1;
    gridConstraints.anchor = GridBagConstraints.WEST;
    getContentPane().add(takeOutRadioButton,
gridConstraints);
    takeOutRadioButton.addActionListener(new ActionListener()
    {
      public void actionPerformed(ActionEvent e)
      {
        whereRadioButtonActionPerformed(e);
      }
    });

    buildButton.setText("Build Pizza");
    gridConstraints = new GridBagConstraints();
    gridConstraints.gridx = 1;
    gridConstraints.gridy = 2;
    getContentPane().add(buildButton, gridConstraints);
    buildButton.addActionListener(new ActionListener()
    {
```

```
      public void actionPerformed(ActionEvent e)
      {
        buildButtonActionPerformed(e);
      }
  });
  exitButton.setText("Exit");
  gridConstraints = new GridBagConstraints();
  gridConstraints.gridx = 2;
  gridConstraints.gridy = 2;
  getContentPane().add(exitButton, gridConstraints);
  exitButton.addActionListener(new ActionListener()
  {
    public void actionPerformed(ActionEvent e)
    {
      exitButtonActionPerformed(e);
    }
  });

  pack();
  Dimension screenSize =
Toolkit.getDefaultToolkit().getScreenSize();
  setBounds((int) (0.5 * (screenSize.width - getWidth())),
(int) (0.5 * (screenSize.height - getHeight())), getWidth(),
getHeight());

  // Initialize parameters
  pizzaSize = smallRadioButton.getText();
  pizzaCrust = thinRadioButton.getText();
  pizzaWhere = eatInRadioButton.getText();
  // Define an array of topping check boxes
  topping[0] = cheeseCheckBox;
  topping[1] = mushroomsCheckBox;
  topping[2] = olivesCheckBox;
  topping[3] = onionsCheckBox;
  topping[4] = peppersCheckBox;
  topping[5] = tomatoesCheckBox;
}

private void sizeRadioButtonActionPerformed(ActionEvent e)
{
  pizzaSize = e.getActionCommand();
}

private void crustRadioButtonActionPerformed(ActionEvent e)
{
  pizzaCrust = e.getActionCommand();
}
```

```java
private void whereRadioButtonActionPerformed(ActionEvent e)
{
  pizzaWhere = e.getActionCommand();
}

private void buildButtonActionPerformed(ActionEvent e)
{
  // This procedure builds a confirm dialog box that
displays your pizza type
  String message;
  message = pizzaWhere + "\n";
  message += pizzaSize + " Pizza" + "\n";
  message += pizzaCrust + "\n";
  // Check each topping using the array we set up
  for (int i = 0; i < 6; i++)
  {
    if (topping[i].isSelected())
    {
      message += topping[i].getText() + "\n";
    }
  }
  JOptionPane.showConfirmDialog(null, message, "Your
Pizza", JOptionPane.DEFAULT_OPTION,
JOptionPane.INFORMATION_MESSAGE);

}

private void exitButtonActionPerformed(ActionEvent e)
{
  System.exit(0);
}

private void exitForm(WindowEvent e)
{
  System.exit(0);
}
}
```

Run the application. There's a lot of code here, you may have to compile a few times to eliminate errors. Notice how the different radio buttons work in their individual groups. Here's a run I made – first, my choices:

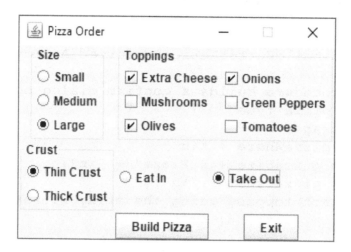

Then, when I click **Build Pizza**, I see:

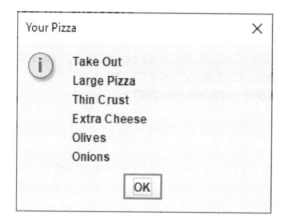

Save your project (saved as **Example3-2** project in the **\LearnJava\LJ Code\Class 3** project group). If you have time, try these modifications:

A. Add a new program button that resets the order form to the initial default values. You'll have to reinitialize the three class level variables, reset all check boxes to unchecked, and reset all three radio button groups to their default values.

B. Modify the code so that if no toppings are selected, the message "Cheese Only" appears on the order form. You'll need to figure out a way to see if no check boxes were checked.

JList Control

Check boxes are useful controls for selecting items from a list. But, what if your list has 100 items? Do you want 100 check boxes? No, but fortunately, there is a tool that solves this problem. A **list** control displays a list of items (with as many items as you like) from which the user can select one or more items. Both single item and multiple item selections are supported.

List Properties:

model	Establishes the items in the list.
font	Font name, style, size.
background	List background color.
foreground	Color of text.
visibleRowCount	Number of rows to display.
selectedIndex	Zero-based index of the currently selected item in a list.
selectedIndices	Zero-based array of indices of all currently selected items in the list.
selectedValue	Currently selected item in the list.
selectedValues	Array of selected items in list.
selectionMode	Gets or sets the method in which items are selected in list (allows single or multiple selections).
selectionEmpty	Boolean variable indicating if any items are selected.

List Methods:

setFont	Sets font name, style, size.
setBackground	Sets the list background color.
setForeground	Sets color of text.
setVisibleRowCount	Sets number of rows to display.
clearSelection	Unselects specified in the list.
getSelectedIndex	Returns a value indicating whether the specified item is selected.
getSelectedIndices	Returns an integer array of indices of selected items.
setSelectedIndex	Selects specified item in a list.
setSelectionMode	Establishes selection mode.
isSelectionEmpty	Checks to see if any items are selected.

List Event:

valueChanged	Event (**ListSelectionEvent**) triggered when any selections in the list change. Added with **ListSelectionListener** (requires importation of **javax.swing.event.*** files).

The **valueChanged** event is new in our work. To add a listener for such an event to a list control named **myList**, use:

```
myList.addListSelectionListener(new
ListSelectionListener()
{
public void valueChanged(ListSelectionEvent e)
{
myListValueChanged(e);
}
});
```

And, the corresponding event code would be placed in a **myListValueChanged** method:

```
private void myListValueChanged(ListSelectionEvent e)
{
[method code]
}
```

The items listed in the list control are defined using the **DefaultListModel** object. This model manages a resizable array of information, such as that used with the list control Such a model (**myListModel**) is created using:

```
DefaultListModel myListModel = new DefaultListModel();
```

Once created, items are added to the list using the **addElement** or **insertElementAt** methods:

```
Add Item:   myListModel.addElement(itemToAdd);
myListModel.insertElementAt(itemToAdd, index);
```

With **addElement**, the item is added to the end of the list. With **insertElementAt** the item will be added at the given **index** value.

List controls normally list string data types, though other types are possible. Many times, you want the items in a list control to be sorted, or in alphabetical order. There are no automatic capabilities within the list control to maintain sorted lists. If you want such capability, you need to do this yourself using your Java coding skills.

To remove items from the list, there are three methods: **removeElement**, **removeElementAt**, or **removeAllElements**. For our example list box, the respective commands are:

```
Delete Item:   myListModel.removeElement(itemToRemove);
myListModel.removeElementAt(index);
Clear list:    myListModel.removeAllElements();
```

Note, when removing items, that indices for subsequent items in the list change following a removal.

To refer to an individual element in the model, use the **getElementAt** method:

```
myListModel.getElementAt(index)
```

and the number of elements in the list is given by the **getSize** method:

```
myListModel.getSize();
```

To view, the last item in this list (zero-based), you would use:

```
myListModel.getElementAt(myListModel.getSize() - 1)
```

Once a list model is established, it is assigned to the list control (**myList**) using the **setModel** method:

```
myList.setModel(myListModel);
```

Always be aware of when to work with the list control and when to work with the list model. The primary thing to remember is that items are added to and deleted from the list model using indices provided by the list control.

The **selectionMode** property specifies whether you want single item selection or multiple selections. The choices are from the **ListSelectionModel** class and there are three possible values:

```
MULTIPLE_INTERVAL_SELECTION    Allows selection of several ranges at
                               a time.
SINGLE_INTERVAL_SELECTION      Allows selection of one range.
SINGLE_SELECTION               Allows selection of one item.
```

The default value allows multiple range selection. To change to single item selection in the **myList** control, use:

```
myList.setSelectionMode(ListSelectionModel.SINGLE_SELECTIO
N);
```

Typical use of **list** control:

> ➢ Declare and create list control, assigning an identifiable **name**. For **myList**, the code is:

```
JList myList = new JList();
```

> ➢ Set **selectionMode** property and populate the list using the list model object (usually in the frame constructor).
> ➢ Add control to layout manager.
> ➢ Monitor **valueChanged** event for individual selections.
> ➢ Use **selectedIndex** and **selectIndices** properties to determine selected items.

Notice one thing we haven't discussed with the list control is what happens when there are more items in the list than the control can display? The answer is nothing – you will not see the items "off the list." The **JList** control does not have any scrolling capabilities. To add such capabilities, we use another Swing component, the **JScrollPane** to implement both horizontal and vertical scroll bars. Let's look at that component.

JScrollPane Control

A very useful container control is the **scroll pane**. This control is like the panel control with the added capability of being able to scroll any component placed on the scroll pane. Hence, a large component can be placed on a small "piece of real estate" in a GUI frame. Several Swing controls rely on the scroll pane to provide scrolling capabilities, including the **JTextArea** control described earlier and the **JList** component just studied. Both horizontal and vertical scrolling of a control is possible.

Scroll Pane Properties:

enabled	Indicates whether the scroll pane is enabled. If false, the component in the pane is disabled.
preferredSize	Specified size (width, height) of scroll pane.
horizontalScrollBarPolicy	Determines how horizontal scroll bar is displayed.
verticalScrollBarPolicy	Determines how vertical scroll bar is displayed.

Scroll Pane Methods:

setEnabled	Sets whether panel is enabled.
setPreferredSize	Establishes size of scroll pane.
setViewportView	Establishes component "hosted" by the scroll pane.
setHorizontalScrollBarPolicy	Establishes how horizontal scroll bar (if any) is displayed.
setVerticalScrollBarPolicy	Establishes how horizontal scroll bar (if any) is displayed.

Using a scroll pane is relatively easy. Since the idea of the pane is to hold a component larger than the pane itself, you need to establish how large you want the pane to be. This is done using the **setPreferredSize** method, which in turn uses the **Dimension** object. What all this means is to set the size of a scroll pane, **myPane**, use:

```
JScrollPane myPane = new JScrollPane();
myPane.setPreferredSize(new Dimension(width, height));
```

where **width** and **height** are the desired dimensions in pixels. Once the pane is established and sized, you can add components to it. A scroll pane can have a layout manager like other controls, but usually you just add a single control to the pane (this control might be a panel control with many controls). A component (**myControl**) is added to the scroll pane using the **setViewportView** method.

```
myPane.setViewportView(myControl);
```

At this point, the added control can be scrolled in the scroll pane - it's that easy! Of course, you need to add the scroll pane to the frame (with associated **gridConstraints**) to make this happen:

```
getContentPane().add(myPane, new gridConstraints());
```

This is the first time we have set "**preferred sizes**" for components. Up to now, we have let the grid layout manager determine component size and it seems to have worked just fine. Once you start setting sizes for components, occasional strange behavior is seen (you'll see it in **Example 3-3**). Sometimes, controls don't show up as you would expect. Many times, if you set the preferred size for a control in one grid location, you need to set sizes for all components on the grid. You'll start developing your own ways to handle these strange behaviors. If something doesn't appear as it should, the preferred size method is a place to start looking.

Scroll bars may or may not appear in the scroll pane, depending on settings for the "**scroll bar policy**." To establish the horizontal scrollbar policy, use the **setHorizontalScrollBarPolicy** with one of three constants from the **ScrollPaneConstants**:

> `HORIZONTAL_SCROLLBAR_AS_NEEDED`   Scroll bar appears when hosted component is wider than allocated space (default).
> `HORIZONTAL_SCROLLBAR_ALWAYS` Scroll bar always appears.
> `HORIZONTAL_SCROLLBAR_NEVER`   Scroll bar never appears.

To establish the vertical scrollbar policy, use the **setVerticalScrollBarPolicy** with one of three constants from the **ScrollPaneConstants**:

> `VERTICAL_SCROLLBAR_AS_NEEDED`   Scroll bar appears when hosted component is wider than allocated space (default).
> `VERTICAL_SCROLLBAR_ALWAYS`   Scroll bar always appears.
> `VERTICAL_SCROLLBAR_NEVER`   Scroll bar never appears.

You don't need any code to make the scroll bars work – that capability comes along with the scroll pane.

Typical use of **scroll pane** control:

> ➢ Declare and create the scroll pane, assigning an identifiable **name**. For **myScrollPane**, the code is:

> `JScrollPane myScrollPane = new JScrollPane();`

> ➢ Set the scroll pane preferred size and, perhaps, set scroll bar policies.
> ➢ Establish the scroll pane viewport view.
> ➢ Add scroll pane to proper layout manager.
> ➢ Monitor events of the hosted control(s) in pane using usual techniques.

JComboBox Control

The **list** control is equivalent to a group of check boxes (allowing multiple selections in a long list of items). The equivalent control for a long list of radio buttons is the **combo box** control. The combo box allows the selection of a single item from a drop-down list. And, if desired, the user can type in an alternate response. The combo box uses its own "list model" allowing direct addition and removal of items from the drop-down list. It also provides its own scrolling capabilities – no need for a scroll pane.

Combo Box Properties:

model	Establishes the items in the drop-down list portion.
itemCount	Number of items in combo box.
font	Font name, style, size.
background	Combo box background color.
foreground	Color of text.
editable	Specifies if selection can be typed by user (default is false).
maximumRowCount	Number of rows to display in drop-down box (scroll bar will automatically appear if there are more items than space).
selectedIndex	Zero-based index of the currently selected item in combo box.
selectedItem	Currently selected item in the combo box.

Combo Box Methods:

setEditable	Establishes whether selected item can be edited.
getItemCount	Gets number of items in combo box.
setMaximumRowCount	Sets number of items to display in drop-down box.
setFont	Sets font name, style, size.
setBackground	Sets the combo box background color.
setForeground	Sets color of text.
getSelectedItem	Retrieves the selected item.
setSelectedIndex	Selects specified item in combo box.

Combo Box Event:

actionPerformed	Event triggered when user makes a selection or presses <Enter>. Added with **ActionListener**.

To add a listener for the **actionPerformed** event for a combo box control named **myComboBox**, use:

```
myComboBox.addActionListener(new ActionListener()
{
  public void actionPerformed(ActionEvent e)
  {
    myComboBoxActionPerformed(e);
  }
});
```

And, the corresponding event code would be placed in a **myComboBoxActionPerformed** method:

```
private void myComboBoxActionPerformed(ActionEvent e)
{
   [method code]
}
```

The combo box has its own list model for adding and removing items from its drop-down list, making list management easier than that of the list control. Items are added to the combo box (**myComboBox**) using the **addItem** or **insertItemAt** methods:

Add Item:
```
myComboBox.addItem(itemToAdd);
myComboBox.insertItemAt(itemToAdd, index);
```

With **addItem**, the item will be added at the end of the list. With **insertItemAt** the item will be added at the given **index** value.

Like list controls, there is no capability for sorted lists – for such lists, you need to add that capability using code.

To remove items from the combo box, there are three methods: **removeItem**, **removeItemAt**, or **removeAllItems**. For our example combo box, the respective commands are:

Delete Item:
```
myComboBox.removeItem(itemToRemove);
myComboBox.removeItemAt(index);
```
Clear list:
```
myComboBox.removeAllItems();
```

Note, when removing items, that indices for subsequent items in the list change following a removal.

To refer to an individual item in the combo box, use the **getItemAt** method:

```
myComboBox.getItemAt(index)
```

and the number of items in the combo box is given by the **getItemCount** method:

```
myComboBox.getItemCount();
```

To view, the last item in this list, you would use:

```
myComboBox.getItemAt(myComboBox.getItemCount() - 1)
```

Typical use of **combo box** control:

> ➢ Declare and create combo box control, assigning an identifiable **name**. For **myComboBox**, the code is:

```
JComboBox myComboBox = new JComboBox();
```

> ➢ Set **editable** property and add items to the combo box (usually in frame constructor).
> ➢ Place control within layout manager.
> ➢ Monitor **actionPerformed** event for selections.
> ➢ Read **selectedItem** property to identify choice.

Let's try to clear up all this new information about list controls, scroll panes and combo boxes with an example.

Example 3-3

Flight Planner

Start a new empty project in **NetBeans**. Name the project **Flight**. Delete default code in Java file named **Flight**. In this example, you select a destination city, a seat location, and a meal preference for airline passengers. The finished product will look like this:

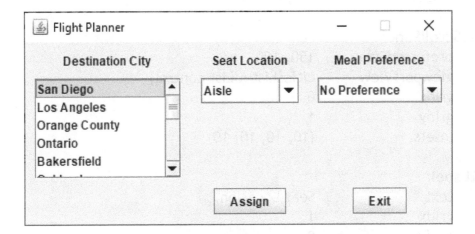

1. Place a scroll pane (which will hold a list control), two combo boxes, three labels and two buttons on the frame. The **GridBagLayout** arrangement for these controls should be:

	gridx = 0	gridx = 1	gridx = 2
gridy = 0	citiesLabel	seatLabel	mealLabel
gridy = 1	citiesScrollPane	seatComboBox	mealComboBox
gridy = 2		assignButton	exitButton

Set the frame and control properties:

Flight Frame:
title	Flight Planner
resizable	false

citiesLabel:
text	Destination City
gridx	0
gridy	0
insets	(10, 0, 0, 0)

citiesScrollPane:
preferredSize	150, 100
viewportView	citiesList (JList control)
gridx	0
gridy	1
insets	(10, 10, 10, 10)

seatLabel:
text	Seat Location
gridx	1
gridy	0
insets	(10, 0, 0, 0)

seatComboBox:
background	WHITE
gridx	1
gridy	1
insets	(10, 10, 0, 10)
anchor	NORTH

mealLabel:
text	Meal Preference
gridx	2
gridy	0
insets	(10, 0, 0, 0);

mealComboBox:

editable	true
gridx	2
gridy	1
insets	(10, 10, 0, 10)
anchor	NORTH

assignButton:

text	Assign
gridx	1
gridy	2
insets	(0, 0, 10, 0)

exitButton:

text	Exit
gridx	2
gridy	2
insets	(0, 0, 10, 0)

2. We will build the project in the usual stages – first code to establish the basic framework:

```
/*
 * Flight.java
 */
package flight;
import javax.swing.*;
import java.awt.*;
import java.awt.event.*;
public class Flight extends JFrame
{
  public static void main(String args[])
  {
    // construct frame
    new Flight().setVisible(true);
  }
  public Flight()
  {
    // create frame
    setTitle("Flight Planner");
    setResizable(false);
    addWindowListener(new WindowAdapter()
    {
      public void windowClosing(WindowEvent e)
      {
        exitForm(e);
      }
    });
    getContentPane().setLayout(new GridBagLayout());

    pack();
    Dimension screenSize =
Toolkit.getDefaultToolkit().getScreenSize();
    setBounds((int) (0.5 * (screenSize.width -
getWidth())), (int) (0.5 * (screenSize.height -
getHeight())), getWidth(), getHeight());
  }
  private void exitForm(WindowEvent e)
  {
    System.exit(0);
  }
}
```

Run to make sure the frame appears.

3. We will first add the scroll pane with the cities list control. Add these class level declarations:

```
JLabel citiesLabel = new JLabel();
JList citiesList = new JList();
JScrollPane citiesScrollPane = new JScrollPane();
```

Position and add each control to the frame (note how the cities list control is placed in scroll pane):

```
GridBagConstraints gridConstraints;
citiesLabel.setText("Destination City");
gridConstraints = new GridBagConstraints();
gridConstraints.gridx = 0;
gridConstraints.gridy = 0;
gridConstraints.insets = new Insets(10, 0, 0, 0);
getContentPane().add(citiesLabel, gridConstraints);
citiesScrollPane.setPreferredSize(new Dimension(150,
100));
citiesScrollPane.setViewportView(citiesList);
gridConstraints = new GridBagConstraints();
gridConstraints.gridx = 0;
gridConstraints.gridy = 1;
gridConstraints.insets = new Insets(10, 10, 10, 10);
getContentPane().add(citiesScrollPane, gridConstraints);
```

Now, at the end of the frame constructor, use this code to add elements to the cities list control and initialize the choice to the top element:

```
DefaultListModel citiesListModel = new DefaultListModel();
citiesListModel.addElement("San Diego");
citiesListModel.addElement("Los Angeles");
citiesListModel.addElement("Orange County");
citiesListModel.addElement("Ontario");
citiesListModel.addElement("Bakersfield");
citiesListModel.addElement("Oakland");
citiesListModel.addElement("Sacramento");
citiesListModel.addElement("San Jose");
citiesListModel.addElement("San Francisco");
citiesListModel.addElement("Eureka");
citiesListModel.addElement("Eugene");
citiesListModel.addElement("Portland");
citiesListModel.addElement("Spokane");
citiesListModel.addElement("Seattle");
citiesList.setModel(citiesListModel);
citiesList.setSelectedIndex(0);
```

Run the project – the city selection list will appear:

Try scrolling through the cities using the scroll pane. Do you see how easy it was to add scrolling capability?

4. Now, we'll add the combo box for picking a seat. Add these class level declarations:

```
JLabel seatLabel = new JLabel();
JComboBox seatComboBox = new JComboBox();
```

Position and add each control to the frame:

```
seatLabel.setText("Seat Location");
gridConstraints = new GridBagConstraints();
gridConstraints.gridx = 1;
gridConstraints.gridy = 0;
gridConstraints.insets = new Insets(10, 0, 0, 0);
getContentPane().add(seatLabel, gridConstraints);
seatComboBox.setBackground(Color.WHITE);
gridConstraints = new GridBagConstraints();
gridConstraints.gridx = 1;
gridConstraints.gridy = 1;
gridConstraints.insets = new Insets(10, 10, 0, 10);
gridConstraints.anchor = GridBagConstraints.NORTH;
getContentPane().add(seatComboBox, gridConstraints);
```

Add code to the frame constructor to "populate" the combo box:

```
seatComboBox.addItem("Aisle");
seatComboBox.addItem("Middle");
seatComboBox.addItem("Window");
seatComboBox.setSelectedIndex(0);
```

Rerun the project. Here's what I get:

Wait a minute!! What happened to the cities list control? As mentioned earlier, when we start setting preferred sizes, odd things can happen. And this is one of them. We set a preferred size for the scroll pane holding the cities list control, but not for the combo box. The **GridBagLayout** has trouble with this. The solution? Set a preferred size for the combo box. I used 100 by 25:

```
seatComboBox.setPreferredSize(new Dimension(100, 25));
```

With this additional property, if you rerun, things should appear properly:

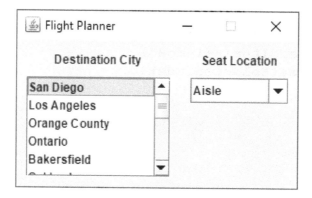

You can now pick a city and a seat. The moral here: when you're setting preferred sizes on some controls, but not others, weird things may happen. Fortunately, the only time we usually need to set preferred sizes is when using scroll panes.

5. Now, let's add the meal combo box and the two buttons (along with their methods). Add the class level declarations:

```
JLabel mealLabel = new JLabel();
JComboBox mealComboBox = new JComboBox();
JButton assignButton = new JButton();
JButton exitButton = new JButton();
```

Use this code to position and add the controls (and events):

```
mealLabel.setText("Meal Preference");
gridConstraints = new GridBagConstraints();
gridConstraints.gridx = 2;
gridConstraints.gridy = 0;
gridConstraints.insets = new Insets(10, 0, 0, 0);
getContentPane().add(mealLabel, gridConstraints);
mealComboBox.setEditable(true);
gridConstraints = new GridBagConstraints();
gridConstraints.gridx = 2;
gridConstraints.gridy = 1;
gridConstraints.insets = new Insets(10, 10, 0, 10);
gridConstraints.anchor = GridBagConstraints.NORTH;
getContentPane().add(mealComboBox, gridConstraints);

assignButton.setText("Assign");
gridConstraints = new GridBagConstraints();
gridConstraints.gridx = 1;
gridConstraints.gridy = 2;
gridConstraints.insets = new Insets(0, 0, 10, 0);
getContentPane().add(assignButton, gridConstraints);
assignButton.addActionListener(new ActionListener()
{
  public void actionPerformed(ActionEvent e)
  {
    assignButtonActionPerformed(e);
  }
});

exitButton.setText("Exit");
gridConstraints = new GridBagConstraints();
gridConstraints.gridx = 2;
gridConstraints.gridy = 2;
gridConstraints.insets = new Insets(0, 0, 10, 0);
getContentPane().add(exitButton, gridConstraints);
exitButton.addActionListener(new ActionListener()
{
```

```
   public void actionPerformed(ActionEvent e)
   {
     exitButtonActionPerformed(e);
   }
});
```

Use this code in the frame constructor to add choices to the meal combo box:

```
mealComboBox.addItem("Chicken");
mealComboBox.addItem("Mystery Meat");
mealComboBox.addItem("Kosher");
mealComboBox.addItem("Vegetarian");
mealComboBox.addItem("Fruit Plate");
mealComboBox.setSelectedItem("No Preference");
```

And, finally, add the two empty button events:

```
private void assignButtonActionPerformed(ActionEvent e)
{
}

private void exitButtonActionPerformed(ActionEvent e)
{
}
```

Rerun to see the finished control arrangement. Notice we didn't need to set a preferred size for the meal combo box – it shows up just as expected without messing up any of the other controls:

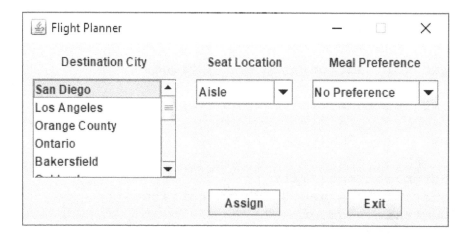

6. We can now add code to the two event methods. First, the
actionPerformed event for the **assignButton**:

```
private void assignButtonActionPerformed(ActionEvent e)
{
  // Build message box that gives your assignment
  String message;
  message = "Destination: " +
citiesList.getSelectedValue() + "\n";
  message += "Seat Location: " +
seatComboBox.getSelectedItem() + "\n";
  message += "Meal: " + mealComboBox.getSelectedItem() +
"\n";
  JOptionPane.showConfirmDialog(null, message, "Your
Assignment", JOptionPane.DEFAULT_OPTION,
JOptionPane.INFORMATION_MESSAGE);
}
```

When the **Assign** button is clicked, this code forms a confirm dialog box message
by concatenating the selected city (from **citiesList**), seat choice (from
seatComboBox), and the meal preference (from **mealComboBox**).

7. And, the code for the **exitButton**:

```
private void exitButtonActionPerformed(ActionEvent e)
{
  System.exit(0);
}
```

For reference purposes, here is the final **Flight.java** code listing (code added to basic framework is shaded):

```
/*
 * Flight.java
 */
package flight;
import javax.swing.*;
import java.awt.*;
import java.awt.event.*;

public class Flight extends JFrame
{
  JLabel citiesLabel = new JLabel();
  JList citiesList = new JList();
  JScrollPane citiesScrollPane = new JScrollPane();
  JLabel seatLabel = new JLabel();
  JComboBox seatComboBox = new JComboBox();
  JLabel mealLabel = new JLabel();
  JComboBox mealComboBox = new JComboBox();
  JButton assignButton = new JButton();
  JButton exitButton = new JButton();

  public static void main(String args[])
  {
    // construct frame
    new Flight().setVisible(true);
  }

  public Flight()
  {
    // create frame
    setTitle("Flight Planner");
    setResizable(false);
    addWindowListener(new WindowAdapter()
    {
      public void windowClosing(WindowEvent e)
      {
        exitForm(e);
      }
    });
    getContentPane().setLayout(new GridBagLayout());

    // position controls
    GridBagConstraints gridConstraints;
    citiesLabel.setText("Destination City");
    gridConstraints = new GridBagConstraints();
```

```java
    gridConstraints.gridx = 0;
    gridConstraints.gridy = 0;
    gridConstraints.insets = new Insets(10, 0, 0, 0);
    getContentPane().add(citiesLabel, gridConstraints);
    citiesScrollPane.setPreferredSize(new Dimension(150,
100));
    citiesScrollPane.setViewportView(citiesList);
    gridConstraints = new GridBagConstraints();
    gridConstraints.gridx = 0;
    gridConstraints.gridy = 1;
    gridConstraints.insets = new Insets(10, 10, 10, 10);
    getContentPane().add(citiesScrollPane, gridConstraints);

    seatLabel.setText("Seat Location");
    gridConstraints = new GridBagConstraints();
    gridConstraints.gridx = 1;
    gridConstraints.gridy = 0;
    gridConstraints.insets = new Insets(10, 0, 0, 0);
    getContentPane().add(seatLabel, gridConstraints);
    seatComboBox.setBackground(Color.WHITE);
    seatComboBox.setPreferredSize(new Dimension(100, 25));
    gridConstraints = new GridBagConstraints();
    gridConstraints.gridx = 1;
    gridConstraints.gridy = 1;
    gridConstraints.insets = new Insets(10, 10, 0, 10);
    gridConstraints.anchor = GridBagConstraints.NORTH;
    getContentPane().add(seatComboBox, gridConstraints);

    mealLabel.setText("Meal Preference");
    gridConstraints = new GridBagConstraints();
    gridConstraints.gridx = 2;
    gridConstraints.gridy = 0;
    gridConstraints.insets = new Insets(10, 0, 0, 0);
    getContentPane().add(mealLabel, gridConstraints);
    mealComboBox.setEditable(true);
    gridConstraints = new GridBagConstraints();
    gridConstraints.gridx = 2;
    gridConstraints.gridy = 1;
    gridConstraints.insets = new Insets(10, 10, 0, 10);
    gridConstraints.anchor = GridBagConstraints.NORTH;
    getContentPane().add(mealComboBox, gridConstraints);

    assignButton.setText("Assign");
    gridConstraints = new GridBagConstraints();
    gridConstraints.gridx = 1;
    gridConstraints.gridy = 2;
    gridConstraints.insets = new Insets(0, 0, 10, 0);
```

```
  getContentPane().add(assignButton, gridConstraints);
  assignButton.addActionListener(new ActionListener()
  {
    public void actionPerformed(ActionEvent e)
    {
      assignButtonActionPerformed(e);
    }
  });


  exitButton.setText("Exit");
  gridConstraints = new GridBagConstraints();
  gridConstraints.gridx = 2;
  gridConstraints.gridy = 2;
  gridConstraints.insets = new Insets(0, 0, 10, 0);
  getContentPane().add(exitButton, gridConstraints);
  exitButton.addActionListener(new ActionListener()
  {
    public void actionPerformed(ActionEvent e)
    {
      exitButtonActionPerformed(e);
    }
  });

  pack();
  Dimension screenSize =
Toolkit.getDefaultToolkit().getScreenSize();
  setBounds((int) (0.5 * (screenSize.width - getWidth())),
(int) (0.5 * (screenSize.height - getHeight())), getWidth(),
getHeight());
  // populate cities
  DefaultListModel citiesListModel = new
DefaultListModel();
  citiesListModel.addElement("San Diego");
  citiesListModel.addElement("Los Angeles");
  citiesListModel.addElement("Orange County");
  citiesListModel.addElement("Ontario");
  citiesListModel.addElement("Bakersfield");
  citiesListModel.addElement("Oakland");
  citiesListModel.addElement("Sacramento");
  citiesListModel.addElement("San Jose");
  citiesListModel.addElement("San Francisco");
  citiesListModel.addElement("Eureka");
  citiesListModel.addElement("Eugene");
  citiesListModel.addElement("Portland");
  citiesListModel.addElement("Spokane");
  citiesListModel.addElement("Seattle");
```

```java
        citiesList.setModel(citiesListModel);
        citiesList.setSelectedIndex(0);

        // populate seats
        seatComboBox.addItem("Aisle");
        seatComboBox.addItem("Middle");
        seatComboBox.addItem("Window");
        seatComboBox.setSelectedIndex(0);

        // meals
        mealComboBox.addItem("Chicken");
        mealComboBox.addItem("Mystery Meat");
        mealComboBox.addItem("Kosher");
        mealComboBox.addItem("Vegetarian");
        mealComboBox.addItem("Fruit Plate");
        mealComboBox.setSelectedItem("No Preference");
    }


    private void assignButtonActionPerformed(ActionEvent e)
    {
        // Build message box that gives your assignment
        String message;
        message = "Destination: " + citiesList.getSelectedValue()
+ "\n";
        message += "Seat Location: " +
seatComboBox.getSelectedItem() + "\n";
        message += "Meal: " + mealComboBox.getSelectedItem() +
"\n";
        JOptionPane.showConfirmDialog(null, message, "Your
Assignment", JOptionPane.DEFAULT_OPTION,
JOptionPane.INFORMATION_MESSAGE);
    }
    private void exitButtonActionPerformed(ActionEvent e)
    {
        System.exit(0);
    }
    private void exitForm(WindowEvent e)
    {
        System.exit(0);
    }
}
```

Run the application. You may have to correct some compilation errors. My finished screen with choices I made shows:

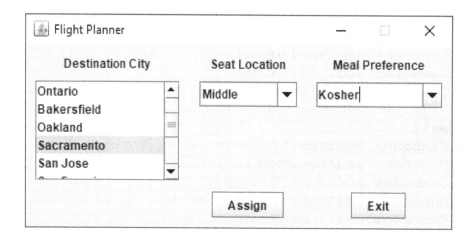

And, after clicking **Assign**, I see:

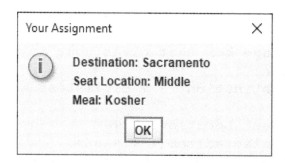

Save the project (saved as **Example3-3** project in **\LearnJava\LJ Code\Class 3** project group).

Class Review

After completing this class, you should understand:

➤ How to use the confirm dialog box (message box), assigning messages, icons and buttons
➤ Useful properties, events, and methods for the frame, button, text field, label, check box, and radio button controls
➤ Where the above listed controls can and should be used
➤ How the panel control is used to group controls, particularly radio buttons
➤ How several events can be handled by a single event procedure
➤ The concept of 'control arrays' and how to use them
➤ How to use list box and combo box controls
➤ How the scroll pane can add scrolling capabilities to a control

Practice Problems 3

Problem 3-1. Message Box Problem. Build an application that lets you see what various message boxes (confirm dialog boxes) look like. Allow selection of icon, buttons displayed, and input message. Provide feedback on button clicked on displayed message box.

Problem 3-2. Tray Problem. Here's a sheet of cardboard (**L** units long and **W** units wide). A square cut **X** units long is made in each corner:

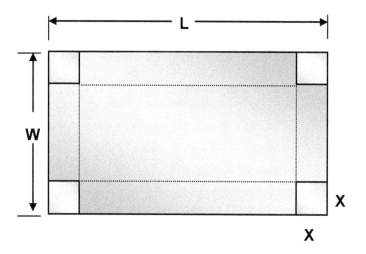

If you cut out the four shaded corners and fold the resulting sides up along the dotted lines, a tray is formed. Build an application that lets a user input the length (L) and width (W). Have the application decide what value X should be such that the tray has the largest volume possible.

Problem 3-3. List Problem. Build an application with two list controls. Select items from one box. Click a button to move selected items to the other list box. If you then click an item in the second list box and click a button, have it return to the first box. Insure the items in the first box are always in alphabetical order.

Problem 3-4. Combo Box Problem. Build an application with an editable combo box. Populate with some kind of information. If the user decides to type in their own selection (that is, they don't choose one of the listed items), add that new item to the drop-down list portion of the combo box.

Exercise 3

Customer Database Input Screen

A new sports store wants you to develop an input screen for its customer database. The required input information is:

1. Name
2. Age
3. City of Residence
4. Sex (Male or Female)
5. Activities (Running, Walking, Biking, Swimming, Skiing and/or In-Line Skating)
6. Athletic Level (Extreme, Advanced, Intermediate, or Beginner)

Set up the screen so that only the Name and Age (use text fields) and, perhaps, City (use a combo box) need to be typed; all other inputs should be set with check boxes and radio buttons. When a screen of information is complete, display the summarized profile in a message box. This profile message box should resemble this:

4

More Java Swing Controls

Review and Preview

In this class, we continue looking at Java Swing controls. We will look at spinners, scroll bars, sliders, labels (again, for displaying graphics) and file chooser dialogs that allow direct interaction with drives, directories, and files.

In the examples, you should start trying to do as much of the building and programming of the applications you can with minimal reference to the notes. This will help you build your programming skills.

JSpinner Control

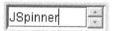

The **spinner** control is like a combo box control with no drop-down list. It is used to choose items from relatively short lists. Using different models, different information can be "spun through." We will look at two cases. We look at a **number spinner**, which uses a number model, and a **list spinner**, which uses a list model.

The **number** spinner looks like a text field control with two small arrows. Clicking the arrows changes the displayed value, which ranges from a specified minimum to a specified maximum. The user can even type in a value, if desired. Such controls are useful for supplying a date in a month or are used as volume controls in some multimedia applications.

The **list** spinner is similar in appearance to the number spinner. The difference is that the list spinner displays a list of string items (rather than numbers) as potential choices. The control is usually reserved for relatively small lists. Examples of use are selecting a state in the United States for an address book, selecting a month for a calendar input or selecting a name from a short list.

Spinner Properties:

model	Model used to supply information for the spinner
value	Current value displayed in spinner control.
font	Font name, style, size.
background	Spinner background color.
foreground	Color of text.

Spinner Methods:

getValue	Determine current value of spinner.
setModel	Establish model to use in spinner control
setFont	Sets font name, style, size.
setBackground	Sets the spinner background color.
setForeground	Sets color of text.

Spinner Event:

stateChanged   Event (**ChangeEvent**) triggered when the spinner
                                value changes. Added with **ChangeEventListener**
                                (requires importation of **javax.swing.event.*** files).

The **stateChanged** event is new in our work. To add a listener for such an event
to a spinner control named **mySpinner**, use:

```
mySpinner.addChangeListener(new ChangeListener()
{
  public void stateChanged(ChangeEvent e)
  {
    mySpinnerStateChanged(e);
  }
});
```

And, the corresponding event code would be placed in a
mySpinnerStateChanged method:

```
private void mySpinnerStateChanged(ChangeEvent e)
{
    [method code]
}
```

Special constructors are used to assign a model to the spinner control. For a
number spinner, the model comes from the **SpinnerNumberModel** class. The
syntax to assign a number model to a spinner (**mySpinner**) is:

```
mySpinner.setModel(new SpinnerNumberModel(value, minimum,
maximum, stepSize));
```

where:

value   Initial number to display
minimum   Minimum value to display
maximum   Maximum value to display
stepSize   Amount to increment or decrement the displayed value
when one of the arrows is clicked.

In our work, all values will be **int** types. The model also allows **double** types for **value**, **minimum**, **maximum**, and **stepSize**. The value for a number spinner can be changed by clicking either of the arrows or, optionally, by typing a value. If using the arrows, the value will always lie between **minimum** and **maximum**. If the user types in a value, you have no control over what value is typed. However, no adjustments to the number spinner can be made as long as the displayed value is outside the acceptable range (between **minimum** and **maximum**).

To recover the numeric value of the spinner (for mathematical operations) requires a bit of tricky code. The value returned by the **getValue** method is an object that can't be converted to an integer type. So, we take a two step process of first converting the object to a string, then converting the string to an **int** type. If the recovered value is **myValue**, the code that does all this for our example spinner (**mySpinner**) is:

```
myValue =
Integer.valueOf(mySpinner.getValue().toString()).intValue(
);
```

For a list spinner, the information to be displayed is stored in a **String** type array. The array is then assigned to the spinner using the **SpinnerListModel** class. The syntax to assign an array (**myArray**) to a spinner (**mySpinner**) is:

```
mySpinner.setModel(new SpinnerListModel(myArray));
```

Like the number spinner, the **value** property (a **String** type here) can be changed by clicking either of the arrows or, optionally, by typing a value. If the user types in a value, you have no control over what value is typed. If an illegal value is typed, no **stateChanged** event is registered until the value displayed matches one of the values in the spinner's list.

You may have noticed that, compared to other controls, the spinner control has <u>no</u> font, background, foreground, or alignment properties. Does this mean we are stuck with default values? No, it just means we need to take another route to change the properties. The display element of the spinner control is a text field managed by the control's **editor**. To change one of the specified properties, we directly access the text field through this editor. For our example spinner (**mySpinner**), to change the font to **myFont**, use:

```
((JSpinner.DefaultEditor)
mySpinner.getEditor()).getTextField().setFont(myFont);
```

To change the background color to **myColor**, use:

```
((JSpinner.DefaultEditor)
mySpinner.getEditor()).getTextField().setBackground(myColo
r);
```

To change the foreground color to **myColor**, use:

```
((JSpinner.DefaultEditor)
mySpinner.getEditor()).getTextField().setForeground(myColo
r);
```

And, to change the alignment to **myAlignment**, use:

```
((JSpinner.DefaultEditor)
mySpinner.getEditor()).getTextField().setHorizontalAlignme
nt(myAlignment);
```

These changes must be made <u>after</u> the spinner model is established.

Typical use of **spinner** control:

> ➤ Declare and create spinner control, assigning an identifiable **name**. For **mySpinner**, the code is:

```
JSpinner mySpinner = new JSpinner();
```

> ➤ Decide whether you are using a **number** or **list** spinner. For a number spinner, choose values for **value**, **minimum**, **maximum** and **stepSize**. Assign number model to spinner control:

```
mySpinner.setModel(new SpinnerNumberModel(value,
minimum, maximum, stepSize);
```

For a list spinner, create an array of the items to display in the list spinner. Assign that array (**myArray**) to spinner control:

```
mySpinner.setModel(new SpinnerListModel(myArray));
```

> ➤ Place control in layout manager.
> ➤ Add listener for and monitor **stateChanged** event for changes in value.
> ➤ Use **getValue** method to determine current value.
> ➤ You may also choose to change the **font**, **background** and **foreground** properties of the spinner control.

Example 4-1

Date Input Device

Start a new project in **NetBeans**. Name the project **DateInput**. Delete code in Java file named **DateInput**. In this project, we'll use two spinner controls to select a month and day of the year. The finished frame will be:

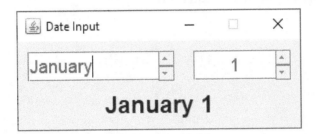

1. Place two spinner controls and a label control on the frame. The **GridBagLayout** arrangement is:

	gridx = 0	gridx = 1
gridy = 0	monthSpinner	daySpinner
gridy = 1	dateLabel	

Properties set in code:

DateInput Frame:

title	Date Input
resizable	false

monthSpinner:

model	SpinnerListModel (array **monthNames**)
preferredSize	(150, 30)
font	Arial, PLAIN, 18
foreground	BLUE
gridx	0
gridy	0
insets	(10, 10, 10, 10)

daySpinner:

model	SpinnerNumberModel
value	1
minimum	1
maximum	31
stepSize	1
preferredSize	(100, 30)
font	Arial, PLAIN, 18
foreground	BLUE
horizontalAlignment	CENTER
gridx	1
gridy	0
insets	(10, 10, 10, 10)

dateLabel:

text	January 1
font	Arial, BOLD, 18
foreground	BLUE
horizontalAlignment	CENTER
gridx	0
gridy	1
gridwidth	2
insets	(0, 0, 10, 0)

2. We first build the framework:

```
/*
 * DateInput.java
 */
package dateinput;
import javax.swing.*;
import javax.swing.event.*;
import java.awt.*;
import java.awt.event.*;

public class DateInput extends JFrame
{
  public static void main(String args[])
  {
    // create frame
    new DateInput().setVisible(true);
  }

  public DateInput()
```

```java
{
  // frame constructor
  setTitle("Date Input");
  setResizable(false);
  addWindowListener(new WindowAdapter()
  {
    public void windowClosing(WindowEvent evt)
    {
      exitForm(evt);
    }
  });
  getContentPane().setLayout(new GridBagLayout());

  pack();
   Dimension screenSize =
Toolkit.getDefaultToolkit().getScreenSize();
    setBounds((int) (0.5 * (screenSize.width - getWidth())),
(int) (0.5 * (screenSize.height - getHeight())), getWidth(),
getHeight());

  }

  private void exitForm(WindowEvent evt)
  {
    System.exit(0);
  }
}
```

Run to make sure the frame appears.

3. Declare the **monthNames** array as a class level variable:

```
String[] monthNames = new String[12];
```

In the frame constructor method, add elements to this array:

```
// add month names
monthNames[0] = "January";
monthNames[1] = "February";
monthNames[2] = "March";
monthNames[3] = "April";
monthNames[4] = "May";
monthNames[5] = "June";
monthNames[6] = "July";
monthNames[7] = "August";
monthNames[8] = "September";
monthNames[9] = "October";
monthNames[10] = "November";
monthNames[11] = "December";
```

4. Next, add the controls and the event method. Declare and create the three controls:

```
JSpinner monthSpinner = new JSpinner();
JSpinner daySpinner = new JSpinner();
JLabel dateLabel = new JLabel();
```

Position and add each control. Add a change event for the two spinner controls:

```
GridBagConstraints gridConstraints;
monthSpinner.setPreferredSize(new Dimension(150, 30));
monthSpinner.setModel(new SpinnerListModel(monthNames));
((JSpinner.DefaultEditor)
monthSpinner.getEditor()).getTextField().setFont(new
Font("Arial", Font.PLAIN, 18));
((JSpinner.DefaultEditor)
monthSpinner.getEditor()).getTextField().setForeground(Col
or.BLUE);
gridConstraints = new GridBagConstraints();
gridConstraints.gridx = 0;
gridConstraints.gridy = 0;
gridConstraints.insets = new Insets(10, 10, 10, 10);
getContentPane().add(monthSpinner, gridConstraints);
monthSpinner.addChangeListener(new ChangeListener()
{
   public void stateChanged(ChangeEvent e)
```

```
    {
      dateStateChanged(e);
    }
});

daySpinner.setPreferredSize(new Dimension(100, 30));
SpinnerNumberModel dayNumberModel = new
SpinnerNumberModel(1, 1, 31, 1);
daySpinner.setModel(dayNumberModel);
((JSpinner.DefaultEditor)
daySpinner.getEditor()).getTextField().setHorizontalAlignm
ent(SwingConstants.CENTER);
((JSpinner.DefaultEditor)
daySpinner.getEditor()).getTextField().setFont(new
Font("Arial", Font.PLAIN, 18));
((JSpinner.DefaultEditor)
daySpinner.getEditor()).getTextField().setForeground(Color
.BLUE);
gridConstraints = new GridBagConstraints();
gridConstraints.gridx = 1;
gridConstraints.gridy = 0;
gridConstraints.insets = new Insets(10, 10, 10, 10);
getContentPane().add(daySpinner, gridConstraints);
daySpinner.addChangeListener(new ChangeListener()
{
  public void stateChanged(ChangeEvent e)
  {
    dateStateChanged(e);
  }
});

dateLabel.setText("January 1");
dateLabel.setFont(new Font("Arial", Font.BOLD, 24));
dateLabel.setHorizontalAlignment(SwingConstants.CENTER);
gridConstraints = new GridBagConstraints();
gridConstraints.gridx = 0;
gridConstraints.gridy = 1;
gridConstraints.gridwidth = 2;
gridConstraints.insets = new Insets(0, 0, 10, 0);
getContentPane().add(dateLabel, gridConstraints);
```

5. We'll skip checking the project at this point and go right to adding the code - there's only one line!! Use this code in the **dateStateChanged** event:

```
private void dateStateChanged(ChangeEvent e)
{
   dateLabel.setText(monthSpinner.getValue() + " " +
daySpinner.getValue());
}
```

This code simply updates the displayed date when either the selected month or day changes.

The final **DateInput.java** code listing (code added to basic framework is shaded):

```
/*
 * DateInput.java
 */
package dateinput;
import javax.swing.*;
import javax.swing.event.*;
import java.awt.*;
import java.awt.event.*;
public class DateInput extends JFrame
{
  JSpinner monthSpinner = new JSpinner();
  JSpinner daySpinner = new JSpinner();
  JLabel dateLabel = new JLabel();
  String[] monthNames = new String[12];
  public static void main(String args[])
  {
    // create frame
    new DateInput().setVisible(true);
  }
  public DateInput()
  {
    // frame constructor
    setTitle("Date Input");
    setResizable(false);
    addWindowListener(new WindowAdapter()
    {
      public void windowClosing(WindowEvent evt)
      {
        exitForm(evt);
      }
    });
```

```java
    getContentPane().setLayout(new GridBagLayout());
    // position controls
    GridBagConstraints gridConstraints;
    monthSpinner.setPreferredSize(new Dimension(150, 30));
    monthSpinner.setModel(new SpinnerListModel(monthNames));
    ((JSpinner.DefaultEditor)
monthSpinner.getEditor()).getTextField().setFont(new
Font("Arial", Font.PLAIN, 18));
    ((JSpinner.DefaultEditor)
monthSpinner.getEditor()).getTextField().setForeground(Color.
BLUE);
    gridConstraints = new GridBagConstraints();
    gridConstraints.gridx = 0;
    gridConstraints.gridy = 0;
    gridConstraints.insets = new Insets(10, 10, 10, 10);
    getContentPane().add(monthSpinner, gridConstraints);
    monthSpinner.addChangeListener(new ChangeListener()
    {
      public void stateChanged(ChangeEvent e)
      {
        dateStateChanged(e);
      }
    });
    daySpinner.setPreferredSize(new Dimension(100, 30));
    SpinnerNumberModel dayNumberModel = new
SpinnerNumberModel(1, 1, 31, 1);
    daySpinner.setModel(dayNumberModel);
    ((JSpinner.DefaultEditor)
daySpinner.getEditor()).getTextField().setHorizontalAlignment
(SwingConstants.CENTER);
    ((JSpinner.DefaultEditor)
daySpinner.getEditor()).getTextField().setFont(new
Font("Arial", Font.PLAIN, 18));
    ((JSpinner.DefaultEditor)
daySpinner.getEditor()).getTextField().setForeground(Color.BL
UE);
    gridConstraints = new GridBagConstraints();
    gridConstraints.gridx = 1;
    gridConstraints.gridy = 0;
    gridConstraints.insets = new Insets(10, 10, 10, 10);
    getContentPane().add(daySpinner, gridConstraints);
    daySpinner.addChangeListener(new ChangeListener()
    {
      public void stateChanged(ChangeEvent e)
      {
        dateStateChanged(e);
      }
```

```java
    });
    dateLabel.setText("January 1");
    dateLabel.setFont(new Font("Arial", Font.BOLD, 24));
    dateLabel.setHorizontalAlignment(SwingConstants.CENTER);
    gridConstraints = new GridBagConstraints();
    gridConstraints.gridx = 0;
    gridConstraints.gridy = 1;
    gridConstraints.gridwidth = 2;
    gridConstraints.insets = new Insets(0, 0, 10, 0);
    getContentPane().add(dateLabel, gridConstraints);
    pack();
    Dimension screenSize =
Toolkit.getDefaultToolkit().getScreenSize();
    setBounds((int) (0.5 * (screenSize.width - getWidth())),
(int) (0.5 * (screenSize.height - getHeight())), getWidth(),
getHeight());
    // add month names
    monthNames[0] = "January";
    monthNames[1] = "February";
    monthNames[2] = "March";
    monthNames[3] = "April";
    monthNames[4] = "May";
    monthNames[5] = "June";
    monthNames[6] = "July";
    monthNames[7] = "August";
    monthNames[8] = "September";
    monthNames[9] = "October";
    monthNames[10] = "November";
    monthNames[11] = "December";
  }
  private void dateStateChanged(ChangeEvent e)
  {
    dateLabel.setText(monthSpinner.getValue() + " " +
daySpinner.getValue());
  }
  private void exitForm(WindowEvent evt)
  {
    System.exit(0);
  }
}
```

Run the program. Scroll through the month names. Scroll through the day values, noticing how the displayed date changes. Here's what I see:

Save the project (saved as **Example4-1** project in the **\LearnJava\LJ Code\Class 4** project group). Do you notice that you could enter April 31 as a date, even though it's not a legal value? Can you think of how to modify this example to make sure you don't exceed the number of days in any particular month? And, how would you handle February – you need to know if it's a leap year.

JScrollBar Control

The number spinner control is useful for relatively small ranges of numeric input. It wouldn't work well for large number ranges – you'd spend a lot of time clicking those little arrows. For large ranges of numbers, we use **scroll bar** controls. Scroll bars are widely used in GUI applications. Scroll bars provide an intuitive way to move through a list of information and make great input devices. Here, we use a scroll bar to obtain a whole number (**int** data type).

Scroll bars are comprised of three areas that can be clicked, or dragged, to change the scroll bar value. Those areas are:

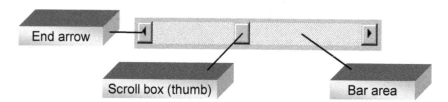

Clicking an **end arrow** increments the **scroll box** a small amount, clicking the **bar area** increments the scroll box a large amount, and dragging the scroll box (thumb) provides continuous motion. Using the properties of scroll bars, we can completely specify how one works. The scroll box position is the only output information from a scroll bar.

Scroll Bar Properties:

preferredSize	Specified size (width, height) of scroll bar.
value	Current position of the scroll box (thumb) within the scroll bar. If you set this in code, Java moves the scroll box to the proper position.
minimum	The minimum possible scroll bar value.
maximum	The maximum possible scroll bar value.
unitIncrement	The increment added to or subtracted from the scroll bar value property when either of the scroll arrows is clicked.
blockIncrement	Increment added to or subtracted from the scroll bar value property when the bar area is clicked.
extent	Width of scroll box.
orientation	Determines whether the scroll bar lies horizontally or vertically.

Scroll Bar Methods:

setPreferredSize	Establishes size of scroll bar.
setValue	Sets current value.
getValue	Determines current value.
setMinimum	Establish minimum value.
setMaximum	Establish minimum value.
setUnitIncrement	Establish unitIncrement property.
setBlockIncrement	Establish blockIncrement property.
setVisibleAmount	Sets width (extent) of scroll box.
getVisibleAmount	Determines width (extent) of scroll box.
setOrientation	Sets orientation of scroll bar (**JScrollBar.HORIZONTAL** for horizontal scroll bar, **JScrollBar.VERTICAL** for vertical scroll bar).

Scroll Bar Event:

adjustmentValueChanged	Event (**AdjustmentEvent**) triggered when the scroll bar value changes. Added with **AdjustmentEventListener** (requires importation of **javax.swing.event.*** files).

Location of properties for **horizontal** scroll bar:

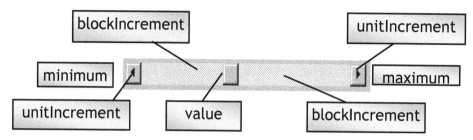

Location of properties for **vertical** scroll bar:

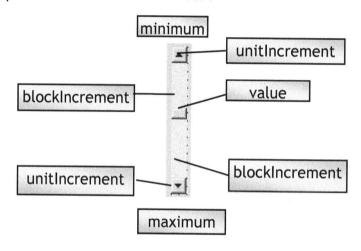

A couple of important notes about scroll bar properties:

1. Notice the vertical scroll bar has its **minimum** at the top and its **maximum** at the bottom. This may be counter-intuitive in some applications. That is, users may expect things to 'go up' as they increase. You can give this appearance of going up by defining another variable that varies 'negatively' with the scroll bar value property.

2. If you ever change the **value**, **minimum**, or **maximum** properties in code, make sure value is at all times between **minimum** and **maximum** or the program will stop with an error message.

To add a listener for the **adjustmentValueChanged** event to a scroll bar control named **myScrollBar**, use:

```
myScrollBar.addAdjustmentListener(new AdjustmentListener()
{
  public void adjustmentValueChanged(AdjustmentEvent e)
  {
    myScrollBarAdjustmentValueChanged(e);
  }
});
```

And, the corresponding event code would be placed in a **myScrollBarAdjustmentValueChanged** method:

```
private void myScrollBarAdjustmentValueChanged
(AdjustmentEvent e)
{
    [method code]
}
```

Typical use of **scroll bar** control:

Declare and create scroll bar control, assigning a meaningful **name**. For **myScrollBar**, the code is:

```
JScrollBar myScrollBar = new JScrollBar();
```

Set the **minimum, maximum, unitIncrement, blockIncrement,** and **orientation** properties. Initialize **value** property.
Place control in grid layout.
Add listener for and monitor **adjustmentValueChanged** event for changes in value.

A Note on the **maximum** Property:

Due to the width of the scroll box (extent), the **maximum** value cannot be achieved by clicking the end arrows, the bar area or moving the scroll box. The maximum achievable **value,** via mouse operations, is given by the relation:

"achievable" maximum = **maximum** – extent

where **extent** is the width of the scroll box. What does this mean? To meet an "achievable" maximum, you need to set the scroll bar **maximum** property using this equation:

maximum = "achievable" maximum + extent

To get the **extent** (or width of the scroll box), use the **getVisibleAmount** method. For example, if you want a scroll bar (**myScrollBar**) to be able to reach 100, set **maximum** using:

```
myScrollBar.setMaximum(100 +
myScrollBar.getVisibleAmount());
```

JSlider Control

The **slider** control is similar to the scroll bar with a different interface. It is used to establish numeric input (usually a fairly small range). It can be oriented either horizontally or vertically. Clicking on the slider, scrolling the pointer, clicking the cursor control keys or pressing <**PgUp**> or <**PgDn**> changes the slider value. The change increments are set by the slider control and cannot be changed. The smallest increment is one. The largest increment is one-tenth of the slider range (this increment is added/subtracted from the value by pressing <**PgUp**> or <**PgDn**>).

Slider Properties:

preferredSize	Specified size (width, height) of slider.
value	Current position of the pointer within the slider. If you set this in code, Java moves the pointer to the proper position.
minimum	The minimum possible slider value.
maximum	The maximum possible slider value.
paintTicks	Used to establish if major and minor tick marks are drawn.
majorTickSpacing	Repetition rate of major tick marks.
minorTickSpacing	Repetition rate of minor tick marks.
paintLabels	Used to add labels to slider values.
inverted	Boolean value indicating direction pointer moves. If false, pointer increments from left to right or from bottom to top; if true, pointer increments from right to left or top to bottom.
orientation	Determines whether the slider lies horizontally or vertically.

Slider Methods:

setPreferredSize	Establishes size of slider.
setValue	Sets current value.
getValue	Determines current value.
setMinimum	Establish minimum value.
setMaximum	Establish minimum value.
setPaintTicks	If true, tick marks are drawn.
setMajorTickSpacing	Set repetition rate of major tick marks (use zero for no major ticks).
setMinorTickSpacing	Set repetition rate of minor tick marks (use zero for no minor ticks).
setPaintLabels	If true, labels are added to slider.
setinverted	Boolean value indicating direction pointer moves. If false, pointer increments from left to right or from **setOrientation** Sets orientation of slider (**JSlider.HORIZONTAL** for horizontal slider, **JScrollBar.VERTICAL** for vertical slider).

Scroll Event:

stateChanged	Event (**ChangeEvent**) triggered when the slider value changes. Added with **ChangeListener** (requires of **javax.swing.event.*** files).

To add a listener for the **stateChanged** event to a slider control named **mySlider**, use:

```
mySlider.addChangeListener(new ChangeListener()
{
  public void stateChanged(ChangeEvent e)
  {
    mySliderStateChanged(e);
  }
});
```

And, the corresponding event code would be placed in a **mySliderStateChanged** method:

```
private void mySliderStateChanged (ChangeEvent e)
{
   [method code]
}
```

A couple of important notes about slider properties:

1. Notice the slider can have the **maximum** or **minimum** at either end of the control. This is different than the scroll bar control.

2. If you ever change the **value**, **minimum**, or **maximum** properties in code, make sure value is at all times between **minimum** and **maximum** or the program will stop with an error message.

3. The track bar **maximum** property can be achieved in code or via mouse operations. It does not exhibit the behavior noted with the scroll bar control (meaning the achievable maximum and **maximum** property value are the same).

Typical use of **slider** control:

➢ Declare and create slider control, assigning a meaningful **name**. For **mySlider**, the code is:

```
JSlider mySlider = new JSlider ();
```

➢ Set the **minimum, maximum,** and **orientation** properties. Initialize **value** property. Choose tick marks and labels, if desired.
➢ Place control in grid layout.
➢ Add listener for and monitor **stateChanged** event for changes in value.

Example 4-2

Temperature Conversion

Start a new project in **NetBeans**. Name the project **Temperature**. Delete code in Java file named **Temperature**. In this project, we convert temperatures in degrees Fahrenheit (set using a horizontal scroll bar) to degrees Celsius. The formula for converting Fahrenheit (F) to Celsius (C) is:

$$C = (F - 32) * 5 / 9$$

Temperatures will be adjusted and displayed in tenths of degrees. The finished frame will look like this:

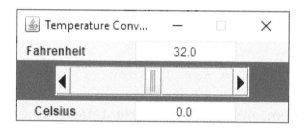

1. Place a panel (will hold the scroll bar and will change colors at a particular temperature), two labels, and two text fields on the frame. The **GridBagLayout** arrangement for the controls is:

	gridx = 0	gridx = 1
gridy = 0	degreesFLabel	degreesFTextField
gridy = 1	colorPanel (holds temperatureScrollBar)	
gridy = 2	degreesCLabel	degreesCTextField

Set the properties of the frame and each control:

Temperature Frame:

title	Temperature Conversion
resizable	false

degreesFLabel:

text	Fahrenheit
gridx	0
gridy	0
insets	(0, 10, 0, 0)

degreesFTextField:

text	32.0
columns	10
editable	false
background	WHITE
horizontalAlignment	CENTER
gridx	1
gridy	0

degreesCLabel:

text	Fahrenheit
gridx	0
gridy	2
insets	(0, 10, 0, 0)

degreesCTextField:

text	0.0
columns	10
editable	false
background	WHITE
horizontalAlignment	CENTER
gridx	1
gridy	2

colorPanel:

preferredSize	(280, 40)
background	BLUE
gridx	0
gridy	1
gridwidth	2

temperatureScrollBar:

preferredSize	(200, 30)
minimum	-600
maximum	1200 ("achievable" maximum)
blockIncrement	10
unitIncrement	1
value	320
orientation	HORIZONTAL

Note the scroll bar properties (**value**, **minimum**, **maximum**, **blockIncrement**, **unitIncrement**) are in tenths of degrees. The initial temperatures are initialized at 32.0 F (value = 320 tenths of degrees) and 0.0 C, known values.

We want an "achievable maximum" of 120.0 degrees or a value of 1200. So, in code we will set the **maximum** using:

```
temperatureScrollBar.setMaximum(1200 +
temperatureScrollBar.getVisibleAmount());
```

2. As usual, build the basic framework:

```
/*
 * Temperature.java
 */
package temperature;
import javax.swing.*;
import javax.swing.event.*;
import java.awt.*;
import java.awt.event.*;
import java.text.*;

public class Temperature extends JFrame
{

  public static void main(String args[])
  {
    // create frame
    new Temperature().setVisible(true);
  }

  public Temperature()
  {
    // frame constructor
    setTitle("Temperature Conversion");
    setResizable(false);
    addWindowListener(new WindowAdapter()
    {
      public void windowClosing(WindowEvent evt)
      {
        exitForm(evt);
      }
    });
    getContentPane().setLayout(new GridBagLayout());
```

```
      pack();
      Dimension screenSize =
Toolkit.getDefaultToolkit().getScreenSize();
      setBounds((int) (0.5 * (screenSize.width -
getWidth())), (int) (0.5 * (screenSize.height -
getHeight())), getWidth(), getHeight());

   }

   private void exitForm(WindowEvent evt)
   {
      System.exit(0);
   }
}
```

Run to make sure things are okay.

3. Now, we add controls. First, declare and create the label and text field for the Fahrenheit temperature:

```
JLabel degreesFLabel = new JLabel();
JTextField degreesFTextField = new JTextField();
```

Position and add these controls to the frame:

```
GridBagConstraints gridConstraints;
degreesFLabel.setText("Fahrenheit");
gridConstraints = new GridBagConstraints();
gridConstraints.gridx = 0;
gridConstraints.gridy = 0;
gridConstraints.insets = new Insets(0, 10, 0, 0);
getContentPane().add(degreesFLabel, gridConstraints);
degreesFTextField.setText("32.0");
degreesFTextField.setColumns(10);
degreesFTextField.setHorizontalAlignment(SwingConstants.CE
NTER);
degreesFTextField.setEditable(false);
degreesFTextField.setBackground(Color.WHITE);
gridConstraints = new GridBagConstraints();
gridConstraints.gridx = 1;
gridConstraints.gridy = 0;
getContentPane().add(degreesFTextField, gridConstraints);
```

Run to see:

4. Now, declare and create the label and text field for the Celsius temperature:

```
JLabel degreesCLabel = new JLabel();
JTextField degreesCTextField = new JTextField();
```

Position and add these controls to the frame:

```
degreesCLabel.setText("Celsius");
gridConstraints = new GridBagConstraints();
gridConstraints.gridx = 0;
gridConstraints.gridy = 2;
gridConstraints.insets = new Insets(0, 10, 0, 0);
getContentPane().add(degreesCLabel, gridConstraints);
degreesCTextField.setText("0.0");
degreesCTextField.setColumns(10);
degreesCTextField.setHorizontalAlignment(SwingConstants.CE
NTER);
degreesCTextField.setEditable(false);
degreesCTextField.setBackground(Color.WHITE);
gridConstraints = new GridBagConstraints();
gridConstraints.gridx = 1;
gridConstraints.gridy = 2;
getContentPane().add(degreesCTextField, gridConstraints);
```

Run to see:

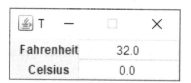

5. Finally, add the panel and scroll bar (with an empty event for the scroll bar). Declare and create the controls:

```
JPanel colorPanel = new JPanel();
JScrollBar temperatureScrollBar = new JScrollBar();
```

Position and add controls to frame. Add scroll bar **adjustmentValueChanged** method:

```
colorPanel.setBackground(Color.BLUE);
colorPanel.setPreferredSize(new Dimension (280, 40));
gridConstraints = new GridBagConstraints();
gridConstraints.gridx = 0;
gridConstraints.gridy = 1;
gridConstraints.gridwidth = 2;
getContentPane().add(colorPanel, gridConstraints);
temperatureScrollBar.setMinimum(-600);
temperatureScrollBar.setMaximum(1200 +
temperatureScrollBar.getVisibleAmount());
temperatureScrollBar.setBlockIncrement(10);
temperatureScrollBar.setUnitIncrement(1);
temperatureScrollBar.setValue(320);
temperatureScrollBar.setOrientation(JScrollBar.HORIZONTAL)
;
temperatureScrollBar.setPreferredSize(new Dimension (200,
30));
colorPanel.add(temperatureScrollBar);
temperatureScrollBar.addAdjustmentListener(new
AdjustmentListener()
{
  public void adjustmentValueChanged(AdjustmentEvent e)
  {
temperatureScrollBarAdjustmentValueChanged(e);
  }
});
```

Add the empty event method:

```
private void
temperatureScrollBarAdjustmentValueChanged(AdjustmentEvent
e)
{
}
```

Run the project to see the finished control arrangement:

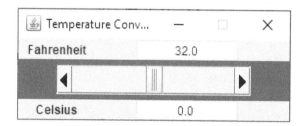

6. Now, we'll write the code. We need a single class level variable:

```
boolean isHot = false;
```

7. Use this code for the **adjustmentValueChanged** event method:

```
private void
temperatureScrollBarAdjustmentValueChanged(AdjustmentEvent
e)
{
   double tempF, tempC;
   // Read F and convert to C - divide by 10 needed since
value is tenths of degrees
   tempF = (double) temperatureScrollBar.getValue() / 10;
   //check to see if changed from hot to cold or vice versa
   if (isHot && tempF < 70)
   {
     // changed to cold
     isHot = false;
     colorPanel.setBackground(Color.BLUE);
   }
   else if (!isHot && tempF >= 70)
   {
     //changed to hot
     isHot = true;
     colorPanel.setBackground(Color.RED);
   }
   degreesFTextField.setText(new
DecimalFormat("0.0").format(tempF));
   tempC = (tempF - 32.0) * 5.0 / 9.0;
   degreesCTextField.setText(new
DecimalFormat("0.0").format(tempC));
}
```

This code determines the scroll bar value as it changes, takes that value as Fahrenheit temperature, computes Celsius temperature, and displays both values. A blue panel is displayed used for cold temperatures, a red panel for warm temperatures (yes, 70 degrees is considered warm in Seattle!).

The complete **Temperature.java** code listing (code added to basic framework is shaded):

```
/*
 * Temperature.java
 */
package temperature;
import javax.swing.*;
import javax.swing.event.*;
import java.awt.*;
import java.awt.event.*;
import java.text.*;
public class Temperature extends JFrame
{
  JLabel degreesFLabel = new JLabel();
  JTextField degreesFTextField = new JTextField();
  JPanel colorPanel = new JPanel();
  JScrollBar temperatureScrollBar = new JScrollBar();
  JLabel degreesCLabel = new JLabel();
  JTextField degreesCTextField = new JTextField();
  boolean isHot = false;
  public static void main(String args[])
  {
    // create frame
    new Temperature().setVisible(true);
  }
  public Temperature()
  {
    // frame constructor
    setTitle("Temperature Conversion");
    setResizable(false);
    addWindowListener(new WindowAdapter()
    {
      public void windowClosing(WindowEvent evt)
      {
        exitForm(evt);
      }
    });
    getContentPane().setLayout(new GridBagLayout());
    // position controls
    GridBagConstraints gridConstraints;
    degreesFLabel.setText("Fahrenheit");
    gridConstraints = new GridBagConstraints();
    gridConstraints.gridx = 0;
    gridConstraints.gridy = 0;
    gridConstraints.insets = new Insets(0, 10, 0, 0);
    getContentPane().add(degreesFLabel, gridConstraints);
```

```
    degreesFTextField.setText("32.0");
    degreesFTextField.setColumns(10);

degreesFTextField.setHorizontalAlignment(SwingConstants.CENTE
R);
    degreesFTextField.setEditable(false);
    degreesFTextField.setBackground(Color.WHITE);
    gridConstraints = new GridBagConstraints();
    gridConstraints.gridx = 1;
    gridConstraints.gridy = 0;
    getContentPane().add(degreesFTextField, gridConstraints);
    degreesCLabel.setText("Celsius");
    gridConstraints = new GridBagConstraints();
    gridConstraints.gridx = 0;
    gridConstraints.gridy = 2;
    gridConstraints.insets = new Insets(0, 10, 0, 0);
    getContentPane().add(degreesCLabel, gridConstraints);
    degreesCTextField.setText("0.0");
    degreesCTextField.setColumns(10);

degreesCTextField.setHorizontalAlignment(SwingConstants.CENTE
R);
    degreesCTextField.setEditable(false);
    degreesCTextField.setBackground(Color.WHITE);
    gridConstraints = new GridBagConstraints();
    gridConstraints.gridx = 1;
    gridConstraints.gridy = 2;
    getContentPane().add(degreesCTextField, gridConstraints);
    colorPanel.setBackground(Color.BLUE);
    colorPanel.setPreferredSize(new Dimension (280, 40));
    gridConstraints = new GridBagConstraints();
    gridConstraints.gridx = 0;
    gridConstraints.gridy = 1;
    gridConstraints.gridwidth = 2;
    getContentPane().add(colorPanel, gridConstraints);
    temperatureScrollBar.setMinimum(-600);
    temperatureScrollBar.setMaximum(1200 +
temperatureScrollBar.getVisibleAmount());
    temperatureScrollBar.setBlockIncrement(10);
    temperatureScrollBar.setUnitIncrement(1);
    temperatureScrollBar.setValue(320);

temperatureScrollBar.setOrientation(JScrollBar.HORIZONTAL);
    temperatureScrollBar.setPreferredSize(new Dimension (200,
30));
    colorPanel.add(temperatureScrollBar);
```

```
        temperatureScrollBar.addAdjustmentListener(new
AdjustmentListener()
        {
          public void adjustmentValueChanged(AdjustmentEvent e)
          {
            temperatureScrollBarAdjustmentValueChanged(e);
          }
        });
      pack();
      Dimension screenSize =
Toolkit.getDefaultToolkit().getScreenSize();
      setBounds((int) (0.5 * (screenSize.width - getWidth())),
(int) (0.5 * (screenSize.height - getHeight())), getWidth(),
getHeight());
    }
  private void
temperatureScrollBarAdjustmentValueChanged(AdjustmentEvent e)
    {
      double tempF, tempC;
      // Read F and convert to C - divide by 10 needed since
value is tenths of degrees
      tempF = (double) temperatureScrollBar.getValue() / 10;
      //check to see if changed from hot to cold or vice versa
      if (isHot && tempF < 70)
      {
        // changed to cold
        isHot = false;
        colorPanel.setBackground(Color.BLUE);
      }
      else if (!isHot && tempF >= 70)
      {
        //changed to hot
        isHot = true;
        colorPanel.setBackground(Color.RED);
      }
      degreesFTextField.setText(new
DecimalFormat("0.0").format(tempF));
      tempC = (tempF - 32.0) * 5.0 / 9.0;
      degreesCTextField.setText(new
DecimalFormat("0.0").format(tempC));
    }
  private void exitForm(WindowEvent evt)
  {
    System.exit(0);
  }
}
```

Run the program. Make sure it provides correct information at obvious points.
For example, 32.0 F better always be the same as 0.0 C! What happens around
70 F? Here's run I made:

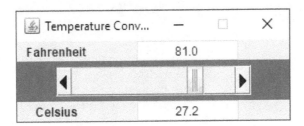

Save the project (saved as **Example4-2** project in the **\LearnJava\LJ Code\Class
4** project group).

Can you find a point where Fahrenheit temperature equals Celsius temperature?
If you don't know this off the top of your head, it's obvious you've never lived in
extremely cold climates. I've actually witnessed one of those bank temperature
signs flashing degrees F and degrees C and seeing the same number! Ever
wonder why body temperature is that odd figure of 98.6 degrees F? Can your
new application give you some insight to an answer to this question?

JLabel Control (Revisited)

Java has powerful features for graphics. In Classes 7 and 8, we will look in detail at most of those features. As an introduction to Java graphics, we look at one capability of the **label control** not examined in the previous class – its ability to **display graphics** files.

The label control **icon** property specifies the graphics file to display. Three types of graphics files can be viewed in a label:

File   Type   Description

JPEG   JPEG   (Joint Photographic Experts Group) is a compressed bitmap format which supports 8 and 24 bit color. It is popular on the Internet and is a common format for digital cameras. JPEG filenames have a **.jpg** extension.

GIF   GIF   (Graphic Interchange Format) is a compressed bitmap format originally developed by CompuServe. It supports up to 256 colors and is also popular on the Internet. GIF filenames have a **.gif** extension.

PNG   PNG   (Portable Network Graphics) format is a popular format for transferring graphics files among different platforms. PNG filenames have **.png** extension.

If you wish to display a graphics file not in one of these formats, there are several commercial products that will convert one format to another. We use Paint Shop Pro by JASC Software.

The displayed images are **ImageIcon** objects. To create an image named **myImage** from a file named **myFile**, use:

```
ImageIcon myImage = new ImageIcon(myFile);
```

The argument (a **String** value) in the **ImageIcon** method must be a legal path to an existing graphics file, or the image will not be created.

When accessing files in Java, references Java are <u>relative</u> to the project directory. Hence, if only a file name is given, it is assumed that file is located in the project directory. For example, say we have graphic of a hamburger (**burger.gif**) stored in the project directory. To load that graphic into **myImage**, you would use:

```
ImageIcon myImage = new ImageIcon("burger.gif");
```

If we have all our graphics stored in a project subfolder named **myGraphics**, the same file would be loaded using:

```
ImageIcon myImage = new
ImageIcon("myGraphics/burger.gif");
```

Or, we could always provide a complete, fully qualified path to the file:

```
ImageIcon myImage = new
ImageIcon("c:/myProject/myGraphics/burger.gif");
```

You will know if your graphics are loading acceptably – they will appear! If they don't appear, check to make sure the path is correct and that the corresponding file is in the correct location. One other thing to notice is that Java uses the slash (/) character to separate folder names and file names. This is contrary to Windows standards of using a backslash (\). If you use the backslash, you will receive an "illegal escape character" error message.

Once created, you often need to know the width and height of the image. These properties are obtained using the **getIconWidth** and **getIconHeight** methods. For our example:

```
width = myImage.getIconWidth();
height = myImage.getIconHeight();
```

To assign an **ImageIcon** object to the label control, you use the **setIcon** method. For a **label** named **myLabel**, the proper code is:

```
myLabel.setIcon(myImage);
```

To clear an image from a label, simply set the icon property to **null** (a Java keyword). This disassociates the icon property from the last loaded image. For our example, the code is:

```
myLabel.setIcon(null);
```

What determines how the image is displayed in the label control? If no preferred size is specified for the label control, it will take on the size of the graphic file. For example, here is a burger graphic (**burger.gif**, 150 pixels x 117 pixels), displayed in a label control in a frame:

If a preferred size is assigned to the label control, the vertical and horizontal alignments specify location of the graphic in the label. If the label is smaller than the graphic, the graphic will be "cropped." For example, here is the burger graphic in a smaller label (with a left, top alignment):

And, if the label is larger than the graphic, there will be "white" space. Here's the burger centered (vertically and horizontally) in a large label:

The label control will only display graphics in their original sizes. In later chapters, we will learn how to shrink/enlarge a graphic to fill any sized space. If you wish to display a large graphic in a small label, one possible approach is to resize and resave (use a different name, if you want) the original file using a commercial product such as Paint Shop Pro mentioned earlier.

A common use for label images is to represent something: a file, a game choice, or a location. And, a common task is to click on this graphic for a selection. Hence, the **mouseClicked** event is monitored to see if a graphic (label) is selected. The code to add the **mouseClicked** event for a label named **myLabel** is:

```
myLabel.addMouseListener(new MouseAdapter()
{
  public void mouseClicked(MouseEvent e)
  {
    myLabelMouseClicked(e);
  }
});
```

And, the **myLabelMouseClicked** method is:

```
private void myLabelMouseClicked(MouseEvent e)
{
   [Method code]
}
```

In this method, you can determine the name of the clicked component (control) using the **getComponent** method:

```
Component clickedComponent = e.getComponent();
```

Typical use of **label** control graphic display:

➢ Declare and create label, assigning an identifiable **name**. For **myLabel**, the statement is:

```
JLabel myLabel = new JLabel();
```

➢ Place control within layout manager.
➢ Assign **ImageIcon** using **setIcon** method.
➢ Add listener for and monitor **mouseClicked** event for label selection.

Example 4-3

"Find the Burger" Game

Start a new project in **NetBeans**. Name the project **FindBurger**. Delete code in Java file named **FindBurger**. In this project, a burger will be hidden behind one of three boxes. You click on the boxes trying to find the burger. The finished game (with the burger uncovered) will look like this:

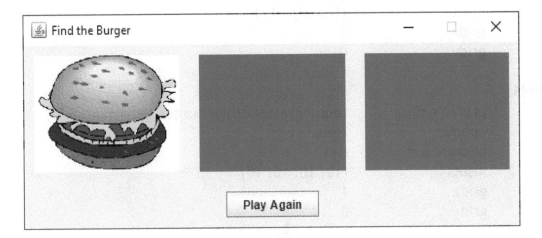

The graphic used for the burger is **burger.gif** and is located in the **\LearnJava\LJ Code\Class 4\Example4-3** folder. Copy this file to your project folder:

burger.gif

1. Place 3 labels and a button control on a frame. The **GridBagLayout** for these controls is:

	gridx = 0	gridx = 1	gridx = 2
gridy = 0	label0	label1	label2
gridy = 1		newButton	

Also add an image icon object (**burger**).

Set the properties of the frame and each control:

FindBurger Frame:
title	Find the Burger
resizable	false

label0:
preferredSize	(burger.getWidth(), burger.getHeight())
opaque	true
background	red
insets	(10, 10, 10, 10)
gridx	0
gridy	0

label1:
preferredSize	(burger.getWidth(), burger.getHeight())
opaque	true
background	red
insets	(10, 10, 10, 10)
gridx	1
gridy	0

label2:
preferredSize	(burger.getWidth(), burger.getHeight())
opaque	true
background	red
insets	(10, 10, 10, 10)
gridx	2
gridy	0

newButton:
text	Play Again
insets	(10, 10, 10, 10)
gridx	1
gridy	1

2. Build the basic framework:

```
/*
 * FindBurger.java
 */
package findburger;
import javax.swing.*;
```

```
import java.awt.*;
import java.awt.event.*;
import java.util.Random;

public class FindBurger extends JFrame
{

  public static void main(String args[])
  {
    // create frame
    new FindBurger().setVisible(true);
  }

  public FindBurger()
  {
    // frame constructor
    setTitle("Find the Burger");
    setResizable(false);
    addWindowListener(new WindowAdapter()
    {
      public void windowClosing(WindowEvent evt)
      {
        exitForm(evt);
      }
    });
    getContentPane().setLayout(new GridBagLayout());

    pack();
    Dimension screenSize =
Toolkit.getDefaultToolkit().getScreenSize();
    setBounds((int) (0.5 * (screenSize.width -
getWidth())), (int) (0.5 * (screenSize.height -
getHeight())), getWidth(), getHeight());
  }

  private void exitForm(WindowEvent evt)
  {
    System.exit(0);
  }
}
```

Run to make sure the frame appears.

3. We now add the controls and establish methods. Add these class level declarations:

```
JLabel label0 = new JLabel();
JLabel label1 = new JLabel();
JLabel label2 = new JLabel();
JLabel[] choiceLabel = new JLabel[3];
ImageIcon burger = new ImageIcon("burger.gif");
JButton newButton = new JButton();
```

Position and add controls, along with events:

```
GridBagConstraints gridConstraints;
choiceLabel[0] = label0;
choiceLabel[1] = label1;
choiceLabel[2] = label2;
for (int i = 0; i < 3; i++)
{
  gridConstraints = new GridBagConstraints();
  choiceLabel[i].setPreferredSize(new
Dimension(burger.getIconWidth(), burger.getIconHeight()));
  choiceLabel[i].setOpaque(true);
  choiceLabel[i].setBackground(Color.RED);
  gridConstraints.gridx = i;
  gridConstraints.gridy = 0;
  gridConstraints.insets = new Insets(10, 10, 10, 10);
  getContentPane().add(choiceLabel[i], gridConstraints);
  choiceLabel[i].addMouseListener(new MouseAdapter()
  {
    public void mouseClicked(MouseEvent e)
    {
      labelMouseClicked(e);
    }
  });
}

newButton.setText("Play Again");
gridConstraints = new GridBagConstraints();
gridConstraints.gridx = 1;
gridConstraints.gridy = 1;
gridConstraints.insets = new Insets(10, 10, 10, 10);
getContentPane().add(newButton, gridConstraints);
newButton.addActionListener(new ActionListener()
{
  public void actionPerformed(ActionEvent e)
  {
```

```
        newButtonActionPerformed(e);
    }
});
```

And, add the two empty event methods:

```
private void labelMouseClicked(MouseEvent e)
{
}

private void newButtonActionPerformed(ActionEvent e)
{
}
```

Run to check the control layout. You should see:

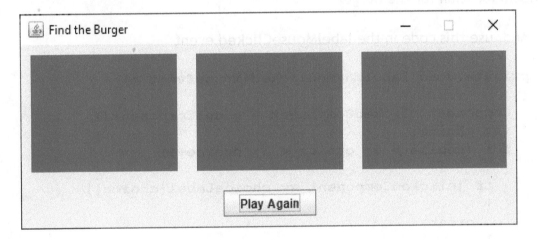

4. Now, we write code for the event methods. We need two class level
    variables, one to track the correct answer and one to generate a random
    number:

```
int burgerLocation;
Random myRandom = new Random();
```

5. Add this code to the **newButtonActionPerformed** event:

```
private void newButtonActionPerformed(ActionEvent e)
{
  // clear boxes and hide burger
  for (int i = 0; i < 3; i++)
  {
    choiceLabel[i].setIcon(null);
    choiceLabel[i].setBackground(Color.RED);
  }
  burgerLocation = myRandom.nextInt(3);
  newButton.setEnabled(false);
}
```

This code clears the three label boxes, restores the color to red and picks a random location for the burger.

6. And, use this code in the **labelMouseClicked** event:

```
private void labelMouseClicked(MouseEvent e)
{
  Component clickedComponent = e.getComponent();
  int choice;
  for (choice = 0; choice < 3; choice++)
  {
    if (clickedComponent == choiceLabel[choice])
    {
      break;
    }
  }
  choiceLabel[choice].setBackground(Color.WHITE);
  if (choice == burgerLocation)
  {
    choiceLabel[choice].setIcon(burger);
    newButton.setEnabled(true);
  }
}
```

This code is executed when any of the three labels is clicked. The code determines which label was clicked and sees if it is the one with the burger hiding behind it. You keep guessing until you fin the burger. Once it is found, you are given the chance to play again.

7. Lastly, add this single line of code in the frame constructor (after creating the frame controls) to initialize the first game:

```
newButton.doClick();
```

Here is the complete **FindBurger.java** file (code added to basic framework is shaded):

```java
/*
 * FindBurger.java
 */
package findburger;
import javax.swing.*;
import java.awt.*;
import java.awt.event.*;
import java.util.Random;

public class FindBurger extends JFrame
{

  JLabel label0 = new JLabel();
  JLabel label1 = new JLabel();
  JLabel label2 = new JLabel();
  JLabel[] choiceLabel = new JLabel[3];
  ImageIcon burger = new ImageIcon("burger.gif");
  JButton newButton = new JButton();
  int burgerLocation;
  Random myRandom = new Random();

  public static void main(String args[])
  {
    // create frame
    new FindBurger().setVisible(true);
  }
  public FindBurger()
  {
    // frame constructor
    setTitle("Find the Burger");
    setResizable(false);
    addWindowListener(new WindowAdapter()
    {
      public void windowClosing(WindowEvent evt)
      {
        exitForm(evt);
      }
    });
```

```
getContentPane().setLayout(new GridBagLayout());

    // position controls
    GridBagConstraints gridConstraints;
    choiceLabel[0] = label0;
    choiceLabel[1] = label1;
    choiceLabel[2] = label2;
    for (int i = 0; i < 3; i++)
    {
      gridConstraints = new GridBagConstraints();
      choiceLabel[i].setPreferredSize(new
Dimension(burger.getIconWidth(), burger.getIconHeight()));
      choiceLabel[i].setOpaque(true);
      choiceLabel[i].setBackground(Color.RED);
      gridConstraints.gridx = i;
      gridConstraints.gridy = 0;
      gridConstraints.insets = new Insets(10, 10, 10, 10);
      getContentPane().add(choiceLabel[i], gridConstraints);
      choiceLabel[i].addMouseListener(new MouseAdapter()
      {
        public void mouseClicked(MouseEvent e)
        {
          labelMouseClicked(e);
        }
      });
    }

    newButton.setText("Play Again");
    gridConstraints = new GridBagConstraints();
    gridConstraints.gridx = 1;
    gridConstraints.gridy = 1;
    gridConstraints.insets = new Insets(10, 10, 10, 10);
    getContentPane().add(newButton, gridConstraints);
    newButton.addActionListener(new ActionListener()
    {
      public void actionPerformed(ActionEvent e)
      {
        newButtonActionPerformed(e);
      }
    });
    pack();
    Dimension screenSize =
Toolkit.getDefaultToolkit().getScreenSize();
    setBounds((int) (0.5 * (screenSize.width - getWidth())),
(int) (0.5 * (screenSize.height - getHeight())), getWidth(),
getHeight());
    // start first game
```

```
      newButton.doClick();
  }

private void labelMouseClicked(MouseEvent e)
{
  Component clickedComponent = e.getComponent();
  int choice;
  for (choice = 0; choice < 3; choice++)
  {
    if (clickedComponent == choiceLabel[choice])
    {
      break;
    }
  }
  choiceLabel[choice].setBackground(Color.WHITE);
  if (choice == burgerLocation)
  {
    choiceLabel[choice].setIcon(burger);
    newButton.setEnabled(true);
  }
}

private void newButtonActionPerformed(ActionEvent e)
{
  // clear boxes and hide burger
  for (int i = 0; i < 3; i++)
  {
    choiceLabel[i].setIcon(null);
    choiceLabel[i].setBackground(Color.RED);
  }
  burgerLocation = myRandom.nextInt(3);
  newButton.setEnabled(false);
}

private void exitForm(WindowEvent evt)
{
  System.exit(0);
}
}
```

Run the application. Click on the boxes trying to find the burger. If the burger graphic does not appear behind any of the boxes, <u>make</u> <u>sure</u> you copied the graphics file to your project directory, as explained in the beginning of this example. Here's a run I made, where I found the burger on my second try:

Save the project (saved as **Example4-3** project in **\LearnJava\LJ Code\Class 4** project group).

JFileChooser Control (Open Files)

Note that to set the **icon** property of the label control, you need the name of a graphics file to load. What if you wanted the user to choose this file from his/her computer? The user would need to provide the path and filename for the graphics file. How can you get this from a user? One possibility would be to use a text field control, asking the user to type in the desired information. This is just asking for trouble. Even the simplest of paths is difficult to type, remembering drive names, proper folder names, file names and extensions, and where all the slashes go. And then you, the programmer, must verify that the information typed contains a valid path and valid file name.

I think you see that asking a user to type a path and file name is a bad idea. We want a 'point and click' type interface to get a file name. Every GUI application provides such an interface for opening files. For example, if I want to open a file in **NetBeans**, this dialog box will appear:

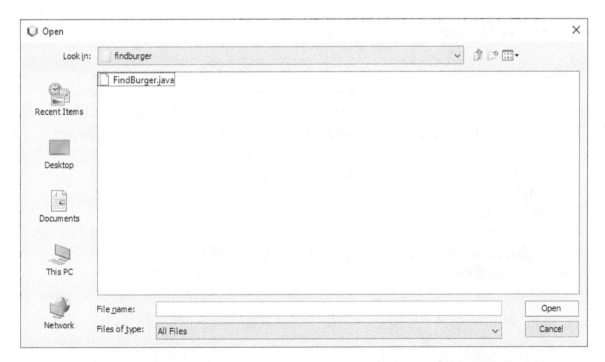

Java lets us use this same interface in our applications via the **JFileChooser** control. This control is one of a suite of dialog controls we can add to our applications. There are also dialog controls to save files (an option of **JFileChooser**), change fonts, change colors, and perform printing operations. We'll look at other dialog controls as we work through the course.

What we learn here is not just limited to opening graphics files for the label control. There are many times in application development where we will need a file name from a user. Applications often require data files, initialization files, configuration files, sound files and other graphic files. The **JFileChooser** control will also be useful in these cases.

File Chooser Properties:

approveButtonText	Text that appears on the 'approve' button – by default, the value is **Open**.
currentDirectory	The selected directory.
dialogTitle	Title that appears in the title area of the dialog.
dialogType	By default, an Open dialog (**JFileChooser.OPEN_DIALOG**), set to **JFileChooser.SAVE_DIALOG** for a save dialog control.
fileFilter	Used to limit types of files displayed.
selectedFile	The currently selected file.

File Chooser Methods:

showOpenDialog	Displays the dialog box for opening files. Returned value indicates which button was clicked by user (**Open** or **Cancel**).
setApproveButtonText	Sets the text that appears on the 'approve' button.
getCurrentDirectory	Retrieves the selected directory.
setDialogTitle	Sets the dialog title.
setDialogType	Sets the dialog type.
setFileFilter	Sets the filter to limit types of files displayed.
addChoosableFileFilter	Add a file filter to file chooser.
getSelectedFile	Retrieves the currently selected file.
listFiles	Used to obtain list of files (File object) from current directory.

File Chooser Events:

actionPerformed	Event (**ActionEvent**) triggered when approve or cancel button is selected. Added with **ActionListener**. Usually monitored when file chooser is embedded in application.
propertyChange	Invoked whenever a property in the file chooser changes. Usually used to detect a change in selected file.

The file chooser control can be added to an application like any control, embedded in the frame. Or, it can be displayed as needed, as a dialog box. You usually only monitor events when the file chooser is embedded in an application.

To add a listener for the **actionPerformed** event for a file chooser named **myChooser**, use:

```
myChooser.addActionListener(new ActionListener()
{
   public void actionPerformed(ActionEvent e)
   {
      myChooserActionPerformed(e);
   }
});
```

And, the corresponding event code would be placed in a **myChooserActionPerformed** method:

```
private void myChooserActionPerformed(ActionEvent e)
{
   [method code]
}
```

In this event, you usually check to see if the approve (**Open**) button has been clicked. The code segment that does this is:

```
if
(e.getActionCommand().equals(JFileChooser.APPROVE_SELECTIO
N))
{
   [code to process]
}
```

The **propertyChange** event is added using the **PropertyChangeListener**. For **myChooser**, use:

```
myChooser.addPropertyChangeListener(new
PropertyChangeListener()
{
  public void propertyChange(PropertyChangeEvent e)
  {
    myChooserPropertyChange(e);
  }
});
```

The corresponding event code would be placed in a **myChooserPropertyChange** method:

```
private void myChooserPropertyChange(PropertyChangeEvent
e)
{
   [method code]
}
```

In this method, we usually want to make sure the changed property is the selected file. To determine the property change that "calls" this event, use:

```
String pName = e.getPropertyName();
```

If **pName** is equal to **JFileChooser.SELECTED_FILE_CHANGED_PROPERTY**, we have the property change we are interested in.

To display the file chooser as an open dialog box, use the **showOpenDialog** method. If the chooser is named **myChooser**, the format is:

```
myChooser.showOpenDialog(this);
```

where **this** is a keyword referring to the current frame. The displayed dialog box is:

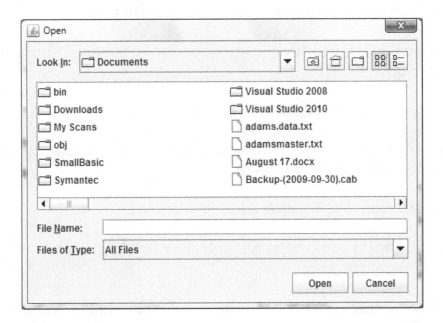

The user selects a file using the dialog control (or types a name in the **File Name** box). The file type is selected from the **Files of Type** box (values here set with the **Filter** property). Once selected, the **Open** button is clicked. **Cancel** can be clicked to cancel the open operation. The **showOpenDialog** method returns the clicked button. This method will return one of two values:

> `JFileChooser.APPROVE_OPTION` – Approve (**Open**) button clicked
> `JFileChooser.CANCEL_OPTION` – **Cancel** button clicked

If the user has selected the **Open** button, we can determine the selected file. This value is given by:

> `myChooser.getSelectedFile()`

Many controls require this name to be a **String** type (the **ImageIcon**, for example). This conversion is done using:

> `myChooser.getSelectedFile().toString()`

The nice thing about this control is that it can validate the file name before it is returned to the application.

The **fileFilter** property is set by the **FileNameExtensionFilter** constructor. The form for this constructor is

`FileNameExtensionFilter(description, extension1, extension2, ... )`

Here, description is the **description** that appears in the file chooser window, each **extension** is an acceptable file extension type to display. Each argument is a **string** type. To use this constructor, you need this **import** statement in your java class:

`import javax.swing.filechooser.*;`

File Filter Example:

Let's do an example for two types of graphics files (**gif**, **jpg**) to illustrate. The code to add such a filter to a file chooser named **myChooser** is:

```
myChooser.addChoosableFileFilter(new
FileNameExtensionFilter("Graphics Files (.gif, .jpg)",
"gif", "jpg"));
```

With such code, the chooser will appear as:

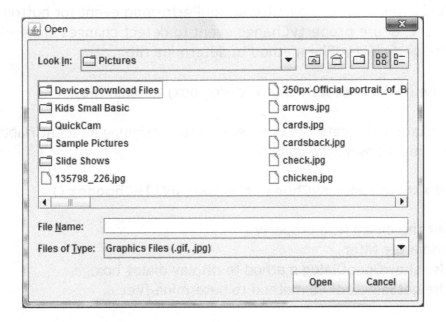

Only files with **gif** and **jpg** extensions are shown.

Typical use of **file chooser** control (embedded) to open files:

> ➢ Declare and create file chooser control, assigning an identifiable **name**. For **myChooser**, the code is:

```
JFileChooser myChooser = new JFileChooser();
```

> ➢ Set the **dialogTitle** property.
> ➢ Add a file filter.
> ➢ Place control in layout manager.
> ➢ Add listener for and monitor **actionPerformed** event for button click event, or use **propertyChange** event to detect changes in selected file.
> ➢ Use **getSelectedFile** method to determine file.

Typical use of **file chooser** control (dialog box) to open files:

> ➢ Declare and create file chooser control, assigning an identifiable **name**. For **myChooser**, the code is:

```
JFileChooser myChooser = new JFileChooser();
```

> ➢ Set the **dialogTitle** property.
> ➢ Add a file filter.
> ➢ Use **showOpenDialog** method to display dialog box.
> ➢ Use **getSelectedFile** method to determine file.

Example 4-4

Image Viewer

Start a new project in **NetBeans**. Name the project **ImageViewer**. Delete default code in Java file named **ImageViewer**. In this application, we search our computer's file structure for graphics files and display the results of our search in an image control. We will use an embedded file chooser. The finished frame will be:

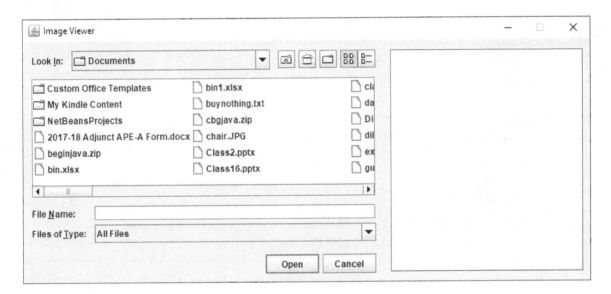

1. The application just needs two controls: a file chooser and a label. The **GridBagLayout** arrangement is:

	gridx = 0	gridx = 1
gridy = 0	**imageChooser**	**imageLabel**

Properties for the controls:

ImageViewer Frame:

title	Image Viewer
resizable	false

imageChooser:

gridx	0
gridy	0

imageLabel:

preferredSize	(270, 300)
border	RED line
opaque	true
background	WHITE
horizontalAlignment	CENTER
verticalAlignment	CENTER
gridx	1
gridy	0
insets	(10, 10, 10, 10);

2. As usual, build a framework to start with:

```
/*
 * ImageViewer.java
 */
package imageviewer;
import javax.swing.filechooser.*;
import javax.swing.*;
import java.awt.*;
import java.awt.event.*;
public class ImageViewer extends JFrame
{
  public static void main(String args[])
  {
    //construct frame
    new ImageViewer().setVisible(true);
  }
  public ImageViewer()
  {
    // create frame
    setTitle("Image Viewer");
    setResizable(false);
    addWindowListener(new WindowAdapter()
    {
      public void windowClosing(WindowEvent e)
      {
        exitForm(e);
      }
    });
    getContentPane().setLayout(new GridBagLayout());

    pack();
    Dimension screenSize =
Toolkit.getDefaultToolkit().getScreenSize();
    setBounds((int) (0.5 * (screenSize.width -
getWidth())), (int) (0.5 * (screenSize.height -
getHeight())), getWidth(), getHeight());
  }
  private void exitForm(WindowEvent e)
  {
    System.exit(0);
  }
}
```

Run to see the frame centered on your screen.

3. Create controls with these class level declarations:

```
JFileChooser imageChooser = new JFileChooser();
JLabel imageLabel = new JLabel();
```

Position controls and add event listener for file chooser:

```
GridBagConstraints gridConstraints = new
GridBagConstraints();
String[] ext = new String[] {"gif", "jpg"};
imageChooser.addChoosableFileFilter(new
ExampleFileFilter(ext, "Graphics
Files"));gridConstraints.gridx = 0;
gridConstraints.gridy = 0;
getContentPane().add(imageChooser, gridConstraints);
imageChooser.addActionListener(new ActionListener()
{
  public void actionPerformed(ActionEvent e)
  {
    imageChooserActionPerformed(e);
  }
});
    imageLabel.setPreferredSize(new Dimension(270, 300));

imageLabel.setBorder(BorderFactory.createLineBorder(Color.
RED));     imageLabel.setOpaque(true);
    imageLabel.setBackground(Color.white);

imageLabel.setHorizontalAlignment(SwingConstants.CENTER);

imageLabel.setVerticalAlignment(SwingConstants.CENTER);
    gridConstraints.gridx = 1;
    gridConstraints.gridy = 0;
    gridConstraints.insets = new Insets(10, 10, 10, 10);
    getContentPane().add(imageLabel, gridConstraints);
```

4. We'll go right to adding code to the **imageChooserActionPerformed** event:

```
private void imageChooserActionPerformed(ActionEvent e)
{
  // create and display graphic if open selected
  if
(e.getActionCommand().equals(JFileChooser.APPROVE_SELECTIO
N))
    {
      ImageIcon myImage = new
ImageIcon(imageChooser.getSelectedFile().toString());
      imageLabel.setIcon(myImage);
    }
}
```

In this code, if the user clicks the **Open** button, the selected file is used to establish the **ImageIcon** to display in the **imageLabel** control.

The complete **ImageViewer.java** code is (code added to framework is shaded):

```
/*
 * ImageViewer.java
 */
package imageviewer;
import javax.swing.filechooser.*;
import javax.swing.*;
import java.awt.*;
import java.awt.event.*;

public class ImageViewer extends JFrame
{
  JFileChooser imageChooser = new JFileChooser();
  JLabel imageLabel = new JLabel();

  public static void main(String args[])
  {
    //construct frame
    new ImageViewer().setVisible(true);
  }

  public ImageViewer()
  {
    // create frame
    setTitle("Image Viewer");
    setResizable(false);
    addWindowListener(new WindowAdapter()
```

```
    {
      public void windowClosing(WindowEvent e)
      {
        exitForm(e);
      }
    });
    getContentPane().setLayout(new GridBagLayout());

    // position controls (establish event methods)
    GridBagConstraints gridConstraints = new
GridBagConstraints();
      imageChooser.addChoosableFileFilter(new
      FileNameExtensionFilter("Graphics Files (.gif, .jpg)",
      "gif", "jpg"));
gridConstraints.gridx = 0;
    gridConstraints.gridy = 0;
    getContentPane().add(imageChooser, gridConstraints);
    imageChooser.addActionListener(new ActionListener()
    {
      public void actionPerformed(ActionEvent e)
      {
        imageChooserActionPerformed(e);
      }
    });


    imageLabel.setPreferredSize(new Dimension(270, 300));

imageLabel.setBorder(BorderFactory.createLineBorder(Color.RED
));
    imageLabel.setOpaque(true);
    imageLabel.setBackground(Color.white);
    imageLabel.setHorizontalAlignment(SwingConstants.CENTER);
    imageLabel.setVerticalAlignment(SwingConstants.CENTER);
    gridConstraints.gridx = 1;
    gridConstraints.gridy = 0;
    gridConstraints.insets = new Insets(10, 10, 10, 10);
    getContentPane().add(imageLabel, gridConstraints);

    pack();
    Dimension screenSize =
Toolkit.getDefaultToolkit().getScreenSize();
    setBounds((int) (0.5 * (screenSize.width - getWidth())),
(int) (0.5 * (screenSize.height - getHeight())), getWidth(),
getHeight());

  }
```

```
  private void imageChooserActionPerformed(ActionEvent e)
  {
    // create and display graphic if open selected
    if
(e.getActionCommand().equals(JFileChooser.APPROVE_SELECTION))
    {
      ImageIcon myImage = new
ImageIcon(imageChooser.getSelectedFile().toString());
      imageLabel.setIcon(myImage);
    }

  }

  private void exitForm(WindowEvent e)
  {
    System.exit(0);
  }
}
```

Run the application. Find gif files and JPEGs (an example of each is included in the project folder). Here's how the form should look when displaying the example JPEG file (a photo from my Mexican vacation):

Save your project (saved as **Example4-4** project in **\LearnJava\LJ Code\Class 4** project group). One possible modification would be to use the **propertyChange** event to detect when a new file is selected and immediately display the new graphics (as opposed to clicking **Open**).

Class Review

After completing this class, you should understand:

➢ Useful properties, events, methods and typical uses for the spinner control, both for numbers and lists

➢ Properties, events, methods, and uses for the scroll bar and slider controls

➢ The three types of graphics files that can be displayed by the label control

➢ How to recognize mouse clicks on label controls

➢ How to load image files as ImageIcon objects

➢ How to use the file chooser control to obtain file names for opening files

Practice Problems 4

Problem 4-1. Number Guess Problem. Build a game where the user guesses a number between 1 and 100. Use a scroll bar for entering the guess and change the extreme limits (**minimum** and **maximum** properties) with each guess to help the user adjust their guess.

Problem 4-2. RGB Color Problem. Build an application with three slider controls and a label control. Use the sliders to adjust the red, green and blue contributions to create a color using the **Color** class. Let the background color of the label control be set by those contributions.

Problem 4-3. Tic-Tac-Toe Problem. Build a simple Tic-Tac-Toe game. Use 'skinny' label controls for the grid and label controls with images for markers (use different pictures to distinguish players). Click the label controls to add the markers. Can you write logic to detect a win?

Problem 4-4. File Times Problem. Use the file chooser control to lists all files in a particular directory. For every file, find what time the file was modified (use the **lastModified** method to get time details). Determine the most popular hours of the day for modifying files.

Exercise 4

Student Database Input Screen

You did so well with last chapter's assignment that, now, a school wants you to develop the beginning structure of an input screen for its students. The required input information is:

1. Student Name
2. Student Grade (1 through 6)
3. Student Sex (Male or Female)
4. Student Date of Birth (Month, Day, Year)
5. Student Picture (Assume they can be loaded as jpeg files)

Set up the screen so that only the name needs to be typed; all other inputs should be set with option buttons, scroll bars, spinners and file choosers. When a screen of information is complete, display the summarized profile in a message box. This profile message box should resemble this:

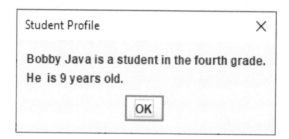

Note the student's age must be computed from the input birth date - watch out for pitfalls in doing the computation. The student's picture does not appear in the profile, only on the input screen.

5

Java GUI Application Design and Distribution

Review and Preview

We've finished looking at many of the Java controls and have been introduced to most of the Java language features. In this class, we learn how to enhance our application design using tabbed panes, general methods and menus. And, we learn some ways to distribute the finished product to our user base.

Application Design Considerations

Before beginning the actual process of building your Java application by designing the GUI interface, setting the control properties, and writing the Java code, many things should be considered to make your application useful. A first consideration should be to determine what processes and functions you want your application to perform. What are the inputs and outputs? Develop a framework or flow chart of all your application's processes.

Decide what controls you need. Do the built-in Java Swing controls and methods meet your needs? Do you need to develop some controls or methods of your own? You can design and build your own controls using Java - a topic beyond the scope of this class, but not that difficult. Appendix II provides an introduction to this topic.

Design your user interface. What do you want your frame to look like? Consider appearance and ease of use. Make the interface consistent with other GUI applications. Familiarity is good in program design. Don't "reinvent the wheel." Many applications you build are similar to other applications. Reuse code whenever possible.

Write your code. Make your code readable and traceable - future code modifiers (including yourself) will thank you. Consider developing reusable code - methods with utility outside your current development. This will save you time in future developments.

Make your code 'user-friendly.' Make operation of your application obvious to the user. Step the user through its use. Try to anticipate all possible ways a user can mess up in using your application. It's fairly easy to write an application that works properly when the user does everything correctly. It's difficult to write an application that can handle all the possible wrong things a user can do and still not bomb out.

Debug your code completely before distributing it. There's nothing worse than having a user call you to point out flaws in your application. A good way to find all the bugs is to let several people try the code - a mini beta-testing program.

JTabbedPane Control

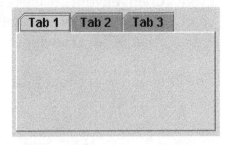

The **tabbed pane** control provides an easy way to present several panels of information in a single frame - it is similar to having a multi-frame application. This is the same interface seen in many commercial GUI applications.

The tabbed pane control provides a group of tabs, each of which can hold a single component (almost always a **panel** control). Only one tab can be active at a time. Navigation from one tab to the next is simple: just click on the corresponding tab. Using this control is easy. Build each tab component as a separate panel: add controls, set properties, and write code like you do for any panel. Then, add each panel to the tabbed pane. Since most of the coding is in the panels attached to the tabbed pane, there are relatively few properties and methods associated with the tabbed pane.

Tabbed Pane Properties:

font	Font used for displayed tab headings.
selectedIndex	Currently "active" tab.
tabLayoutPolicy	Controls how tabs are displayed when there are many tabs.

Tabbed Pane Methods:

setFont	Used to set font property.
setSelectedIndex	Used to programmatically change displayed tab.
getSelectedIndex	Used to determine "active" tab.
addTab	Adds tabs and associated components to control.
setTabLayoutPolicy	Used to establish tab layout (JTabbedPane.SCROLL_TAB_LAYOUT restricts tabs to a single, scrollable row, JTabbedPane.WRAP_TAB_LAYOUT will stack tabs.)

Tabbed Pane Event:

stateChanged   Event (**ChangeEvent**) triggered when the selected tab
                                changes. Added with **ChangeEventListener** (requires
                                importation of **javax.swing.event.*** files).

 To add a listener for the **stateChanged** event to a tabbed pane control named
myTabbedPane, use:

```
myTabbedPane.addChangeListener(new ChangeListener()
{
  public void stateChanged(ChangeEvent e)
  {
    myTabbedPaneStateChanged(e);
  }
});
```

And, the corresponding event code would be placed in a
myTabbedPaneStateChanged method:

```
private void myTabbedPaneStateChanged(ChangeEvent e)
{
   [method code]
}
```

Using the tabbed pane control is straightforward. It is created and placed on a
frame in the usual manner. The tabbed pane can take up the entire frame of be
one of several displayed controls.

As mentioned, each tab on the control is a separate panel control. Recall panel
controls are containers for other controls and have their own grid layout
manager for control placement. The process for using a tabbed pane control is
to create a separate panel for each tab. The panels are then added to the
tabbed pane using the **addTab** method. For example, to add a panel named
myPanel to a tabbed pane control named **myTabbedPane**, you would use:

```
myTabbedPane.addTab(tabTitle, myPanel);
```

where **tabTitle** is a string value representing the text that will appear on the tab
associated with **myPanel**. The tabbed pane control will "grow" to fit the largest
panel added to it.

As the programmer, you need to know which tab is active. To do this, use the **getSelectedIndex** method in the **stateChanged** event for the tabbed pane control.   And, you need to keep track of which controls are available with each tab page (panel).

Typical use of **tabbed pane** control:

> Declare and create the tabbed pane control, assigning an identifiable **name**. The code to create **myTabbedPane** is:

```
JTabbedPane myTabbedPane = new JTabbedPane();
```

> Create a panel control for each tab. Add controls and write code for each panel.
> Add panels to tabbed pane.
> Add listener for and monitor **stateChanged** event to determine when active tab is changed.

Example 5-1

Shopping Cart

Start a new empty project in **NetBeans**. Name the project **ShoppingCart**.
Delete default code in Java file named **ShoppingCart**. We will build a tabbed
pane application that provides a good start for a simple 'on-line' commerce
system. One tab will be used to enter a mailing address and add items to a
shopping cart. Other tabs will display the current contents of the shopping cart
and display a mailing label. We'll build each tab panel separately. The finished
product will look like this:

1. The frame will hold a single tabbed pane (**shoppingPane**) control. The tabbed pane will hold three panels (**orderPanel**, **cartPanel** and **addressPanel**). We design each panel separately. First, we design the panel (**orderPanel**) to obtain the order information. The **GridBagLayout** is:

	gridx = 0
gridy = 0	orderLabel
gridy = 1	orderTextArea
gridy = 2	orderSpinner
gridy = 3	addButton
gridy = 4	numberTextField
gridy = 5	newButton
gridy = 6	exitButton

Properties:

orderLabel:

text	Order Address:
anchor	WEST
gridx	0
gridy	0
insets	(10, 10, 0, 0)

orderTextArea:

columns	30
rows	6
gridx	0
gridy	1
insets	(10, 10, 10, 10)

orderSpinner:

model	SpinnerListModel (array **product**)
preferredSize	(150, 25)
gridx	0
gridy	2

addButton:

text	Add to Order
gridx	0
gridy	3
insets	(5, 0, 5, 0)

numberTextField:

setText	Items Ordered: 0
columns	20
editable	false
background	WHITE
horizontalAlignment	CENTER
gridx	0
gridy	4
insets	(5, 0, 5, 0)

newButton:

text	New Order
gridx	0
gridy	5
insets	(5, 0, 5, 0)

exitButton:

text	Exit
gridx	0
gridy	6
insets	(5, 0, 5, 0)

Now, we design the panel (**cartPanel**) that will display the shopping cart contents. Its **GridBagLayout** is:

	gridx = 0
gridy = 0	**cartPane**
gridy = 1	**costTextField**

Properties:

cartPane:

preferredSize	(250, 150)
viewportView	cartTextArea (JTextArea control)
gridx	0
gridy	0
insets	(10, 10, 10, 10)

costTextField:

text	Total Cost:
columns	20
editable	false
background	WHITE
gridx	0
gridy	1
insets	(5, 0, 5, 0)

Lastly, we design the panel (**addressPanel**) that will display the mailing label. Its **GridBagLayout** is:

	gridx = 0
gridy = 0	**addressPane**

Properties:

addressPane:

preferredSize	(250, 150)
viewportView	addressTextArea (JTextArea control)
gridx	0
gridy	0
insets	(10, 10, 10, 10)

2. Now, we'll write the code. First, we build the basic framework with the single tabbed pane (**shoppingPane**) control. The tabbed pane will have an empty **stateChanged** event. The code to do this is:

```
/*
 * ShoppingCart.java
 */
package shoppingcart;
import javax.swing.*;
import javax.swing.event.*;
import java.awt.*;
import java.awt.event.*;
import java.text.*;

public class ShoppingCart extends JFrame
{

  JTabbedPane shoppingPane = new JTabbedPane();
  public static void main(String args[])
  {
    //construct frame
    new ShoppingCart().setVisible(true);
  }

  public ShoppingCart()
  {
```

```
      // code to build the form
      setTitle("Shopping Cart");
      setResizable(false);
      addWindowListener(new WindowAdapter()
      {
        public void windowClosing(WindowEvent e)
        {
          exitForm(e);
        }
      });
      getContentPane().setLayout(new GridBagLayout());

      // position tabbed pane
      GridBagConstraints gridConstraints = new
GridBagConstraints();
      gridConstraints.gridx = 0;
      gridConstraints.gridy = 0;
      getContentPane().add(shoppingPane, gridConstraints);
      shoppingPane.addChangeListener(new ChangeListener()
      {
        public void stateChanged(ChangeEvent e)
        {
          shoppingPaneStateChanged(e);
        }
      });

      pack();
      Dimension screenSize =
Toolkit.getDefaultToolkit().getScreenSize();
      setBounds((int) (0.5 * (screenSize.width -
getWidth())), (int) (0.5 * (screenSize.height -
getHeight())), getWidth(), getHeight());
    }
    private void shoppingPaneStateChanged(ChangeEvent e)
    {
    }

    private void exitForm(WindowEvent e)
    {
      System.exit(0);
    }
  }
}
```

Run the code to make sure the frame appears (the tabbed pane will be very small).

3. We'll now add the **orderPanel**. Add these class level declarations for controls and variables:

```
JPanel orderPanel= new JPanel();
JLabel orderLabel = new JLabel();
JTextArea orderTextArea = new JTextArea();
JSpinner orderSpinner = new JSpinner();
JButton addButton = new JButton();
JTextField numberTextField = new JTextField();
JButton newButton = new JButton();
JButton exitButton = new JButton();

final int numberProducts = 10;
String[] product = new String[numberProducts];
double[] cost = new double[numberProducts];
int[] ordered = new int[numberProducts];
int itemsOrdered;
```

Add these lines of code (establish product names and costs) at the top of the frame constructor method:

```
product[0] = "Tricycle" ; cost[0] = 50;
product[1] = "Skateboard" ; cost[1] = 60;
product[2] = "In-Line Skates" ; cost[2] = 100;
product[3] = "Magic Set" ; cost[3] = 15;
product[4] = "Video Game" ; cost[4] = 45;
product[5] = "Helmet" ; cost[5] = 25;
product[6] = "Building Kit" ; cost[6] = 35;
product[7] = "Artist Set" ; cost[7] = 40;
product[8] = "Doll Baby" ; cost[8] = 25;
product[9] = "Bicycle" ; cost[9] = 150;
```

Now, in the constructor code, position the controls, add event listeners and add the panel to the tabbed pane:

```
// order panel
orderPanel.setLayout(new GridBagLayout());
gridConstraints = new GridBagConstraints();
orderLabel.setText("Order Address:");
gridConstraints.gridx = 0;
gridConstraints.gridy = 0;
gridConstraints.insets = new Insets(10, 10, 0, 0);
gridConstraints.anchor = GridBagConstraints.WEST;
orderPanel.add(orderLabel, gridConstraints);
gridConstraints = new GridBagConstraints();
orderTextArea.setColumns(30);
```

```java
orderTextArea.setRows(6);
gridConstraints.gridx = 0;
gridConstraints.gridy = 1;
gridConstraints.insets = new Insets(10, 10, 10, 10);
orderPanel.add(orderTextArea, gridConstraints);
gridConstraints = new GridBagConstraints();
orderSpinner.setModel(new SpinnerListModel(product));
orderSpinner.setPreferredSize(new Dimension(150, 25));
gridConstraints.gridx = 0;
gridConstraints.gridy = 2;
orderPanel.add(orderSpinner, gridConstraints);
gridConstraints = new GridBagConstraints();
addButton.setText("Add to Order");
gridConstraints.gridx = 0;
gridConstraints.gridy = 3;
gridConstraints.insets = new Insets(5, 0, 5, 0);
orderPanel.add(addButton, gridConstraints);
addButton.addActionListener(new ActionListener()
{
  public void actionPerformed(ActionEvent e)
  {
    addButtonActionPerformed(e);
  }
});
gridConstraints = new GridBagConstraints();
numberTextField.setColumns(20);
numberTextField.setEditable(false);
numberTextField.setBackground(Color.WHITE);
numberTextField.setHorizontalAlignment(SwingConstants.CENT
ER);
numberTextField.setText("Items Ordered: 0");
gridConstraints.gridx = 0;
gridConstraints.gridy = 4;
gridConstraints.insets = new Insets(5, 0, 5, 0);
orderPanel.add(numberTextField, gridConstraints);
newButton.setText("New Order");
gridConstraints.gridx = 0;
gridConstraints.gridy = 5;
gridConstraints.insets = new Insets(5, 0, 5, 0);
orderPanel.add(newButton, gridConstraints);
newButton.addActionListener(new ActionListener()
{
  public void actionPerformed(ActionEvent e)
  {
    newButtonActionPerformed(e);
  }
});
```

```
exitButton.setText("Exit");
gridConstraints.gridx = 0;
gridConstraints.gridy = 6;
gridConstraints.insets = new Insets(5, 0, 5, 0);
orderPanel.add(exitButton, gridConstraints);
exitButton.addActionListener(new ActionListener()
{
  public void actionPerformed(ActionEvent e)
  {
    exitButtonActionPerformed(e);
  }
});
shoppingPane.addTab("Order Form", orderPanel);
```

And, three empty event methods for the three button controls:

```
private void addButtonActionPerformed(ActionEvent e)
{
}
private void newButtonActionPerformed(ActionEvent e)
{
}
private void exitButtonActionPerformed(ActionEvent e)
{
}
```

Run to see the first tabbed panel:

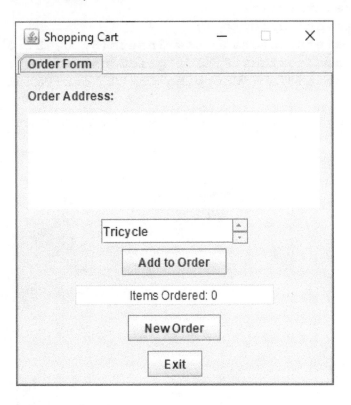

4. Now, we follow similar steps to add the **cartPanel**. Add class level declarations for the needed controls:

```
JPanel cartPanel = new JPanel();
JScrollPane cartPane = new JScrollPane();
JTextArea cartTextArea = new JTextArea();
JTextField costTextField = new JTextField();
```

Add positioning code:

```
// cart panel
cartPanel.setLayout(new GridBagLayout());
cartPane.setPreferredSize(new Dimension (250, 150));
cartPane.setViewportView(cartTextArea);
gridConstraints.gridx = 0;
gridConstraints.gridy = 0;
gridConstraints.insets = new Insets(10, 10, 10, 10);
cartPanel.add(cartPane, gridConstraints);
gridConstraints = new GridBagConstraints();
costTextField.setColumns(20);
costTextField.setEditable(false);
costTextField.setBackground(Color.WHITE);
```

```
costTextField.setText("Total Cost:");
gridConstraints.gridx = 0;
gridConstraints.gridy = 1;
gridConstraints.insets = new Insets(5, 0, 5, 0);
cartPanel.add(costTextField, gridConstraints);
shoppingPane.addTab("Shopping Cart", cartPanel);
```

Resave, recompile and rerun. Click the newly added tab to see:

5. Now, the **addressPanel** to complete the project controls. The class level declarations:

```
JPanel addressPanel = new JPanel();
JScrollPane addressPane = new JScrollPane();
JTextArea addressTextArea = new JTextArea();
```

And, the positioning code:

```
// address panel
addressPanel.setLayout(new GridBagLayout());
addressPane.setPreferredSize(new Dimension (250, 150));
addressPane.setViewportView(addressTextArea);
gridConstraints.gridx = 0;
gridConstraints.gridy = 0;
gridConstraints.insets = new Insets(10, 10, 10, 10);
addressPanel.add(addressPane, gridConstraints);
shoppingPane.addTab("Mailing Label", addressPanel);
```

Resave, recompile, rerun to see the newly added tab:

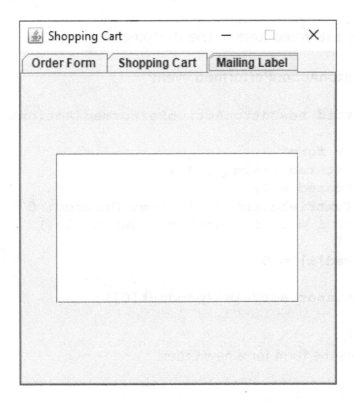

6. Now, let's write the code. First the **addButtonActionPerformed** event:

```
private void addButtonActionPerformed(ActionEvent e)
{
  int selectedProduct;
   // increment selected product by one
   for (selectedProduct = 0; selectedProduct <
numberProducts; selectedProduct++)
   {
     if
(product[selectedProduct].equals(orderSpinner.getValue().t
oString()))
     {
        break;
     }
   }
  ordered[selectedProduct]++;
  itemsOrdered++;
  numberTextField.setText("Items Ordered: " +
itemsOrdered);
}
```

This code adds a selected item to the shopping cart.

7. The **newButtonActionPerformed** event:

```
private void newButtonActionPerformed(ActionEvent e)
{
  // clear form
  orderTextArea.setText("");
  itemsOrdered = 0;
  numberTextField.setText("Items Ordered: 0");
  for (int i = 0; i < numberProducts; i++)
  {
    ordered[i] = 0;
  }
  orderSpinner.setValue(product[0]);
}
```

This code clears the form for a new order.

8. Use this code in the **exitButtonActionPerformed** procedure which stops the application:

```java
private void exitButtonActionPerformed(ActionEvent e)
{
    System.exit(0);
}
```

9. The last event method is **shoppingPaneStateChanged** (this replaces the empty method added when we first built the frame):

```java
private void shoppingPaneStateChanged(ChangeEvent e)
{
    switch (shoppingPane.getSelectedIndex())
    {
        case 0:
            break;
        case 1:
            if (itemsOrdered == 0)
            {
                JOptionPane.showConfirmDialog(null, "No items have
been ordered.", "Error", JOptionPane.DEFAULT_OPTION,
JOptionPane.ERROR_MESSAGE);
                shoppingPane.setSelectedIndex(0);
            }
            else
            {
                double totalCost = 0.00;
                String order = "";
                //load in ordered items
                for (int i = 0; i < numberProducts; i++)
                {
                    if (ordered[i] != 0)
                    {
                        order += ordered[i] + " " +
product[i].toString() + "\n";
                        totalCost += ordered[i] * cost[i];
                    }
                }
                cartTextArea.setText(order);
                costTextField.setText("Total Cost: $" + new
DecimalFormat("0.00").format(totalCost));
            }
            break;
        case 2:
            // establish address and show label form
```

```
      if (orderTextArea.getText().equals(""))
      {
         JOptionPane.showConfirmDialog(null, "Address is
blank.", "Error", JOptionPane.DEFAULT_OPTION,
JOptionPane.ERROR_MESSAGE);
         shoppingPane.setSelectedIndex(0);
      }
      else
      {
         //form label
         addressTextArea.setText("My Company\n" + "My
Address\n" + "My City, State, Zip\n\n\n" +
orderTextArea.getText());
      }
      break;
   }
}
```

In this code, if the cart tab is selected, the contents of the shopping cart are
displayed. If the label tab is selected, the mailing label is formed.

The application is, at long last, complete. The complete **ShoppingCart.java** code listing is (code added to framework is shaded):

```java
/*
 * ShoppingCart.java
*/
package shoppingcart;
import javax.swing.*;
import javax.swing.event.*;
import java.awt.*;
import java.awt.event.*;
import java.text.*;
public class ShoppingCart extends JFrame
{
    JTabbedPane shoppingPane = new JTabbedPane();
    JPanel orderPanel  = new JPanel();
    JLabel orderLabel = new JLabel();
    JTextArea orderTextArea = new JTextArea();
    JSpinner orderSpinner = new JSpinner();
    JButton addButton = new JButton();
    JTextField numberTextField = new JTextField();
    JButton newButton = new JButton();
    JButton exitButton = new JButton();
    JPanel cartPanel = new JPanel();
    JScrollPane cartPane = new JScrollPane();
    JTextArea cartTextArea = new JTextArea();
    JTextField costTextField = new JTextField();
    JPanel addressPanel = new JPanel();
    JScrollPane addressPane = new JScrollPane();
    JTextArea addressTextArea = new JTextArea();
    final int numberProducts = 10;
    String[] product = new String[numberProducts];
    double[] cost = new double[numberProducts];
    int[] ordered = new int[numberProducts];
    int itemsOrdered;
    public static void main(String args[])
    {
        //construct frame
        new ShoppingCart().setVisible(true);
    }
    public ShoppingCart()
    {
        // define products and cost
        product[0] = "Tricycle" ; cost[0] = 50;
        product[1] = "Skateboard" ; cost[1] = 60;
        product[2] = "In-Line Skates" ; cost[2] = 100;
        product[3] = "Magic Set" ; cost[3] = 15;
```

```
product[4] = "Video Game" ; cost[4] = 45;
product[5] = "Helmet" ; cost[5] = 25;
product[6] = "Building Kit" ; cost[6] = 35;
product[7] = "Artist Set" ; cost[7] = 40;
product[8] = "Doll Baby" ; cost[8] = 25;
product[9] = "Bicycle" ; cost[9] = 150;
// code to build the form
setTitle("Shopping Cart");
setResizable(false);
addWindowListener(new WindowAdapter()
{
  public void windowClosing(WindowEvent e)
  {
    exitForm(e);
  }
});
getContentPane().setLayout(new GridBagLayout());
// position controls (establish event methods)
GridBagConstraints gridConstraints = new
GridBagConstraints();
gridConstraints.gridx = 0;
gridConstraints.gridy = 0;
getContentPane().add(shoppingPane, gridConstraints);
shoppingPane.addChangeListener(new ChangeListener()
{
  public void stateChanged(ChangeEvent e)
  {
    shoppingPaneStateChanged(e);
  }
});
// order panel
orderPanel.setLayout(new GridBagLayout());
gridConstraints = new GridBagConstraints();
orderLabel.setText("Order Address:");
gridConstraints.gridx = 0;
gridConstraints.gridy = 0;
gridConstraints.insets = new Insets(10, 10, 0, 0);
gridConstraints.anchor = GridBagConstraints.WEST;
orderPanel.add(orderLabel, gridConstraints);
gridConstraints = new GridBagConstraints();
orderTextArea.setColumns(30);
orderTextArea.setRows(6);
gridConstraints.gridx = 0;
gridConstraints.gridy = 1;
gridConstraints.insets = new Insets(10, 10, 10, 10);
orderPanel.add(orderTextArea, gridConstraints);
gridConstraints = new GridBagConstraints();
```

```
orderSpinner.setModel(new SpinnerListModel(product));
orderSpinner.setPreferredSize(new Dimension(150, 25));
gridConstraints.gridx = 0;
gridConstraints.gridy = 2;
orderPanel.add(orderSpinner, gridConstraints);
gridConstraints = new GridBagConstraints();
addButton.setText("Add to Order");
gridConstraints.gridx = 0;
gridConstraints.gridy = 3;
gridConstraints.insets = new Insets(5, 0, 5, 0);
orderPanel.add(addButton, gridConstraints);
addButton.addActionListener(new ActionListener()
{
  public void actionPerformed(ActionEvent e)
  {
    addButtonActionPerformed(e);
  }
});
gridConstraints = new GridBagConstraints();
numberTextField.setColumns(20);
numberTextField.setEditable(false);
numberTextField.setBackground(Color.WHITE);

numberTextField.setHorizontalAlignment(SwingConstants.CENTER)
;
numberTextField.setText("Items Ordered: 0");
gridConstraints.gridx = 0;
gridConstraints.gridy = 4;
gridConstraints.insets = new Insets(5, 0, 5, 0);
orderPanel.add(numberTextField, gridConstraints);
newButton.setText("New Order");
gridConstraints.gridx = 0;
gridConstraints.gridy = 5;
gridConstraints.insets = new Insets(5, 0, 5, 0);
orderPanel.add(newButton, gridConstraints);
newButton.addActionListener(new ActionListener()
{
  public void actionPerformed(ActionEvent e)
  {
    newButtonActionPerformed(e);
  }
});
exitButton.setText("Exit");
gridConstraints.gridx = 0;
gridConstraints.gridy = 6;
gridConstraints.insets = new Insets(5, 0, 5, 0);
orderPanel.add(exitButton, gridConstraints);
```

```
exitButton.addActionListener(new ActionListener()
{
  public void actionPerformed(ActionEvent e)
  {
    exitButtonActionPerformed(e);
  }
});
shoppingPane.addTab("Order Form", orderPanel);
// cart panel
cartPanel.setLayout(new GridBagLayout());
cartPane.setPreferredSize(new Dimension (250, 150));
cartPane.setViewportView(cartTextArea);
gridConstraints.gridx = 0;
gridConstraints.gridy = 0;
gridConstraints.insets = new Insets(10, 10, 10, 10);
cartPanel.add(cartPane, gridConstraints);
gridConstraints = new GridBagConstraints();
costTextField.setColumns(20);
costTextField.setEditable(false);
costTextField.setBackground(Color.WHITE);
costTextField.setText("Total Cost:");
gridConstraints.gridx = 0;
gridConstraints.gridy = 1;
gridConstraints.insets = new Insets(5, 0, 5, 0);
cartPanel.add(costTextField, gridConstraints);
 shoppingPane.addTab("Shopping Cart", cartPanel);
 // address panel
addressPanel.setLayout(new GridBagLayout());
addressPane.setPreferredSize(new Dimension (250, 150));
addressPane.setViewportView(addressTextArea);
gridConstraints.gridx = 0;
gridConstraints.gridy = 0;
gridConstraints.insets = new Insets(10, 10, 10, 10);
addressPanel.add(addressPane, gridConstraints);
shoppingPane.addTab("Mailing Label", addressPanel);
pack();
Dimension screenSize =
Toolkit.getDefaultToolkit().getScreenSize();
setBounds((int) (0.5 * (screenSize.width - getWidth())),
(int) (0.5 * (screenSize.height - getHeight())), getWidth(),
getHeight());
  }

  private void shoppingPaneStateChanged(ChangeEvent e)
  {
    switch (shoppingPane.getSelectedIndex())
    {
```

```java
      case 0:
        break;
      case 1:
        if (itemsOrdered == 0)
        {
          JOptionPane.showConfirmDialog(null, "No items have
been ordered.", "Error", JOptionPane.DEFAULT_OPTION,
JOptionPane.ERROR_MESSAGE);
          shoppingPane.setSelectedIndex(0);
        }
        else
        {
          double totalCost = 0.00;
          String order = "";
          //load in ordered items
          for (int i = 0; i < numberProducts; i++)
          {
            if (ordered[i] != 0)
            {
              order += ordered[i] + " " +
product[i].toString() + "\n";
              totalCost += ordered[i] * cost[i];
            }
          }
          cartTextArea.setText(order);
          costTextField.setText("Total Cost: $" + new
DecimalFormat("0.00").format(totalCost));
        }
        break;
      case 2:
        // establish address and show label form
        if (orderTextArea.getText().equals(""))
        {
          JOptionPane.showConfirmDialog(null, "Address is
blank.", "Error", JOptionPane.DEFAULT_OPTION,
JOptionPane.ERROR_MESSAGE);
          shoppingPane.setSelectedIndex(0);
        }
        else
        {
          //form label
          addressTextArea.setText("My Company\n" + "My
Address\n" + "My City, State, Zip\n\n\n" +
orderTextArea.getText());
        }
        break;
    }
```

```java
  }

  private void exitForm(WindowEvent e)
  {
    System.exit(0);
  }

  private void addButtonActionPerformed(ActionEvent e)
  {
    int selectedProduct;
    // increment selected product by one
    for (selectedProduct = 0; selectedProduct <
numberProducts; selectedProduct++)
    {
      if
(product[selectedProduct].equals(orderSpinner.getValue().toSt
ring()))
      {
        break;
      }
    }
    ordered[selectedProduct]++;
    itemsOrdered++;
    numberTextField.setText("Items Ordered: " +
itemsOrdered);
  }

  private void newButtonActionPerformed(ActionEvent e)
  {
    // clear form
    orderTextArea.setText("");
    itemsOrdered = 0;
    numberTextField.setText("Items Ordered: 0");
    for (int i = 0; i < numberProducts; i++)
    {
      ordered[i] = 0;
    }
    orderSpinner.setValue(product[0]);
  }

  private void exitButtonActionPerformed(ActionEvent e)
  {
    System.exit(0);
  }
}
```

Run the project. Notice how the shopping cart works and how the different tabs work together. Here's a run I made, first entering an order:

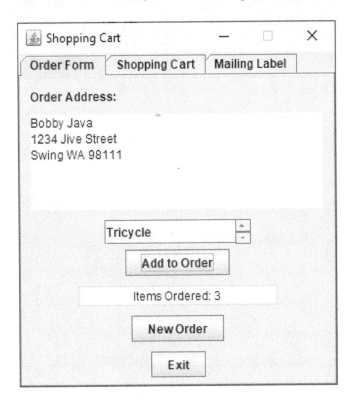

With such an order, the shopping cart appears as:

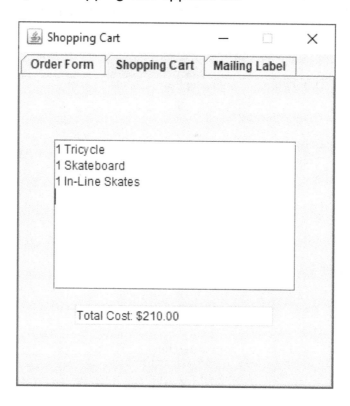

And, the mailing label is:

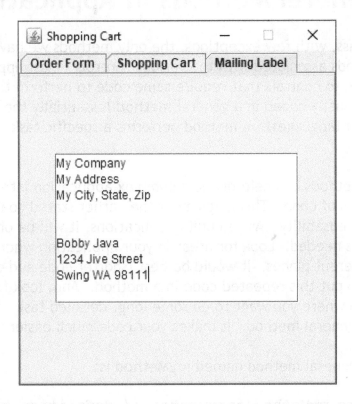

Save the project (saved as **Example5-1** project in the **\LearnJava\LJ Code\Class 5** project group).

As mentioned, this is a start to an e-commerce type system. If you're interested in such projects, you can expand this to meet your needs.

Using General Methods in Applications

So far in this class, with few exceptions, the only methods we have studied are the event methods associated with the various controls. Most applications have tasks not related to controls that require some code to perform these tasks. Such tasks are usually coded in a general **method** (essentially the same as a function in other languages). A method performs a specific task, returning some value.

Using general methods can help divide a complex application into more manageable units of code. This helps meet the earlier stated goals of readability and reusability. As you build applications, it will be obvious where such a method is needed. Look for areas in your application where code is repeated in different places. It would be best (shorter code and easier maintenance) to put this repeated code in a method. And, look for places in your application where you want to do some long, detailed task – this is another great use for a general method. It makes your code much easier to follow.

The form for a general method named **myMethod** is:

```
public type myMethod(arguments)  // definition header
{
   [method code]
   return(returnedValue)
}
```

The definition header names the **method**, specifies its **type** (the type of the returned value – if no value is returned, use the keyword **void**) and defines any input **arguments** passed to the method. The keyword **public** indicates the method can be called from anywhere in the project.

Arguments are a comma-delimited list of variables passed to the method. If there are arguments, we need to take care in how they are declared in the header statement. In particular, we need to be concerned with:

➢ Number of arguments
➢ Order of arguments
➢ Type of arguments

We will address each point separately.

The **number** of arguments is dictated by how many variables the method needs to do its job. You need a variable for each piece of input information. You then place these variables in a particular **order** for the argument list.

Each variable in the argument list will be a particular **data type**. This must be known for each variable. In Java, all variables are passed by value, meaning their value cannot be changed in the method. Variables are declared in the argument list using standard notation:

```
type variableName
```

The variable name (**variableName**) is treated as a local variable in the method.

Arrays can also be used as input arguments. To declare an array as an argument, use:

```
type[] arrayName
```

The brackets indicate an array is being passed.

To use a general method, simply refer to it, by name, in code (with appropriate arguments). Wherever it is used, it will be replaced by the computed value. A function can be used to return a value:

```
rtnValue = myFunction(arguments);
```

or in an expression:

```
thisNumber = 7 * myFunction(arguments) / anotherNumber;
```

Let's build a quick example that converts Fahrenheit temperatures to Celsius (remember the example in Class 4?) Here's such a function:

```
public double degFTodegC(double tempF)
{
  double tempC;
  tempC = (tempF - 32) * 5 / 9;
  return(tempC);
}
```

The method is named **degFTodegC**. It has a single argument, **tempF**, of type **double**. It returns a **double** data type. This code segment converts 45.7 degrees Fahrenheit to the corresponding Celsius value:

```
double t;
.
.
t = degFTodegC(45.7);
```

After this, **t** will have a value of **7.61 degrees C**.

To put a general method in a Java application, simply type it with the event methods associated with controls. Just make sure it is <u>before</u> the final closing brace for the Java class defining the project. Type the header, the opening left brace, the code and the closing right brace.

Every method developed in this class that has some general purpose, that is can be used outside of a particular application, is listed in **Appendix I**. The method **degFTodegC** can be found in that appendix. You will also find two methods developed in Class 2 to validate decimal (**validateDecimalNumber** - **Example 2-3**) and integer (**validateIntegerNumber** - **Exercise 2-2**) numbers in text field controls. And, there is a copy of the code for the **ExampleFileFilter** class used in Class 4. We will be adding more.

Example 5-2

Average Value

Start a new empty project in **NetBeans**. Name the project **Average**. Delete default code in Java file named **Average**. This will be an application where a user inputs a list of numbers. Once complete, the average value of the input numbers is computed using a general method. This example illustrates the use of arrays in argument lists. The finished project will look like this:

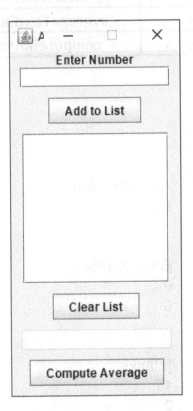

1. Place label, two text fields, three button controls and a scroll pane control on the frame. The **GridBagLayout** arrangement for the controls is:

	gridx = 0
gridy = 0	enterLabel
gridy = 1	enterTextField
gridy = 2	addButton
gridy = 3	listPane
gridy = 4	clearButton
gridy = 5	averageTextField
gridy = 6	computeButton

Properties:

Average Frame:

title	Average Value
resizable	false

enterLabel:

text	Enter Number
gridx	0
gridy	0

enterTextField:

text	[blank]
columns	15
gridx	0
gridy	1
insets	(0, 10, 0, 10);

addButton:

text	Add to List
gridx	0
gridy	2
insets	(10, 0, 0, 0);

listPane:

preferredSize	(150, 150)
viewportView	valueList (JList control)
gridx	0
gridy	3
insets	(10, 10, 10, 10);

clearButton:

text	Clear List
gridx	0
gridy	4

averageTextField:

text	[blank]
columns	15
editable	false
background	WHITE
horizontalAlignment	CENTER
gridx	0
gridy	5
insets	(10, 0, 0, 0)

computeButton:

text	Compute Average
gridx	0
gridy	6
insets	(10, 0, 10, 0)

2. First, build the basic framework. The code to do this is:

```java
/*
 * Average.java
 */
package average;
import javax.swing.*;
import java.awt.*;
import java.awt.event.*;
import java.text.*;
public class Average extends JFrame
{

  public static void main(String args[])
  {
    //construct frame
    new Average().setVisible(true);
  }
  public Average()
  {
    // code to build the form
    setTitle("Average Value");
    setResizable(false);
    addWindowListener(new WindowAdapter()
    {
      public void windowClosing(WindowEvent e)
      {
        exitForm(e);
      }
    });
    getContentPane().setLayout(new GridBagLayout());

    pack();
    Dimension screenSize =
Toolkit.getDefaultToolkit().getScreenSize();
    setBounds((int) (0.5 * (screenSize.width -
getWidth())), (int) (0.5 * (screenSize.height -
getHeight())), getWidth(), getHeight());
  }
  private void exitForm(WindowEvent e)
  {
    System.exit(0);
  }
}
```

3. Now, add controls and events. Add these class level declarations:

```
JLabel enterLabel = new JLabel();
JTextField enterTextField = new JTextField();
JButton addButton = new JButton();
JScrollPane listPane = new JScrollPane();
JList valueList = new JList();
DefaultListModel valueListModel = new DefaultListModel();
JButton clearButton = new JButton();
JTextField averageTextField = new JTextField();
JButton computeButton = new JButton();
```

Position and add each control and events to the frame:

```
// position controls (establish event methods)
GridBagConstraints gridConstraints = new
GridBagConstraints();
enterLabel.setText("Enter Number");
gridConstraints.gridx = 0;
gridConstraints.gridy = 0;
getContentPane().add(enterLabel, gridConstraints);

enterTextField.setText("");
enterTextField.setColumns(15);
gridConstraints = new GridBagConstraints();
gridConstraints.gridx = 0;
gridConstraints.gridy = 1;
gridConstraints.insets = new Insets(0, 10, 0, 10);
getContentPane().add(enterTextField, gridConstraints);
enterTextField.addActionListener(new ActionListener()
{
   public void actionPerformed(ActionEvent e)
   {
enterTextFieldActionPerformed(e);
   }
});

addButton.setText("Add to List");
gridConstraints = new GridBagConstraints();
gridConstraints.gridx = 0;
gridConstraints.gridy = 2;
gridConstraints.insets = new Insets(10, 0, 0, 0);
getContentPane().add(addButton, gridConstraints);
addButton.addActionListener(new ActionListener()
{
   public void actionPerformed(ActionEvent e)
```

```
          {
addButtonActionPerformed(e);
     }
});

valueList.setModel(valueListModel);
listPane.setPreferredSize(new Dimension (150, 150));
listPane.setViewportView(valueList);
gridConstraints = new GridBagConstraints();
gridConstraints.gridx = 0;
gridConstraints.gridy = 3;
gridConstraints.insets = new Insets(10, 10, 10, 10);
getContentPane().add(listPane, gridConstraints);

clearButton.setText("Clear List");
gridConstraints = new GridBagConstraints();
gridConstraints.gridx = 0;
gridConstraints.gridy = 4;
getContentPane().add(clearButton, gridConstraints);
clearButton.addActionListener(new ActionListener()
{
   public void actionPerformed(ActionEvent e)
   {
clearButtonActionPerformed(e);
   }
});

averageTextField.setText("");
averageTextField.setColumns(15);
averageTextField.setEditable(false);
averageTextField.setBackground(Color.WHITE);
averageTextField.setHorizontalAlignment(SwingConstants.CEN
TER);
gridConstraints = new GridBagConstraints();
gridConstraints.gridx = 0;
gridConstraints.gridy = 5;
gridConstraints.insets = new Insets(10, 0, 0, 0);
getContentPane().add(averageTextField, gridConstraints);

computeButton.setText("Compute Average");
gridConstraints = new GridBagConstraints();
gridConstraints.gridx = 0;
gridConstraints.gridy = 6;
gridConstraints.insets = new Insets(10, 0, 10, 0);
getContentPane().add(computeButton, gridConstraints);
computeButton.addActionListener(new ActionListener()
{
```

```
    public void actionPerformed(ActionEvent e)
    {
computeButtonActionPerformed(e);
    }
});
```

And, add the empty event methods:

```
    private void enterTextFieldActionPerformed(ActionEvent e)
    {
    }

    private void addButtonActionPerformed(ActionEvent e)
    {
    }

    private void clearButtonActionPerformed(ActionEvent e)
    {
    }

    private void computeButtonActionPerformed(ActionEvent e)
    {
    }
```

Run to make sure all the controls appear as desired.

4. Now, we add code. First, the general method that computes an average. The numbers it averages are in the 0-based array **values**. There are **numberValues** elements in the array:

```
    public double average(int numberValues, double[] values)
    {
      // find average
      double sum = 0.0;
       for (int i = 0; i < numberValues; i++)
       {
        sum += values[i];
       }
      return(sum / numberValues);
    }
```

Type this after the event methods. Notice how the array (values) is passed into the method. This method has been placed in **Appendix I**.

5. Use this code in the **enterTextFieldActionPerformed** event:

```
private void enterTextFieldActionPerformed(ActionEvent e)
{
  addButton.doClick();
}
```

This code simply 'clicks' the **Add to List** button when <**Enter**> is pressed.

6. Use this code for the **addButtonActionPerformed** event:

```
private void addButtonActionPerformed(ActionEvent e)
{
  // check for valid number
  if (!validateDecimalNumber(enterTextField))
  {
    return;
  }
  // add value to list control
  valueListModel.addElement(enterTextField.getText());
  enterTextField.setText("");
  enterTextField.requestFocus();
}
```

This adds the validated, entered value to the list box. The validation is done with the **validateDecimalNumber** method (copy from **Appendix I**):

```
public boolean validateDecimalNumber(JTextField tf)
{
  // checks to see if text field contains
  // valid decimal number with only digits and a single
decimal point
  // or negative sign
  String s = tf.getText().trim();
  boolean hasDecimal = false;
  boolean valid = true;
  if (s.length() == 0)
  {
    valid = false;
  }
  else
  {
    for (int i = 0; i < s.length(); i++)
    {
      char c = s.charAt(i);
      if ((c >= '0' && c <= '9') || (c == '-' && i == 0))
```

```
      {
        continue;
      }
      else if (c == '.' && !hasDecimal)
      {
        hasDecimal = true;
      }
      else
      {
        // invalid character found
        valid = false;
      }
    }
  }
  if (valid)
  {
    tf.setText(s);
  }
  else
  {
    tf.setText("");
    tf.requestFocus();
  }
  return (valid);
}
```

7. Use this code in the **clearButtonActionPerformed** event – it clears the list box for another average:

```
private void clearButtonActionPerformed(ActionEvent e)
{
  // resets form for another average
  valueListModel.removeAllElements();
  averageTextField.setText("");
  enterTextField.setText("");
  enterTextField.requestFocus();
}
```

8. Use this code for the **computeButtonActionPerformed** event:

```
private void computeButtonActionPerformed(ActionEvent e)
{
  int count = valueListModel.getSize();
  // make sure numbers have been entered
  if (count != 0)
  {
     double[] myValues = new double[count];
    double myAverage;
    // load values in array and compute average
    for (int i = 0; i < count; i++)
    {
      myValues[i] =
Double.valueOf(valueListModel.getElementAt(i).toString()).
doubleValue();
    }
    myAverage = average(count, myValues);
    averageTextField.setText(new
DecimalFormat("0.00").format(myAverage));
  }
  enterTextField.requestFocus();
}
```

This takes the values from the list control and finds the average value.

Here is the complete **Average.java** code (code added to basic framework is shaded):

```
/*
 * Average.java
*/
package average;
import javax.swing.*;
import java.awt.*;
import java.awt.event.*;
import java.text.*;

public class Average extends JFrame
{

  JLabel enterLabel = new JLabel();
  JTextField enterTextField = new JTextField();
  JButton addButton = new JButton();
  JScrollPane listPane = new JScrollPane();
  JList valueList = new JList();
```

```java
DefaultListModel valueListModel = new DefaultListModel();
JButton clearButton = new JButton();
JTextField averageTextField = new JTextField();
JButton computeButton = new JButton();

public static void main(String args[])
{
  //construct frame
  new Average().setVisible(true);
}

public Average()
{
  // code to build the form
  setTitle("Average Value");
  setResizable(false);
  addWindowListener(new WindowAdapter()
  {
    public void windowClosing(WindowEvent e)
    {
      exitForm(e);
    }
  });
  getContentPane().setLayout(new GridBagLayout());

  // position controls (establish event methods)
  GridBagConstraints gridConstraints = new
GridBagConstraints();
  enterLabel.setText("Enter Number");
  gridConstraints.gridx = 0;
  gridConstraints.gridy = 0;
  getContentPane().add(enterLabel, gridConstraints);

  enterTextField.setText("");
  enterTextField.setColumns(15);
  gridConstraints = new GridBagConstraints();
  gridConstraints.gridx = 0;
  gridConstraints.gridy = 1;
  gridConstraints.insets = new Insets(0, 10, 0, 10);
  getContentPane().add(enterTextField, gridConstraints);
  enterTextField.addActionListener(new ActionListener()
  {
    public void actionPerformed(ActionEvent e)
    {
      enterTextFieldActionPerformed(e);
    }
  });
```

```
addButton.setText("Add to List");
gridConstraints = new GridBagConstraints();
gridConstraints.gridx = 0;
gridConstraints.gridy = 2;
gridConstraints.insets = new Insets(10, 0, 0, 0);
getContentPane().add(addButton, gridConstraints);
addButton.addActionListener(new ActionListener()
{
  public void actionPerformed(ActionEvent e)
  {
    addButtonActionPerformed(e);
  }
});

valueList.setModel(valueListModel);
listPane.setPreferredSize(new Dimension (150, 150));
listPane.setViewportView(valueList);
gridConstraints = new GridBagConstraints();
gridConstraints.gridx = 0;
gridConstraints.gridy = 3;
gridConstraints.insets = new Insets(10, 10, 10, 10);
getContentPane().add(listPane, gridConstraints);

clearButton.setText("Clear List");
gridConstraints = new GridBagConstraints();
gridConstraints.gridx = 0;
gridConstraints.gridy = 4;
getContentPane().add(clearButton, gridConstraints);
clearButton.addActionListener(new ActionListener()
{
  public void actionPerformed(ActionEvent e)
  {
    clearButtonActionPerformed(e);
  }
});

averageTextField.setText("");
averageTextField.setColumns(15);
averageTextField.setEditable(false);
averageTextField.setBackground(Color.WHITE);
averageTextField.setHorizontalAlignment(SwingConstants.CENTER
);
gridConstraints = new GridBagConstraints();
gridConstraints.gridx = 0;
gridConstraints.gridy = 5;
```

```
      gridConstraints.insets = new Insets(10, 0, 0, 0);
      getContentPane().add(averageTextField, gridConstraints);

      computeButton.setText("Compute Average");
      gridConstraints = new GridBagConstraints();
      gridConstraints.gridx = 0;
      gridConstraints.gridy = 6;
      gridConstraints.insets = new Insets(10, 0, 10, 0);
      getContentPane().add(computeButton, gridConstraints);
      computeButton.addActionListener(new ActionListener()
      {
        public void actionPerformed(ActionEvent e)
        {
          computeButtonActionPerformed(e);
        }
      });

    pack();
    Dimension screenSize =
Toolkit.getDefaultToolkit().getScreenSize();
      setBounds((int) (0.5 * (screenSize.width - getWidth())),
(int) (0.5 * (screenSize.height - getHeight())), getWidth(),
getHeight());
  }


  private void enterTextFieldActionPerformed(ActionEvent e)
  {
    addButton.doClick();
  }

  private void addButtonActionPerformed(ActionEvent e)
  {
    // check for valid number
    if (!validateDecimalNumber(enterTextField))
    {
      return;
    }
    // add value to list control
    valueListModel.addElement(enterTextField.getText());
    enterTextField.setText("");
    enterTextField.requestFocus();
  }

  private void clearButtonActionPerformed(ActionEvent e)
  {
    // resets form for another average
```

```
    valueListModel.removeAllElements();
    averageTextField.setText("");
    enterTextField.setText("");
    enterTextField.requestFocus();
  }

  private void computeButtonActionPerformed(ActionEvent e)
  {
    int count = valueListModel.getSize();
    // make sure numbers have been entered
    if (count != 0)
    {
      double[] myValues = new double[count];
      double myAverage;
      // load values in array and compute average
      for (int i = 0; i < count; i++)
      {
        myValues[i] =
Double.valueOf(valueListModel.getElementAt(i).toString()).dou
bleValue();
      }
      myAverage = average(count, myValues);
      averageTextField.setText(new
DecimalFormat("0.00").format(myAverage));
    }
    enterTextField.requestFocus();
  }

  private void exitForm(WindowEvent e)
  {
    System.exit(0);
  }

  public double average(int numberValues, double[] values)
  {
    // find average
    double sum = 0.0;
     for (int i = 0; i < numberValues; i++)
     {
      sum += values[i];
    }
    return(sum / numberValues);
  }

  public boolean validateDecimalNumber(JTextField tf)
  {
    // checks to see if text field contains
```

```java
    // valid decimal number with only digits and a single
decimal point
    // or negative sign
    String s = tf.getText().trim();
    boolean hasDecimal = false;
    boolean valid = true;
    if (s.length() == 0)
    {
      valid = false;
    }
    else
    {
      for (int i = 0; i < s.length(); i++)
      {
        char c = s.charAt(i);
        if ((c >= '0' && c <= '9') || (c == '-' && i == 0))
        {
          continue;
        }
        else if (c == '.' && !hasDecimal)
        {
          hasDecimal = true;
        }
        else
        {
          // invalid character found
          valid = false;
        }
      }
    }
    if (valid)
    {
      tf.setText(s);
    }
    else
    {
      tf.setText("");
      tf.requestFocus();
    }
    return (valid);
  }
}
```

Run the application and try different values. This averaging method might come in handy for some task you may have.   Here's a run I made averaging the first 10 integers:

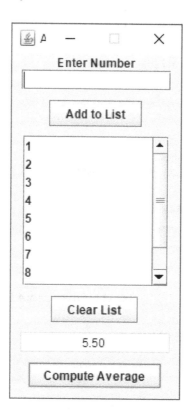

Save the application (saved as **Example5-2** project in **\LearnJava\LJ Code\Class 5** project group).

Returning Multiple Values from General Methods

You may have noticed a general method can only return a single value (or no value). What if you need to **compute** and **return multiple values**? Can a method still be used? There are two possible approaches to this situation, depending on the types of information being returned.

If the returned values are of different types, you would need to add class level variables for all additional computed values. Then, these values would be available where needed in the project. This works, but is not ideal since it tends to destroy the "portability" of a method. This portability is destroyed because you need to make sure users of your method know what the class level variables are and make sure they include the needed declarations in their project.

If the returned values are all of the same type, there is a better solution that maintains the portability of methods. In this situation, simply return an array of output values. With such an approach, no class level variables are needed and the users don't need to add any extra declarations. They just need to use the method.

An example of this second approach should make things clearer. Assume you are a carpet layer and always need the perimeter and area for a rectangle. We'll build a method that helps you with the computations. We need, for inputs, the length and width of the rectangle. The output information will be an array with the perimeter and area. Here is the method that does the job:

```
public double[] rectangleInfo(double length, double width)
{
   double[] info = new double[2];
   info[0] = 2 * (length + width); // perimeter
   info[1] = length * width; // area
   return(info);
}
```

The method is named **rectangleInfo**. It has two arguments, both of type **double**. The two arguments are **length** and **width**. Notice how the computed perimeter and area are placed in the **info** array returned by the method. Make sure the type in the header statement indicates an array is returned (**double[]** in this case). This method is in **Appendix I**.

This code segment will call our method:

```
double l;
double w;
double[] carpet = new double[2];
     .
     .
     .
l = 6.2;
w = 2.3;
carpet = rectangleInfo(l, w);
```

Once this code is executed, the variable **carpet[0]** will have the perimeter of a rectangle of length 6.2 and width 2.3 (17.0). The variable **carpet[1]** will have the area of the same rectangle (14.26). Notice there is no reason for the variables in the calling argument sequence to have the same names assigned in the method declaration. The location of each variable in the calling sequence defines which variable is which (that's why order of arguments is important).

Example 5-3

Circle Geometry

Start a new empty project in **NetBeans**. Name the project **Circle**. Delete default code in Java file named **Circle**. This will be a simple application that illustrates use of a method that returns an array. The procedure will compute the area and circumference of a circle, given its diameter. The finished project will look like this:

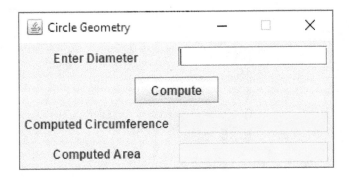

1. Add three labels, three text fields and a button control to the frame. The **GridBagLayout** is:

	gridx = 0	gridx = 1
gridy = 0	diameterLabel	diameterTextField
gridy = 1	computeButton	
gridy = 2	circumferenceLabel	circumferenceTextField
gridy = 3	areaLabel	areaTextField

Properties:

Circle Frame:

title	Circle Geometry
resizable	false

diameterLabel:

text	Enter Diameter
gridx	0
gridy	0
insets	(5, 5, 5, 5)

diameterTextField:

text	[blank]
columns	15
gridx	1
gridy	0
insets	(5, 5, 5, 5)

computeButton:

text	Compute
gridx	0
gridy	1
gridwidth	2
insets	(5, 5, 5, 5)

circumferenceLabel:

text	Computed Circumference
gridx	0
gridy	2
insets	(5, 5, 5, 5)

circumferenceTextField:

text	[blank]
columns	15
editable	false
background	YELLOW
horizontalAlignment	CENTER
gridx	1
gridy	2
insets	(5, 5, 5, 5)

areaLabel:

text	Computed Area
gridx	0
gridy	3
insets	(5, 5, 5, 5)

areaTextField:

text	[blank]
columns	15
editable	false
background	YELLOW
horizontalAlignment	CENTER
gridx	1
gridy	3
insets	(5, 5, 5, 5)

2. Build the basic framework:

```java
/*
 * Circle.java
 * KIDware
 */
package circle;
import javax.swing.*;
import java.awt.*;
import java.awt.event.*;
import java.text.*;

public class Circle extends JFrame
{

  public static void main(String args[])
  {
    //construct frame
    new Circle().setVisible(true);
  }

  public Circle()
  {
    // code to build the form
    setTitle("Circle Geometry");
    setResizable(false);
    addWindowListener(new WindowAdapter()
    {
      public void windowClosing(WindowEvent e)
```

```
        {
          exitForm(e);
        }
      });
      getContentPane().setLayout(new GridBagLayout());



      pack();
      Dimension screenSize =
   Toolkit.getDefaultToolkit().getScreenSize();
      setBounds((int) (0.5 * (screenSize.width -
   getWidth())), (int) (0.5 * (screenSize.height -
   getHeight())), getWidth(), getHeight());
      }

    private void exitForm(WindowEvent e)
    {
      System.exit(0);
    }
  }
```

Run to check things out.

3. Now, add controls and events. Class level declarations for controls:

```
    JLabel diameterLabel = new JLabel();
    JTextField diameterTextField = new JTextField();
    JButton computeButton = new JButton();
    JLabel circumferenceLabel = new JLabel();
    JTextField circumferenceTextField = new JTextField();
    JLabel areaLabel = new JLabel();
    JTextField areaTextField = new JTextField();
```

Position controls and add event methods:

```
    GridBagConstraints gridConstraints = new
    GridBagConstraints();
    diameterLabel.setText("Enter Diameter");
    gridConstraints.gridx = 0;
    gridConstraints.gridy = 0;
    gridConstraints.insets = new Insets(5, 5, 5, 5);
    getContentPane().add(diameterLabel, gridConstraints);

    diameterTextField.setText("");
    diameterTextField.setColumns(15);
```

```
gridConstraints = new GridBagConstraints();
gridConstraints.gridx = 1;
gridConstraints.gridy = 0;
gridConstraints.insets = new Insets(5, 5, 5, 5);
getContentPane().add(diameterTextField, gridConstraints);
diameterTextField.addActionListener(new ActionListener()
{
  public void actionPerformed(ActionEvent e)
  {
    diameterTextFieldActionPerformed(e);
  }
});

computeButton.setText("Compute");
gridConstraints = new GridBagConstraints();
gridConstraints.gridx = 0;
gridConstraints.gridy = 1;
gridConstraints.gridwidth = 2;
gridConstraints.insets = new Insets(5, 5, 5, 5);
getContentPane().add(computeButton, gridConstraints);
computeButton.addActionListener(new ActionListener()
{
  public void actionPerformed(ActionEvent e)
  {
    computeButtonActionPerformed(e);
  }
});

circumferenceLabel.setText("Computed Circumference");
gridConstraints = new GridBagConstraints();
gridConstraints.gridx = 0;
gridConstraints.gridy = 2;
gridConstraints.insets = new Insets(5, 5, 5, 5);
getContentPane().add(circumferenceLabel, gridConstraints);

circumferenceTextField.setText("");
circumferenceTextField.setColumns(15);
circumferenceTextField.setEditable(false);
circumferenceTextField.setBackground(Color.YELLOW);
circumferenceTextField.setHorizontalAlignment(SwingConstan
ts.CENTER);
gridConstraints = new GridBagConstraints();
gridConstraints.gridx = 1;
gridConstraints.gridy = 2;
gridConstraints.insets = new Insets(5, 5, 5, 5);
getContentPane().add(circumferenceTextField,
gridConstraints);
```

```
areaLabel.setText("Computed Area");
gridConstraints = new GridBagConstraints();
gridConstraints.gridx = 0;
gridConstraints.gridy = 3;
gridConstraints.insets = new Insets(5, 5, 5, 5);
getContentPane().add(areaLabel, gridConstraints);

areaTextField.setText("");
areaTextField.setColumns(15);
areaTextField.setEditable(false);
areaTextField.setBackground(Color.YELLOW);
areaTextField.setHorizontalAlignment(SwingConstants.CENTER
);
gridConstraints = new GridBagConstraints();
gridConstraints.gridx = 1;
gridConstraints.gridy = 3;
gridConstraints.insets = new Insets(5, 5, 5, 5);
getContentPane().add(areaTextField, gridConstraints);
```

Add two empty event methods (one for the diameter text field and one for the compute button):

```
private void diameterTextFieldActionPerformed(ActionEvent
e)
{
}

private void computeButtonActionPerformed(ActionEvent e)
{
}
```

Run to check the control alignment.

4. Let's add the code. Add a general method (**circleGeometry**) that computes the circumference and area of a circle:

```
public double[] circleGeometry(double diameter)
{
   double [] geometry = new double[2];
   geometry[0] = Math.PI * diameter; // circumference
   geometry[1] = Math.PI * diameter * diameter / 4; // area
   return(geometry);
}
```

Notice the variable **diameter** is input and an array (**geometry**) contains the outputs. **geometry[0]** holds the circumference and **geometry[1]** holds the area. This procedure can be found in **Appendix I**.

5. Use this code in the **diameterTextFieldActionPerformed** event:

```
private void diameterTextFieldActionPerformed(ActionEvent
e)
{
   computeButton.doClick();
}
```

This code simply 'clicks' the **Compute** button when <**Enter**> is pressed.

6. Use this code for the **computeButtonActionPerformed** event:

```
private void computeButtonActionPerformed(ActionEvent e)
{
  // check for valid number
  if (!validateDecimalNumber(diameterTextField))
  {
    return;
  }
  double[] info = new double[2];
  double d =
Double.valueOf(diameterTextField.getText()).doubleValue();
  info = circleGeometry(d);
  circumferenceTextField.setText(new
DecimalFormat("0.00").format(info[0]));
  areaTextField.setText(new
DecimalFormat("0.00").format(info[1]));
}
```

This reads the validated diameter and computes the circle geometry. The validation is done with the **validateDecimalNumber** method (copy from **Appendix I**):

```
public boolean validateDecimalNumber(JTextField tf)
{
  // checks to see if text field contains
  // valid decimal number with only digits and a single
decimal point
  // or negative sign
  String s = tf.getText().trim();
   oolean hasDecimal = false;
   oolean valid = true;
  if (s.length() == 0)
  {
    valid = false;
  }
  else
  {
    for (int i = 0; i < s.length(); i++)
    {
      char c = s.charAt(i);
      if ((c >= '0' && c <= '9') || (c == '-' && i == 0))
      {
        continue;
      }
      else if (c == '.' && !hasDecimal)
```

```
          {
            hasDecimal = true;
          }
          else
          {
            // invalid character found
            valid = false;
          }
        }
      }
   if (valid)
   {
      tf.setText(s);
   }
   else
   {
      tf.setText("");
      tf.requestFocus();
   }
   return (valid);
}
```

The final **Circle.java** code listing (with code added to basic framework shaded):

```
/*
 * Circle.java
*/
package circle;
import javax.swing.*;
import java.awt.*;
import java.awt.event.*;
import java.text.*;

public class Circle extends JFrame
{
   JLabel diameterLabel = new JLabel();
   JTextField diameterTextField = new JTextField();
   JButton computeButton = new JButton();
   JLabel circumferenceLabel = new JLabel();
   JTextField circumferenceTextField = new JTextField();
   JLabel areaLabel = new JLabel();
   JTextField areaTextField = new JTextField();

   public static void main(String args[])
   {
     //construct frame
     new Circle().setVisible(true);
   }

   public Circle()
   {
     // code to build the form
     setTitle("Circle Geometry");
     setResizable(false);
     addWindowListener(new WindowAdapter()
     {
       public void windowClosing(WindowEvent e)
       {
         exitForm(e);
       }
     });
     getContentPane().setLayout(new GridBagLayout());

     // position controls (establish event methods)
     GridBagConstraints gridConstraints = new
GridBagConstraints();
     diameterLabel.setText("Enter Diameter");
     gridConstraints.gridx = 0;
     gridConstraints.gridy = 0;
```

```java
    gridConstraints.insets = new Insets(5, 5, 5, 5);
    getContentPane().add(diameterLabel, gridConstraints);

    diameterTextField.setText("");
    diameterTextField.setColumns(15);
    gridConstraints = new GridBagConstraints();
    gridConstraints.gridx = 1;
    gridConstraints.gridy = 0;
    gridConstraints.insets = new Insets(5, 5, 5, 5);
    getContentPane().add(diameterTextField, gridConstraints);
    diameterTextField.addActionListener(new ActionListener()
    {
      public void actionPerformed(ActionEvent e)
      {
        diameterTextFieldActionPerformed(e);
      }
    });

    computeButton.setText("Compute");
    gridConstraints = new GridBagConstraints();
    gridConstraints.gridx = 0;
    gridConstraints.gridy = 1;
    gridConstraints.gridwidth = 2;
    gridConstraints.insets = new Insets(5, 5, 5, 5);
    getContentPane().add(computeButton, gridConstraints);
    computeButton.addActionListener(new ActionListener()
    {
      public void actionPerformed(ActionEvent e)
      {
        computeButtonActionPerformed(e);
      }
    });

    circumferenceLabel.setText("Computed Circumference");
    gridConstraints = new GridBagConstraints();
    gridConstraints.gridx = 0;
    gridConstraints.gridy = 2;
    gridConstraints.insets = new Insets(5, 5, 5, 5);
    getContentPane().add(circumferenceLabel,
gridConstraints);

    circumferenceTextField.setText("");
    circumferenceTextField.setColumns(15);
    circumferenceTextField.setEditable(false);
    circumferenceTextField.setBackground(Color.YELLOW);
```

```
circumferenceTextField.setHorizontalAlignment(SwingConstants.
CENTER);
    gridConstraints = new GridBagConstraints();
    gridConstraints.gridx = 1;
    gridConstraints.gridy = 2;
    gridConstraints.insets = new Insets(5, 5, 5, 5);
    getContentPane().add(circumferenceTextField,
gridConstraints);

    areaLabel.setText("Computed Area");
    gridConstraints = new GridBagConstraints();
    gridConstraints.gridx = 0;
    gridConstraints.gridy = 3;
    gridConstraints.insets = new Insets(5, 5, 5, 5);
    getContentPane().add(areaLabel, gridConstraints);

    areaTextField.setText("");
    areaTextField.setColumns(15);
    areaTextField.setEditable(false);
    areaTextField.setBackground(Color.YELLOW);

areaTextField.setHorizontalAlignment(SwingConstants.CENTER);
    gridConstraints = new GridBagConstraints();
    gridConstraints.gridx = 1;
    gridConstraints.gridy = 3;
    gridConstraints.insets = new Insets(5, 5, 5, 5);
    getContentPane().add(areaTextField, gridConstraints);


    pack();
    Dimension screenSize =
Toolkit.getDefaultToolkit().getScreenSize();
    setBounds((int) (0.5 * (screenSize.width - getWidth())),
(int) (0.5 * (screenSize.height - getHeight())), getWidth(),
getHeight());
  }

  private void diameterTextFieldActionPerformed(ActionEvent
e)
  {
    computeButton.doClick();
  }

  private void computeButtonActionPerformed(ActionEvent e)
  {
    // check for valid number
```

```java
    if (!validateDecimalNumber(diameterTextField))
    {
      return;
    }
    double[] info = new double[2];
    double d =
Double.valueOf(diameterTextField.getText()).doubleValue();
    info = circleGeometry(d);
    circumferenceTextField.setText(new
DecimalFormat("0.00").format(info[0]));
    areaTextField.setText(new
DecimalFormat("0.00").format(info[1]));
  }

  public double[] circleGeometry(double diameter)
  {
    double [] geometry = new double[2];
    geometry[0] = Math.PI * diameter; // circumference
    geometry[1] = Math.PI * diameter * diameter / 4; // area
    return(geometry);
  }

  public boolean validateDecimalNumber(JTextField tf)
  {
    // checks to see if text field contains
    // valid decimal number with only digits and a single
decimal point
    // or negative sign
    String s = tf.getText().trim();
    boolean hasDecimal = false;
    boolean valid = true;
    if (s.length() == 0)
    {
      valid = false;
    }
    else
    {
      for (int i = 0; i < s.length(); i++)
      {
        char c = s.charAt(i);
        if ((c >= '0' && c <= '9') || (c == '-' && i == 0))
        {
          continue;
        }
        else if (c == '.' && !hasDecimal)
        {
          hasDecimal = true;
```

```
        }
        else
        {
          // invalid character found
          valid = false;
        }
      }
    }
    if (valid)
    {
      tf.setText(s);
    }
    else
    {
      tf.setText("");
      tf.requestFocus();
    }
    return (valid);
  }

  private void exitForm(WindowEvent e)
  {
    System.exit(0);
  }
}
```

Run the application and try some different diameters. Here's what I got when I used a diameter of 23.24:

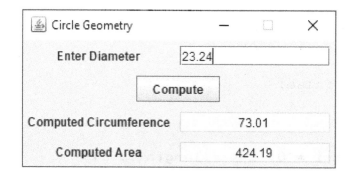

Save the project (saved as **Example5-3** project in **\LearnJava\LJ Code\Class 5** project group).

Adding Menus to Java Applications

As the applications you build become more and more detailed, with more features for the user, you will need some way to organize those features. A **menu** provides such organization. Menus are a part of most applications. They provide ways to navigate within an application and access desired features. Menus are easily incorporated into Java GUI programs using three Swing objects: **menu bars**, **menus**, and **menu items**.

The **JMenuBar** object is placed at the top of a frame and is used to hold the menu. The **JMenu** object is a labeled menu item, within the menu bar, that when clicked displays a pull-down menu. And, a **JMenuItem** is a simple menu item that when clicked results in some program action. **JMenuItem** objects appear in the pull-down menus of **JMenu** objects. Menu items can be simply text or even radio buttons and check boxes.

A good way to think about elements of a menu structure is to consider them as a hierarchical list of button-type controls that only appear when pulled down from the menu. When you click on a menu item, some action is taken. Like buttons, menu items are named, have properties and events. The best way to learn to use all these objects is to build an example menu. The menu structure we will build is:

File	Edit	Format
New	Cut	Bold
Open	Copy	Italic
Save	Paste	Size
————		10
Exit		15
		20

The level of indentation indicates position of a menu item within the hierarchy. For example, **New** is a sub-element of the **File** menu. The line under **Save** in the **File** menu is a separator bar (separates menu items).

The three headings, **File**, **Edit** and **Format**, will be **JMenu** objects within a **JMenuBar** object. With this structure, the menu would display as:

    File   **Edit**   **Format**

The sub-menus appear when one of these 'top' level menu items is selected. Note the **Size** sub-menu under **Format** has another level of hierarchy. It is good practice to not use more than two levels in menus. Each menu item will have an **actionPerformed** event associated with it. This event is invoked when the user clicks the corresponding item.

When designing your menus, follow formats used by standard GUI applications. For example, if your application works with files, the first heading should be **File** and the last element in the sub-menu under **File** should be **Exit**. If your application uses editing features (cutting, pasting, copying), there should be an **Edit** heading. By doing this, you insure your user will be comfortable with your application. Of course, there will be times your application has unique features that do not fit a 'standard' menu item. In such cases, choose headings that accurately describe such unique features.

We're ready to build this sample menu, step-by-step. Start a new project in **NetBeans**. Name the project **MenuExample**. Delete default code in file named **MenuExample**. Use this code to create an empty frame:

```java
/*
 * MenuExample.java
 */
package menuexample;
import javax.swing.*;
import java.awt.*;
import java.awt.event.*;
public class MenuExample extends JFrame
{
  public static void main(String args[])
  {
    // construct frame
    new MenuExample().setVisible(true);
  }
  public MenuExample()
  {
    // frame constructor
    setTitle("Menu Example");
    setSize(400, 200);
    addWindowListener(new WindowAdapter()
    {
      public void windowClosing(WindowEvent e)
      {
        exitForm(e);
      }
    });
  }
  private void exitForm(WindowEvent evt)
  {
    System.exit(0);
  }
}
```

Run to make sure the empty frame appears:

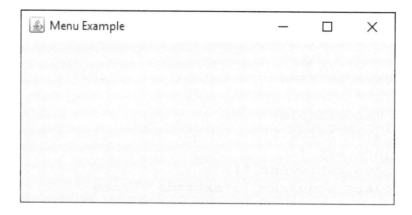

We first add a menu bar and the three main headings. We will name our menu bar **exampleMenuBar**. To create this, use:

```
JMenuBar exampleMenuBar = new JMenuBar();
```

This declaration and creation is usually at class level. To add this menu bar to the existing frame, use the JFrame **setJMenuBar** method:

```
setJMenuBar(exampleMenuBar);
```

Then, each heading (**JMenu** object) needs a declaration and creation statement. When the heading is created, you add the text that is displayed in the heading. For our three headings, the statements (again, class level declarations) would be:

```
JMenu fileMenu = new JMenu("File");
JMenu editMenu = new JMenu("Edit");
JMenu formatMenu = new JMenu("Format");
```

These menu objects are added to the menu bar with the add method:

```
exampleMenuBar.add(fileMenu);
exampleMenuBar.add(editMenu);
exampleMenuBar.add(formatMenu);
```

Here is the frame code modified (modifications shaded) to add the menu bar and three headings:

```java
/*
 * MenuExample.java
 */
package menuexample;
import javax.swing.*;
import java.awt.*;
import java.awt.event.*;
public class MenuExample extends JFrame
{
  JMenuBar exampleMenuBar = new JMenuBar();
  JMenu fileMenu = new JMenu("File");
  JMenu editMenu = new JMenu("Edit");
  JMenu formatMenu = new JMenu("Format");
  public static void main(String args[])
  {
    // construct frame
    new MenuExample().setVisible(true);
  }
  public MenuExample()
  {
    // frame constructor
    setTitle("Menu Example");
    setSize(400, 200);
    addWindowListener(new WindowAdapter()
    {
      public void windowClosing(WindowEvent e)
      {
        exitForm(e);
      }
    });
    // build menu
    setJMenuBar(exampleMenuBar);
    exampleMenuBar.add(fileMenu);
    exampleMenuBar.add(editMenu);
    exampleMenuBar.add(formatMenu);
  }
  private void exitForm(WindowEvent evt)
  {
    System.exit(0);
  }
}
```

Run the project to see the menu appear:

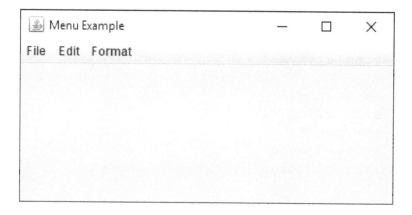

Now, we add menu items to each of the main headings. Each element is added in the same manner. Say we have an item named **myItem** with a label **myText**. To declare and create this item, use:

```
JMenuItem myItem = new JMenuItem(myText);
```

Then, this is added to the desired menu object (**myMenu**) using the **add** method:

```
myMenu.add(myItem);
```

Add the items in the order you want them to appear in the pull-down menu. To add a separator bar to a menu, use the **addSeparator** method:

```
myMenu.addSeparator();
```

Here is the modified code (modifications shaded) with pull-down menus added to the **File** and **Edit** menus (we will do the **Format** menu separately):

```
/*
 * MenuExample.java
 */
package menuexample;
import javax.swing.*;
import java.awt.*;
import java.awt.event.*;
public class MenuExample extends JFrame
{
  JMenuBar exampleMenuBar = new JMenuBar();
  JMenu fileMenu = new JMenu("File");
  JMenuItem newMenuItem = new JMenuItem("New");
```

```java
JMenuItem openMenuItem = new JMenuItem("Open");
JMenuItem saveMenuItem = new JMenuItem("Save");
JMenuItem exitMenuItem = new JMenuItem("Exit");
JMenu editMenu = new JMenu("Edit");
JMenuItem cutMenuItem = new JMenuItem("Cut");
JMenuItem copyMenuItem = new JMenuItem("Copy");
JMenuItem pasteMenuItem = new JMenuItem("Paste");
JMenu formatMenu = new JMenu("Format");

public static void main(String args[])
{
  // construct frame
  new MenuExample().setVisible(true);
}
public MenuExample()
{
  // frame constructor
  setTitle("Menu Example");
  setSize(400, 200);
  addWindowListener(new WindowAdapter()
  {
    public void windowClosing(WindowEvent e)
    {
      exitForm(e);
    }
  });

  // build menu
  setJMenuBar(exampleMenuBar);
  exampleMenuBar.add(fileMenu);
  fileMenu.add(newMenuItem);
  fileMenu.add(openMenuItem);
  fileMenu.add(saveMenuItem);
  fileMenu.addSeparator();
  fileMenu.add(exitMenuItem);
  exampleMenuBar.add(editMenu);
  editMenu.add(cutMenuItem);
  editMenu.add(copyMenuItem);
  editMenu.add(pasteMenuItem);
  exampleMenuBar.add(formatMenu);

}
private void exitForm(WindowEvent evt)
{
  System.exit(0);
}
}
```

Run. Here is the expanded **File** menu:

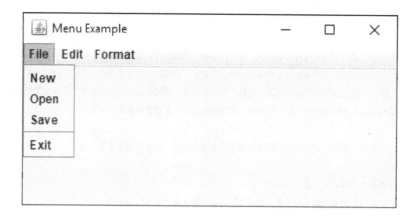

And, here is the expanded **Edit** menu:

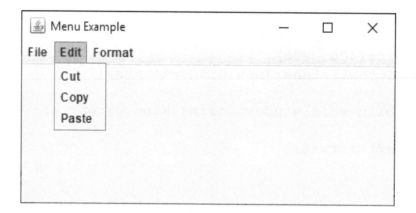

The **Format** menu will be different in several ways. Recall it has options for **Bold**, **Italic** and **Size**. The **Size** menu has another pull-down menu. When a user selects either **Bold** or **Italic**, we would like some indication if either of these has already been selected. To do this, we will use **check boxes** as the menu items (**JCheckBoxMenuItem**). Two arguments are used in creating such an object – the menu item label and a **boolean** value indicating if the box should be initially checked. To create the **Bold** menu item (with no check mark), use:

```
JCheckBoxMenuItem boldMenuItem = new
JCheckBoxMenuItem("Bold", false);
```

Once created, the menu item is added to the desired menu object (**formatMenu** in this case) with the same **add** method. Similar code is used to create the **Italic** menu item.

The **Size** element in the **Format** menu is another menu object. It is created using:

```
JMenu sizeMenu = new JMenu("Size");
```

Then, it is added to the **Format** menu object using the **add** method. But, now it needs a pull-down menu. The pull-down menu offers three choices for size: **10**, **15** or **20**. Only one size can be selected – we will use radio button menu items (**JRadioButtonMenuItem**). Such menu items are created similarly to radio buttons. Like the check box menu item, two arguments are used in creating such an object – the menu item label and a **boolean** value indicating if the box should be initially selected. To create the **10** menu item (initially selected), use:

```
JRadioButtonMenuItem size10MenuItem = new
JRadioButtonMenuItem("10", true);
```

Once created, the menu item is added to the **sizeMenu** menu object with the same **add** method. You also need to add the radio buttons to a button group to insure they act as a group. The modifications to our example should make all this clear.

The modified code adding the **Format** menu is:

```
/*
 * MenuExample.java
 */
package menuexample;
import javax.swing.*;
import java.awt.*;
import java.awt.event.*;
public class MenuExample extends JFrame
{
   JMenuBar exampleMenuBar = new JMenuBar();
   JMenu fileMenu = new JMenu("File");
   JMenuItem newMenuItem = new JMenuItem("New");
   JMenuItem openMenuItem = new JMenuItem("Open");
   JMenuItem saveMenuItem = new JMenuItem("Save");
   JMenuItem exitMenuItem = new JMenuItem("Exit");
   JMenu editMenu = new JMenu("Edit");
   JMenuItem cutMenuItem = new JMenuItem("Cut");
   JMenuItem copyMenuItem = new JMenuItem("Copy");
   JMenuItem pasteMenuItem = new JMenuItem("Paste");
   JMenu formatMenu = new JMenu("Format");
```

```
   JCheckBoxMenuItem boldMenuItem = new
JCheckBoxMenuItem("Bold", false);
   JCheckBoxMenuItem italicMenuItem = new
JCheckBoxMenuItem("Italic", false);
   JMenu sizeMenu = new JMenu("Size");
   ButtonGroup sizeGroup = new ButtonGroup();
   JRadioButtonMenuItem size10MenuItem = new
JRadioButtonMenuItem("10", true);
   JRadioButtonMenuItem size15MenuItem = new
JRadioButtonMenuItem("15", false);
   JRadioButtonMenuItem size20MenuItem = new
JRadioButtonMenuItem("20", false);
  public static void main(String args[])
  {
    // construct frame
    new MenuExample().setVisible(true);
  }
  public MenuExample()
  {
    // frame constructor
    setTitle("Menu Example");
    setSize(400, 200);
    addWindowListener(new WindowAdapter()
    {
      public void windowClosing(WindowEvent e)
      {
        exitForm(e);
      }
    });
    // build menu
    setJMenuBar(exampleMenuBar);
    exampleMenuBar.add(fileMenu);
    fileMenu.add(newMenuItem);
    fileMenu.add(openMenuItem);
    fileMenu.add(saveMenuItem);
    fileMenu.addSeparator();
    fileMenu.add(exitMenuItem);
    exampleMenuBar.add(editMenu);
    editMenu.add(cutMenuItem);
    editMenu.add(copyMenuItem);
    editMenu.add(pasteMenuItem);
    exampleMenuBar.add(formatMenu);
    formatMenu.add(boldMenuItem);
    formatMenu.add(italicMenuItem);
    formatMenu.add(sizeMenu);
    sizeMenu.add(size10MenuItem);
    sizeMenu.add(size15MenuItem);
```

```
      sizeMenu.add(size20MenuItem);
      sizeGroup.add(size10MenuItem);
      sizeGroup.add(size15MenuItem);
      sizeGroup.add(size20MenuItem);
    }
  private void exitForm(WindowEvent evt)
  {
    System.exit(0);
  }
}
```

Run the application. See how the check boxes and radio buttons in the **Format** menu work. Here's the expanded menu, where I've selected **Italic** and size **15**:

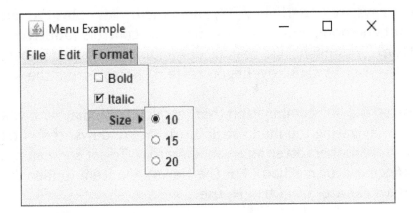

We're getting close to finishing the menu structure, but there are still a few things to consider. Most menus feature **shortcuts** that allow a user to select a menu from the menu bar using the keyboard. In Windows, a typical shortcut would be to hold the <**Alt**> key while pressing some letter. To access the **File** menu here, we would use <**Alt**>-**F**. A shortcut is added to a menu using the **setMnemonic** method. Three shortcuts assigned for our menu would be:

```
fileMenu.setMnemonic('F');
editMenu.setMnemonic('E');
formatMenu.setMnemonic('O');
```

Note a unique letter must be selected for each shortcut.

Add these three lines after the code setting the menu bar, then rerun to see:

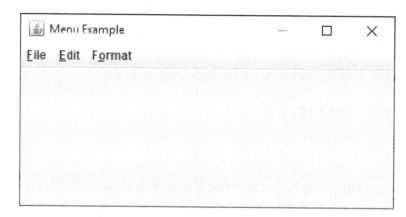

The shortcut keys are underlined. Try them (hold <**Alt**> plus the underlined key). The **setMnemonic** method works on other controls (**JButton**, **JCheckBox**, **JRadioButton**). You might like to consider adding shortcuts to these controls. This allows the user to cause events on certain controls from the keyboard.

An **accelerator** is a key combination that lets you immediately invoke a menu item without navigating the menu structure). In Windows, the <**Ctrl**> key is often used with another letter as an accelerator. To set such an accelerator, use the **setAccelerator** method. For the **New** menu item (under the **File** menu), to assign an accelerator of <**Ctrl**>-**N**, use:

```
newMenuItem.setAccelerator(KeyStroke.getKeyStroke('N',
Event.CTRL_MASK));
```

In this expression, the **KeyStroke** class defines a key combination. **getKeyStroke** returns the key stroke corresponding to the two arguments. The first argument is the key and the second is the key being held down.

Adding this single line of code to our example and expanding the **File** menu (try the <**Alt**>-**F** combination) shows:

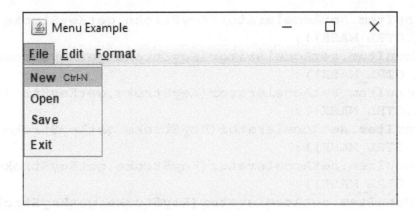

Notice how the accelerator combination is shown next to the menu item.

For our example menu structure (**exampleMenuBar**), I used these accelerators:

Text	Name	Accelerator
File	fileMenu	N/A
New	newMenuItem	<Ctrl>-N
Open	openMenuItem	<Ctrl>-O
Save	saveMenuItem	<Ctrl>-S
Exit	exitMenuItem	None
Edit	editMenu	N/A
Cut	cutMenuItem	<Ctrl>-X
Copy	copyMenuItem	<Ctrl>-C
Paste	pasteMenuItem	<Ctrl>-V
Format	formatMenu	N/A
Bold	boldMenuItem (CheckBox)	<Ctrl>-B
Italic	italicMenuItem (CheckBox)	<Ctrl>-I
Size	sizeMenu	N/A
10	size10MenuItem (RadioButton)	<Ctrl>-0
15	size15MenuItem (RadioButton)	<Ctrl>-1
20	size20MenuItem (RadioButton)	<Ctrl>-2

Make sure all accelerator keys are unique.

These are the lines of code that add these accelerators (place this after the lines setting the shortcuts):

```
newMenuItem.setAccelerator(KeyStroke.getKeyStroke('N',
Event.CTRL_MASK));
openMenuItem.setAccelerator(KeyStroke.getKeyStroke('O',
Event.CTRL_MASK));
saveMenuItem.setAccelerator(KeyStroke.getKeyStroke('S',
Event.CTRL_MASK));
cutMenuItem.setAccelerator(KeyStroke.getKeyStroke('X',
Event.CTRL_MASK));
copyMenuItem.setAccelerator(KeyStroke.getKeyStroke('C',
Event.CTRL_MASK));
pasteMenuItem.setAccelerator(KeyStroke.getKeyStroke('V',
Event.CTRL_MASK));
boldMenuItem.setAccelerator(KeyStroke.getKeyStroke('B',
Event.CTRL_MASK));
italicMenuItem.setAccelerator(KeyStroke.getKeyStroke('I',
Event.CTRL_MASK));
size10MenuItem.setAccelerator(KeyStroke.getKeyStroke('0',
Event.CTRL_MASK));
size15MenuItem.setAccelerator(KeyStroke.getKeyStroke('1',
Event.CTRL_MASK));
size20MenuItem.setAccelerator(KeyStroke.getKeyStroke('2',
Event.CTRL_MASK));
```

Rerun. I've expanded the **Format** menu to show the accelerators:

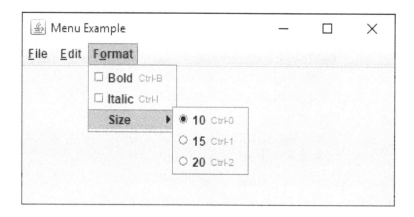

Try the accelerator keys to see how options can be selected and unselected using keystroke combinations.

You might think we're finally done, but we're not. We still need to write code for menu item events. You need to add a listener for the **actionPerformed** event for each menu item. This event is invoked whenever a menu item is selected (via mouse or via an accelerator). For a menu item named **myMenuItem**, use:

```
myMenuItem.addActionListener(new ActionListener()
{
   public void actionPerformed(ActionEvent e)
   {
      myMenuItemActionPerformed(e);
   }
});
```

And, the corresponding event code would be placed in a **myMenuItemActionPerformed** method:

```
private void myMenuItemActionPerformed(ActionEvent e)
{
    [method code]
}
```

You often assign several menu items to the same method, using the event's **getActionCommand** to determine which menu item was selected.

We will not add any methods at this point. See **Example 5-1** for typical ways to add methods to menu items. For reference, the menu example is saved as **MenuExample** in the **\LearnJava\LJ Code\Class 5** project group.

Example 5-4

Note Editor

Start a new empty project in **NetBeans**. Name the project **NoteEditor**. Delete default code in Java file named **NoteEditor**. We will use this application the rest of this class. We will build a note editor with a menu structure that allows us to control the appearance of the text in the editor box. The finished product will look like this:

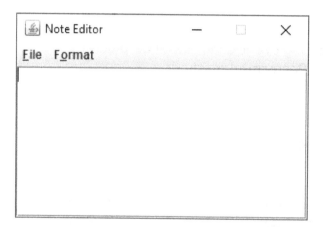

1. Place a scroll pane and text area on the frame. The **GridBagLayout** is very simple:

	gridx = 0
gridy = 0	**editorScrollPane**

Properties:

NoteEditor Frame:
       title   Note Editor
       resizable   false

editorScrollPane:
       preferredSize   (300, 150)
       viewportView   editorTextArea (JTextArea control)
       gridx   0
       gridy   0
editorTextArea:

font	Arial, PLAIN, 18
lineWrap	true
wrapStyleWord	true

We will add this menu structure to the **Note Editor**:

File	Format
New	Bold
———	Italic
Exit	Size
	Small
	Medium
	Large

Names and accelerator keys for this menu bar (**editorMenuBar**):

Text	Name	Accelerator
File	fileMenu	N/A
New	newMenuItem	<Ctrl>-N
Exit	exitMenuItem	None
Format	formatMenu	N/A
Bold	boldMenuItem (CheckBox)	<Ctrl>-B
Italic	italicMenuItem (CheckBox)	<Ctrl>-I
Size	sizeMenu	N/A
Small	smallMenuItem (RadioButton - sizeGroup)	<Ctrl>-S
Medium	mediumMenuItem (RadioButton - sizeGroup)	<Ctrl>-M
Large	largeMenuItem (RadioButton - sizeGroup)	<Ctrl>-L

2. Let's build the usual basic framework. You have probably started to notice that many GUI applications look like other GUI applications. Look how similar the menu structure here is to the menu structure we built in our example menu. The differences? There are no **Open** and **Save** options under the **File** menu, there is no **Edit** menu at all, and the names and accelerators on the **Size** choices are different.

Rather than start from scratch, we will modify the **MenuExample** to build the framework for our **Note Editor** project. In NetBeans, open the **MenuExample** and open the **MenuExample.java** file. Select the entire file and copy it (choose **Edit**, then **Copy**). Now, move to the empty **NoteEditor.java** file in the **NoteEditorProject**. Paste the copied code into this file (choose **Edit**, then **Paste**). Now, make these changes:

> ➤ Change all instances of **MenuExample** to **NoteEditor** (there are 4 places you need to do this).
> ➤ Change the frame **title** to **Note Editor**.
> ➤ Set the frame **resizable** property to **false**.
> ➤ Rename **exampleMenuBar** to **editorMenuBar** and change code where needed.
> ➤ Delete code creating and adding **openMenuItem** and **saveMenuItem**.
> ➤ Delete code creating and adding **editMenu** and associated menu items (**cutMenuItem**, **copyMenuItem**, **pasteMenuItem**).
> ➤ Change names and accelerators (as noted above) of font size menu items.

After these changes, the basic framework code (modifications are shaded and lines associated with **openMenuItem**, **saveMenuItem**, **editMenu** and its menu items have been deleted):

```
/*
 * NoteEditor.java
 */
package noteeditor;
import javax.swing.*;
import java.awt.*;
import java.awt.event.*;
public class NoteEditor extends JFrame
{
  JMenuBar editorMenuBar = new JMenuBar();
  JMenu fileMenu = new JMenu("File");
  JMenuItem newMenuItem = new JMenuItem("New");
  JMenuItem exitMenuItem = new JMenuItem("Exit");
  JMenu formatMenu = new JMenu("Format");
  JCheckBoxMenuItem boldMenuItem = new
JCheckBoxMenuItem("Bold", false);
  JCheckBoxMenuItem italicMenuItem = new
JCheckBoxMenuItem("Italic", false);
  JMenu sizeMenu = new JMenu("Size");
  ButtonGroup sizeGroup = new ButtonGroup();
  JRadioButtonMenuItem smallMenuItem = new
JRadioButtonMenuItem("Small", true);
  JRadioButtonMenuItem mediumMenuItem = new
JRadioButtonMenuItem("Medium", false);
  JRadioButtonMenuItem largeMenuItem = new
JRadioButtonMenuItem("Large", false);
  public static void main(String args[])
  {
    // construct frame
    new NoteEditor().setVisible(true);
  }
  public NoteEditor()
  {
    // frame constructor
    setTitle("Note Editor");
    setResizable(false);
    setSize(400, 200);
    addWindowListener(new WindowAdapter()
    {
      public void windowClosing(WindowEvent e)
      {
        exitForm(e);
```

```
        }
    });

    // build menu
    setJMenuBar(editorMenuBar);
    fileMenu.setMnemonic('F');
    formatMenu.setMnemonic('O');
    newMenuItem.setAccelerator(KeyStroke.getKeyStroke('N',
Event.CTRL_MASK));

boldMenuItem.setAccelerator(KeyStroke.getKeyStroke('B',
Event.CTRL_MASK));

italicMenuItem.setAccelerator(KeyStroke.getKeyStroke('I',
Event.CTRL_MASK));

smallMenuItem.setAccelerator(KeyStroke.getKeyStroke('S',
Event.CTRL_MASK));

mediumMenuItem.setAccelerator(KeyStroke.getKeyStroke('M',
Event.CTRL_MASK));

largeMenuItem.setAccelerator(KeyStroke.getKeyStroke('L',
Event.CTRL_MASK));
    editorMenuBar.add(fileMenu);
    fileMenu.add(newMenuItem);
    fileMenu.addSeparator();
    fileMenu.add(exitMenuItem);
    editorMenuBar.add(formatMenu);
    formatMenu.add(boldMenuItem);
    formatMenu.add(italicMenuItem);
    formatMenu.add(sizeMenu);
    sizeMenu.add(smallMenuItem);
    sizeMenu.add(mediumMenuItem);
    sizeMenu.add(largeMenuItem);
    sizeGroup.add(smallMenuItem);
    sizeGroup.add(mediumMenuItem);
    sizeGroup.add(largeMenuItem);

  }
  private void exitForm(WindowEvent evt)
  {
    System.exit(0);
  }
}
```

Run to view the modified menu structure:

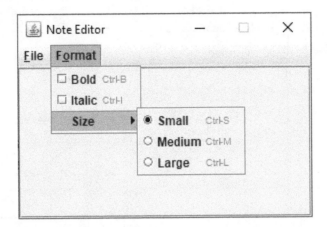

I've expanded the **Format** menu. Make sure all shortcuts and accelerator keys work as needed. Do you see how much easier it is to adapt an existing application rather than start over from scratch? Always look for applications that look similar to any new ones you build. Much of the work may have already been done for you. We briefly addressed this "don't reinvent the wheel" concept at the beginning of this class.

3. Now, let's add the two controls. Delete the line of code setting the frame size. The controls will now establish size. The class level declarations:

```
JScrollPane editorPane = new JScrollPane();
JTextArea editorTextArea = new JTextArea();
```

And the code adding the layout manager and positioning the controls:

```
getContentPane().setLayout(new GridBagLayout());
// position scroll pane and text box
GridBagConstraints gridConstraints = new
GridBagConstraints();
editorPane.setPreferredSize(new Dimension(300, 150));
editorPane.setViewportView(editorTextArea);
gridConstraints.gridx = 0;
gridConstraints.gridy = 0;
getContentPane().add(editorPane, gridConstraints);
pack();
```

Run again to see the finished frame.

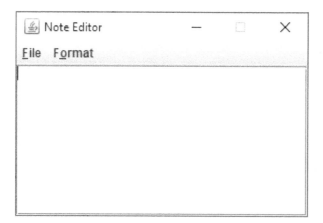

4. Now, we need add listeners (and code) for event methods we need when corresponding menu items are selected. We need listeners for events for: **newMenuItem, exitMenuItem, boldMenuItem, italicMenuItem, smallMenuItem, mediumMenuItem** and **largeMenuItem**. We'll do the two items under the **File** menu first. Code to add listeners for the **newMenuItem** and **exitMenuItem** (place after code positioning the controls):

```
newMenuItem.addActionListener(new ActionListener()
{
  public void actionPerformed(ActionEvent e)
  {
    newMenuItemActionPerformed(e);
  }
});
    exitMenuItem.addActionListener(new ActionListener()
{
  public void actionPerformed(ActionEvent e)
  {
    exitMenuItemActionPerformed(e);
  }
});
```

If **newMenuItem** is clicked, the program checks to see if the user really wants a new file and, if so (the default response), clears out the text box. That method is:

```
private void newMenuItemActionPerformed(ActionEvent e)
{
  // if user wants new file, clear out text
  if (JOptionPane.showConfirmDialog(null, "Are you sure
you want to start a new file?", "New File",
JOptionPane.YES_NO_OPTION, JOptionPane.QUESTION_MESSAGE)
== JOptionPane.YES_OPTION)
  {
    editorTextArea.setText("");
  }
}
```

If **exitMenuItem** is clicked, the program ends:

```
private void exitMenuItemActionPerformed(ActionEvent e)
{
  System.exit(0);
}
```

If you want, rerun at this time to make sure these two menu items work properly.

5. Now, we need events and code for items under the **Format** menu. Items here will be changing the appearance (**Font**) of the text displayed in the editor. They will all refer to the same event method (**formatMenuItemActionPerformed**). The listeners are added using:

```
boldMenuItem.addActionListener(new ActionListener()
{
  public void actionPerformed(ActionEvent e)
  {
    formatMenuItemActionPerformed(e);
  }
});

italicMenuItem.addActionListener(new ActionListener()
{
  public void actionPerformed(ActionEvent e)
  {
    formatMenuItemActionPerformed(e);
  }
});

smallMenuItem.addActionListener(new ActionListener()
{
  public void actionPerformed(ActionEvent e)
  {
    formatMenuItemActionPerformed(e);
  }
});

mediumMenuItem.addActionListener(new ActionListener()
{
  public void actionPerformed(ActionEvent e)
  {
    formatMenuItemActionPerformed(e);
  }
});

largeMenuItem.addActionListener(new ActionListener()
{
  public void actionPerformed(ActionEvent e)
  {
    formatMenuItemActionPerformed(e);
  }
});
```

And, the event method code is:

```
private void formatMenuItemActionPerformed(ActionEvent e)
{
  // Put together font based on menu selections
  int newFont = Font.PLAIN;
  int fontSize = 12;
  if (boldMenuItem.isSelected())
  {
    newFont += Font.BOLD;
  }
  if (italicMenuItem.isSelected())
  {
    newFont += Font.ITALIC;
  }
  if (smallMenuItem.isSelected())
  {
    fontSize = 12;
  }
  else if (mediumMenuItem.isSelected())
  {
    fontSize = 18;
  }
  else
  {
    fontSize = 24;
  }
  editorTextArea.setFont(new Font("Arial", newFont,
fontSize));
}
```

This routine sets the text area font based on the choices under the **Format** menu.

The final **NoteEditor.java** code listing (with modifications since basic framework shaded):

```
/*
 * NoteEditor.java
 */
package noteeditor;
import javax.swing.*;
import java.awt.*;
import java.awt.event.*;
public class NoteEditor extends JFrame
{
  JMenuBar editorMenuBar = new JMenuBar();
  JMenu fileMenu = new JMenu("File");
  JMenuItem newMenuItem = new JMenuItem("New");
  JMenuItem exitMenuItem = new JMenuItem("Exit");
  JMenu formatMenu = new JMenu("Format");
  JCheckBoxMenuItem boldMenuItem = new
JCheckBoxMenuItem("Bold", false);
  JCheckBoxMenuItem italicMenuItem = new
JCheckBoxMenuItem("Italic", false);
  JMenu sizeMenu = new JMenu("Size");
  ButtonGroup sizeGroup = new ButtonGroup();
  JRadioButtonMenuItem smallMenuItem = new
JRadioButtonMenuItem("Small", true);
  JRadioButtonMenuItem mediumMenuItem = new
JRadioButtonMenuItem("Medium", false);
  JRadioButtonMenuItem largeMenuItem = new
JRadioButtonMenuItem("Large", false);
  JScrollPane editorPane = new JScrollPane();
  JTextArea editorTextArea = new JTextArea();

  public static void main(String args[])
  {
    // construct frame
    new NoteEditor().setVisible(true);
  }
  public NoteEditor()
  {
    // frame constructor
    setTitle("Note Editor");
    setResizable(false);
    addWindowListener(new WindowAdapter()
    {
      public void windowClosing(WindowEvent e)
      {
        exitForm(e);
```

```
        }
    });

    // build menu
    setJMenuBar(editorMenuBar);
    fileMenu.setMnemonic('F');
    formatMenu.setMnemonic('O');
    newMenuItem.setAccelerator(KeyStroke.getKeyStroke('N',
Event.CTRL_MASK));
        boldMenuItem.setAccelerator(KeyStroke.getKeyStroke('B',
Event.CTRL_MASK));
        italicMenuItem.setAccelerator(KeyStroke.getKeyStroke('I',
Event.CTRL_MASK));
        smallMenuItem.setAccelerator(KeyStroke.getKeyStroke('S',
Event.CTRL_MASK));
        mediumMenuItem.setAccelerator(KeyStroke.getKeyStroke('M',
Event.CTRL_MASK));
        largeMenuItem.setAccelerator(KeyStroke.getKeyStroke('L',
Event.CTRL_MASK));
    editorMenuBar.add(fileMenu);
    fileMenu.add(newMenuItem);
    fileMenu.addSeparator();
    fileMenu.add(exitMenuItem);
    editorMenuBar.add(formatMenu);
    formatMenu.add(boldMenuItem);
    formatMenu.add(italicMenuItem);
    formatMenu.add(sizeMenu);
    sizeMenu.add(smallMenuItem);
    sizeMenu.add(mediumMenuItem);
    sizeMenu.add(largeMenuItem);
    sizeGroup.add(smallMenuItem);
    sizeGroup.add(mediumMenuItem);
    sizeGroup.add(largeMenuItem);
```

```
    newMenuItem.addActionListener(new ActionListener()
    {
      public void actionPerformed(ActionEvent e)
      {
        newMenuItemActionPerformed(e);
      }
    });
    exitMenuItem.addActionListener(new ActionListener()
    {
      public void actionPerformed(ActionEvent e)
      {
        exitMenuItemActionPerformed(e);
      }
```

```
  });
    boldMenuItem.addActionListener(new ActionListener()
    {
      public void actionPerformed(ActionEvent e)
      {
        formatMenuItemActionPerformed(e);
      }
    });
    italicMenuItem.addActionListener(new ActionListener()
    {
      public void actionPerformed(ActionEvent e)
      {
        formatMenuItemActionPerformed(e);
      }
    });
    smallMenuItem.addActionListener(new ActionListener()
    {
      public void actionPerformed(ActionEvent e)
      {
        formatMenuItemActionPerformed(e);
      }
    });
    mediumMenuItem.addActionListener(new ActionListener()
    {
      public void actionPerformed(ActionEvent e)
      {
        formatMenuItemActionPerformed(e);
      }
    });
    largeMenuItem.addActionListener(new ActionListener()
    {
      public void actionPerformed(ActionEvent e)
      {
        formatMenuItemActionPerformed(e);
      }
    });

    getContentPane().setLayout(new GridBagLayout());
    // position scroll pane and text box
    GridBagConstraints gridConstraints = new
GridBagConstraints();
    editorPane.setPreferredSize(new Dimension(300, 150));
    editorPane.setViewportView(editorTextArea);
    editorTextArea.setFont(new Font("Arial", Font.PLAIN,
12));
    editorTextArea.setLineWrap(true);
    editorTextArea.setWrapStyleWord(true);
```

```
    gridConstraints.gridx = 0;
    gridConstraints.gridy = 0;
    getContentPane().add(editorPane, gridConstraints);

    pack();
    Dimension screenSize =
Toolkit.getDefaultToolkit().getScreenSize();
    setBounds((int) (0.5 * (screenSize.width - getWidth())),
(int) (0.5 * (screenSize.height - getHeight())), getWidth(),
getHeight());

  }
  private void newMenuItemActionPerformed(ActionEvent e)
  {
    // if user wants new file, clear out text
    if (JOptionPane.showConfirmDialog(null, "Are you sure you
want to start a new file?", "New File",
JOptionPane.YES_NO_OPTION, JOptionPane.QUESTION_MESSAGE) ==
JOptionPane.YES_OPTION)
    {
      editorTextArea.setText("");
    }
  }

  private void exitMenuItemActionPerformed(ActionEvent e)
  {
    System.exit(0);
  }

  private void formatMenuItemActionPerformed(ActionEvent e)
  {
    // Put together font based on menu selections
    int newFont = Font.PLAIN;
    int fontSize = 12;
    if (boldMenuItem.isSelected())
    {
      newFont += Font.BOLD;
    }
    if (italicMenuItem.isSelected())
    {
      newFont += Font.ITALIC;
    }
    if (smallMenuItem.isSelected())
    {
      fontSize = 12;
    }
    else if (mediumMenuItem.isSelected())
```

```
   {
     fontSize = 18;
   }
   else
   {
     fontSize = 24;
   }
   editorTextArea.setFont(new Font("Arial", newFont,
fontSize));
   }

  private void exitForm(WindowEvent e)
  {
    System.exit(0);
  }

}
```

Run the application. Test out all the options. Notice how the toggling of the check marks works. Try the shortcut and accelerator keys. Here's some text I wrote – note the appearance of the scroll bar since the text exceeds the size allotted to the pane:

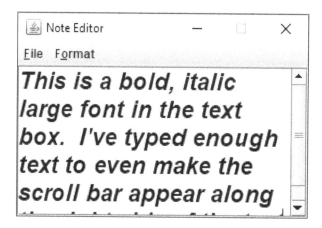

Save your application (saved as **Example5-4** project in **\LearnJava\LJ Code\Class 5** project group). We will use it again in Class 6 where we'll learn how to save and open text files created with the Note Editor.

Notice whatever formatting is selected is applied to all text in the control. You cannot selectively format text in a text box control. In Class 9, we look at another control that allows selective formatting.

Distribution of a Java GUI Application

I bet you're ready to show your friends and colleagues some of the applications you have built using Java. Just give them a copy of all your project files, ask them to download and install the Java Development Kit, download and install NetBeans and learn how to open and run a project. Then, have them open your project and run the application.

I think you'll agree this is asking a lot of your friends, colleagues, and, ultimately, your user base. Fortunately, there are other solutions. In this section, we will look at one possibility. We'll use the **NoteEditor** program just built as an example. You can easily make needed modifications for other projects. The example is built using Windows. Similar steps can be taken using other operating systems (Linux, UNIX, MacOS).

Executable (jar) Files

A simple way to run a Java application outside of the IDE environment is with an executable version of the application, a so-called **jar** (**j**ava **ar**chive) file. With such a file, a user can simply double-click the file and the corresponding application will run. As mentioned, we will work with the **NoteEditor** saved as **Example5-4** project in **\LearnJava\LJ Code\Class 5**

jar files are created using the Java **jar.exe** application. You can make your jar file runnable by telling **jar.exe** which class has **main**. To do that, you first need to create a **manifest** file. A manifest is a one-line text file with a "Main-Class" directive.

Creating a Manifest File in NetBeans

Using the **Note Editor** project,

1. Right-click the project's name and choose **Properties**.
2. Select the **Run** category and **noteeditor.NoteEditor** in the **Main Class** field.
3. Click **OK** to close the **Project Properties** dialog box.

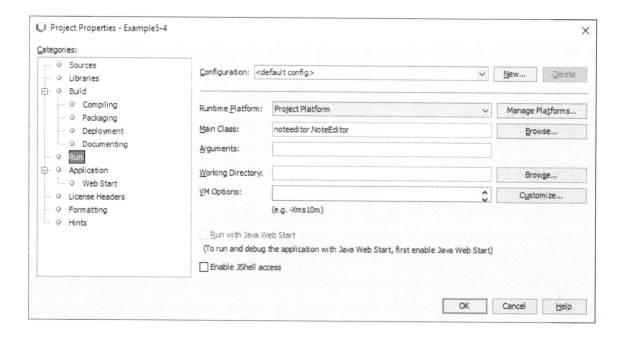

Creating a jar File in NetBeans

Now that you have your sources ready and your project configured, it is time to build your project. To build the project:

- Choose **Run** > **Build Project**
- Alternatively, right-click the project's name in the **Projects** window and choose **Build**.

When you build your project, a **jar** file containing your project is created inside the project's **/dist** folder.

With Windows Explorer, go to your project folder. Open the **dist** folder. The **NoteEditor.jar** file will be there. Double-click that file and the **NoteEditor** program will appear:

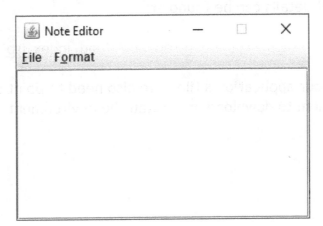

Notice the file has a "plain vanilla" Java frame icon in the title bar area – we will change that soon.

So, to distribute a Java project to other users, you need to give them a copy of the project's **jar** file and copies of any additional files the project needs to run (data files, graphics files, sound files). These files can be copied to a CD-ROM or uploaded to a server and transferred to other users.

For another user to run the project on his/her computer, they need to copy the files you give them to a folder they create. To run the project, they would then navigate to that folder and double-click the **jar** file (just like we did for the **NoteEditor**). Alternatively, the user could create a shortcut to the **jar** file and place it on their desktop or **Programs** file menu. We will see how to do this soon, but first let's "dress up" our application a bit.

One more thing before moving on - Note Editor runs on my computer (and will work on yours) because I have the **Java Run-Time Environment** (JRE) installed (it is installed when Java is installed). Every Java application needs the JRE to be installed on the hosting computer. Installing the JRE is similar to installing the Java SDK. Full details can be found at:

http://java.com/en/download/index.jsp

So, in addition to our application's files, we also need to point potential users to the JRE and ask them to download and install the environment on their computer.

Application Icons

Recall there is a plain Java icon that appears in the upper left hand corner of the frame. Icons are also used to represent programs in the **Programs** menu and to represent programs on the desktop. The default icons are ugly! We need the capability to change them. The icon associated with the frame is different from the icons used to represent the application in the Windows menu and desktop. We discuss both.

The icon associated with a frame is based on a graphics file. Changing this icon is simple. The idea is to assign a unique icon to indicate the frame's function. To assign an icon, use this line of code when the frame (**myFrame** in this example) is first created:

```
myFrame.setIconImage(new ImageIcon(icon).getImage());
```

where **icon** is some graphics file.

Open the **NoteEditor** project in NetBeans. We will use the **notepad.gif** graphic (in **Example5-4** folder in **\LearnJava\LJ Code\Class 5**) for the icon. Add the shaded line of code to the top of the frame constructor code:

```
public NoteEditor()
{
  // frame constructor
  setTitle("Note Editor");
  setIconImage(new ImageIcon("notepad.gif").getImage());
  setResizable(false);
  addWindowListener(new WindowAdapter()
  {
    public void windowClosing(WindowEvent e)
    {
      exitForm(e);
    }
  });

  // build menu
  setJMenuBar(editorMenuBar);
    .
    .
```

Save, run the project again. The cute little icon appears:

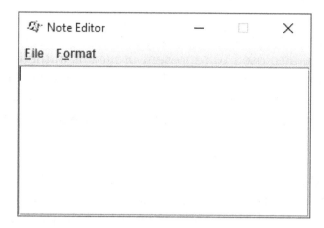

At this point, rebuild the jar file for the project so the icon is included.   To do this in **NetBeans**, just click the tool button defined earlier.

Icons associated with the program menu and desktop are Windows icon files (**ico** extension). They are special 32 x 32 graphics. The Internet and other sources offer a wealth of such icon files from which you can choose. But, it's also fun to design your own icon to add that personal touch.

Using IconEdit

Many years ago, *PC Magazine* offered a free utility called **IconEdit** that allows you to design and save icons. Included with these notes is this program and other files (folder **\LearnJava\LJ Code\IconEdit**). To run **IconEdit**, click **Start** on the Windows task bar, then click **Run**. Find the **IconEdit** program (use **Browse** mode), then click **OK**. When the **IconEdit** program window appears, click the **File** menu heading, then choose **New** (we are creating a new icon). The following editor window will appear:

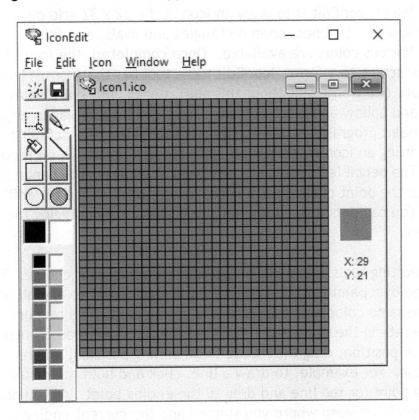

The editor window displays two representations of the icon: a large zoomed-in square (a 32 x 32 grid) that's eight times bigger than the actual icon, and a small square to its right that's actual size. The zoomed square is where the editing takes place. New icons appear as solid green with a black square surrounding each pixel representation. The **pixels** (small squares) are, of course, eight times actual size like the square itself for ease of editing. The green color is not actually the starting color of the icon, but instead represents the transparent "color" (whatever is behind this green color on the screen will be seen).

The basic idea of **IconEdit** is to draw an icon in the 32 x 32 grid displayed. You can draw single points, lines, open rectangles and ovals, and filled rectangles and ovals. Various colors are available. Once completed, the icon file can be saved for attaching to a form. **IconEdit** has a tool bar that consists of eight tools: capture (we won't talk about this one), pencil, fill, line, hollow and filled rectangle, and hollow and filled ellipse. These will be familiar to anyone who has used a paint program and on-line help is available. The default tool when you start editing an icon is the pencil, since this is the tool you'll probably use the most. The pencil let's you color one pixel at a time. To change a pixel, simply place the point of the pencil cursor over a pixel in the big editing square and click. You can pencil-draw several pixels at once by dragging the pencil over an area.

To change editing tools, simply click the tool button of your choice. The fill tool (represented by a paint can) will color the pixel you point to and all adjacent pixels of the same color with the color you've selected. The remaining five tools all operate in the same way. You click and hold the mouse button at the starting pixel position, drag the mouse to an ending position, and release the mouse button. For example, to draw a line, click and hold the mouse button on the starting point for the line and drag to the ending point. As you drag, the line will stretch between where you started and the current ending position. Only when you release the mouse button will the line be permanently drawn. For a rectangle or an ellipse, drag from one corner to the opposite corner. You control the color that the tool uses by pressing either the left or right mouse button.

The two large color squares right under the tools are the current colors for the left and right mouse buttons, respectively. When you start **IconEdit**, the left mouse button color is black and the right mouse button color is white. If you click with the left mouse button on a pixel with the pencil tool, for example, the pixel will turn black. Click with the right mouse button and the pixel will turn white. To change the default colors, click on one of the 16 colors in the palette just below the current color boxes with either the left or right mouse button. Clicking on a palette color with the left button will change the left button color and a right button click will change the right button color. You can pick the transparent "color" at the bottom of the editor if you want a pixel to be transparent.

Try drawing an icon using **IconEdit**. It's really pretty easy. Once you have finished your icon, save it. Click **File**, then **Save**. Icon files are special graphics files saved with an **ico** extension. The save window is just like the window you've used to save files in other Windows programs. Remember where you saved your icon (usually in your project folder).

With **IconEdit**, you can now customize your programs with your own icons. And, another fun thing to do is load in other icon files you find (click **File**, then **Open**) and see how much artistic talent really goes into creating an icon. You can even modify these other icons and save them for your use.

I found an icon on the Internet to use with the **NoteEditor** project. The file
note.ico is included in **Example5-4** folder in **\LearnJava\LJ Code\Class 5**
folder. When you open this file in **IconEdit**, you can see the detail in the icon:

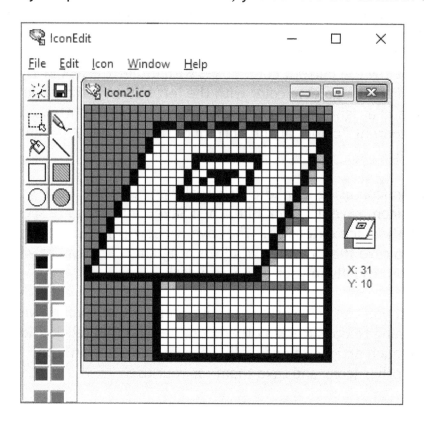

We'll now use this icon to help your user run the program.

Running a Project on Another Computer

As mentioned, users of your program need to copy the files you give them into a folder of their choice. Once done, they should do one or both of these steps to make it easier to run the project:

1. Add a shortcut to the computer desktop.
2. Add a shortcut on the **Start** menu.

Let's see how to do both of these steps with our example. We do this for Windows.

I copied all the needed files to a folder named **My Editor** (in this case, the **gif** file, the **ico** file and the **jar** file) on my computer. Examining the files in that folder, I see:

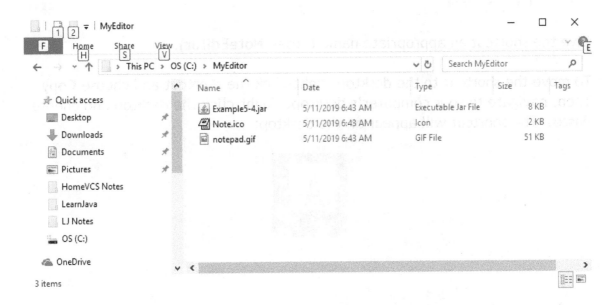

To create a shortcut to the executable file, right-click **NoteEditor.jar** and choose **Create Shortcut**. The shortcut will appear in the folder:

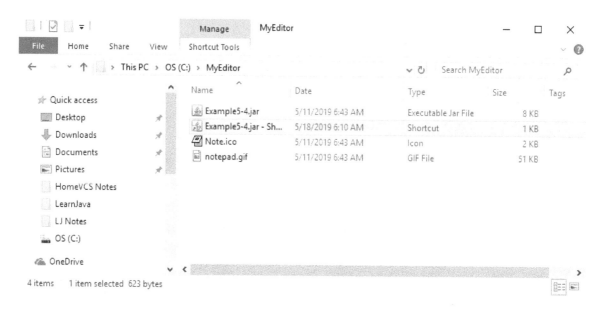

Give the shortcut an appropriate name (I used **NoteEditor**).

To move the shortcut to the desktop, right-click the shortcut and choose **Copy**. Then, navigate to your computer's desktop. Right-click the desktop and choose **Paste**. The shortcut will appear on the desktop:

Let's change the icon. Right-click the shortcut and choose **Properties**. This window appears:

Click the **Change Icon** button. Navigate to your project folder and select the **note.ico** file. Close out the properties window and the desktop shortcut should now appear as:

If you double-click this icon, the **NoteEditor** will begin.

To add the program shortcut to the **Start** menu, you need to open a folder deep within your computer. Open **File Explorer**, click View and make sure there is a check mark next to **Hidden Items**. Choose **Users**. Select your user folder. Navigate to this folder **AppData/Roaming/Microsoft/Windows/Start Menu/Programs**

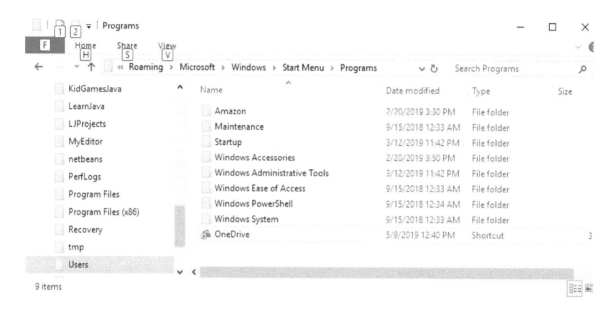

Copy and paste the desktop shortcut to **NoteEditor** into this folder.

The **Start** menu will now contain the project shortcut. To see it, click **Start**, and scroll down a bit:

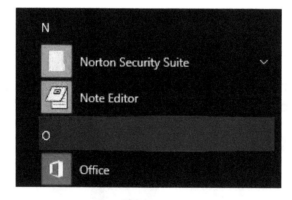

Click **NoteEditor** and the program begins.

Your user now has two ways to run the project on their computer – via the desktop or via the **Programs** menu. If you ever modify your program, you will need to provide your user with a new copy of the **jar** file (and any additional files that may have changed).

Class Review

After completing this class, you should understand:

➢ How to work with the **JTabbedPane** control in a Java application
➢ How to use general methods in a Java application
➢ How to add a menu structure to a Java application using the **JMenuBar**, **JMenu** and **JMenuItem** objects.
➢ Potential ways to distribute a Java application to your user base.

Practice Problems 5

Problem 5-1. Tabbed Pane Problem. Build an application with three tabs on a tabbed pane. On each tab, have radio buttons that set the background color of the corresponding tab panel.

Problem 5-2. Note Editor About Box Problem. Most applications have a **Help** menu heading. When you click on this heading, at the bottom of the menu is an **About** item. Choosing this item causes a dialog box to appear that provides the user with copyright and other application information. Prepare and implement such an About box for the Note Editor we build in this chapter (Example 5-4).

Problem 5-3. Normal Numbers Problem. There are other random number generators in Java. One is **nextDouble** that returns a double type number between 0 and 1. These numbers produce what is known as a uniform distribution, meaning each number comes up with equal probability. Statisticians often need a 'bell-shaped curve' to do their work. This curve is what is used in schools when they 'grade on a curve.' Such a 'probability distribution' is spread about a **mean** with some values very likely (near the mean) and some not very likely (far from the mean). Such distributions (called **normal** or **Gaussian** distributions) have a specified mean and a specified **standard deviation** (measure of how far spread out possible values are). To simulate a single 'normally distributed' number using the 'uniformly distributed' random number generator, we sum twelve random numbers (from the **nextDouble** method) and subtract six from the sum. That value is approximately 'normal' with a mean of zero and a standard deviation of one. See if such an approximation really works by first writing a general method that computes a single 'normally distributed number.' Then, write general methods to compute the mean (average) and standard deviation of an array of values (the equations are found back in **Exercise 2-1**). See if the described approximation is good by computing a large number of 'normally approximate' numbers. If you do a little research, you will find there is actually a Java method that returns normally distributed numbers (**nextGaussian**), so the approximation method used here is not really needed!

Exercise 5

US/World Capitals Quiz

Develop an application that quizzes a user on states and capitals in the United States or capitals of world countries. Or, if desired, quiz a user on any matching pairs of items – for example, words and meanings, books and authors, or inventions and inventors. Use a menu structure that allows the user to decide whether they want to name states (countries) or capitals and whether they want multiple choice or type-in answers. Thoroughly test your application. If you want, give your program to someone else (with the JRE on their computer) and let him or her enjoy your nifty little program.

6

Exception Handling, Debugging, Sequential Files

Review and Preview

In this class, we expand our Java knowledge from past classes and examine a few new topics. We first look at what to do about errors (also called exceptions) in programs, using both exception handling and debugging techniques. We then study reading and writing sequential disk files.

Program Errors

No matter how hard we try, **errors** do creep into our programs. These errors can be grouped into three categories:

1. **Syntax** errors
2. **Run-time** errors (also called **exceptions**)
3. **Logic** errors

Syntax errors occur when you mistype a command, leave out an expected argument, use improper case in variable or method names or omit needed punctuation. You cannot run a Java program until all syntax errors have been corrected. Syntax errors are the easiest to identify and eliminate. The **NetBeans** development environment is a big help in finding syntax errors. When you try to compile a program with a syntax error, NetBeans will point out the offending line and provide some explanation of the problem. Probably the most common syntax error is a 'cannot resolve symbol error.' It means one of just a few things. If involving a variable, it means you have misspelled a properly declared variable (check upper and lower case letters) or you have forgotten to declare a variable. If the message involves a method or function, it means you have misspelled the function name (again, check upper and lower case letters) or have not provided it to your class. Other common syntax errors are forgetting semicolons, having unmatched parentheses and having unmatched curly braces.

Run-time errors (or **exceptions**) are usually beyond your program's control. Examples include: when a variable takes on an unexpected value (divide by zero), when a disk is not accessible, or when a file is not found. Java lets us handle such errors (using the concept of **exception handling**) and make attempts to correct them. Doing so precludes our program from unceremoniously stopping. Users do not like programs that stop unexpectedly!

Logic errors are the most difficult to find. With logic errors, the program will usually run, but will produce incorrect or unexpected results. Logic errors must be eliminated using **debugging** techniques.

Some ways to minimize errors in programs are:

➤ Design your application carefully. More design time means less debugging time.

➤ Use comments where applicable to help you remember what you were trying to do.

➤ Use consistent and meaningful naming conventions for your variables, controls, objects, and methods.

Exception Handling

Run-time errors (referred to in Java as **exceptions**) are "catchable." That is, Java recognizes an error has occurred and enables you to catch it and take corrective action (handle the error). As mentioned, if an error occurs and is not caught, your program will usually end in a rather unceremonious manner. Most run-time errors occur when your application is working with files, either trying to open, read, write or save a file. Other common run-time errors are divide by zero, overflow (exceeding a data type's range) and improper data types.

Java uses a structured approach to catching and handling exceptions. The structure is referred to as a **try/catch/finally** block. And the annotated syntax for using this block is:

```
try
{
  // here is code you try where some kind of
  // error may occur

}
catch (ExceptionType ex)
{
  // if error described by exception of ExceptionType
  // occurs, process this code

}
catch (Exception ex)
{
  // if any other error occurs, process this code

}
finally
{
  // Execute this code whether error occurred or not
  // this block is optional

}
// Execution continues here
```

The above code works from the top, down. It 'tries' the code between **try** and the first **catch** statement. If no error is encountered, any code in the **finally** block will be executed and the program will continue after the right brace closing the **try/catch/finally** block. If an exception (error) occurs, the program will look to find, if any, the first **catch** statement (you can have multiple **catch** statements and must have at least one) that matches the exception that occurred. If one is found, the code in that respective block is executed (code to help clear up the error – the exception handling), then the code in the **finally** block, then program execution continues after the closing brace. If an error occurs that doesn't match a particular exception, the code in the 'generic' **catch** block is executed, followed by the code in the **finally** block. And, program execution continues after the closing brace.

This structure can be used to catch and handle any of the exceptions defined in the Java **Exception** class. There are hundreds of possible exceptions related to data access, input and output functions, graphics functions, data types and numerical computations. Here is a list of example exception types (their names are descriptive of the corresponding error condition):

```
IllegalArgumentException        NullPointerException
IndexOutofBoundsException        ArithmeticException
NegativeArraySizeException       Exception
EOFException                     FileNotFoundException
IOException                      RunTimeException
```

Let's take a closer look at the **catch** block. When you define a **catch** block, you define the exception type you want to catch. For example, if want to catch a divide by zero condition, an **ArithmeticException**, we use:

```
catch (ArithmeticException ex)
{
   // Code to execute if divide by zero occurs
}
```

If in the **try** block, a divide by zero occurs, the code following this **catch** statement will be executed. You would probably put a message box here to tell the user what happened and provide him or her with options of how to fix the problem. To help with the messaging capability, the variable you define as the exception (**ex**, in this case) has a **message** property you can use. The message is retrieved using **ex.getMessage().**

A **try** block may be exited using the **break** statement. Be aware any code in the **finally** block will still be executed even if **break** is encountered. Once the **finally** code is executed, program execution continues after the brace closing the **try** block.

Example of **try** block to catch a "file not found" error:

```
try
{
  // Code to open file
}
catch (FileNotFoundException ex)
{
  // message box describing the error
  JOptionPane.showConfirmDialog(null, ex.getMessage(),
"Error", JOptionPane.DEFAULT_OPTION,
JOptionPane.ERROR_MESSAGE);
}
finally
{
  //Code to close file (even if error occurred)
}
```

Example of a **generic** error catching routine:

```
try
{
  // Code to try
}
catch (Exception ex)
{
  // message box describing the error
  JOptionPane.showConfirmDialog(null, ex.getMessage(),
"Error", JOptionPane.DEFAULT_OPTION,
JOptionPane.ERROR_MESSAGE);
}
finally
{
  //Code to finish the block
}
```

We've only taken a brief look at the structured run-time exception handling capabilities of Java. It is difficult to be more specific without knowing just what an application's purpose is. You need to know what type of errors you are looking for and what corrective actions should be taken if these errors are encountered. As you build and run your own applications, you will encounter run-time errors. These errors may be due to errors in your code. If so, fix them. But, they may also be errors that arise due to some invalid inputs from your user, because a file does not meet certain specifications or because a disk drive is not ready. You need to use exception handling to keep such errors from shutting down your application, leaving your user in a frustrated state.

You will find many Java methods (for instance, file methods studied next) must be used within **try** blocks. This helps to minimize errors. In such methods, you will know the types of exceptions you are looking for. The method will define them for you.

Debugging Java Programs

We now consider the search for, and elimination of, **logic errors**. These are errors that don't prevent an application from running, but cause incorrect or unexpected results. Logic errors are sometimes difficult to find; they may be very subtle. Eliminating logic errors is known as debugging your program.

A typical logic error could involve an **if** structure. Look at this example:

```
if (a > 5 && b < 4)
{
../ // do this code
}
else if (a == 6)
{
  // do this code
}
```

In this example, if **a** is 6 and **b** is 2, the **else if** statement (which you wanted executed if **a** is 6) will never be seen. In this case, swap the two **if** clauses to get the desired behavior. Or, another possible source of a logic error:

```
ImageIcon myImage = new
ImageIcon(imageChooser.getSelectedFile().toString());
```

In this little 'snippet' from Class 4, the user has selected a file to display as an image. The code looks okay, but what if the user selected a file that really wasn't meant to be used as an image. You would not see anything displayed – another logic error.

Debugging code is an art, not a science. There are no prescribed processes that you can follow to eliminate all logic errors in your program. The usual approach is to eliminate them as they are discovered. We will look at two approaches to debugging a Java program – a **simple** method that prints out information from a program and a more involved method which uses the Java **debugger** that was installed on your computer when you installed Java.

Simple Debugging

The simplest approach to debugging a Java program is to print information (usually variable values) directly to the **output** window while an application is running. Sometimes, this is all the debugging you may need. A few carefully placed print statements can sometimes clear up all logic errors, especially in small applications.

The output window is used in Java <u>console</u> applications to display output results. It can also be used in GUI applications. To write to the output window, use the **println** method of the **System.out** object (the output window):

```
System.out.println(stringData);
```

This will write the string information **stringData** as a line in the output window. Hence, the output window can be used as a kind of scratch pad for your application. If the argument in the **println** method contains numeric information, Java will convert it to strings. Be careful using concatenation operators however. Sometimes, there is confusion between numeric addition and string concatenation.

Example 6-1

Debugging Example

This example simply has a frame with two button controls used to execute some code. There is no need to build this example - just load the project from the course notes (saved as **Example6-1** project in **\LearnJava\LJ Code\Class 6** project group). The finished project is simply:

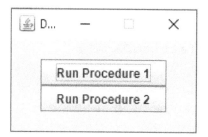

Here is the complete **Debugging.java** code listing:

```
/*
 * Debugging.java
 */
package debugging;
import javax.swing.*;
import java.awt.*;
import java.awt.event.*;
public class Debugging extends JFrame
{
  JButton procedure1Button = new JButton();
  JButton procedure2Button = new JButton();
  int xCount = 0, ySum = 0;
  public static void main(String args[])
  {
    // construct frame
    new Debugging().show();
  }

  public Debugging()
  {
    // frame constructor
    setTitle("Debug");
    setResizable(false);
```

```
    addWindowListener(new WindowAdapter()
    {
      public void windowClosing(WindowEvent e)
      {
        exitForm(e);
      }
    });
    getContentPane().setLayout(new GridBagLayout());

    // add buttons and method listeners
    GridBagConstraints gridConstraints = new
GridBagConstraints();
    procedure1Button.setText("Run Procedure 1");
    gridConstraints.gridx = 0;
    gridConstraints.gridy = 0;
    gridConstraints.insets = new Insets(20, 30, 0, 30);
    getContentPane().add(procedure1Button, gridConstraints);
    procedure1Button.addActionListener(new ActionListener()
    {
      public void actionPerformed(ActionEvent e)
      {
        procedure1ButtonActionPerformed(e);
      }
    });
    procedure2Button.setText("Run Procedure 2");
    gridConstraints.gridx = 0;
    gridConstraints.gridy = 1;
    gridConstraints.insets = new Insets(0, 30, 20, 30);
    getContentPane().add(procedure2Button, gridConstraints);
    procedure2Button.addActionListener(new ActionListener()
    {
      public void actionPerformed(ActionEvent e)
      {
        procedure2ButtonActionPerformed(e);
      }
    });

    pack();
     Dimension screenSize =
Toolkit.getDefaultToolkit().getScreenSize();
    setBounds((int) (0.5 * (screenSize.width - getWidth())),
(int) (0.5 * (screenSize.height - getHeight())), getWidth(),
getHeight());

  }
```

```java
private void procedure1ButtonActionPerformed(ActionEvent e)
{
  int x1 = -1, y1;
  do
  {
    x1++;
    y1 = fcn(x1);
    xCount++;
    ySum += y1;
  }
  while (x1 < 20);
}

private void procedure2ButtonActionPerformed(ActionEvent e)
{
  int x2, y2;
  for (x2 = -10; x2 <= 10; x2++)
  {
     y2 = 5 * fcn(x2);
    xCount++;
    ySum += y2;
  }
}

private void exitForm(WindowEvent e)
{
  System.exit(0);
}

public int fcn(int x)
{
  double value;
  value = 0.1 * x * x;
  return ((int) value);
}

}
```

A few notes about the program:

The application has two variables with class level scope: **xCount** and **ySum**. **xCount** keeps track of the number of times each of two counter variables is incremented. **ySum** sums all computed y values.

Procedure 1 uses a **do/while** structure to increment the counter variable **x1** from 0 to 20. For each x1, a corresponding **y1** is computed using the general method **fcn**. In each cycle of the **do/while** loop, the class level variables **xCount** and **ySum** are adjusted accordingly.

The general method (**fcn**) used by this procedure computes an 'integer parabola.' No need to know what that means. Just recognize, given an x value, it computes and returns a y.

Procedure 2 is similar to **Procedure 1**. It uses a **for** structure to increment the counter variable **x2** from -10 to 10. For each **x2**, a corresponding **y2** is computed using the same general method **fcn**. In each cycle of the **for** loop, the class level variables **xCount** and **ySum** are adjusted accordingly.

Run the application code to make sure it works. The running application looks like this:

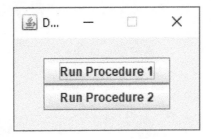

Notice not much happens if you click either button. Admittedly, this code doesn't do much, especially without any output, but it makes a good example for debugging practice.

System.out.println Example:

1. Modify the **Procedure 1** code in **Example 6-1** by including the shaded line:

```
private void procedure1ButtonActionPerformed(ActionEvent
e)
{
  int x1 = -1, y1;
  do
  {
    x1++;
    y1 = fcn(x1);
    System.out.println(x1 + " " + y1);
    xCount++;
    ySum += y1;
  }
  while (x1 < 20);
}
```

Run the application. Click the **Run Procedure 1** button.

2. Examine the output window. You should see this:

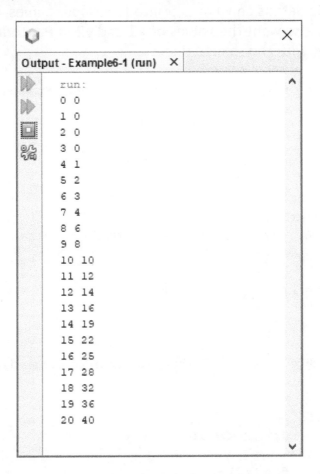

Note how, at each iteration of the loop, the program prints the value of **x1** and **y1**. You can use this information to make sure **x1** is incrementing correctly, ending at the proper value and that **y1** values look acceptable. You can get a lot of information using **println**.

3. If needed, you can add additional text information in the **println** argument to provide specific details on what is printed (variable names, procedure names, etc.). Say, we also want the values of **x2** and **y2** in **Procedure 2**. Modify the two procedures with the shaded lines:

```
private void procedure1ButtonActionPerformed(ActionEvent
e)
{
  int x1 = -1, y1;
  do
  {
    x1++;
    y1 = fcn(x1);
    System.out.println("In Procedure 1, x1=" + x1 + " y1="
+ y1);
    xCount++;
    ySum += y1;
  }
  while (x1 < 20);
}
private void procedure2ButtonActionPerformed(ActionEvent
e)
{
  int x2, y2;
  for (x2 = -10; x2 <= 10; x2++)
  {
    y2 = 5 * fcn(x2);
    System.out.println("In Procedure 2, x2=" + x2 + " y2="
+ y2);
    xCount++;
    ySum += y2;
  }
}
```

Run. Click both buttons and notice how you get a listing of the variable values.
Here is a segment of that output window:

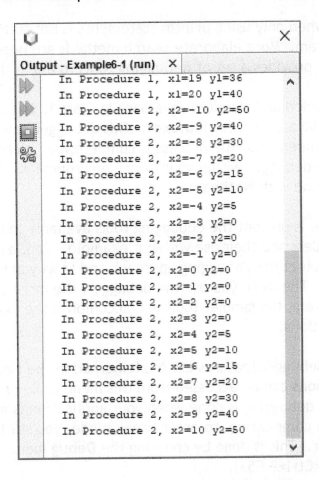

```
Output - Example6-1 (run)    X
        In Procedure 1, x1=19 y1=36
        In Procedure 1, x1=20 y1=40
        In Procedure 2, x2=-10 y2=50
        In Procedure 2, x2=-9 y2=40
        In Procedure 2, x2=-8 y2=30
        In Procedure 2, x2=-7 y2=20
        In Procedure 2, x2=-6 y2=15
        In Procedure 2, x2=-5 y2=10
        In Procedure 2, x2=-4 y2=5
        In Procedure 2, x2=-3 y2=0
        In Procedure 2, x2=-2 y2=0
        In Procedure 2, x2=-1 y2=0
        In Procedure 2, x2=0 y2=0
        In Procedure 2, x2=1 y2=0
        In Procedure 2, x2=2 y2=0
        In Procedure 2, x2=3 y2=0
        In Procedure 2, x2=4 y2=5
        In Procedure 2, x2=5 y2=10
        In Procedure 2, x2=6 y2=15
        In Procedure 2, x2=7 y2=20
        In Procedure 2, x2=8 y2=30
        In Procedure 2, x2=9 y2=40
        In Procedure 2, x2=10 y2=50
```

Again, notice how you can get a lot of information from just two **println**
statements. Stop the program and delete the **println** statements.

Using the Java Debugger

There are times when only using **println** statements is not sufficient for finding bugs in your program. More elaborate search methods are needed to find subtle logic errors. Java provides a set of **debugging** tools to aid in this search.

When you downloaded and installed Java back in Class 1, you also downloaded and installed the Java debugger (**jdb.exe**). This debugger can be used outside of a design environment, but the process is cumbersome. More desirable is to be able to use the debugger within your design environment. The good news is that this can be done with **NetBeans**.

What we'll do here is present the debugging tools available in the Java environment and describe their use with our example. You, as the program designer, should select the debugging approach and tools you feel most comfortable with. The more you use the debugger, the more you will learn about it. Fortunately, the simpler tools will accomplish the tasks for most debugging applications.

Most of the Java debugger features are implemented in the NetBeans **Debug** menu. Debug options can be accessed from this menu or by pressing certain function keys. All debugging is done when your application is in **break** mode. Following program compilation, to enter **break** mode, you start your application using the debugger. This is done by choosing the **Debug** menu, then **Debug Main Project** (or press <Ctrl>-<F5>).

The debugger can be used to:

> Set breakpoints
> Determine values of variables
> Manually control the application
> Determine which procedures have been called

To stop the debugger, press <**Shift**>-<**F5**> or choose **Finish Debug Session** under the NetBeans **Debug** menu. The best way to learn proper debugging is do an example. We'll continue with the same example program.

Using the Debugging Tools

There are several **debugging tools** available for use in Java. Access to these tools is provided via both menu options and function keys:

> ➢ **Breakpoints** which let us stop our application.
> ➢ **'Mouse hover'** that lets you examine variable values by holding your mouse over a variable name.
> ➢ **Step into**, **step over** and **step out** which provide manual execution of our code.

Breakpoints:

Notice when we used **println** for debugging, the program ran to completion before we could look at the output window. In many applications, we want to stop the application while it is running, examine variables and then continue running. This can be done with **breakpoints.** A breakpoint marks a line in code where you want to stop (temporarily) program execution, that is force the program into **break** mode. One way to set a breakpoint is to put the cursor in the line of code you want to break at and press **<Ctrl>-<F8>** (or select the **Debug** menu, then **Toggle Breakpoint**). Or, right-click the desired line of code and choose **Toggle Breakpoint** from the drop-down menu. Or simply click the line number in the left side of the editor. Once set, a red square marks the line:

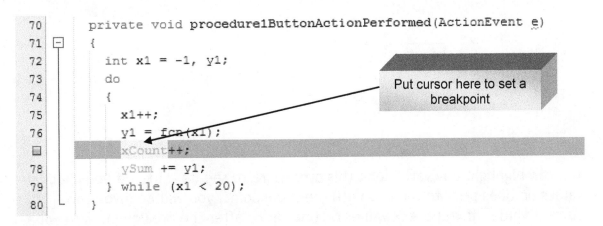

```
70      private void procedure1ButtonActionPerformed(ActionEvent e)
71      {
72          int x1 = -1, y1;
73          do
74          {
75              x1++;
76              y1 = fcn(x1);
                xCount++;
78              ySum += y1;
79          } while (x1 < 20);
80      }
```

Put cursor here to set a breakpoint

To remove a breakpoint, repeat the above process. Breakpoints can be added/deleted at any time. When you run your application in the debugger (press **<Ctrl>-<F5>** or choose **Debug** from the menu, then **Debug Main Project**), Java will stop when it reaches lines with breakpoints and allow you to check variables and expressions. To continue program operation after a breakpoint, press **<F5>** or choose **Continue** from the **Debug** menu.

Breakpoint Example:

1. Set a breakpoint on the **xCount++;** line in **Procedure 1** (as demonstrated above). Run the debugger (**<Ctrl>-<F5>**) and click the **Run Procedure 1** button. A **Debug Output** window will appear in NetBeans and the program will stop at the desired line (it will have a little arrow and be highlighted):

```
70        private void procedure1ButtonActionPerformed(ActionEvent e)
71   ⊟    {
72          int x1 = -1, y1;
73          do
74          {
75            x1++;
76            y1 = fcn(x1);
⇨            xCount++;
78            ySum += y1;
79          } while (x1 < 20);
80        }
```

At this point, you can determine the value of any variable by simply hovering over the variable name with the mouse. Try it with **x1**, you should see **x1 = 0**:

```
70        private void procedure1ButtonActionPerformed(ActionEvent e)
71   ⊟    {
72          int x1 = -1, y1;
73          do
74          {
75            x1++;
76            y1 =  xCount = (int) 0
⇨            xCount++;
78            ySum += y1;
79          } while (x1 < 20);
80        }
```

You can highlight any variable in this procedure to see its value. If you check values on lines prior to the line with the breakpoint, you will be given the current value. If you check values on lines at or after the breakpoint, you will get their last computed value.

2. Continue running the program (choose **Continue** from the **Debug** menu button or press **<F5>**). The program will again stop at this line, but **x1** will now be equal to **1**. Check it:

```
70        private void procedure1ButtonActionPerformed(ActionEvent e)
71   ⊟    {
72          int x1 = -1, y1;
73          do
74          {
75            x1++;
76            y1  | xCount = (int) 1 |
⬛          xCount++;
78            ySum += y1;
79          } while (x1 < 20);
80   └    }
```

3. Continue running the program, examining **x1** and **y1** (and **xCount** and **ySum** too). Procedure level variable values can also be viewed in the **Variables Window**:

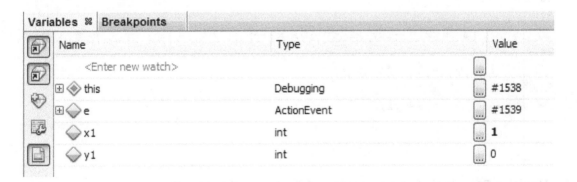

Variables ✖	Breakpoints		
Name		Type	Value
<Enter new watch>			...
⊞ ◈ this		Debugging	... #1538
⊞ ◇ e		ActionEvent	... #1539
◇ x1		int	... 1
◇ y1		int	... 0

4. Try other breakpoints in the application if you have time. Once done, make sure you clear all the breakpoints you used. To stop the debugger, choose **Debug** and **Finish Debugger Session**, or press **<Shift>-<F5>**.

Single Stepping (Step Into) An Application:

A powerful feature of the Java debugger is the ability to manually control execution of the code in your application. The **Step Into** option lets you execute your program one line at a time. It lets you watch how variables change or how your code executes, one step at a time. This feature is very useful for making sure loop and decision structures are implemented correctly.

Once in break mode (at a breakpoint), you can use **Step Into** by pressing **<F7>**, choosing the **Step Into** option in the **Debug** menu.

Step Into Example:

1. Set a breakpoint at the **For X2 = - 10 To 10** line in **Procedure 2**. Run the application in the debugger. Click **Run Procedure 2**. The program will stop and the line will be marked:

```
82        private void procedure2ButtonActionPerformed(ActionEvent e)
83    ⊟    {
84           int x2, y2;
 ⏎>          for (x2 = -10; x2 <= 10; x2++)
86           {
87             y2 = 5 * fcn(x2);
88             xCount++;
89             ySum += y2;
90           }
91         }
```

2. Use the **Step Into** feature (press <F7> to single step through the program. It's fun to see the program logic being followed. At any point, you may use the mouse or **Variables** window to check a variable value. When you are in **Procedure 2**, you can check **x2** and **y2**. When in the function, you can check **x** and **value**.

3. At some point, remove the breakpoint and continue (<F5>). The procedure will finish its **for** loop without stopping again and the frame will reappear.

Method Stepping (Step):

Did you notice in the example just studied that, after a while, it became annoying to have to single step through the function evaluation at every step of the **for** loop? While single stepping your program, if you come to a method call that you know operates properly, you can perform **method stepping**. This simply executes the entire method at once, treating as a single line of code, rather than one step at a time.

To move through a method in this manner, while in break mode, press **<F8>**, or choose **Step Over** from the **Debug** menu.

Step Example:

1. Run the previous example. Single step through it a couple of times.

2. One time through, when you are at the line calling the **Fcn** method, press <F8> button. Notice how the program did not single step through the method as it did previously.

Method Exit (Step Out):

While stepping through your program, if you wish to complete the execution of a method you are in, without stepping through it line-by-line, choose the **Step Out** option. The method will be completed and you will be returned to the method accessing that method.

To perform this step out, press **<Ctrl>+<F7>** or choose **Step Out** from the **Debug** menu.

Step Out Example:

1. Run the previous example. Single step through it a couple of times. Also, try stepping over the method.

2. At some point, while single stepping through the method, press <Ctrl>-<F7> (**Step Out**). Notice how control is immediately returned to the calling procedure (**Procedure 2**).

3. At some point, while in **Procedure 2**, press <Ctrl>-<F7>. The procedure will be completed.

Debugging Strategies

We've looked at each debugging feature briefly. Be aware this is a cursory introduction. Other useful debugging features are the **Call Stack** and **Watch** points. Go to the Java and NetBeans websites to delve into the details of each feature described.

Only through lots of use and practice can you become a proficient debugger. There are some common sense guidelines to follow when debugging. My first suggestion is: keep it **simple**. Many times, you only have one or two bad lines of code. And you, knowing your code best, can usually quickly narrow down the areas with bad lines. Don't set up some elaborate debugging procedure if you haven't tried a simple approach to find your error(s) first. Many times, just a few intelligently-placed **println** statements or a few examinations of variable values with debugger, will solve the problem.

A tried and true approach to debugging can be called **Divide and Conquer**. If you're not sure where your error is, guess somewhere in the middle of your application code. Set a breakpoint there. If the error hasn't shown up by then, you know it's in the second half of your code. If it has shown up, it's in the first half. Repeat this division process until you've narrowed your search.

And, of course, the best debugging strategy is to be careful when you first design and write your application to minimize searching for errors later.

Sequential Files

In many applications, it is helpful to have the capability to read and write information to a disk file. This information could be some computed data or perhaps information needed by your Java project. Java supports several file formats. We will look at the most common format: **sequential files.**

A sequential file is a line-by-line list of data that can be viewed with any text editor. Sequential access easily works with files that have lines with mixed information of different lengths. Hence, sequential files can include both variables and text data. When using sequential files, it is helpful, but not necessary, to know the order data was written to the file to allow easy retrieval.

The ability to read and generate sequential files is a very powerful capability of Java. This single capability is the genesis of many applications I've developed. Let's examine a few possible applications where we could use such files. One possibility is to use sequential files to provide initialization information for a project. Such a file is called a **configuration or initialization file** and almost all applications use such files. Here is the idea:

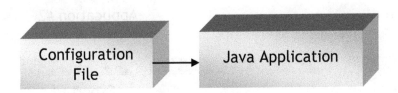

In this diagram, the configuration file (a sequential file) contains information that can be used to initialize different parameters (control properties, variable values) within the Java application. The file is opened when the application begins, the file values are read and the various parameters established. Similarly, when we exit an application, we could have it write out current parameter values to an output configuration file:

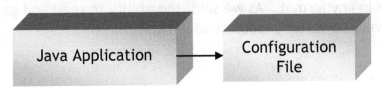

This output file could then become an input file the next time the application is executed. We will look at how to implement such a configuration file in a Java application.

Many data-intensive, or not-so intensive, applications provide file export capabilities. For example, you can save data from a spreadsheet program to an external file. The usual format for such an exported data file is a **CSV** (comma separated variables) sequential file. You can write a Java application that reads this exported file and performs some kind of analysis or further processing of the data:

In the above example, the results of the Java program could be displayed using GUI controls (text areas, list controls, labels) or the program could also write another sequential file that could be used by some other application (say a database application or word processor). This task is actually more common than you might think. Many applications support exporting data. And, many applications support importing data from other sources. A big problem is that the output file from one application might not be an acceptable input file to another application. Java to the rescue:

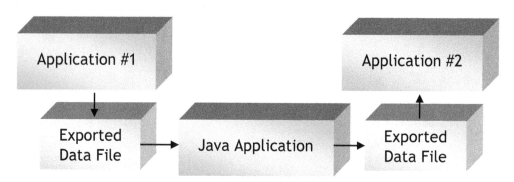

In this diagram, **Application #1** writes an exported data file that is read by the Java application. This application writes a data file in an input format required by **Application #2**.

You will find that you can use Java to read a sequential file in any format and, likewise, write a file in any format. As we said, the ability to read and generate sequential files is a very powerful capability of Java.

Sequential File Output (Variables)

We will first look at **writing** values of **variables** to sequential files. The initial step in accessing any sequential file (either for input or output) is to open the file, knowing the name of the file. To open a file for output requires the "nesting" of three different Java classes. To use these classes requires importing the **java.io.*** package. The innermost class is the **FileWriter** – a useful class for writing character data (such as variables). The **FileWriter** constructor we will use is:

```
new FileWriter(myFile)
```

where **myFile** is a legal filename. Recall file references are relative to the project directory. Hence, if only a filename is given, the file will be located in the project directory. For our work, this is acceptable. For other tasks, you may need to use fully qualified filename paths, including drive and directory structure.

The next class used is the **BufferedWriter** – this class provides optimized writing of data to files. Its constructor uses the **FileWriter** object as an argument:

```
new BufferedWriter(new FileWriter(myFile))
```

The "outside" class that controls the writing of information to the file is the **PrintWriter** class. It uses the **BufferedWriter** object as its argument. Hence, the complete constructor for opening a sequential file (**myFile**) for output is:

```
PrintWriter outputFile = new PrintWriter(new
BufferedWriter(new FileWriter(myFile)));
```

where **myFile** is the name (a **String**) of the file to open and **outputFile** is the returned **PrintWriter** object used to write variables to disk.

A word of warning - when you open a file using the **PrintWriter** method, if the file already exists, it will be erased immediately! So, make sure you really want to overwrite the file. Using the **JFileChooser** control (discussed in Class 4) can prevent accidental overwriting. Just be careful.

You can append to an existing sequential file by opening it using a **boolean append** argument. That syntax is:

```
PrintWriter outputFile = new PrintWriter(new
BufferedWriter(new FileWriter(myFile, append)));
```

If **append** is true, the file will be opened in an 'append' mode. If the file to append doesn't exist or can't be found, it will be created as an empty file.

The code opening a file for output <u>must</u> be within a **try** block for exception handling or you will receive a syntax error. For our example, a minimum structure for handling potential input/output exceptions (**IOException**) is:

```
// open file
try
{
   PrintWriter outputFile = new PrintWriter(new
BufferedWriter(new FileWriter(myFile)));
   // code to write to file

}
catch (IOException ex)
{
  // print any error encountered
  System.out.println(ex.getMessage());
}
```

When done writing to a sequential file, it must be flushed (information placed on disk) and closed. The syntax for our example file is:

```
outputFile.flush();
outputFile.close();
```

Once a file is closed, it is saved on the disk under the path (if different from the project path) and filename used to open the file.

Information (variables or text) is written to a sequential file in an appended fashion. Separate Java statements are required for each appending. There are two different ways to write variables to a sequential file. You choose which method you want based on your particular application.

The first method uses the **print** method. For a file opened as **outputFile**, the syntax is to print a variable named **myVariable** is:

```
outputFile.print(myVariable);
```

This statement will append the specified variable to the current line in the sequential file. If you only use **print** for output, everything will be written in one very long line. And, if no other characters (**delimiters**) are entered to separate variables, they will all be concatenated together.

Example using **print** method:

```
int a;
String b;
double c, e;
boolean d;
try
{
   PrintWriter outputFile = new PrintWriter(new
BufferedWriter(new FileWriter("testout.txt")));
   outputFile.print(a);
   outputFile.print(b);
   outputFile.print(c);
   outputFile.print(d);
   outputFile.print(e);
   outputFile.flush();
   outputFile.close();
}
catch (IOException ex)
{
   System.out.println(ex.getMessage());
}
```

After this code runs, the file **testout.txt** (in the project directory) will have a single line with all five variables (a, b, c, d, e) concatenated together.

The other way to write variables to a sequential file is **println**, the companion to **print**. Its syntax is:

```
outputFile.println(myVariable);
```

This method works identically to the **print** method with the exception that a 'carriage return' is added, placing the variables on a single line in the file. It can be used to insert blank lines by omitting the variable.

Example using **PrintLine** function:

```
int a;
String b;
double c, e;
boolean d;
try
{
  PrintWriter outputFile = new PrintWriter(new
BufferedWriter(new FileWriter("testout.txt")));
  outputFile.println (a);
  outputFile.println (b);
  outputFile.println (c);
  outputFile.println (d);
  outputFile.println (e);
  outputFile.flush();
  outputFile.close();
}
catch (IOException ex)
{
  System.out.println(ex.getMessage());
}
```

After this code runs, the file **testout.txt** will have five lines, each of the variables (a, b, c, d, e) on a separate line.

Example 6-2

Writing Variables to Sequential Files

Start a new empty project in **NetBeans**. Name the project **VariableWriting**. Delete default code in Java file named **VariableWriting**. We will build a simple Java console application that writes data to sequential files using each of the methods for doing such writing.

The complete code for **VariableWriting.java**:

```java
/*
 * VariableWriting.java
*/
package variablewriting;
import java.io.*;
public class VariableWriting
{

  public static void main(String args[])
  {
    // variables
    int v1 = 5;
    String v2 = "Learn Java is fun";
    double v3 = 1.23;
    int v4 = -4;
    boolean v5 = true;
    String v6 = "Another string type";

    // open and write file for print method
    try
    {
      PrintWriter outputFile1 = new PrintWriter(new
BufferedWriter(new FileWriter("test1.txt")));
      outputFile1.print(v1);
      outputFile1.print(v2);
      outputFile1.print(v3);
      outputFile1.print(v4);
      outputFile1.print(v5);
      outputFile1.print(v6);
      outputFile1.flush();
      outputFile1.close();
    }
```

```
      catch (IOException ex)
      {
        System.out.println(ex.getMessage());
      }
      // open and write file for println method
      try
      {
        PrintWriter outputFile2 = new PrintWriter(new
BufferedWriter(new FileWriter("test2.txt")));
        outputFile2.println(v1);
        outputFile2.println(v2);
        outputFile2.println(v3);
        outputFile2.println(v4);
        outputFile2.println(v5);
        outputFile2.println(v6);
        outputFile2.flush();
        outputFile2.close();
      }
      catch (IOException ex)
      {
        System.out.println(ex.getMessage());
      }
    }
}
```

This code writes six variables of different types to two different sequential files (using the two different printing methods).

Save the application (saved as **Example6-2** project in **\LearnJava\LJ Code\Class 6** project group). Then, run it. If no exceptions occurred, two files will be written to the project folder. In that folder will be two files: **test1.txt** (written using **print** method) and **test2.txt** (written using **println** method). Open each file using a text editor (Notepad in Windows works fine) and notice how each file is different.

My files look like this:

test1.txt (uses **print**)

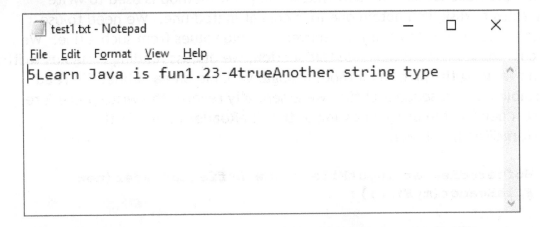

Notice how the variables are just "glommed" together. To read these variables back into an application would require a bit of tricky programming. Later, we discuss the use of delimiters to separate variables, so individual variables can be easily identified.

test2.txt (uses **println**)

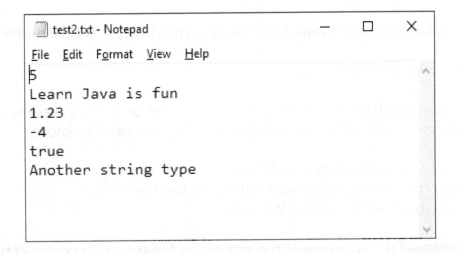

Having each variable on a separate line makes each variable easily identifiable. This is the preferred way of writing variables to disk.

Sequential File Input (Variables)

In the previous section, we saw that if the **print** method is used to write variables to disk, you obtain one long concatenated line. We need to use special techniques (parsing) to recover variable values from such a line. We discuss those methods next. In this section, we discuss reading variables written to a file using the **println** method, a single variable on each line. To **read variables** from a sequential file, we essentially reverse the write procedure. First, open the file using a nesting of the **FileReader** object in the **BufferedReader** object:

```
BufferedReader inputFile = new BufferedReader(new
FileReader(myFile));
```

where **inputFile** is the returned file object and **myFile** is a valid path to the file (whether relative to the project file or a complete qualified path).

If the file you are trying to open does not exist, an error will occur. Like the output file, opening an input file must be within a **try** structure, hence such an exception will be caught. A way to minimize errors is to use the **JFileChooser** control to insure the file exists before trying to open it.

When all values have been read from the sequential file, it is closed using:

```
inputFile.close();
```

Variables are read from a sequential file in the same order they were written. Hence, to read in variables from a sequential file, you need to know:

> How many variables are in the file
> The order the variables were written to the file
> The type of each variable in the file

If you developed the structure of the sequential file (say for a configuration file), you obviously know all of this information. And, if it is a file you generated from another source (spreadsheet, database), the information should be known. If the file is from an unknown source, you may have to do a little detective work. Open the file in a text editor and look at the data. See if you can figure out what is in the file.

Many times, you may know the order and type of variables in a sequential file, but the number of variables may vary. For example, you may export monthly sales data from a spreadsheet. One month may have 30 variables, the next 31 variables, and February would have 28 or 29. In such a case, you can examine the **ready** property of the **BufferedReader** object. If the property is **true**, there are still values to read. If **false**, you have reached the end-of-file. If you don't do such a check, an **EOFException** is "thrown." You can use a **catch** block to know when this occurs.

Variables are read from a sequential file using the **readLine** method. The syntax for our example file is:

```
myVariableString = inputFile.readLine();
```

where **myVariableString** is the **String** representation of the variable being read. To retrieve the variable value from this string, we need to convert the string to the proper type. Conversions for **int**, **double** and **boolean** variables are:

```
myintVariable =
Integer.valueOf(myVariableString).intValue();
mydoubleVariable =
Double.valueOf(myVariableString).doubleValue();
mybooleanVariable =
Boolean.valueOf(myVariableString).booleanValue();
```

Example using **readLine** method:

```
int a;
String b;
double c, e;
boolean d;
try
{
  BufferedReader inputfile = new BufferedReader(new
FileReader("testout.txt"));
  a = Integer.valueOf(inputFile.readLine()).intValue();
  b = inputFile.readLine();
  c = Double.valueOf(inputFile.readLine()).doubleValue();
  d =
Boolean.valueOf(inputFile.readLine()).booleanValue();
  e = Double.valueOf(inputFile.readLine()).doubleValue();
  inputFile.close();
}
catch (IOException ex)
{
  System.out.println(ex.getMessage());
}
```

This code opens the file **testout.txt** (in the project folder) and sequentially reads five variables. Notice how the **readLine** method is nested in the conversions. Also notice, the string variable **b** (obviously) requires no conversion.

Example 6-3

Reading Variables from Sequential Files

Start a new empty project in **NetBeans**. Name the project **VariableReading**. Delete default code in Java file named **VariableReading**. We will build a console application that opens and reads in the data file written with **println** in **Example 6-2**.

The complete **VariableReading.java** code listing is:

```java
/*
 * VariableReading.java
*/
package variablereading;
import java.io.*;
public class VariableReading
{

  public static void main(String args[])
  {
    int v1;
    String v2;
    double v3;
    int v4;
    boolean v5;
    String v6;

    // open file
    try
    {
      BufferedReader inputFile = new BufferedReader(new
FileReader("test2.txt"));
      v1 = Integer.valueOf(inputFile.readLine()).intValue();
      v2 = inputFile.readLine();
      v3 =
Double.valueOf(inputFile.readLine()).doubleValue();
      v4 = Integer.valueOf(inputFile.readLine()).intValue();
      v5 =
Boolean.valueOf(inputFile.readLine()).booleanValue();
      v6 = inputFile.readLine();
      System.out.println("v1 = " + v1);
      System.out.println("v2 = " + v2);
```

```
    System.out.println("v3 = " + v3);
    System.out.println("v4 = " + v4);
    System.out.println("v5 = " + v5);
    System.out.println("v6 = " + v6);
    inputFile.close();

  }
  catch (IOException ex)
  {
    System.out.println(ex.getMessage());
  }
 }
}
```

This code opens the file, then reads and converts the six variables. The variable values are written in the output window.

Save the application (saved as **Example6-3** project in **\LearnJava\LJ Code\Class 6** project group). Run the application. You will probably get this error message in the output window:

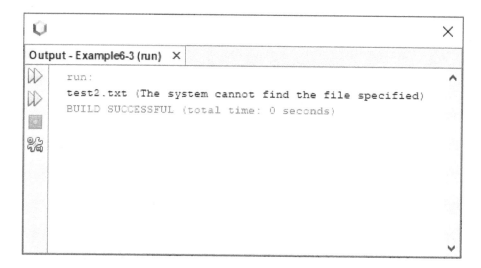

Exception handling works! Remember that the project expects the input file to be in the project directory. We need to copy that file (from our previous example's directory) into this example's directory. Do that now. Copy **test2.text** (from **Example 6-2**) into the project folder for **Example 6-3**.

Now, try running again. You should see:

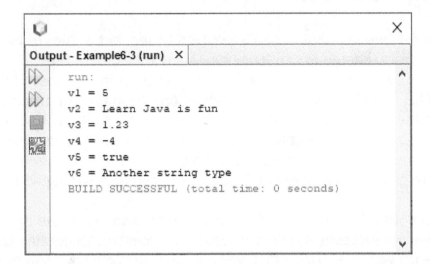

Notice how each of the six variables was read in and properly converted.

Parsing Data Lines

In **Example 6-2**, we saw that variables written to sequential files using the **print** method are concatenated in one long line. Many times, data files you receive from other applications will also have several variables in one line. How can we read variables in such formats? One possible correction for this problem is to restructure the file so each variable is on a single line and it can be read using techniques like those in **Example 6-3**. But, many times this is not possible. If the file is coming from a source you have no control over, you need to work with what you are given. But, there's still hope. You can do anything with Java!

The approach we take is called **parsing** a line. We read in a single line as a long string. Then, we successively remove substrings from this longer line that represent each variable. To do this, we still need to know how many variables are in a line, their types and their location in the line. The location can be specified by some kind of delimiter (a quote, a space, a slash) or by an exact position within the line. All of this can be done with the Java string functions (you may want to review these - they are in Class 2). Though here we are concerned with lines read from a sequential file, note these techniques can be applied to any string data type in Java.

The first thing we need to do is open the file with the lines to be parsed and read in each line as a string. This is <u>exactly</u> what we did in reading variables written to a file using the **println** method. The file is opened using **BufferedReader** and **FileReader** objects. Once the file (**inputFile**) is opened a line is read using the **readLine** method:

```
myLine = inputFile.readLine();
```

Once we have the line (**myLine**) to parse, what we do with it depends on what we know. The basic idea is to determine the bounding character positions of each variable within the line. Character location is zero-based, hence the first character in a string is character 0.   If the first position is **fp** and the last position is **lp**, the substring representation of this variable (**variableString**) can be found using the Java **substring** method:

```
variableString = myLine.substring(fp, lp + 1);
```

Recall this says return the **substring** in **myLine** that starts at position **fp** and ends at character **lp** (the method requires you input the character one beyond the last character, **lp +1**). Once we have extracted **variableString**, we convert it to the proper data type.

So, how do you determine the starting and ending positions for a variable in a line? The easiest case is when you are told by those providing the file what 'columns' bound certain data. This is common in engineering data files. Otherwise, you must know what 'delimits' variables. You can search for these delimiters using the **indexOf** and **lastIndexOf** methods. A common delimiter is just a lot of space between each variable (you may have trouble retrieving strings containing space). Other delimiters include slashes, commas, pound signs and even exclamation points. The power of Java allows you to locate any delimiters and extract the needed information

As variables are extracted from the input data line, we sometimes shorten the line (excluding the extracted substring) before looking for the next variable To do this, we use another version of the **substring** method. If **lp** was the last position of the substring removed from left side of **myLine**, we shorten this line using:

```
myLine = myLine.substring(lp + 1);
```

This removes the first **lp** characters from the left side of **myLine**. Notice by shortening the string in this manner, the first position for finding each subsequent substring will always be 0 (**fp** = 0).

Example 6-4

Parsing Data Lines

Start a new empty project in **NetBeans**. Name the project **Parsing**. Delete default code in Java file named **Parsing**. We will build an application that opens and reads in the single line data file written with the print method in **Example 6-2**. We will then parse that line to extract all the variables. As a first step, copy the **test1.txt** file from that example into your new project's folder.

The **Parsing.java** code listing is:

```java
/*
 * Parsing.java
 */
package parsing;
import java.io.*;

public class Parsing
{
  public static void main(String args[])
  {
    int v1;
    String v2;
    double v3;
    int v4;
    boolean v5;
    String v6;
    String myLine = "";

    // open file
    try
    {
      BufferedReader inputFile = new BufferedReader(new FileReader("test1.txt"));
      myLine = inputFile.readLine();
      inputFile.close();

    }
    catch (IOException ex)
    {
      System.out.println(ex.getMessage());
```

```
    }
    v1 = Integer.valueOf(myLine.substring(0, 1)).intValue();
    v2 = myLine.substring(1, 18);
    v3 = Double.valueOf(myLine.substring(18,
22)).doubleValue();
    v4 = Integer.valueOf(myLine.substring(22,
24)).intValue();
    v5 = Boolean.valueOf(myLine.substring(24,
28)).booleanValue();
    v6 = myLine.substring(28);
   System.out.println("v1 = " + v1);
   System.out.println("v2 = " + v2);
   System.out.println("v3 = " + v3);
   System.out.println("v4 = " + v4);
   System.out.println("v5 = " + v5);
   System.out.println("v6 = " + v6);
  }
}
```

This code opens the file and reads the single line as a string data type. It then extracts each variable from that line. It uses position within the data line to extract the variables. You should be able to figure out this code. Look at the single data line (**test1.txt**) and see how I determined the arguments used in the substring methods.

Save the application (saved as **Example6-4** project in **\LearnJava\LJ Code\Class 6** project group). Run the application. If you get a 'file not found,' error, make sure the data file is in your project folder. Once the program runs, you should see the six variables display correctly in the output window:

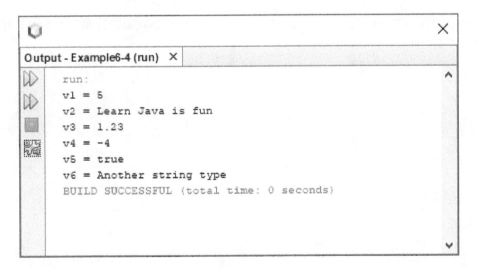

Parsing a data line using character positions is tedious and assumes the variables are always the same length – not necessarily a good assumption. It would be preferable if multiple variable values in a single line were separated by some kind of delimiter. Then, these delimiters could be used to identify where variables start and end. Let's try that. Open **test1.txt** in a text editor and place exclamation points (!) between each of the variables. My file looks like this:

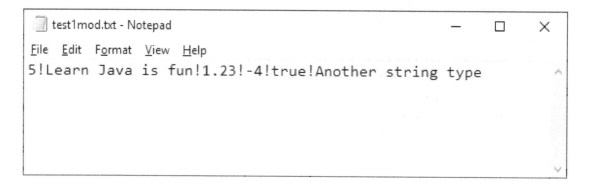

Resave the file as **test1mod.txt**. We could have also added these exclamation points when we originally wrote the file to disk by inserting **print** statements (printing exclamation points) between each **print** statement printing a variable.

The exclamation points (delimiters) now define starting and ending positions for each variable. By locating successive delimiters, we can retrieve the variables. To determine the location of an exclamation point in a string (**myString**), use the **indexOf** method:

```
myString.indexOf("!", sp)
```

This returns the character location of the exclamation point, starting at **sp** (a –1 is returned if none is found).

To parse the new line, modify the **Parsing.java** code as shaded (we essentially replace the 'hard-coded' string positions with the locations of exclamation points):

```
/*
 * Parsing.java
*/
package parsing;
import java.io.*;
import java.text.*;

public class Parsing
{

  public static void main(String args[])
  {
    int v1;
    String v2;
    double v3;
    int v4;
    boolean v5;
    String v6;
    String myLine = "";
    int ep1, ep2;

    // open file
    try
    {
      BufferedReader inputFile = new BufferedReader(new
FileReader("test1mod.txt"));
      myLine = inputFile.readLine();
      inputFile.close();

    }
    catch (IOException ex)
    {
      System.out.println(ex.getMessage());
    }
    ep2 = myLine.indexOf("!");
    v1 = Integer.valueOf(myLine.substring(0,
ep2)).intValue();
    ep1 = ep2;
    ep2 = myLine.indexOf("!", ep1 + 1);
    v2 = myLine.substring(ep1 + 1, ep2);
    ep1 = ep2;
    ep2 = myLine.indexOf("!", ep1 + 1);
```

```
    v3 = Double.valueOf(myLine.substring(ep1 + 1,
ep2)).doubleValue();
    ep1 = ep2;
    ep2 = myLine.indexOf("!", ep1 + 1);
    v4 = Integer.valueOf(myLine.substring(ep1 + 1,
ep2)).intValue();
    ep1 = ep2;
    ep2 = myLine.indexOf("!", ep1 + 1);
    v5 = Boolean.valueOf(myLine.substring(ep1 + 1,
ep2)).booleanValue();
    ep1 = ep2;
    v6 = myLine.substring(ep1 + 1);
    System.out.println("v1 = " + v1);
    System.out.println("v2 = " + v2);
    System.out.println("v3 = " + v3);
    System.out.println("v4 = " + v4);
    System.out.println("v5 = " + v5);
    System.out.println("v6 = " + v6);
  }
}
```

This code simply finds delimiters (exclamation points) bounding the six variables. The variables **ep1** and **ep2** are used to identify left and right delimiter locations, respectively. Recompile and rerun to see the variables. Notice there are no specific numbers in the method arguments. This makes your job easier, especially when variables may have different lengths in different files. You still need to know how many variables and what type of variables are in each line, but the coding is simpler. Next, we'll look at another way to find variables in 'tokenized' lines – those with variables separated by delimiters.

Reading Tokenized Lines

The parsing methods just discussed will work with any data line and any token, even if there are different tokens in a data line. The process uses the **indexOf** method to identify the bounding tokens, then the **substring** method to extract the variable. If a data line contains the same delimiter to bound variable values, there is another set of Java methods that will make your programming tasks easier.

Assume we have a line of text with the variables separated by some delimiter. Such lines are easily created using the **print** method, just 'print' a delimiter between each variable. We call each variable in such a line a **token** – something to be retrieved. If this line is **myLine** and the delimiter is a character **d**, the tokenized version of the line (**myLineToken**) is formed using the **StringTokenizer** object:

```
StringTokenizer myLineToken = new StringTokenizer(myLine,
d);
```

The tokens (string representations of the variables) can now be retrieved from **myLineToken**. To use these tokenizers, you need to import the **java.util.*** package.

The number of variables (tokens) in the line is given by:

```
myLineToken.countTokens()
```

You need to be careful using this result. The count will decrease as you extract tokens.

Subsequent variables (tokens) are extracted from the tokenized string using the **nextToken** method:

```
variableString = myLineToken.nextToken();
```

You repeat this extraction for each token in the line (**myLineToken.countTokens()** times). Once extracted, the string (**variableString**) must still be converted to the proper type.

Example 6-5

Reading Tokenized Data Lines

Start a new empty project in **NetBeans**. Name the project **Tokens**. Delete default code in Java file named **Tokens**. We will modify the previous application that opens and reads in the single line data file (**test1mod.txt**, the one with variables separated by exclamation points).. The modifications will use token methods to extract all the variables. As a first step, copy the **test1mod.txt** file from that example into your new project's folder.

The **Tokens.java** code listing is (modifications to Example 6-4 are shaded):

```java
/*
 * Tokens.java
 */
package tokens;
import java.io.*;
import java.util.*;
public class Tokens
{

  public static void main(String args[])
  {
    int v1;
    String v2;
    double v3;
    int v4;
    boolean v5;
    String v6;
    String myLine = "";

    // open file
    try
    {
      BufferedReader inputFile = new BufferedReader(new
FileReader("test1mod.txt"));
      myLine = inputFile.readLine();
      inputFile.close();
    }
    catch (IOException ex)
    {
      System.out.println(ex.getMessage());
```

```
    }

    StringTokenizer myLineToken = new StringTokenizer(myLine,
"!");

    v1 =
Integer.valueOf(myLineToken.nextToken()).intValue();
    v2 = myLineToken.nextToken();
    v3 =
Double.valueOf(myLineToken.nextToken()).doubleValue();
    v4 = Integer.valueOf(myLineToken.nextToken()).intValue();
    v5 =
Boolean.valueOf(myLineToken.nextToken()).booleanValue();
    v6 = myLineToken.nextToken();

    System.out.println("v1 = " + v1);
    System.out.println("v2 = " + v2);
    System.out.println("v3 = " + v3);
    System.out.println("v4 = " + v4);
    System.out.println("v5 = " + v5);
    System.out.println("v6 = " + v6);
  }
}
```

Notice how much easier the code is to read. The tokenizers take care of determining where all the exclamation points (delimiters) are located.

Run to see that this, too, extracts all six variables correctly. We suggest that you always use these tokenizer methods if each data line has the same delimiter. Save this project (saved as **Example6-5** project in **\LearnJava\LJ Code\Class 6** project group).

Building Data Lines

Code similar to that used to parse, or break up, a line of data can also be used to build a line of data that can then be used in a control such as a text area or written to a sequential file. A primary application for such lines is to write precisely formatted data files. It allows left justification, centering and right justification of values. It also allows positioning data in any 'column' desired.

You might think you could just directly modify the contents of some string variable to accomplish this task. Unfortunately, string variables in Java are **immutable** – they cannot be modified directly. We take another approach. We will build the data line as an array of characters. Then, we will convert that array to a string for output. We will build a couple of general methods that help in building data lines.

A first step in building data lines is to choose the maximum number of characters that will be in each line. This length is usually established by the width of a displaying control or the width of a printed page (we'll look at this in Class 9). Once this maximum width is selected, each line is initialized as a blank character array of that length. We will use a general method to initialize such an array to all blank spaces. The method (**blankLine**) is:

```
public void blankLine(char[] charLine)
{
  for (int i = 0; i < charLine.length; i++)
  {
    charLine[i] = ' ';
  }
}
```

The method simply takes an input character array (**charLine**) and changes each element in the array to a blank character (space).

Once the blank line is established, the spaces are replaced with specified substrings at specific locations. We create a general method (**midLine**) to accomplish this task:

```
public void midLine(String inString, char[] charLine, int
pos)
{
  for (int i = pos; i < pos + inString.length(); i++)
  {
    charLine[i] = inString.charAt(i - pos);
  }
}
```

This method takes the contents of the string **inString** and places its characters in the array **charLine**, starting at position **pos**. Hence, to left justify **mySubString** in **myCharLine** at position **lp**, use:

```
midLine(mySubString, myCharLine, lp);
```

When doing these replacements, always make sure you are within the bounding length of the **myCharLine** array.

Once the line of data represented by the character array is as desired, it is converted to a **String** type line (**myLine**) using:

```
myLine = String.copyValueOf(myCharLine);
```

This line can then be printed for a sequential file or used for other purposes. The general methods **blankLine** and **midLine** have been added to **Appendix I**.

So, to build a line of variable data, we decide what variables we want in each line and where we want to position them. We then successively convert each variable to a string and place it in a character array using the **midLine** method. When this array is complete, it is converted to a data line, and, if it is for a sequential file, it is printed to the file (**outputFile**) using the **println** method:

```
outputFile.println(myLine);
```

We don't have to use the newly constructed line in a data file. It could also be added to the **text** property of any control. In such a case, if you want the new line on its own separate line, be sure to append the proper line feed character (**\n**).

We saw how to left justify a substring in a data line represented by a character array. We can also center justify and right justify. To right justify **mySubString** in **myCharLine** at location **rp**, use:

```
midLine(mySubString, myCharLine, rp + 1 -
mySubString.Length());
```

And to center **mySubString** in **myCharLine**, use:

```
midLine(mySubString, myCharLine, (int) (0.5 *
(myCharLine.length - mySubString.length())));
```

Of course, to center justify a substring, the substring must be shorter than the line it is being centered in. To see how both of these replacements work, just go through an example and you'll see the logic.

Most of what is presented here works best with fixed width fonts (each character is the same width). I usually use **Courier New**. You will have to experiment if using proportional fonts to obtain desired results.

Example 6-6

Building Data Lines

Start a new empty project in **NetBeans**. Name the project **BuildingData**. Delete default code in Java file named **BuildingData**. We will build an application that lets a user enter a minimum and maximum circle diameter. The program then computes perimeter and area for twenty circles between those two input values. We will use the **circleGeometry** procedure developed in **Example 5-3** for the computations. The computed results are displayed in tabular form. The finished frame looks like this:

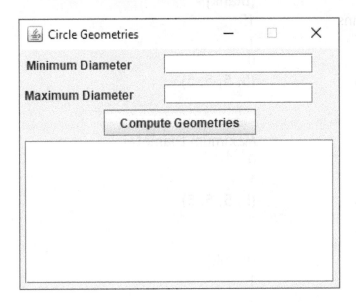

Place two labels, two text fields, a button and a scroll pane in the frame. The **GridBagLayout** will look like this:

	gridx = 0	gridx = 1
gridy = 0	minLabel	minTextField
gridy = 1	minLabel	minTextField
gridy = 2	computeButton	
gridy = 3	resultsScrollPane	

Properties:

Building Frame:
        title   Circle Geometries
        resizable   false

minLabel:
        text   Minimum Diameter
        gridx   0
        gridy   0
        insets   (5, 5, 5, 5)

minTextField:
        text   [Blank]
        columns   15
        gridx   1
        gridy   0
        insets   (5, 5, 5, 5)

maxLabel:
        text   Maximum Diameter
        gridx   0
        gridy   1
        insets   (5, 5, 5, 5)

maxTextField:
        text   [Blank]
        gridx   1
        gridy   1
        insets   (5, 5, 5, 5)

computeButton:
        text   Compute Geometries
        gridx   0
        gridy   2
        insets   (5, 5, 5, 5)

resultsScrollPane:

viewPortView	resultsTextArea
gridx	0
gridy	3
gridwidth	2
insets	(5, 5, 5, 5)

resultsTextArea

columns	45
rows	10
font	Courier New, PLAIN, 12

Build the basic framework with this code:

```java
/*
 * BuildingData.java
*/
package buildingdata;
import javax.swing.*;
import java.awt.*;
import java.awt.event.*;
import java.text.*;

public class BuildingData extends JFrame
{

  public static void main(String args[])
  {
    //construct frame
    new BuildingData().show();
  }

  public BuildingData()
  {
    // code to build the form
    setTitle("Circle Geometries");
    setResizable(false);
    addWindowListener(new WindowAdapter()
    {
      public void windowClosing(WindowEvent e)
      {
        exitForm(e);
      }
    });
    getContentPane().setLayout(new GridBagLayout());
```

```
      pack();
      Dimension screenSize =
Toolkit.getDefaultToolkit().getScreenSize();
      setBounds((int) (0.5 * (screenSize.width -
getWidth())), (int) (0.5 * (screenSize.height -
getHeight())), getWidth(), getHeight());
   }

  private void exitForm(WindowEvent e)
  {
     System.exit(0);
  }
}
```

Run to test the code.

Next, we'll add the controls and associated event methods. Use these class level declarations:

```
JLabel minLabel = new JLabel();
JTextField minTextField = new JTextField();
JLabel maxLabel = new JLabel();
JTextField maxTextField = new JTextField();
JButton computeButton = new JButton();
JScrollPane resultsScrollPane = new JScrollPane();
JTextArea resultsTextArea = new JTextArea();
```

And, this code to place all the controls and establish methods:

```
// position controls (establish event methods)
GridBagConstraints gridConstraints = new
GridBagConstraints();
minLabel.setText("Minimum Diameter");
gridConstraints.gridx = 0;
gridConstraints.gridy = 0;
gridConstraints.insets = new Insets(5, 5, 5, 5);
getContentPane().add(minLabel, gridConstraints);
minTextField.setText("");
minTextField.setColumns(15);
gridConstraints = new GridBagConstraints();
gridConstraints.gridx = 1;
gridConstraints.gridy = 0;
gridConstraints.insets = new Insets(5, 5, 5, 5);
getContentPane().add(minTextField, gridConstraints);

maxLabel.setText("Maximum Diameter");
```

```
gridConstraints.gridx = 0;
gridConstraints.gridy = 1;
gridConstraints.insets = new Insets(5, 5, 5, 5);
getContentPane().add(maxLabel, gridConstraints);
maxTextField.setText("");
maxTextField.setColumns(15);
gridConstraints = new GridBagConstraints();
gridConstraints.gridx = 1;
gridConstraints.gridy = 1;
gridConstraints.insets = new Insets(5, 5, 5, 5);
getContentPane().add(maxTextField, gridConstraints);

computeButton.setText("Compute Geometries");
gridConstraints = new GridBagConstraints();
gridConstraints.gridx = 0;
gridConstraints.gridy = 2;
gridConstraints.gridwidth = 2;
getContentPane().add(computeButton, gridConstraints);
computeButton.addActionListener(new ActionListener()
{
   public void actionPerformed(ActionEvent e)
   {
     computeButtonActionPerformed(e);
   }
});

resultsTextArea.setColumns(45);
resultsTextArea.setRows(10);
resultsTextArea.setFont(new Font("Courier New",
Font.PLAIN, 12));
resultsScrollPane.setViewportView(resultsTextArea);
gridConstraints.gridx = 0;
gridConstraints.gridy = 3;
gridConstraints.gridwidth = 2;
gridConstraints.insets = new Insets(5, 5, 5, 5);
getContentPane().add(resultsScrollPane, gridConstraints);
```

Lastly, an empty method for clicking on the button control:

```
private void computeButtonActionPerformed(ActionEvent e)
{
}
```

Run to see the finished control layout:

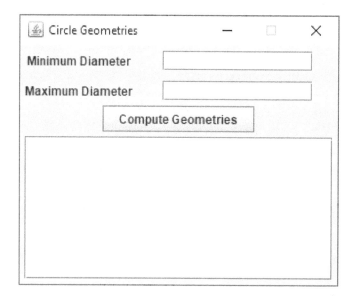

Lastly, we write the code. Add the two general methods developed earlier (**blankLine** and **midLine**) for building the data lines using a character array:

```java
public void blankLine(char[] charLine)
{
  for (int i = 0; i < charLine.length; i++)
  {
    charLine[i] = ' ';
  }
}

public void midLine(String inString, char[] charLine, int pos)
{
  for (int i = pos; i < pos + inString.length(); i++)
  {
    charLine[i] = inString.charAt(i - pos);
  }
}
```

Add the **circleGeometries** general method from **Example 5-3** (in **Appendix I**):

```
public double[] circleGeometry(double diameter)
{
  double [] geometry = new double[2];
  geometry[0] = Math.PI * diameter; // circumference
  geometry[1] = Math.PI * diameter * diameter / 4; // area
  return(geometry);
}
```

Use this code in the **computeButtonActionPerformed** event:

```
private void computeButtonActionPerformed(ActionEvent e)
{
  double d, delta;
  double[] values = new double[2];
  String myLine;
  String mySubString;
  final int numberValues = 20;
  final int lineWidth = 36;
  char[] buildLine = new char[lineWidth];
  // read min/max and increment
  double dMin =
Double.valueOf(minTextField.getText()).doubleValue();
  double dMax =
Double.valueOf(maxTextField.getText()).doubleValue();
  if (dMin >= dMax)
  {
    JOptionPane.showConfirmDialog(null, "Maximum must be
less than minimum.", "Error", JOptionPane.DEFAULT_OPTION,
JOptionPane.ERROR_MESSAGE);
    minTextField.requestFocus();
    return;
  }
  delta = (dMax - dMin) / numberValues;
  // center header
  blankLine(buildLine);
  mySubString = "Circle Geometries";
  midLine(mySubString, buildLine, (int) (0.5 * (lineWidth
- mySubString.length())));
  myLine = String.copyValueOf(buildLine);
  resultsTextArea.setText(myLine + "\n");
  resultsTextArea.setText(resultsTextArea.getText() +
"Diameter      Perimeter          Area\n");
  for (d = dMin; d <= dMax; d += delta)
  {
```

```
      values = circleGeometry(d);
      // right justify three values with two decimals
      blankLine(buildLine);
      mySubString = new DecimalFormat("0.00").format(d);
      midLine(mySubString, buildLine, 8 -
mySubString.length());
      mySubString = new
DecimalFormat("0.00").format(values[0]);
      midLine(mySubString, buildLine, 22 -
mySubString.length());
      mySubString = new
DecimalFormat("0.00").format(values[1]);
      midLine(mySubString, buildLine, 36 -
mySubString.length());
      myLine = String.copyValueOf(buildLine);
      resultsTextArea.setText(resultsTextArea.getText() +
myLine + "\n");
    }
  minTextField.requestFocus();
}
```

This code reads the input values and determines the diameter range. It writes some header information and then, for each diameter, computes and prints geometries. Values are right justified.

The complete **BuildingData.java** code listing (changes to original framework are shaded):

```
/*
 * BuildingData.java
*/
package buildingdata;
import javax.swing.*;
import java.awt.*;
import java.awt.event.*;
import java.text.*;

public class BuildingData extends JFrame
{
  JLabel minLabel = new JLabel();
  JTextField minTextField = new JTextField();
  JLabel maxLabel = new JLabel();
  JTextField maxTextField = new JTextField();
  JButton computeButton = new JButton();
  JScrollPane resultsScrollPane = new JScrollPane();
  JTextArea resultsTextArea = new JTextArea();
```

```java
public static void main(String args[])
{
  //construct frame
  new BuildingData().show();
}

public BuildingData()
{
  // code to build the form
  setTitle("Circle Geometries");
  setResizable(false);
  addWindowListener(new WindowAdapter()
  {
    public void windowClosing(WindowEvent e)
    {
      exitForm(e);
    }
  });
  getContentPane().setLayout(new GridBagLayout());

  // position controls (establish event methods)
  GridBagConstraints gridConstraints = new
GridBagConstraints();
  minLabel.setText("Minimum Diameter");
  gridConstraints.gridx = 0;
  gridConstraints.gridy = 0;
  gridConstraints.insets = new Insets(5, 5, 5, 5);
  getContentPane().add(minLabel, gridConstraints);
  minTextField.setText("");
  minTextField.setColumns(15);
  gridConstraints = new GridBagConstraints();
  gridConstraints.gridx = 1;
  gridConstraints.gridy = 0;
  gridConstraints.insets = new Insets(5, 5, 5, 5);
  getContentPane().add(minTextField, gridConstraints);

  maxLabel.setText("Maximum Diameter");
  gridConstraints.gridx = 0;
  gridConstraints.gridy = 1;
  gridConstraints.insets = new Insets(5, 5, 5, 5);
  getContentPane().add(maxLabel, gridConstraints);
  maxTextField.setText("");
  maxTextField.setColumns(15);
  gridConstraints = new GridBagConstraints();
  gridConstraints.gridx = 1;
  gridConstraints.gridy = 1;
```

```
    gridConstraints.insets = new Insets(5, 5, 5, 5);
    getContentPane().add(maxTextField, gridConstraints);

    computeButton.setText("Compute Geometries");
    gridConstraints = new GridBagConstraints();
    gridConstraints.gridx = 0;
    gridConstraints.gridy = 2;
    gridConstraints.gridwidth = 2;
    getContentPane().add(computeButton, gridConstraints);
    computeButton.addActionListener(new ActionListener()
    {
      public void actionPerformed(ActionEvent e)
      {
        computeButtonActionPerformed(e);
      }
    });

    resultsTextArea.setColumns(45);
    resultsTextArea.setRows(10);
    resultsTextArea.setFont(new Font("Courier New",
Font.PLAIN, 12));
    resultsScrollPane.setViewportView(resultsTextArea);
    gridConstraints.gridx = 0;
    gridConstraints.gridy = 3;
    gridConstraints.gridwidth = 2;
    gridConstraints.insets = new Insets(5, 5, 5, 5);
    getContentPane().add(resultsScrollPane, gridConstraints);


    pack();
    Dimension screenSize =
Toolkit.getDefaultToolkit().getScreenSize();
    setBounds((int) (0.5 * (screenSize.width - getWidth())),
(int) (0.5 * (screenSize.height - getHeight())), getWidth(),
getHeight());
  }


  private void computeButtonActionPerformed(ActionEvent e)
  {
    double d, delta;
    double[] values = new double[2];
    String myLine;
    String mySubString;
    final int numberValues = 20;
    final int lineWidth = 36;
    char[] buildLine = new char[lineWidth];
```

```
    // read min/max and increment
    double dMin =
Double.valueOf(minTextField.getText()).doubleValue();
    double dMax =
Double.valueOf(maxTextField.getText()).doubleValue();
    if (dMin >= dMax)
    {
        JOptionPane.showConfirmDialog(null, "Maximum must be
less than minimum.", "Error", JOptionPane.DEFAULT_OPTION,
JOptionPane.ERROR_MESSAGE);
        minTextField.requestFocus();
        return;
    }
    delta = (dMax - dMin) / numberValues;
    // center header
    blankLine(buildLine);
    mySubString = "Circle Geometries";
    midLine(mySubString, buildLine, (int) (0.5 * (lineWidth -
mySubString.length())));
    myLine = String.copyValueOf(buildLine);
    resultsTextArea.setText(myLine + "\n");
    resultsTextArea.setText(resultsTextArea.getText() +
"Diameter      Perimeter        Area\n");
    for (d = dMin; d <= dMax; d += delta)
    {
        values = circleGeometry(d);
        // right justify three values with two decimals
        blankLine(buildLine);
        mySubString = new DecimalFormat("0.00").format(d);
        midLine(mySubString, buildLine, 8 -
mySubString.length());
        mySubString = new
DecimalFormat("0.00").format(values[0]);
        midLine(mySubString, buildLine, 22 -
mySubString.length());
        mySubString = new
DecimalFormat("0.00").format(values[1]);
        midLine(mySubString, buildLine, 36 -
mySubString.length());
        myLine = String.copyValueOf(buildLine);
        resultsTextArea.setText(resultsTextArea.getText() +
myLine + "\n");
    }
    minTextField.requestFocus();
}

private void exitForm(WindowEvent e)
```

```
    {
      System.exit(0);
    }


  public double[] circleGeometry(double diameter)
  {
    double [] geometry = new double[2];
    geometry[0] = Math.PI * diameter; // circumference
    geometry[1] = Math.PI * diameter * diameter / 4; // area
    return(geometry);
  }

  public void blankLine(char[] charLine)
  {
    for (int i = 0; i < charLine.length; i++)
    {
      charLine[i] = ' ';
    }
  }

  public void midLine(String inString, char[] charLine, int
pos)
  {
    for (int i = pos; i < pos + inString.length(); i++)
    {
      charLine[i] = inString.charAt(i - pos);
    }
  }
}
```

Run the project. When I used 30 and 70 for minimum and maximum diameters, respectively, I obtain this neatly formatted table of results:

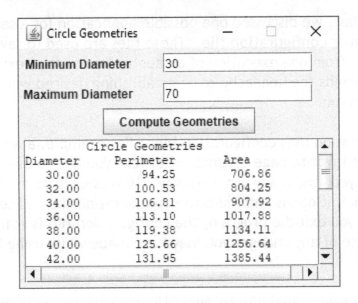

Save the application (saved as **Example6-6** project in **\LearnJava\LJ Code\Class 6** project group).

Configuration Files

Earlier in this class, we discussed one possible application for a sequential file - an **initialization** or **configuration file**. These files are used to save user selected options from one execution of an application to the next. With such files, the user avoids the headache of re-establishing desired values each time an application is run.

Every GUI application uses configuration files. For example, a word processor remembers your favorite page settings, what font you like to use, what toolbars you want displayed, and many other options. How does it do this? When you start the program, it opens and reads the configuration file and sets your choices. When you exit the program, the configuration file is written back to disk, making note of any changes you may have made while using the word processor.

You can add the same capability to Java GUI applications. How do you decide what your configuration file will contain and how it will be formatted? That is completely up to you, the application designer. Typical information stored in a **configuration** file includes: current dates and times, check box settings, radio button settings, selected colors, font name, font style, font size, and selected menu options. You decide what is important in your application. You develop variables to save information and read and write these variables from and to the sequential configuration file. There is usually one variable (numeric, string, date, **boolean**) for each option being saved. And, I usually place each variable on its own line in the configuration file. That way, no 'tokenizing' is required.

Once you've decided on values to save and the format of your file, how do you proceed? A first step is to create an initial file using a text editor. Save your configuration file in your application's project folder. Configuration files will always be kept in the application path. And, the usual three letter file extension for a configuration file is **ini** (for initialization). When distributing your application to other users, be sure to include a copy of the configuration file.

Once you have developed the configuration file, you need to write code to fit this framework:

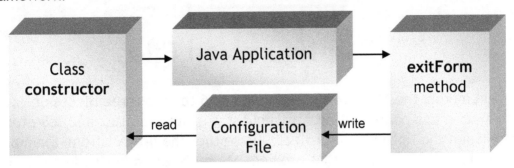

When your application begins (in the class **constructor**; after code adding controls to frame), open and read the configuration file and use the variables to establish the respective options. Establishing options involves things like setting font objects, establishing colors, simulating click events on check boxes and radio buttons, and setting properties.

When your application ends (**exitForm** method in our applications), examine all options to be saved, establish respective variables to represent these options, and open and write (**println** method, usually) the configuration file. And, we will need to make one other change (perhaps) to our applications. Many times, an application will have an **Exit** button or an **Exit** option in the menu structure. We need to make sure the event method for this option is always:

```
exitForm(null);
```

and not a direct call to close the form. That way, no matter how the application is stopped, either with the **Exit** button or by clicking the **X** in the upper right corner of the frame, the code in the **exitForm** event method (including writing the configuration file) will be executed.

Example 6-7

Configuration Files

We will modify the **Note Editor** built in Class 5 to save three pieces of
information in a configuration file: bold status, italic status, and selected font
size. Open the **Note Editor** project. Use either the project from **Example 5-4**
or **Problem 5-1**, if you did that problem. I use **Problem 5-1** (it includes an
About message box). The needed modifications are listed.

1. Add this line to import the **java.io.*** package:

```
import java.io.*;
```

2. Use this code at the end of the frame constructor::

```
int fontSize;
try
{
  // Open configuration file and set font values
  BufferedReader inputFile = new BufferedReader(new
FileReader("note.ini"));

boldMenuItem.setSelected(Boolean.valueOf(inputFile.readLin
e()).booleanValue());

italicMenuItem.setSelected(Boolean.valueOf(inputFile.readL
ine()).booleanValue());
  fontSize =
Integer.valueOf(inputFile.readLine()).intValue();
  inputFile.close();
}
catch (IOException ex)
{
  JOptionPane.showConfirmDialog(null, ex.getMessage(),
"Error Reading Configuration File",
JOptionPane.DEFAULT_OPTION, JOptionPane.ERROR_MESSAGE);
  System.exit(0);
}
```

```
switch (fontSize)
{
  case 1:
    smallMenuItem.doClick();
    break;
  case 2:
    mediumMenuItem.doClick();
    break;
  case 3:
    largeMenuItem.doClick();
    break;
}
```

In this code, the configuration file (named **note.ini**) is opened. We first read two **boolean** values. These establish whether checks should be next to bold and/or italic in the menu structure. Then, an integer is read and used to set font size (1-small, 2-medium, 3-large). Note use of the **doClick** method to simulate clicking on the corresponding font size menu option. If an error occurs, a message appears and the application stops.

3. Use this code in the **exitForm** event method (again, modifications are shaded):

```
private void exitForm(WindowEvent e)
{
   try
   {
     // Open configuration file and write
     PrintWriter outputFile = new PrintWriter(new
BufferedWriter(new FileWriter("note.ini")));
     outputFile.println(boldMenuItem.isSelected());
     outputFile.println(italicMenuItem.isSelected());
     if (smallMenuItem.isSelected())
     {
       outputFile.println("1");
     }
     else if (mediumMenuItem.isSelected())
     {
       outputFile.println("2");
     }
     else if (largeMenuItem.isSelected())
     {
       outputFile.println("3");
     }
     outputFile.flush();
     outputFile.close();
   }
   catch (IOException ex)
   {
     JOptionPane.showConfirmDialog(null, ex.getMessage(),
"Error Writing Configuration File",
JOptionPane.DEFAULT_OPTION, JOptionPane.ERROR_MESSAGE);
   }
   finally
   {
     System.exit(0);
   }
}
```

This code does the 'inverse' of the procedure followed in the constructor method. The configuration file is opened for output. Two **boolean** variables representing current status of the bold and italic menu options are written to the file. Then, an integer representing the selected font size is written prior to closing and saving the file.

4. Lastly, modify the **exitMenuItemActionPerformed** method. Rather than exit, this routine now calls the **exitForm** method:

```
private void exitMenuItemActionPerformed(ActionEvent e)
{
   exitForm(null);
}
```

Save the application (saved as **Example6-7** project in **\LearnJava\LJ Code\Class 6** project group). Run and compile the modified project. You will see this error message:

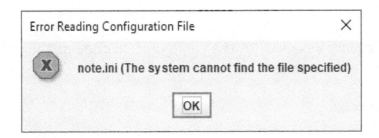

This message is telling us that the configuration file cannot be found. Of course, it can't – we forgot to create it! If you are using configuration files, you must always create an initial version. Open a text editor (With Windows, **Notepad** will work) and type these three lines:

```
false
false
1
```

This says that bold and italic will be unchecked (false) and the font size will be small (represented by the 1 in last line). Save this file as **note.ini** in the project folder. Try running it again and things should be fine. Try changing any of the saved options and exit the program. Run it again and you should see the selected options are still there. Any text typed will have disappeared. We'll solve the 'disappearing text' problem next when we look at how to save text in a sequential file.

Let's look at one other way to solve the 'missing configuration file' problem. Many times, program users looking around in their computer directories will delete any file they don't recognize. Configuration files may sometimes fall victim to these haphazard deletions. If the configuration file in our note editor is deleted, a message is displayed to that effect. But, that message may have no meaning to a user. A better solution would be to just 'reconstruct' the configuration file without the user even knowing anything.

Let's modify the **Note Editor** application (again) so that if the configuration file cannot be found, the program will still run. If the file can't be found (causing an exception), we'll establish values for the three missing format variables and continue.

The modified (changes shaded) to the configuration code at the end of the constructor that accomplishes this task is:

```
int fontSize;
try
{
  // Open configuration file and set font values
  BufferedReader inputFile = new BufferedReader(new
FileReader("note.ini"));

boldMenuItem.setSelected(Boolean.valueOf(inputFile.readLin
e()).booleanValue());

italicMenuItem.setSelected(Boolean.valueOf(inputFile.readL
ine()).booleanValue());
  fontSize =
Integer.valueOf(inputFile.readLine()).intValue();
  inputFile.close();
}
catch (IOException e)
{
   JOptionPane.showConfirmDialog(null, e.getMessage(),
"Error Reading Configuration File",
JOptionPane.DEFAULT_OPTION, JOptionPane.ERROR_MESSAGE);
  boldMenuItem.setSelected(false);
  italicMenuItem.setSelected(false);
  fontSize = 1;
}
switch (fontSize)
{
  case 1:
    smallMenuItem.doClick();
```

```
      break;
   case 2:
     mediumMenuItem.doClick();
     break;
   case 3:
     largeMenuItem.doClick();
     break;
 }
```

In this code, if the file is not found, the **catch** block establishes values for the bold and italic status (both false) and a font size (1 is small). This allows the program to run to completion.

Delete the **note.ini** file from the project directory (you need to do this to test our new reconstruction code). Resave, recompile and rerun the project. You should see:

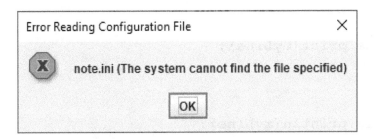

If you don't get this message and the program runs, stop the application and delete the **note.ini** file from the project folder. Then, run again and you should see the above message box generated in the **catch** block.

Choose some formatting features, stop the application and run it again. The error message box will not be seen – why? The reason you don't see the error message again is that when you exited the program, it wrote the **note.ini** file in the proper folder. The neat thing about such code is that we fixed a problem without the user even knowing there was a problem. In fact, you can delete the code displaying the message box – the user doesn't need to know anything has happened!

Writing and Reading Text Using Sequential Files

In many applications, we would like to be able to save text information and retrieve it for later reference. This information could be a **text file** created by an application or the contents of a Swing **text area** control. Writing and reading text using sequential files involves methods we have already seen and a few new ones.

To **write** a sequential text file, we follow the simple procedure: open the file for output, write the file, close the file. If the file is a line-by-line text file, each line of the file is written to disk using a single **print** or **println** statement. Use **print** if a line already has a new line (\n) character appended to it. Use **println** if there is no such character. So, to write **myLine** to **outputFile**, use either:

```
outputFile.print(myLine);
```

or

```
outputFile.println(myLine);
```

This assumes you have somehow generated the string **myLine**. How you generate this data depends on your particular application. You may have lines of text or may form the lines using techniques just discussed. The **print** or **println** statement should be in a loop that encompasses all lines of the file. You must know the number of lines in your file, beforehand. A typical code segment to accomplish this task is:

```
PrintWriter outputFile = new PrintWriter(new
BufferedWriter(new FileWriter(myFile)));
for (int i = o; i < numberLines; i++)
{
..// need code here to generate string data myLine
..outputFile.println(myLine);
}
outputFile.flush();
outputFile.close();
```

This code writes **numberLines** text lines to the sequential file **myFile**, located in the project folder.

If we want to write the contents of the **text** property of a Swing **text area**, we use some special properties of that control (these properties requires importing the **javax.swing.text.*** package):

`lineCount`	Number of lines in text area control
`lineStartOffset(i)`	Starting character position of line i
`lineEndOffset(i)`	Ending character position of line i

So, we recover each line from the control's **text** property using character positions and the **substring** method. These recovered lines are then written to the file (using **print**, since each line will have a new line character). A sample code snippet that accomplishes this task for **myTextArea** is:

```
PrintWriter outputFile = new PrintWriter(new
BufferedWriter(new FileWriter(myFile)));
for (int i = 0; i < myTextArea.getLineCount(); i++)
{
  fp = myTextArea.getLineStartOffset(i);
  lp = myTextArea.getLineEndOffset(i);
  outputFile.print(myTextArea.getText().substring(fp,
lp));
}
outputFile.flush();
outputFile.close();
```

This code opens **myFile** for output. It then cycles through each line in the **text area** control. For each line, it finds the first position (**fp**) and last position (**lp**). The bounded substring is then extracted from the text property to form the line for output to **outputFile**. This code must be in a **try** block that handles a **BadLocationException** error (in case a bad position is referenced).

To **read** the contents of a previously-saved text file, we follow similar steps to the writing process: open the file, read the file, close the file. If the file is a text file, we read each individual line with the **readLine** method:

```
myline = inputFile.readLine();
```

This line is usually placed in a **while** structure that is repeated until all lines of the file are read in. A **null** line can be used to detect an end-of-file condition, if you don't know, beforehand, how many lines are in the file. A typical code segment to accomplish this task is:

```
BufferedReader inputFile = new BufferedReader(new
FileReader(myFile));
editorTextArea.setText("");
while ((myLine = inputFile.readLine()) != null)
{
   // do something with myLine here
}
inputFile.close();
```

This code reads text lines from the sequential file **myFile** until the end-of-file is reached. You could put a counter in the loop to count lines if you like.

To place the contents of a sequential text file into a **text area** control, a similar process is followed: open the file, read the lines, place the lines in the control, close the file. When the lines are added to the control (using the **append** method), you need to add a new line character (**\n**) to each line because the **readLine** method ignores such characters if they are there. So, to place the contents of a previously saved sequential file (**myFile**) into the **text** property of a text area control named **myTextArea**, we need this code:

```
BufferedReader inputFile = new BufferedReader(new
FileReader(myFile));
myTextArea.setText("");
while ((myLine = inputFile.readLine()) != null)
{
   myTextArea.append(myLine + "\n");
}
inputFile.close();
```

JFileChooser Control (Save Files)

As mentioned when we first discussed sequential files, when a file is opened for output, if the file being opened already exists, it is first erased. This is fine for files like configuration files. We want to overwrite these files. But, for other files, this might not be desirable behavior. Hence, prior to overwriting a sequential file, we want to make sure it is acceptable. Using the **JFileChooser** control (introduced in Class 4) to obtain filenames for saving will provide this "safety factor." This control, along with a bit of coding, insures that any path selected for saving a file exists and that if an existing file is selected, the user has agreed to overwriting that file.

File Chooser Properties:

approveButtonText   Text that appears on the 'approve' button – for a save dialog, the value is **Save**.
currentDirectory   The selected directory.
dialogTitle   Title that appears in the title area of the dialog.
dialogType   By default, an Open dialog, set to **JFileChooser.SAVE_DIALOG** for a save dialog control.
fileFilter   Used to limit types of files displayed.
selectedFile   The currently selected file.

File Chooser Methods:

showSaveDialog   Displays the dialog box for saving files. Returned value indicates which button was clicked by user (**Save** or **Cancel**).
setApproveButtonText   Sets the text that appears on the 'approve' button.
getCurrentDirectory   Retrieves the selected directory.
setDialogTitle   Sets the dialog title.
setDialogType   Sets the dialog type.
setFileFilter   Sets the filter to limit types of files displayed.
addChoosableFileFilter Add a file filter to file chooser.
getSelectedFile   Retrieves the currently selected file.

File Chooser Events:

actionPerformed   Event (**ActionEvent**) triggered when approve or cancel button is selected. Added with **ActionListener**. Usually monitored when file chooser is embedded in application.

The file chooser control can be added to an application like any control, embedded in the frame. Or, it can be displayed as needed, as a dialog box. You usually only monitor events when the file chooser is embedded in an application.

To add a listener for the **actionPerformed** event for a file chooser named **myChooser**, use:

```
myChooser.addActionListener(new ActionListener()
{
  public void actionPerformed(ActionEvent e)
  {
    myChooserActionPerformed(e);
  }
});
```

And, the corresponding event code would be placed in a **myChooserActionPerformed** method:

```
private void myChooserActionPerformed(ActionEvent e)
{
   [method code]
}
```

In this event, you usually check to see if the approve (**Save**) button has been clicked. The code segment that does this is:

```
if
(e.getActionCommand().equals(JFileChooser.APPROVE_SELECTIO
N))
{
   [code to process]
}
```

To display the file chooser as a **save dialog** box, use the **showSaveDialog** method. If the chooser is named **myChooser**, the format is:

```
myChooser.showSaveDialog(this);
```

where **this** is a keyword referring to the current frame. The displayed dialog box is:

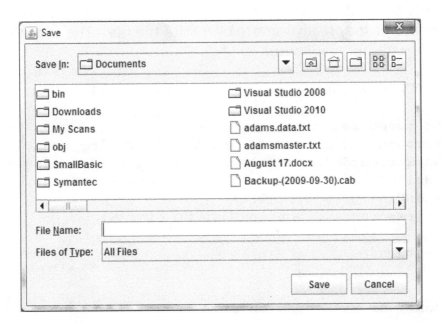

The user selects a file using the dialog control (or types a name in the **File Name** box). The file type is selected from the **Files of Type** box (values here set with the **Filter** property). Once selected, the **Save** button is clicked. **Cancel** can be clicked to cancel the open operation. The **showSaveDialog** method returns the clicked button. This method will return one of two values:

```
JFileChooser.APPROVE_OPTION
```
– Approve (**Save**) button clicked
```
JFileChooser.CANCEL_OPTION
```
– **Cancel** button clicked

If the user has selected the **Save** button, we can determine the selected file. This value is given by:

```
myChooser.getSelectedFile()
```

Many methods require this name to be a **String** type. This conversion is done using:

```
myChooser.getSelectedFile().toString()
```

There is no built-in capability to prevent a user from overwriting an existing file. You need to write code to do this. The **exists** method can be applied to the selected file to see if it already exists. If it does, you display a message box asking the user if they really want to overwrite the file. The code that accomplishes this for **myChooser** is:

```
if (myChooser.getSelectedFile().exists())
{
  int response;
  response = JOptionPane.showConfirmDialog(null,
myChooser.getSelectedFile().toString() + " exists.
Overwrite?", "Confirm Save", JOptionPane.YES_NO_OPTION,
JOptionPane.QUESTION_MESSAGE);
  if (response == JOptionPane.NO_OPTION)
  {
    return;
  }
}
// continue with code to save file
```

If you try to save a file that exists, you will see a dialog similar to this:

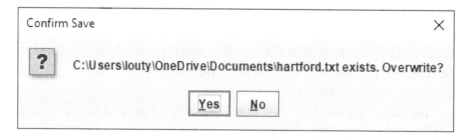

The types of files that can be saved can be established using the **fileFilter** property. The **fileFilter** property is set by the **FileNameExtensionFilter** constructor. If you choose to limit the extensions used to save a file, you need to write code to insure the extension added by the user is acceptable. And, you may want to add an extension if one is not included. The Java string methods can be used to accomplish these tasks.

Typical use of **file chooser** control (embedded) to save files:

> ➤ Declare and create file chooser control, assigning an identifiable **name**. For **myChooser**, the code is:

```
JChooser myChooser = new JChooser();
```

> ➤ Set the **dialogTitle** property.
> ➤ Add a file filter (if desired).
> ➤ Place control in layout manager.
> ➤ Add listener for and monitor **actionPerformed** event for button click event (**actionPerformed**).
> ➤ Use **getSelectedFile** method to determine file. If file exists, ask user if overwriting is desired.

Typical use of **file chooser** control (dialog box) to save files:

> ➤ Declare and create file chooser control, assigning an identifiable **name**. For **myChooser**, the code is:

```
JChooser myChooser = new JChooser();
```

> ➤ Set the **dialogTitle** property.
> ➤ Add a file filter (if desired).
> ➤ Use **showSaveDialog** method to display dialog box.
> ➤ Use **getSelectedFile** method to determine file. If file exists, ask user if overwriting is desired.

Example 6-8

Note Editor - Reading and Saving Text Files

We'll now add the capability to read in and save the contents of the text area in the **Note Editor** application we modified in **Example 6-7**. Load that application (saved as **Example6-7** project in **\LearnJava\LJ Code\Class 6** project group).

1. Add these lines to import the needed packages:

```
import javax.swing.text.*;
import javax.swing.filechooser.*;
```

2. Modify the **File** menu in your application, such that **Open** and **Save** options are included. The File menu should now read:

File
    New
    Open (**openMenuItem**)
    Save (**saveMenuItem**)
    ‾‾‾‾‾‾‾
    Exit

These new menu options (plus the needed file chooser object) require the class level declarations:

```
JMenuItem openMenuItem = new JMenuItem("Open");
JMenuItem saveMenuItem = new JMenuItem("Save");
JFileChooser myChooser = new JFileChooser();
```

and code to place the options in the menu (in frame constructor):

```
fileMenu.add(openMenuItem);
fileMenu.add(saveMenuItem);
```

and code to add the event methods (also, in frame constructor):

```
openMenuItem.addActionListener(new ActionListener()
{
  public void actionPerformed(ActionEvent e)
  {
    openMenuItemActionPerformed(e);
  }
});

saveMenuItem.addActionListener(new ActionListener()
{
  public void actionPerformed(ActionEvent e)
  {
    saveMenuItemActionPerformed(e);
  }
});
```

3. The two new menu options need code. Use this code in the
    openMenuItemActionPerformed method:

```
private void openMenuItemActionPerformed(ActionEvent e)
{
  String myLine;
  myChooser.setDialogType(JFileChooser.OPEN_DIALOG);
  myChooser.setDialogTitle("Open Text File");
  myChooser.addChoosableFileFilter(new
FileNameExtensionFilter("Text Files", "txt"));
  if (myChooser.showOpenDialog(this) ==
JFileChooser.APPROVE_OPTION)
  {
    try
    {
      // Open input file
      BufferedReader inputFile = new BufferedReader(new
FileReader(myChooser.getSelectedFile().toString()));
      editorTextArea.setText("");
      while ((myLine = inputFile.readLine()) != null)
      {
          editorTextArea.append(myLine + "\n");
      }
      inputFile.close();
    }
    catch (IOException ex)
    {
        JOptionPane.showConfirmDialog(null,
ex.getMessage(), "Error Opening File",
JOptionPane.DEFAULT_OPTION, JOptionPane.ERROR_MESSAGE);
    }
  }
}
```

This code uses a file chooser to select a file name, then the file is read into the
text area control one line at a time.

4. And for the **saveMenuItemActionPerformed** method, use this code:

```
private void saveMenuItemActionPerformed(ActionEvent e)
{
  myChooser.setDialogType(JFileChooser.SAVE_DIALOG);
  myChooser.setDialogTitle("Save Text File");
  myChooser.addChoosableFileFilter(new
FileNameExtensionFilter("Text Files", "txt"));
  int fp, lp;
  if (myChooser.showSaveDialog(this) ==
JFileChooser.APPROVE_OPTION)
  {
    // see if file already exists
    if (myChooser.getSelectedFile().exists())
    {
      int response;
      response = JOptionPane.showConfirmDialog(null,
myChooser.getSelectedFile().toString() + " exists.
Overwrite?", "Confirm Save", JOptionPane.YES_NO_OPTION,
JOptionPane.QUESTION_MESSAGE);
      if (response == JOptionPane.NO_OPTION)
      {
        return;
      }
    }
    // make sure file has txt extension
    // strip off any extension that might be there
    // then tack on txt
    String fileName =
myChooser.getSelectedFile().toString();
    int dotlocation = fileName.indexOf(".");
    if (dotlocation == -1)
    {
      // no extension
      fileName += ".txt";
    }
    else
    {
      // make sure extension is txt
      fileName = fileName.substring(0, dotlocation) +
".txt";
    }
    try
    {
      // Open output file and write
      PrintWriter outputFile = new PrintWriter(new
BufferedWriter(new FileWriter(fileName)));
```

```
      for (int i = 0; i < editorTextArea.getLineCount();
i++)
      {
        fp = editorTextArea.getLineStartOffset(i);
        lp = editorTextArea.getLineEndOffset(i);

outputFile.print(editorTextArea.getText().substring(fp,
lp));
      }
      outputFile.flush();
      outputFile.close();
    }
    catch (BadLocationException ex)
    {
    }
    catch (IOException ex)
    {
      JOptionPane.showConfirmDialog(null,
ex.getMessage(),"Error Writing File",
JOptionPane.DEFAULT_OPTION, JOptionPane.ERROR_MESSAGE);
    }
  }
}
```

There's lots going on here. Make sure you understand each step. Once a file is selected from the file chooser control, if it exists, the user is asked if overwriting is acceptable. Then, the **txt** extension is added. Then, each line of the text area control is retrieved and written to the selected file.

For reference, here is the complete **NoteEditor.java** code listing (modifications made to include the configuration file and open/save features have been shaded):

```
/*
 * NoteEditor.java
 */
package noteeditor;
import javax.swing.*;
import javax.swing.text.*;
import javax.swing.filechooser.*;
import java.awt.*;
import java.awt.event.*;
import java.io.*;
public class NoteEditor extends JFrame
{
  JMenuBar editorMenuBar = new JMenuBar();
  JMenu fileMenu = new JMenu("File");
  JMenuItem newMenuItem = new JMenuItem("New");
  JMenuItem openMenuItem = new JMenuItem("Open");
  JMenuItem saveMenuItem = new JMenuItem("Save");
  JMenuItem exitMenuItem = new JMenuItem("Exit");
  JMenu formatMenu = new JMenu("Format");
  JCheckBoxMenuItem boldMenuItem = new
JCheckBoxMenuItem("Bold", false);
  JCheckBoxMenuItem italicMenuItem = new
JCheckBoxMenuItem("Italic", false);
  JMenu sizeMenu = new JMenu("Size");
  ButtonGroup sizeGroup = new ButtonGroup();
  JRadioButtonMenuItem smallMenuItem = new
JRadioButtonMenuItem("Small", true);
  JRadioButtonMenuItem mediumMenuItem = new
JRadioButtonMenuItem("Medium", false);
  JRadioButtonMenuItem largeMenuItem = new
JRadioButtonMenuItem("Large", false);
  JMenu helpMenu = new JMenu("Help");
  JMenuItem aboutMenuItem = new JMenuItem("About Note
Editor");
  JScrollPane editorPane = new JScrollPane();
  JTextArea editorTextArea = new JTextArea();
  JFileChooser myChooser = new JFileChooser();

  public static void main(String args[])
  {
    // construct frame
    new NoteEditor().show();
```

```
  }

  public NoteEditor()
  {
    // frame constructor
    setTitle("Note Editor");

    setResizable(false);
    addWindowListener(new WindowAdapter()
    {
      public void windowClosing(WindowEvent e)
      {
        exitForm(e);
      }
    });

    // build menu
    setJMenuBar(editorMenuBar);
    fileMenu.setMnemonic('F');
    formatMenu.setMnemonic('O');
    helpMenu.setMnemonic('H');
    newMenuItem.setAccelerator(KeyStroke.getKeyStroke('N',
Event.CTRL_MASK));
    boldMenuItem.setAccelerator(KeyStroke.getKeyStroke('B',
Event.CTRL_MASK));
    italicMenuItem.setAccelerator(KeyStroke.getKeyStroke('I',
Event.CTRL_MASK));
    smallMenuItem.setAccelerator(KeyStroke.getKeyStroke('S',
Event.CTRL_MASK));
    mediumMenuItem.setAccelerator(KeyStroke.getKeyStroke('M',
Event.CTRL_MASK));
    largeMenuItem.setAccelerator(KeyStroke.getKeyStroke('L',
Event.CTRL_MASK));
    editorMenuBar.add(fileMenu);
    fileMenu.add(newMenuItem);
    fileMenu.add(openMenuItem);
    fileMenu.add(saveMenuItem);
    fileMenu.addSeparator();
    fileMenu.add(exitMenuItem);
    editorMenuBar.add(formatMenu);
    formatMenu.add(boldMenuItem);
    formatMenu.add(italicMenuItem);
    formatMenu.add(sizeMenu);
    sizeMenu.add(smallMenuItem);
    sizeMenu.add(mediumMenuItem);
    sizeMenu.add(largeMenuItem);
    sizeGroup.add(smallMenuItem);
```

```java
sizeGroup.add(mediumMenuItem);
sizeGroup.add(largeMenuItem);
editorMenuBar.add(helpMenu);
helpMenu.add(aboutMenuItem);

newMenuItem.addActionListener(new ActionListener()
{
  public void actionPerformed(ActionEvent e)
  {
    newMenuItemActionPerformed(e);
  }
});
openMenuItem.addActionListener(new ActionListener()
{
  public void actionPerformed(ActionEvent e)
  {
    openMenuItemActionPerformed(e);
  }
});
saveMenuItem.addActionListener(new ActionListener()
{
  public void actionPerformed(ActionEvent e)
  {
    saveMenuItemActionPerformed(e);
  }
});
exitMenuItem.addActionListener(new ActionListener()
{
  public void actionPerformed(ActionEvent e)
  {
    exitMenuItemActionPerformed(e);
  }
});
boldMenuItem.addActionListener(new ActionListener()
{
  public void actionPerformed(ActionEvent e)
  {
    formatMenuItemActionPerformed(e);
  }
});
italicMenuItem.addActionListener(new ActionListener()
{
  public void actionPerformed(ActionEvent e)
  {
    formatMenuItemActionPerformed(e);
  }
});
```

```java
    smallMenuItem.addActionListener(new ActionListener()
    {
      public void actionPerformed(ActionEvent e)
      {
        formatMenuItemActionPerformed(e);
      }
    });
    mediumMenuItem.addActionListener(new ActionListener()
    {
      public void actionPerformed(ActionEvent e)
      {
        formatMenuItemActionPerformed(e);
      }
    });
    largeMenuItem.addActionListener(new ActionListener()
    {
      public void actionPerformed(ActionEvent e)
      {
        formatMenuItemActionPerformed(e);
      }
    });
    aboutMenuItem.addActionListener(new ActionListener()
    {
      public void actionPerformed(ActionEvent e)
      {
        aboutMenuItemActionPerformed(e);
      }
    });

    getContentPane().setLayout(new GridBagLayout());
    // position scroll pane and text box
    GridBagConstraints gridConstraints = new
GridBagConstraints();
    editorPane.setPreferredSize(new Dimension(300, 150));
    editorPane.setViewportView(editorTextArea);
    editorTextArea.setFont(new Font("Arial", Font.PLAIN,
12));
    editorTextArea.setLineWrap(true);
    editorTextArea.setWrapStyleWord(true);
    gridConstraints.gridx = 0;
    gridConstraints.gridy = 0;
    getContentPane().add(editorPane, gridConstraints);

    pack();
    Dimension screenSize =
Toolkit.getDefaultToolkit().getScreenSize();
```

```
        setBounds((int) (0.5 * (screenSize.width - getWidth())),
(int) (0.5 * (screenSize.height - getHeight())), getWidth(),
getHeight());


     int fontSize;
     try
     {
       // Open configuration file and set font values
       BufferedReader inputFile = new BufferedReader(new
FileReader("note.ini"));

boldMenuItem.setSelected(Boolean.valueOf(inputFile.readLine()
).booleanValue());

italicMenuItem.setSelected(Boolean.valueOf(inputFile.readLine
()).booleanValue());
       fontSize =
Integer.valueOf(inputFile.readLine()).intValue();
       inputFile.close();
     }
     catch (IOException ex)
     {
        JOptionPane.showConfirmDialog(null, ex.getMessage(),
"Error Reading Configuration File",
JOptionPane.DEFAULT_OPTION, JOptionPane.ERROR_MESSAGE);
       boldMenuItem.setSelected(false);
       italicMenuItem.setSelected(false);
       fontSize = 1;
     }
     switch (fontSize)
     {
       case 1:
         smallMenuItem.doClick();
         break;
       case 2:
         mediumMenuItem.doClick();
         break;
       case 3:
         largeMenuItem.doClick();
         break;
     }
  }
  private void newMenuItemActionPerformed(ActionEvent e)
  {
     // if user wants new file, clear out text
     if (JOptionPane.showConfirmDialog(null, "Are you sure you
want to start a new file?", "New File",
```

```
JOptionPane.YES_NO_OPTION, JOptionPane.QUESTION_MESSAGE) ==
JOptionPane.YES_OPTION)
    {
       editorTextArea.setText("");
    }
  }
  private void openMenuItemActionPerformed(ActionEvent e)
  {
    String myLine;
    myChooser.setDialogType(JFileChooser.OPEN_DIALOG);
    myChooser.setDialogTitle("Open Text File");
  myChooser.addChoosableFileFilter(new
FileNameExtensionFilter("Text Files", "txt"));
    if (myChooser.showOpenDialog(this) ==
JFileChooser.APPROVE_OPTION)
      try
      {
        // Open input file
        BufferedReader inputFile = new BufferedReader(new
FileReader(myChooser.getSelectedFile().toString()));
        editorTextArea.setText("");
        while ((myLine = inputFile.readLine()) != null)
        {
            editorTextArea.append(myLine + "\n");
        }
        inputFile.close();
      }
      catch (IOException ex)
      {
          JOptionPane.showConfirmDialog(null, ex.getMessage(),
"Error Opening File", JOptionPane.DEFAULT_OPTION,
JOptionPane.ERROR_MESSAGE);
      }
    }
  }

  private void saveMenuItemActionPerformed(ActionEvent e)
  {
    myChooser.setDialogType(JFileChooser.SAVE_DIALOG);
    myChooser.setDialogTitle("Save Text File");
    myChooser.addChoosableFileFilter(new
FileNameExtensionFilter("Text Files", "txt"));
    int fp, lp;
    if (myChooser.showSaveDialog(this) ==
JFileChooser.APPROVE_OPTION)
    {
      // see if file already exists
```

```java
        if (myChooser.getSelectedFile().exists())
        {
            int response;
            response = JOptionPane.showConfirmDialog(null,
myChooser.getSelectedFile().toString() + " exists.
Overwrite?", "Confirm Save", JOptionPane.YES_NO_OPTION,
JOptionPane.QUESTION_MESSAGE);
            if (response == JOptionPane.NO_OPTION)
            {
                return;
            }
        }
        // make sure file has txt extension
        // strip off any extension that might be there
        // then tack on txt
        String fileName =
myChooser.getSelectedFile().toString();
        int dotlocation = fileName.indexOf(".");
        if (dotlocation == -1)
        {
            // no extension
            fileName += ".txt";
        }
        else
        {
            // make sure extension is txt
            fileName = fileName.substring(0, dotlocation) +
".txt";
        }
        try
        {
            // Open output file and write
            PrintWriter outputFile = new PrintWriter(new
BufferedWriter(new FileWriter(fileName)));
            for (int i = 0; i < editorTextArea.getLineCount();
i++)
            {
                fp = editorTextArea.getLineStartOffset(i);
                lp = editorTextArea.getLineEndOffset(i);

outputFile.print(editorTextArea.getText().substring(fp, lp));
            }
            outputFile.flush();
            outputFile.close();
        }
        catch (BadLocationException ex)
        {
```

```
      }
      catch (IOException ex)
      {
        JOptionPane.showConfirmDialog(null, ex.getMessage(),
"Error Writing File", JOptionPane.DEFAULT_OPTION,
JOptionPane.ERROR_MESSAGE);
      }
    }
  }

  private void exitMenuItemActionPerformed(ActionEvent e)
  {
    exitForm(null);
  }

  private void formatMenuItemActionPerformed(ActionEvent e)
  {
    // Put together font based on menu selections
    int newFont = Font.PLAIN;
    int fontSize = 12;
    if (boldMenuItem.isSelected())
    {
      newFont += Font.BOLD;
    }
    if (italicMenuItem.isSelected())
    {
      newFont += Font.ITALIC;
    }
    if (smallMenuItem.isSelected())
    {
      fontSize = 12;
    }
    else if (mediumMenuItem.isSelected())
    {
      fontSize = 18;
    }
    else
    {
      fontSize = 24;
    }
    editorTextArea.setFont(new Font("Arial", newFont,
fontSize));
  }

  private void aboutMenuItemActionPerformed(ActionEvent e)
  {
```

```
    JOptionPane.showConfirmDialog(null, "About Note
Editor\nCopyright 2003", "Note Editor",
JOptionPane.DEFAULT_OPTION, JOptionPane.INFORMATION_MESSAGE);
  }

  private void exitForm(WindowEvent e)
  {
    try
    {
      // Open configuration file and write
      PrintWriter outputFile = new PrintWriter(new
BufferedWriter(new FileWriter("note.ini")));
      outputFile.println(boldMenuItem.isSelected());
      outputFile.println(italicMenuItem.isSelected());
      if (smallMenuItem.isSelected())
      {
        outputFile.println("1");
      }
      else if (mediumMenuItem.isSelected())
      {
        outputFile.println("2");
      }
      else if (largeMenuItem.isSelected())
      {
        outputFile.println("3");
      }
      outputFile.flush();
      outputFile.close();
    }
    catch (IOException ex)
    {
      JOptionPane.showConfirmDialog(null, ex.getMessage(),
"Error Writing Configuration File",
JOptionPane.DEFAULT_OPTION, JOptionPane.ERROR_MESSAGE);
    }
    finally
    {
      System.exit(0);
    }
  }
}
```

Save your application (saved as **Example6-8** project in the **\LearnJava\LJ Code\Class 6** project group). Run it and test the **Open** and **Save** functions. Check out the "overwrite protection" when saving an existing file. Note you have to save a file before you can open one. Here's a run with the new **File** menu expanded:

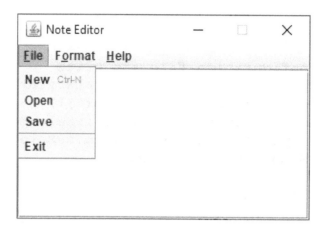

Note, too, that after opening a file, text is displayed based on current format settings. It would be nice to save formatting information along with the text. You could do this by saving an additional file with the format settings (bold, italic status and font size). Then, when opening the text file, open the accompanying format file and set the saved format. Note this is much like having a configuration file for each saved text file. See if you can make these modifications.

Another thing you could try: Add a message box that appears when you try to **Exit**. Have it ask if you wish to save your file before exiting - provide **Yes, No, Cancel** buttons. Program the code corresponding to each possible response. Use calls to existing methods, if possible.

Class Review

After completing this class, you should understand:

➤ How to implement run-time exception handling in a Java method
➤ How to use the various capabilities of the Java debugger to find and eliminate logic errors
➤ How to read and write sequential files (and the difference between using **print** and **println** functions)
➤ How to parse and build a text string
➤ How to read tokenized lines of data
➤ How to use configuration files in an application
➤ How to use the **JFileChooser** control to save files
➤ How to save and write the text property of a text area control

Practice Problems 6

Problem 6-1. Debugging Problem. Load the **Problem6-1** project in the **\LearnJava\LJ Code\Class 6** project group. It's the temperature conversion example from Class 4 with some errors introduced. Run the application. It shouldn't run. Debug the program and get it running correctly.

Problem 6-2. Option Saving Problem. Load **Problem3-1** project (in the **\LearnJava\LJ Code\Class 3** project group), the practice problem used to examine sample message boxes. Modify this program to allow saving of the user inputs when application ends. Use a text file to save the information. When the application begins, it should reflect this set of saved inputs.

Problem 6-3. Text File Problem. Build an application that lets you look through your computer directories for text files (.txt extension) and view those files in a text area control. The image viewer (Example 4-4) built in Class 4 is a good starting point.

Problem 6-4. Data File Problem. In the **\LearnJava\LJ Code\Class 6\Problem6-4** project folder is a file entitled **MAR95.DAT**. Open this file using the a text editor. The first several lines of the file are:

```
144
"4/27/95","Detroit        ",2,3,0,"Opening Night  "
"4/28/95","Detroit        ",2,8,2,"               "
"4/29/95","Detroit        ",2,11,1,"              "
"4/30/95","Detroit        ",2,1,10,"              "
"5/1/95","Texas           ",1,4,1,"            "
"5/2/95","Texas           ",1,15,3,"             "
"5/3/95","Texas           ",1,5,1,"            "
"5/5/95","California       ",1,0,10,"             "
"5/6/95","California       ",1,5,7,"            "
"5/7/95","California       ",1,3,2,"            "
```

This file chronicles the strike-shortened 1995 season of the Seattle Mariners baseball team, their most exciting year up until 2001. (Our apologies to foreign readers who don't understand the game of baseball!) The first line tells how many lines are in the file. Each subsequent line represents a single game.

There are six variables on each line:

Variable Number	Variable Type	Description
1	String	Date of Game
2	String	Opponent
3	Integer	(1-Away game, 2-Home game)
4	Integer	Mariners runs
5	Integer	Opponent runs
6	String	Comment

Write an application that reads this file, determines which team won each game and outputs to another file (a comma-separated, or **csv**, file) the game number and current Mariners winning or losing streak (consecutive wins or losses). Use positive integers for wins, negative integers for losses.

As an example, the corresponding output file for the lines displayed above would be:

1,1 (a win)
2,2 (a win)
3,3 (a win)
4,-1 (a loss)
5,1 (a win)
6,2 (a win)
7,3 (a win)
8,-1 (a loss)
9,-2 (a loss)
10,1 (a win)

There will be 144 lines in this output file. Load the resulting file in a spreadsheet application (Excel will work) and obtain a bar chart for the output data.

Exercise 6-1

Information Tracking

Design and develop an application that allows the user to enter (on a daily basis) some piece of information that is to be saved for future review and reference. Examples could be stock price, weight, or high temperature for the day. The input screen should display the current date and an input box for the desired information. All values should be saved on disk for future retrieval and update. A scroll bar should be available for reviewing all previously-stored values.

Exercise 6-2

'Recent Files' Menu Option

Under the **File** menu on nearly every application (that opens files) is a list of the four most recently-used files (usually right above the **Exit** option). Modify your information tracker to implement such a feature. This is not trivial -- there are lots of things to consider. For example, you'll need a file to store the last four file names. You need to open that file and initialize the corresponding menu entries when you run the application -- you need to rewrite that file when you exit the application. You need logic to re-order file names when a new file is opened or saved. You need logic to establish new menu items as new files are used. You'll need additional exception handling in the open procedure, in case a file selected from the menu no longer exists. Like I said, a lot to consider here.

7

Graphics Techniques with Java

Review and Preview

In Class 4, we looked at using the label control to display graphics files. In this class, we extend our graphics programming skills to learn how to perform simple animations, build little games, draw lines, rectangles and ellipses and do some basic plotting of lines, bars and pie segments.

Most of the examples in this class will be relatively short. We show you how to do many graphics tasks. You can expand the examples to fit your needs.

Simple Animation

One of the more fun things to do with Java programs is to create animated graphics. We'll look at a few simple **animation** techniques here. In Class 8, we look at more detailed animations.

One of the simplest animation effects is achieved by **toggling** between two **images**. For example, you may have a picture of a stoplight with a red light. By quickly changing this picture to one with a green light, we achieve a dynamic effect - animation. Other two image animations could be open and closed file drawers, open and closed mail or smiling and frowning faces. The **label** control is used to achieve this animated effect using **ImageIcon** objects.

The idea here is simple. The approach is to create an **image icon** object for each picture in the animation sequence (here, just two pictures). Recall (from Class 4) the code to do this (for object **myImage**) is:

```
ImageIcon myImage = new ImageIcon(myFile);
```

where **myFile** is the file with the displayed graphic (either a **gif** or **jpg** file). Initialize the "viewing" label control's icon property to the first **image icon** object. The code to do this for a label control named **myLabel** is:

```
myLabel.setIcon(myImage);
```

Upon detection of some toggling event (clicking on the label control or a button), simply set the **icon** property of this displaying control to the **image icon** object of the other picture.

The Java code for 'two-state' simple animation is straightforward. Define a class level scope variable (**pictureNumber**) that keeps track of the currently displayed picture (either a 0 or 1).

```
int pictureNumber;
```

Then, in the toggling event procedure use this code (**myLabel** is the displaying control, **myImage0** is the first graphic (an **ImageIcon** object), **myImage1** is the 'toggled' graphic):

```
if (pictureNumber == 0)
{
  myLabel.setIcon(myImage0);
  pictureNumber = 1;
}
else
{
  myLabel.setIcon(myImage1);
  pictureNumber = 0;
}
```

One question you may be asking is where do I get the graphics for toggling pictures? Search web sites and find graphics files available for purchase. You've probably seen the CD-ROM sets with 100,000 graphics! Also, look for **gif** and **jpg** files installed on your computer by other applications.

Example 7-1

Simple Animation

Start a new empty project in **NetBeans**. Name the project **SimpleAnimation**.
Delete the default code in Java file named **SimpleAnimation**. We'll build a
simple two-picture animation example showing mail entering a mailbox. The
initial finished frame looks like this:

The graphics used are **image0.gif** and **image1.gif** and are located in the
\LearnJava\LJ Code\Class 7\Example7-1 folder. Copy these graphic files into
your project's folder:

image0.gif   image1.gif

Place a single label control in a frame. The **GridBagLayout** is:

	gridx = 0
gridy = 0	**displayLabel**

Also include two image icon objects (**image0** and **image1**). Set the following properties:

SimpleAnimation Frame:

resizable	false

image0:

ImageIcon	image0.gif

image1:

ImageIcon	image1.gif

displayLabel:

preferredSize	(image0.getIconWidth(), image0.getIconHeight())
icon	image0
gridx	0
gridy	0
insets	(10, 10, 10, 10)

Build the basic framework:

```java
/*
 * SimpleAnimation.java
 */
package simpleanimation;
import javax.swing.*;
import java.awt.*;
import java.awt.event.*;
public class SimpleAnimation extends JFrame
{
  public static void main(String args[])
  {
    // create frame
    new SimpleAnimation().show();
  }
  public SimpleAnimation()
  {
    // frame constructor
    setResizable(false);
    addWindowListener(new WindowAdapter()
    {
      public void windowClosing(WindowEvent evt)
      {
        exitForm(evt);
      }
    });
    getContentPane().setLayout(new GridBagLayout());
    pack();
    Dimension screenSize =
Toolkit.getDefaultToolkit().getScreenSize();
    setBounds((int) (0.5 * (screenSize.width -
getWidth())), (int) (0.5 * (screenSize.height -
getHeight())), getWidth(), getHeight());
  }
  private void exitForm(WindowEvent evt)
  {
    System.exit(0);
  }
}
```

Run to test.

We will add the controls and write all the code at once (since the code is very simple). Use these class level scope declarations:

```
JLabel displayLabel = new JLabel();
ImageIcon image0 = new ImageIcon("image0.gif");
ImageIcon image1 = new ImageIcon("image1.gif");
int pictureNumber = 0;
```

This establishes the displaying label control and the images to display. Now, position and initialize the label control:

```
GridBagConstraints gridConstraints = new
GridBagConstraints();
displayLabel.setPreferredSize(new
Dimension(image0.getIconWidth(), image0.getIconHeight()));
displayLabel.setIcon(image0);
gridConstraints.gridx = 0;
gridConstraints.gridy = 0;
gridConstraints.insets = new Insets(10, 10, 10, 10);
getContentPane().add(displayLabel, gridConstraints);
displayLabel.addMouseListener(new MouseAdapter()
{
  public void mouseClicked(MouseEvent e)
  {
    displayMouseClicked(e);
  }
});
```

Use the following code in the **displayMouseClicked** method that toggles the
display:

```
private void displayMouseClicked(MouseEvent e)
{
  if (pictureNumber == 0)
  {
    displayLabel.setIcon(image0);
    pictureNumber = 1;
  }
  else
  {
    displayLabel.setIcon(image1);
    pictureNumber = 0;
  }
}
```

The final **SimpleAnimation.java** code listing (changes to framework are shaded):

```
/*
 * SimpleAnimation.java
 */
package simpleanimation;
import javax.swing.*;
import java.awt.*;
import java.awt.event.*;
public class SimpleAnimation extends JFrame
{
  JLabel displayLabel = new JLabel();
  ImageIcon image0 = new ImageIcon("image0.gif");
  ImageIcon image1 = new ImageIcon("image1.gif");
  int pictureNumber = 0;
  public static void main(String args[])
  {
    // create frame
    new SimpleAnimation().show();
  }
  public SimpleAnimation()
  {
    // frame constructor
    setResizable(false);
    addWindowListener(new WindowAdapter()
    {
      public void windowClosing(WindowEvent evt)
      {
        exitForm(evt);
```

```
      }
    });
    getContentPane().setLayout(new GridBagLayout());
    // position controls
    GridBagConstraints gridConstraints = new
GridBagConstraints();
    displayLabel.setPreferredSize(new
Dimension(image0.getIconWidth(), image0.getIconHeight()));
    displayLabel.setIcon(image0);
    gridConstraints.gridx = 0;
    gridConstraints.gridy = 0;
    gridConstraints.insets = new Insets(10, 10, 10, 10);
    getContentPane().add(displayLabel, gridConstraints);
    displayLabel.addMouseListener(new MouseAdapter()
    {
      public void mouseClicked(MouseEvent e)
      {
        displayMouseClicked(e);
      }
    });
    pack();
    Dimension screenSize =
Toolkit.getDefaultToolkit().getScreenSize();
    setBounds((int) (0.5 * (screenSize.width - getWidth())),
(int) (0.5 * (screenSize.height - getHeight())), getWidth(),
getHeight());
  }
  private void displayMouseClicked(MouseEvent e)
  {
    if (pictureNumber == 0)
    {
      displayLabel.setIcon(image0);
      pictureNumber = 1;
    }
    else
    {
      displayLabel.setIcon(image1);
      pictureNumber = 0;
    }
  }
  private void exitForm(WindowEvent evt)
  {
    System.exit(0);
  }
}
```

Run the project. Click the mailbox graphic and watch the letter go in and out. Here's the sequence:

Save the project (saved as **Example7-1** project in **\LearnJava\LJ Code\Class 7** program group).

Timer Object

If want to expand simple animation to more than two graphics, the first step is to add additional images to the sequence. But, then how do we cycle through the images? We could ask a user to keep clicking on a button or image to see all the images. That's one solution, but perhaps not a desirable one. What would be nice is to have the images cycle without user interaction. To do this, we need to have the capability to generate events without user interaction. The Java **timer** object (looked at very briefly way back in a Class 1 problem) provides such a capability.

A timer generates an event every **delay** milliseconds. The code in the timer's corresponding **actionPerformed** method is executed with each such event. The timer object is very easy to implement and provides useful functionality beyond simple animation tasks. Other control events can be detected while the timer control processes events in the background. This multi-tasking allows more than one thing to be happening in your application.

Timer Properties:

> **delay**   Number of milliseconds (there are 1000 milliseconds in one second) between each invocation of the timer object's **actionPerformed** method.
> **running**   Boolean value indicating if timer is running.

Timer Methods:

> **start**   Used to start timer object.
> **stop**   Used to stop timer.
> **isRunning**   Method that returns **boolean** value indicating whether timer is running (generating events).

Timer Events:

> **actionPerformed**   Event method invoked every **delay** milliseconds while timer object's **running** property is **true**.

To use a timer object, you first declare it using the standard syntax. For a timer named **myTimer**, the code is:

```
Timer myTimer;
```

The constructor for the timer object specifies the **delay** and adds the event (**actionPerformed**) method, using an **ActionListener**, in a single step. The syntax is:

```
myTimer = new Timer(delay, new ActionListener()
{
  public void actionPerformed(ActionEvent e)
  {
    myTimerActionPerformed(e);
  }
});
```

And, the corresponding event code would be placed in a **myTimerActionPerformed** method:

```
private void myTimerActionPerformed(ActionEvent e)
{
    [method code]
}
```

To use the **timer** object, we add it to our application the same as any object. You write code in the timer object's **actionPerformed** method. This is the code you want to repeat every **delay** milliseconds. In the animation-sequencing example, this is where you would change the label control's **icon** property.

You 'turn on' a timer in code using the **start** method:

```
myTimer.start();
```

and it is turned off using the **stop** method:

```
myTimer.stop();
```

To check if the timer is on, use the **isRunning** method:

```
myTimer.isRunning();
```

If this method returns a **boolean** true, the timer is on. When first created, the timer is off.

Applications can (and many times do) have multiple timer objects. You need separate timer objects (and event methods) if you have events that occur with different regularity (different **delay** values). Timer objects are used for two primary purposes. First, you use timer objects to periodically repeat some code segment. This is like our animation example. Second, you can use a timer object to implement some 'wait time' established by the **delay** property. In this case, you simply start the timer and when the delay is reached, have the **actionPerformed** event turn its corresponding timer off.

Typical use of **timer** object:

> Declare timer, assigning an identifiable **name**. For **myTimer**, the statement is:

```
Timer myTimer;
```

> Establish a **delay** value. Create the timer using specified constructor, adding the **actionPerformed** method. Write the method code.
> At some point in your application, start the timer. Also, have capability to turn the timer off, when desired.

Example 7-2

Timer Example

Start a new empty project in **NetBeans**. Name it **TimerExample**. Delete the
default code in Java file named **TimerExample**. We want an application that
generates a beep every second. The finished frame appears as:

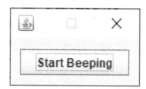

1. Place a single button control on the frame. The **GridBagLayout** is:

	gridx = 0
gridy = 0	**beepButton**

Also include a timer object (**beepTimer**). Set the following properties:

TimerExample Frame:
      resizable   false

beepButton:
      text   Start Beeping
      gridx   0
      gridy   0
      insets   (10, 10, 10, 10)

beepTimer:
      delay   1000

We don't build this short example in steps. We just present the code, shading the portions establishing the timer and button control, with their corresponding methods. You should be able to follow this code. The complete **TimerExample.java** code listing:

```java
/*
 * TimerExample.java
 */
package timerexample;
import javax.swing.*;
import java.awt.*;
import java.awt.event.*;
public class TimerExample extends JFrame
{
  Timer beepTimer;
  JButton beepButton = new JButton();
  public static void main(String args[])
  {
    // create frame
    new TimerExample().show();
  }
  public TimerExample()
  {
    // frame constructor
    setResizable(false);
    addWindowListener(new WindowAdapter()
    {
      public void windowClosing(WindowEvent evt)
      {
        exitForm(evt);
      }
    });
    getContentPane().setLayout(new GridBagLayout());
    // position controls

    GridBagConstraints gridConstraints = new
GridBagConstraints();
    beepButton.setText("Start Beeping");
    gridConstraints.gridx = 0;
    gridConstraints.gridy = 0;
    gridConstraints.insets = new Insets(10, 10, 10, 10);
    getContentPane().add(beepButton, gridConstraints);
    beepButton.addActionListener(new ActionListener()
    {
    public void actionPerformed(ActionEvent e)
    {
```

```
        beepButtonActionPerformed(e);
      }
    });
    beepTimer = new Timer(1000, new ActionListener()
    {
    public void actionPerformed(ActionEvent e)
    {
      beepTimerActionPerformed(e);
    }
    });
    pack();
    Dimension screenSize =
Toolkit.getDefaultToolkit().getScreenSize();
    setBounds((int) (0.5 * (screenSize.width - getWidth())),
(int) (0.5 * (screenSize.height - getHeight())), getWidth(),
getHeight());
  }
  private void beepButtonActionPerformed(ActionEvent e)
  {
    // toggle timer and button text
    if (beepTimer.isRunning())
    {
      beepTimer.stop();
      beepButton.setText("Start Beeping");
    }
    else
    {
      beepTimer.start();
      beepButton.setText("Stop Beeping");
    }
  }
  private void beepTimerActionPerformed(ActionEvent e)
  {
    Toolkit.getDefaultToolkit().beep();
  }
  private void exitForm(WindowEvent evt)
  {
    System.exit(0);
  }
}
```

In particular, notice the code constructing the timer (**beepTimer**) with a delay of one second (1000 milliseconds):

```
beepTimer = new Timer(1000, new ActionListener()
{
  public void actionPerformed(ActionEvent e)
  {
    beepTimerActionPerformed(e);
  }
});
```

And notice how the timer is toggled on and off in the **beepButtonActionPerformed** method:

```
private void beepButtonActionPerformed(ActionEvent e)
{
  // toggle timer and button text
  if (beepTimer.isRunning())
  {
    beepTimer.stop();
    beepButton.setText("Start Beeping");
  }
  else
  {
    beepTimer.start();
    beepButton.setText("Stop Beeping");
  }
}
```

Run the project. Start and stop the beeping until you get tired of hearing it. If you don't hear a beep, it's probably because your computer has no internal speaker. The beep sound does not usually play through sound cards. Save the application (saved as **Example7-2** project in **\LearnJava\LJ Code\Class 7** program group).

Basic Animation

We return to the question of how to do animation with more than two images. More detailed animations are obtained by rotating through several images - each a slight change in the previous picture. This is the principle motion pictures are based on. In a movie, pictures flash by us at 24 frames per second and our eyes are tricked into believing things are smoothly moving.

Basic animation is done in a Java application by creating **image icon** objects for each picture in the animation sequence. A timer object changes the display in a label control. With each **actionPerformed** event, a new image is seen. Once the end of the sequence is reached, you can 'loop' back to the first image and repeat or you can simply stop. To achieve this effect in code, we have a class level scope variable that keeps track of the currently displayed **pictureNumber**:

```
int pictureNumber;
```

You need to initialize this at some point, either in this declaration or when you start the timer.

Assume we have **n** pictures to cycle through. We will have **n** image icon objects with the respective animation pictures (from graphics files, numbered **0** to **n-1**). If **displayLabel** is the displaying label control and **image0** through **imagen-1** are the animation images, the code in the timer object's **actionPerformed** method is:

```
switch (pictureNumber)
{
  case 0:
    displayLabel.setIcon(image0);
    break;
  case 1:
    displayLabel.setIcon(image1);
    break;
  case 2:
    displayLabel.setIcon(image2);
    break;
    .
  // there will be a case for each image up to n-1
    .
}
pictureNumber++;
```

You need to check when **pictureNumber** reaches n. When it does, you can stop the sequence (stop the timer). Or, you can reset **pictureNumber** to **0** to repeat the animation sequence.

Example 7-3

Basic Animation

Start a new empty project in **NetBeans**. Name the project **SpinningEarth**. Delete the default code in Java file named **SpinningEarth**. We'll build an animation example that uses the timer control to display a spinning earth! The frame will look like this:

The graphics used are **earth0.gif**, **earth1.gif**, **earth2.gif**, **earth3.gif**, **earth4.gif**, and **earth5.gif** and are located in the **\LearnJava\LJ Code\Class 7\Example7-3** folder. Copy these graphic files into your project's folder:

| earth0.gif | earth1.gif | earth2.gif | earth3.gif | earth4.gif | earth5.gif |

1. Place a label control and a button control on the frame. The **GridBagLayout** is:

	gridx = 0
gridy = 0	**displayLabel**
gridy = 1	**earthButton**

Add a timer object (**earthTimer**) and six image icon objects (**image0**, **image1**, **image2**, **image3**, **image4**, **image5**).

Set the following properties:

SpinningEarth Frame:

resizable	false

displayLabel:

preferredSize	(image0.getIconWidth(), image0.getIconHeight())
icon	image0
gridx	0
gridy	0
insets	(10, 10, 10, 10)

earthButton:

text	Start Spinning
gridx	0
gridy	1
insets	(10, 10, 10, 10)

earthTimer:

delay	500

image0:

ImageIcon	earth0.gif

image1:

ImageIcon	earth1.gif

image2:

ImageIcon	earth2.gif

image3:

ImageIcon	earth3.gif

image4:

ImageIcon	earth4.gif

image5:

ImageIcon	earth5.gif

2. Build the basic framework:

```
/*
 * SpinningEarth.java
 */
package spinningearth;
import javax.swing.*;
import java.awt.*;
import java.awt.event.*;
public class SpinningEarth extends JFrame
{
  public static void main(String args[])
  {
    // create frame
    new SpinningEarth().show();
  }
  public SpinningEarth()
  {
    // frame constructor
    setResizable(false);
    addWindowListener(new WindowAdapter()
    {
      public void windowClosing(WindowEvent evt)
      {
        exitForm(evt);
      }
    });
    getContentPane().setLayout(new GridBagLayout());

    pack();
    Dimension screenSize =
  Toolkit.getDefaultToolkit().getScreenSize();
    setBounds((int) (0.5 * (screenSize.width -
  getWidth())), (int) (0.5 * (screenSize.height -
  getHeight())), getWidth(), getHeight());
  }
  private void exitForm(WindowEvent evt)
  {
    System.exit(0);
  }
}
```

Run to test.

3. Now, add controls and other objects and establish methods. Add these class level declarations:

```
JLabel displayLabel = new JLabel();
JButton earthButton = new JButton();
ImageIcon image0 = new ImageIcon("earth0.gif");
ImageIcon image1 = new ImageIcon("earth1.gif");
ImageIcon image2 = new ImageIcon("earth2.gif");
ImageIcon image3 = new ImageIcon("earth3.gif");
ImageIcon image4 = new ImageIcon("earth4.gif");
ImageIcon image5 = new ImageIcon("earth5.gif");
Timer earthTimer;
```

Position and add controls; create timer object:

```
GridBagConstraints gridConstraints = new
GridBagConstraints();
displayLabel.setPreferredSize(new
Dimension(image0.getIconWidth(), image0.getIconHeight()));
displayLabel.setIcon(image0);
gridConstraints.gridx = 0;
gridConstraints.gridy = 0;
gridConstraints.insets = new Insets(10, 10, 10, 10);
getContentPane().add(displayLabel, gridConstraints);
gridConstraints = new GridBagConstraints();
earthButton.setText("Start Spinning");
gridConstraints.gridx = 0;
gridConstraints.gridy = 1;
gridConstraints.insets = new Insets(10, 10, 10, 10);
getContentPane().add(earthButton, gridConstraints);
earthButton.addActionListener(new ActionListener()
{
  public void actionPerformed(ActionEvent e)
  {
    earthButtonActionPerformed(e);
  }
});
earthTimer = new Timer(500, new ActionListener()
{
  public void actionPerformed(ActionEvent e)
  {
    earthTimerActionPerformed(e);
  }
});
```

And, add two empty event methods:

```
private void earthButtonActionPerformed(ActionEvent e)
{
}

private void earthTimerActionPerformed(ActionEvent e)
{
}
```

Run to check the control layout:

4. Now, we write code for the event methods: Use this class level scope declaration that declares and initializes **pictureNumber**:

```
int pictureNumber = 0;
```

5. Use the following code in the **earthButtonActionPerformed** method to toggle the timer:

```
private void earthButtonActionPerformed(ActionEvent e)
{
  // toggle timer and button text
  if (earthTimer.isRunning())
  {
    earthTimer.stop();
    earthButton.setText("Start Spinning");
  }
  else
  {
    earthTimer.start();
    earthButton.setText("Stop Spinning");
  }
}
```

6. Use this code in the **earthTimerActionPerformed** method to cycle through the different pictures (I choose to repeat the sequence when the end is reached):

```java
private void earthTimerActionPerformed(ActionEvent e)
{
  switch (pictureNumber)
  {
  case 0:
    displayLabel.setIcon(image0);
    break;
  case 1:
    displayLabel.setIcon(image1);
    break;
  case 2:
    displayLabel.setIcon(image2);
    break;
  case 3:
    displayLabel.setIcon(image3);
    break;
  case 4:
    displayLabel.setIcon(image4);
    break;
  case 5:
    displayLabel.setIcon(image5);
    break;
  }
  pictureNumber++;
  if (pictureNumber == 6)
  {
    pictureNumber = 0;
  }
}
```

The complete **SpinningEarth.java** code (code added to framework is shaded):

```java
/*
 * SpinningEarth.java
 */
package spinningearth;
import javax.swing.*;
import java.awt.*;
import java.awt.event.*;

public class SpinningEarth extends JFrame
{

  JLabel displayLabel = new JLabel();
  JButton earthButton = new JButton();
  ImageIcon image0 = new ImageIcon("earth0.gif");
  ImageIcon image1 = new ImageIcon("earth1.gif");
  ImageIcon image2 = new ImageIcon("earth2.gif");
  ImageIcon image3 = new ImageIcon("earth3.gif");
  ImageIcon image4 = new ImageIcon("earth4.gif");
  ImageIcon image5 = new ImageIcon("earth5.gif");
  Timer earthTimer;
  int pictureNumber = 0;

  public static void main(String args[])
  {
    // create frame
    new SpinningEarth().show();
  }

  public SpinningEarth()
  {
    // frame constructor
    setResizable(false);
    addWindowListener(new WindowAdapter()
    {
      public void windowClosing(WindowEvent evt)
      {
        exitForm(evt);
      }
    });
    getContentPane().setLayout(new GridBagLayout());

    // position controls

    GridBagConstraints gridConstraints = new
GridBagConstraints();
```

```
    displayLabel.setPreferredSize(new
Dimension(image0.getIconWidth(), image0.getIconHeight()));
    displayLabel.setIcon(image0);
    gridConstraints.gridx = 0;
    gridConstraints.gridy = 0;
    gridConstraints.insets = new Insets(10, 10, 10, 10);
    getContentPane().add(displayLabel, gridConstraints);

    gridConstraints = new GridBagConstraints();
    earthButton.setText("Start Spinning");
    gridConstraints.gridx = 0;
    gridConstraints.gridy = 1;
    gridConstraints.insets = new Insets(10, 10, 10, 10);
    getContentPane().add(earthButton, gridConstraints);
    earthButton.addActionListener(new ActionListener()
    {
    public void actionPerformed(ActionEvent e)
    {
      earthButtonActionPerformed(e);
    }
    });
    earthTimer = new Timer(500, new ActionListener()
    {
    public void actionPerformed(ActionEvent e)
    {
      earthTimerActionPerformed(e);
    }
    });
    pack();
    Dimension screenSize =
Toolkit.getDefaultToolkit().getScreenSize();
    setBounds((int) (0.5 * (screenSize.width - getWidth())),
(int) (0.5 * (screenSize.height - getHeight())), getWidth(),
getHeight());
  }
```

```
  private void earthButtonActionPerformed(ActionEvent e)
  {
    // toggle timer and button text
    if (earthTimer.isRunning())
    {
      earthTimer.stop();
      earthButton.setText("Start Spinning");
    }
    else
    {
      earthTimer.start();
```

```
      earthButton.setText("Stop Spinning");
    }
  }

  private void earthTimerActionPerformed(ActionEvent e)
  {
    switch (pictureNumber)
    {
    case 0:
      displayLabel.setIcon(image0);
      break;
    case 1:
      displayLabel.setIcon(image1);
      break;
    case 2:
      displayLabel.setIcon(image2);
      break;
    case 3:
      displayLabel.setIcon(image3);
      break;
    case 4:
      displayLabel.setIcon(image4);
      break;
    case 5:
      displayLabel.setIcon(image5);
      break;
    }
    pictureNumber++;
    if (pictureNumber == 6)
    {
      pictureNumber = 0;
    }

  }

  private void exitForm(WindowEvent evt)
  {
    System.exit(0);
  }
}
```

Run the application. Start and stop the timer and watch the earth spin! Here is my spinning earth showing Australia:

Save the project (saved as **Example7-3** project in **\LearnJava\LJ Code\Class 7** program group).

Random Numbers (Revisited) and Games

A fun thing to do with Java is to create **games**. You can write games that you play against the computer or against another opponent. Graphics and animations play a big part in most games. And each time we play a game, we want the response to be different. It would be boring playing a game like Solitaire if the same cards were dealt each time you played. Here, we review the random number generator introduced back in Class 2.

To introduce chaos and randomness into games, we use **random numbers**. Random numbers are used to have the computer roll a die, deal a deck of cards, and draw bingo numbers. Java develops random numbers using a built-in **random number generator**. There are several such generators in Java – we use one that generates random **integer** values. All random generators are part of the **java.util.Random** package.

The random number generator in Java must be initialized by creating a **Random** object. The statement to do this is:

```
Random myRandom = new Random();
```

This statement is placed with the variable declaration statements.

Once created, when you need a random integer value, use the **nextInt** method of this **Random** object:

```
myRandom.nextInt(limit)
```

This statement generates a random integer value that is greater than or equal to 0 and less than **limit**. Note it is less than limit, not equal to. For example, the method:

```
myRandom.nextInt(5)
```

will generate random numbers from 0 to 4. The possible values will be 0, 1, 2, 3 and 4.

Random **Examples:**

To roll a six-sided die, the number of spots would be computed using:

```
numberSpots = myRandom.nextInt(6) + 1;
```

To randomly choose a card from a deck of 52 cards (indexed from 0 to 51), use:

```
cardValue = myRandom.nextInt(52);
```

To pick a number from 0 to 100, use:

```
number = myRandom.nextInt(101);
```

Let's use our new animation skills and random numbers to build a little game.

Randomly Sorting Integers

In many games, we have the need to randomly sort a sequence of integers. For example, to shuffle a deck of cards, we sort the integers from 0 to 51 (giving us 52 integers to represent the cards). To randomly sort the state names in a states/capitals game, we would randomize the values from 0 to 49.

Randomly sorting **n** integers is a common task. Here is a general method that does that task. The method has a single argument - **n** (the number of integers to be sorted). The method (**sortIntegers**) returns an integer array containing the random integers. The returned array is zero-based, returning random integers from 0 to n - 1, not 1 to n. If you need integers from 1 to n, just simply add 1 to each value in the returned array! The code is:

```
public int[] sortIntegers(int n)
{
  /*
  *  Returns n randomly sorted integers 0 -> n - 1
  */
  int nArray[] = new int[n];
  int temp, s;
  Random myRandom = new Random();
  //  initialize array from 0 to n - 1
  for (int i = 0; i < n; i++)
  {
    nArray[i] = i;
  }
  //  i is number of items remaining in list
  for (int i = n; i >= 1; i--)
  {
    s = myRandom.nextInt(i);
    temp = nArray[s];
    nArray[s] = nArray[i - 1];
    nArray[i - 1] = temp;
  }
  return(nArray);
}
```

Look at the code, one number is pulled from the original sorted array and put at the bottom of the array. Then a number is pulled from the remaining unsorted values and put at the 'new' bottom. This selection continues until all the numbers have been sorted. This routine has been called a 'one card shuffle' because it's like shuffling a deck of cards by pulling one card out of the deck at a time and laying it aside in a pile.

Note this method uses a random number object; hence the **java.util.Random** package must be imported to projects using this method. This method has been added to **Appendix I**, our collection of general methods. This procedure has a wide range of applications. I've used it to randomize the letters of the alphabet, scramble words in spelling games, randomize answers in multiple choice tests, and even playback compact disc songs in random order (yes, you can build a CD player with Java).

Example 7-4

Random Integers

Start a new empty project in **NetBeans**. Name the project **RandomIntegers**.
Delete the default code in Java file named **RandomIntegers**. We want an
application that randomly sorts a selected number of integers. The finished
frame will look like this:

1. Add a scroll pane, a spinner control and a button control to the frame. The
   GridBagLayout looks like this:

	gridx = 0
gridy = 0	**randomScrollPane**
gridy = 1	**randomSpinner**
gridy = 2	**randomButton**

Set the following properties:

RandomIntegers Frame:
resizable	false

randomScrollPane:
viewPortView	randomTextArea
gridx	0
gridy	0
insets	(5, 5, 5, 5)

randomTextArea:
columns	6
rows	10
lineWrap	true

randomSpinner:
model	SpinnerNumberModel
value	2
minimum	2
maximum	100
stepSize	1
gridx	0
gridy	1
insets	(5, 0, 5, 0)

randomButton:
text	Sort Integers
gridx	0
gridy	2
insets	(5, 0, 5, 0)

2. Build the basic framework:

```
/*
 * RandomIntegers.java
*/
package randomintegers;
import javax.swing.*;
import java.awt.*;
import java.awt.event.*;
import java.util.Random;
public class RandomIntegers extends JFrame
{
  public static void main(String args[])
  {
    //construct frame
    new RandomIntegers().show();
  }
  public RandomIntegers()
  {
    // code to build the form
    setResizable(false);
    addWindowListener(new WindowAdapter()
    {
      public void windowClosing(WindowEvent e)
      {
        exitForm(e);
      }
    });
    getContentPane().setLayout(new GridBagLayout());

    pack();
    Dimension screenSize =
Toolkit.getDefaultToolkit().getScreenSize();
    setBounds((int) (0.5 * (screenSize.width -
getWidth())), (int) (0.5 * (screenSize.height -
getHeight())), getWidth(), getHeight());
  }
  private void exitForm(WindowEvent e)
  {
    System.exit(0);
  }
}
```

Run to test the framework.

3. Establish the class level control declarations:

```
JScrollPane randomScrollPane = new JScrollPane();
JTextArea randomTextArea = new JTextArea();
JSpinner randomSpinner = new JSpinner();
JButton randomButton = new JButton();
```

Position controls and add events:

```
GridBagConstraints gridConstraints = new
GridBagConstraints();
randomTextArea.setColumns(6);
randomTextArea.setRows(10);
randomTextArea.setLineWrap(true);
randomScrollPane.setViewportView(randomTextArea);
gridConstraints.gridx = 0;
gridConstraints.gridy = 0;
gridConstraints.insets = new Insets(5, 5, 5, 5);
getContentPane().add(randomScrollPane, gridConstraints);

randomSpinner.setModel(new SpinnerNumberModel(2, 2, 100,
1));
gridConstraints = new GridBagConstraints();
gridConstraints.gridx = 0;
gridConstraints.gridy = 1;
gridConstraints.insets = new Insets(5, 0, 5, 0);
getContentPane().add(randomSpinner, gridConstraints);

randomButton.setText("Sort Integers");
gridConstraints = new GridBagConstraints();
gridConstraints.gridx = 0;
gridConstraints.gridy = 2;
gridConstraints.insets = new Insets(5, 0, 5, 0);
getContentPane().add(randomButton, gridConstraints);
randomButton.addActionListener(new ActionListener()
{
  public void actionPerformed(ActionEvent e)
  {
    randomButtonActionPerformed(e);
  }
});
```

Add the one empty event method:

```
private void randomButtonActionPerformed(ActionEvent e)
{
}
```

Run to test the control layout:

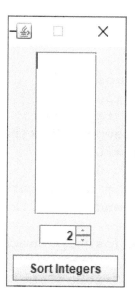

4. Now, we add the code. First, add the **sortIntegers** general method

```java
public int[] sortIntegers(int n)
{
  /*
   *  Returns n randomly sorted integers 0 -> n - 1
   */
  int nArray[] = new int[n];
  int temp, s;
  Random myRandom = new Random();
  //  initialize array from 0 to n - 1
  for (int i = 0; i < n; i++)
  {
    nArray[i] = i;
  }
  //  i is number of items remaining in list
  for (int i = n; i >= 1; i--)
  {
    s = myRandom.nextInt(i);
    temp = nArray[s];
    nArray[s] = nArray[i - 1];
    nArray[i - 1] = temp;
  }
  return(nArray);
}
```

5. Use this code in the **randomButtonActionPerformed** event method:

```
private void randomButtonActionPerformed(ActionEvent e)
{
  int arraySize =
Integer.valueOf(randomSpinner.getValue().toString()).intVa
lue();
  int[] integerArray = new int[arraySize];
  // Clear text area
  randomTextArea.setText("");
  // sort  integers
  integerArray = sortIntegers(arraySize);
  // display sorted integers
  for (int i = 0 ; i < arraySize; i++)
  {
    randomTextArea.append(String.valueOf(integerArray[i])
+ "\n");
  }
}
```

This code reads the value of the spinner control, establishes the array
(**integerArray**) and calls **sortIntegers**. The sorted values are displayed in the
text area.

The complete **RandomIntegers.java** code listing (additions to framework are
shaded):

```
/*
 * RandomIntegers.java
*/
package randomintegers;
import javax.swing.*;
import java.awt.*;
import java.awt.event.*;
import java.util.Random;

public class RandomIntegers extends JFrame
{

  JScrollPane randomScrollPane = new JScrollPane();
  JTextArea randomTextArea = new JTextArea();
  JSpinner randomSpinner = new JSpinner();
  JButton randomButton = new JButton();

  public static void main(String args[])
  {
```

```java
    //construct frame
    new RandomIntegers().show();
  }

  public RandomIntegers()
  {
    // code to build the form
    setResizable(false);
    addWindowListener(new WindowAdapter()
    {
      public void windowClosing(WindowEvent e)
      {
        exitForm(e);
      }
    });
    getContentPane().setLayout(new GridBagLayout());

    // position controls (establish event methods)
    GridBagConstraints gridConstraints = new
GridBagConstraints();
    randomTextArea.setColumns(6);
    randomTextArea.setRows(10);
    randomTextArea.setLineWrap(true);
    randomScrollPane.setViewportView(randomTextArea);
    gridConstraints.gridx = 0;
    gridConstraints.gridy = 0;
    gridConstraints.insets = new Insets(5, 5, 5, 5);
    getContentPane().add(randomScrollPane, gridConstraints);

    randomSpinner.setModel(new SpinnerNumberModel(2, 2, 100,
1));
    gridConstraints = new GridBagConstraints();
    gridConstraints.gridx = 0;
    gridConstraints.gridy = 1;
    gridConstraints.insets = new Insets(5, 0, 5, 0);
    getContentPane().add(randomSpinner, gridConstraints);

    randomButton.setText("Sort Integers");
    gridConstraints = new GridBagConstraints();
    gridConstraints.gridx = 0;
    gridConstraints.gridy = 2;
    gridConstraints.insets = new Insets(5, 0, 5, 0);
    getContentPane().add(randomButton, gridConstraints);
    randomButton.addActionListener(new ActionListener()
    {
      public void actionPerformed(ActionEvent e)
```

```
      {
        randomButtonActionPerformed(e);
      }
    });

    pack();
    Dimension screenSize =
Toolkit.getDefaultToolkit().getScreenSize();
    setBounds((int) (0.5 * (screenSize.width - getWidth())),
(int) (0.5 * (screenSize.height - getHeight())), getWidth(),
getHeight());
  }

  private void randomButtonActionPerformed(ActionEvent e)
  {
    int arraySize =
Integer.valueOf(randomSpinner.getValue().toString()).intValue
();
    int[] integerArray = new int[arraySize];
    // Clear text area
    randomTextArea.setText("");
    // sort  integers
    integerArray = sortIntegers(arraySize);
    // display sorted integers
    for (int i = 0 ; i < arraySize; i++)
    {
      randomTextArea.append(String.valueOf(integerArray[i]) +
"\n");
    }
  }

  private void exitForm(WindowEvent e)
  {
    System.exit(0);
  }

  public int[] sortIntegers(int n)
  {
    /*
     *  Returns n randomly sorted integers 0 -> n - 1
     */
    int nArray[] = new int[n];
    int temp, s;
    Random myRandom = new Random();
    //  initialize array from 0 to n - 1
    for (int i = 0; i < n; i++)
    {
```

```
      nArray[i] = i;
    }
    //  i is number of items remaining in list
    for (int i = n; i >= 1; i--)
    {
      s = myRandom.nextInt(i);
      temp = nArray[s];
      nArray[s] = nArray[i - 1];
      nArray[i - 1] = temp;
    }
    return(nArray);
  }
}
```

Run the project. Try sorting different numbers of integers. Notice you get different results every time you do a sort. Here's a few runs I made to sort 10 integers (0 to 9):

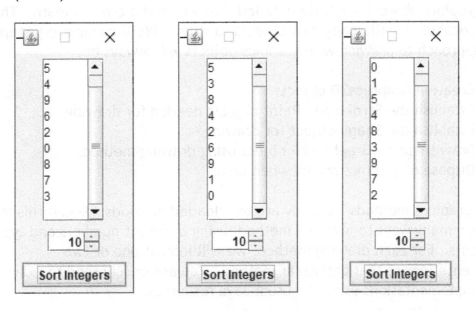

Save the project (saved as **Example7-4** project in **\LearnJava\LJ Code\Class 7** program group).

Java 2D Graphics

We now know how to display graphics files (images) in Java applications and how to do basic animations. Java also offers a wealth of **graphics methods** that let us draw lines, rectangles, ellipses, pie shapes and polygons. With these methods, you can draw anything!

Graphics can be created using either or both the Java **Graphics** class and the Java 2D **Graphics2D** class, an improved graphics environment. In these notes, we work solely with the **Graphics2D** class, meaning graphics methods are applied to **Graphics2D** objects. Be aware that Java references to graphics objects are usually passed as **Graphics** objects, so casting to **Graphics2D** objects will often be required. This will all become clear as we delve further into graphics.

Using graphics objects is a little detailed, but worth the time to learn. There is a new vocabulary with many new objects to study. We'll cover every step. The basic approach to drawing with graphics objects will always be:

> ➤ Create a **Graphics2D** object.
> ➤ Establish the **Stroke** and **Paint** objects needed for drawing.
> ➤ Establish the **Shape** object for drawing.
> ➤ Draw shape to **Graphics2D** object using drawing methods
> ➤ Dispose of graphics object when done.

All the graphics methods we study are **overloaded** methods. Recall this means there are many ways to invoke a method, using different numbers and types of arguments. For each drawing method, we will look at one or two implementations of that particular method. You are encouraged to examine other implementations using the usual Java resources.

In this class, we will learn about **Graphics2D** objects, **Stroke** and **Paint** objects (use of **colors**) and **Shape** objects. We'll learn how to draw **lines**, draw and fill **rectangles**, draw and fill **ellipses** and draw and fill **arc** segments. We'll use these skills to build basic plotting packages and, in Class 8, a simple paintbrush program. There's a lot to learn here, so let's get started.

Graphics2D Object

As mentioned, graphics methods (drawing methods) are applied to graphics objects. **Graphics2D objects** provide the "surface" for drawing methods. You can draw on many of the Swing components. In this course, we will use the panel control for drawing.

A **Graphics2D object** (**g2D**) is created using:

```
Graphics g2D = (Graphics2D) hostControl.getGraphics();
```

where **hostControl** is the control hosting the graphics object. Note the **getGraphics** method returns a **Graphics** object that must be cast (converted) to a **Graphics2D** object. Placement of this statement depends on scope. Place it in a method for method level scope. Place it with other class level declarations for class level scope.

Once a graphics object is created, all graphics methods are applied to this object. Hence, to apply a drawing method named **drawingMethod** to the **g2D** object, use:

```
g2D.drawingMethod(arguments);
```

where **arguments** are any needed arguments.

Once you are done drawing to an object and need it no longer, it should be properly disposed to clear up system resources. The syntax for disposing of our example graphics object uses the **dispose** method:

```
g2D.dispose();
```

Stroke and Paint Objects

The attributes of lines (either lines or borders of shapes) drawn using **Graphics2D** objects are specified by the **stroke**. Stroke can be used to establish line style, such as solid, dashed or dotted lines, line thickness and line end styles. By default, a solid line, one pixel in width is drawn. In this class, we will only look at how to change the line thickness. Stroke is changed using the **setStroke** method. To set the thickness (**width**) of the line for a graphics object **g2D**, use a **BasicStroke** object:

```
g2D.setStroke(new BasicStroke(width));
```

After this method, all lines will be drawn with the new **width** attribute.

To change the color of lines being drawn, use the **setPaint** method. For our example graphics object, the color is changed using:

```
g2D.setPaint(color);
```

where **color** is either a built-in color or one set using RGB values. After this line of code, all lines are drawn with the new color.

The **setPaint** method can also be used to establish the color and pattern used to fill a graphics region. In this class, we will fill such regions with solid colors. Simply specifying the desired color in the **setPaint** method will accomplish this. In Class 8, we will look at ways to fill a region with textures and patterns.

Shapes and Drawing Methods

We will learn to draw various **shapes**. Shapes will include lines, rectangles, ellipses and arcs. The classes used to do this drawing are in the **java.awt.geom.*** package, so we need to include an import statement for this package.

Shape objects are specified with the **user coordinates** of the hosting control:

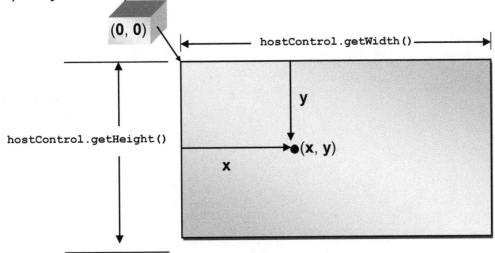

The host dimensions, **hostControl.getWidth()** and **hostControl.getHeight()** represent the "graphics" region of the control hosting the graphics object.

Points in user coordinates are referred to by a Cartesian pair, **(x, y)**. In the diagram, note the **x** (horizontal) coordinate runs from left to right, starting at **0** and extending to **hostControl.getWidth() - 1**. The **y** (vertical) coordinate goes from top to bottom, starting at **0** and ending at **hostControl.getHeight() - 1**. All measurements are integers and in units of **pixels**. Later, we will see how we can use any coordinate system we want.

Once a **shape** object is created (we will see how to do that next), the shape is drawn using the **draw** method. For a shape **myShape** using our example graphics object (**g2D**), the code is:

```
g2D.draw(myShape);
```

The shape will be drawn using the current **stroke** and **paint** attributes.

For shape objects that encompass some two-dimensional region, that region can be filled using the **fill** method. For our example, the code is:

```
g2D.fill(myShape);
```

The shape will be filled using the current **paint** attribute.

Let's define our first shape – a **line** – yes, a line is a shape.

Line2D Shape

The first shape we learn to draw is a line, or the **Line2D** shape. This shape is used to connect two Cartesian points with a straight-line segment:

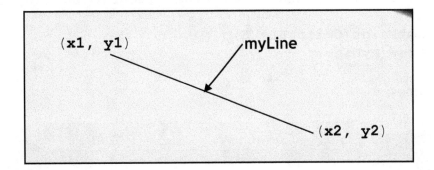

If we wish to connect the point (**x1, y1**) with (**x2, y2**), the shape (**myLine**) is created using:

```
Line2D.Double myLine = new Line2D.Double(x1, y1, x2, y2);
```

Each coordinate value is a **double** type (there is also a **Line2D.Float** shape, where each coordinate is a **float** type). Once created, the line is drawn (in a previously created **Graphics2D** object, **g2D**) using the **draw** method:

```
g2D.draw(myLine);
```

The line will be drawn using the current **stroke** and **paint** attributes.

Say we have a panel control (**myPanel**) of dimension (300, 200). To draw a **black** line (**myLine**) in that panel, with a line **width** of **1** (the default **stroke**) from (**20, 20**) to (**280, 180**), the Java code would be:

```
Graphics2D g2D = (Graphics2D) myPanel.getGraphics();
Line2D.Double myLine = new Line2D.Double(20, 20, 280,
180);
g2D.setPaint(Color.BLACK);
g2D.draw(myLine);
```

This produces:

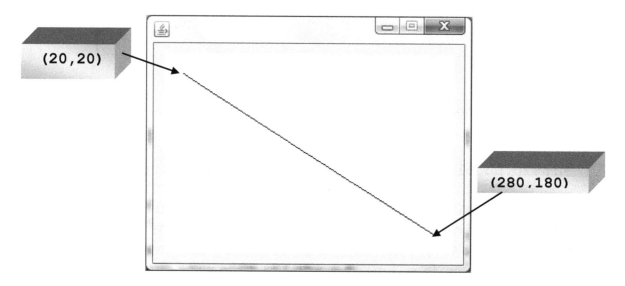

For every line segment you need to draw, you will need a separate **Line2D** shape and **draw** statement. Of course, you can choose to change color (**setPaint**) or width (**setStroke**) at any time you wish.

Graphics Demonstration

Before continuing, let's look at a little example to demonstrate some of the things we've learned about 2D graphics in Java. Open the **\LearnJava\LJ Code\Class 7** program group in **NetBeans**. Make **GraphicsDemo1** the active project. Open the **GraphicsDemonstration.java** file. The finished interface for this application has a panel for drawing and a button control:

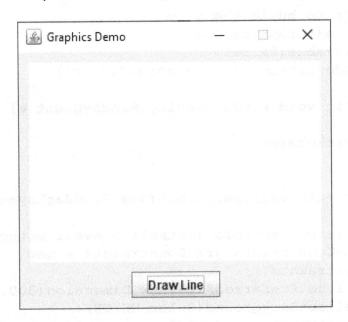

When we click the button, we want to draw a blue line on the panel from the upper left corner to the lower right corner. When we click the button again, we want the line to disappear. The complete code listing is:

```java
/*
 * GraphicsDemonstration.java
 */
package graphicsdemonstration;
import javax.swing.*;
import java.awt.*;
import java.awt.geom.*;
import java.awt.event.*;

public class GraphicsDemonstration extends JFrame
{

    JPanel myPanel = new JPanel();
    JButton myButton = new JButton();
    boolean lineThere = false;
```

```
public static void main(String args[])
{
  //construct frame
  new GraphicsDemonstration().show();
}

public GraphicsDemonstration()
{
  // code to build the form
  setTitle("Graphics Demo");
  setResizable(false);
  addWindowListener(new WindowAdapter()
  {
    public void windowClosing(WindowEvent e)
    {
      exitForm(e);
    }
  });
  getContentPane().setLayout(new GridBagLayout());

  // position controls (establish event methods)
  GridBagConstraints gridConstraints = new
GridBagConstraints();
  myPanel.setPreferredSize(new Dimension(300, 200));
  myPanel.setBackground(Color.WHITE);
  gridConstraints.gridx = 0;
  gridConstraints.gridy = 0;
  gridConstraints.insets = new Insets(10, 10, 10, 10);
  getContentPane().add(myPanel, gridConstraints);

  myButton.setText("Draw Line");
  gridConstraints = new GridBagConstraints();
  gridConstraints.gridx = 0;
  gridConstraints.gridy = 1;
  gridConstraints.insets = new Insets(0, 0, 10, 0);
  getContentPane().add(myButton, gridConstraints);
  myButton.addActionListener(new ActionListener()
  {
    public void actionPerformed(ActionEvent e)
    {
      myButtonActionPerformed(e);
    }
  });

  pack();
```

```
    Dimension screenSize =
Toolkit.getDefaultToolkit().getScreenSize();
    setBounds((int) (0.5 * (screenSize.width -
getWidth())), (int) (0.5 * (screenSize.height -
getHeight())), getWidth(), getHeight());
  }
```

```
  private void myButtonActionPerformed(ActionEvent e)
  {
    // toggle button text property
    if (myButton.getText().equals("Draw Line"))
    {
      myButton.setText("Clear Line");
      lineThere = true;
    }
    else
    {
      myButton.setText("Draw Line");
      lineThere = false;
    }
    Graphics2D g2D = (Graphics2D) myPanel.getGraphics();
    Line2D.Double myLine = new Line2D.Double(0, 0,
myPanel.getWidth(), myPanel.getHeight());
    if (lineThere)
    {
      g2D.setPaint(Color.BLUE);
    }
    else
    {
      g2D.setPaint(myPanel.getBackground());
    }
    g2D.draw(myLine);
    g2D.dispose();
  }
  private void exitForm(WindowEvent e)
  {
    System.exit(0);
  }
}
```

Since this is the first graphics code we've seen, let's look at it closely. You should recognize all the code that creates and places the controls. Especially, note the line importing **java.awt.geom.***. The code that does the drawing is in the **myButtonActionPerformed** method (shaded in the listing). This code first 'toggles' the button's **text** property and establishes a value for **lineThere**. It then creates the **Graphics2D** object **g2D** using the panel (**myPanel**) as the host control. The **Line2D** shape (**myLine**) is then created (the line starts in the upper left corner of the panel and ends in the lower right corner). Next, the code checks the status of **lineThere** to determine if we're drawing a line or clearing the line. If drawing (**lineThere** is **true**), a blue line is drawn. If clearing, a line the same color as the background of the panel is drawn, essentially erasing the line. Before leaving the method, the object is disposed.

Run this little project and click the button one time. You should see something like this:

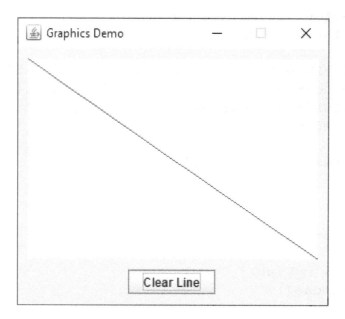

Your first line!! Click the button to watch the line disappear. Click the button a few times to see the toggling feature.

After all this hard work, let's look at a "feature" of graphics methods. Make sure a line appears on the panel and reduce the frame to an icon by clicking the **Minimize** button (the one with an underscore character) in the upper right-hand corner of the form. Or, cover the frame with another window. Now, restore the frame to the screen by clicking the corresponding entry on your task bar (or make the window appear again). Here's what you should see:

The button control is still there, but the line we carefully drew has disappeared! What happened? We'll answer that question next.

Persistent Graphics

Why did the line disappear in our little example when the frame went away for a bit? Java graphics objects have <u>no</u> memory. They only display what has been last drawn on them. If you reduce your frame to an icon (or it becomes obscured by another frame) and restore it, the graphics object cannot remember what was displayed previously – it will be cleared. Similarly, if you switch from an active Java application to some other application, your Java form may become partially or fully obscured. When you return to your Java application, the obscured part of any graphics object will be erased. Again, there is no memory. Notice in both these cases, however, all controls are automatically restored to the form. Your application remembers these, fortunately! The controls are persistent. We also want **persistent graphics**.

To maintain persistent graphics, we need to build memory into our graphics objects using code. In this code, we must be able to recreate, when needed, the current state of a graphics object. This 'custom' code is placed in the host control's **paintComponent** method. This event method is called whenever an obscured object becomes unobscured. The **paintComponent** method will be called for each object when a frame is first activated and when a frame is restored from an icon or whenever an obscured object is viewable again.

How do we access the **paintComponent** method for a control? For such access, we need to create a separate **class** for the control that **extends** the particular control. Creating the class is a simple task (see **Appendix II** for a brief primer on the subject). We define a **GraphicsPanel** class (a **JPanel** control hosting a graphics object) using the following code segment:

```
class GraphicsPanel extends JPanel
{
  public GraphicsPanel()
  {
  }
  public void paintComponent(Graphics g)
  {
      [Painting code goes here]
  }
}
```

This class is placed after the main class in our program. A **GraphicsPanel** object is then declared and created using:

```
GraphicsPanel myPanel = new GraphicsPanel();
```

With this declaration, the "painting" of the control is now handled by the **paintComponent** method. Notice this method passes a **Graphics** object **g**. The first step in painting the component is to cast this object to a **Graphics2D** object:

```
Graphics2D g2D = (Graphics2D) g;
```

After this, we place code in the **paintComponent** method that describes the current state of the graphics object. In particular, make sure the first statement is:

```
super.paintComponent(g2D);
```

This will reestablish any background color (the keyword **super** refers to the 'inherited' control, the panel in this case).

Maintaining persistent graphics does require a bit of work on your part. You need to always know what is in your graphics objects and how to recreate the objects, when needed. This usually involves developing some program variables that describe how to recreate the graphics object. And, you usually need to develop some ad hoc rules for recreation. As you build your first few **paintComponent** events, you will begin to develop your own ways for maintaining persistent graphics. At certain times, you'll need to force a "repaint" of your control. To do this, for a host control named **hostControl** use:

```
hostControl.repaint();
```

You will often need to have your **paintComponent** method access variables from your **main** class. If your main class is named **mainClass** and you want the value of **myVariable**, the variable is accessed using:

```
mainClass.myVariable
```

Any variables accessed in this manner must have class level scope and, when declared, be prefaced with the keyword **static**. This is due to the way the **paintComponent** method works.

This all may sound difficult, but it really isn't and an example should clear things up. Let's see how to maintain persistent graphics in our graphics demonstration. First, add the framework for the **GraphicsPanel** class at the end of the main class (**GraphicsDemonstration**) code:

```
class GraphicsPanel extends JPanel
{
  public GraphicsPanel()
  {
  }
  public void paintComponent(Graphics g)
  {
    Graphics2D g2D = (Graphics2D) g;
    super.paintComponent(g2D);
  }
}
```

Change the line of code creating **myPanel** to:

```
GraphicsPanel myPanel = new GraphicsPanel();
```

Next, <u>move</u> all the graphics statements out of the **myButtonActionPerformed** event method into the **paintComponent** method. The **paintComponent** method will be (the added lines are shaded – make sure these lines are no longer in the button action method):

```
public void paintComponent(Graphics g)
{
  Graphics2D g2D = (Graphics2D) g;
  super.paintComponent(g2D);
  Graphics2D g2D = (Graphics2D) myPanel.getGraphics();
  Line2D.Double myLine = new Line2D.Double(0, 0,
myPanel.getWidth(), myPanel.getHeight());
  if (lineThere)
  {
    g2D.setPaint(Color.BLUE);
  }
  else
  {
    g2D.setPaint(myPanel.getBackground());
  }
  g2D.draw(myLine);
  g2D.dispose();
}
```

We need to make a few modifications to make this code work:

> Delete the line creating **g2D** using **myPanel**. This line is not needed because the graphics object is provided when the method is called.

> Remove the references to **myPanel** in code creating the **Line2D** object and code setting the background color. The use of this control is implicit in the class definition.

> The **lineThere** variable is from the main class. Hence, change the **lineThere** reference to **GraphicsDemonstration.lineThere**. Also, in the main class, preface the declaration for **lineThere** with **static**.

The modified method is (changes are shaded):

```
public void paintComponent(Graphics g)
{
  Graphics2D g2D = (Graphics2D) g;
  super.paintComponent(g2D);
  Line2D.Double myLine = new Line2D.Double(0, 0,
getWidth(), getHeight());
  if (GraphicsDemonstration.lineThere)
  {
    g2D.setPaint(Color.BLUE);
  }
  else
  {
    g2D.setPaint(getBackground());
  }
  g2D.draw(myLine);
  g2D.dispose();
}
```

With this code, the line will be drawn when **lineThere** is **true**, else the line object will be cleared.

Run the application with these changes in place. Click the button. There's no line there! Keep clicking the button. No matter what you do, a line is never drawn. Why? Look at the modified **myButtonActionPerformed** method:

```
private void myButtonActionPerformed(ActionEvent e)
{
  // toggle button text property
  if (myButton.getText().equals("Draw Line"))
  {
    myButton.setText("Clear Line");
    lineThere = true;
  }
  else
  {
    myButton.setText("Draw Line");
    lineThere = false;
  }
}
```

We have moved the commands to draw and clear the line into the **paintComponent** method, but there is no code in the **myButtonActionPerformed** method that can access that code. Add this line as the last line in this method (before the closing brace, of course):

```
myPanel.repaint();
```

This will force a "repaint" of the frame before toggling, meaning the **paintComponent** method will be invoked. This is just what we were doing before adding the **paintComponent** method – we toggled the button **text** property, set the **lineThere** property, then drew or cleared the line.

Run the application again. No line – yeah! Things should be working like they should. Click the button a few times to become convinced that this is the case. Then, try minimizing or obscuring the form. Restore the form. The graphics should be persistent, meaning the line will be there when it's supposed to and not there when it's not supposed to be there. The last incarnation of this little graphics example is saved as the **GraphicsDemo2** project in the **\LearnJava\LJ Code\Class 7** program group.

So, to use persistent graphics, you need to do a little work. Once you've done that work, make sure you truly have persistent graphics. Perform checks similar to those we did for our little example here. The NetBeans environment makes doing these checks very easy. It's simple to make changes and immediately see the effects of those changes. A particular place to check is to make sure the initial loading of graphics objects display correctly. Sometimes, **paintComponent** events cause incorrect results the first time they are invoked.

And, though, including **paintComponent** methods in a Java application require extra coding, it also has the advantage of centralizing all graphics operations in one procedure. This usually helps to simplify the tasks of code modification and maintenance. I've found that the persistent graphics problem makes me look more deeply at my code. In the end, I write better code. I believe you'll find the same is true with your applications. Most graphics applications we build will use a **GraphicsPanel** object with corresponding **paintComponent** methods. Study these examples to become familiar with the idea of persistent graphics. A basic framework for the **GraphicsPanel** class has been added to **Appendix I** to these notes. If you have an application that uses more than one panel to host graphics, you will need to create **GraphicsPanel** type objects for each. Each panel would have a different class name, but the same structure as the **GraphicsPanel** used here, each with a unique **paintComponent** method.

Example 7-5

Drawing Lines

Start a new empty project in **NetBeans**. Name the project **DrawingLines**.
Delete the default code in Java file named **DrawingLines**. In this application,
we will draw random line segments in a panel control using **Line2D** shapes. The
finished frame looks like this:

1. Add a panel control and two button controls to the frame. The
   GridBagLayout is:

	gridx = 0
gridy = 0	drawPanel
gridy = 1	drawButton
gridy = 2	clearButton

PictureBox1

Set the following properties:

DrawingLines Frame:
title	Drawing Lines
resizable	false

panelDraw (a GraphicsPanel object):
preferredSize	(300, 200)
background	WHITE
gridx	0
gridy	0
insets	(10, 10, 10, 10)

drawButton:
text	Draw Lines
gridx	0
gridy	1

clearButton:
text	Clear Lines
gridx	0
gridy	2
insets	(5, 0, 5, 0)

2. Build the basic framework code:

```
/*
 * DrawingLines.java
*/
package drawinglines;
import javax.swing.*;
import java.awt.*;
import java.awt.geom.*;
import java.awt.event.*;
import java.util.Random;

public class DrawingLines extends JFrame
{
  public static void main(String args[])
  {
    //construct frame
    new DrawingLines().show();
  }
```

```
    public DrawingLines()
    {
      // code to build the form
      setTitle("Drawing Lines");
      setResizable(false);
      addWindowListener(new WindowAdapter()
      {
        public void windowClosing(WindowEvent e)
        {
          exitForm(e);
        }
      });
      getContentPane().setLayout(new GridBagLayout());

      pack();
      Dimension screenSize =
  Toolkit.getDefaultToolkit().getScreenSize();
      setBounds((int) (0.5 * (screenSize.width -
  getWidth())), (int) (0.5 * (screenSize.height -
  getHeight())), getWidth(), getHeight());
    }
    private void exitForm(WindowEvent e)
    {
      System.exit(0);
    }
  }
```

Run to check the code.

3. Now, we add controls and methods. Add these class level declarations:

```
GraphicsPanel drawPanel = new GraphicsPanel();
JButton drawButton = new JButton();
JButton clearButton = new JButton();
```

Position and add controls and event methods:

```
GridBagConstraints gridConstraints = new
GridBagConstraints();
drawPanel.setPreferredSize(new Dimension(300, 200));
drawPanel.setBackground(Color.WHITE);
gridConstraints.gridx = 0;
gridConstraints.gridy = 0;
gridConstraints.insets = new Insets(10, 10, 10, 10);
getContentPane().add(drawPanel, gridConstraints);
```

```
drawButton.setText("Draw Lines");
gridConstraints = new GridBagConstraints();
gridConstraints.gridx = 0;
gridConstraints.gridy = 1;
getContentPane().add(drawButton, gridConstraints);
drawButton.addActionListener(new ActionListener()
{
  public void actionPerformed(ActionEvent e)
  {
    drawButtonActionPerformed(e);
  }
});

clearButton.setText("Clear Lines");
gridConstraints = new GridBagConstraints();
gridConstraints.gridx = 0;
gridConstraints.gridy = 2;
gridConstraints.insets = new Insets(5, 0, 5, 0);
getContentPane().add(clearButton, gridConstraints);
clearButton.addActionListener(new ActionListener()
{
  public void actionPerformed(ActionEvent e)
  {
    clearButtonActionPerformed(e);
  }
});
```

And, add the two empty event methods:

```
private void drawButtonActionPerformed(ActionEvent e)
{
}

private void clearButtonActionPerformed(ActionEvent e)
{
}
```

4. Add the **GraphicsPanel** class (from **Appendix I**) after the main class to allow for persistent graphics using the **paintComponent** method:

```
class GraphicsPanel extends JPanel
{
  public GraphicsPanel()
  {
  }
  public void paintComponent(Graphics g)
  {
  }
}
```

Run to check control layout:

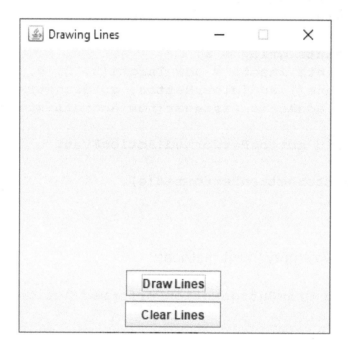

The panel appears gray because we haven't coded the **paintComponent** method yet. We'll do that now.

5. Use these class level variable declarations (to keep track of what has been drawn):

```
static int numberPoints = 0;
static int[] x = new int[50];
static int[] y = new int[50];
final int maxPoints = 50;
Random myRandom = new Random();
```

Note three variables (**numberPoints, x, y**) are prefaced with **static** since they will be used in the **paintComponent** method.

6. Use this code in the **drawButtonActionPerformed** event method:

```
private void drawButtonActionPerformed(ActionEvent e)
{
   // add new random point to line array and redraw
   // create two points first time through
   do
   {
      x[numberPoints] =
myRandom.nextInt(drawPanel.getWidth());
      y[numberPoints] =
myRandom.nextInt(drawPanel.getHeight());
      numberPoints++;
   }
   while (numberPoints < 2);
   drawPanel.repaint();
   // no more clicks if maxpoints exceeded
   if (numberPoints == maxPoints)
   {
      drawButton.setEnabled(false);
   }
}
```

With each click of the button, a new point is added to the array to draw.

7. Use this code in **clearButtonActionPerformed** event – this clears the graphics object and allows new line segments to be drawn:

```java
private void clearButtonActionPerformed(ActionEvent e)
{
  // clear region
  numberPoints = 0;
  drawButton.setEnabled(true);
  drawPanel.repaint();
}
```

8. Use this code in the **paintComponent** method in the **GraphicsPanel** class. This code draws the line segments defined by the **x** and **y** arrays:

```java
public void paintComponent(Graphics g)
{
  // create graphics object and connect points in x, y
arrays
  Line2D.Double myLine;
  Graphics2D g2D = (Graphics2D) g;
  super.paintComponent(g2D);
  g2D.setPaint(Color.BLUE);
  g2D.setStroke(new BasicStroke(3));
  if (DrawingLines.numberPoints != 0)
  {
    for (int i = 1; i < DrawingLines.numberPoints; i++)
    {
      myLine = new Line2D.Double(DrawingLines.x[i - 1],
DrawingLines.y[i - 1], DrawingLines.x[i],
DrawingLines.y[i]);
      g2D.draw(myLine);
    }
  }
  g2D.dispose();
}
```

Notice we draw blue lines (**setPaint**), 3 pixels wide (**setStroke**).

The final **DrawingLines.java** code listing (code added to framework is shaded):

```
/*
 * DrawingLines.java
*/
package drawinglines;
import javax.swing.*;
import java.awt.*;
import java.awt.geom.*;
import java.awt.event.*;
import java.util.Random;
public class DrawingLines extends JFrame
{
  GraphicsPanel drawPanel = new GraphicsPanel();
  JButton drawButton = new JButton();
  JButton clearButton = new JButton();
  static int numberPoints = 0;
  static int[] x = new int[50];
  static int[] y = new int[50];
  final int maxPoints = 50;
  Random myRandom = new Random();
  public static void main(String args[])
  {
    //construct frame
    new DrawingLines().show();
  }
  public DrawingLines()
  {
    // code to build the form
    setTitle("Drawing Lines");
    setResizable(false);
    addWindowListener(new WindowAdapter()
    {
      public void windowClosing(WindowEvent e)
      {
        exitForm(e);
      }
    });
    getContentPane().setLayout(new GridBagLayout());
    // position controls (establish event methods)
    GridBagConstraints gridConstraints = new
GridBagConstraints();
    drawPanel.setPreferredSize(new Dimension(300, 200));
    drawPanel.setBackground(Color.WHITE);
    gridConstraints.gridx = 0;
    gridConstraints.gridy = 0;
    gridConstraints.insets = new Insets(10, 10, 10, 10);
```

```
    getContentPane().add(drawPanel, gridConstraints);
    drawButton.setText("Draw Lines");
    gridConstraints = new GridBagConstraints();
    gridConstraints.gridx = 0;
    gridConstraints.gridy = 1;
    getContentPane().add(drawButton, gridConstraints);
    drawButton.addActionListener(new ActionListener()
    {
      public void actionPerformed(ActionEvent e)
      {
        drawButtonActionPerformed(e);
      }
    });
    clearButton.setText("Clear Lines");
    gridConstraints = new GridBagConstraints();
    gridConstraints.gridx = 0;
    gridConstraints.gridy = 2;
    gridConstraints.insets = new Insets(5, 0, 5, 0);
    getContentPane().add(clearButton, gridConstraints);
    clearButton.addActionListener(new ActionListener()
    {
      public void actionPerformed(ActionEvent e)
      {
        clearButtonActionPerformed(e);
      }
    });
    pack();
    Dimension screenSize =
Toolkit.getDefaultToolkit().getScreenSize();
    setBounds((int) (0.5 * (screenSize.width - getWidth())),
(int) (0.5 * (screenSize.height - getHeight())), getWidth(),
getHeight());
  }
  private void drawButtonActionPerformed(ActionEvent e)
  {
    // add new random point to line array and redraw
    // create two points first time through
    do
    {
      x[numberPoints] =
myRandom.nextInt(drawPanel.getWidth());
      y[numberPoints] =
myRandom.nextInt(drawPanel.getHeight());
      numberPoints++;
    }
    while (numberPoints < 2);
    drawPanel.repaint();
```

```
      // no more clicks if maxpoints exceeded
      if (numberPoints == maxPoints)
      {
        drawButton.setEnabled(false);
      }
  }
  private void clearButtonActionPerformed(ActionEvent e)
  {
      // clear region
      numberPoints = 0;
      drawButton.setEnabled(true);
      drawPanel.repaint();
  }
  private void exitForm(WindowEvent e)
  {
      System.exit(0);
  }
}
class GraphicsPanel extends JPanel
{
  public GraphicsPanel()
  {
  }
  public void paintComponent(Graphics g)
  {
      // create graphics object and connect points in x, y
arrays
      Line2D.Double myLine;
      Graphics2D g2D = (Graphics2D) g;
      super.paintComponent(g2D);
      g2D.setPaint(Color.BLUE);
      g2D.setStroke(new BasicStroke(3));
      if (DrawingLines.numberPoints != 0)
      {
        for (int i = 1; i < DrawingLines.numberPoints; i++)
        {
          myLine = new Line2D.Double(DrawingLines.x[i - 1],
DrawingLines.y[i - 1], DrawingLines.x[i], DrawingLines.y[i]);
          g2D.draw(myLine);
        }
      }
      g2D.dispose();
  }
}
```

Run the project. Try drawing (click **Draw Lines** several times) and clearing random line segments. Note that the graphics are persistent. Try obscuring the form to prove this. Here's a run I made drawing several line segments:

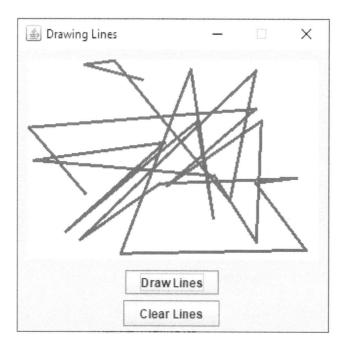

Save the project application (saved as **Example 7-5** project in **\LearnJava\LJ Code\Class 7** program group).

Rectangle2D Shape

We now begin looking at two-dimensional shapes. The first is a rectangle, represented by the **Rectangle2D** shape. To specify this shape, you need to know the Cartesian location of the upper left corner of the rectangle (**x, y**), the width of the rectangle, **w**, and the rectangle height, **h**:

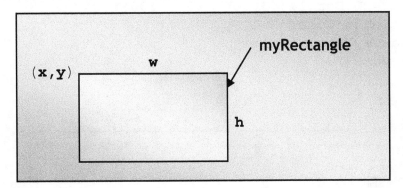

If the rectangle is named **myRectangle**, the corresponding shape is created using:

```
Rectangle2D.Double myRectangle = new Rectangle2D.Double(x,
y, w, h);
```

Each argument value is a **double** type (there is also a **Rectangle2D.Float** shape, where each argument is a **float** type). Once created, the rectangle is drawn (in a previously created **Graphics2D** object, **g2D**) using the **draw** method:

```
g2D.draw(myRectangle);
```

The rectangle will be drawn using the current **stroke** and **paint** attributes.

Say we have a panel (**myPanel**) of dimension (300, 200). To draw a **black** rectangle (**myRectangle**) in that panel, with a line **width** of **1** (the default **stroke**), starting at (**40, 40**), with **width 150** and **height 100**, the Java code would be:

```
Graphics2D g2D = (Graphics2D) myPanel.getGraphics();
Rectangle2D.Double myRectangle = new
Rectangle2D.Double(40, 40, 150, 100);
g2D.setPaint(Color.BLACK);
g2D.draw(myRectangle);
g2D.dispose();
```

This produces:

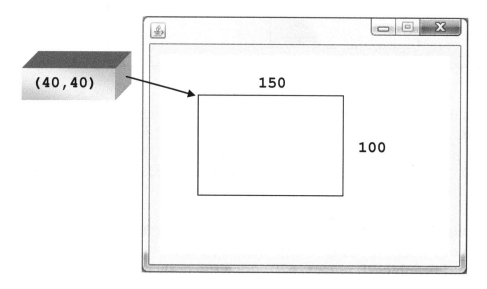

The rectangle we just drew is pretty boring. It would be nice to have the capability to fill it with a color and/or pattern. Filling of shapes in Java 2D graphics is done with the **fill** method. If the graphics object is **g2D**, and the shape **myShape**, the syntax to fill the shape is:

```
g2D.fill(myRectangle);
```

The rectangle will be filled with the current **paint** attribute. For now, we will just fill the shapes with solid colors. In Class 8, we will learn how to fill with patterns and textures.

To fill our example rectangle with red, we use this code:

```
Graphics2D g2D = (Graphics2D) myPanel.getGraphics();
Rectangle2D.Double myRectangle = new
Rectangle2D.Double(40, 40, 150, 100);
g2D.setPaint(Color.RED);
g2D.fill(myRectangle);
g2D.dispose();
```

This produces:

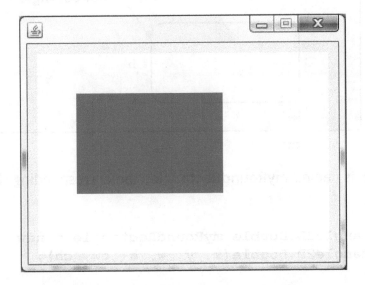

Notice the **fill** method fills the entire region with the selected color. If you had previously used the **draw** method to form a bordered rectangle, the **fill** will blot out that border. If you want a bordered, filled region, do the **fill** operation **first, then** the **draw** operation.

RoundRectangle2D Shape

There is one other 'rectangle' shape, the **RoundRectangle2D**. It is like the rectangle, with rounded corners. It is created with a constructor similar to **Rectangle2D** with two additional arguments, the corner width (**cw**) and corner height (**cw**):

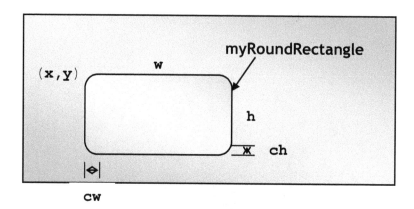

If the rectangle is named **myRoundRectangle**, the corresponding shape is created using:

```
RoundRectangle2D.Double myRoundRectangle = new
RoundRectangle2D.Double(x, y, w, h, cw, ch);
```

Each argument value is a **double** type (there is also a **RoundRectangle2D.Float** shape, where each argument is a **float** type).

Once created, the round rectangle is drawn (in a previously created **Graphics2D** object, **g2D**) using the **draw** method:

```
g2D.draw(myRoundRectangle);
```

The rectangle will be drawn using the current **stroke** and **paint** attributes. The rectangle is filled with the **fill** method:

```
g2D.fill(myRoundRectangle);
```

The rectangle is filled using the current **paint** attribute.

Let's return to our example panel (**myPanel**) of dimension (300, 200). To draw a **black** bordered, **green** filled round rectangle (**myRectangle**) in that panel, with a line **width** of **3**, starting at (**40, 40**), with **width 150** and **height 100**, **corner width 30** and **corner height 20**, the Java code would be:

```
Graphics2D g2D = (Graphics2D) myPanel.getGraphics();
RoundRectangle2D.Double myRoundRectangle = new
RoundRectangle2D.Double(40, 40, 150, 100, 30, 20);
g2D.setPaint(Color.GREEN);
g2D.fill(myRoundRectangle);
g2D.setStroke(new BasicStroke(3));
g2D.setPaint(Color.BLACK);
g2D.draw(myRoundRectangle);
g2D.dispose();
```

This produces:

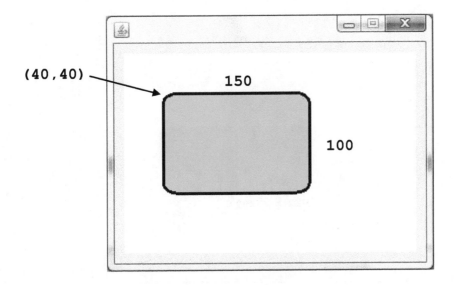

Notice we filled the shape before drawing it to maintain the border.

Example 7-6

Drawing Rectangles

Start a new empty project in **NetBeans**. Name the project **DrawingRectangles**. Delete the default code in Java file named **DrawingRectangles**. In this application, we will draw and fill random rectangles and round rectangles in a panel control. The rectangles will be filled with random colors. The finished frame:

1. Add a panel control and three button controls to the frame. The **GridBagLayout** is:

	gridx = 0
gridy = 0	**drawPanel**
gridy = 1	**drawButton**
gridy = 2	**fillButton**
gridy = 3	**clearButton**

Set the following properties:

DrawingRectangles Frame:
title	Drawing Rectangles
resizable	false

panelDraw (a GraphicsPanel class):
preferredSize	(300, 200)
background	WHITE
gridx	0
gridy	0
insets	(10, 10, 10, 10)

drawButton:
text	Draw Rectangle
gridx	0
gridy	1

fillButton:
text	Fill Rectangle
enabled	false
gridx	0
gridy	2
insets	(5, 0, 0, 0)

clearButton:
text	Clear Rectangle
enabled	false
gridx	0
gridy	2
insets	(5, 0, 5, 0)

2. Build the basic framework code:

```
/*
 * DrawingRectangles.java
 */
package drawingrectangles;
import javax.swing.*;
import java.awt.*;
import java.awt.geom.*;
import java.awt.event.*;
import java.util.Random;
public class DrawingRectangles extends JFrame
{
  public static void main(String args[])
  {
    //construct frame
    new DrawingRectangles().show();
  }
  public DrawingRectangles()
  {
    // code to build the form
    setTitle("Drawing Rectangles");
    setResizable(false);
    addWindowListener(new WindowAdapter()
    {
      public void windowClosing(WindowEvent e)
      {
        exitForm(e);
      }
    });
    getContentPane().setLayout(new GridBagLayout());

    pack();
    Dimension screenSize =
Toolkit.getDefaultToolkit().getScreenSize();
    setBounds((int) (0.5 * (screenSize.width -
getWidth())), (int) (0.5 * (screenSize.height -
getHeight())), getWidth(), getHeight());
  }
  private void exitForm(WindowEvent e)
  {
    System.exit(0);
  }
}
```

Run to check the code.

3. Now, we add controls and methods. Add these class level declarations:

```
GraphicsPanel drawPanel = new GraphicsPanel();
JButton drawButton = new JButton();
JButton fillButton = new JButton();
JButton clearButton = new JButton();
static Rectangle2D.Double myRectangle;
static RoundRectangle2D.Double myRoundRectangle;
```

Position and add controls and event methods:

```
GridBagConstraints gridConstraints = new
GridBagConstraints();
drawPanel.setPreferredSize(new Dimension(300, 200));
drawPanel.setBackground(Color.WHITE);
gridConstraints.gridx = 0;
gridConstraints.gridy = 0;
gridConstraints.insets = new Insets(10, 10, 10, 10);
getContentPane().add(drawPanel, gridConstraints);

drawButton.setText("Draw Rectangle");
gridConstraints = new GridBagConstraints();
gridConstraints.gridx = 0;
gridConstraints.gridy = 1;
getContentPane().add(drawButton, gridConstraints);
drawButton.addActionListener(new ActionListener()
{
  public void actionPerformed(ActionEvent e)
  {
    drawButtonActionPerformed(e);
  }
});

fillButton.setText("Fill Rectangle");
fillButton.setEnabled(false);
gridConstraints = new GridBagConstraints();
gridConstraints.gridx = 0;
gridConstraints.gridy = 2;
gridConstraints.insets = new Insets(5, 0, 0, 0);
getContentPane().add(fillButton, gridConstraints);
fillButton.addActionListener(new ActionListener()
{
  public void actionPerformed(ActionEvent e)
  {
```

```
      fillButtonActionPerformed(e);
    }
});

    clearButton.setText("Clear Rectangle");
    clearButton.setEnabled(false);
    gridConstraints = new GridBagConstraints();
    gridConstraints.gridx = 0;
    gridConstraints.gridy = 3;
    gridConstraints.insets = new Insets(5, 0, 5, 0);
    getContentPane().add(clearButton, gridConstraints);
    clearButton.addActionListener(new ActionListener()
    {
      public void actionPerformed(ActionEvent e)
      {
        clearButtonActionPerformed(e);
      }
    });
```

And, add the three empty event methods:

```
    private void drawButtonActionPerformed(ActionEvent e)
    {
    }

    private void fillButtonActionPerformed(ActionEvent e)
    {
    }

    private void clearButtonActionPerformed(ActionEvent e)
    {
    }
```

4. Add the **GraphicsPanel** class (from **Appendix I**) after the main class to allow for persistent graphics using the **paintComponent** method:

```
class GraphicsPanel extends JPanel
{
  public GraphicsPanel()
  {
  }
  public void paintComponent(Graphics g)
  {
  }
}
```

Run to test the control layout:

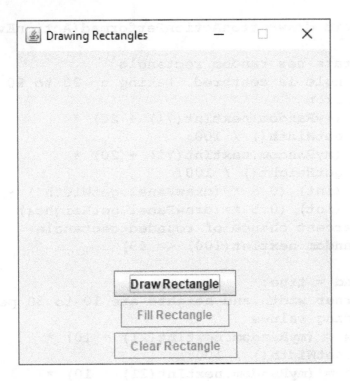

The panel appears gray because we haven't coded the **paintComponent** method yet. We'll do that now.

5. Use these class level variable declarations:

```
static boolean isRound = false;
static boolean isDrawn = false;
static boolean isFilled = false;
static int fillRed, fillGreen, fillBlue;
Random myRandom = new Random();
```

6. Use this code in the **drawButtonActionPerformed** event method:

```java
private void drawButtonActionPerformed(ActionEvent e)
{
  // generate new random rectangle
  // rectangle is centered, taking up 20 to 90 percent of
each dimension
  int w = (myRandom.nextInt(71) + 20) *
drawPanel.getWidth() / 100;
  int h = (myRandom.nextInt(71) + 20) *
drawPanel.getHeight() / 100;
  int x = (int) (0.5 * (drawPanel.getWidth() - w));
  int y = (int) (0.5 * (drawPanel.getHeight() - h));
  // 50 percent chance of rounded rectangle
  if (myRandom.nextInt(100) <= 49)
  {
    isRound = true;
    // corner width and heights are 10 to 30 percent of
corresponding values
    int cw = (myRandom.nextInt(21) + 10) *
drawPanel.getWidth() / 100;
    int ch = (myRandom.nextInt(21) + 10) *
drawPanel.getHeight() / 100;
    myRoundRectangle = new RoundRectangle2D.Double(x, y,
w, h, cw, ch);
  }
  else
  {
    isRound = false;
    myRectangle = new Rectangle2D.Double(x, y, w, h);
  }
  isDrawn = true;
  isFilled = false;
  drawButton.setEnabled(false);
  fillButton.setEnabled(true);
  clearButton.setEnabled(true);
  drawPanel.repaint();
}
```

This code establishes either a rectangle or round rectangle shape and draws that shape.

7. Use this code in the **fillButtonActionPerformed** event method:

```
private void fillButtonActionPerformed(ActionEvent e)
{
  // fill rectangle
  isFilled = true;
  drawButton.setEnabled(false);
  // pick colors at random
  fillRed = myRandom.nextInt(256);
  fillGreen = myRandom.nextInt(256);
  fillBlue = myRandom.nextInt(256);
  drawPanel.repaint();
}
```

Here, random colors are picked and the existing rectangle is filled.

8. Use this code in **clearButtonActionPerformed** method - this clears the graphics object and allows another rectangle to be drawn:

```
private void clearButtonActionPerformed(ActionEvent e)
{
  // clear region
  isDrawn = false;
  isFilled = false;
  drawButton.setEnabled(true);
  fillButton.setEnabled(false);
  clearButton.setEnabled(false);
  drawPanel.repaint();
}
```

9. Use this code in the **paintComponent** method in the **GraphicsPanel** class. This code draws/fills the rectangle if it is in the panel control:

```
public void paintComponent(Graphics g)
{
  Graphics2D g2D = (Graphics2D) g;
  super.paintComponent(g2D);
  // fill before draw to keep border
  if (DrawingRectangles.isFilled)
  {
    // fill with random color
    g2D.setPaint(new Color(DrawingRectangles.fillRed,
DrawingRectangles.fillGreen, DrawingRectangles.fillBlue));
    if (DrawingRectangles.isRound)
    {
      g2D.fill(DrawingRectangles.myRoundRectangle);
```

```
      }
      else
      {
        g2D.fill(DrawingRectangles.myRectangle);
      }
    }
    if (DrawingRectangles.isDrawn)
    {
      // draw with pen 3 pixels wide
      g2D.setStroke(new BasicStroke(3));
      g2D.setPaint(Color.BLACK);
      if (DrawingRectangles.isRound)
      {
        g2D.draw(DrawingRectangles.myRoundRectangle);
      }
      else
      {
        g2D.draw(DrawingRectangles.myRectangle);
      }
    }
    g2D.dispose();
  }
```

Notice we draw black border lines (**setPaint**), 3 pixels wide (**setStroke**).

The final **DrawingRectangles.java** code listing (code added to framework is shaded):

```
/*
 * DrawingRectangles.java
 */
package drawingrectangles;
import javax.swing.*;
import java.awt.*;
import java.awt.geom.*;
import java.awt.event.*;
import java.util.Random;
public class DrawingRectangles extends JFrame
{
  GraphicsPanel drawPanel = new GraphicsPanel();
  JButton drawButton = new JButton();
  JButton fillButton = new JButton();
  JButton clearButton = new JButton();
  static Rectangle2D.Double myRectangle;
  static RoundRectangle2D.Double myRoundRectangle;
  static boolean isRound = false;
```

```java
static boolean isDrawn = false;
static boolean isFilled = false;
static int fillRed, fillGreen, fillBlue;
Random myRandom = new Random();
public static void main(String args[])
{
  //construct frame
  new DrawingRectangles().show();
}
public DrawingRectangles()
{
  // code to build the form
  setTitle("Drawing Rectangles");
  setResizable(false);
  addWindowListener(new WindowAdapter()
  {
    public void windowClosing(WindowEvent e)
    {
      exitForm(e);
    }
  });
  getContentPane().setLayout(new GridBagLayout());
  // position controls (establish event methods)
  GridBagConstraints gridConstraints = new
GridBagConstraints();
  drawPanel.setPreferredSize(new Dimension(300, 200));
  drawPanel.setBackground(Color.WHITE);
  gridConstraints.gridx = 0;
  gridConstraints.gridy = 0;
  gridConstraints.insets = new Insets(10, 10, 10, 10);
  getContentPane().add(drawPanel, gridConstraints);
   drawButton.setText("Draw Rectangle");
  gridConstraints = new GridBagConstraints();
  gridConstraints.gridx = 0;
  gridConstraints.gridy = 1;
  getContentPane().add(drawButton, gridConstraints);
  drawButton.addActionListener(new ActionListener()
  {
    public void actionPerformed(ActionEvent e)
    {
      drawButtonActionPerformed(e);
    }
  });
   fillButton.setText("Fill Rectangle");
   fillButton.setEnabled(false);
  gridConstraints = new GridBagConstraints();
  gridConstraints.gridx = 0;
```

```
   gridConstraints.gridy = 2;
   gridConstraints.insets = new Insets(5, 0, 0, 0);
   getContentPane().add(fillButton, gridConstraints);
   fillButton.addActionListener(new ActionListener()
   {
     public void actionPerformed(ActionEvent e)
     {
       fillButtonActionPerformed(e);
     }
   });
    clearButton.setText("Clear Rectangle");
    clearButton.setEnabled(false);
   gridConstraints = new GridBagConstraints();
   gridConstraints.gridx = 0;
   gridConstraints.gridy = 3;
   gridConstraints.insets = new Insets(5, 0, 5, 0);
   getContentPane().add(clearButton, gridConstraints);
   clearButton.addActionListener(new ActionListener()
   {
     public void actionPerformed(ActionEvent e)
     {
       clearButtonActionPerformed(e);
     }
   });

   pack();
   Dimension screenSize =
Toolkit.getDefaultToolkit().getScreenSize();
    setBounds((int) (0.5 * (screenSize.width - getWidth())),
(int) (0.5 * (screenSize.height - getHeight())), getWidth(),
getHeight());
  }
  private void drawButtonActionPerformed(ActionEvent e)
  {
    // generate new random rectangle
    // rectangle is centered, taking up 20 to 90 percent of
each dimension
    int w = (myRandom.nextInt(71) + 20) *
drawPanel.getWidth() / 100;
    int h = (myRandom.nextInt(71) + 20) *
drawPanel.getHeight() / 100;
    int x = (int) (0.5 * (drawPanel.getWidth() - w));
    int y = (int) (0.5 * (drawPanel.getHeight() - h));
    // 50 percent chance of rounded rectangle
    if (myRandom.nextInt(100) <= 49)
    {
      isRound = true;
```

```
        // corner width and heights are 10 to 30 percent of
corresponding values
        int cw = (myRandom.nextInt(21) + 10) *
drawPanel.getWidth() / 100;
        int ch = (myRandom.nextInt(21) + 10) *
drawPanel.getHeight() / 100;
        myRoundRectangle = new RoundRectangle2D.Double(x, y, w,
h, cw, ch);
      }
      else
      {
        isRound = false;
        myRectangle = new Rectangle2D.Double(x, y, w, h);
      }
      isDrawn = true;
      isFilled = false;
      drawButton.setEnabled(false);
      fillButton.setEnabled(true);
      clearButton.setEnabled(true);
      drawPanel.repaint();
  }
  private void fillButtonActionPerformed(ActionEvent e)
  {
      // fill rectangle
      isFilled = true;
      drawButton.setEnabled(false);
      // pick colors at random
      fillRed = myRandom.nextInt(256);
      fillGreen = myRandom.nextInt(256);
      fillBlue = myRandom.nextInt(256);
      drawPanel.repaint();
  }
  private void clearButtonActionPerformed(ActionEvent e)
  {
      // clear region
      isDrawn = false;
      isFilled = false;
      drawButton.setEnabled(true);
      fillButton.setEnabled(false);
      clearButton.setEnabled(false);
      drawPanel.repaint();
  }
  private void exitForm(WindowEvent e)
  {
      System.exit(0);
  }
}
```

```
class GraphicsPanel extends JPanel
{
  public GraphicsPanel()
  {
  }
  public void paintComponent(Graphics g)
  {
    Graphics2D g2D = (Graphics2D) g;
    super.paintComponent(g2D);
    // fill before draw to keep border
    if (DrawingRectangles.isFilled)
    {
      // fill with random color
      g2D.setPaint(new Color(DrawingRectangles.fillRed,
DrawingRectangles.fillGreen, DrawingRectangles.fillBlue));
      if (DrawingRectangles.isRound)
      {
        g2D.fill(DrawingRectangles.myRoundRectangle);
      }
      else
      {
        g2D.fill(DrawingRectangles.myRectangle);
      }
    }
    if (DrawingRectangles.isDrawn)
    {
      // draw with pen 3 pixels wide
      g2D.setStroke(new BasicStroke(3));
      g2D.setPaint(Color.BLACK);
      if (DrawingRectangles.isRound)
      {
        g2D.draw(DrawingRectangles.myRoundRectangle);
      }
      else
      {
        g2D.draw(DrawingRectangles.myRectangle);
      }
    }
    g2D.dispose();
  }
}
```

Run the project. Try drawing and filling rectangles. Notice how the random colors work. Notice how the button controls are enabled and disabled at different points. Note that the graphics are persistent. Here's a rounded rectangle I drew and filled:

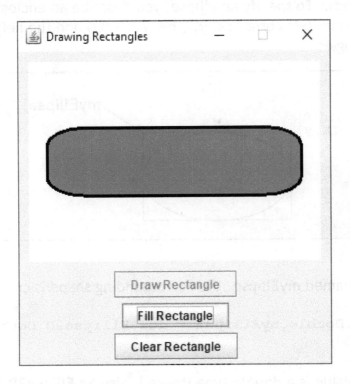

Save the project (saved as **Example7-6** project in **\LearnJava\LJ Code\Class 7** program group

Ellipse2D Shape

Ellipses can be defined, drawn and filled using methods nearly identical to the rectangle methods. To specify an ellipse, you describe an enclosing rectangle, specifying the upper left corner (**x, y**), the width (**w**) and the height (**h**) of the enclosing rectangle:

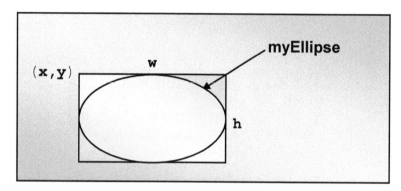

If the ellipse is named **myEllipse**, the corresponding shape is created using:

```
Ellipse2D.Double myEllipse = new Ellipse2D.Double(x, y, w,
h);
```

Each argument value is a **double** type (there is also an **Ellipse2D.Float** shape, where each argument is a **float** type). Once created, the ellipse is drawn (in a previously created **Graphics2D** object, **g2D**) using the **draw** method:

```
g2D.draw(myEllipse);
```

The ellipse will be drawn using the current **stroke** and **paint** attributes.

Again, we have a panel (**myPanel**) of dimension (300, 200). To draw a **black** ellipse (**myEllipse**) in that panel, with a line **width** of **1** (the default **stroke**), starting at (**40, 40**), with **width 150** and **height 100**, the Java code would be:

```
Graphics2D g2D = (Graphics2D) myPanel.getGraphics();
Ellipse2D.Double myEllipse = new Ellipse2D.Double(40, 40,
150, 100);
g2D.setPaint(Color.BLACK);
g2D.draw(myEllipse);
g2D.dispose();
```

This produces:

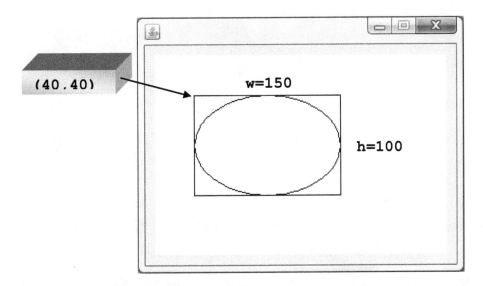

The surrounding rectangle is not drawn. It is shown to display how the ellipse fits.

The ellipse is filled with the **fill** method:

```
g2D.fill(myEllipse);
```

The shape will be filled with the current **paint** attribute.

To **fill** our example ellipse with **yellow**, we use this code:

```
Graphics2D g2D = (Graphics2D) myPanel.getGraphics();
Ellipse2D.Double myEllipse = new Ellipse2D.Double(40, 40,
150, 100);
g2D.setPaint(Color.YELLOW);
g2D.fill(myEllipse);
g2D.dispose();
```

This produces:

Like the rectangle methods, notice the **fill** operation erases any border that may have been there after a **draw** operation. For a bordered, filled ellipse, do the **fill**, then the **draw**.

Example 7-7

Drawing Ellipses

Start a new empty project in **NetBeans**. Name the project **DrawingEllipses**. Delete the default code in Java file named **DrawingEllipses**. This example will be nearly identical to **Example 7-6**, so rather than build everything from scratch, we will modify that example. In this project, we will draw and fill random ellipses in a panel control. The ellipses will be filled with random colors. The finished frame will look like this:

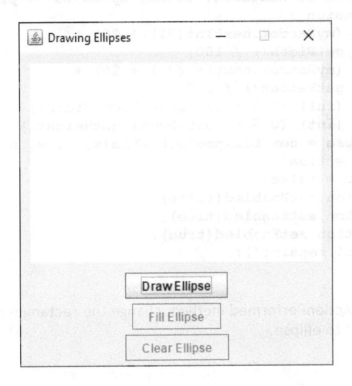

Copy the code from **DrawingRectangles.java** into the empty **DrawingEllipses.java** file. Make these changes:

➤ Change all instances of **DrawingRectangles** to **DrawingEllipses**. I found fifteen such instances.

➤ Replace the two statements creating rectangle shapes with one creating an ellipse shape:

```
static Ellipse2D.Double myEllipse;
```

➤ Delete the statement declaring the **isRound** variable.

➤ Change the frame **title** to **Drawing Ellipses**.

➤ Change the word **Rectangle** to **Ellipse** on the three button controls.

➤ Change the **drawButtonActionPerformed** method (we removed code for round rectangles and changed rectangle references to ellipse references):

```
private void drawButtonActionPerformed(ActionEvent e)
{
  // generate new random ellipse
  // ellipse is centered, taking up 20 to 90 percent of
each dimension
  int w = (myRandom.nextInt(71) + 20) *
drawPanel.getWidth() / 100;
  int h = (myRandom.nextInt(71) + 20) *
drawPanel.getHeight() / 100;
  int x = (int) (0.5 * (drawPanel.getWidth() - w));
  int y = (int) (0.5 * (drawPanel.getHeight() - h));
   myEllipse = new Ellipse2D.Double(x, y, w, h);
  isDrawn = true;
  isFilled = false;
  drawButton.setEnabled(false);
  fillButton.setEnabled(true);
  clearButton.setEnabled(true);
  drawPanel.repaint();
}
```

➤ In **fillButtonActionPerformed** method, change the **rectangle** reference in the comment to **ellipse**.

➢ Modify the **paintComponent** method (again, round rectangle drawing is deleted and rectangle references are changed to ellipse references):

```java
public void paintComponent(Graphics g)
{
  Graphics2D g2D = (Graphics2D) g;
  super.paintComponent(g2D);
  // fill before draw to keep border
  if (DrawingEllipses.isFilled)
  {
    // fill with random color
    g2D.setPaint(new Color(DrawingEllipses.fillRed,
DrawingEllipses.fillGreen, DrawingEllipses.fillBlue));
    g2D.fill(DrawingEllipses.myEllipse);
  }
  if (DrawingEllipses.isDrawn)
  {
    // draw with pen 3 pixels wide
    g2D.setStroke(new BasicStroke(3));
    g2D.setPaint(Color.BLACK);
    g2D.draw(DrawingEllipses.myEllipse);
  }
  g2D.dispose();
}
```

The complete **DrawingEllipses.java** code (modifications to DrawingRectangles.java are shaded):

```java
/*
 * DrawingEllipses.java
 */
package drawingellipses;
import javax.swing.*;
import java.awt.*;
import java.awt.geom.*;
import java.awt.event.*;
import java.util.Random;

public class DrawingEllipses extends JFrame
{

  GraphicsPanel drawPanel = new GraphicsPanel();
  JButton drawButton = new JButton();
  JButton fillButton = new JButton();
  JButton clearButton = new JButton();
  static Ellipse2D.Double myEllipse;
```

```java
static boolean isDrawn = false;
static boolean isFilled = false;
static int fillRed, fillGreen, fillBlue;
Random myRandom = new Random();

public static void main(String args[])
{
  //construct frame
  new DrawingEllipses().show();
}


public DrawingEllipses()
{
  // code to build the form
  setTitle("Drawing Ellipses");
  setResizable(false);
  addWindowListener(new WindowAdapter()
  {
    public void windowClosing(WindowEvent e)
    {
      exitForm(e);
    }
  });
  getContentPane().setLayout(new GridBagLayout());

  // position controls (establish event methods)
  GridBagConstraints gridConstraints = new
GridBagConstraints();
  drawPanel.setPreferredSize(new Dimension(300, 200));
  drawPanel.setBackground(Color.WHITE);
  gridConstraints.gridx = 0;
  gridConstraints.gridy = 0;
  gridConstraints.insets = new Insets(10, 10, 10, 10);
  getContentPane().add(drawPanel, gridConstraints);

  drawButton.setText("Draw Ellipse");
  gridConstraints = new GridBagConstraints();
  gridConstraints.gridx = 0;
  gridConstraints.gridy = 1;
  getContentPane().add(drawButton, gridConstraints);
  drawButton.addActionListener(new ActionListener()
  {
    public void actionPerformed(ActionEvent e)
    {
      drawButtonActionPerformed(e);
    }
  });
```

```
    fillButton.setText("Fill Ellipse");
    fillButton.setEnabled(false);
  gridConstraints = new GridBagConstraints();
  gridConstraints.gridx = 0;
  gridConstraints.gridy = 2;
  gridConstraints.insets = new Insets(5, 0, 0, 0);
  getContentPane().add(fillButton, gridConstraints);
  fillButton.addActionListener(new ActionListener()
  {
    public void actionPerformed(ActionEvent e)
    {
      fillButtonActionPerformed(e);
    }
  });

    clearButton.setText("Clear Ellipse");
    clearButton.setEnabled(false);
  gridConstraints = new GridBagConstraints();
  gridConstraints.gridx = 0;
  gridConstraints.gridy = 3;
  gridConstraints.insets = new Insets(5, 0, 5, 0);
  getContentPane().add(clearButton, gridConstraints);
  clearButton.addActionListener(new ActionListener()
  {
    public void actionPerformed(ActionEvent e)
    {
      clearButtonActionPerformed(e);
    }
  });

  pack();
  Dimension screenSize =
Toolkit.getDefaultToolkit().getScreenSize();
  setBounds((int) (0.5 * (screenSize.width - getWidth())),
(int) (0.5 * (screenSize.height - getHeight())), getWidth(),
getHeight());
  }

 private void drawButtonActionPerformed(ActionEvent e)
 {
    // generate new random ellipse
    // ellipse is centered, taking up 20 to 90 percent of
each dimension
    int w = (myRandom.nextInt(71) + 20) *
drawPanel.getWidth() / 100;
```

```
    int h = (myRandom.nextInt(71) + 20) *
drawPanel.getHeight() / 100;
    int x = (int) (0.5 * (drawPanel.getWidth() - w));
    int y = (int) (0.5 * (drawPanel.getHeight() - h));
     myEllipse = new Ellipse2D.Double(x, y, w, h);
    isDrawn = true;
    isFilled = false;
    drawButton.setEnabled(false);
    fillButton.setEnabled(true);
    clearButton.setEnabled(true);
    drawPanel.repaint();
  }

  private void fillButtonActionPerformed(ActionEvent e)
  {
    // fill ellipse
    isFilled = true;
    drawButton.setEnabled(false);
    // pick colors at random
    fillRed = myRandom.nextInt(256);
    fillGreen = myRandom.nextInt(256);
    fillBlue = myRandom.nextInt(256);
    drawPanel.repaint();
  }

  private void clearButtonActionPerformed(ActionEvent e)
  {
    // clear region
    isDrawn = false;
    isFilled = false;
    drawButton.setEnabled(true);
    fillButton.setEnabled(false);
    clearButton.setEnabled(false);
    drawPanel.repaint();
  }

  private void exitForm(WindowEvent e)
  {
    System.exit(0);
  }
}

class GraphicsPanel extends JPanel
{
  public GraphicsPanel()
  {
  }
```

```java
public void paintComponent(Graphics g)
{
   Graphics2D g2D = (Graphics2D) g;
   super.paintComponent(g2D);
   // fill before draw to keep border
   if (DrawingEllipses.isFilled)
   {
     // fill with random color
     g2D.setPaint(new Color(DrawingEllipses.fillRed,
DrawingEllipses.fillGreen, DrawingEllipses.fillBlue));
     g2D.fill(DrawingEllipses.myEllipse);
   }
   if (DrawingEllipses.isDrawn)
   {
     // draw with pen 3 pixels wide
     g2D.setStroke(new BasicStroke(3));
     g2D.setPaint(Color.BLACK);
     g2D.draw(DrawingEllipses.myEllipse);
   }
   g2D.dispose();
  }
}
```

Run the project. Try drawing and filling ellipses. Notice how the random colors work. Notice how the button controls are enabled and disabled at different points. Note that the graphics are persistent. Here's a blue filled ellipse I drew:

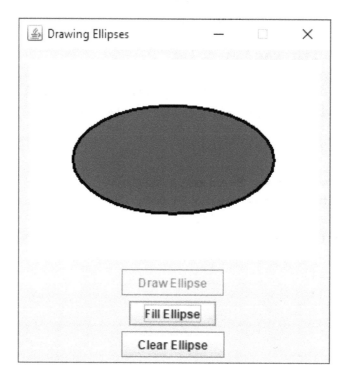

Save the project (saved as **Example7-7** project in **\LearnJava\LJ Code\Class 7** program group).

Arc2D Shape

Arc segments can be defined using the **Arc2D** shape. To specify an arc, you first describe an enclosing rectangle, specifying the upper left corner (**x, y**), the width (**w**) and the height (**h**) of the enclosing rectangle. You then specify a **start** angle (in degrees), the angular **extent** of the arc (in degrees) and the **arcType**. A diagram illustrates:

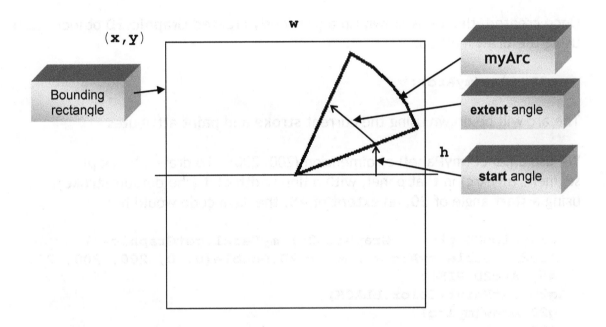

If the arc is named **myArc**, the corresponding shape is created using:

```
Arc2D.Double myArc = new Arc2D.Double(x, y, w, h, start,
extent, arcType);
```

Each argument value is a **double** type (there is also an **Arc2D.Float** shape, where each argument is a **float** type).

The **start** angle is measured counter-clockwise from the horizontal axis to the first side of the arc. **extent** is the counter-clockwise angle starting at start and ending at the second side of the arc. Notice if **start = 0** and **extent = 360**, the **Arc2D** shape is the same figure as **Ellipse2D** (you get the whole ellipse!).

There are three different values for the **arcType**:

> `Arc2D.OPEN`   Ends of arc are not connected
> `Arc2D.CHORD`   Ends of arc are connected by a straight line
> `Arc2D.PIE`   Ends of arc are connected by straight lines to center of
> bounding ellipse forming a pie segment.

We will usually use **Arc2D.PIE** to draw and fill pie segments.

Once created, the arc is drawn (in a previously created **Graphics2D** object, **g2D**) using the **draw** method:

```
g2D.draw(myArc);
```

The arc will be drawn using the current **stroke** and **paint** attributes.

We use a panel (**myPanel**) of dimension (200, 200). To draw a **black** pie segment (**myArc**) in that panel, with a line **width** of **1** (the default **stroke**), using a **start** angle of **20**, an **extent** of **45**, the Java code would be:

```
Graphics2D g2D = (Graphics2D) myPanel.getGraphics();
Arc2D.Double myArc = new Arc2D.Double(0, 0, 200, 200, 20,
45, Arc2D.PIE);
g2D.setPaint(Color.BLACK);
g2D.draw(myArc);
g2D.dispose();
```

This produces:

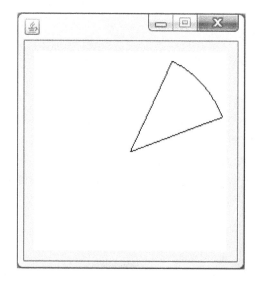

The pie segment (arc) is filled with the **fill** method:

```
g2D.fill(myArc);
```

The shape will be filled with the current **paint** attribute.

To **fill** our example segment with **magenta**, we use this code:

```
Graphics2D g2D = (Graphics2D) myPanel.getGraphics();
Arc2D.Double myArc = new Arc2D.Double(0, 0, 200, 200, 20,
45, Arc2D.PIE);
g2D.setPaint(Color.MAGENTA);
g2D.fill(myArc);
g2D.dispose();
```

This produces:

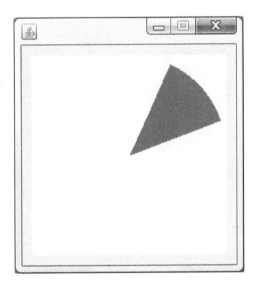

Like the rectangle and ellipse methods, notice the **fill** operation erases any border that may have been there after a **draw** operation. For a bordered, filled pie segment, do the **fill**, then the **draw**.

Example 7-8

Drawing Pie Segments

Start a new empty project in **NetBeans**. Name the project **DrawingPie**. Delete the default code in Java file named **DrawingPie**. In this application, we will draw an ellipse (in a panel control) and fill it with a random number (2 to 6) of pie segments. Each segment will be a different color. The finished frame looks like this:

1. Add a panel control and two button controls to the frame. The **GridBagLayout** is:

	gridx = 0
gridy = 0	**drawPanel**
gridy = 1	**drawButton**
gridy = 2	**clearButton**

PictureBox1

Set the following properties:

DrawingPie Frame:

title	Drawing Pie Segments
resizable	false

panelDraw (a GraphicsPanel class):

preferredSize	(250, 250)
background	WHITE
gridx	0
gridy	0
insets	(10, 10, 10, 10)

drawButton:

text	Draw/Fill Pie
gridx	0
gridy	1

clearButton:

text	Clear Pie
enabled	false
gridx	0
gridy	2
insets	(5, 0, 5, 0)

2. Build the basic framework code:

```
/*
 * DrawingPie.java
 */
package drawingpie;
import javax.swing.*;
import java.awt.*;
import java.awt.geom.*;
import java.awt.event.*;
import java.util.Random;

public class DrawingPie extends JFrame
{


  public static void main(String args[])
  {
    //construct frame
```

```
      new DrawingPie().show();
    }

  public DrawingPie()
  {
    // code to build the form
    setTitle("Drawing Pie Segments");
    setResizable(false);
    addWindowListener(new WindowAdapter()
    {
      public void windowClosing(WindowEvent e)
      {
        exitForm(e);
      }
    });
    getContentPane().setLayout(new GridBagLayout());

    pack();
    Dimension screenSize =
Toolkit.getDefaultToolkit().getScreenSize();
    setBounds((int) (0.5 * (screenSize.width -
getWidth())), (int) (0.5 * (screenSize.height -
getHeight())), getWidth(), getHeight());
  }

  private void exitForm(WindowEvent e)
  {
    System.exit(0);
  }
}
```

Run to check the code.

3. Now, we add controls and methods. Add these class level declarations:

```
GraphicsPanel drawPanel = new GraphicsPanel();
JButton drawButton = new JButton();
JButton clearButton = new JButton();
```

Position and add controls and event methods:

```
GridBagConstraints gridConstraints = new
GridBagConstraints();
drawPanel.setPreferredSize(new Dimension(250, 250));
drawPanel.setBackground(Color.WHITE);
gridConstraints.gridx = 0;
```

```
gridConstraints.gridy = 0;
gridConstraints.insets = new Insets(10, 10, 10, 10);
getContentPane().add(drawPanel, gridConstraints);

drawButton.setText("Draw/Fill Pie");
gridConstraints = new GridBagConstraints();
gridConstraints.gridx = 0;
gridConstraints.gridy = 1;
getContentPane().add(drawButton, gridConstraints);
drawButton.addActionListener(new ActionListener()
{
  public void actionPerformed(ActionEvent e)
  {
    drawButtonActionPerformed(e);
  }
});

clearButton.setText("Clear Pie");
clearButton.setEnabled(false);
gridConstraints = new GridBagConstraints();
gridConstraints.gridx = 0;
gridConstraints.gridy = 3;
gridConstraints.insets = new Insets(5, 0, 5, 0);
getContentPane().add(clearButton, gridConstraints);
clearButton.addActionListener(new ActionListener()
{
  public void actionPerformed(ActionEvent e)
  {
    clearButtonActionPerformed(e);
  }
});
```

And, add the two empty event methods:

```
private void drawButtonActionPerformed(ActionEvent e)
{
}

private void clearButtonActionPerformed(ActionEvent e)
{
}
```

4. Add the **GraphicsPanel** class (from **Appendix I**) after the main class to allow for persistent graphics using the **paintComponent** method:

```
class GraphicsPanel extends JPanel
{
  public GraphicsPanel()
  {
  }
  public void paintComponent(Graphics g)
  {
  }
}
```

Run to check control layout:

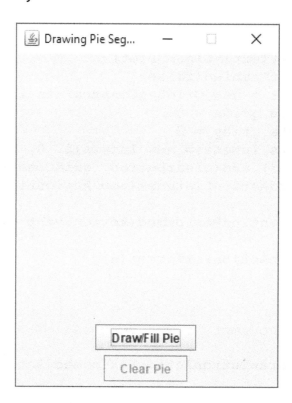

The panel appears gray because we haven't coded the **paintComponent** method yet. We'll do that now.

5. Use these class level variable declarations:

```
static Ellipse2D.Double myEllipse;
static int numberSlices;
static double[] extent = new double[6];
static Color[] myColors = new Color[6];
static boolean isDrawn = false;
Random myRandom = new Random();
```

6. Add these lines of code at the end of the constructor code to initialize the bounding ellipse and set colors:

```
myEllipse = new Ellipse2D.Double(20, 20,
drawPanel.getWidth() - 40, drawPanel.getHeight() - 40);
myColors[0] = Color.RED;
myColors[1] = Color.GREEN;
myColors[2] = Color.YELLOW;
myColors[3] = Color.BLUE;
myColors[4] = Color.MAGENTA;
myColors[5] = Color.CYAN;
```

7. Use this code in the **drawButtonActionPerformed** event method:

```java
private void drawButtonActionPerformed(ActionEvent e)
{
  // new pie - get number of slices (2-6), sweep angles
and draw it
  double degreesRemaining = 360;
  // choose 2 to 6 slices at random
  numberSlices = myRandom.nextInt(5) + 2;
  // for each slice choose an extent angle
  for (int n = 0; n < numberSlices; n++)
  {
    if (n < numberSlices - 1)
    {
      extent[n] = myRandom.nextInt((int) (degreesRemaining
- 1)) + 1;
    }
    else
    {
      extent[n] = degreesRemaining;
    }
    degreesRemaining -= extent[n];
  }
  isDrawn = true;
  drawButton.setEnabled(false);
  clearButton.setEnabled(true);
  drawPanel.repaint();
}
```

This code establishes the pie segments and draws them.

8. Use this code in **clearButtonActionPerformed** event - this clears the graphics object and allows new pie segments to be drawn:

```java
private void clearButtonActionPerformed(ActionEvent e)
{
  // clear region
  isDrawn = false;
  drawButton.setEnabled(true);
  clearButton.setEnabled(false);
  drawPanel.repaint();
}
```

9. Use this code in the **paintComponent** method in the **GraphicsPanel** class. This code draws/fills an ellipse with pie segments if it is in the panel control:

```java
public void paintComponent(Graphics g)
{
  Graphics2D g2D = (Graphics2D) g;
  super.paintComponent(g2D);
  if (DrawingPie.isDrawn)
  {
    // draw pie
    double startAngle = 0;
    // for each slice fill and draw
    for (int n = 0; n < DrawingPie.numberSlices; n++)
    {
      Arc2D.Double myArc = new
Arc2D.Double(DrawingPie.myEllipse.x,
DrawingPie.myEllipse.y, DrawingPie.myEllipse.width,
DrawingPie.myEllipse.height, startAngle,
DrawingPie.extent[n], Arc2D.PIE);
      g2D.setPaint(DrawingPie.myColors[n]);
      g2D.fill(myArc);
      g2D.setPaint(Color.BLACK);
      g2D.draw(myArc);
      startAngle += DrawingPie.extent[n];
    }
    // draw bounding ellipse
    g2D.draw(DrawingPie.myEllipse);
  }
  g2D.dispose();
}
```

Notice how we accessed the bounding ellipse geometry.

The final **DrawingPie.java** code listing (code added to framework is shaded):

```java
/*
 * DrawingPie.java
 */
package drawingpie;
import javax.swing.*;
import java.awt.*;
import java.awt.geom.*;
import java.awt.event.*;
import java.util.Random;

public class DrawingPie extends JFrame
{

    GraphicsPanel drawPanel = new GraphicsPanel();
    JButton drawButton = new JButton();
    JButton clearButton = new JButton();
    static Ellipse2D.Double myEllipse;
    static int numberSlices;
    static double[] extent = new double[6];
    static Color[] myColors = new Color[6];
    static boolean isDrawn = false;
    Random myRandom = new Random();

    public static void main(String args[])
    {
      //construct frame
      new DrawingPie().show();
    }

    public DrawingPie()
    {
      // code to build the form
      setTitle("Drawing Pie Segments");
      setResizable(false);
      addWindowListener(new WindowAdapter()
      {
        public void windowClosing(WindowEvent e)
        {
          exitForm(e);
        }
      });
      getContentPane().setLayout(new GridBagLayout());

      // position controls (establish event methods)
```

```
      GridBagConstraints gridConstraints = new
GridBagConstraints();
    drawPanel.setPreferredSize(new Dimension(250, 250));
    drawPanel.setBackground(Color.WHITE);
    gridConstraints.gridx = 0;
    gridConstraints.gridy = 0;
    gridConstraints.insets = new Insets(10, 10, 10, 10);
    getContentPane().add(drawPanel, gridConstraints);

     drawButton.setText("Draw/Fill Pie");
    gridConstraints = new GridBagConstraints();
    gridConstraints.gridx = 0;
    gridConstraints.gridy = 1;
    getContentPane().add(drawButton, gridConstraints);
    drawButton.addActionListener(new ActionListener()
    {
      public void actionPerformed(ActionEvent e)
      {
        drawButtonActionPerformed(e);
      }
    });

     clearButton.setText("Clear Pie");
     clearButton.setEnabled(false);
    gridConstraints = new GridBagConstraints();
    gridConstraints.gridx = 0;
    gridConstraints.gridy = 3;
    gridConstraints.insets = new Insets(5, 0, 5, 0);
    getContentPane().add(clearButton, gridConstraints);
    clearButton.addActionListener(new ActionListener()
    {
      public void actionPerformed(ActionEvent e)
      {
        clearButtonActionPerformed(e);
      }
    });

    pack();
    Dimension screenSize =
Toolkit.getDefaultToolkit().getScreenSize();
    setBounds((int) (0.5 * (screenSize.width - getWidth())),
(int) (0.5 * (screenSize.height - getHeight())), getWidth(),
getHeight());
    // define bounding ellipse and colors
    myEllipse = new Ellipse2D.Double(20, 20,
drawPanel.getWidth() - 40, drawPanel.getHeight() - 40);
    myColors[0] = Color.RED;
```

```
  myColors[1] = Color.GREEN;
  myColors[2] = Color.YELLOW;
  myColors[3] = Color.BLUE;
  myColors[4] = Color.MAGENTA;
  myColors[5] = Color.CYAN;
}

private void drawButtonActionPerformed(ActionEvent e)
{
  // new pie - get number of slices (2-6), sweep angles and
draw it
  double degreesRemaining = 360;
  // choose 2 to 6 slices at random
  numberSlices = myRandom.nextInt(5) + 2;
  // for each slice choose an extent angle
  for (int n = 0; n < numberSlices; n++)
  {
    if (n < numberSlices - 1)
    {
      extent[n] = myRandom.nextInt((int) (degreesRemaining
- 1)) + 1;
    }
    else
    {
      extent[n] = degreesRemaining;
    }
    degreesRemaining -= extent[n];
  }
  isDrawn = true;
  drawButton.setEnabled(false);
  clearButton.setEnabled(true);
  drawPanel.repaint();
}

private void clearButtonActionPerformed(ActionEvent e)
{
  // clear region
  isDrawn = false;
  drawButton.setEnabled(true);
  clearButton.setEnabled(false);
  drawPanel.repaint();
}

private void exitForm(WindowEvent e)
{
  System.exit(0);
}
```

```
}

class GraphicsPanel extends JPanel
{
  public GraphicsPanel()
  {
  }
  public void paintComponent(Graphics g)
  {
    Graphics2D g2D = (Graphics2D) g;
    super.paintComponent(g2D);
    if (DrawingPie.isDrawn)
    {
      // draw pie
      double startAngle = 0;
      // for each slice fill and draw
      for (int n = 0; n < DrawingPie.numberSlices; n++)
      {
        Arc2D.Double myArc = new
Arc2D.Double(DrawingPie.myEllipse.x, DrawingPie.myEllipse.y,
DrawingPie.myEllipse.width, DrawingPie.myEllipse.height,
startAngle, DrawingPie.extent[n], Arc2D.PIE);
        g2D.setPaint(DrawingPie.myColors[n]);
        g2D.fill(myArc);
        g2D.setPaint(Color.BLACK);
        g2D.draw(myArc);
        startAngle += DrawingPie.extent[n];
      }
      // draw bounding ellipse
      g2D.draw(DrawingPie.myEllipse);
    }
    g2D.dispose();
  }
}
```

Run the project. Click **Draw/Fill Pie** to draw a segmented pie. Try several – each will be different. Note that the graphics are persistent. Here's a run I made:

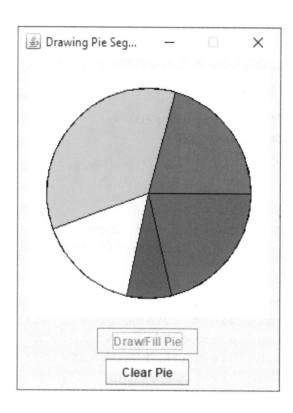

Save the project application (saved as **Example7-8** project in **\LearnJava\LJ Code\Class 7** program group).

Pie Charts

The example just discussed suggests an immediate application for such capabilities – drawing **pie charts**. Pie charts are used to compare values of like information or to show what makes up a particular quantity. For example, a pie chart could illustrate what categories your monthly expenses fit into. Or, here is a pie chart with 12 segments illustrating monthly rainfall (in inches) for my hometown of Seattle (the segments for the winter months are very big!):

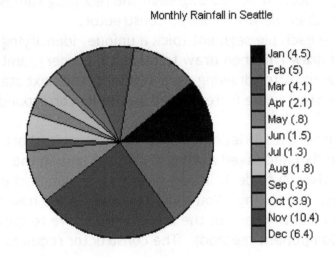

This chart was created with Java, by the way.

The steps for drawing a pie chart are straightforward. Assume you have **n** pieces of data (monthly rainfall, categorized expenditures, seasonal air traffic, various income sources). Follow these steps to create a pie chart using the Java graphics methods:

> Generate **n** pieces of data to be plotted. Store this data in an n element array **y** (a 0-based array).
> Sum the **n** elements of the **y** array to obtain a total value.
> Divide each **y** element by the computed total to obtain the proportional contributions of each.
> Multiply each proportion by 360 degrees – the resulting values will be the **extent** arguments in the **Arc2D** shape constructor.
> Define and draw each pie segment (pick a unique, identifying color) using **Arc2D**, **fill** and **draw** (**fill** then **draw** to maintain border). Initialize the **start** angle at zero. After drawing each segment, the next **start** angle will be the previous **start** value incremented by the its corresponding **extent**.

The following is a general class (**PieChartPanel**) to draw a pie chart in a panel control (it is in **Appendix I** and saved as **PieChartPanel.java** in the **\LearnJava\LJ Code\Class 7** folder). It is a simple extension of the **GraphicsPanel** we have been using. You should be able to see how input variables are used and identify each of the steps listed above to draw a pie chart (see the **paintComponent** method). The constructor requires four arguments:

border   Rectangle (within the panel) describing the border region for the pie chart (**Rectangle2D.Double** type). Using such a rectangle leaves space, if desired, in the panel for labeling and other information.
nSegments   Number of pie segments (**int** data type)
yValues   Array of data (**double** data type)
colorValues   Array of pie segment colors (**Color** type)

The class code (**PieChartPanel.java**) is:

```java
import javax.swing.*;
import java.awt.geom.*;
import java.awt.*;
public class PieChartPanel extends JPanel
{
  private Rectangle2D.Double borderRectangle;
  private int n;
  private double[] y;
  private Color[] c;

  public PieChartPanel()
  {
    // default constructor for initialization
  }
  public PieChartPanel(Rectangle2D.Double border, int
nSegments, double[] yValues, Color[] colorValues)
  {
    this.borderRectangle = border;
    this.n = nSegments;
    this.y = yValues;
    this.c = colorValues;
  }
  public void paintComponent(Graphics g)
  {
    // Draws a pie chart
    // borderRectangle - rectangle object to draw chart
    // n - number of pie segments to draw
    // y - array of points (Double type) to chart (lower
index is 1, upper index is N)
    // c - color of pie segments
    Graphics2D g2D = (Graphics2D) g;
    super.paintComponent(g2D);
    double sum = 0.0;
    for (int i = 0; i < n; i++)
    {
      sum += y[i];
    }
    // draw pie
    double startAngle = 0;
    Arc2D.Double myArc;
    // for each slice fill and draw
    for (int i = 0; i < n; i++)
    {
        myArc = new Arc2D.Double(borderRectangle.x,
borderRectangle.y, borderRectangle.width,
```

```
borderRectangle.height, startAngle, 360 * y[i] / sum,
Arc2D.PIE);
        g2D.setPaint(c[i]);
        g2D.fill(myArc);
        g2D.setPaint(Color.BLACK);
        g2D.draw(myArc);
        startAngle += 360 * y[i] / sum;
    }
    g2D.dispose();
  }
}
```

Using this class to draw a pie chart is simple. First, include the class code in your project. Second, declare and initialize a **PieChartPanel** object using the usual syntax. If that panel is **myPieChart**, the code is:

```
PieChartPanel myPieChart = new PieChartPanel();
```

Placement of this declaration depends on the desired scope for the panel. The panel is positioned in a frame (and properties are set) just like any **JPanel** control, since we are extending that class. It seems to work best when positioned within another **JPanel** control.

Once you have decided on the input arguments (bounding rectangle **myBorder**, number of segments **n**, data value array **y**, and color array **c**), the pie chart object is constructed using:

```
myPieChart = new PieChartPanel(myBorder, n, y, c);
```

After this line of code, the pie chart will appear in the corresponding **PieChartPanel** object. See **Example 7-9** for an example of using this class and corresponding object.

Line Charts and Bar Charts

In addition to pie charts, two other useful data display tools are **line charts** and **bar charts**. Line charts are used to plot Cartesian pairs of data (x, y) generated using some function. They are useful for seeing trends in data. As an example, you could plot your weight while following a diet and exercise regime. And, here is a line chart (created with Java) of yearly attendance at the Seattle Mariners baseball games:

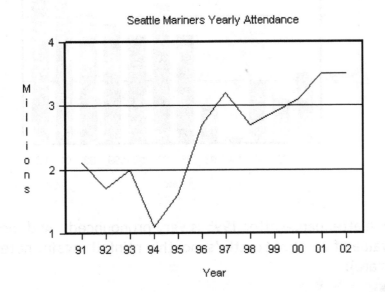

You can see there was increased interest in the team after the 1995 year (that's the exciting year we've alluded to in some of our problems – for example, see **Problem 7-4** at the end of this class).

The Java **Line2D** shape and **draw** method can be used to create line charts. The steps for generating such a chart are simple:

➤ Generate **n** Cartesian pairs of data to be plotted. Store the horizontal values in an **n** element array **x** and the corresponding vertical values in an **n** element array **y** (both 0-based arrays).

➤ Loop through all **n** points, connecting consecutive points using **Line2D** shapes and the **draw** method.

Bar charts plot values as horizontal or vertical bars (referenced to some base value, many times zero). They can also be used to see trends and to compare values, like pie charts. Here's a vertical bar chart (drawn with Java methods) of the same attendance data in the line chart above (the base value is 1 million):

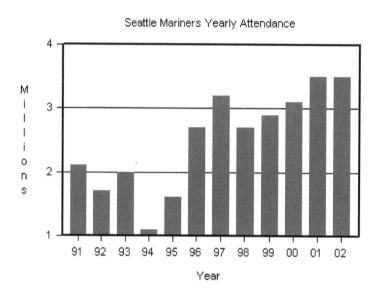

The increase in attendance after 1995 is very pronounced. And, here's a bar chart (base value of zero) of Seattle's monthly rainfall (again, note how big the 'winter' bars are):

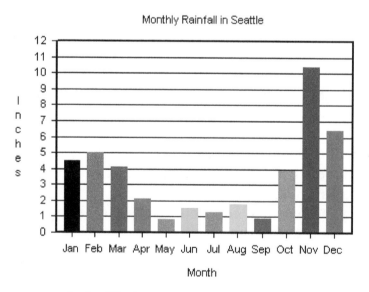

Yes, this, too, was created with Java.

The **Rectangle2D** shape and **fill** method can be used for bar charts. The steps for generating a vertical bar chart:

> ➢ Generate **n** pieces of data to be plotted. Store this data in an **n** element array **y** (a 0-based array).
> ➢ Determine the width of each bar, using width of the plotting area as a guide. I usually allow some space between each bar.
> ➢ Select a **base** value (the value at the bottom of the bar). This is often zero.
> ➢ For each bar, determine horizontal position based on bar width and current bar being drawn. Draw each bar (pick a unique, identifying color, if desired) using **Rectangle2D** shapes and the **fill** method. The bar height begins at the **base** value and ends at the respective **y** value.

At this point, similar to what we did for pie charts, we could write code to implement general classes for drawing line and bar charts. But, there's a problem. And, that problem relates to the **user coordinates** used by the graphics objects. Let me illustrate. Say we wanted to draw a very simple line chart described by the four Cartesian points given by:

x = 0, y = 2
x = 2, y = 7
x = 5, y = 11
x = 6, y = 13

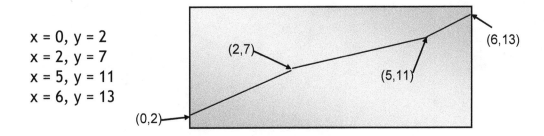

In this plot, the horizontal axis (which increases from left to right) value (**x**) begins at 0 and reaches a maximum of 6. The vertical axis value (**y**) has a minimum value of 2, a maximum of 13. And, **y** increases in an upward direction.

Say, we want to plot this in a **Rectangle2D** object, **myRectangle**, within a panel (a typical thing to do). Graphically, we have:

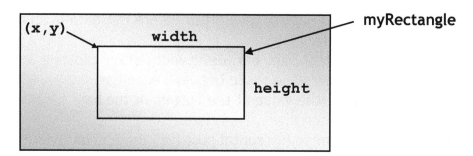

Note the user coordinates of the rectangle object have an origin of **(myRectangle.x, myRectangle.y)** at the upper left corner. The maximum **x** value is **myRectangle.x + myRectangle.width – 1**, the maximum **y** value is **myRectangle.y + myRectangle.height –1** and **y** increases in a downward direction. Hence, to plot our data, we need to first compute where each **(x, y)** pair in our 'physical-coordinates' fits within the dimensions of the rectangle object specified by the **myRectangle** object properties. This is a straightforward coordinate conversion computation.

Coordinate Conversions

Drawing in graphics object is done in **user coordinates** (measured in pixels). Data for plotting line and bar charts is usually in some physically meaningful units (inches, degrees, dollars) we'll call **physical coordinates**. In order to draw a line or bar chart, we need to be able to convert from physical coordinates to user coordinates. We will assume the 'user' space is a rectangle object (**r**) with upper left corner at (**x, y**) and **w** by **h** in size. We will do each axis (horizontal and vertical) separately.

The horizontal (**xUser** axis) in **user coordinates** is **w** pixels wide. The far left pixel is at **xUser = r.x** and the far right is at **xUser = r.x + r.w – 1**. **xUser** increases from left to right:

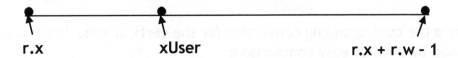

Assume the horizontal data (**xPhysical** axis) in our physical coordinates runs from a minimum, **xMin**, at the left to a maximum, **xMax,** at the right. Thus, the first pixel on the horizontal axis of our physical coordinates will be **xMin** and the last will be **xMax**:

With these two depictions, we can compute the **xUser** value corresponding to a given **xPhysical** value using simple **proportions,** dividing the distance from some point on the axis to the minimum value by the total distance. The process is also called **linear interpolation.** These proportions show:

$$\frac{xPhysical - xMin}{xMax - xMin} = \frac{xUser - r.x}{r.x + r.w - 1 - r.x}$$

Solving this for **xUser** yields the desired conversion from a physical value on the horizontal axis (**xUser**) to a user value for plotting:

xUser = r.x + (xPhysical - xMin)(r.w - 1)/(xMax - Xmin)

You can see this is correct at each extreme value. When **xPhysical = Xmin**, **xUser = r.x**. When **xPhysical = xMax, xUser = r.x + r.w - 1.**

Now, we find the corresponding conversion for the vertical axis. We'll place the two axes side-by-side for easy comparison:

User Axis: **Physical Axis:**

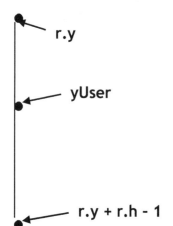
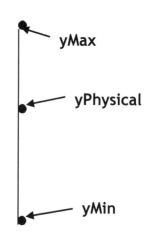

The vertical (**yUser** axis) in **user coordinates** is r.h pixels high. The topmost pixel is at **yUser = r.y** and the bottom is at **yUser = r.y + r.h - 1.** yUser increases from top to bottom. The vertical data (**yPhysical** axis) in our physical coordinates, runs from a minimum, **yMin**, at the bottom, to a maximum, **yMax**, at the top. Thus, the top pixel on the vertical axis of our physical coordinates will be **yMax** and the bottom will be **yMin** (note our physical axis increases up, rather than down).

With these two depictions, we can compute the **yUser** value corresponding to a given **yPhysical** value using linear interpolation. The computations show:

$$\frac{yPhysical - Ymin}{Ymax - Ymin} = \frac{yUser - (r.y + r.h - 1)}{r.y - (r.y + r.h - 1)}$$

Solving this for **yUser** yields the desired conversion from a physical value on the horizontal axis (**yPhysical**) to a user value for plotting (this requires a bit algebra, but it's straightforward):

yUser = r.y + (yMax - yPhysical)(r.h - 1)/(yMax - yMin)

Again, check the extremes. When **yPhysical = yMin, yUser = r.y + r.h - 1**. When **yPhysical = yMax, yUser = r.y**. It looks good.

Whenever we need to plot real, physical data in a graphics object, we will need coordinate conversions. In these notes, we use two general methods to do the conversions (both of these functions are in **Appendix I**). First, for the horizontal axis, we use **xPhysicaltoxUser**. This function has four input arguments: **r** the rectangle object (**Rectangle2D** object) that the conversion is based on, the **xPhysical** value, the minimum physical value, **xMin**, and the maximum value, **xMax**. All values are of **double** data type. The method returns the user coordinate (a **double** type):

```
private double xPhysicalToxUser(Rectangle2D.Double r,
double xPhysical, double xMin, double xMax)
{
  return(r.x + (xPhysical - xMin) * (r.width - 1) / (xMax
- xMin));
}
```

For the vertical axis, we use **yPhysicalToyUser**. This function has four input arguments: **r** the rectangle object (**Rectangle2D** object) that the conversion is based on, the **yPhysical** value, the minimum physical value, **yMin**, and the maximum value, **yMax**. All values are of **double** data type. The method returns the user coordinate (a **double** type):

```
private double yPhysicalToyUser(Rectangle2D.Double r,
double yPhysical, double yMin, double yMax)
{
  return(r.y + (yMax - yPhysical) * (r.height - 1) / (yMax
- yMin));
}
```

With the ability to transform coordinates, we can now develop general-purpose line and bar chart classes, similar to that developed for the pie chart. The modified steps to create a line chart are:

> Generate **n** Cartesian pairs of data to be plotted. Store the horizontal values in an **n** element array **x**, the corresponding vertical values in an **n** element array **y** (both 0-based arrays).
> Loop through all **n** points to determine the **minimum** and **maximum x** and **y** values.
> Again, loop through all **n** points. For each point, convert the **x** and **y** values to user coordinates, then connect the current point with the previous point using the **Line2D** shape and **draw** method.

The following is a general class (**LineChartPanel**) to draw a line chart in a panel control (it is in **Appendix I** and saved as **LineChartPanel.java** in the **\LearnJava\LJ Code\Class 7** folder). You should be able to identify the chart building steps (most involve finding minimum and maximum values). The class includes the coordinate conversions. The constructor requires five arguments:

border   Rectangle (within the panel) describing the border region for the line chart (**Rectangle2D.Double** type). Using such a rectangle leaves space, if desired, in the panel for labeling and other information.
nPoints   Number of data points (**int** data type)
xValues   Array of horizontal values (**double** data type)
yValues   Array of vertical values, corresponding to xValues array (**double** data type)
colorValue   Color of line in chart (**Color** type)

The class code (**LineChartPanel.java**) is:

```
import javax.swing.*;
import java.awt.geom.*;
import java.awt.*;
public class LineChartPanel extends JPanel
{
  private Rectangle2D.Double borderRectangle;
  private int n;
  private double[] x;
  private double[] y;
  private Color c;
  public LineChartPanel()
  {
    // default constructor for initialization
  }
  public LineChartPanel(Rectangle2D.Double border, int
nPoints, double[] xValues, double[] yValues, Color
colorValue)
  {
    this.borderRectangle = border;
    this.n = nPoints;
    this.x = xValues;
    this.y = yValues;
    this.c = colorValue;
  }
  public void paintComponent(Graphics g)
  {
    // Draws a  line chart - pairs of (x,y) coordinates
    // borderRectangle - rectangle region to draw plot
```

```
    // n - number of points to plot
    // x - array of x points (lower index is 0, upper
index is n-1)
    // y - array of y points (lower index is 0, upper
index is n-1)
    // c - color of line
    // Need at least 2 points to plot
    if (n < 2)
    {
      return;
    }
    double xMin = x[0]; double xMax = x[0];
    double yMin = y[0]; double yMax = y[0];
    // find minimums and maximums
    for (int i = 1; i < n; i++)
    {
      xMin = Math.min(xMin, x[i]);
      xMax = Math.max(xMax, x[i]);
      yMin = Math.min(yMin, y[i]);
      yMax = Math.max(yMax, y[i]);
    }
    // Extend y values a bit so lines are not right on
borders
    yMin = (1 - 0.05 * Double.compare(yMin, 0)) * yMin;
    yMax = (1 + 0.05 * Double.compare(yMax, 0)) * yMax;
    Graphics2D g2D = (Graphics2D) g;
    super.paintComponent(g2D);
    Line2D.Double myLine;
    g2D.setPaint(c);
    for (int i = 0; i < n - 1; i++)
    {
      // plot in user coordinates
      myLine = new
Line2D.Double(xPhysicalToxUser(borderRectangle, x[i],
xMin, xMax), yPhysicalToyUser(borderRectangle, y[i], yMin,
yMax), xPhysicalToxUser(borderRectangle, x[i + 1], xMin,
xMax), yPhysicalToyUser(borderRectangle, y[i + 1], yMin,
yMax));
      g2D.draw(myLine);
    }
    // draw border
    g2D.setPaint(Color.BLACK);
    g2D.draw(borderRectangle);
    g2D.dispose();
  }
  private double xPhysicalToxUser(Rectangle2D.Double r,
double xPhysical, double xMin, double xMax)
```

```
    {
        return(r.x + (xPhysical - xMin) * (r.width - 1) /
(xMax - xMin));
    }
    private double yPhysicalToyUser(Rectangle2D.Double r,
double yPhysical, double yMin, double yMax)
    {
        return(r.y + (yMax - yPhysical) * (r.height - 1) /
(yMax - yMin));
    }
}
```

To use this class to draw a line chart, first, include the class code in your project. Second, declare and initialize a **LineChartPanel** object using the usual syntax. If that panel is **myLineChart**, the code is:

```
LineChartPanel myLineChart = new LineChartPanel();
```

Placement of this declaration depends on the desired scope for the panel. The panel is positioned in a frame (and properties are set) just like any **JPanel** control, since we are extending that class. It seems to work best when positioned within another **JPanel** control.

Once you have decided on the input arguments (bounding rectangle **myBorder**, number of points **n**, data value arrays **x** and **y**, and line color **c**), the line chart object is constructed using:

```
myLineChart = new LineChartPanel(myBorder, n, x, y, c);
```

After this line of code, the line chart will appear in the corresponding **LineChartPanel** object. See **Example 7-9** for an example of using this class and corresponding object.

The modified steps to create a bar chart are:

➢ Generate **n** pieces of data to be plotted. Store this data in an **n** element array **y** (a 0-based array).
➢ Determine the width of each bar, using width of the plotting area as a guide. I usually allow some space between each bar.
➢ Loop through all **n** points to determine the **minimum** and **maximum y** value.
➢ Select a **base** value (the value at the bottom of the bar). This is often zero. Convert the **base** value to user coordinates.
➢ For each bar, determine horizontal position based on bar width and current bar being drawn. Draw each bar (pick a unique, identifying color, if desired) using **Rectangle2D** objects and the **fill** method. The bar height begins at the **base** value and ends at the respective **y** value (converted to user coordinates.

The following is a general class (**BarChartPanel**) to draw a bar chart in a panel control (it is in **Appendix I** and saved as **BarChartPanel.java** in the **\LearnJava\LJ Code\Class 7** folder). You should be able to identify the chart building steps (most involve finding minimum and maximum values). Note different coding is needed depending whether the bar value is higher or lower than the base value (i.e., whether the bar goes up or down).The class includes the coordinate conversions. The constructor requires five arguments:

border   Rectangle (within the panel) describing the border region for the bar chart (**Rectangle2D.Double** type). Using such a rectangle leaves space, if desired, in the panel for labeling and other information.
nPoints   Number of data points (**int** data type)
yValues   Array of data values (**double** data type)
base   Base value (**double** type)
colorValue   Color of line in chart (**Color** type)

The class code (**BarChartPanel.java**) is:

```
import javax.swing.*;
import java.awt.geom.*;
import java.awt.*;
public class BarChartPanel extends JPanel
{
  private Rectangle2D.Double borderRectangle;
  private int n;
  private double[] y;
  private double b;
  private Color c;
```

```
   public BarChartPanel()
   {
     // default constructor for initialization
   }
   public BarChartPanel(Rectangle2D.Double border, int
nPoints, double[] yValues, double base, Color colorValue)
   {
     this.borderRectangle = border;
     this.n = nPoints;
     this.y = yValues;
     this.b = base;
     this.c = colorValue;
   }
   public void paintComponent(Graphics g)
   {
     // Draws a  bar chart
     // borderRectangle - rectangle region to draw plot
     // n - number of points to plot
     // y - array of y points (lower index is 0, upper
index is n-1)
     // c - color of bars
     double yMin = y[0]; double yMax = y[0];
     // find minimums and maximums
     for (int i = 1; i < n; i++)
     {
       yMin = Math.min(yMin, y[i]);
       yMax = Math.max(yMax, y[i]);
     }
     // Extend y values a bit so bars are not right on
borders
     yMin = (1 - 0.05 * Double.compare(yMin, 0)) * yMin;
     yMax = (1 + 0.05 * Double.compare(yMax, 0)) * yMax;
     Graphics2D g2D = (Graphics2D) g;
     super.paintComponent(g2D);
     // Find bar width in client coordinates
     // use half bar-width as margins between bars
     double barWidth = 2 * (borderRectangle.width - 1) / (3
* n + 1);
     double clientBase = yPhysicalToyUser(borderRectangle,
b, yMin, yMax);
     Rectangle2D.Double myRectangle;
     for (int i = 0; i < n; i++)
     {
       // draw bars
       if (y[i] > b)
       {
```

```
          myRectangle = new
Rectangle2D.Double(borderRectangle.x + (1.5 * i + 0.5) *
barWidth, yPhysicalToyUser(borderRectangle, y[i], yMin,
yMax), barWidth, clientBase -
yPhysicalToyUser(borderRectangle, y[i], yMin, yMax));
        }
        else
        {
          myRectangle = new
Rectangle2D.Double(borderRectangle.x + (1.5 * i + 0.5) *
barWidth, clientBase, barWidth,
yPhysicalToyUser(borderRectangle, y[i], yMin, yMax) -
clientBase);
        }
        g2D.setPaint(c);
        g2D.fill(myRectangle);
      }
      // draw border
      g2D.setPaint(Color.BLACK);
      g2D.draw(borderRectangle);
      // line at base
      g2D.draw(new Line2D.Double(borderRectangle.x,
clientBase, borderRectangle.x + borderRectangle.width - 1,
clientBase));
      g2D.dispose();
    }
    private double xPhysicalToxUser(Rectangle2D.Double r,
double xPhysical, double xMin, double xMax)
    {
      return(r.x + (xPhysical - xMin) * (r.width - 1) /
(xMax - xMin));
    }
    private double yPhysicalToyUser(Rectangle2D.Double r,
double yPhysical, double yMin, double yMax)
    {
      return(r.y + (yMax - yPhysical) * (r.height - 1) /
(yMax - yMin));
    }
}
```

To use this class to draw a bar chart, first, include the class code in your project. Second, declare and initialize a **BarChartPanel** object using the usual syntax. If that panel is **myBarChart**, the code is:

```
BarChartPanel myBarChart = new BarChartPanel();
```

Placement of this declaration depends on the desired scope for the panel. The panel is positioned in a frame (and properties are set) just like any **JPanel** control, since we are extending that class. It seems to work best when positioned within another **JPanel** control.

Once you have decided on the input arguments (bounding rectangle **myBorder**, number of points **n**, data value array **y**, base value **b** and line color **c**), the bar chart object is constructed using:

```
myBarChart = new BarChartPanel(myBorder, n, y, b, c);
```

After this line of code, the bar chart will appear in the corresponding **BarChartPanel** object. See **Example 7-9** for an example of using this class and corresponding object.

Example 7-9

Line, Bar and Pie Charts

Start a new empty project in **NetBeans**. Name the project **ChartExamples**.
Delete the default code in Java file named **ChartExamples**. Here, we'll use the
classes we developed and presented to plot line, bar and pie charts. The data
for the plots will be random.

Copy the three class files, **PieChartPanel.java, LineChartPanel.java** and
BarChartPanel.java (from **\LearnJava\LJ Code\Class 7** folder) to your project's
source folder (the one where **ChartExamples.java** is located). Open each of the
added files and place this line at the top of each file

```
package chartexamples;
```

This "connects" these classes to your project.

The finished frame will appear as:

1. Put a panel control and four buttons on a frame. The **GridBagLayout** is:

	gridx = 0	gridx = 1	gridx = 2	gridx = 3
gridy = 0	myPanel			
gridy = 1	lineButton	spiralButton	barButton	pieButton

Set these properties:

ChartExamples Frame:

title	Chart Examples
resizable	false

myPanel:

preferredSize	(400, 300)
background	WHITE
gridx	0
gridy	0
gridwidth	4
insets	(10, 10, 10, 10)

lineButton:

text	Line
preferredSize	(100, 25)
gridx	0
gridy	1
insets	(5, 5, 5, 5)

spiralButton:

text	Spiral
preferredSize	(100, 25)
gridx	1
gridy	1
insets	(5, 5, 5, 5)

barButton:

text	Bar
preferredSize	(100, 25)
gridx	2
gridy	1
insets	(5, 5, 5, 5)

pieButton:

text	Pie
preferredSize	(100, 25)
gridx	3
gridy	1
insets	(5, 5, 5, 5)

2. Build the basic framework:

```
/*
 * ChartExamples.java
 */
package chartexamples;
import javax.swing.*;
import java.awt.*;
import java.awt.event.*;
import java.util.Random;
import java.awt.geom.*;
public class ChartExamples extends JFrame
{
  public static void main(String args[])
  {
    // create frame
    new ChartExamples().show();
  }
  public ChartExamples()
  {
    // frame constructor
    setTitle("Chart Examples");
    setResizable(false);
    addWindowListener(new WindowAdapter()
    {
      public void windowClosing(WindowEvent evt)
      {
        exitForm(evt);
      }
    });
    getContentPane().setLayout(new GridBagLayout());

    pack();
    Dimension screenSize =
Toolkit.getDefaultToolkit().getScreenSize();
    setBounds((int) (0.5 * (screenSize.width -
getWidth())), (int) (0.5 * (screenSize.height -
getHeight())), getWidth(), getHeight());
  }
```

```
    private void exitForm(WindowEvent e)
    {
      System.exit(0);
    }
}
```

Run to check the framework.

3. Class level control declarations:

```
JPanel myPanel = new JPanel();
JButton lineButton = new JButton();
JButton spiralButton = new JButton();
JButton barButton = new JButton();
JButton pieButton = new JButton();
```

Position controls and add event methods:

```
myPanel.setPreferredSize(new Dimension(400, 300));
myPanel.setBackground(Color.WHITE);
GridBagConstraints gridConstraints = new
GridBagConstraints();
gridConstraints.gridx = 0;
gridConstraints.gridy = 0;
gridConstraints.gridwidth = 4;
gridConstraints.insets = new Insets(10, 10, 10, 10);
getContentPane().add(myPanel, gridConstraints);

lineButton.setText("Line");
lineButton.setPreferredSize(new Dimension (100,25));
gridConstraints = new GridBagConstraints();
gridConstraints.gridx = 0;
gridConstraints.gridy = 1;
gridConstraints.insets = new Insets(5, 5, 5, 5);
getContentPane().add(lineButton, gridConstraints);
lineButton.addActionListener(new ActionListener()
{
  public void actionPerformed(ActionEvent e)
  {
    lineButtonActionPerformed(e);
  }
});

spiralButton.setText("Spiral");
spiralButton.setPreferredSize(new Dimension (100,25));
gridConstraints = new GridBagConstraints();
```

```
gridConstraints.gridx = 1;
gridConstraints.gridy = 1;
gridConstraints.insets = new Insets(5, 5, 5, 5);
getContentPane().add(spiralButton, gridConstraints);
spiralButton.addActionListener(new ActionListener()
{
  public void actionPerformed(ActionEvent e)
  {
    lineButtonActionPerformed(e);
  }
});

barButton.setText("Bar");
barButton.setPreferredSize(new Dimension (100,25));
gridConstraints = new GridBagConstraints();
gridConstraints.gridx = 2;
gridConstraints.gridy = 1;
gridConstraints.insets = new Insets(5, 5, 5, 5);
getContentPane().add(barButton, gridConstraints);
barButton.addActionListener(new ActionListener()
{
  public void actionPerformed(ActionEvent e)
  {
    barButtonActionPerformed(e);
  }
});

pieButton.setText("Pie");
pieButton.setPreferredSize(new Dimension (100,25));
gridConstraints = new GridBagConstraints();
gridConstraints.gridx = 3;
gridConstraints.gridy = 1;
gridConstraints.insets = new Insets(5, 5, 5, 5);
getContentPane().add(pieButton, gridConstraints);
pieButton.addActionListener(new ActionListener()
{
  public void actionPerformed(ActionEvent e)
  {
    pieButtonActionPerformed(e);
  }
});
```

Add three empty methods:

```
private void lineButtonActionPerformed(ActionEvent e)
{
}

private void barButtonActionPerformed(ActionEvent e)
{
}

private void pieButtonActionPerformed(ActionEvent e)
{
}
```

Run to check the control layout:

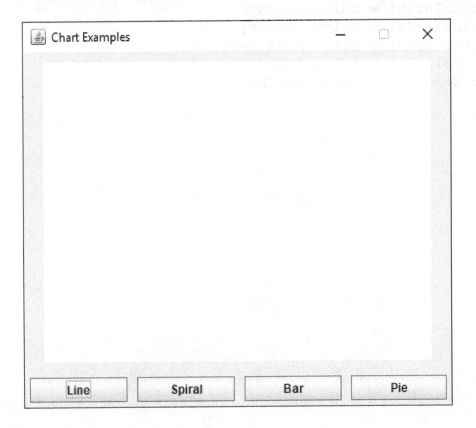

4. Now, we add code. Class level variable declarations:

```
double[] x = new double[200];
double[] y = new double[200];
double[] yd = new double[200];
Color[] plotColor = new Color[10];
Random myRandom = new Random();
```

5. Add this code to the constructor code. This sets colors to use:

```
plotColor[0] = Color.YELLOW;
plotColor[1] = Color.BLUE;
plotColor[2] = Color.GREEN;
plotColor[3] = Color.CYAN;
plotColor[4] = Color.RED;
plotColor[5] = Color.MAGENTA;
plotColor[6] = Color.ORANGE;
plotColor[7] = Color.DARK_GRAY;
plotColor[8] = Color.GRAY;
plotColor[9] = Color.BLACK;
```

6. Add this code to the **lineButtonActionPerformed** method (handles both drawing of line and spiral plots). This code generates random data to plot using the **LineChartPanel** class:

```java
private void lineButtonActionPerformed(ActionEvent e)
{
  // Draws line and spiral charts
  // Create a sinusoid with 200 points
  double alpha = 0.1 - myRandom.nextDouble() * 0.2;
  double beta = myRandom.nextDouble() * 10 + 5;
  for (int i = 0; i < 200; i++)
  {
    x[i] = i;
    y[i] = Math.exp(-alpha * i) * Math.sin(Math.PI * i /
beta);
    yd[i] = Math.exp(-alpha * i) * (Math.PI *
Math.cos(Math.PI * i / beta) / beta - alpha *
Math.sin(Math.PI * i / beta));
  }
  // Draw plots
  Rectangle2D.Double borderRectangle = new
Rectangle2D.Double(20, 20, 360, 260);
  LineChartPanel myLineChart = new LineChartPanel();
  if (e.getActionCommand().equals(lineButton.getText()))
  {
    myLineChart = new LineChartPanel(borderRectangle, 200,
x, y, plotColor[myRandom.nextInt(10)]);
  }
  else
  {
    myLineChart = new LineChartPanel(borderRectangle, 200,
y, yd, plotColor[myRandom.nextInt(10)]);
  }
  myLineChart.setPreferredSize(new Dimension (400, 300));
  myLineChart.setBackground(Color.WHITE);
  myPanel.removeAll();
  myPanel.add(myLineChart);
  this.pack();
}
```

Note, in particular, how, once the line chart object is created, it is placed on the panel control (**myPanel**).

7. Add this code to the **barButtonActionPerformed** method. This code generates random data to plot using the **BarChartPanel** class:

```
private void barButtonActionPerformed(ActionEvent e)
{
  // generate 5-10 bars with values from -10 to 10 and
draw bar chart
  int numberBars = myRandom.nextInt(6) + 5;
  for (int i = 0; i < numberBars; i++)
  {
    y[i] = myRandom.nextDouble() * 20 - 10;
  }
  // Draw chart
  Rectangle2D.Double borderRectangle = new
Rectangle2D.Double(20, 20, 360, 260);
  BarChartPanel myBarChart = new
BarChartPanel(borderRectangle, numberBars, y, 0.0,
plotColor[myRandom.nextInt(10)]);
  myBarChart.setPreferredSize(new Dimension (400, 300));
  myBarChart.setBackground(Color.WHITE);
  myPanel.removeAll();
  myPanel.add(myBarChart);
  this.pack();
}
```

8. Add this code to the **pieButtonActionPerformed** method. This code generates random data to plot using the **PieChartPanel** class:

```
private void pieButtonActionPerformed(ActionEvent e)
{
  // Generate 3 to 10 slices at random with values from 1
to 5
  int numberSlices = myRandom.nextInt(8) + 3;
  for (int i = 0; i < numberSlices; i++)
  {
    y[i] = myRandom.nextDouble() * 5 + 1;
  }
  Rectangle2D.Double borderRectangle = new
Rectangle2D.Double(70, 20, 260, 260);
  PieChartPanel myPieChart = new
PieChartPanel(borderRectangle, numberSlices, y,
plotColor);
  myPieChart.setPreferredSize(new Dimension (400, 300));
  myPieChart.setBackground(Color.WHITE);
  myPanel.removeAll();
  myPanel.add(myPieChart);
  this.pack();
}
```

The complete **ChartExamples.java** code listing (code added to framework is shaded):

```
/*
 * ChartExamples.java
 */

package chartexamples;
import javax.swing.*;
import java.awt.*;
import java.awt.event.*;
import java.util.Random;
import java.awt.geom.*;

public class ChartExamples extends JFrame
{
  JPanel myPanel = new JPanel();
  JButton lineButton = new JButton();
  JButton spiralButton = new JButton();
  JButton barButton = new JButton();
  JButton pieButton = new JButton();
  // data arrays
```

```java
    double[] x = new double[200];
    double[] y = new double[200];
    double[] yd = new double[200];
    Color[] plotColor = new Color[10];
    Random myRandom = new Random();

  public static void main(String args[])
  {
    // create frame
    new ChartExamples().show();
}

  public ChartExamples()
  {
    // frame constructor
    setTitle("Chart Examples");
    setResizable(false);
    addWindowListener(new WindowAdapter()
    {
      public void windowClosing(WindowEvent evt)
      {
        exitForm(evt);
      }
    });
    getContentPane().setLayout(new GridBagLayout());

    myPanel.setPreferredSize(new Dimension(400, 300));
    myPanel.setBackground(Color.WHITE);
    GridBagConstraints gridConstraints = new
GridBagConstraints();
    gridConstraints.gridx = 0;
    gridConstraints.gridy = 0;
    gridConstraints.gridwidth = 4;
    gridConstraints.insets = new Insets(10, 10, 10, 10);
    getContentPane().add(myPanel, gridConstraints);

    lineButton.setText("Line");
    lineButton.setPreferredSize(new Dimension (100,25));
    gridConstraints = new GridBagConstraints();
    gridConstraints.gridx = 0;
    gridConstraints.gridy = 1;
    gridConstraints.insets = new Insets(5, 5, 5, 5);
    getContentPane().add(lineButton, gridConstraints);
    lineButton.addActionListener(new ActionListener()
    {
      public void actionPerformed(ActionEvent e)
      {
```

```
      lineButtonActionPerformed(e);
    }
});

spiralButton.setText("Spiral");
spiralButton.setPreferredSize(new Dimension (100,25));
gridConstraints = new GridBagConstraints();
gridConstraints.gridx = 1;
gridConstraints.gridy = 1;
gridConstraints.insets = new Insets(5, 5, 5, 5);
getContentPane().add(spiralButton, gridConstraints);
spiralButton.addActionListener(new ActionListener()
{
  public void actionPerformed(ActionEvent e)
  {
    lineButtonActionPerformed(e);
  }
});

barButton.setText("Bar");
barButton.setPreferredSize(new Dimension (100,25));
gridConstraints = new GridBagConstraints();
gridConstraints.gridx = 2;
gridConstraints.gridy = 1;
gridConstraints.insets = new Insets(5, 5, 5, 5);
getContentPane().add(barButton, gridConstraints);
barButton.addActionListener(new ActionListener()
{
  public void actionPerformed(ActionEvent e)
  {
    barButtonActionPerformed(e);
  }
});

pieButton.setText("Pie");
pieButton.setPreferredSize(new Dimension (100,25));
gridConstraints = new GridBagConstraints();
gridConstraints.gridx = 3;
gridConstraints.gridy = 1;
gridConstraints.insets = new Insets(5, 5, 5, 5);
getContentPane().add(pieButton, gridConstraints);
pieButton.addActionListener(new ActionListener()
{
  public void actionPerformed(ActionEvent e)
  {
    pieButtonActionPerformed(e);
  }
```

```
    });

    pack();
    Dimension screenSize =
Toolkit.getDefaultToolkit().getScreenSize();
    setBounds((int) (0.5 * (screenSize.width - getWidth())),
(int) (0.5 * (screenSize.height - getHeight())), getWidth(),
getHeight());
    // colors to use
    plotColor[0] = Color.YELLOW;
    plotColor[1] = Color.BLUE;
    plotColor[2] = Color.GREEN;
    plotColor[3] = Color.CYAN;
    plotColor[4] = Color.RED;
    plotColor[5] = Color.MAGENTA;
    plotColor[6] = Color.ORANGE;
    plotColor[7] = Color.DARK_GRAY;
    plotColor[8] = Color.GRAY;
    plotColor[9] = Color.BLACK;


  }



  private void lineButtonActionPerformed(ActionEvent e)
  {
    // Draws line and spiral charts
    // Create a sinusoid with 200 points
    double alpha = 0.1 - myRandom.nextDouble() * 0.2;
    double beta = myRandom.nextDouble() * 10 + 5;
    for (int i = 0; i < 200; i++)
    {
      x[i] = i;
      y[i] = Math.exp(-alpha * i) * Math.sin(Math.PI * i /
beta);
      yd[i] = Math.exp(-alpha * i) * (Math.PI *
Math.cos(Math.PI * i / beta) / beta - alpha *
Math.sin(Math.PI * i / beta));
    }
    // Draw plots
    Rectangle2D.Double borderRectangle = new
Rectangle2D.Double(20, 20, 360, 260);
    LineChartPanel myLineChart = new LineChartPanel();
    if (e.getActionCommand().equals(lineButton.getText()))
    {
      myLineChart = new LineChartPanel(borderRectangle, 200,
x, y, plotColor[myRandom.nextInt(10)]);
    }
```

```
    else
    {
      myLineChart = new LineChartPanel(borderRectangle, 200,
y, yd, plotColor[myRandom.nextInt(10)]);
    }
    myLineChart.setPreferredSize(new Dimension (400, 300));
    myLineChart.setBackground(Color.WHITE);
    myPanel.removeAll();
    myPanel.add(myLineChart);
    this.pack();
  }

  private void barButtonActionPerformed(ActionEvent e)
  {
    // generate 5-10 bars with values from -10 to 10 and draw
bar chart
    int numberBars = myRandom.nextInt(6) + 5;
    for (int i = 0; i < numberBars; i++)
    {
      y[i] = myRandom.nextDouble() * 20 - 10;
    }
    // Draw chart
    Rectangle2D.Double borderRectangle = new
Rectangle2D.Double(20, 20, 360, 260);
    BarChartPanel myBarChart = new
BarChartPanel(borderRectangle, numberBars, y, 0.0,
plotColor[myRandom.nextInt(10)]);
    myBarChart.setPreferredSize(new Dimension (400, 300));
    myBarChart.setBackground(Color.WHITE);
    myPanel.removeAll();
    myPanel.add(myBarChart);
    this.pack();
  }

  private void pieButtonActionPerformed(ActionEvent e)
  {
    // Generate 3 to 10 slices at random with values from 1
to 5
    int numberSlices = myRandom.nextInt(8) + 3;
    for (int i = 0; i < numberSlices; i++)
    {
      y[i] = myRandom.nextDouble() * 5 + 1;
    }
    Rectangle2D.Double borderRectangle = new
Rectangle2D.Double(70, 20, 260, 260);
    PieChartPanel myPieChart = new
PieChartPanel(borderRectangle, numberSlices, y, plotColor);
```

```
    myPieChart.setPreferredSize(new Dimension (400, 300));
    myPieChart.setBackground(Color.WHITE);
    myPanel.removeAll();
    myPanel.add(myPieChart);
    this.pack();
  }

  private void exitForm(WindowEvent e)
  {
    System.exit(0);
  }
}
```

Run the project. Try all the plotting options. Each time you draw any plot it will be different because of the randomness programmed in. Here's an example of each plot type:

Line Chart:

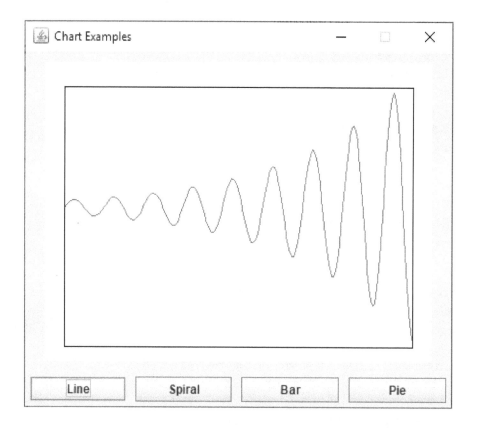

Spiral Chart:

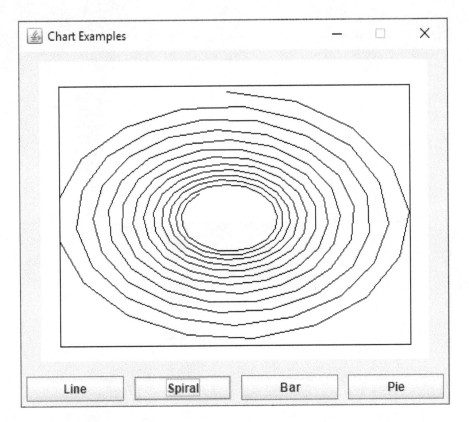

Bar Chart:

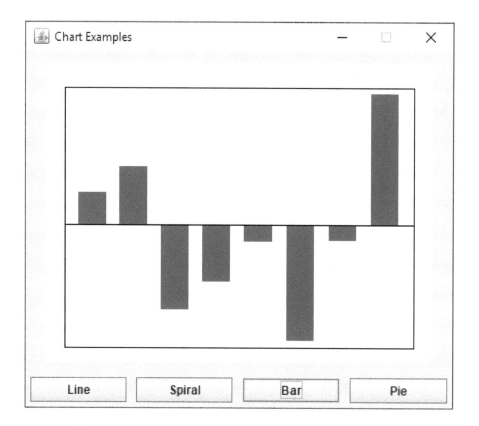

Pie Chart:

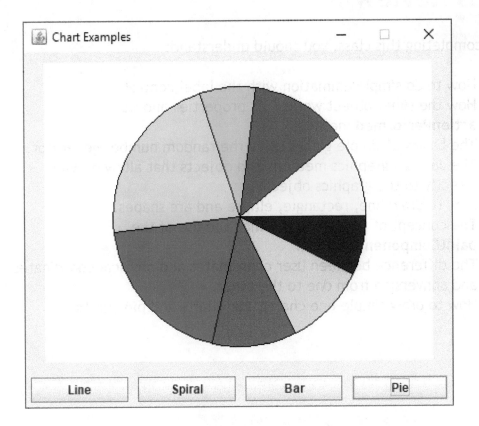

You're ready to tackle any plotting job now. Save the project (saved as **Example7-9** project in **\LearnJava\LJ Code\Class 7** program group).

These routines just call out for enhancements. Some things you might try:

a. Draw grid lines on the plots. Use dotted or dashed lines at regular intervals.

b. Modify the line and chart routines to allow plotting more than one function. Use colors or different line styles to differentiate the lines and bars. Add a legend defining each plot.

c. Label the plot axes. Put titling information on the axes and the plot. Consult the **drawString** method described in Class 8.

Class Review

After completing this class, you should understand:

➤ How to do simple animation with the label control.

➤ How the timer object works – its properties and its **actionPerformed** method.

➤ The basics of simple games using the random number generator.

➤ The Java 2D graphics methods and objects that allow drawing directly to the graphics object.

➤ How to draw line, rectangle, ellipse and arc shapes.

➤ The concept of persistent graphics and use of the **paintComponent** method.

➤ The difference between user coordinates and physical coordinates and conversion from one to the other.

➤ How to draw simple line charts, bar charts and pie charts.

Practice Problems 7

Problem 7-1. Dice Rolling Problem. Build an application that rolls two dice and displays the results (graphics of the six die faces are included in the **\LearnJava\LJ Code\Class 7\Problem7-1** folder). Have each die 'stop rolling' at different times.

Problem 7-2. Shape Guessing Problem. Build a game where the user is presented with three different shapes. Give the user one shape name and have them identify the matching shape.

Problem 7-3. Pie Chart Problem. Build an application where the user can enter a list of numbers and build a pie chart from that list.

Problem 7-4. Plotting Problem. Build an application that opens the output file created in **Problem 6-4** (the Mariners win streak file - saved as **MAR95.CSV** in the **\LearnJava\LJ Code\Class 6\Problem6-4** folder) and plots the information as a bar chart in a panel control. You'll want to first copy the **CSV** file into the project folder of this new application.

Exercise 7-1

Information Tracking Plotting

Add plotting capabilities to the information tracker you developed in Class 6. Plot whatever information you stored versus the date. Use a line or bar chart.

8

More Graphics Techniques, Multimedia Effects

Review and Preview

In the last class, we learned a lot about graphics methods in Java. Yet, everything we drew was static; there was no user interaction. In this class, we extend our graphics methods knowledge by learning how to detect mouse events. An example paintbrush program is built. We look at new paint methods and how to 'draw' text.

We then are introduced to concepts needed for multimedia (game) programming – animation, collision detection, and sounds. Like Class 7, we will build lots of relatively short examples to demonstrate concepts. You'll learn to modify the examples for your needs.

Mouse Events

In Class 7, we learned about the **Graphics2D** object, the shape object and many drawing methods. We learned how to draw lines, rectangles, ellipses and pie segments. We learned how to incorporate these drawing elements into procedures for line charts, bar charts and pie charts. Everything drawn with these elements was static; there was no user interaction. We set the parameters in code and drew our shapes or plots. We (the users) just sat there and watched pretty things appear.

In this class, the user becomes involved. To provide user interaction with an application, we can use the mouse as an interface for drawing graphics with Java. To do this, we need to understand **mouse events**. Mouse events are similar to control events. Certain event procedures are invoked when certain mouse actions are detected. Here, we see how to use mouse events for drawing on panel controls.

We've used the mouse to click on controls in past applications. For example, we've written code for many events resulting from clicking on button controls. And we've used the **mouseClicked** event in some games. To use the mouse for drawing purposes, however, a simple click event is not sufficient. We need to know not only that a control was clicked, but also need to know where it was clicked to provide a point to draw to. The mouse event that provides this information is the **mousePressed** event. The **mousePressed** event method is triggered whenever a mouse button is pressed while the mouse cursor is over a control. The form of this method must be:

```
public void mousePressed(MouseEvent e)
{
   [Java code]
}
```

The **MouseEvent** argument **e** reveals which button was clicked and the coordinate of mouse cursor when button was pressed. Useful methods are:

> `e.getButton()`   Returns mouse button pressed. Possible values are: `MouseEvent.BUTTON1` (left button), `MouseEvent.BUTTON2` (middle button), `MouseEvent.BUTTON3` (right button)
>
> `e.getX()`   Returns X coordinate of mouse cursor when mouse was clicked
>
> `e.getY()`   Returns Y coordinate of mouse cursor when mouse was clicked

To add a listener for the **mousePressed** event for a control named **myControl** (usually a panel), use:

```
myPanel.addMouseListener(new MouseAdapter()
{
  public void mousePressed(MouseEvent e)
  {
    myControlMousePressed(e);
  }
});
```

And, the corresponding event code is placed in the **myControlMousePressed** method:

```
private void myControlMousePressed(MouseEvent e)
{
   [method code]
}
```

In drawing applications, the **mousePressed** method is used to initialize a drawing process. The point clicked is used to start drawing a line and the button clicked is often used to select line color.

Another common task for drawing with the mouse is moving the mouse while holding down a mouse button. The mouse event that provides this information is the **mouseDragged** event. The **mouseDragged** event method is continuously triggered whenever the mouse is being dragged over a control. The form of this method is:

```
public void mouseDragged(MouseEvent e)
{
   [Java code]
}
```

The methods associated with the **MouseEvent e** are identical to those of the **mousePressed** event:

e.getButton()   Returns mouse button held while mouse is dragging. Possible values are: **MouseEvent.BUTTON1** (left button), **MouseEvent.BUTTON2** (middle button), **MouseEvent.BUTTON3** (right button)

e.getX()   Returns X coordinate of mouse cursor when drag event invoked.

e.getY()   Returns Y coordinate of mouse cursor when drag event invoked.

To add a listener for the **mouseDragged** event for a control named **myControl**, use:

```
myPanel.addMouseMotionListener(new MouseMotionAdapter()
{
  public void mouseDragged(MouseEvent e)
  {
    myControlMouseDragged(e);
  }
});
```

And, the corresponding event code is placed in the **myControlMouseDragged** method:

```
private void myControlMouseDragged(MouseEvent e)
{
    [method code]
}
```

In drawing processes, the **mouseDragged** event is used to detect the continuation of a previously started line. If drawing is continuing, the current point is connected to the previous point using a line shape object.

Lastly, we would like to be able to detect the release of a mouse button. The **mouseReleased** event is the opposite of the **mousePressed** event. It is triggered whenever a previously pressed mouse button is released. The method outline is:

```
public void mouseReleased(MouseEvent e)
{
    [Java code]
}
```

The methods associated with the **MouseEvent e** are identical to those of the other mouse events:

e.getButton()	Returns mouse button released. Possible values are: **MouseEvent.BUTTON1** (left button), **MouseEvent.BUTTON2** (middle button), **MouseEvent.BUTTON3** (right button)
e.getX()	Returns X coordinate of mouse cursor when mouse button released.
e.getY()	Returns Y coordinate of mouse cursor when mouse button released.

To add a listener for the **mouseReleased** event for a control named **myControl**, use:

```
myPanel.addMouseListener(new MouseAdapter()
{
  public void mouseReleased(MouseEvent e)
  {
    myControlMouseReleased(e);
  }
});
```

And, the corresponding event code is placed in the **myControlMouseReleased** method:

```
private void myControlMouseReleased(MouseEvent e)
{
   [method code]
}
```

In a drawing program, the **mouseReleased** event signifies the halting of the current drawing process. We'll find the **mousePressed**, **mouseDragged** and **mouseReleased** events are integral parts of any Java drawing program. We use them now (in conjunction with the **Line2D** shape and **draw** method) to build a paintbrush program called the **Blackboard**.

Example 8-1

Blackboard

Start a new empty project in **NetBeans**. Name the project **Blackboard**. Delete default code in Java file named **Blackboard**. Here, we will build a blackboard we can scribble on with the mouse (using colored 'chalk'). The left and right mouse buttons will draw with different (selectable) colors. The finished project will look like this:

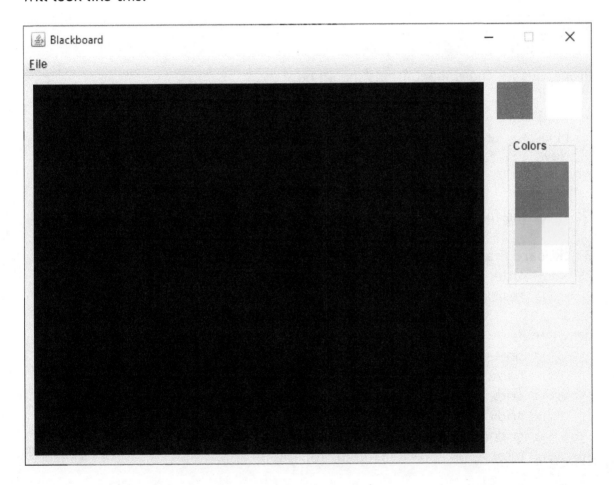

1. Place a large panel control, two label controls and a panel (with 8 small label controls). The **GridBagLayout** is:

	gridx = 0	gridx = 1	gridx = 2
gridy = 0	drawPanel	leftColorLabel	rightColorLabel
gridy = 1		colorPanel	

Add a Menu Bar control (**mainMenuBar**) with this simple structure:

<u>F</u>ile
   New
   ———
   Exit

Properties for these menu items should be:

Text	Name
File	fileMenu
New	newMenuItem
Exit	exitMenuItem

Now, set the following properties:

Blackboard Frame:

title	Blackboard
resizable	false

drawPanel:

preferredSize	(500, 400)
background	BLACK
gridx	0
gridy	0
gridheight	2
insets	(10, 10, 10, 10)

leftColorLabel:

preferredSize	(40, 40)
opaque	true
gridx	1
gridy	0
anchor	NORTH
insets	(10, 5, 10, 10)

rightColorLabel:

preferredSize	(40, 40)
opaque	true
gridx	2
gridy	0
anchor	NORTH
insets	(10, 5, 10, 10)

colorPanel:

preferredSize	(80, 160)
border	TitledBorder("Colors")
gridx	1
gridy	1
gridwidth	2
anchor	NORTH
insets	(10, 10, 10, 10)

The layout of **colorPanel:**

	gridx = 0	gridx = 1
gridy = 0	**colorLabel[0]**	**colorLabel[4]**
gridy = 1	**colorLabel[1]**	**colorLabel[5]**
gridy = 2	**colorLabel[2]**	**colorLabel[6]**
gridy = 3	**colorLabel[3]**	**colorLabel[7]**

colorLabel[0]:

preferredSize	(30, 30)
opaque	true
background	GRAY
gridx	0
gridy	0

colorLabel[1]:

preferredSize	(30, 30)
opaque	true
background	BLUE
gridx	0
gridy	1

colorLabel[2]:

preferredSize	(30, 30)
opaque	true
background	GREEN
gridx	0
gridy	2

colorLabel[3]:

preferredSize	(30, 30)
opaque	true
background	CYAN
gridx	0
gridy	3

colorLabel[4]:

preferredSize	(30, 30)
opaque	true
background	RED
gridx	1
gridy	0

colorLabel[5]:

preferredSize	(30, 30)
opaque	true
background	MAGENTA
gridx	1
gridy	1

colorLabel[6]:

preferredSize	(30, 30)
opaque	true
background	YELLOW
gridx	1
gridy	2

colorLabel[7]:

preferredSize	(30, 30)
opaque	true
background	WHITE
gridx	1
gridy	3

2. Build the basic framework:

```
/*
 * Blackboard.java
 */
package blackboard;
import javax.swing.*;
import java.awt.*;
import java.awt.event.*;
import java.awt.geom.*;
public class Blackboard extends JFrame
{
  public static void main(String args[])
  {
    // construct frame
    new Blackboard().show();
  }
  public Blackboard()
  {
    // frame constructor
    setTitle("Blackboard");
    setResizable(false);
    addWindowListener(new WindowAdapter()
    {
      public void windowClosing(WindowEvent e)
      {
        exitForm(e);
      }
    });
    getContentPane().setLayout(new GridBagLayout());

    pack();
    Dimension screenSize =
  Toolkit.getDefaultToolkit().getScreenSize();
      setBounds((int) (0.5 * (screenSize.width -
  getWidth())), (int) (0.5 * (screenSize.height -
  getHeight())), getWidth(), getHeight());
  }
  private void exitForm(WindowEvent e)
  {
    System.exit(0);
  }
}
```

Run to check.

3. Add declarations for controls and menu items:

```
JMenuBar mainMenuBar = new JMenuBar();
JMenu fileMenu = new JMenu("File");
JMenuItem newMenuItem = new JMenuItem("New");
JMenuItem exitMenuItem = new JMenuItem("Exit");
JPanel drawPanel = new JPanel();
JLabel leftColorLabel = new JLabel();
JLabel rightColorLabel = new JLabel();
JPanel colorPanel = new JPanel();
JLabel[] colorLabel = new JLabel[8];
```

Add menu, position and add controls, including event methods:

```
setJMenuBar(mainMenuBar);
fileMenu.setMnemonic('F');
mainMenuBar.add(fileMenu);
fileMenu.add(newMenuItem);
fileMenu.addSeparator();
fileMenu.add(exitMenuItem);
newMenuItem.addActionListener(new ActionListener()
{
  public void actionPerformed(ActionEvent e)
  {
    newMenuItemActionPerformed(e);
  }
});
exitMenuItem.addActionListener(new ActionListener()
{
  public void actionPerformed(ActionEvent e)
  {
    exitMenuItemActionPerformed(e);
  }
});

drawPanel.setPreferredSize(new Dimension(500, 400));
drawPanel.setBackground(Color.BLACK);
GridBagConstraints gridConstraints = new
GridBagConstraints();
gridConstraints.gridx = 0;
gridConstraints.gridy = 0;
gridConstraints.gridheight = 2;
gridConstraints.insets = new Insets(10, 10, 10, 10);
getContentPane().add(drawPanel, gridConstraints);
drawPanel.addMouseListener(new MouseAdapter()
{
```

```java
      public void mousePressed(MouseEvent e)
      {
        drawPanelMousePressed(e);
      }
});
drawPanel.addMouseMotionListener(new MouseMotionAdapter()
{
    public void mouseDragged(MouseEvent e)
    {
      drawPanelMouseDragged(e);
    }
});
drawPanel.addMouseListener(new MouseAdapter()
{
    public void mouseReleased(MouseEvent e)
    {
      drawPanelMouseReleased(e);
    }
});

leftColorLabel.setPreferredSize(new Dimension(40, 40));
leftColorLabel.setOpaque(true);
gridConstraints = new GridBagConstraints();
gridConstraints.gridx = 1;
gridConstraints.gridy = 0;
gridConstraints.anchor = GridBagConstraints.NORTH;
gridConstraints.insets = new Insets(10, 5, 10, 10);
getContentPane().add(leftColorLabel, gridConstraints);
rightColorLabel.setPreferredSize(new Dimension(40, 40));
rightColorLabel.setOpaque(true);
gridConstraints = new GridBagConstraints();
gridConstraints.gridx = 2;
gridConstraints.gridy = 0;
gridConstraints.anchor = GridBagConstraints.NORTH;
gridConstraints.insets = new Insets(10, 5, 10, 10);
getContentPane().add(rightColorLabel, gridConstraints);

colorPanel.setPreferredSize(new Dimension(80, 160));
colorPanel.setBorder(BorderFactory.createTitledBorder("Col
ors"));
gridConstraints = new GridBagConstraints();
gridConstraints.gridx = 1;
gridConstraints.gridy = 1;
gridConstraints.gridwidth = 2;
gridConstraints.anchor = GridBagConstraints.NORTH;
gridConstraints.insets = new Insets(10, 10, 10, 10);
getContentPane().add(colorPanel, gridConstraints);
```

```
colorPanel.setLayout(new GridBagLayout());
int j = 0;
for (int i = 0; i < 8; i++)
{
  colorLabel[i] = new JLabel();
  colorLabel[i].setPreferredSize(new Dimension(30, 30));
  colorLabel[i].setOpaque(true);
  gridConstraints = new GridBagConstraints();
  gridConstraints.gridx = j;
  gridConstraints.gridy = i - j * 4;
  colorPanel.add(colorLabel[i], gridConstraints);
  if (i == 3)
  {
    j++;
  }
  colorLabel[i].addMouseListener(new MouseAdapter()
  {
    public void mousePressed(MouseEvent e)
    {
      colorMousePressed(e);
    }
  });
}
// set color labels
colorLabel[0].setBackground(Color.GRAY);
colorLabel[1].setBackground(Color.BLUE);
colorLabel[2].setBackground(Color.GREEN);
colorLabel[3].setBackground(Color.CYAN);
colorLabel[4].setBackground(Color.RED);
colorLabel[5].setBackground(Color.MAGENTA);
colorLabel[6].setBackground(Color.YELLOW);
colorLabel[7].setBackground(Color.WHITE);
leftColor = colorLabel[0].getBackground();
leftColorLabel.setBackground(leftColor);
rightColor = colorLabel[7].getBackground();
rightColorLabel.setBackground(rightColor);
```

And, add these empty methods:

```
private void newMenuItemActionPerformed(ActionEvent e)
{
}

private void exitMenuItemActionPerformed(ActionEvent e)
{
}

private void colorMousePressed(MouseEvent e)
{
}

private void drawPanelMousePressed(MouseEvent e)
{
}

private void drawPanelMouseDragged(MouseEvent e)
{
}

private void drawPanelMouseReleased(MouseEvent e)
{
}
```

Run to check control layout.

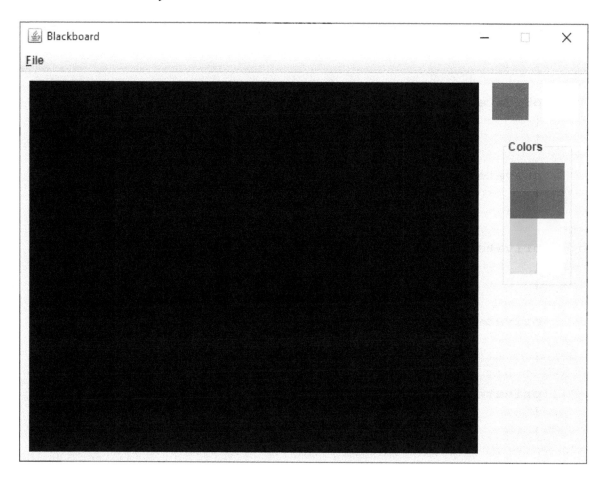

4. Now, we write code. Use these class level variables:

```
Graphics2D g2D;
double xPrevious, yPrevious;
Color drawColor, leftColor, rightColor;
```

These are used to do the drawing.

5. Use this code in each indicated method.

Add this code at the end of the constructor to establish graphics object:

```
// create graphics object
g2D = (Graphics2D) drawPanel.getGraphics();
```

Code for **newFileMenuActionPerformed** method where we check to see if the drawing should be erased.

```
private void newMenuItemActionPerformed(ActionEvent e)
{
  int response;
  response = JOptionPane.showConfirmDialog(null, "Are you
sure you want to start a new drawing?", "New Drawing",
JOptionPane.YES_NO_OPTION, JOptionPane.QUESTION_MESSAGE);
  if (response == JOptionPane.YES_OPTION)
  {
    g2D.setPaint(drawPanel.getBackground());
    g2D.fill(new Rectangle2D.Double(0, 0,
drawPanel.getWidth(), drawPanel.getHeight()));
  }
}
```

In **exitMenuItemActionPerformed**, make sure the user really wants to stop the application.

```
private void exitMenuItemActionPerformed(ActionEvent e)
{
  int response;
  response = JOptionPane.showConfirmDialog(null, "Are you
sure you want to exit the Blackboard program?", "Exit
Program", JOptionPane.YES_NO_OPTION,
JOptionPane.QUESTION_MESSAGE);
  if (response == JOptionPane.NO_OPTION)
  {
    return;
  }
  else
  {
    exitForm(null);
  }
}
```

Add a single line (shaded) to the **exitForm** method to dispose of the graphics object:

```
private void exitForm(WindowEvent e)
{
  g2D.dispose();
  System.exit(0);
}
```

Code for **colorMousePressed** method to select color (handles clicking on any of eight color choice label controls).

```
private void colorMousePressed(MouseEvent e)
{
  // decide which color was selected and which button was
used
  Component clickedColor = e.getComponent();
  // Make audible tone and set drawing color
  Toolkit.getDefaultToolkit().beep();
  if (e.getButton() == MouseEvent.BUTTON1)
  {
    leftColor = clickedColor.getBackground();
    leftColorLabel.setBackground(leftColor);
  }
  else if (e.getButton() == MouseEvent.BUTTON3)
  {
    rightColor = clickedColor.getBackground();
    rightColorLabel.setBackground(rightColor);
  }
}
```

When a mouse button is clicked (left or right button), drawing is initialized at the mouse cursor location with the respective color in the **drawPanelMousePressed** method.

```
private void drawPanelMousePressed(MouseEvent e)
{
  // if left button or right button clicked, set color and
start drawing process
  if (e.getButton() == MouseEvent.BUTTON1 || e.getButton()
== MouseEvent.BUTTON3)
  {
    xPrevious = e.getX();
    yPrevious = e.getY();
    if (e.getButton() == MouseEvent.BUTTON1)
    {
      drawColor = leftColor;
    }
    else
    {
      drawColor = rightColor;
    }
  }
}
```

While mouse is being dragged, draw lines in current color in
drawPanelMouseDragged method.

```
    private void drawPanelMouseDragged(MouseEvent e)
    {
      // if drawing, connect previous point with new point
      Line2D.Double myLine = new Line2D.Double(xPrevious,
yPrevious, e.getX(), e.getY());
      g2D.setPaint(drawColor);
      g2D.draw(myLine);
      xPrevious = e.getX();
      yPrevious = e.getY();
    }
```

When a mouse button is released, stop drawing current line in the
drawPanelMouseReleased method.

```
    private void drawPanelMouseReleased(MouseEvent e)
    {
      // if left or button released,connect last point
      if (e.getButton() == MouseEvent.BUTTON1 || e.getButton()
== MouseEvent.BUTTON3)
      {
        Line2D.Double myLine = new Line2D.Double(xPrevious,
yPrevious, e.getX(), e.getY());
        g2D.setPaint(drawColor);
        g2D.draw(myLine);
      }
    }
```

The complete **Blackboard.java** code listing (additions to framework code are
shaded):

```
/*
 * Blackboard.java
 */
package blackboard;
import javax.swing.*;
import java.awt.*;
import java.awt.event.*;
import java.awt.geom.*;
public class Blackboard extends JFrame
{
  JMenuBar mainMenuBar = new JMenuBar();
  JMenu fileMenu = new JMenu("File");
  JMenuItem newMenuItem = new JMenuItem("New");
```

```java
JMenuItem exitMenuItem = new JMenuItem("Exit");
JPanel drawPanel = new JPanel();
JLabel leftColorLabel = new JLabel();
JLabel rightColorLabel = new JLabel();
JPanel colorPanel = new JPanel();
JLabel[] colorLabel = new JLabel[8];
Graphics2D g2D;
double xPrevious, yPrevious;
Color drawColor, leftColor, rightColor;
public static void main(String args[])
{
  // construct frame
  new Blackboard().show();
}
public Blackboard()
{
  // frame constructor
  setTitle("Blackboard");
  setResizable(false);
  addWindowListener(new WindowAdapter()
  {
    public void windowClosing(WindowEvent e)
    {
      exitForm(e);
    }
  });
  getContentPane().setLayout(new GridBagLayout());

  // build menu
  setJMenuBar(mainMenuBar);
  fileMenu.setMnemonic('F');
  mainMenuBar.add(fileMenu);
  fileMenu.add(newMenuItem);
  fileMenu.addSeparator();
  fileMenu.add(exitMenuItem);
  newMenuItem.addActionListener(new ActionListener()
  {
    public void actionPerformed(ActionEvent e)
    {
      newMenuItemActionPerformed(e);
    }
  });
  exitMenuItem.addActionListener(new ActionListener()
  {
    public void actionPerformed(ActionEvent e)
    {
      exitMenuItemActionPerformed(e);
```

```
      }
   });

   drawPanel.setPreferredSize(new Dimension(500, 400));
   drawPanel.setBackground(Color.BLACK);
   GridBagConstraints gridConstraints = new
GridBagConstraints();
   gridConstraints.gridx = 0;
   gridConstraints.gridy = 0;
   gridConstraints.gridheight = 2;
   gridConstraints.insets = new Insets(10, 10, 10, 10);
   getContentPane().add(drawPanel, gridConstraints);
    drawPanel.addMouseListener(new MouseAdapter()
   {
     public void mousePressed(MouseEvent e)
     {
       drawPanelMousePressed(e);
     }
   });
    drawPanel.addMouseMotionListener(new
MouseMotionAdapter()
   {
     public void mouseDragged(MouseEvent e)
     {
       drawPanelMouseDragged(e);
     }
   });
    drawPanel.addMouseListener(new MouseAdapter()
   {
     public void mouseReleased(MouseEvent e)
     {
       drawPanelMouseReleased(e);
     }
   });

   leftColorLabel.setPreferredSize(new Dimension(40, 40));
   leftColorLabel.setOpaque(true);
   gridConstraints = new GridBagConstraints();
   gridConstraints.gridx = 1;
   gridConstraints.gridy = 0;
   gridConstraints.anchor = GridBagConstraints.NORTH;
   gridConstraints.insets = new Insets(10, 5, 10, 10);
   getContentPane().add(leftColorLabel, gridConstraints);
   rightColorLabel.setPreferredSize(new Dimension(40, 40));
   rightColorLabel.setOpaque(true);
   gridConstraints = new GridBagConstraints();
   gridConstraints.gridx = 2;
```

```
    gridConstraints.gridy = 0;
    gridConstraints.anchor = GridBagConstraints.NORTH;
    gridConstraints.insets = new Insets(10, 5, 10, 10);
    getContentPane().add(rightColorLabel, gridConstraints);

    colorPanel.setPreferredSize(new Dimension(80, 160));

colorPanel.setBorder(BorderFactory.createTitledBorder("Colors
"));
    gridConstraints = new GridBagConstraints();
    gridConstraints.gridx = 1;
    gridConstraints.gridy = 1;
    gridConstraints.gridwidth = 2;
    gridConstraints.anchor = GridBagConstraints.NORTH;
    gridConstraints.insets = new Insets(10, 10, 10, 10);
    getContentPane().add(colorPanel, gridConstraints);

    colorPanel.setLayout(new GridBagLayout());
    int j = 0;
    for (int i = 0; i < 8; i++)
    {
      colorLabel[i] = new JLabel();
      colorLabel[i].setPreferredSize(new Dimension(30, 30));
      colorLabel[i].setOpaque(true);
      gridConstraints = new GridBagConstraints();
      gridConstraints.gridx = j;
      gridConstraints.gridy = i - j * 4;
      colorPanel.add(colorLabel[i], gridConstraints);
      if (i == 3)
      {
        j++;
      }
      colorLabel[i].addMouseListener(new MouseAdapter()
      {
        public void mousePressed(MouseEvent e)
        {
          colorMousePressed(e);
        }
      });
    }
    // set color labels
    colorLabel[0].setBackground(Color.GRAY);
    colorLabel[1].setBackground(Color.BLUE);
    colorLabel[2].setBackground(Color.GREEN);
    colorLabel[3].setBackground(Color.CYAN);
    colorLabel[4].setBackground(Color.RED);
    colorLabel[5].setBackground(Color.MAGENTA);
```

```
colorLabel[6].setBackground(Color.YELLOW);
colorLabel[7].setBackground(Color.WHITE);
leftColor = colorLabel[0].getBackground();
leftColorLabel.setBackground(leftColor);
rightColor = colorLabel[7].getBackground();
rightColorLabel.setBackground(rightColor);

    pack();
    Dimension screenSize =
Toolkit.getDefaultToolkit().getScreenSize();
    setBounds((int) (0.5 * (screenSize.width - getWidth())),
(int) (0.5 * (screenSize.height - getHeight())), getWidth(),
getHeight());
    // create graphics object
    g2D = (Graphics2D) drawPanel.getGraphics();
  }


  private void newMenuItemActionPerformed(ActionEvent e)
  {
    int response;
    response = JOptionPane.showConfirmDialog(null, "Are you
sure you want to start a new drawing?", "New Drawing",
JOptionPane.YES_NO_OPTION, JOptionPane.QUESTION_MESSAGE);
    if (response == JOptionPane.YES_OPTION)
    {
      g2D.setPaint(drawPanel.getBackground());
      g2D.fill(new Rectangle2D.Double(0, 0,
drawPanel.getWidth(), drawPanel.getHeight()));
    }
  }


  private void exitMenuItemActionPerformed(ActionEvent e)
  {
    int response;
    response = JOptionPane.showConfirmDialog(null, "Are you
sure you want to exit the Blackboard program?", "Exit
Program", JOptionPane.YES_NO_OPTION,
JOptionPane.QUESTION_MESSAGE);
    if (response == JOptionPane.NO_OPTION)
    {
      return;
    }
    else
    {
      exitForm(null);
    }
  }
```

```
  private void colorMousePressed(MouseEvent e)
  {
    // decide which color was selected and which button was
used
    Component clickedColor = e.getComponent();
    // Make audible tone and set drawing color
    Toolkit.getDefaultToolkit().beep();
    if (e.getButton() == MouseEvent.BUTTON1)
    {
      leftColor = clickedColor.getBackground();
      leftColorLabel.setBackground(leftColor);
    }
    else if (e.getButton() == MouseEvent.BUTTON3)
    {
      rightColor = clickedColor.getBackground();
      rightColorLabel.setBackground(rightColor);
    }
  }

  private void drawPanelMousePressed(MouseEvent e)
  {
    // if left button or right button clicked, set color and
start drawing process
    if (e.getButton() == MouseEvent.BUTTON1 || e.getButton()
== MouseEvent.BUTTON3)
    {
      xPrevious = e.getX();
      yPrevious = e.getY();
      if (e.getButton() == MouseEvent.BUTTON1)
      {
        drawColor = leftColor;
      }
      else
      {
        drawColor = rightColor;
      }
    }
  }

  private void drawPanelMouseDragged(MouseEvent e)
  {
    // if drawing, connect previous point with new point
    Line2D.Double myLine = new Line2D.Double(xPrevious,
yPrevious, e.getX(), e.getY());
    g2D.setPaint(drawColor);
    g2D.draw(myLine);
```

```
      xPrevious = e.getX();
      yPrevious = e.getY();
  }

  private void drawPanelMouseReleased(MouseEvent e)
  {
      // if left or button released,connect last point
      if (e.getButton() == MouseEvent.BUTTON1 || e.getButton()
== MouseEvent.BUTTON3)
      {
        Line2D.Double myLine = new Line2D.Double(xPrevious,
yPrevious, e.getX(), e.getY());
        g2D.setPaint(drawColor);
        g2D.draw(myLine);
      }
  }

  private void exitForm(WindowEvent e)
  {
    g2D.dispose();
    System.exit(0);
  }
}
```

Run the project. Try drawing. The left mouse button draws with one color and the right button draws with another. The current drawing colors are displayed at the top right corner of the form. To change a color, left or right click on the desired color in the **Colors** panel. Fun, huh? Here's one of my sketches:

Save the application (saved as **Example8-1** project in **\LearnJava\LJ Code\Class 8** program group). This is a neat application, but there's a problem. Draw a little something and then reduce the project to an icon. When the frame is restored, your masterpiece is gone! The graphics here are not persistent. To add persistence (as we did in Class 7), we need to use the panel control's **paintComponent** method (using the **GraphicsPanel** class we created). We need a way to somehow store every point and every color used in the picture. Then, in the **paintComponent** method, every drawing step taken by the user would need to be reproduced. This is a slightly difficult problem. Fortunately, Java provides a class that provides a solution. We'll look at that next.

Persistent Graphics, Revisited (Vector Class)

To add persistence to our **Blackboard** example, we need to do two things (well, more than two, but two for now). First, we create the drawing area from the **GraphicsPanel** class (in **Appendix I**) developed in Class 7. Recall this class extends the **JPanel** control, adding a **paintComponent** method:

```
class GraphicsPanel extends JPanel
{
  public GraphicsPanel()
  {
  }
  public void paintComponent(Graphics g)
  {
  }
}
```

Second, in the **paintComponent** method, we need to be able to describe the current contents of the panel. To do this, we need to know every line drawn on the blackboard and every color used. This may sound like a daunting task, but it's not too bad (fortunately).

The Java **Vector** class stores a collection of objects that works like an array, but has a special feature of being able to grow and shrink as needed. We will use a **Vector** object to store every colored line drawn in our blackboard example. Then, when needed, the **paintComponent** method will use this vector object to recreate the colored lines. Let's look at how to use the **Vector** class. First, you need to import the **java.util.*** package which contains the **Vector** class.

If I am storing a vector of lines called **myLines**, the required vector object is created using this constructor:

```
Vector myLines = new Vector(200, 100);
```

This will create a vector of 200 initial elements, with 100 elements added every time new elements are needed (these numbers can be changed if desired). The size of **myLines** is handled by Java - you never have to worry about it, unlike arrays.

Once created, a line is added to the vector using the **add** method. If the line object to add is named **myColoredLine**, the syntax is:

```
myLines.add(myColoredLine);
```

The vector object (**myLines**) keeps every object stored and accounted for.

In the **paintComponent** method, we need to recover all of the colored lines we have stored so they can be redrawn on the graphics panel. To do this, we need to know how many objects there are and how to recover each one. The number of elements in a vector object is given by the **size** property. For our example object (**myLines**), that value is found using:

```
myLines.size()
```

The objects are stored like a zero-based array, ranging from object **0** to object **size - 1**. To retrieve object **n** from our example, use the **elementAt** method:

```
myColoredLine = myLines.elementAt(n);
```

Having retrieved the colored line object, we can redraw it in the graphics panel control.

One last thing you might like to do with the vector object is to remove all the elements to do a reinitialization. We would do this in our blackboard when we erase. The code that does this is:

```
myLine.removeAllElements();
```

This line should be followed by a **repaint** of the control hosting the graphics panel.

So, we can now use a vector object to store and retrieve colored lines in our blackboard example. One question that remains is how to specify a 'colored line' object. We draw our lines using a **Line2D** object. This object specifies the coordinates used to draw a line, but has no color information. To store (and retrieve) a colored line, we will define a **ColoredLine** class. The **ColoredLine** class defines a colored line object with two arguments: a **Line2D** object (**theLine**) that defines the connecting points and a **Color** object (**theColor**) that defines the color. That class is:

```
class ColoredLine
{
  public Line2D.Double theLine;
  public Color theColor;
  public ColoredLine(Line2D.Double theLine, Color
theColor)
  {
    this.theLine = theLine;
    this.theColor = theColor;
  }
}
```

To use this class in a project, place it after the main class. In our blackboard example, we will also add the **GraphicsPanel** class.

Note the constructor for a colored line object has two arguments:

```
public ColoredLine(Line2D.Double theLine, Color theColor)
```

Hence, to create a colored line object (made up of **myLine**, a **Line2D** object, and **myColor**), use:

```
ColoredLine myColoredLine = new ColoredLine(myLine,
myColor);
```

In our blackboard example, every time a line is drawn, we will create such a colored line object and store it in our vector class.

To reconstruct a blackboard drawing, in the **paintComponent** method, we retrieve the **Line2D** object (**theLine**) and **Color** object (**theColor**) from the array of colored lines objects to redraw the graphics panel. If the retrieved colored line is **myColoredLine**, the corresponding **Line2D** and **Color** objects are defined by:

```
myLine = myColoredLine.theLine;
myColor = myColoredLine.theColor;
```

This information is then used to redraw **myLine** in **myColor** using graphics methods.

Storing the colored lines in a vector object also makes it possible to save and retrieve previous drawings from disk files. This requires something called **serializable objects**. Using such objects is beyond the scope of this course, but you might like to study their use if you want to save drawings. For now, let's modify our **Blackboard** to add persistence.

Example 8-2

Blackboard (Revisited)

Here, we will modify the **Blackboard** example so the graphics are persistent. That way, you'll never lose your masterpiece! The modifications are fairly simple. Load the project from **Example 8-1**.

➢ First, add the **GraphicsPanel** (in **Appendix I**) and **ColoredLine** classes to the project (after the main class). Also, add a line importing the **java.util.*** package.

➢ Change the declaration for the **drawPanel** object to a **GraphicsPanel**:

```
GraphicsPanel drawPanel = new GraphicsPanel();
```

➢ Add a class level declaration for the vector class:

```
static Vector myLines = new Vector(200, 100);
```

The **static** preface is needed because it is used in the **paintComponent** method.

➢ Modify the 'erase' procedure in the **newMenuItemActionPerformed** method so it removes all elements from the **myLines** vector object and repaints (new lines are shaded):

```
private void newMenuItemActionPerformed(ActionEvent e)
{
  int response;
  response = JOptionPane.showConfirmDialog(null, "Are you
sure you want to start a new drawing?", "New Drawing",
JOptionPane.YES_NO_OPTION, JOptionPane.QUESTION_MESSAGE);
  if (response == JOptionPane.YES_OPTION)
  {
    myLines.removeAllElements();
    drawPanel.repaint();
  }
}
```

➢ Add a single line (shaded) to the **drawPanelMouseDragged** and
drawPanelMouseReleased methods to save the colored line object:

```
private void drawPanelMouseDragged(MouseEvent e)
{
  // if drawing, connect previous point with new point
  Line2D.Double myLine = new Line2D.Double(xPrevious,
yPrevious, e.getX(), e.getY());
  g2D.setPaint(drawColor);
  g2D.draw(myLine);
  xPrevious = e.getX();
  yPrevious = e.getY();
  myLines.add(new ColoredLine(myLine, drawColor));
}

private void drawPanelMouseReleased(MouseEvent e)
{
  // if left or button released,connect last point
  if (e.getButton() == MouseEvent.BUTTON1 || e.getButton()
== MouseEvent.BUTTON3)
  {
    Line2D.Double myLine = new Line2D.Double(xPrevious,
yPrevious, e.getX(), e.getY());
    g2D.setPaint(drawColor);
    g2D.draw(myLine);
    myLines.add(new ColoredLine(myLine, drawColor));
  }
}
```

➢ Use this **paintComponent** method in the **GraphicsPanel** class to recreate all colored line objects when needed:

```
public void paintComponent(Graphics g)
{
   Graphics2D g2D = (Graphics2D) g;
   super.paintComponent(g2D);
   for (int i = 0; i < Blackboard.myLines.size(); i++)
   {
      ColoredLine thisLine = (ColoredLine)
Blackboard.myLines.elementAt(i);
      g2D.setColor(thisLine.theColor);
      g2D.draw(thisLine.theLine);
   }
   g2D.dispose();
}
```

Study this code. It goes through all elements of the **myLines** object (note it is prefaced with the main class name **Blackboard** since it is an object from that class). In each step, it retrieves a colored line from the vector object. It uses the corresponding **Line2D** and **Color** objects to draw the line in the proper color.

That's all the changes needed. The modified **Blackboard.java** code listing (changes are shaded):

```
/*
 * Blackboard.java
 */
package blackboard;
import javax.swing.*;
import java.awt.*;
import java.awt.event.*;
import java.awt.geom.*;
import java.util.*;

public class Blackboard extends JFrame
{
   JMenuBar mainMenuBar = new JMenuBar();
   JMenu fileMenu = new JMenu("File");
   JMenuItem newMenuItem = new JMenuItem("New");
   JMenuItem exitMenuItem = new JMenuItem("Exit");
   GraphicsPanel drawPanel = new GraphicsPanel();
   JLabel leftColorLabel = new JLabel();
   JLabel rightColorLabel = new JLabel();
   JPanel colorPanel = new JPanel();
```

```
JLabel[] colorLabel = new JLabel[8];

Graphics2D g2D;
double xPrevious, yPrevious;
Color drawColor, leftColor, rightColor;
static Vector myLines = new Vector(200, 100);

public static void main(String args[])
{
  // construct frame
  new Blackboard().show();
}
public Blackboard()
{
  // frame constructor
  setTitle("Blackboard");
  setResizable(false);
  addWindowListener(new WindowAdapter()
  {
    public void windowClosing(WindowEvent e)
    {
      exitForm(e);
    }
  });
  getContentPane().setLayout(new GridBagLayout());

  // build menu
  setJMenuBar(mainMenuBar);
  fileMenu.setMnemonic('F');
  mainMenuBar.add(fileMenu);
  fileMenu.add(newMenuItem);
  fileMenu.addSeparator();
  fileMenu.add(exitMenuItem);
  newMenuItem.addActionListener(new ActionListener()
  {
    public void actionPerformed(ActionEvent e)
    {
      newMenuItemActionPerformed(e);
    }
  });
  exitMenuItem.addActionListener(new ActionListener()
  {
    public void actionPerformed(ActionEvent e)
    {
      exitMenuItemActionPerformed(e);
    }
  });
```

```
      drawPanel.setPreferredSize(new Dimension(500, 400));
      drawPanel.setBackground(Color.BLACK);
      GridBagConstraints gridConstraints = new
GridBagConstraints();
      gridConstraints.gridx = 0;
      gridConstraints.gridy = 0;
      gridConstraints.gridheight = 2;
      gridConstraints.insets = new Insets(10, 10, 10, 10);
      getContentPane().add(drawPanel, gridConstraints);
       drawPanel.addMouseListener(new MouseAdapter()
      {
        public void mousePressed(MouseEvent e)
        {
          drawPanelMousePressed(e);
        }
      });
       drawPanel.addMouseMotionListener(new
MouseMotionAdapter()
      {
        public void mouseDragged(MouseEvent e)
        {
          drawPanelMouseDragged(e);
        }
      });
       drawPanel.addMouseListener(new MouseAdapter()
      {
        public void mouseReleased(MouseEvent e)
        {
          drawPanelMouseReleased(e);
        }
      });

      leftColorLabel.setPreferredSize(new Dimension(40, 40));
      leftColorLabel.setOpaque(true);
      gridConstraints = new GridBagConstraints();
      gridConstraints.gridx = 1;
      gridConstraints.gridy = 0;
      gridConstraints.anchor = GridBagConstraints.NORTH;
      gridConstraints.insets = new Insets(10, 5, 10, 10);
      getContentPane().add(leftColorLabel, gridConstraints);
      rightColorLabel.setPreferredSize(new Dimension(40, 40));
      rightColorLabel.setOpaque(true);
      gridConstraints = new GridBagConstraints();
      gridConstraints.gridx = 2;
      gridConstraints.gridy = 0;
      gridConstraints.anchor = GridBagConstraints.NORTH;
```

```
    gridConstraints.insets = new Insets(10, 5, 10, 10);
    getContentPane().add(rightColorLabel, gridConstraints);

    colorPanel.setPreferredSize(new Dimension(80, 160));

colorPanel.setBorder(BorderFactory.createTitledBorder("Colors
"));
    gridConstraints = new GridBagConstraints();
    gridConstraints.gridx = 1;
    gridConstraints.gridy = 1;
    gridConstraints.gridwidth = 2;
    gridConstraints.anchor = GridBagConstraints.NORTH;
    gridConstraints.insets = new Insets(10, 10, 10, 10);
    getContentPane().add(colorPanel, gridConstraints);

    colorPanel.setLayout(new GridBagLayout());
    int j = 0;
    for (int i = 0; i < 8; i++)
    {
      colorLabel[i] = new JLabel();
      colorLabel[i].setPreferredSize(new Dimension(30, 30));
      colorLabel[i].setOpaque(true);
      gridConstraints = new GridBagConstraints();
      gridConstraints.gridx = j;
      gridConstraints.gridy = i - j * 4;
      colorPanel.add(colorLabel[i], gridConstraints);
      if (i == 3)
      {
        j++;
      }
      colorLabel[i].addMouseListener(new MouseAdapter()
      {
        public void mousePressed(MouseEvent e)
        {
          colorMousePressed(e);
        }
      });
    }
    // set color labels
    colorLabel[0].setBackground(Color.GRAY);
    colorLabel[1].setBackground(Color.BLUE);
    colorLabel[2].setBackground(Color.GREEN);
    colorLabel[3].setBackground(Color.CYAN);
    colorLabel[4].setBackground(Color.RED);
    colorLabel[5].setBackground(Color.MAGENTA);
    colorLabel[6].setBackground(Color.YELLOW);
    colorLabel[7].setBackground(Color.WHITE);
```

```
    leftColor = colorLabel[0].getBackground();
    leftColorLabel.setBackground(leftColor);
    rightColor = colorLabel[7].getBackground();
    rightColorLabel.setBackground(rightColor);

    pack();
    Dimension screenSize =
Toolkit.getDefaultToolkit().getScreenSize();
    setBounds((int) (0.5 * (screenSize.width - getWidth())),
(int) (0.5 * (screenSize.height - getHeight())), getWidth(),
getHeight());
    // create graphics object
    g2D = (Graphics2D) drawPanel.getGraphics();
  }

  private void newMenuItemActionPerformed(ActionEvent e)
  {
    int response;
    response = JOptionPane.showConfirmDialog(null, "Are you
sure you want to start a new drawing?", "New Drawing",
JOptionPane.YES_NO_OPTION, JOptionPane.QUESTION_MESSAGE);
    if (response == JOptionPane.YES_OPTION)
    {
      myLines.removeAllElements();
      drawPanel.repaint();
    }
  }

  private void exitMenuItemActionPerformed(ActionEvent e)
  {
    int response;
    response = JOptionPane.showConfirmDialog(null, "Are you
sure you want to exit the Blackboard program?", "Exit
Program", JOptionPane.YES_NO_OPTION,
JOptionPane.QUESTION_MESSAGE);
    if (response == JOptionPane.NO_OPTION)
    {
      return;
    }
    else
    {
      exitForm(null);
    }
  }

  private void colorMousePressed(MouseEvent e)
  {
```

```
      // decide which color was selected and which button was
used
      Component clickedColor = e.getComponent();
      // Make audible tone and set drawing color
      Toolkit.getDefaultToolkit().beep();
      if (e.getButton() == MouseEvent.BUTTON1)
      {
        leftColor = clickedColor.getBackground();
        leftColorLabel.setBackground(leftColor);
      }
      else if (e.getButton() == MouseEvent.BUTTON3)
      {
        rightColor = clickedColor.getBackground();
        rightColorLabel.setBackground(rightColor);
      }
    }


  private void drawPanelMousePressed(MouseEvent e)
    {
      // if left button or right button clicked, set color and
start drawing process
      if (e.getButton() == MouseEvent.BUTTON1 || e.getButton()
== MouseEvent.BUTTON3)
      {
        xPrevious = e.getX();
        yPrevious = e.getY();
        if (e.getButton() == MouseEvent.BUTTON1)
        {
          drawColor = leftColor;
        }
        else
        {
          drawColor = rightColor;
        }
      }
    }


  private void drawPanelMouseDragged(MouseEvent e)
    {
      // if drawing, connect previous point with new point
      Line2D.Double myLine = new Line2D.Double(xPrevious,
yPrevious, e.getX(), e.getY());
      g2D.setPaint(drawColor);
      g2D.draw(myLine);
      xPrevious = e.getX();
      yPrevious = e.getY();
      myLines.add(new ColoredLine(myLine, drawColor));
```

```
    }

    private void drawPanelMouseReleased(MouseEvent e)
    {
      // if left or button released,connect last point
      if (e.getButton() == MouseEvent.BUTTON1 || e.getButton()
== MouseEvent.BUTTON3)
      {
        Line2D.Double myLine = new Line2D.Double(xPrevious,
yPrevious, e.getX(), e.getY());
        g2D.setPaint(drawColor);
        g2D.draw(myLine);
        myLines.add(new ColoredLine(myLine, drawColor));
      }
    }

    private void exitForm(WindowEvent e)
    {
      g2D.dispose();
      System.exit(0);
    }
}

class GraphicsPanel extends JPanel
{
  public GraphicsPanel()
  {
  }
  public void paintComponent(Graphics g)
  {
    Graphics2D g2D = (Graphics2D) g;
    super.paintComponent(g2D);
    for (int i = 0; i < Blackboard.myLines.size(); i++)
    {
      ColoredLine thisLine = (ColoredLine)
Blackboard.myLines.elementAt(i);
      g2D.setColor(thisLine.theColor);
      g2D.draw(thisLine.theLine);
    }
    g2D.dispose();
  }
}

class ColoredLine
{
  public Line2D.Double theLine;
  public Color theColor;
```

```
  public ColoredLine(Line2D.Double theLine, Color theColor)
  {
    this.theLine = theLine;
    this.theColor = theColor;
  }
}
```

Rerun the project. Try drawing. Once you have a few lines (with different colors) on the blackboard, reduce the program to an icon. Restore the application. Your picture is still there! The graphics are persistent. As more lines are drawn, you may notice the redraw process may slow – this is a result of needing to store and retrieve lots of information. Save the project (saved as **Example8-2** project in **\LearnJava\LJ Code\Class 8** program group).

More Graphics Methods

In Class 7, we learned about the Java 2D graphics object and several shapes and drawing methods. We learned how to draw lines, rectangles, ellipses and pie segments. We learned how to incorporate these drawing elements into procedures for line charts, bar charts and pie charts. The Java 2D graphics package is vast and offers many graphics methods.

Here, we look a few more graphics methods to use in our applications. We learn how to draw and fill more complex shapes like polygons and closed curves. And, we learn about non-solid fills and how to add text to a graphics object.

The steps for drawing here are exactly the same as those followed in Class 7:

> ➤ Create a **Graphics2D** object.
> ➤ Establish the **Stroke** and **Paint** objects needed for drawing.
> ➤ Establish the **Shape** object for drawing.
> ➤ Draw shape to **Graphics2D** object using drawing methods
> ➤ Dispose of graphics object when done.

Before studying the new methods, we look at another graphics object, the **Point2D** object.

Point2D Object

We will look at shape objects that describe line and curve segments by connecting points. In order to reconstruct such shapes using a **paintComponent** method, it is helpful to have a convenient way to store points in a **Vector** collection. The **Point2D** object, which specifies a Cartesian point, offers this convenience. The **Point2D** object has just two properties: **x**, the horizontal coordinate, and **y**, the vertical coordinate. To create a point object named **myPoint**, you use:

```
Point2D.Double myPoint = new Point2D.Double(x, y);
```

Each argument value is a **double** type (there is also a **Point2D.Float** object with **float** type arguments).

To retrieve the **x** and **y** coordinates of a **Point2D** object (**myPoint**), you use one of two methods. To retrieve the **x** coordinate, use:

```
myPoint.getX()
```

and to retrieve the **y** coordinate:

```
myPoint.getY()
```

GeneralPath Object

In Class 7, we looked at how to draw 'normal' shapes like rectangles and ellipses. To draw more complex shapes, we use a **GeneralPath** object. Such an object is used to specify segments of a path to follow. These segments can be straight lines (for drawing polygons) or curves (for drawing free form shapes).

A general path object named **myPath** is created using:

```
GeneralPath myPath = new GeneralPath();
```

As always, placement of such a statement depends on desired scope for the object.

Once created, the first point in the path is specified using the **moveTo** method. If the desired point is (**x**, **y**), the syntax is:

```
myPath.moveTo(x, y);
```

Note the coordinates here (and for all path methods) are of type **float**. If your application uses some other type for coordinates, the arguments need to be cast to **float** type.

Following this initialization, segments can be added to the path using several different methods. The syntax for each method is (again, all arguments are **float** type):

Method	Description
`lineTo(x,y)`	Connects current path point to (**x**, **y**) using a straight line segment.
`quadTo(x1,y1,x2,y2)`	Connects current path point to (**x2**, **y2**) using a quadratic curve segment with 'control point' (**x1**, **y1**)
`curveTo(x1,y1,x2,y2,x3,y3)`	Connects current path point to (**x3**, **y3**) using a cubic curve segment with 'control points' (**x1**, **y1**) and (**x2**, **y2**)
`closePath()`	Connects current point to point established by last **moveTo** method with a straight line segment. To close with a curve, use **quadTo** or **curveTo**.

The meanings and uses of each of these drawing methods will be explained in more detail in the next few sections. Once a **GeneralPath** object (a shape) is complete, it is drawn with the usual **Graphics2D draw** and **fill** methods. If our object is **myPath** and the graphics object is **g2D**, the proper syntax for drawing and filling is:

```
g2D.draw(myPath);
g2D.fill(myPath);
```

When general path objects have intersecting sides, a **winding rule** is used to decide which areas should be filled and which shouldn't. There are just two such rules. We use the default rule, called the **non-zero** winding rule. To use the other rule (**even-odd** rule), you need to use a different constructor for the path object. We won't go into details here about the different rules. They don't even matter if your shapes don't have many areas to fill. Consult the usual Java references for more information on the two possible rules.

Drawing Polygons

Using the general path methods for constructing straight-line segments allows us to create and draw polygons as shapes. The process is for a path named **myPolygon** is:

> Declare path using:

```
GeneralPath myPolygon = new GeneralPath();
```

> Initialize polygon at one of its vertices (corners):

```
myPolygon.moveTo(x, y);
```

> For each side of the polygon, draw a line to the next vertex using:

```
myPolygon.lineTo(x, y);
```

> Once, you have drawn a line to the last vertex, complete the path using:

```
myPolygon.closePath();
```

> Draw the path (after setting **stroke** and **paint** attributes, if needed), assuming a graphics object g2D:

```
g2D.draw(myPolygon);
```

Let's draw a polygon in a panel (**myPanel**) of dimension (300, 200). The **polygon** will have a **red** outline with a line **width** of **1** (the default **stroke**). The vertices of the polygon (five sides, a pentagon) are:

```
(50, 100), (100, 20), (270, 80), (250, 150), (100, 170)
```

Following the steps outlined above, the Java code would be:

```
Graphics2D g2D = (Graphics2D) myPanel.getGraphics();
GeneralPath myPolygon = new GeneralPath();
myPolygon.moveTo(50, 100);
myPolygon.lineTo(100, 20);
myPolygon.lineTo(270, 80);
myPolygon.lineTo(250, 150);
myPolygon.lineTo(100, 170);
myPolygon.closePath();
g2D.setPaint(Color.RED);
g2D.draw(myPolygon);
```

This produces:

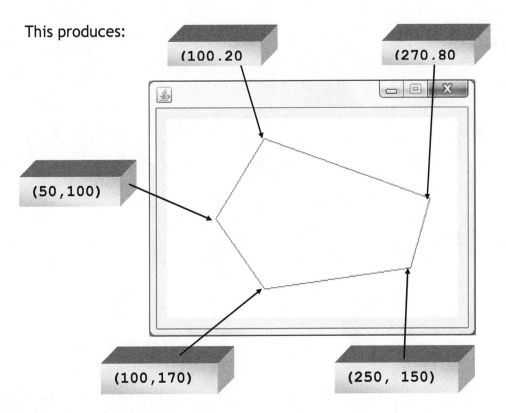

The polygon is filled with the fill method:

```
g2D.fill(myPolygon);
```

The shape will be filled with the current **paint** attribute.

To **fill** our example polygon with **yellow**, the shaded code is added:

```
Graphics2D g2D = (Graphics2D) myPanel.getGraphics();
GeneralPath myPolygon = new GeneralPath();
myPolygon.moveTo(50, 100);
myPolygon.lineTo(100, 20);
myPolygon.lineTo(270, 80);
myPolygon.lineTo(250, 150);
myPolygon.lineTo(100, 170);
myPolygon.closePath();
g2D.setPaint(Color.YELLOW);
g2D.fill(myPolygon);
g2D.setPaint(Color.RED);
g2D.draw(myPolygon);
g2D.dispose();
```

This produces:

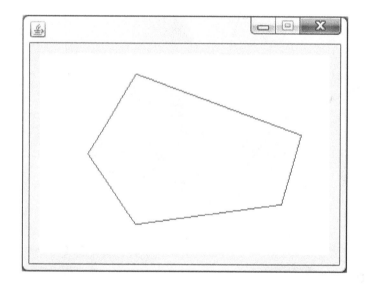

Notice that, to preserve the red border, we did the **fill** operation before the **draw.**

Example 8-3

Drawing Polygons

Start a new empty project in **NetBeans**. Name the project **DrawingPolygons**.
Delete default code in Java file named **DrawingPolygons**. In this application,
the user will click on a panel specifying a set of points. These points will be
used to draw a polygon or a filled (random color) polygon. The finished frame
is:

1. Add a panel control and two button controls to the frame. The
    GridBagLayout is:

	gridx = 0
gridy = 0	**drawPanel**
gridy = 1	**drawButton**
gridy = 2	**fillButton**

Set the following properties:

DrawingPolygons Frame:

title	Drawing Polygons
resizable	false

panelDraw (a GraphicsPanel class):

preferredSize	(350, 250)
background	WHITE
gridx	0
gridy	0
insets	(10, 10, 10, 10)

drawButton:

text	Draw Polygon
enabled	false
gridx	0
gridy	1

fillButton:

text	Fill Polygon
enabled	false
gridx	0
gridy	2
insets	(5, 0, 0, 0)

2. Build the basic framework:

```
/*
 * DrawingPolygons.java
*/
package drawingpolygons;
import javax.swing.*;
import java.awt.*;
import java.awt.geom.*;
import java.awt.event.*;
import java.util.*;
import java.util.Random;

public class DrawingPolygons extends JFrame
{

  public static void main(String args[])
  {
```

```
      //construct frame
      new DrawingPolygons().show();
  }

  public DrawingPolygons()
  {
    // code to build the form
    setTitle("Drawing Polygons");
    setResizable(false);
    addWindowListener(new WindowAdapter()
    {
      public void windowClosing(WindowEvent e)
      {
        exitForm(e);
      }
    });
    getContentPane().setLayout(new GridBagLayout());

    pack();
    Dimension screenSize =
Toolkit.getDefaultToolkit().getScreenSize();
    setBounds((int) (0.5 * (screenSize.width -
getWidth())), (int) (0.5 * (screenSize.height -
getHeight())), getWidth(), getHeight());
  }

  private void exitForm(WindowEvent e)
  {
    System.exit(0);
  }
}
```

Run to check the framework.

3. Now, we add controls and methods. Add class level declarations:

```
GraphicsPanel drawPanel = new GraphicsPanel();
JButton drawButton = new JButton();
JButton fillButton = new JButton();
```

Positon and add controls and event methods:

```
GridBagConstraints gridConstraints = new
GridBagConstraints();
drawPanel.setPreferredSize(new Dimension(350, 250));
drawPanel.setBackground(Color.WHITE);
```

```
gridConstraints.gridx = 0;
gridConstraints.gridy = 0;
gridConstraints.insets = new Insets(10, 10, 10, 10);
getContentPane().add(drawPanel, gridConstraints);
 drawPanel.addMouseListener(new MouseAdapter()
{
  public void mousePressed(MouseEvent e)
  {
drawPanelMousePressed(e);
  }
});

 drawButton.setText("Draw Polygon");
 drawButton.setEnabled(false);
gridConstraints = new GridBagConstraints();
gridConstraints.gridx = 0;
gridConstraints.gridy = 1;
getContentPane().add(drawButton, gridConstraints);
drawButton.addActionListener(new ActionListener()
{
  public void actionPerformed(ActionEvent e)
  {
drawButtonActionPerformed(e);
  }
});

 fillButton.setText("Fill Polygon");
 fillButton.setEnabled(false);
gridConstraints = new GridBagConstraints();
gridConstraints.gridx = 0;
gridConstraints.gridy = 2;
gridConstraints.insets = new Insets(5, 0, 5, 0);
getContentPane().add(fillButton, gridConstraints);
fillButton.addActionListener(new ActionListener()
{
  public void actionPerformed(ActionEvent e)
  {
fillButtonActionPerformed(e);
  }
});
```

Add three empty methods.

```
private void drawPanelMousePressed(MouseEvent e)
{
}

private void drawButtonActionPerformed(ActionEvent e)
{
}

private void fillButtonActionPerformed(ActionEvent e)
{
}
```

4. Add the **GraphicsPanel** class (from **Appendix I**) after the main class to allow for persistent graphics in the **paintComponent** method:

```
class GraphicsPanel extends JPanel
{
  public GraphicsPanel()
  {
  }
  public void paintComponent(Graphics g)
  {
  }
}
```

Run to check control layout:

The panel is gray because we haven't coded the **paintComponent** method. And, yes, the buttons should not be enabled.

5. Now, we write code. Use these class level scope declarations:

```
static boolean shapeDrawn = true; //set to true for proper
initialization
static boolean shapeFilled = false;
static Color fillColor;
static Vector myPoints = new Vector(50, 10);
Random myRandom = new Random();
```

6. Use this code in the **drawPanelMousePressed** method. It saves the clicked points and marks them with a red dot:

```
private void drawPanelMousePressed(MouseEvent e)
{
  if (shapeDrawn)
  {
    // starting over with new drawing
    drawButton.setEnabled(false);
    fillButton.setEnabled(false);
    shapeDrawn = false;
    shapeFilled = false;
    myPoints.removeAllElements();
  }
  // Save clicked point and mark with red dot
  Point2D.Double myPoint = new Point2D.Double(e.getX(),
e.getY());
  myPoints.add(myPoint);
  if (myPoints.size() > 2)
  {
    drawButton.setEnabled(true);
  }
  drawPanel.repaint();
}
```

7. Use this code in the **drawButtonActionPerformed** event method:

```
private void drawButtonActionPerformed(ActionEvent e)
{
  // connect lines
  drawButton.setEnabled(false);
  fillButton.setEnabled(true); // allow filling polygon
  shapeDrawn = true;
  drawPanel.repaint();
}
```

This code connects the points and draws a polygon.

8. Use this code in the **fillButtonActionPerformed** event method:

```
private void fillButtonActionPerformed(ActionEvent e)
{
  // fill polygon
  fillColor = new Color(myRandom.nextInt(256),
myRandom.nextInt(256), myRandom.nextInt(256));
  shapeFilled = true;
  drawPanel.repaint();
}
```

The closed polygon is filled with a random color.

9. Use this code in the **paintComponent** method in the **GraphicsPanel** class. This code draws and fills the polygon, as needed. Note, in particular, how the saved points (**Point2D** objects) are retrieved from the **myPoints** vector collection:

```
public void paintComponent(Graphics g)
{
  // create graphics object and connect points in x, y
arrays
  GeneralPath myShape = new GeneralPath();
  Graphics2D g2D = (Graphics2D) g;
  super.paintComponent(g2D);
  if (DrawingPolygons.myPoints.size() == 0)
  {
    return;
  }
  for (int i = 0; i < DrawingPolygons.myPoints.size();
i++)
  {
    Point2D.Double myPoint = (Point2D.Double)
DrawingPolygons.myPoints.elementAt(i);
    if (!DrawingPolygons.shapeDrawn)
    {
      // points only
      g2D.setPaint(Color.RED);
      g2D.fill(new Ellipse2D.Double(myPoint.getX() - 1,
myPoint.getY() - 1, 3, 3));
    }
    else
    {
      // build the path for drawing and or filling
      if (i == 0)
      {
```

```
              myShape.moveTo((float) myPoint.getX(), (float)
myPoint.getY());
          }
          else
          {
              myShape.lineTo((float) myPoint.getX(), (float)
myPoint.getY());
          }
      }
  }
  if (DrawingPolygons.shapeDrawn)
  {
    // fill then redraw
    myShape.closePath();
    if (DrawingPolygons.shapeFilled)
    {
      g2D.setPaint(DrawingPolygons.fillColor);
      g2D.fill(myShape);
    }
    g2D.setStroke(new BasicStroke(2));
    g2D.setPaint(Color.BLUE);
    g2D.draw(myShape);
  }
  g2D.dispose();
}
```

The complete **DrawingPolygons.java** code (additions to basic framework are shaded):

```
/*
 * DrawingPolygons.java
*/
package drawingpolygons;
import javax.swing.*;
import java.awt.*;
import java.awt.geom.*;
import java.awt.event.*;
import java.util.*;
import java.util.Random;

public class DrawingPolygons extends JFrame
{
  GraphicsPanel drawPanel = new GraphicsPanel();
  JButton drawButton = new JButton();
  JButton fillButton = new JButton();
```

```
  static boolean shapeDrawn = true; //set to true for proper
initialization
  static boolean shapeFilled = false;
  static Color fillColor;
  static Vector myPoints = new Vector(50, 10);
  Random myRandom = new Random();

  public static void main(String args[])
  {
    //construct frame
    new DrawingPolygons().show();
  }

  public DrawingPolygons()
  {
    // code to build the form
    setTitle("Drawing Polygons");
    setResizable(false);
    addWindowListener(new WindowAdapter()
    {
      public void windowClosing(WindowEvent e)
      {
        exitForm(e);
      }
    });
    getContentPane().setLayout(new GridBagLayout());

    // position controls (establish event methods)
    GridBagConstraints gridConstraints = new
GridBagConstraints();
    drawPanel.setPreferredSize(new Dimension(350, 250));
    drawPanel.setBackground(Color.WHITE);
    gridConstraints.gridx = 0;
    gridConstraints.gridy = 0;
    gridConstraints.insets = new Insets(10, 10, 10, 10);
    getContentPane().add(drawPanel, gridConstraints);
     drawPanel.addMouseListener(new MouseAdapter()
    {
      public void mousePressed(MouseEvent e)
      {
        drawPanelMousePressed(e);
      }
    });

    drawButton.setText("Draw Polygon");
    drawButton.setEnabled(false);
    gridConstraints = new GridBagConstraints();
```

```
   gridConstraints.gridx = 0;
   gridConstraints.gridy = 1;
   getContentPane().add(drawButton, gridConstraints);
   drawButton.addActionListener(new ActionListener()
   {
     public void actionPerformed(ActionEvent e)
     {
       drawButtonActionPerformed(e);
     }
   });

    fillButton.setText("Fill Polygon");
    fillButton.setEnabled(false);
   gridConstraints = new GridBagConstraints();
   gridConstraints.gridx = 0;
   gridConstraints.gridy = 2;
   gridConstraints.insets = new Insets(5, 0, 5, 0);
   getContentPane().add(fillButton, gridConstraints);
   fillButton.addActionListener(new ActionListener()
   {
     public void actionPerformed(ActionEvent e)
     {
       fillButtonActionPerformed(e);
     }
   });

   pack();
   Dimension screenSize =
Toolkit.getDefaultToolkit().getScreenSize();
   setBounds((int) (0.5 * (screenSize.width - getWidth())),
(int) (0.5 * (screenSize.height - getHeight())), getWidth(),
getHeight());
  }

  private void drawPanelMousePressed(MouseEvent e)
  {
    if (shapeDrawn)
    {
      // starting over with new drawing
      drawButton.setEnabled(false);
      fillButton.setEnabled(false);
      shapeDrawn = false;
      shapeFilled = false;
      myPoints.removeAllElements();
    }
    // Save clicked point and mark with red dot
```

```
      Point2D.Double myPoint = new Point2D.Double(e.getX(),
e.getY());
    myPoints.add(myPoint);
    if (myPoints.size() > 2)
    {
      drawButton.setEnabled(true);
    }
    drawPanel.repaint();
  }

  private void drawButtonActionPerformed(ActionEvent e)
  {
    // connect lines
    drawButton.setEnabled(false);
    fillButton.setEnabled(true); // allow filling polygon
    shapeDrawn = true;
    drawPanel.repaint();
  }

  private void fillButtonActionPerformed(ActionEvent e)
  {
    // fill polygon
    fillColor = new Color(myRandom.nextInt(256),
myRandom.nextInt(256), myRandom.nextInt(256));
    shapeFilled = true;
    drawPanel.repaint();
  }

  private void exitForm(WindowEvent e)
  {
    System.exit(0);
  }
}


class GraphicsPanel extends JPanel
{
  public GraphicsPanel()
  {
  }
  public void paintComponent(Graphics g)
  {
    // create graphics object and connect points in x, y
arrays
    GeneralPath myShape = new GeneralPath();
    Graphics2D g2D = (Graphics2D) g;
    super.paintComponent(g2D);
    if (DrawingPolygons.myPoints.size() == 0)
```

```
    {
      return;
    }
    for (int i = 0; i < DrawingPolygons.myPoints.size(); i++)
    {
      Point2D.Double myPoint = (Point2D.Double)
DrawingPolygons.myPoints.elementAt(i);
      if (!DrawingPolygons.shapeDrawn)
      {
        // points only
        g2D.setPaint(Color.RED);
        g2D.fill(new Ellipse2D.Double(myPoint.getX() - 1,
myPoint.getY() - 1, 3, 3));
      }
      else
      {
        // build the path for drawing and or filling
        if (i == 0)
        {
          myShape.moveTo((float) myPoint.getX(), (float)
myPoint.getY());
        }
        else
        {
          myShape.lineTo((float) myPoint.getX(), (float)
myPoint.getY());
        }
      }
    }
    if (DrawingPolygons.shapeDrawn)
    {
      // fill then redraw
      myShape.closePath();
      if (DrawingPolygons.shapeFilled)
      {
        g2D.setPaint(DrawingPolygons.fillColor);
        g2D.fill(myShape);
      }
      g2D.setStroke(new BasicStroke(2));
      g2D.setPaint(Color.BLUE);
      g2D.draw(myShape);
    }
    g2D.dispose();
  }
}
```

Run the application. Try drawing points (just click the frame with any button of the mouse) and polygons. Fill the polygons. Notice how the random colors work. Notice how the button controls are enabled and disabled at different points. To start a new drawing, just click the frame with a new starting point. Try overlapping points to see some nice effects. Here's a polygon I drew:

Save the project (saved as **Example8-3** project in **\LearnJava\LJ Code\Class 8** program group)

Drawing Curves

The **GeneralPath** object can also be used to draw curved segments. Drawing **curves** is a little more detailed than drawing polygons and involves a little mathematical jargon. We'll try not to overwhelm you with the math. We'll develop the steps needed to fill a polygonal region with a smooth curve.

There are two methods that allow the drawing of curved segments: **quadTo** and **curveTo**. First, let's look at **quadTo**. For the mathematically inclined, **quadTo** constructs a quadratic (second-order polynomial – you may remember the quadratic formula from ninth grade algebra) curve segment between the current path point and a new point using a specified 'control' point. The segment is constructed such that tangents (straight lines just touching the curve) to the two curve points intersect at the control point. You don't have to know what all this means – here's a picture of what **quadTo** does:

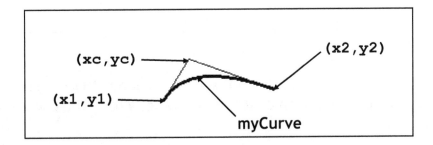

In this picture, (**x1, y1**) is the current path point (last point drawn to), (**x2, y2**) is the new point to add to the path and (**xc, yc**) is the control point. If the **GeneralPath** object we are constructing is **myCurve**, the code to draw this quadratic segment is:

```
myCurve.quadTo(xc, yc, x2, y2);
```

Notice (**x1, y1**) does not appear in the method – it is assumed to be the last point drawn to in the path construction. Quadratic curves smoothly transition from one point to the next.

The **curveTo** method requires two control points for each curve segment. In mathematical terms, **curveTo** constructs a cubic (third-order) curve, also known as a Bezier curve, between the current path point and a new point using the two control points. The segment is constructed such that the tangent from each curve point goes through its corresponding control point. Pictorially, the resulting segment is:

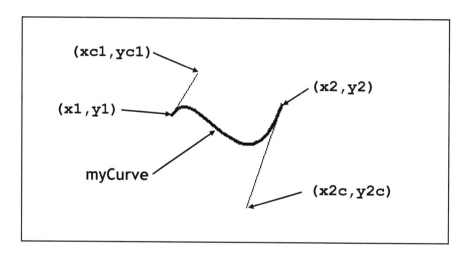

where (**x1, y1**) is the current path point with control point (**x1c, y1c**) and (**x2, y2**) is the new point to add with control point (**x2c, y2c**). The code to draw this cubic segment is:

```
myCurve.curveTo(x1c, y1c, x2c, y2c, x2, y2);
```

Again, (**x1, y1**) is implicit in the path construction. Cubic curves are seen to be a bit "curvier." This is because we can work with two control points.

As mentioned earlier, we don't want to overwhelm you with the mathematics behind quadratic and cubic curves. To draw general curved shapes requires some knowledge of calculus and optimization techniques for proper placement of curve and control points. We'll show you how to draw a general shape (using **quadTo**) using only addition and division skills. The approach we take is fit a curved shape within a polygon. The **vertices** of the polygon will be the **control points** for the curved path. The **midpoints** of the sides of the polygon will be the **curve points**. You'll see that this technique draws a pretty nice closed curve.

Let's work through an example. Here's the polygon we used as a previous example, with the vertices labeled:

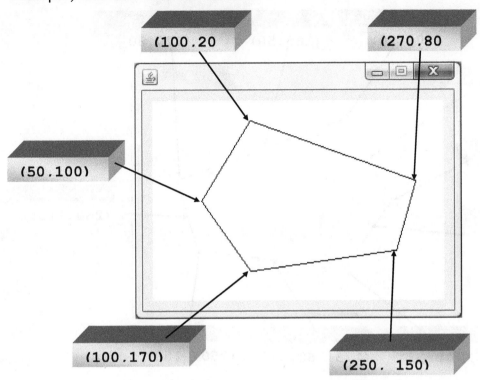

We want to draw a curve in the interior of this polygon. As mentioned, the identified vertices will be the control points to use with the **quadTo** method.

The curve points will be the midpoints of the sides of the polygon. How do you find these points? This is where the addition and division skills are needed. If (**x1, y1**) is the coordinate at one end of a side and (**x2, y2**) is the coordinate at the other end, the midpoint (**xm, ym**) is just the average of the x values and y values:

```
(xm, ym) = (0.5 * (x1 + x2), 0.5 * (y1 + y2))
```

So, here is the polygon with all midpoints added and labeled:

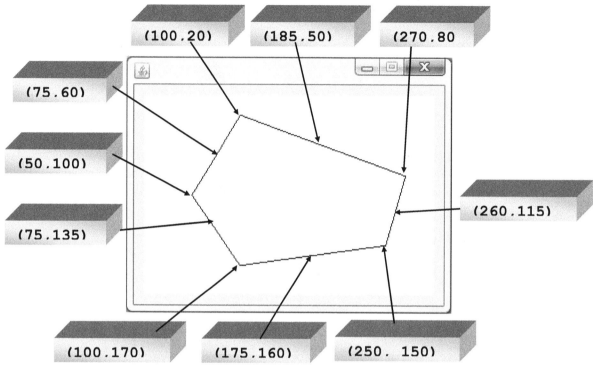

Make sure you see how we got all these values.

With all these points, we can now construct the interior curve. Recall the vertices are control points and the midpoints are curve points. We will start at (**75, 60**) and move counterclockwise, connecting the curve points using the control points in a **quadTo** method. The code to draw the interior curve (in a panel **myPanel**, in **red** with **width 3**) is:

```
Graphics2D g2D = (Graphics2D) myPanel.getGraphics();
GeneralPath myCurve = new GeneralPath();
g2D.setStroke(new BasicStroke(3));
myCurve.moveTo(75, 60);
myCurve.quadTo(100, 20, 185, 50);
myCurve.quadTo(270, 80, 260, 115);
myCurve.quadTo(250, 150, 175, 160);
myCurve.quadTo(100, 170, 75, 135);
myCurve.quadTo(50, 100, 75, 60);
g2D.setColor(Color.RED);
g2D.draw(myCurve);
g2D.dispose();
```

This yields (we also drew the border so you can see how the curve fits):

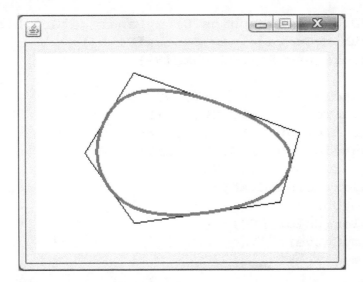

For clarity, we didn't relabel all the points, but you should be able to see how the curve travels through the specified midpoints. Notice we don't use the **closePath** method here to connect the last point with the first point (like we did for a polygon). The **closePath** method uses a straight line for connection. Instead, we need one last **quadTo** method to connect the points using the corresponding control point.

The curve can be filled with the fill method:

```
g2D.fill(myCurve);
```

The shape will be filled with the current **paint** attribute.

To **fill** our example curve with **cyan**, the shaded code is added:

```
Graphics2D g2D = (Graphics2D) myPanel.getGraphics();
GeneralPath myCurve = new GeneralPath();
g2D.setStroke(new BasicStroke(3));
myCurve.moveTo(75, 60);
myCurve.quadTo(100, 20, 185, 50);
myCurve.quadTo(270, 80, 260, 115);
myCurve.quadTo(250, 150, 175, 160);
myCurve.quadTo(100, 170, 75, 135);
myCurve.quadTo(50, 100, 75, 60);
g2D.setColor(Color.CYAN);
g2D.fill(myCurve);
g2D.setColor(Color.RED);
g2D.draw(myCurve);
g2D.dispose();
```

This produces (again, we've left the bordering polygon):

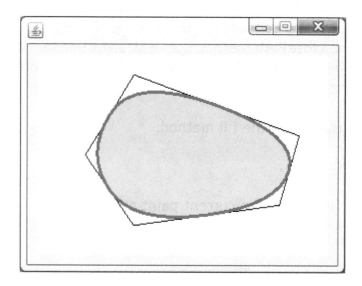

Notice that, to preserve the red border, we did the **fill** operation before the **draw**.

I think you'll agree this simple approach (no calculus!) yields a pretty nice curved shape. Even if the segments of the surrounding polygon overlap, you get a neat curve. Let's summarize the steps to create a curved region (**myCurve**):

> ➢ Declare path using:

```
GeneralPath myCurve = new GeneralPath();
```

> ➢ Determine vertices and midpoints of surrounding polygon.

> ➢ Initialize the curve at some midpoint (this establishes the 'current' drawing point):

```
myCurve.moveTo(x, y);
```

> ➢ Following the path of the surrounding polygon, for each subsequent midpoint, including the initial point, draw a curve segment using:

```
myPolygon.quadTo(xc, yc, x, y);
```

where (**xc, yc**) (the control point) is the vertex between the midpoint (**x, y**) and the previous curve point.

> ➢ Draw the curve (after setting **stroke** and **paint** attributes, if needed), assuming a graphics object **g2D**:

```
g2D.draw(myCurve);
```

You should be able to identify each of these steps in the little example we did. Now, let's use this technique to replicate **Example 8-3** with curves instead of polygons.

Example 8-4

Drawing Curves

Start a new empty project in **NetBeans**. Name the project **DrawingCurves**. Delete default code in Java file named **DrawingCurves**. In this application, the user will click on a panel control specifying a set of points. These points will be used to a curve or a filled (random color) curve. This example is essentially the same as **Example 8-3**. Because of this, we will simply modify that example.

Open **Example 8-3** (DrawingPolygons) and open the **DrawingPolygons.java** file. Copy the contents of that file into the **DrawingCurves.java** file. Make these changes:

➢ Change all instances of **DrawingPolygons** to **DrawingCurves** – I found 11 such instances.

➢ Change the frame title to **Drawing Curves**.

➢ Change the **drawButton** text to **Draw Curve**

➢ Change the **fillButton** text to **Fill Curve**.

➢ Change the **paintComponent** method in **GraphicsClass**:

```
public void paintComponent(Graphics g)
{
  // create graphics object and connect points in x, y
arrays
  GeneralPath myCurve = new GeneralPath();
  Graphics2D g2D = (Graphics2D) g;
  super.paintComponent(g2D);
  int numberPoints = DrawingCurves.myPoints.size();
  if (numberPoints == 0)
  {
    return;
  }
  // array for control points
  Point2D[] controlPoint = new Point2D[numberPoints];
  for (int i = 0; i < numberPoints; i++)
  {
```

```
        controlPoint[i] = (Point2D.Double)
DrawingCurves.myPoints.elementAt(i);
      if (!DrawingCurves.shapeDrawn)
      {
        // points only
        g2D.setPaint(Color.RED);
        g2D.fill(new Ellipse2D.Double(controlPoint[i].getX()
- 1, controlPoint[i].getY() - 1, 3, 3));
      }
    }
    if (DrawingCurves.shapeDrawn)
    {
      // array for curve points
      Point2D[] curvePoint = new Point2D[numberPoints];
      // establish last point first
      curvePoint[numberPoints - 1] = new Point2D.Double(0.5
* (controlPoint[numberPoints - 1].getX() +
controlPoint[0].getX()), 0.5 * (controlPoint[numberPoints
- 1].getY() + controlPoint[0].getY()));
      myCurve.moveTo((float) curvePoint[numberPoints -
1].getX(), (float) curvePoint[numberPoints - 1].getY());
      for (int i = 0; i < numberPoints; i++)
      {
        if (i < numberPoints - 1)
        {
          curvePoint[i] = new Point2D.Double(0.5 *
(controlPoint[i].getX() + controlPoint[i + 1].getX()), 0.5
* (controlPoint[i].getY() + controlPoint[i + 1].getY()));
        }
        myCurve.quadTo((float) controlPoint[i].getX(),
(float) controlPoint[i].getY(), (float)
curvePoint[i].getX(), (float) curvePoint[i].getY());
      }
      if (DrawingCurves.shapeFilled)
      {
        g2D.setPaint(DrawingCurves.fillColor);
        g2D.fill(myCurve);
      }
      g2D.setStroke(new BasicStroke(2));
      g2D.setPaint(Color.BLUE);
      g2D.draw(myCurve);
    }
    g2D.dispose();
}
```

The complete **DrawingCurves.java** code listing (changes to
DrawingPolygons.java are shaded):

```
/*
 * DrawingCurves.java
 */
package drawingcurves;
import javax.swing.*;
import java.awt.*;
import java.awt.geom.*;
import java.awt.event.*;
import java.util.*;
import java.util.Random;

public class DrawingCurves extends JFrame
{

  GraphicsPanel drawPanel = new GraphicsPanel();
  JButton drawButton = new JButton();
  JButton fillButton = new JButton();

  static boolean shapeDrawn = true; //set to true for proper
initialization
  static boolean shapeFilled = false;
  static Color fillColor;
  static Vector myPoints = new Vector(50, 10);
  Random myRandom = new Random();

  public static void main(String args[])
  {
    //construct frame
    new DrawingCurves().show();
  }

  public DrawingCurves()
  {
    // code to build the form
    setTitle("Drawing Curves");
    setResizable(false);
    addWindowListener(new WindowAdapter()
    {
      public void windowClosing(WindowEvent e)
      {
        exitForm(e);
      }
    });
    getContentPane().setLayout(new GridBagLayout());
```

```
   // position controls (establish event methods)
   GridBagConstraints gridConstraints = new
GridBagConstraints();
   drawPanel.setPreferredSize(new Dimension(350, 250));
   drawPanel.setBackground(Color.WHITE);
   gridConstraints.gridx = 0;
   gridConstraints.gridy = 0;
   gridConstraints.insets = new Insets(10, 10, 10, 10);
   getContentPane().add(drawPanel, gridConstraints);
    drawPanel.addMouseListener(new MouseAdapter()
   {
     public void mousePressed(MouseEvent e)
     {
       drawPanelMousePressed(e);
     }
   });

     drawButton.setText("Draw Curve");
    drawButton.setEnabled(false);
   gridConstraints = new GridBagConstraints();
   gridConstraints.gridx = 0;
   gridConstraints.gridy = 1;
   getContentPane().add(drawButton, gridConstraints);
   drawButton.addActionListener(new ActionListener()
   {
     public void actionPerformed(ActionEvent e)
     {
       drawButtonActionPerformed(e);
     }
   });

     fillButton.setText("Fill Curve");
    fillButton.setEnabled(false);
   gridConstraints = new GridBagConstraints();
   gridConstraints.gridx = 0;
   gridConstraints.gridy = 2;
   gridConstraints.insets = new Insets(5, 0, 5, 0);
   getContentPane().add(fillButton, gridConstraints);
   fillButton.addActionListener(new ActionListener()
   {
     public void actionPerformed(ActionEvent e)
     {
       fillButtonActionPerformed(e);
     }
   });
```

```
      pack();
      Dimension screenSize =
Toolkit.getDefaultToolkit().getScreenSize();
      setBounds((int) (0.5 * (screenSize.width - getWidth())),
(int) (0.5 * (screenSize.height - getHeight())), getWidth(),
getHeight());
   }

   private void drawPanelMousePressed(MouseEvent e)
   {
      if (shapeDrawn)
      {
        // starting over with new drawing
        drawButton.setEnabled(false);
        fillButton.setEnabled(false);
        shapeDrawn = false;
        shapeFilled = false;
        myPoints.removeAllElements();
      }
      // Save clicked point and mark with red dot
      Point2D.Double myPoint = new Point2D.Double(e.getX(),
e.getY());
      myPoints.add(myPoint);
      if (myPoints.size() > 2)
      {
        drawButton.setEnabled(true);
      }
      drawPanel.repaint();
   }

   private void drawButtonActionPerformed(ActionEvent e)
   {
      // connect lines
      drawButton.setEnabled(false);
      fillButton.setEnabled(true); // allow filling polygon
      shapeDrawn = true;
      drawPanel.repaint();
   }

   private void fillButtonActionPerformed(ActionEvent e)
   {
      // fill polygon
      fillColor = new Color(myRandom.nextInt(256),
myRandom.nextInt(256), myRandom.nextInt(256));
      shapeFilled = true;
      drawPanel.repaint();
   }
```

```
  private void exitForm(WindowEvent e)
  {
    System.exit(0);
  }
}

class GraphicsPanel extends JPanel
{
  public GraphicsPanel()
  {
  }
  public void paintComponent(Graphics g)
  {
    // create graphics object and connect points in x, y
arrays
    GeneralPath myCurve = new GeneralPath();
    Graphics2D g2D = (Graphics2D) g;
    super.paintComponent(g2D);
    int numberPoints = DrawingCurves.myPoints.size();
    if (numberPoints == 0)
    {
      return;
    }
    // array for control points
    Point2D[] controlPoint = new Point2D[numberPoints];
    for (int i = 0; i < numberPoints; i++)
    {
      controlPoint[i] = (Point2D.Double)
DrawingCurves.myPoints.elementAt(i);
      if (!DrawingCurves.shapeDrawn)
      {
        // points only
        g2D.setPaint(Color.RED);
        g2D.fill(new Ellipse2D.Double(controlPoint[i].getX()
- 1, controlPoint[i].getY() - 1, 3, 3));
      }
    }
    if (DrawingCurves.shapeDrawn)
    {
      // array for curve points
      Point2D[] curvePoint = new Point2D[numberPoints];
      // establish last point first
      curvePoint[numberPoints - 1] = new Point2D.Double(0.5
* (controlPoint[numberPoints - 1].getX() +
controlPoint[0].getX()), 0.5 * (controlPoint[numberPoints -
1].getY() + controlPoint[0].getY()));
```

```
      myCurve.moveTo((float) curvePoint[numberPoints -
1].getX(), (float) curvePoint[numberPoints - 1].getY());
      for (int i = 0; i < numberPoints; i++)
      {
        if (i < numberPoints - 1)
        {
          curvePoint[i] = new Point2D.Double(0.5 *
(controlPoint[i].getX() + controlPoint[i + 1].getX()), 0.5 *
(controlPoint[i].getY() + controlPoint[i + 1].getY()));
        }
        myCurve.quadTo((float) controlPoint[i].getX(),
(float) controlPoint[i].getY(), (float) curvePoint[i].getX(),
(float) curvePoint[i].getY());
      }

      if (DrawingCurves.shapeFilled)
      {
        g2D.setPaint(DrawingCurves.fillColor);
        g2D.fill(myCurve);
      }
      g2D.setStroke(new BasicStroke(2));
      g2D.setPaint(Color.BLUE);
      g2D.draw(myCurve);
    }
    g2D.dispose();
  }
}
```

Run the project. Try drawing closed curves. Fill the closed curves. Notice how the random colors work. Notice how the button controls are enabled and disabled at different points. To start a new drawing once complete, just click the form with a new starting point. Try overlapping points to see some nice effects. Here's a curve I drew:

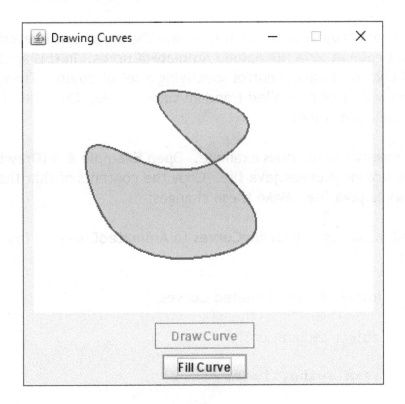

Save the project (saved as **Example8-4** project in **\LearnJava\LJ Code\Class 8** program group). Try the next example if you want to see something cool!!

Example 8-5

Animated Curves

Start a new empty project in **NetBeans**. Name the project **AnimatedCurves**. Delete default code in Java file named **AnimatedCurves**. In this application, the user will click on a panel control specifying a set of points. These points will be used to draw a curve or a filled (random color) curve. Once filled, the shape will change itself over time!

We will just modify the previous example. Open **Example 8-4** (**DrawingCurves**) and open the **DrawingCurves.java** file. Copy the contents of that file into the **AnimatedCurves.java** file. Make these changes:

➢ Change all instances of **DrawingCurves** to **AnimatedCurves**- I found 10 such instances.

➢ Change the frame title to **Animated Curves**.

➢ Add a timer object declaration:

```
myTimer javax.swing.Timer;
```

We need to preface this with **javax.swing** because there is also a timer object in the **java.util package**.

➢ In the frame constructor, create and add a method for the **myTimer** object.

```
myTimer = new javax.swing.Timer(100, new ActionListener()
{
  public void actionPerformed(ActionEvent e)
  {
    myTimerActionPerformed(e);
  }
});
```

➢ In the **drawPanelMousePressed** method, when a new drawing is started, add a line of code to turn off the timer:

```
myTimer.stop();
```

➤ In the **fillButtonActionPerformed** method, add a line of code to turn on the timer object:

```
myTimer.start();
```

➤ Add this **myTimerActionPerformed** method:

```
private void myTimerActionPerformed(ActionEvent e)
{
   // tweak all the control points a bit
   for (int i = 0; i < myPoints.size(); i++)
   {
      Point2D.Double myPoint = (Point2D.Double)
myPoints.elementAt(i);
      myPoint.x += myRandom.nextDouble() * 20.0 - 10.0;
      myPoint.y += myRandom.nextDouble() * 20.0 - 10.0;
      myPoints.setElementAt(myPoint,i);
   }
   drawPanel.repaint();
}
```

In this method, we go through the list of control points and randomly change them. This will 'perturb' the displayed curve a little and give the effect of animation.

The complete **AnimatedCurves.java** code (changes to DrawingCurves.java are shaded):

```
/*
 * AnimatedCurves.java
 */
package animatedcurves;
import javax.swing.*;
import java.awt.*;
import java.awt.geom.*;
import java.awt.event.*;
import java.util.*;
import java.util.Random;

public class AnimatedCurves extends JFrame
{

   GraphicsPanel drawPanel = new GraphicsPanel();
   JButton drawButton = new JButton();
   JButton fillButton = new JButton();
   javax.swing.Timer myTimer;
```

```
static boolean shapeDrawn = true; //set to true for proper
initialization
  static boolean shapeFilled = false;
  static Color fillColor;
  static Vector myPoints = new Vector(50, 10);
  Random myRandom = new Random();

  public static void main(String args[])
  {
    //construct frame
    new AnimatedCurves().show();
  }

  public AnimatedCurves()
  {
    // code to build the form
    setTitle("Animated Curves");
    setResizable(false);
    addWindowListener(new WindowAdapter()
    {
      public void windowClosing(WindowEvent e)
      {
        exitForm(e);
      }
    });
    getContentPane().setLayout(new GridBagLayout());

    // position controls (establish event methods)
    GridBagConstraints gridConstraints = new
GridBagConstraints();
    drawPanel.setPreferredSize(new Dimension(350, 250));
    drawPanel.setBackground(Color.WHITE);
    gridConstraints.gridx = 0;
    gridConstraints.gridy = 0;
    gridConstraints.insets = new Insets(10, 10, 10, 10);
    getContentPane().add(drawPanel, gridConstraints);
     drawPanel.addMouseListener(new MouseAdapter()
    {
      public void mousePressed(MouseEvent e)
      {
        drawPanelMousePressed(e);
      }
    });

    drawButton.setText("Draw Curve");
    drawButton.setEnabled(false);
```

```
    gridConstraints = new GridBagConstraints();
    gridConstraints.gridx = 0;
    gridConstraints.gridy = 1;
    getContentPane().add(drawButton, gridConstraints);
    drawButton.addActionListener(new ActionListener()
    {
      public void actionPerformed(ActionEvent e)
      {
        drawButtonActionPerformed(e);
      }
    });

     fillButton.setText("Fill Curve");
     fillButton.setEnabled(false);
    gridConstraints = new GridBagConstraints();
    gridConstraints.gridx = 0;
    gridConstraints.gridy = 2;
    gridConstraints.insets = new Insets(5, 0, 5, 0);
    getContentPane().add(fillButton, gridConstraints);
    fillButton.addActionListener(new ActionListener()
    {
      public void actionPerformed(ActionEvent e)
      {
        fillButtonActionPerformed(e);
      }
    });

      myTimer = new javax.swing.Timer(100, new
ActionListener()
    {
    public void actionPerformed(ActionEvent e)
    {
      myTimerActionPerformed(e);
    }
    });

    pack();
    Dimension screenSize =
Toolkit.getDefaultToolkit().getScreenSize();
    setBounds((int) (0.5 * (screenSize.width - getWidth())),
(int) (0.5 * (screenSize.height - getHeight())), getWidth(),
getHeight());
  }

  private void drawPanelMousePressed(MouseEvent e)
  {
    if (shapeDrawn)
```

```
    {
      // starting over with new drawing
      myTimer.stop();
      drawButton.setEnabled(false);
      fillButton.setEnabled(false);
      shapeDrawn = false;
      shapeFilled = false;
      myPoints.removeAllElements();
    }
    // Save clicked point and mark with red dot
    Point2D.Double myPoint = new Point2D.Double(e.getX(),
e.getY());
    myPoints.add(myPoint);
    if (myPoints.size() > 2)
    {
      drawButton.setEnabled(true);
    }
    drawPanel.repaint();
  }

  private void drawButtonActionPerformed(ActionEvent e)
  {
    // connect lines
    drawButton.setEnabled(false);
    fillButton.setEnabled(true); // allow filling polygon
    shapeDrawn = true;
    drawPanel.repaint();
  }

  private void fillButtonActionPerformed(ActionEvent e)
  {
    // fill polygon
    myTimer.start();
    fillColor = new Color(myRandom.nextInt(256),
myRandom.nextInt(256), myRandom.nextInt(256));
    shapeFilled = true;
    drawPanel.repaint();
  }

  private void myTimerActionPerformed(ActionEvent e)
  {
    // tweak all the control points a bit
    for (int i = 0; i < myPoints.size(); i++)
    {
      Point2D.Double myPoint = (Point2D.Double)
myPoints.elementAt(i);
      myPoint.x += myRandom.nextDouble() * 20.0 - 10.0;
```

```
            myPoint.y += myRandom.nextDouble() * 20.0 - 10.0;
            myPoints.setElementAt(myPoint,i);
        }
        drawPanel.repaint();
    }
```

```
    private void exitForm(WindowEvent e)
    {
        System.exit(0);
    }
}

class GraphicsPanel extends JPanel
{
    public GraphicsPanel()
    {
    }
    public void paintComponent(Graphics g)
    {
        // create graphics object and connect points in x, y
arrays
        GeneralPath myCurve = new GeneralPath();
        Graphics2D g2D = (Graphics2D) g;
        super.paintComponent(g2D);
        int numberPoints = AnimatedCurves.myPoints.size();
        if (numberPoints == 0)
        {
            return;
        }
        // array for control points
        Point2D[] controlPoint = new Point2D[numberPoints];
        for (int i = 0; i < numberPoints; i++)
        {
            controlPoint[i] = (Point2D.Double)
AnimatedCurves.myPoints.elementAt(i);
            if (!AnimatedCurves.shapeDrawn)
            {
                // points only
                g2D.setPaint(Color.RED);
                g2D.fill(new Ellipse2D.Double(controlPoint[i].getX()
- 1, controlPoint[i].getY() - 1, 3, 3));
            }
        }
        if (AnimatedCurves.shapeDrawn)
        {
            // array for curve points
            Point2D[] curvePoint = new Point2D[numberPoints];
```

```
      // establish last point first
      curvePoint[numberPoints - 1] = new Point2D.Double(0.5
* (controlPoint[numberPoints - 1].getX() +
controlPoint[0].getX()), 0.5 * (controlPoint[numberPoints -
1].getY() + controlPoint[0].getY()));
      myCurve.moveTo((float) curvePoint[numberPoints -
1].getX(), (float) curvePoint[numberPoints - 1].getY());
      for (int i = 0; i < numberPoints; i++)
      {
        if (i < numberPoints - 1)
        {
          curvePoint[i] = new Point2D.Double(0.5 *
(controlPoint[i].getX() + controlPoint[i + 1].getX()), 0.5 *
(controlPoint[i].getY() + controlPoint[i + 1].getY()));
        }
        myCurve.quadTo((float) controlPoint[i].getX(),
(float) controlPoint[i].getY(), (float) curvePoint[i].getX(),
(float) curvePoint[i].getY());
      }

      if (AnimatedCurves.shapeFilled)
      {
        g2D.setPaint(AnimatedCurves.fillColor);
        g2D.fill(myCurve);
      }
      g2D.setStroke(new BasicStroke(2));
      g2D.setPaint(Color.BLUE);
      g2D.draw(myCurve);
    }
    g2D.dispose();
  }
}
```

Run. Create and fill a curve. Once filled, be amazed at its animated
performance. You might like to also change colors as the animation is going on.
Save the project (saved as **Example8-5** project in **\LearnJava\LJ Code\Class 8**
program group).

GradientPaint Object

The filled polygons and filled curves are pretty, but it would be nice to have them filled with something other than a solid color. Java provides other paint classes that provide interesting fill effects. The **GradientPaint** class fills a shape with a blending of two colors. It starts with one color and gradually 'becomes' the other color in a specified direction. You specify the colors and direction of the 'gradient.'

To create a **GradientPaint** object, you specify a **gradient line**, which begins at a **Point2D** object **p1** with color **c1**, and ends at a **Point2D** object **p2** with color **c2**. Then, as you move along this gradient line from **p1** to **p2**, the color transitions from **c1** to **c2**. The **GradientPaint** object creates parallel bands of color perpendicular to the gradient line. Here is a gradient line that runs diagonally from **p1**, color **yellow**, to **p2**, color **dark gray**:

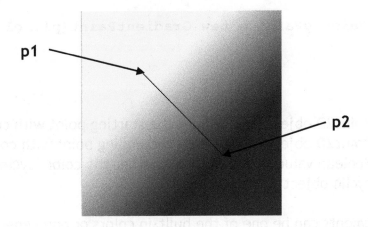

By changing **p1** and **p2**, you can set up gradients in any direction you desire. The paint displayed above is **acyclic**. In an **acyclic** gradient paint object, any points beyond the ends of the gradient line are the same color as the endpoints.

The **GradientPaint** object can also be **cyclic**. In a **cyclic** object, the gradient line is repeated in both directions of the extended gradient line. Here is the previous gradient with cyclic behavior:

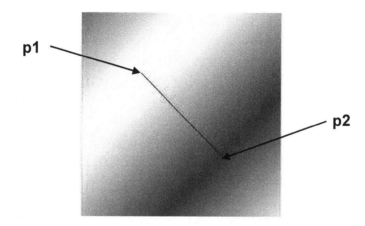

To create a **GradientPaint** object (**gPaint**), we use this constructor:

```
GradientPaint gPaint = new GradientPaint(p1, c1, p2, c2,
cyclic);
```

where:

p1   **Point2D** object that defines the starting point with color **c1**
p2   **Point2D** object that defines the ending point with color **c2**
cyclic   Boolean value that specifies whether the color 'cycles.' If true, a
          cyclic object is created.

The color arguments can be one of the built-in colors or one generated with red, green and blue contributions. Once established, use the new paint with the **setPaint** method and it becomes the new paint attribute.

Example 8-6

Gradient Paint

Start a new empty project in **NetBeans**. Name the project **GradientPainting**. Delete default code in Java file named **GradientPainting**. In this application, we will view gradient paint directions, colors and sizes. The finished frame is:

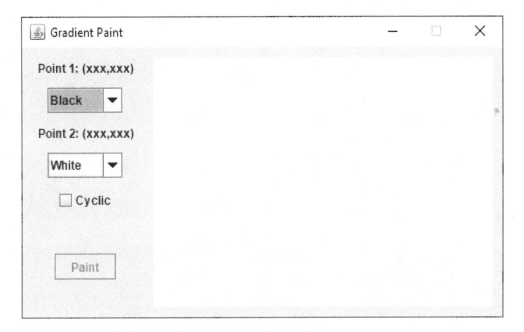

1. Add two labels, two combo box controls, a check box, a button and a panel control to the frame. The **GridBagLayout** is:

	gridx = 0	gridx = 1
gridy = 0	point1Label	
gridy = 1	color1ComboBox	
gridy = 2	point2Label	paintPanel
gridy = 3	color2ComboBox	
gridy = 4	cyclicCheckBox	
gridy = 5	paintButton	

Set the following properties:

GradientPainting Frame:
title	Gradient Painting
resizable	false

point1Label:
text	Point 1: (xxx,xxx)
preferredSize	(120, 20)
horizontalAlignment	CENTER
gridx	0
gridy	0
insets	(10, 5, 0, 0)

color1ComboBox:
background	WHITE
gridx	0
gridy	1
insets	(10, 5, 0, 0)

point2Label:
text	Point 2: (xxx,xxx)
preferredSize	(120, 20)
horizontalAlignment	CENTER
gridx	0
gridy	2
insets	(10, 5, 0, 0)

color2ComboBox:
background	WHITE
gridx	0
gridy	3
insets	(10, 5, 0, 0)

cyclicCheckBox:
text	Cyclic
gridx	0
gridy	4
insets	(10, 5, 0, 0)

paintButton:

text	Paint
enabled	false
gridx	0
gridy	5
insets	(5, 5, 0, 0)

paintPanel:

preferredSize	(350, 250)
background	WHITE
gridx	1
gridy	0
gridheight	6
insets	(10, 10, 10, 10)

2. Build the basic framework:

```
/*
 * GradientPainting.java
 */
package gradientpainting;
import javax.swing.*;
import javax.swing.event.*;
import java.awt.*;
import java.awt.geom.*;
import java.awt.event.*;

public class GradientPainting extends JFrame
{

  public static void main(String args[])
  {
    //construct frame
    new GradientPainting().show();
  }

  public GradientPainting()
  {

    // code to build the form
    setTitle("Gradient Paint");
    setResizable(false);
    addWindowListener(new WindowAdapter()
    {
      public void windowClosing(WindowEvent e)
```

```
            {
              exitForm(e);
            }
        });
        getContentPane().setLayout(new GridBagLayout());

        pack();
        Dimension screenSize =
Toolkit.getDefaultToolkit().getScreenSize();
        setBounds((int) (0.5 * (screenSize.width -
getWidth())), (int) (0.5 * (screenSize.height -
getHeight())), getWidth(), getHeight());
    }

    private void exitForm(WindowEvent e)
    {
      System.exit(0);
    }
}
```

Run to check.

3. Add these class level declarations for the controls:

```
JLabel point1Label = new JLabel();
JLabel point2Label = new JLabel();
JComboBox color1ComboBox = new JComboBox();
JComboBox color2ComboBox = new JComboBox();
JCheckBox cyclicCheckBox = new JCheckBox();
JButton paintButton = new JButton();
JPanel paintPanel = new JPanel();
```

Position and add controls and methods in frame constructor:

```
point1Label.setText("Point 1: (xxx,xxx)");
point1Label.setPreferredSize(new Dimension(120, 20));
point1Label.setHorizontalAlignment(SwingConstants.CENTER);
GridBagConstraints gridConstraints = new
GridBagConstraints();
gridConstraints.gridx = 0;
gridConstraints.gridy = 0;
gridConstraints.insets = new Insets(10, 5, 0, 0);
getContentPane().add(point1Label, gridConstraints);

color1ComboBox.setBackground(Color.WHITE);
gridConstraints = new GridBagConstraints();
```

```
gridConstraints.gridx = 0;
gridConstraints.gridy = 1;
gridConstraints.insets = new Insets(10, 5, 0, 0);
getContentPane().add(color1ComboBox, gridConstraints);
color1ComboBox.addActionListener(new ActionListener()
{
  public void actionPerformed(ActionEvent e)
  {
    paintButtonActionPerformed(e);
  }
});

point2Label.setPreferredSize(new Dimension(120, 20));
point2Label.setText("Point 2: (xxx,xxx)");
point2Label.setHorizontalAlignment(SwingConstants.CENTER);
gridConstraints = new GridBagConstraints();
gridConstraints.gridx = 0;
gridConstraints.gridy = 2;
gridConstraints.insets = new Insets(10, 5, 0, 0);
getContentPane().add(point2Label, gridConstraints);

color2ComboBox.setBackground(Color.WHITE);
gridConstraints = new GridBagConstraints();
gridConstraints.gridx = 0;
gridConstraints.gridy = 3;
gridConstraints.insets = new Insets(10, 5, 0, 0);
getContentPane().add(color2ComboBox, gridConstraints);
color2ComboBox.addActionListener(new ActionListener()
{
  public void actionPerformed(ActionEvent e)
  {
    paintButtonActionPerformed(e);
  }
});

cyclicCheckBox.setText("Cyclic");
gridConstraints = new GridBagConstraints();
gridConstraints.gridx = 0;
gridConstraints.gridy = 4;
gridConstraints.insets = new Insets(10, 5, 0, 0);
getContentPane().add(cyclicCheckBox, gridConstraints);
cyclicCheckBox.addActionListener(new ActionListener()
{
  public void actionPerformed(ActionEvent e)
  {
    paintButtonActionPerformed(e);
  }
```

```
});

paintButton.setText("Paint");
paintButton.setEnabled(false);
gridConstraints = new GridBagConstraints();
gridConstraints.gridx = 0;
gridConstraints.gridy = 5;
gridConstraints.insets = new Insets(5, 5, 0, 0);
getContentPane().add(paintButton, gridConstraints);
paintButton.addActionListener(new ActionListener()
{
  public void actionPerformed(ActionEvent e)
  {
    paintButtonActionPerformed(e);
  }
});

paintPanel.setPreferredSize(new Dimension(350, 250));
paintPanel.setBackground(Color.WHITE);
gridConstraints = new GridBagConstraints();
gridConstraints.gridx = 1;
gridConstraints.gridy = 0;
gridConstraints.gridheight = 6;
gridConstraints.insets = new Insets(10, 10, 10, 10);
getContentPane().add(paintPanel, gridConstraints);
paintPanel.addMouseListener(new MouseAdapter()
{
  public void mousePressed(MouseEvent e)
  {
    paintPanelMousePressed(e);
  }
});
```

Add empty methods:

```
private void paintPanelMousePressed(MouseEvent e)
{
}

private void paintButtonActionPerformed(ActionEvent e)
{
}
```

Run to check control layout. My frame looks like this:

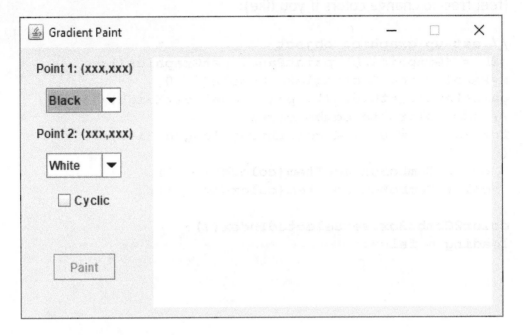

4. Now, write code. Use these class level variables:

```
Graphics2D g2D;
Rectangle2D.Double myPanel;
Color[] colorArray = {Color.BLACK, Color.BLUE,
Color.GREEN, Color.CYAN, Color.RED, Color.MAGENTA,
Color.YELLOW, Color.WHITE};
String[] colorName = {"Black", "Blue", "Green", "Cyan",
"Red", "Magenta", "Yellow", "White"};
int pointNumber = 0;
Point2D.Double p1;
Point2D.Double p2;
boolean loading = true;
```

5. Add this code at the end of the constructor. This sets up the combo boxes (feel free to change colors if you like):

```
// set up graphics object
g2D = (Graphics2D) paintPanel.getGraphics();
myPanel = new Rectangle2D.Double(0, 0,
paintPanel.getWidth(), paintPanel.getHeight());
// add colors to combo boxes
for (int i = 0; i < colorArray.length; i++)
{
  color1ComboBox.addItem(colorName[i]);
  color2ComboBox.addItem(colorName[i]);
}
color2ComboBox.setSelectedIndex(7);
loading = false;
```

6. Use this code in the **paintPanelMousePressed** method. This code detects mouse clicks that define the gradient line:

```
private void paintPanelMousePressed(MouseEvent e)
{
  if (pointNumber == 0)
  {
    // getting first gradient point
    g2D.setPaint(paintPanel.getBackground());
    g2D.fill(myPanel);
    point1Label.setText("Point 1: (" + e.getX() + "," +
e.getY() + ")");
    point2Label.setText("Point 2: (xxx,xxx)");
    p1 = new Point2D.Double(e.getX(), e.getY());
    g2D.setPaint(Color.RED);
    g2D.fill(new Ellipse2D.Double(e.getX() - 1, e.getY() -
1, 3, 3));
    paintButton.setEnabled(false);
    pointNumber = 1;
  }
  else if (pointNumber == 1)
  {
    // getting second gradient point
    point2Label.setText("Point 2: (" + e.getX() + "," +
e.getY() + ")");
    p2 = new Point2D.Double(e.getX(), e.getY());
    g2D.setPaint(Color.RED);
    g2D.fill(new Ellipse2D.Double(e.getX() - 1, e.getY() -
1, 3, 3));
    Line2D.Double gradientLine = new Line2D.Double(p1,
p2);
    g2D.setPaint(Color.BLACK);
    g2D.draw(gradientLine);
    paintButton.setEnabled(true);
    pointNumber = 0;
  }
}
```

7. Use this code in the **paintButtonActionPerformed** method (also handles a change to any of the combo boxes or check box). This paints the frame using the specified choices:

```
private void paintButtonActionPerformed(ActionEvent e)
{
  // don't try painting when loading array elements
  if (loading)
  {
    return;
  }
  // paint the panel
  Color c1 =
colorArray[color1ComboBox.getSelectedIndex()];
  Color c2 =
colorArray[color2ComboBox.getSelectedIndex()];
  GradientPaint gPaint = new GradientPaint(p1, c1, p2, c2,
cyclicCheckBox.isSelected());
  g2D.setPaint(gPaint);
  g2D.fill(myPanel);
}
```

The final **GradientPainting.java** code (additions to framework are shaded):

```
/*
 * GradientPainting.java
 */
package gradientpainting;
import javax.swing.*;
import javax.swing.event.*;
import java.awt.*;
import java.awt.geom.*;
import java.awt.event.*;
public class GradientPainting extends JFrame
{
  JLabel point1Label = new JLabel();
  JLabel point2Label = new JLabel();
  JComboBox color1ComboBox = new JComboBox();
  JComboBox color2ComboBox = new JComboBox();
  JCheckBox cyclicCheckBox = new JCheckBox();
  JButton paintButton = new JButton();
  JPanel paintPanel = new JPanel();

  Graphics2D g2D;
  Rectangle2D.Double myPanel;
```

```
  Color[] colorArray = {Color.BLACK, Color.BLUE, Color.GREEN,
Color.CYAN, Color.RED, Color.MAGENTA, Color.YELLOW,
Color.WHITE};
  String[] colorName = {"Black", "Blue", "Green", "Cyan",
"Red", "Magenta", "Yellow", "White"};
 int pointNumber = 0;
 Point2D.Double p1;
 Point2D.Double p2;
 boolean loading = true;

public static void main(String args[])
{
  //construct frame
  new GradientPainting().show();
}
public GradientPainting()
{
  // code to build the form
  setTitle("Gradient Paint");
  setResizable(false);
  addWindowListener(new WindowAdapter()
  {
    public void windowClosing(WindowEvent e)
    {
      exitForm(e);
    }
  });
  getContentPane().setLayout(new GridBagLayout());

  // position controls (establish event methods)
   point1Label.setText("Point 1: (xxx,xxx)");
   point1Label.setPreferredSize(new Dimension(120, 20));

point1Label.setHorizontalAlignment(SwingConstants.CENTER);
    GridBagConstraints gridConstraints = new
GridBagConstraints();
    gridConstraints.gridx = 0;
    gridConstraints.gridy = 0;
    gridConstraints.insets = new Insets(10, 5, 0, 0);
    getContentPane().add(point1Label, gridConstraints);

    color1ComboBox.setBackground(Color.WHITE);
    gridConstraints = new GridBagConstraints();
    gridConstraints.gridx = 0;
    gridConstraints.gridy = 1;
    gridConstraints.insets = new Insets(10, 5, 0, 0);
    getContentPane().add(color1ComboBox, gridConstraints);
```

```
    color1ComboBox.addActionListener(new ActionListener()
    {
      public void actionPerformed(ActionEvent e)
      {
        paintButtonActionPerformed(e);
      }
    });

     point2Label.setPreferredSize(new Dimension(120, 20));
     point2Label.setText("Point 2: (xxx,xxx)");

point2Label.setHorizontalAlignment(SwingConstants.CENTER);
    gridConstraints = new GridBagConstraints();
    gridConstraints.gridx = 0;
    gridConstraints.gridy = 2;
    gridConstraints.insets = new Insets(10, 5, 0, 0);
    getContentPane().add(point2Label, gridConstraints);

    color2ComboBox.setBackground(Color.WHITE);
    gridConstraints = new GridBagConstraints();
    gridConstraints.gridx = 0;
    gridConstraints.gridy = 3;
    gridConstraints.insets = new Insets(10, 5, 0, 0);
    getContentPane().add(color2ComboBox, gridConstraints);
    color2ComboBox.addActionListener(new ActionListener()
    {
      public void actionPerformed(ActionEvent e)
      {
        paintButtonActionPerformed(e);
      }
    });

     cyclicCheckBox.setText("Cyclic");
    gridConstraints = new GridBagConstraints();
    gridConstraints.gridx = 0;
    gridConstraints.gridy = 4;
    gridConstraints.insets = new Insets(10, 5, 0, 0);
    getContentPane().add(cyclicCheckBox, gridConstraints);
    cyclicCheckBox.addActionListener(new ActionListener()
    {
      public void actionPerformed(ActionEvent e)
      {
        paintButtonActionPerformed(e);
      }
    });

     paintButton.setText("Paint");
```

```
     paintButton.setEnabled(false);
  gridConstraints = new GridBagConstraints();
  gridConstraints.gridx = 0;
  gridConstraints.gridy = 5;
  gridConstraints.insets = new Insets(5, 5, 0, 0);
  getContentPane().add(paintButton, gridConstraints);
  paintButton.addActionListener(new ActionListener()
  {
    public void actionPerformed(ActionEvent e)
    {
      paintButtonActionPerformed(e);
    }
  });

  paintPanel.setPreferredSize(new Dimension(350, 250));
  paintPanel.setBackground(Color.WHITE);
  gridConstraints = new GridBagConstraints();
  gridConstraints.gridx = 1;
  gridConstraints.gridy = 0;
  gridConstraints.gridheight = 6;
  gridConstraints.insets = new Insets(10, 10, 10, 10);
  getContentPane().add(paintPanel, gridConstraints);
   paintPanel.addMouseListener(new MouseAdapter()
  {
    public void mousePressed(MouseEvent e)
    {
      paintPanelMousePressed(e);
    }
  });

  pack();
  Dimension screenSize =
Toolkit.getDefaultToolkit().getScreenSize();
  setBounds((int) (0.5 * (screenSize.width - getWidth())),
(int) (0.5 * (screenSize.height - getHeight())), getWidth(),
getHeight());
  // set up graphics object
  g2D = (Graphics2D) paintPanel.getGraphics();
  myPanel = new Rectangle2D.Double(0, 0,
paintPanel.getWidth(), paintPanel.getHeight());
  // add colors to combo boxes
  for (int i = 0; i < colorArray.length; i++)
  {
    color1ComboBox.addItem(colorName[i]);
    color2ComboBox.addItem(colorName[i]);
  }
  color2ComboBox.setSelectedIndex(7);
```

```
        loading = false;
    }


    private void paintPanelMousePressed(MouseEvent e)
    {
        if (pointNumber == 0)
        {
            // getting first gradient point
            g2D.setPaint(paintPanel.getBackground());
            g2D.fill(myPanel);
            point1Label.setText("Point 1: (" + e.getX() + "," +
e.getY() + ")");
            point2Label.setText("Point 2: (xxx,xxx)");
            p1 = new Point2D.Double(e.getX(), e.getY());
            g2D.setPaint(Color.RED);
            g2D.fill(new Ellipse2D.Double(e.getX() - 1, e.getY() -
1, 3, 3));
            paintButton.setEnabled(false);
            pointNumber = 1;
        }
        else if (pointNumber == 1)
        {
            // getting second gradient point
            point2Label.setText("Point 2: (" + e.getX() + "," +
e.getY() + ")");
            p2 = new Point2D.Double(e.getX(), e.getY());
            g2D.setPaint(Color.RED);
            g2D.fill(new Ellipse2D.Double(e.getX() - 1, e.getY() -
1, 3, 3));
            Line2D.Double gradientLine = new Line2D.Double(p1,
p2);
            g2D.setPaint(Color.BLACK);
            g2D.draw(gradientLine);
            paintButton.setEnabled(true);
            pointNumber = 0;
        }
    }


    private void paintButtonActionPerformed(ActionEvent e)
    {
        // don't try painting when loading array elements
        if (loading)
        {
            return;
        }
        // paint the panel
        Color c1 = colorArray[color1ComboBox.getSelectedIndex()];
```

```
    Color c2 = colorArray[color2ComboBox.getSelectedIndex()];
    GradientPaint gPaint = new GradientPaint(p1, c1, p2, c2,
cyclicCheckBox.isSelected());
    g2D.setPaint(gPaint);
    g2D.fill(myPanel);
  }

  private void exitForm(WindowEvent e)
  {
    System.exit(0);
  }
}
```

Run the project. Choose colors and decide on the cyclic value. Click the panel in two places to define the gradient line (direction and size of gradient) – the coordinates of the two points will be displayed. Click **Paint** to see the painted effect. Select different gradient directions (just click panel to redefine the gradient line) and colors. Notice how the gradient line size and cyclic selection can provide interesting effects. Once any combo box is active, you can use the cursor arrows on the keyboard to 'scroll' through the colors. Here's one of my results:

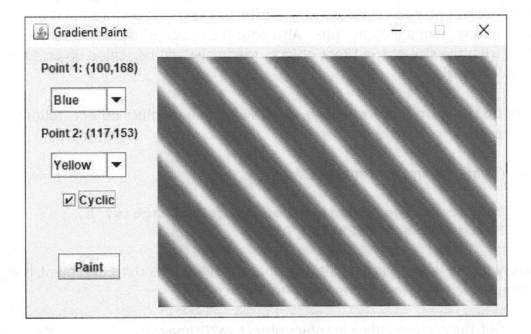

Save the project (saved as **Example8-6** project in **\LearnJava\LJ Code\Class 8** program group). Note for this simple example, we did not use a graphics panel; hence the painting is <u>not persistent</u>.

TexturePaint Object

Another painting object available in Java 2D is the **TexturePaint** object. This object paints an area with a repeated rectangular region (a **BufferedImage** – we'll see what this is). This gives the filled region a 'tiled' effect like a kitchen floor. The rectangular tile can be something you create using drawing methods or a graphic file (**gif** or **jpg** file).

To create a **TexturePaint** object (**tPaint**), we use this constructor:

```
TexturePaint tPaint = new TexturePaint(tImage, tRect);
```

where:

tImage   **BufferedImage** object that defines painting 'tile'
tRect   **Rectangle2D** object the size of the tile when painted in the graphics object.

We won't go into a lot of details about a **BufferedImage**, just think of it as a rectangular picture (use requires the **java.awt.image.*** package be imported). We will look at how to create our own **BufferedImage** for texture paint and how to create one from a graphics file. Also note if the size of the image object differs from the size of the **tRect** object, the image will be scaled up or down in size, accordingly.

To create your own **BufferedImage**, by drawing to a graphics object, follow these steps:

> Create the image (**tImage**) using:

```
BufferedImage tImage = new BufferedImage(w, h,
BufferedImage.TYPE_INT_RGB);
```

where **w** is the image width and **h** the image height. The third argument is a constant specifying we are drawing with 8 bit colors.

> Get the corresponding graphics object (**g2DtImage**):

```
Graphics2D g2DtImage = (Graphics2D)
tImage.getGraphics();
```

> Draw to the graphics object using **path** objects, **shape** objects, **stroke** objects and **paint** objects. Create whatever tile you want.

Once you are done drawing to the buffered image (**tImage**) graphic object (**g2DtImage**), you create the **TexturePaint** object. Decide on a size (**tRect**) for your tile when it is painted (usually the same size as the **BufferedImage** object). Create the **TexturePaint** object using:

```
TexturePaint tPaint = new TexturePaint(tImage, tRect);
```

This paint object can be used in the **setPaint** method to establish a paint attribute (usually used for filling a region).

Let's do an example to illustrate the steps. We will build a tile 30 x 30 in size. It will be filled with a gradient paint (yellow to red) running diagonally from top, left to bottom, right. There will be a small, dark gray ellipse in the middle of the tile. An expanded version of the tile is:

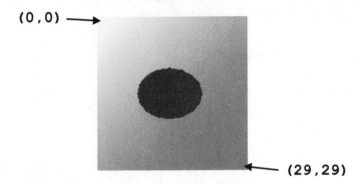

Here are the steps:

➢ Create the **BufferedImage** and **Graphics2D** object, 30 units wide by 30 units high:

```
BufferedImage tImage = new BufferedImage(30, 30,
BufferedImage.TYPE_INT_RGB);
Graphics2D g2DtImage = (Graphics2D)
tImage.getGraphics();
```

➢ Create a **Rectangle2D** object the size of the image:

```
Rectangle2D.Double tRect = new Rectangle2D.Double(0, 0,
tImage.getWidth(), tImage.getHeight());
```

> Establish a gradient paint, as described, and fill the image:

```
g2DtImage.setPaint(new GradientPaint(0, 0, Color.YELLOW,
tImage.getWidth() - 1, tImage.getHeight() - 1,
Color.RED, false));
g2DtImage.fill(tRect);
```

Note we have used a **GradientPaint** constructor that allows direct specification of the coordinates (without using **Point** objects).

> Draw a small, dark gray ellipse near the center of the image:

```
Ellipse2D.Double tEllipse = new Ellipse2D.Double(8, 10,
13, 10);
g2DtImage.setPaint(Color.DARK_GRAY);
g2DtImage.fill(tEllipse);
```

> Establish the **TexturePaint** object:

```
TexturePaint tPaint = new TexturePaint(tImage, tRect);
```

Here's a frame painted with our new tiles:

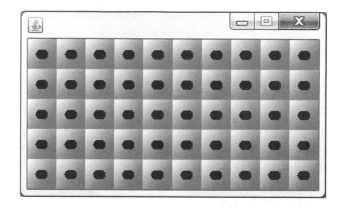

Creating a **TexturePaint** object from a graphics file involves a few more steps. To create the buffered image object:

> Load the image (**myImage**) from a file (**imageFile**, a **gif** or **jpg** file), then create the buffered image (**tImage**):

```
Image myImage = new ImageIcon(imageFile).getImage();
BufferedImage tImage = new
BufferedImage(myImage.getWidth(this),
myImage.getHeight(this), BufferedImage.TYPE_INT_RGB);
```

> Get the corresponding graphics object (**g2DtImage**):

```
Graphics2D g2DtImage = (Graphics2D)
tImage.getGraphics();
```

> Draw the image (**myImage**) to the graphics object using the **drawImage** method:

```
g2DtImage.drawImage(myImage, 0, 0, this);
```

This completes creation of the buffered image object. Now, create the **TexturePaint** object. Decide on a size (**tRect**) for your tile when it is painted (for graphics files, this is many times a scaling of the **BufferedImage** object size). Create the **TexturePaint** object using:

```
TexturePaint tPaint = new TexturePaint(tImage, tRect);
```

This paint object can be used in the **setPaint** method to establish a paint attribute (usually used for filling a region).

Let's do an example to illustrate the steps. We will build a texture paint made up of small hamburgers (**burger.gif**):

Here are the steps:

> Create the **BufferedImage** and **Graphics2D** object:

```
Image myImage = new ImageIcon("burger.gif").getImage();
BufferedImage tImage = new
BufferedImage(myImage.getWidth(this),
myImage.getHeight(this), BufferedImage.TYPE_INT_RGB);
Graphics2D g2DtImage = (Graphics2D)
tImage.getGraphics();
g2DtImage.drawImage(myImage, 0, 0, this);
```

> Create a **Rectangle2D** object 40 by 40 units in size:

```
Rectangle2D.Double tRect = new Rectangle2D.Double(0, 0,
40, 40);
```

> Establish the **TexturePaint** object:

```
TexturePaint tPaint = new TexturePaint(tImage, tRect);
```

Here's a frame painted with our new tiles:

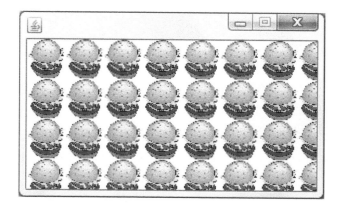

Example 8-7

Texture Paint

Start a new empty project in **NetBeans**. Name the project **TexturePainting**.
Delete default code in Java file named **TexturePainting**.

In this application, we will view different texture paints (using **gif** and **jpg**
images). The finished frame appears as:

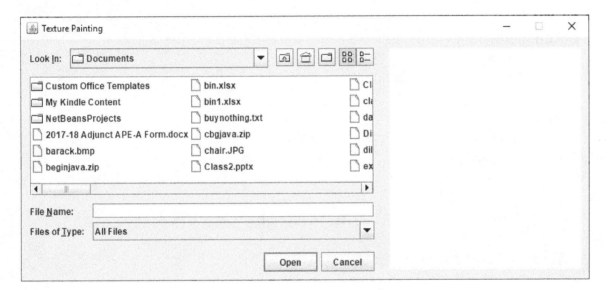

1. The application just needs two controls: a file chooser and a panel. The **GridBagLayout** arrangement is:

	gridx = 0	gridx = 1
gridy = 0	**paintChooser**	**paintPanel**

Properties for the controls:

TexturePainting Frame:

	title	Texture Painting
	resizable	false

paintChooser:

	gridx	0
	gridy	0

paintPanel:

	preferredSize	(270, 300)
	background	WHITE
	gridx	1
	gridy	0
	insets	(10, 10, 10, 10);

2. As usual, build a framework to start with:

```
/*
 * TexturePainting.java
 */
package texturepainting;
import javax.swing.*;
import java.awt.*;
import java.awt.event.*;
import java.awt.image.*;
import java.awt.geom.*;

public class TexturePainting extends JFrame
{
  public static void main(String args[])
  {
    //construct frame
    new TexturePainting().show();
  }
```

```
  public TexturePainting()
  {
    // create frame
    setTitle("Texture Painting");
    setResizable(false);
    addWindowListener(new WindowAdapter()
    {
      public void windowClosing(WindowEvent e)
      {
        exitForm(e);
      }
    });
    getContentPane().setLayout(new GridBagLayout());

    pack();
    Dimension screenSize =
Toolkit.getDefaultToolkit().getScreenSize();
    setBounds((int) (0.5 * (screenSize.width -
getWidth())), (int) (0.5 * (screenSize.height -
getHeight())), getWidth(), getHeight());

  }
  private void exitForm(WindowEvent e)
  {
    System.exit(0);
  }
}
```

Run to see the frame centered on your screen.

3. Create controls with these class level declarations:

```
JFileChooser paintChooser = new JFileChooser();
JPanel paintPanel = new JPanel();
```

Position controls and add event listener for file chooser:

```
GridBagConstraints gridConstraints = new
GridBagConstraints();
paintChooser.addChoosableFileFilter(new
FileNameExtensionFilter("Graphics Files", "gif", "jpg"));
gridConstraints.gridx = 0;
gridConstraints.gridy = 0;
getContentPane().add(paintChooser, gridConstraints);
paintChooser.addActionListener(new ActionListener()
{
  public void actionPerformed(ActionEvent e)
  {
    paintChooserActionPerformed(e);
  }
});

paintPanel.setPreferredSize(new Dimension(270, 300));
paintPanel.setBackground(Color.white);
gridConstraints.gridx = 1;
gridConstraints.gridy = 0;
gridConstraints.insets = new Insets(10, 10, 10, 10);
getContentPane().add(paintPanel, gridConstraints);
```

4. We'll go right to adding code to the **paintChooserActionPerformed** event:

```
private void paintChooserActionPerformed(ActionEvent e)
{
  // create paint
  if
(e.getActionCommand().equals(JFileChooser.APPROVE_SELECTIO
N))
  {
    Image myImage = new
ImageIcon(paintChooser.getSelectedFile().toString()).getIm
age();
    BufferedImage tImage = new
BufferedImage(myImage.getWidth(this),
myImage.getHeight(this), BufferedImage.TYPE_INT_RGB);
    Graphics2D g2DtImage = (Graphics2D)
tImage.getGraphics();
    g2DtImage.drawImage(myImage, 0, 0, this);
    // use full size graphic for paint
    Rectangle2D.Double tRect = new Rectangle2D.Double(0,
0, myImage.getWidth(this), myImage.getHeight(this));
    TexturePaint tPaint = new TexturePaint(tImage, tRect);
    // paint panel
    Graphics2D g2D = (Graphics2D)
paintPanel.getGraphics();
    Rectangle2D.Double myRectangle = new
Rectangle2D.Double(0, 0, paintPanel.getWidth(),
paintPanel.getHeight());
    g2D.setPaint(tPaint);
    g2D.fill(myRectangle);
  }
}
```

In this code, if the user clicks the **Open** button, the selected file is used to establish the **BufferedImage** to use as a textured paint in the **paintPanel** control.

The complete **TexturePainting.java** code is (code added to framework is shaded):

```
/*
 * TexturePainting.java
 */
package texturepainting;
import javax.swing.*;
import javax.swing.filechooser.*;
import java.awt.*;
import java.awt.event.*;
import java.awt.image.*;
import java.awt.geom.*;

public class TexturePainting extends JFrame
{
  JFileChooser paintChooser = new JFileChooser();
  JPanel paintPanel = new JPanel();

  public static void main(String args[])
  {
    //construct frame
    new TexturePainting().show();
  }

  public TexturePainting()
  {
    // create frame
    setTitle("Texture Painting");
    setResizable(false);
    addWindowListener(new WindowAdapter()
    {
      public void windowClosing(WindowEvent e)
      {
        exitForm(e);
      }
    });
    getContentPane().setLayout(new GridBagLayout());

    // position controls (establish event methods)
    GridBagConstraints gridConstraints = new
GridBagConstraints();
    paintChooser.addChoosableFileFilter(new
FileNameExtensionFilter("Graphics Files", "gif", "jpg"));
    gridConstraints.gridx = 0;
    gridConstraints.gridy = 0;
    getContentPane().add(paintChooser, gridConstraints);
```

```
      paintChooser.addActionListener(new ActionListener()
      {
        public void actionPerformed(ActionEvent e)
        {
          paintChooserActionPerformed(e);
        }
      });

      paintPanel.setPreferredSize(new Dimension(270, 300));
      paintPanel.setBackground(Color.white);
      gridConstraints.gridx = 1;
      gridConstraints.gridy = 0;
      gridConstraints.insets = new Insets(10, 10, 10, 10);
      getContentPane().add(paintPanel, gridConstraints);

      pack();
      Dimension screenSize =
Toolkit.getDefaultToolkit().getScreenSize();
      setBounds((int) (0.5 * (screenSize.width - getWidth())),
(int) (0.5 * (screenSize.height - getHeight())), getWidth(),
getHeight());

    }
  private void paintChooserActionPerformed(ActionEvent e)
  {
    // create paint
    if
(e.getActionCommand().equals(JFileChooser.APPROVE_SELECTION))
    {
      Image myImage = new
ImageIcon(paintChooser.getSelectedFile().toString()).getImage
();
      BufferedImage tImage = new
BufferedImage(myImage.getWidth(this),
myImage.getHeight(this), BufferedImage.TYPE_INT_RGB);
      Graphics2D g2DtImage = (Graphics2D)
tImage.getGraphics();
      g2DtImage.drawImage(myImage, 0, 0, this);
      // use full size graphic for paint
      Rectangle2D.Double tRect = new Rectangle2D.Double(0, 0,
myImage.getWidth(this), myImage.getHeight(this));
      TexturePaint tPaint = new TexturePaint(tImage, tRect);
      // paint panel
      Graphics2D g2D = (Graphics2D) paintPanel.getGraphics();
      Rectangle2D.Double myRectangle = new
Rectangle2D.Double(0, 0, paintPanel.getWidth(),
paintPanel.getHeight());
```

```
        g2D.setPaint(tPaint);
        g2D.fill(myRectangle);
    }
 }

  private void exitForm(WindowEvent e)
  {
     System.exit(0);
  }
}
```

Run the project. Choose a **gif** or **jpg** file (there are a few in the **\LearnJava\LJ Code\Class 8\Example8-7** folder). Click **Open** to see the panel painted with the selected graphic. Here's some "beany wallpaper":

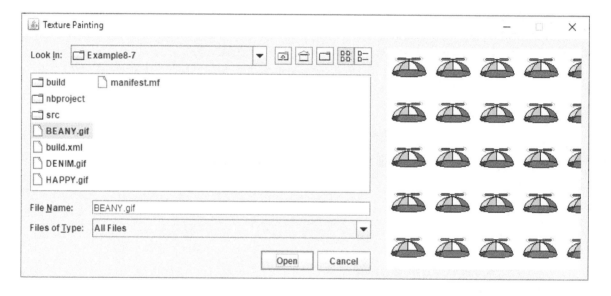

Save the project (saved as **Example8-7** project in **\LearnJava\LJ Code\Class 8** program group). Note the graphics are <u>not</u> persistent.

drawString Method

The last drawing method we study 'draws' text information on a graphics object. Text adds useful information to graphics objects, especially for plots. The line, bar and pie chart examples built in Class 7 are rather boring without the usual titles, labels and legends. The **drawString** method will let us add text to any graphic object.

The **drawString** method is easy to use. You need to know what text you want to draw (**myString**, a **String** type) and where you want to locate the text (**x, y**). The method operates on a previously created graphics object (**g2D**). The syntax is:

```
g2D.drawString(myString, x, y);
```

The string will be drawn using the current font and paint attributes. Note (**x, y**) is the Cartesian coordinate (**int** type) specifying location of the <u>lower</u> left corner of the text string's "baseline":

(x,y) ⟶ **myString**

The baseline is the line we were taught to write on in grade school. Notice some letters may descend below the baseline.

Let's look at an example. Can you see what this code will produce?

```
g2D.setFont(new Font("Arial", Font.BOLD, 48));
g2D.setPaint(Color.RED);
g2D.drawString("Hello Java!", 10, 40);
```

This says print the string **"Hello Java!"** using an **Arial, BOLD,** Size **48** font with a **red** paint attribute. The baseline begins at (**x = 10, y = 40**) of the graphics object **g2D**.

Using this code with a panel form as the graphics object, we would see

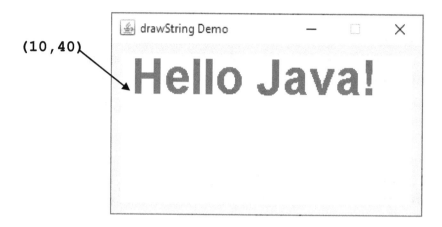

(10,40)

Simple, huh? This example is saved as the **DrawStringDemo** project in the **\LearnJava\LJ Code\Class 8** program group.

A key decision in using **drawString** is placement. That is, what **x** and **y** values should you use? To help in this decision, it is helpful to know what size a particular text string is. If we know how wide and how tall (in pixels) a string is, we can perform precise placements, including left, center and right justifications.

The Java method **getStringBounds** gives us the width and height of a particular string. The method returns a **Rectangle2D** object that bounds the given string. If the current font is **myFont**, the graphics object **g2D**, and the string we are measuring is **myString**, the bounding rectangle (**stringRect**) is returned with:

```
Rectangle2D stringRect = myFont.getStringBounds(myString,
g2D.getFontRenderContext());
```

This particular method requires importation of the **java.awt.font.*** package. The **getFontRenderContext** method provides information about the current font. Once the bounding rectangle is obtained, the height of **myString** is given by:

```
stringRect.getHeight()
```

and the width is given by:

```
stringRect.getWidth()
```

The height of a string lets us know how much to increment the desired vertical position after printing each line in multiple lines of text. Or, it can be used to 'vertically justify' a string within a control hosting a graphics object. For example, assume we have found the height of a string (**stringRect.getHeight()**) using the **getStringBounds** method. To vertically justify this string in a host control (**myControl**) for a graphics object, the **y** coordinate (converted to an **int** type needed by **drawString**) would be:

```
y = (int) (0.5 * (myControl.getHeight() +
stringRect.getHeight()));
```

This assumes the string is 'shorter' than **myControl**.

Similarly, the width of a string lets us define margins and left, right or center justify a string within the client rectangle of a graphics object. For left justification, establish a left margin and set the x coordinate to this value in the **drawString** method. If we know the width of a string (**stringRect.getWidth()**), it is centered justified in a graphics object's host control **myControl** using an **x** value of (again converted to **int**):

```
x = (int) (0.5 * (myControl.getWidth() -
stringRect.getWidth()));
```

To right justify the same string, use:

```
x = (int) (myControl.getWidth() - stringRect.getWidth());
```

Both of the above equations, of course, assume the string is 'narrower' than **myControl**.

Let's go back and apply these relations to our "Hello Java!" example. The text **vertically** and **center** justified looks like this:

The text is a little below the perceived center line because the bounding rectangle includes space above the string for potential "ascent" characters (such as carets, apostrophes, asterisks).

Right justified with y = 40, the text appears like this:

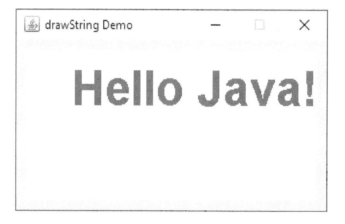

Even more interesting effects can be obtained using other paint attributes. Try drawing strings with **gradient** and **texture** paints. Here's the "Hello Java!" example with a **gradient** paint:

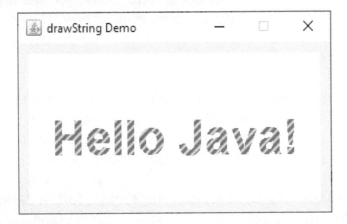

And, here's the "Hello Java!" example with a 'denim' **textured** paint:

Modify the **DrawStringDemo** project to see if you can achieve the above effects. A 'denim' graphic (**denim.gif**) is included in the **DrawStringDemo** folder.

We won't do much more with the **drawString** method here. You will, however, see the **drawString** method again in Class 9. This method is integral in obtaining printed information from a Java application. And, you will see its use is identical. You need to determine what to print, in what font, with what paint and where on the page it needs to be.

Multimedia Effects

Everywhere you look in the world of computers today, you see **multimedia effects**. Computer games, web sites and meeting presentations are filled with animated graphics and fun sounds. It is relatively easy to add such effects to our Java applications.

In Class 7, we achieved simple animation effects by changing the image in a label control. Sophisticated animation relies on the ability to change <u>and</u> move several changing objects over a changing background. To achieve more sophisticated animation, we will use the Java **drawImage** method.

Animation requires the moving of rectangular regions (often defined by **Rectangle2D** objects). We need ways to move these rectangular regions. The mouse (using mouse methods) is one option. Another option considered is movement using **keyboard methods**. And, many times we want to know if these rectangular regions overlap to detect things like files reaching trash cans, balls hitting paddles or little creatures eating power pellets. We will learn how to detect if two **rectangles intersect**.

Multimedia presentations also use **sounds**. We will see how to use Java to play sounds represented by **au** and **wav** files.

Animation with drawImage Method

To achieve animation in a Java application, whether it is background scrolling, sprite animation, or other special effects, we use the **drawImage** graphics method. In its simplest form, this method draws an **image** object at a particular position in a graphics object. Changing and/or moving the image within the graphics object achieves animation. And, multiple images can be moved/changed within the graphics object. There are many overloaded versions of **drawImage**. We will look a few of them in this class. We encourage you to study the other forms, as you need them.

Before using **drawImage**, you need two things: a **graphics** object (**g2D**) to draw to and an **image** object to draw. We create the graphics object (assume **myControl** is the host control):

```
Graphics2D g2D = (Graphics2D) myControl.getGraphics();
```

The **Image** object (**myImage**) is usually created from a graphics file:

```
Image myImage = new ImageIcon(imageFile).getImage();
```

where **imageFile** is the graphics file describing the image to draw. At this point, we can draw **myImage** in **g2D**. To retrieve the width and height of this object, use:

```
width = myImage.getWidth(this);
height = myImage.getHeight(this);
```

One form of the **drawImage** method is:

```
g2D.drawImage(myImage, x, y, w, h, this);
```

In this method, the image will be positioned at (**x**, **y**) with width **w** and height **h**. The final argument refers to the **ImageObserver** object used to draw the image – we use the keyword **this** to indicate the current graphics object is the observer. The width and height arguments are optional and can be the original image size or scaled up or down. It's your choice. To draw the image at (**x**, **y**) in its original size, simply use:

```
g2D.drawImage(myImage, x, y, this);
```

A picture illustrates what's going on with **drawImage**:

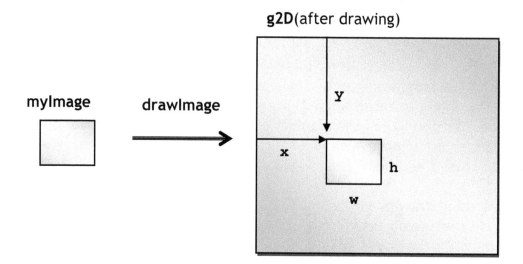

Note how the transfer of the rectangular region occurs. Successive transfers gives the impression of motion, or animation. Recall **w** and **h** in the graphics object do not have to necessarily match the width and height of the **image** object. Scaling (up or down) is possible.

Example 8-8

Bouncing Ball

Start a new empty project in NetBeans. Name the project **BouncingBall**.
Delete default code in Java file named **BouncingBall**. We'll build an application
with a ball bouncing from the top to the bottom (and back) as an illustration of
the use of **drawImage**. The finished frame will look like this:

The graphic file used is **earth.gif** and is located in the **\LearnJava\LJ Code\Class
8\Example8-8** folder. Copy this graphic file into your project's folder:

1. Add a panel control (will display the animation) and a button to the frame. The **GridBagLayout** is:

	gridx = 0
gridy = 0	**displayPanel**
gridy = 1	**startButton**

Also include an image object (**myBall**) and a timer object (**ballTimer**). Set these properties:

BouncingBall Frame:

      resizable   false

displayPanel (a GraphicsPanel class)::

      preferredSize   (100, 400)
      background   WHITE
      gridx   0
      gridy   0
      insets   (10, 10, 10, 10)

startButton:

      text   Start
      gridx   0
      gridy   1
      insets   (10, 10, 10, 10)

ballTimer:

      delay   100

myBall:

      image   earth.gif

2. Build the basic framework:

```
/*
 * BouncingBall.java
 */
package bouncingball;
import javax.swing.*;
import java.awt.*;
import java.awt.event.*;
import java.awt.geom.*;
public class BouncingBall extends JFrame
{
  public static void main(String args[])
  {
    // create frame
    new BouncingBall().show();
  }
  public BouncingBall()
  {
    // frame constructor
    setResizable(false);
    addWindowListener(new WindowAdapter()
    {
      public void windowClosing(WindowEvent evt)
      {
        exitForm(evt);
      }
    });
    getContentPane().setLayout(new GridBagLayout());

    pack();
    Dimension screenSize =
Toolkit.getDefaultToolkit().getScreenSize();
    setBounds((int) (0.5 * (screenSize.width -
getWidth())), (int) (0.5 * (screenSize.height -
getHeight())), getWidth(), getHeight());
  }
  private void exitForm(WindowEvent evt)
  {
    System.exit(0);
  }
}
```

Run to test.

3. Now, we add controls and methods. Add these class level declarations:

```
GraphicsPanel displayPanel = new GraphicsPanel();
JButton startButton = new JButton();
static Image myBall = new
ImageIcon("earth.gif").getImage();
static Timer ballTimer;
```

myBall is used in the **paintComponent** method, hence is prefaced with **static**.

Position and add controls and methods:

```
GridBagConstraints gridConstraints = new
GridBagConstraints();
 displayPanel.setPreferredSize(new Dimension(100, 400));
 displayPanel.setBackground(Color.WHITE);
 gridConstraints.gridx = 0;
gridConstraints.gridy = 0;
gridConstraints.insets = new Insets(10, 10, 10, 10);
getContentPane().add(displayPanel, gridConstraints);

gridConstraints = new GridBagConstraints();
 startButton.setText("Start");
 gridConstraints.gridx = 0;
gridConstraints.gridy = 1;
gridConstraints.insets = new Insets(10, 10, 10, 10);
getContentPane().add(startButton, gridConstraints);
startButton.addActionListener(new ActionListener()
{
  public void actionPerformed(ActionEvent e)
  {
    startButtonActionPerformed(e);
  }
});
ballTimer = new Timer(100, new ActionListener()
{
  public void actionPerformed(ActionEvent e)
  {
    ballTimerActionPerformed(e);
  }
});
```

And, add two empty event methods:

```
private void startButtonActionPerformed(ActionEvent e)
{
}

private void ballTimerActionPerformed(ActionEvent e)
{
}
```

4. Add the **GraphicsPanel** class (from **Appendix I**) after the main class:

```
class GraphicsPanel extends JPanel
{
  public GraphicsPanel()
  {
  }
  public void paintComponent(Graphics g)
  {
  }
}
```

Run to check control layout:

The panel is gray because we have no code in the **paintComponent** method.

5. Use these class level variable declarations (declares movement variables):

```
static int ballSize, ballX, ballY, ballDir;
```

6. Add these lines of code to the constructor (initializes ball position):

```
ballSize = 50;
ballX = (int) (0.5 * (displayPanel.getWidth() -
ballSize));
ballY = 0;
ballDir = 1;
displayPanel.repaint();
```

7. Write a **startButtonActionPerformed** event method to toggle the timer:

```
private void startButtonActionPerformed(ActionEvent e)
{
  if (ballTimer.isRunning())
  {
    ballTimer.stop();
    startButton.setText("Start");
  }
  else
  {
    ballTimer.start();
    startButton.setText("Stop");
  }
}
```

8. The **ballTimerActionPerformed** method controls the bouncing ball position:

```
private void ballTimerActionPerformed(ActionEvent e)
{
  // determine ball position and draw it
  ballY = (int) (ballY + ballDir *
displayPanel.getHeight() / 50);
  //check for bounce
  if (ballY < 0)
  {
    ballY = 0;
    ballDir = 1;
  }
  else if (ballY + ballSize > displayPanel.getHeight())
  {
    ballY = displayPanel.getHeight() - ballSize;
    ballDir = -1;
  }
  displayPanel.repaint();
}
```

9. And, the **paintComponent** method in the **GraphicsPanel** class does the actual image drawing:

```java
public void paintComponent(Graphics g)
{
  Graphics2D g2D = (Graphics2D) g;
  super.paintComponent(g2D);
  // draw ball
  g2D.drawImage(BouncingBall.myBall, BouncingBall.ballX,
BouncingBall.ballY, BouncingBall.ballSize,
BouncingBall.ballSize, this);
  g2D.dispose();
}
```

The complete **BouncingBall.java** code listing (changes to framework are shaded):

```java
/*
 * BouncingBall.java
 */
package bouncingball;
import javax.swing.*;
import java.awt.*;
import java.awt.event.*;
import java.awt.geom.*;
public class BouncingBall extends JFrame
{
  GraphicsPanel displayPanel = new GraphicsPanel();
  JButton startButton = new JButton();
  static Image myBall = new
ImageIcon("earth.gif").getImage();
  Timer ballTimer;

  static int ballSize, ballX, ballY, ballDir;
  public static void main(String args[])
  {
    // create frame
    new BouncingBall().show();
}
  public BouncingBall()
  {
    // frame constructor
    setResizable(false);
    addWindowListener(new WindowAdapter()
    {
      public void windowClosing(WindowEvent evt)
```

```
    {
      exitForm(evt);
    }
  });
    getContentPane().setLayout(new GridBagLayout());
    // position controls

    GridBagConstraints gridConstraints = new
GridBagConstraints();
     displayPanel.setPreferredSize(new Dimension(100, 400));
     displayPanel.setBackground(Color.WHITE);
     gridConstraints.gridx = 0;
    gridConstraints.gridy = 0;
    gridConstraints.insets = new Insets(10, 10, 10, 10);
    getContentPane().add(displayPanel, gridConstraints);

    gridConstraints = new GridBagConstraints();
     startButton.setText("Start");
     gridConstraints.gridx = 0;
    gridConstraints.gridy = 1;
    gridConstraints.insets = new Insets(10, 10, 10, 10);
    getContentPane().add(startButton, gridConstraints);
    startButton.addActionListener(new ActionListener()
    {
      public void actionPerformed(ActionEvent e)
      {
        startButtonActionPerformed(e);
      }
    });
    ballTimer = new Timer(100, new ActionListener()
    {
      public void actionPerformed(ActionEvent e)
      {
        ballTimerActionPerformed(e);
      }
    });
    pack();
    Dimension screenSize =
Toolkit.getDefaultToolkit().getScreenSize();
    setBounds((int) (0.5 * (screenSize.width - getWidth())),
(int) (0.5 * (screenSize.height - getHeight())), getWidth(),
getHeight());
    // initialize variables/set up graphics objects
    // horizontally center ball in display panel
    ballSize = 50;
    ballX = (int) (0.5 * (displayPanel.getWidth() -
ballSize));
```

```
    ballY = 0;
    ballDir = 1;
    displayPanel.repaint();
  }
  private void startButtonActionPerformed(ActionEvent e)
  {
    if (ballTimer.isRunning())
    {
      ballTimer.stop();
      startButton.setText("Start");
    }
    else
    {
      ballTimer.start();
      startButton.setText("Stop");
    }
  }
  private void ballTimerActionPerformed(ActionEvent e)
  {
    // determine ball position and draw it
    ballY = (int) (ballY + ballDir * displayPanel.getHeight()
/ 50);
    //check for bounce
    if (ballY < 0)
    {
      ballY = 0;
      ballDir = 1;
    }
    else if (ballY + ballSize > displayPanel.getHeight())
    {
      ballY = displayPanel.getHeight() - ballSize;
      ballDir = -1;
    }
    displayPanel.repaint();
  }
  private void exitForm(WindowEvent evt)
  {
    System.exit(0);
  }
}
class GraphicsPanel extends JPanel
{
  public GraphicsPanel()
  {
  }
  public void paintComponent(Graphics g)
  {
```

```
    Graphics2D g2D = (Graphics2D) g;
    super.paintComponent(g2D);
    // draw ball
    g2D.drawImage(BouncingBall.myBall, BouncingBall.ballX,
BouncingBall.ballY, BouncingBall.ballSize,
BouncingBall.ballSize, this);
    g2D.dispose();
 }
}
```

Run and compile the finished project. Follow the bouncing ball!!

Save the project (saved as **Example8-8** project in the **\LearnJava\LJ Code\Class 8** program group).

Scrolling Backgrounds

Most action arcade games employ scrolling or moving backgrounds. What looks like a very sophisticated effect is really just a simple application of the **drawImage** method. The idea is that we have a large image representing the background "world" we want to move around in. At any point, we can view a small region of that world in our graphics object. Pictorially, we have:

The boxed area represents the area of our world we can see at any one time. By varying **x** and **y** (leaving **w** and **h** fixed), we can move around in this world. As **x** and **y** vary, if we draw the "viewable area" into a graphics object of the same size, we obtain the moving background effect. To accomplish this task, we need a form of the **drawImage** method that allows drawing a portion of a "source" image. But, first, we need to review the steps needed to use **drawImage**.

Before using **drawImage**, we need: a **graphics** object to draw to and an **image** object to draw from. We create the graphics object (**g2D** - assume **myControl** is the host control):

```
Graphics2D g2D = (Graphics2D) myControl.getGraphics();
```

The **image** object (**myImage**) is usually created from a graphics file:

```
Image myImage = new ImageIcon(imageFile).getImage();
```

where **imageFile** is the graphics file describing the image to draw.

To draw a portion of the source image (**myImage**) in the graphics object (**g2D**), we use another version of the **drawImage** method:

```
g2D.DrawImage(myImage, dx1, dy1, dx2, dy2, sx1, sy1, sx2,
sy2, this);
```

where:

(**dx1,dy1**)	Coordinate of the upper left corner within the graphics object (the **destination** rectangle) where the image will be drawn.
(**dx2,dy2**)	Coordinate of the lower right corner within the graphics object (the **destination** rectangle) where the image will be drawn.
(**sx1,sy1**)	Coordinate of the upper left corner of the image object (the **source** rectangle) defining the portion of the image to draw in the graphics object.
(**sx2,sy2**)	Coordinate of the upper right corner of the image object (the **source** rectangle) defining the portion of the image to draw in the graphics object.

For scrolling backgrounds, the 'destination' rectangle encompasses the entire control (**myControl**) hosting the graphics object used as the viewing area. Hence, the corresponding coordinates are:

```
(dx1,dy1) = (0, 0)
(dx2,dy2) = (myControl.getWidth() -1,
myControl.getHeight() - 1)
```

The 'source' rectangle contains the portion of the image we want to copy into the graphics object. This rectangle has the same dimensions (width and height) as the destination rectangle, with the corners shifted by a desired position (x, y) within the source image:

```
(sx1,sy1) = (x, y)
(sx2,sy2) = (x + myControl.getWidth() - 1, y +
myControl.getHeight() - 1)
```

An example using our beach photo should clear things up (hopefully). Applying the **drawImage** method using **myImage** will result in the following display in **g2D:**

In this picture, **w** is the width (**myControl.getWidth()**) of the graphics object host control and **h** is the height of that control (**myControl.getHeight()**).

Hence, the process for moving (or scrolling) backgrounds is simple (once the image is available):

> ➢ Decide on the desired viewing area (set width **w** and height **h**).
> ➢ Choose a mechanism for varying **x** and **y**. Scroll bars and cursor control keys are often used, or they can be varied using timer objects.
> ➢ As **x** and **y** vary, use **drawImage** to draw the current "viewable area" of the source image into the viewer (graphics object).

Example 8-9

Horizontally Scrolling Background

Start a new empty project in **NetBeans**. Name the project **Scrolling**. Delete default code in Java file named **Scrolling**. In this project, we'll view a horizontally scrolling seascape. The finished frame will appear as:

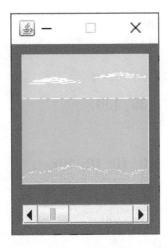

The graphic file used for the background is **undersea.gif** and is located in the **\LearnJava\LJ Code\Class 8\Example8-9** folder. Copy this graphic file into your project's folder:

As **x** increases, the background appears to scroll to the left. Note as **x** reaches the end of this source image, we need to copy a little of both ends to the destination graphics object to have the background "wrap-around." The graphic is 500 x 130 in size. The "viewing area" will be a square 130 x 130 in size.

1. Add a panel and scroll bar to a frame. The **GridBagLayout** will be:

	gridx = 0
gridy = 0	**displayPanel**
gridy = 1	**backgroundScrollBar**

Also include an image object (**backgroundImage**) and a timer object (**scrollTimer**). Set these properties:

Scrolling Frame:

resizable	false
background	BLUE

displayPanel:

preferredSize	(130, 130)
gridx	0
gridy	0
insets	(10, 10, 10, 10)

backgroundScrollBar:

preferredSize	(130, 20)
minimum	0
maximum	20 ("achievable" maximum)
blockIncrement	2
unitIncrement	1
value	0
orientation	HORIZONTAL
gridx	0
gridy	1
insets	(10, 10, 10, 10)

scrollTimer:

delay	50

backgroundImage:

image	undersea.gif

2. Build the framework:

```java
/*
 * Scrolling.java
 */
package scrolling;
import javax.swing.*;
import java.awt.*;
import java.awt.event.*;
import java.awt.geom.*;
public class Scrolling extends JFrame
{
  public static void main(String args[])
  {
    // create frame
    new Scrolling().show();
  }
  public Scrolling()
  {
    // frame constructor
    setResizable(false);
    getContentPane().setBackground(Color.BLUE);
    addWindowListener(new WindowAdapter()
    {
      public void windowClosing(WindowEvent evt)
      {
        exitForm(evt);
      }
    });
    getContentPane().setLayout(new GridBagLayout());

    pack();
    Dimension screenSize =
Toolkit.getDefaultToolkit().getScreenSize();
    setBounds((int) (0.5 * (screenSize.width -
getWidth())), (int) (0.5 * (screenSize.height -
getHeight())), getWidth(), getHeight());
  }
  private void exitForm(WindowEvent evt)
  {
    System.exit(0);
  }
}
```

Run to check.

3. Add class level object declarations:

```
JPanel displayPanel = new JPanel();
JScrollBar backgroundScrollBar = new JScrollBar();
Image backgroundImage = new
ImageIcon("undersea.gif").getImage();
Timer scrollTimer;
```

Position and add controls.

```
GridBagConstraints gridConstraints = new
GridBagConstraints();
 displayPanel.setPreferredSize(new Dimension(imageSize,
imageSize));
gridConstraints.gridx = 0;
gridConstraints.gridy = 0;
gridConstraints.insets = new Insets(10, 10, 10, 10);
getContentPane().add(displayPanel, gridConstraints);

gridConstraints = new GridBagConstraints();
backgroundScrollBar.setPreferredSize(new
Dimension(imageSize, 20));
backgroundScrollBar.setMinimum(0);
backgroundScrollBar.setMaximum(20 +
backgroundScrollBar.getVisibleAmount());
backgroundScrollBar.setBlockIncrement(2);
backgroundScrollBar.setUnitIncrement(1);
backgroundScrollBar.setValue(0);
backgroundScrollBar.setOrientation(JScrollBar.HORIZONTAL);
gridConstraints.gridx = 0;
gridConstraints.gridy = 1;
gridConstraints.insets = new Insets(10, 10, 10, 10);
getContentPane().add(backgroundScrollBar,
gridConstraints);

scrollTimer = new Timer(50, new ActionListener()
{
  public void actionPerformed(ActionEvent e)
  {
    scrollTimerActionPerformed(e);
  }
});
```

Add a single empty method:

```
private void scrollTimerActionPerformed(ActionEvent e)
{
}
```

Run to check control layout:

4. Now, add code. Use these class level declarations (declares objects and movement variables):

```
int scrollX = 0;
int imageSize = 130;
Graphics2D g2D;
```

5. Add two lines of code to the end of the constructor (creates graphics object and starts timer) after frame is created:

```
g2D = (Graphics2D) displayPanel.getGraphics();
scrollTimer.start();
```

6. The **scrollTimerActionPerformed** method controls scrolling. At each program cycle, we update the position on the background image and draw the result.

```
private void scrollTimerActionPerformed(ActionEvent e)
{
  int addedWidth;
  // Find next location on background
  scrollX += backgroundScrollBar.getValue();
  if (scrollX > backgroundImage.getWidth(this))
  {
    scrollX = 0;
  }
  // When x is near right edge, we need to copy
  // two segments of the background into display panel
  if (scrollX > (backgroundImage.getWidth(this) -
imageSize))
  {
    addedWidth = backgroundImage.getWidth(this) - scrollX;
    g2D.drawImage(backgroundImage, 0, 0, addedWidth - 1,
imageSize - 1, scrollX, 0, scrollX + addedWidth - 1,
imageSize - 1, this);
    g2D.drawImage(backgroundImage, addedWidth, 0,
imageSize - 1, imageSize - 1, 0, 0, imageSize - addedWidth
- 1, imageSize - 1, this);
  }
  else
  {
    g2D.drawImage(backgroundImage, 0, 0, imageSize - 1,
imageSize - 1, scrollX, 0, scrollX + imageSize - 1,
imageSize - 1, this);
  }
}
```

Note how the "wrap around" is implemented.

The complete **Scrolling.java** code listing (changes to framework are shaded):

```java
/*
 * Scrolling.java
 */
package scrolling;
import javax.swing.*;
import java.awt.*;
import java.awt.event.*;
import java.awt.geom.*;

public class Scrolling extends JFrame
{

  JPanel displayPanel = new JPanel();
  JScrollBar backgroundScrollBar = new JScrollBar();
  Image backgroundImage = new
ImageIcon("undersea.gif").getImage();
  Timer scrollTimer;

  int scrollX = 0;
  int imageSize = 130;
  Graphics2D g2D;

  public static void main(String args[])
  {
    // create frame
    new Scrolling().show();
}

  public Scrolling()
  {
    // frame constructor
    setResizable(false);
    getContentPane().setBackground(Color.BLUE);
    addWindowListener(new WindowAdapter()
    {
      public void windowClosing(WindowEvent evt)
      {
        exitForm(evt);
      }
    });
    getContentPane().setLayout(new GridBagLayout());

    // position controls
```

```
        GridBagConstraints gridConstraints = new
GridBagConstraints();
        displayPanel.setPreferredSize(new Dimension(imageSize,
imageSize));
        gridConstraints.gridx = 0;
        gridConstraints.gridy = 0;
        gridConstraints.insets = new Insets(10, 10, 10, 10);
        getContentPane().add(displayPanel, gridConstraints);

        gridConstraints = new GridBagConstraints();
        backgroundScrollBar.setPreferredSize(new
Dimension(imageSize, 20));
        backgroundScrollBar.setMinimum(0);
        backgroundScrollBar.setMaximum(20 +
backgroundScrollBar.getVisibleAmount());
        backgroundScrollBar.setBlockIncrement(2);
        backgroundScrollBar.setUnitIncrement(1);
        backgroundScrollBar.setValue(0);

backgroundScrollBar.setOrientation(JScrollBar.HORIZONTAL);
        gridConstraints.gridx = 0;
        gridConstraints.gridy = 1;
        gridConstraints.insets = new Insets(10, 10, 10, 10);
        getContentPane().add(backgroundScrollBar,
gridConstraints);

        scrollTimer = new Timer(50, new ActionListener()
        {
          public void actionPerformed(ActionEvent e)
          {
            scrollTimerActionPerformed(e);
          }
        });

        pack();
        Dimension screenSize =
Toolkit.getDefaultToolkit().getScreenSize();
        setBounds((int) (0.5 * (screenSize.width - getWidth())),
(int) (0.5 * (screenSize.height - getHeight())), getWidth(),
getHeight());

        g2D = (Graphics2D) displayPanel.getGraphics();
        scrollTimer.start();
    }


    private void scrollTimerActionPerformed(ActionEvent e)
```

```
   {
     int addedWidth;
     // Find next location on background
     scrollX += backgroundScrollBar.getValue();
     if (scrollX > backgroundImage.getWidth(this))
     {
       scrollX = 0;
     }
     // When x is near right edge, we need to copy
     // two segments of the background into display panel
     if (scrollX > (backgroundImage.getWidth(this) -
imageSize))
     {
       addedWidth = backgroundImage.getWidth(this) - scrollX;
       g2D.drawImage(backgroundImage, 0, 0, addedWidth - 1,
imageSize - 1, scrollX, 0, scrollX + addedWidth - 1,
imageSize - 1, this);
       g2D.drawImage(backgroundImage, addedWidth, 0, imageSize
- 1, imageSize - 1, 0, 0, imageSize - addedWidth - 1,
imageSize - 1, this);
     }
     else
     {
       g2D.drawImage(backgroundImage, 0, 0, imageSize - 1,
imageSize - 1, scrollX, 0, scrollX + imageSize - 1, imageSize
- 1, this);
     }
   }

  private void exitForm(WindowEvent evt)
  {
    System.exit(0);
  }

}
```

Run the project. Watch the sea go by. The scroll bar is used to control the speed of the scrolling (the amount x increases each time a timer event occurs). Here's my sea scrolling:

Save the project (saved as **Example8-9** project in the **\LearnJava\LJ Code\Class 8** program group). Notice the graphics appear persistent, even though there is no **paintComponent** method. The reason this occurs is because the timer object is automatically updating the displayed picture 20 times each second.

Sprite Animation

Using the **drawImage** method to draw a scrolling background leads us to an obvious question. Can we make an object move across the background – the kind of effect you see in video games? Yes we can – it just takes a little more effort. The moving picture is called a **sprite**. Working with the previous example, say we want a fish to bob up and down through the moving waters. The first thing we need is a picture of a fish – draw one with a painting program or borrow one from somewhere and convert it to **gif** format (**gif** extension). Here's one (**fish.gif**) I came up with:

This is included in the **\LearnJava\LJ Code\Example8-10** folder. If you copy this picture onto the background using the **drawImage** method, the fish will be there, but the background will be gray. We could paint the background the same color as the water and things would look OK, but what if the fish jumps out of the water or swims near the rocks? The background is obliterated. We want whatever background the fish is swimming in to "come through." To do this, we want to define the gray color in the background to be transparent. Let's look at two ways of doing this.

Many graphics programs allow you to define a color within a **gif** image to be transparent. A program I use to do this is Corel's Paint Shop Pro. If you have such software, you can load the fish image and define the gray background to be transparent, the resave the image.

We'll take another approach - using Java code to define an image with a transparent color. Doing an Internet search turned up this cool Java class (**Transparency.java**, saved in the **\LearnJava\LJ Code\Class 8** folder):

```
/*
 *   From:
 *http://www.rgagnon.com/javadetails/java-0265.html
 *
 */

import java.awt.*;
import java.awt.image.*;

public class Transparency
{
```

```
    public static Image makeColorTransparent(Image im, final
Color color)
    {
      ImageFilter filter = new RGBImageFilter()
      {
        // the color we are looking for... Alpha bits are
set to opaque
        public int markerRGB = color.getRGB() | 0xFF000000;
        public final int filterRGB(int x, int y, int rgb)
        {
          if ( ( rgb | 0xFF000000 ) == markerRGB )
          {
            // Mark the alpha bits as zero - transparent
            return 0x00FFFFFF & rgb;
          }
          else
          {
            // nothing to do
            return rgb;
          }
        }
      };
      ImageProducer ip = new
FilteredImageSource(im.getSource(), filter);
      return Toolkit.getDefaultToolkit().createImage(ip);
    }
}
```

This **Transparency** class allows the creation of an **Image** object with a transparent color. Look through the code if you'd like. It does some 'bitwise' math to define a transparent color in an image.

To use the **Transparency** class, assume you have an image (**myImage**) with a background color (**myColor**) you want changed to transparent. The following line of code will return the same image, with the input background color set to transparent (**myTransparentImage**):

```
myTransparentImage =
Transparency.makeColorTransparent(myImage, myColor);
```

We have noted one problem with using the **Transparency** class. Though the returned image retains the size of the original image, the **width** and **height** information are destroyed. So, to obtain the width and height of your image, always refer to the original image.

One question is lingering – how do you determine the desired color to make transparent? In our fish example, it is a gray, but that's not a real definite specification. The argument used in the **makeColorTransparent** method must be a Java **Color** object, using values for the red, green and blue contributions. How do you come up with such values? I'll give you one approach using the little fish image as an example.

Here's a snippet of code to identify the background color in the fish image (I also found this code on the Internet – there's lots of neat code out there):

```
Image fishTemp= new ImageIcon("fish.gif").getImage();
BufferedImage fishTempB = new
BufferedImage(fishTemp.getWidth(null),
fishTemp.getHeight(null), BufferedImage.TYPE_INT_RGB);
// Copy image to buffered image
Graphics g = fishTempB.createGraphics();
// Paint the image onto the buffered image
g.drawImage(fishTemp, 0, 0, null);
int c = fishTempB.getRGB(0, 0);
int  red = (c & 0x00ff0000) >> 16;
int  green = (c & 0x0000ff00) >> 8;
int  blue = c & 0x000000ff;
System.out.println("red " + red);
System.out.println("green " + green);
System.out.println("blue " + blue);
```

First, the fish image is loaded from its file. Next, the **Image** object (**fishTemp**) is converted to a **BufferedImage** object (**fishTempB**). We can determine the color of individual pixels in such objects. That is what is done in the remaining lines of code – we read the color, using **getRGB**, of the pixel in the upper left corner of **fishTempB** (part of the background), convert it to its red, green and blue components and print these to the output window.

Running this snippet results in:

```
General Output
-------------------Configuration: Exa
red 192
green 192
blue 192


Process completed.
```

This tells us the red, green and blue contributions are each 192. Hence, the transparent background color can be represented by:

new Color(192, 192, 192)

This is the color argument we would use in the **makeColorTransparent** method to make the background of the fish transparent.

We'll place the fish in our scrolling background soon, but first let's look at ways to move the fish once it's in the picture.

Keyboard Methods

In multimedia applications, particularly games, you often need to move objects around. This movement can be automatic (using the **timer** object) for animation effects. But then there are times you want the user to have the ability to move objects. One possibility (studied earlier in this class) is using the mouse and the corresponding mouse methods. Here, we consider an alternate movement technique: **keyboard methods.** Just one keyboard method is studied: the **keyPressed** method, which we will see is very similar to the **mousePressed** method.

In a GUI application, many objects can recognize keyboard events. Yet, only the object that has **focus** can receive a keyboard event. When trying to detect a keyboard event for a particular control, we need to make sure the control has focus. Recall the code to apply focus, assuming a control named **myControl**, is:

```
myControl.requestFocus();
```

This command in Java will give the control focus, allowing it to recognize keyboard events. We use the **requestFocus** method with the **keyPressed** method to insure proper execution of each event.

A control's **keyPressed** event has the ability to detect the pressing of <u>any</u> key on the computer keyboard. It can detect:

Special combinations of the **Shift**, **Ctrl**, and **Alt** keys
Insert, **Del**, **Home**, **End**, **PgUp**, **PgDn** keys
Cursor control keys
Numeric keypad keys (it can distinguish these numbers from those on the top row of the keyboard)
Function keys
Letter, number and character keys

The **keyPressed** event is triggered whenever a key is pressed. The form of the corresponding method must be:

```
public void keyPressed(KeyEvent e)
{
      [Java code for keyPressed event]
}
```

The **KeyEvent** argument **e** tells us which key was pressed by providing what is called a **key code**. There is a key code value for each key on the keyboard. By evaluating the **e.getKeyCode()** argument, we can determine which key was pressed. There are over 100 values, some of which are:

e.getKeyCode()	Description
e.VK_BACK_SPACE	The BACKSPACE key.
e.VK_CANCEL	The CANCEL key.
e.VK_DELETE	The DEL key.
e.VK_DOWN	The DOWN ARROW key.
e.VK_ENTER	The ENTER key.
e.VK_ESCAPE	The ESC key.
e.VK_F1	The F1 key.
e.VK_HOME	The HOME key.
e.VK_LEFT	The LEFT ARROW key.
e.VK_NUMPAD0	The 0 key on the numeric keypad.
e.VK_PAGE_DOWN	The PAGE DOWN key.
e.VK_PAGE_UP	The PAGE UP key.
e.VK_RIGHT	The RIGHT ARROW key.
e.VK_SPACE	The SPACEBAR key.
e.VK_TAB	The TAB key.
e.VK_UP	The UP ARROW key.
e.VK_G	The letter G.
e.VK_4	The number 4.

The status of other keys (**Alt**, **Ctrl**, **Shift** and others) can be determined using the **e.getModifiers()** method. The values are:

e.getKeyModifiers()	Description
e.ALT_MASK	The ALT key.
e.CTRL_MASK	The CTRL key.
e.SHIFT_MASK	The SHIFT key.

To add a listener for the **keyPressed** event for a control named **myControl** (often a panel), use:

```
myControl.addKeyListener(new KeyAdapter()
{
  public void keyPressed(KeyEvent e)
  {
    myControlKeyPressed(e)
  }
});
```

And, the corresponding event code is placed in the **myControlKeyPressed** method:

```
private void myControlKeyPressed(KeyEvent e)
{
    [method code]
}
```

There is often a lot of work involved in interpreting the information provided in the **keyPressed** event. For example, the **keyPressed** event cannot distinguish between an upper and lower case letter. You need to make that distinction in your Java code. You usually use an **if** structure (based on **e.getKeyCode()** and **e.getKeyModifiers()**) to determine which key was pressed.

Example 8-10

Sprite Animation

1. In this application, we will add a swimming fish to the scrolling background implemented in **Example 8-9**. And, we use cursor control keys to move the fish up and down. We just need to make a couple of changes to the code. Open **Example 8-9**.

2. Add the **Transparency.java** file (in **\LearnJava\LJ Code\Class 8** folder) to the project source folder. Include a `package scrolling;` statement at the top of the file.

3. In the **\LearnJava\LJ Code\Class 9\Example8-10** folder is a graphics file named **fish.gif**. This is the fish graphics. Copy this file into your project folder.

4. Add these 'fish' variables to the class level declarations:

```
Image fishTemp= new ImageIcon("fish.gif").getImage();
Image fishImage =
Transparency.makeColorTransparent(fishTemp, new Color(192,
192, 192));
int fishW = 37, fishH=38;
int fishX, fishY;
```

These lines load in a temporary image (**fishTemp**). Then we create the image (**fishImage**) with a transparent background using the **Transparency** class. Next, dimensions and position of the fish (**width**, **height**, **x** position and **y** position) are declared.

5. Add this code to the frame constructor after code placing **displayPanel** on the frame (adds a listener for the cursor keys):

```
displayPanel.addKeyListener(new KeyAdapter()
{
  public void keyPressed(KeyEvent e)
  {
    displayPanelKeyPressed(e);
  }
});
```

6. Add this code to the frame constructor prior to the line starting the timer. This code is used to initialize the 'fish' variables and give the display panel focus to recognize cursor keys:

```
fishX = (int) (0.5 * (displayPanel.getWidth() - fishW));
fishY = (int) (0.5 * (displayPanel.getHeight() - fishH));
displayPanel.requestFocus();
```

7. Add this line at the end of the **scrollTimerActionPerformed** method to draw the fish on the background:

```
g2D.drawImage(fishImage, fishX, fishY, this);
```

8. Use this code in the **displayPanelKeyPressed** method (new code):

```
private void displayPanelKeyPressed(KeyEvent e)
{
  if (e.getKeyCode() == e.VK_UP)
  {
    fishY -= 5;
  }
  else if (e.getKeyCode() == e.VK_DOWN)
  {
    fishY += 5;
  }
}
```

This moves the fish up (up cursor key) and down (down cursor key).

The modified **Scrolling.java** code listing (changes are shaded):

```
/*
 * Scrolling.java
 */
package scrolling;
import javax.swing.*;
import java.awt.*;
import java.awt.event.*;
import java.awt.geom.*;

public class Scrolling extends JFrame
{

  JPanel displayPanel = new JPanel();
  JScrollBar backgroundScrollBar = new JScrollBar();
  Image backgroundImage = new
ImageIcon("undersea.gif").getImage();
  Timer scrollTimer;
  Image fishTemp= new ImageIcon("fish.gif").getImage();
  Image fishImage =
Transparency.makeColorTransparent(fishTemp, new Color(192,
192, 192));
  int fishW = 37, fishH=38;
  int fishX, fishY;
  int scrollX = 0;
  int imageSize = 130;
  Graphics2D g2D;

  public static void main(String args[])
  {
    // create frame
    new Scrolling().show();
  }

  public Scrolling()
  {
    // frame constructor
    setResizable(false);
    getContentPane().setBackground(Color.BLUE);
    addWindowListener(new WindowAdapter()
    {
      public void windowClosing(WindowEvent evt)
      {
        exitForm(evt);
      }
    });
```

```
    getContentPane().setLayout(new GridBagLayout());

  // position controls

  GridBagConstraints gridConstraints = new
GridBagConstraints();
    displayPanel.setPreferredSize(new Dimension(imageSize,
imageSize));
    gridConstraints.gridx = 0;
    gridConstraints.gridy = 0;
    gridConstraints.insets = new Insets(10, 10, 10, 10);
    getContentPane().add(displayPanel, gridConstraints);
    displayPanel.addKeyListener(new KeyAdapter()
    {
      public void keyPressed(KeyEvent e)
      {
        displayPanelKeyPressed(e);
      }
    });

    gridConstraints = new GridBagConstraints();
    backgroundScrollBar.setPreferredSize(new
Dimension(imageSize, 20));
    backgroundScrollBar.setMinimum(0);
    backgroundScrollBar.setMaximum(20 +
backgroundScrollBar.getVisibleAmount());
    backgroundScrollBar.setBlockIncrement(2);
    backgroundScrollBar.setUnitIncrement(1);
    backgroundScrollBar.setValue(0);

backgroundScrollBar.setOrientation(JScrollBar.HORIZONTAL);
    gridConstraints.gridx = 0;
    gridConstraints.gridy = 1;
    gridConstraints.insets = new Insets(10, 10, 10, 10);
    getContentPane().add(backgroundScrollBar,
gridConstraints);

    scrollTimer = new Timer(50, new ActionListener()
    {
      public void actionPerformed(ActionEvent e)
      {
        scrollTimerActionPerformed(e);
      }
    });

    pack();
```

```
      Dimension screenSize =
Toolkit.getDefaultToolkit().getScreenSize();
      setBounds((int) (0.5 * (screenSize.width - getWidth())),
(int) (0.5 * (screenSize.height - getHeight())), getWidth(),
getHeight());
      g2D = (Graphics2D) displayPanel.getGraphics();
      fishX = (int) (0.5 * (displayPanel.getWidth() - fishW));
      fishY = (int) (0.5 * (displayPanel.getHeight() - fishH));
      displayPanel.requestFocus();
      scrollTimer.start();
  }

  private void scrollTimerActionPerformed(ActionEvent e)
  {
    int addedWidth;
    // Find next location on background
    scrollX += backgroundScrollBar.getValue();
    if (scrollX > backgroundImage.getWidth(this))
    {
      scrollX = 0;
    }
    // When x is near right edge, we need to copy
    // two segments of the background into display panel
    if (scrollX > (backgroundImage.getWidth(this) -
imageSize))
    {
      addedWidth = backgroundImage.getWidth(this) - scrollX;
      g2D.drawImage(backgroundImage, 0, 0, addedWidth - 1,
imageSize - 1, scrollX, 0, scrollX + addedWidth - 1,
imageSize - 1, this);
      g2D.drawImage(backgroundImage, addedWidth, 0, imageSize
- 1, imageSize - 1, 0, 0, imageSize - addedWidth - 1,
imageSize - 1, this);
    }
    else
    {
      g2D.drawImage(backgroundImage, 0, 0, imageSize - 1,
imageSize - 1, scrollX, 0, scrollX + imageSize - 1, imageSize
- 1, this);
    }
    g2D.drawImage(fishImage, fishX, fishY, this);
  }

  private void exitForm(WindowEvent evt)
  {
    System.exit(0);
  }
```

```
private void displayPanelKeyPressed(KeyEvent e)
{
  if (e.getKeyCode() == e.VK_UP)
  {
    fishY -= 5;
  }
  else if (e.getKeyCode() == e.VK_DOWN)
  {
    fishY += 5;
  }
}
}
```

Run the application and save it (saved as **Example8-10** project in the
\LearnJava\LJ Code\Class 8** program group). Use the **up cursor key to move
the fish up and the **down** cursor key to move the fish down. Notice that, no
matter where the fish is, the background shows through. Here's the fish in the
middle of the water:

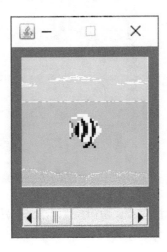

Here's the fish down by the rocks:

And, here's a fabulous flying fish:

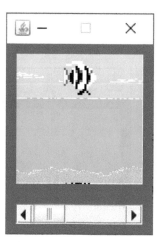

You now know the secrets of doing animations in video games – scrolling backgrounds and the use of sprites.

Collision Detection

As objects move in a multimedia presentation or video game, we need some way to see if two items **collide** or **overlap**. For example, in a basketball game, you need to see if the ball goes in the hoop. In a solitaire card game, you need to see if a card is placed on another card properly. In a file disposal application, you want to know when the file reaches the trashcan. Rectangular regions describe all the moving objects in a multimedia application. Hence, we want to know if two rectangles **intersect**. In Java, this test can be accomplished using the **createIntersection** method of the **Rectangle2D** shape we've seen before.

To use the **createIntersection** method, we need three **Rectangle2D** shapes. The first two (call them **rectangle1** and **rectangle2**) describe the rectangles being checked for intersection. The rectangle describing the intersection of these two rectangles (**collided**) is then defined by:

```
collided = rectangle1.createIntersection(rectangle2);
```

Once the intersection (or collision) rectangle is created using **createIntersection**, we check the intersection by examining the **isEmpty** Boolean property:

```
collided.isEmpty()
```

If this property is **true**, there is no intersection or collision. If **isEmpty** is **false**, there is intersection and properties (**x**, **y**, **width**, **height**) of the **collided** rectangle define that intersection region.

Just because two rectangles intersect, you may not want to declare a collision. In many cases, it is prudent to check for intersection and, once detected, see how large the intersection area is. If this intersection area is small compared to the size of the compared rectangles, you might not allow the collision. Or, you might want different response depending on location of the intersection region. For example, if a ball hits (collides with) a paddle on one side, the ball will go in one direction. If the ball hits the paddle on the other side, a different rebound direction is assumed.

Example 8-11

Collision Detection

Start a new empty project in **NetBeans**. Name the project **Collision**. Delete default code in Java file named **Collision**. In this application, we will use cursor control keys to move one rectangle around and see when it collides with a second rectangle. The finished frame appears as:

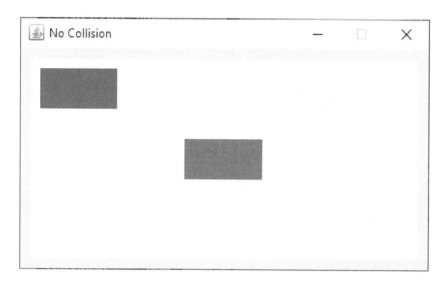

1. Place a panel control on a frame, a very simple **GridBagLayout**:

	gridx = 0
gridy = 0	**displayPanel**

Set these properties:

Intersection Frame:
        title   No Collision
        resizable   false

displayPanel:
        preferredSize   (400, 200)
        background   WHITE
        gridx   0
        gridy   0
        insets   (10, 10, 10, 10)

2. Build a basic framework to establish the frame:

```
/*
 * Collision.java
 */
package collision;
import javax.swing.*;
import java.awt.*;
import java.awt.event.*;
import java.awt.geom.*;
public class Collision extends JFrame
{
  public static void main(String args[])
  {
    // create frame
    new Collision().show();
  }
  public Collision()
  {
    // frame constructor
    setTitle("No Collision");
    setResizable(false);
    addWindowListener(new WindowAdapter()
    {
      public void windowClosing(WindowEvent evt)
      {
        exitForm(evt);
      }
    });
    getContentPane().setLayout(new GridBagLayout());

    pack();
    Dimension screenSize =
Toolkit.getDefaultToolkit().getScreenSize();
    setBounds((int) (0.5 * (screenSize.width -
getWidth())), (int) (0.5 * (screenSize.height -
getHeight())), getWidth(), getHeight());
  }
  private void exitForm(WindowEvent evt)
  {
    System.exit(0);
  }
}
```

Run to check the code.

3. Add controls and methods. Add this class level declaration:

```
JPanel displayPanel = new JPanel();
```

Position panel control and create method:

```
GridBagConstraints gridConstraints = new
GridBagConstraints();
displayPanel.setPreferredSize(new Dimension(400, 200));
displayPanel.setBackground(Color.WHITE);
gridConstraints.gridx = 0;
gridConstraints.gridy = 0;
gridConstraints.insets = new Insets(10, 10, 10, 10);
getContentPane().add(displayPanel, gridConstraints);
displayPanel.addKeyListener(new KeyAdapter()
{
  public void keyPressed(KeyEvent e)
  {
    displayPanelKeyPressed(e);
  }
});
```

Add empty **keyPressed** method:

```
private void displayPanelKeyPressed(KeyEvent e)
{
}
```

Run to check the control (one panel) layout:

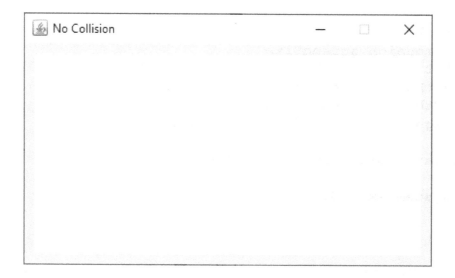

4. Use these class level variable declarations (declaring the rectangles and graphics object):

```
Rectangle2D.Double rect1;
Rectangle2D.Double rect2;
Graphics2D g2D;
```

5. Use this code at the end of the constructor to initialize the rectangle objects:

```
g2D = (Graphics2D) displayPanel.getGraphics();
rect1 = new Rectangle2D.Double(10, 10, 80, 40);
g2D.setPaint(Color.BLUE);
g2D.fill(rect1);
rect2 = new Rectangle2D.Double(160, 80, 80, 40);
g2D.setPaint(Color.RED);
g2D.fill(rect2);
displayPanel.requestFocus();
```

6. Use this code in the **displayPanelKeyPressed** method. This moves the blue rectangle around and checks for collisions. Collision status (including the area of the intersection region) is displayed in the **title** property of the frame. This is the information appearing in the title bar area.

```
private void displayPanelKeyPressed(KeyEvent e)
{
  double rectX = rect1.getX();
  double rectY = rect1.getY();
  // erase blue rectangle
  g2D.setColor(displayPanel.getBackground());
  g2D.fill(rect1);
  // see which way box moved
  if (e.getKeyCode() == e.VK_LEFT)
  {
    rectX -= 5;
  }
  else if (e.getKeyCode() == e.VK_RIGHT)
  {
    rectX += 5;
  }
  else if (e.getKeyCode() == e.VK_UP)
  {
    rectY -= 5;
  }
  else if (e.getKeyCode() == e.VK_DOWN)
  {
```

```
            rectY += 5;
        }
        g2D.setPaint(Color.RED);
        g2D.fill(rect2);
        // establish rectangle position and redraw
        rect1.setRect(rectX, rectY, 80, 40);
        g2D.setPaint(Color.BLUE);
        g2D.fill(rect1);
        Rectangle2D.Double rect3 = (Rectangle2D.Double)
    rect1.createIntersection(rect2);
        // check for collision
        if (rect3.isEmpty())
        {
            this.setTitle("No Collision");
        }
        else
        {
            // determine percentage of overlap
            double overlap = 100 * rect3.getWidth() *
    rect3.getHeight() / (rect1.getWidth() *
    rect1.getHeight());
            this.setTitle(overlap + "% Collision!!");
        }
    }
```

The complete **Collision.java** code listing (changes to framework are shaded):

```
/*
 * Collision.java
 */
package collision;
import javax.swing.*;
import java.awt.*;
import java.awt.event.*;
import java.awt.geom.*;
public class Collision extends JFrame
{
    JPanel displayPanel = new JPanel();
    Rectangle2D.Double rect1;
    Rectangle2D.Double rect2;
    Graphics2D g2D;
    public static void main(String args[])
    {
        // create frame
        new Collision().show();
    }
    public Collision()
```

```
  {
    // frame constructor
    setTitle("No Collision");
    setResizable(false);
    addWindowListener(new WindowAdapter()
    {
      public void windowClosing(WindowEvent evt)
      {
        exitForm(evt);
      }
    });
    getContentPane().setLayout(new GridBagLayout());
    // position controls
    GridBagConstraints gridConstraints = new
GridBagConstraints();
    displayPanel.setPreferredSize(new Dimension(400, 200));
    displayPanel.setBackground(Color.WHITE);
    gridConstraints.gridx = 0;
    gridConstraints.gridy = 0;
    gridConstraints.insets = new Insets(10, 10, 10, 10);
    getContentPane().add(displayPanel, gridConstraints);
    displayPanel.addKeyListener(new KeyAdapter()
    {
      public void keyPressed(KeyEvent e)
      {
        displayPanelKeyPressed(e);
      }
    });
    pack();
    Dimension screenSize =
Toolkit.getDefaultToolkit().getScreenSize();
    setBounds((int) (0.5 * (screenSize.width - getWidth())),
(int) (0.5 * (screenSize.height - getHeight())), getWidth(),
getHeight());
    g2D = (Graphics2D) displayPanel.getGraphics();
    rect1 = new Rectangle2D.Double(10, 10, 80, 40);
    g2D.setPaint(Color.BLUE);
     g2D.fill(rect1);
    rect2 = new Rectangle2D.Double(160, 80, 80, 40);
    g2D.setPaint(Color.RED);
    g2D.fill(rect2);
    displayPanel.requestFocus();
  }
  private void displayPanelKeyPressed(KeyEvent e)
  {
    double rectX = rect1.getX();
    double rectY = rect1.getY();
```

```
    // erase blue rectangle
    g2D.setColor(displayPanel.getBackground());
    g2D.fill(rect1);
    // see which way box moved
    if (e.getKeyCode() == e.VK_LEFT)
    {
      rectX -= 5;
    }
    else if (e.getKeyCode() == e.VK_RIGHT)
    {
      rectX += 5;
    }
    else if (e.getKeyCode() == e.VK_UP)
    {
      rectY -= 5;
    }
    else if (e.getKeyCode() == e.VK_DOWN)
    {
      rectY += 5;
    }
    g2D.setPaint(Color.RED);
    g2D.fill(rect2);
    // establish rectangle position and redraw
    rect1.setRect(rectX, rectY, 80, 40);
    g2D.setPaint(Color.BLUE);
    g2D.fill(rect1);
    Rectangle2D.Double rect3 = (Rectangle2D.Double)
rect1.createIntersection(rect2);
    // check for collision
    if (rect3.isEmpty())
    {
      this.setTitle("No Collision");
    }
    else
    {
      // determine percentage of overlap
      double overlap = 100 * rect3.getWidth() *
rect3.getHeight() / (rect1.getWidth() * rect1.getHeight());
      this.setTitle(overlap + "% Collision!!");
    }
  }
  private void exitForm(WindowEvent evt)
  {
    System.exit(0);
  }
}
```

Run the project. Notice we haven't bothered to make the graphics persistent.
If the boxes don't appear initially, press a cursor control key and they'll show
up. Use the keyboard cursor control arrows to move the blue rectangle around
the frame. We check to see when the blue rectangle collides with the red
rectangle (see title bar of frame). Notice how collisions are detected no matter
which direction you approach the red rectangle from. Here's a collision I made:

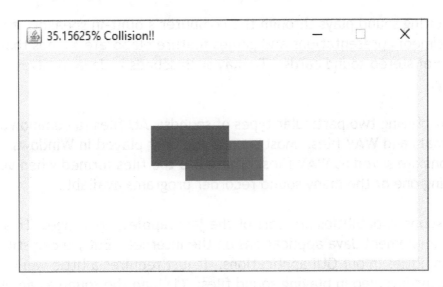

Save the project (saved as **Example8-11** project in the **\LearnJava\LJ
Code\Class 8** program group).

Sounds in Java

There is only one sound available with Java, a simple beep generated using:

```
Toolkit.getDefaultToolkit().beep();
```

This unexciting sound plays through the computer's built-in speaker, if there is one. Multimedia presentations and games feature elaborate sounds that take advantage of stereo sound cards. To play such sounds in Java involves just a bit of trickery.

We look at playing two particular types of sounds: **AU** files (a common Java audio format) and **WAV** files. Most sounds you hear played in Windows applications are saved as **WAV** files. These are the files formed when you record using one of the many sound recorder programs available.

The Java sound capabilities are part of the **java.applet.*** package. This package is used to implement Java applications on the Internet. But we can still use these capabilities in our GUI applications. It just requires a little work. There are two steps involved in playing sound files: (1) load the sound as an audio clip and (2) play the sound.

A sound file is loaded using the **newAudioClip** method. If we name the sound **mySound**, the sound is loaded using:

```
mySound = Applet.newAudioClip(mySoundURL);
```

where **mySoundURL** is the "address" of the sound file. You may note that URL is an Internet address (universal resource locator) – this is because the sound utilities are part of the applet package. Does this mean our sounds must be stored on the Internet somewhere? No. By forming a special URL as the argument, we can load sound files from our project folder, just like we have loaded graphics files.

A URL for use in the **newAudioClip** method is formed using the Java **URL** method (in the **java.net.URL** package). If the sound file is **mySoundFile** (**String** type), the URL is formed with:

```
mySoundURL = new URL("file: " + mySoundFile);
```

The addition of the **"file:"** string tells Java the sound is loaded from a file rather than the Internet. This assumes the sound file is located in the project folder. If it is in another folder, you need to "prepend" the file name with the appropriate directory information.

We need to consider one last thing. The URL can only be formed within a **try/catch** loop to catch potential exceptions. Hence, the complete code segment to load a sound (**mySound**) from a file (**mySoundFile**) is:

```
try
{
    mySound = Applet.newAudioClip(new URL("file: " +
mySoundFile));
}
catch (Exception ex)
{
    [Error message]
}
```

Such code to create sounds is usually placed at the end of the class constructor code with all sounds declared as class level variables.

Once we have created a sound clip, there are three methods used to play or stop the corresponding sound. To play **mySound** one time, use the **play** method:

```
mySound.play();
```

To play the sound in a continuous loop, use the **loop** method:

```
mySound.loop();
```

To stop the sound from playing, use the **stop** method:

```
mySound.stop();
```

It's that easy.

It is normal practice to include any sound files an application uses in the project folder. This makes them easily accessible. As such, when distributing your application to other users, you must remember to include the sound files in the package.

Example 8-12

Playing Sounds

Start a new empty project in **NetBeans**. Name the project **PlaySounds**. Delete default code in Java file named **PlaySounds**.

We'll build a little example that lets us hear **AU** and **WAV** files. We will use an embedded file chooser. The finished frame will be:

1. The application just needs one control: a file chooser. The **GridBagLayout** arrangement is:

	gridx = 0
gridy = 0	**soundChooser**

PlaySounds Frame:

title	Playing Sounds
resizable	false

soundChooser:

gridx	0
gridy	0

2. As usual, build a framework to start with:

```
/*
 * PlaySounds.java
 */
package playsounds;
import javax.swing.*;
import java.awt.*;
import java.awt.event.*;
import java.net.URL;
import java.applet.*;
public class PlaySounds extends JFrame
{
  public static void main(String args[])
  {
    //construct frame
    new PlaySounds().show();
  }
  public PlaySounds()
  {
    // create frame
    setTitle("Playing Sounds");
    setResizable(false);
    addWindowListener(new WindowAdapter()
    {
      public void windowClosing(WindowEvent e)
      {
        exitForm(e);
      }
```

```
    });
    getContentPane().setLayout(new GridBagLayout());

    pack();
    Dimension screenSize =
Toolkit.getDefaultToolkit().getScreenSize();
    setBounds((int) (0.5 * (screenSize.width -
getWidth())), (int) (0.5 * (screenSize.height -
getHeight())), getWidth(), getHeight());
  }
  private void exitForm(WindowEvent e)
  {
    System.exit(0);
  }
}
```

Run to see the frame centered on your screen.

3. Create control with this class level declarations:

```
JFileChooser soundChooser = new JFileChooser();
```

Position controls and add event listener for file chooser:

```
GridBagConstraints gridConstraints = new
GridBagConstraints();
soundChooser.addChoosableFileFilter(new
FileNameExtensionFilter("Sound Files", "au", "wav"));
gridConstraints.gridx = 0;
gridConstraints.gridy = 0;
getContentPane().add(soundChooser, gridConstraints);
soundChooser.addActionListener(new ActionListener()
{
  public void actionPerformed(ActionEvent e)
  {
    soundChooserActionPerformed(e);
  }
});
```

4. We'll go right to adding code to the **soundChooserActionPerformed** event:

```
private void soundChooserActionPerformed(ActionEvent e)
{
  // load and play sound if open selected
  if
(e.getActionCommand().equals(JFileChooser.APPROVE_SELECTIO
N))
  {
    AudioClip mySound = null;
    try
    {
      mySound = Applet.newAudioClip(new URL("file:"+
soundChooser.getSelectedFile().toString()));
    }
    catch (Exception ex)
    {
      System.out.println("Error loading sound.");
    }
    mySound.play();
  }
}
```

In this code, if the user clicks the **Open** button, the selected file is used to establish a sound clip that is played.

The complete **PlaySounds.java** code is (code added to framework is shaded):

```
/*
 * PlaySounds.java
 */
package playsounds;
import javax.swing.*;
import javax.swing.filechooser.*;
import java.awt.*;
import java.awt.event.*;
import java.net.URL;
import java.applet.*;
public class PlaySounds extends JFrame
{
  JFileChooser soundChooser = new JFileChooser();

  public static void main(String args[])
  {
    //construct frame
    new PlaySounds().show();
```

```
  }
public PlaySounds()
{
  // create frame
  setTitle("Playing Sounds");
  setResizable(false);
  addWindowListener(new WindowAdapter()
  {
    public void windowClosing(WindowEvent e)
    {
      exitForm(e);
    }
  });
  getContentPane().setLayout(new GridBagLayout());

  // position controls (establish event methods)
  GridBagConstraints gridConstraints = new
GridBagConstraints();
  soundChooser.addChoosableFileFilter(new
FileNameExtensionFilter("Sound Files", "au", "wav"));
  gridConstraints.gridx = 0;
  gridConstraints.gridy = 0;
  getContentPane().add(soundChooser, gridConstraints);
  soundChooser.addActionListener(new ActionListener()
  {
    public void actionPerformed(ActionEvent e)
    {
      soundChooserActionPerformed(e);
    }
  });

  pack();
  Dimension screenSize =
Toolkit.getDefaultToolkit().getScreenSize();
  setBounds((int) (0.5 * (screenSize.width - getWidth())),
(int) (0.5 * (screenSize.height - getHeight())), getWidth(),
getHeight());
  }
private void soundChooserActionPerformed(ActionEvent e)
{
  // load and play sound if open selected
  if
(e.getActionCommand().equals(JFileChooser.APPROVE_SELECTION))
  {
    AudioClip mySound = null;
    try
    {
```

```
        mySound = Applet.newAudioClip(new URL("file:"+
soundChooser.getSelectedFile().toString()));
      }
      catch (Exception ex)
      {
        System.out.println("Error loading sound.");
      }
      mySound.play();
    }
  }
  private void exitForm(WindowEvent e)
  {
    System.exit(0);
  }
}
```

Run the project. Find a sound file and listen to the lovely results. There are several **WAV** files in the project folder (**\LearnJava\LJ Code\Class 8\Example8-12**) to listen to. Here's the screen when I played the cheering sound:

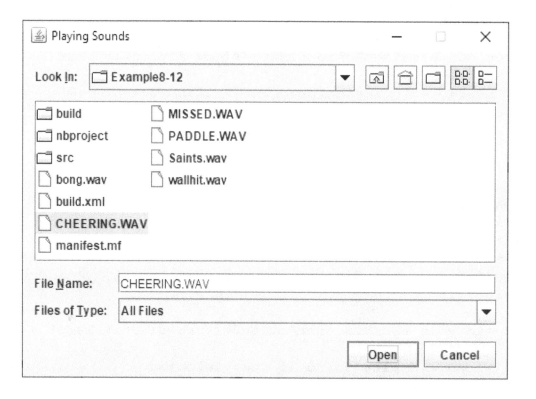

Save the application and run it (saved as **Example8-12** project in the **\LearnJava\LJ Code\Class 8** program group).

Example 8-13

Bouncing Ball with Sound!

Let's add sound to the bouncing ball example (**Example 8-8**). Start a new empty project in **NetBeans**. Name the project **BallSound**. Delete default code in Java file named **BallSound** and rename the file **BouncingBall**. Copy the code from **BouncingBall.java** (in **Example 8-8**) to this empty file. We will modify the file to add sound when the ball bounces. In the **\LearnJava\LJ Code\Class 8\Example8-13** is a bouncing sound (**bong.wav**). Copy the file to your project's folder. Also copy the **earth.gif** file (the bouncing ball) to the same folder.

Make these changes to **BouncingBall.java** to add sound:

1. Add the needed import statements:

```
import java.net.URL;
import java.applet.*;
```

2. Declare a class level variable (**bounceSound**) for the sound clip:

```
static AudioClip bounceSound;
```

3. Add code to the constructor to load the sound (place code before line repainting the panel):

```
try
{
  bounceSound = Applet.newAudioClip(new
URL("file:"+"bong.wav"));
}
catch (Exception ex)
{
  System.out.println("Error loading sound");
}
```

4. Add code to the **ballTimerActionPerformed** method to play the 'bounce' sound when needed (added code is shaded):

```
private void ballTimerActionPerformed(ActionEvent e)
{
  // determine ball position and draw it
  ballY = (int) (ballY + ballDir *
displayPanel.getHeight() / 50);
  //check for bounce
  if (ballY < 0)
  {
    ballY = 0;
    ballDir = 1;
    bounceSound.play();
  }
  else if (ballY + ballSize > displayPanel.getHeight())
  {
    ballY = displayPanel.getHeight() - ballSize;
    ballDir = -1;
    bounceSound.play();
  }
  displayPanel.repaint();
}
```

For reference, here is the modified **BouncingBall.java** code listing (modifications are shaded):

```
/*
 * BouncingBall.java
 */
package bouncingball;
import javax.swing.*;
import java.awt.*;
import java.awt.event.*;
import java.awt.geom.*;
import java.net.URL;
import java.applet.*;
public class BouncingBall extends JFrame
{
  GraphicsPanel displayPanel = new GraphicsPanel();
  JButton startButton = new JButton();
  static Image myBall = new
ImageIcon("earth.gif").getImage();
  Timer ballTimer;
  AudioClip bounceSound;
  static int ballSize, ballX, ballY, ballDir;
```

```
  public static void main(String args[])
  {
    // create frame
    new BouncingBall().show();
}

  public BouncingBall()
  {
    // frame constructor
    setResizable(false);
    addWindowListener(new WindowAdapter()
    {
      public void windowClosing(WindowEvent evt)
      {
        exitForm(evt);
      }
    });
    getContentPane().setLayout(new GridBagLayout());

    // position controls
    GridBagConstraints gridConstraints = new
GridBagConstraints();
      displayPanel.setPreferredSize(new Dimension(100, 400));
      displayPanel.setBackground(Color.WHITE);
      gridConstraints.gridx = 0;
    gridConstraints.gridy = 0;
    gridConstraints.insets = new Insets(10, 10, 10, 10);
    getContentPane().add(displayPanel, gridConstraints);

    gridConstraints = new GridBagConstraints();
     startButton.setText("Start");
     gridConstraints.gridx = 0;
    gridConstraints.gridy = 1;
    gridConstraints.insets = new Insets(10, 10, 10, 10);
    getContentPane().add(startButton, gridConstraints);
    startButton.addActionListener(new ActionListener()
    {
      public void actionPerformed(ActionEvent e)
      {
        startButtonActionPerformed(e);
      }
    });
    ballTimer = new Timer(100, new ActionListener()
    {
      public void actionPerformed(ActionEvent e)
      {
        ballTimerActionPerformed(e);
```

```
      }
    });

    pack();
    Dimension screenSize =
Toolkit.getDefaultToolkit().getScreenSize();
    setBounds((int) (0.5 * (screenSize.width - getWidth())),
(int) (0.5 * (screenSize.height - getHeight())), getWidth(),
getHeight());
    // initialize variables/set up graphics objects
    // horizontally center ball in display panel
    ballSize = 50;
    ballX = (int) (0.5 * (displayPanel.getWidth() -
ballSize));
    ballY = 0;
    ballDir = 1;
    try
    {
      bounceSound = Applet.newAudioClip(new
URL("file:"+"bong.wav"));
    }
    catch (Exception ex)
    {
      System.out.println("Error loading sound");
    }
    displayPanel.repaint();
  }
  private void startButtonActionPerformed(ActionEvent e)
  {
    if (ballTimer.isRunning())
    {
      ballTimer.stop();
      startButton.setText("Start");
    }
    else
    {
      ballTimer.start();
      startButton.setText("Stop");
    }
  }
  private void ballTimerActionPerformed(ActionEvent e)
  {
    // determine ball position and draw it
    ballY = (int) (ballY + ballDir * displayPanel.getHeight()
/ 50);
    //check for bounce
    if (ballY < 0)
```

```
      {
        ballY = 0;
        ballDir = 1;
        bounceSound.play();
      }
      else if (ballY + ballSize > displayPanel.getHeight())
      {
        ballY = displayPanel.getHeight() - ballSize;
        ballDir = -1;
        bounceSound.play();
      }
      displayPanel.repaint();
  }
  private void exitForm(WindowEvent evt)
  {
      System.exit(0);
  }

}
class GraphicsPanel extends JPanel
{
  public GraphicsPanel()
  {
  }
  public void paintComponent(Graphics g)
  {
      Graphics2D g2D = (Graphics2D) g;
      super.paintComponent(g2D);
      // draw ball
      g2D.drawImage(BouncingBall.myBall, BouncingBall.ballX,
BouncingBall.ballY, BouncingBall.ballSize,
BouncingBall.ballSize, this);
      g2D.dispose();
  }
}
```

Rerun the project.   Each time the ball bounces, you should hear a bonk! Save the project (saved as **Example8-13** project in the **\LearnJava\LJ Code\Class 8** program group).

Class Review

After completing this class, you should understand:

> ➢ How to detect and use mouse methods
> ➢ How to draw lines, polygons and filled polygons
> ➢ How to draw curves, closed curves and filled closed curves
> ➢ How to use gradient and texture paints
> ➢ How to add text to a graphics object
> ➢ How to do animation using **drawImage**
> ➢ How to work with scrolling backgrounds
> ➢ How to use keyboard events and detect collision of two rectangular regions
> ➢ How to play sound files

Practice Problems 8

Problem 8-1. Blackboard Problem. Modify the **Blackboard** application (**Example 8-2**) to allow adjustable line width while drawing.

Problem 8-2. Rubber Band Problem. Build an application where the user draws a 'rubber band' rectangle in a panel. Let a left-click start drawing (defining upper left corner). Then move the mouse until the rectangle is as desired and release the mouse button. When the 'rubber band' is complete, draw an ellipse in the defined region.

Problem 8-3. Plot Labels Problem. In **Problem 7-4**, we built a project that plotted the win streak for the Seattle Mariners 1995 season. Use the **drawString** method to add any labeling information desired.

Problem 8-4. Bouncing Balls Problem. Build an application with two bouncing balls. When they collide make them disappear with some kind of sound. Add any other effects you might like.

Problem 8-5. Moon Problem. In the \LearnJava\Java Code\Class 8\Problem8-5\ folder is a graphics file named **THEMOON.GIF**. It is a large (450 pixels high, 640 pixels wide) lunar landscape. Build an application that lets you traverse this landscape in a small viewing window. Use cursor control keys to move horizontally and vertically.

Exercise 8

The Original Video Game - Pong!

In the early 1970's, Nolan Bushnell began the video game revolution with Atari's **Pong** game -- a very simple Ping-Pong kind of game. Try to replicate this game using Java. In the game, a ball bounces from one end of a court to another, bouncing off sidewalls. Players try to deflect the ball at each end using a controllable paddle. Use sounds where appropriate.

9

Other Java Topics

Review and Preview

In this final class, we conclude our discussion of Java GUI applications. We look at some other controls, action objects, and how to print from an application.

Other Controls

In the past several classes, we've looked at many of the controls in the Java Swing library. But, there are still others. We will look at a couple of these **controls** in this class. For each control, we will build a short example to demonstrate its use. With your programming skills, you should be able to expand these examples to fit your particular needs.

What if you can't find the exact Swing control you need for a particular task? There are two possible answers to this question. First, a skill you can develop, using the knowledge gained in this course, is the ability to build and deploy your own Java controls. You can modify an existing control, build a control made up of several existing controls or create an entirely new control. Building your own controls is beyond the scope of this course. There are several excellent texts and websites that address this topic.

Another way to find other controls is to take advantage of other programmers' work. Many Java programmers create controls and make them available to the Java community via downloads from the Internet. These controls are usually very low cost or even free. We'll look how to use one of these controls.

JTextPane Control

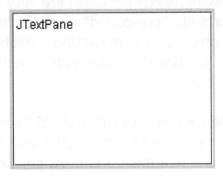

In Class 5, we built a note editor (using a text area control) that allowed formatting of the typed text. The formatting, though, affected all displayed text. The **JTextPane** control allows the user to enter and edit text, providing more advanced formatting features than the conventional text area control. You can use different fonts and font styles for different text sections. You can even change alignment, control indents, hanging indents, and bulleted paragraphs. Possible uses for this control include: reading and viewing large text files (including HTML files) or implementing a full-featured text editor into any applications. Hosting the text pane in a scroll pane control provides scrolling capabilities.

Text Pane Properties:

text	String displayed in text pane.
background	Text pane background color.
editable	Indicates whether text in the text pane is read-only.

Text Pane Methods:

setText	Sets the text pane text.
getText	Retrieves the text pane text.
setBackground	Sets the text pane background color.
setEditable	If set to false, text pane cannot be edited.

Notice that the text pane control has relatively few properties and methods. The formatting features of the control are handled using **Action** objects. These objects (from the **javax.swing.text.*** package) are very convenient when using menus and toolbars and provide "pre-coded" methods for common editing events. The text pane control hosts many action objects. We will look at a few of the action objects associated with certain editing features: bold, italic, underline and setting font size.

By default, the **JTextPane** control uses the **StyledEditorKit** class to implement its actions (there are other editor kits, too). Let's look at the steps needed to create an action and assign it to a menu item. As an example, we will add an action and menu item to make selected text bold face. The steps:

  ➢ Create the action object:

```
Action boldAction = new StyledEditorKit.BoldAction();
```

  ➢ Assign a text value (**NAME**) to the action (for display in the menu item):

```
boldAction.putValue(Action.NAME, "Bold");
```

  ➢ Add action object to the desired menu object (**myMenu**):

```
myMenu.add(boldAction);
```

Using action objects eliminates the need for menu item objects and associated **actionPerformed** methods. Once an action object is added to a menu, use is simple: select some text in the text pane and choose a menu item with an assigned action. Once chosen, the indicated action is taken – you don't need to write any code!!

The above example shows hold to set text to bold. Other actions we can use are:

```
ItalicAction()        italicize text
UnderlineAction()     underline text
```

Note we couldn't underline text with the text area control.

To change the selected text font size, we use the **FontSizeAction**. There are two steps (here, we change the **size** to **12**):

> ➢ Create the action object (include text value for menu item):

```
Action smallAction = new
StyledEditorKit.FontSizeAction("Small", 12);
```

> ➢ Add action object to your desired menu (**myMenu**):

```
myMenu.add(smallAction);
```

Action objects can also have assigned accelerator keys. The syntax uses the **putValue** method. If the action is **myAction**, an accelerator key is assigned using

```
myAction.putValue(Action.ACCELERATOR_KEY, keyStroke);
```

where **keyStroke** is the desired **KeyStroke** object.

Saving and opening files with the text pane control uses simple coding when compared to the text area, where we needed to count lines. To save the text in a text pane control (**myTextPane**) in a file named as **myFile**, use (in a **try/catch** loop, of course):

```
myWriter = new FileWriter(myFile);
myTextPane.write(myWriter);
```

and to open such a file and load the contents into the control, use:

```
myReader = new FileReader(myFile);
myTextPane.read(myReader, null);
```

But, wait there is a problem! This code will not preserve any formatting applied to the text, it will only save and read the actual text. Some tricky code is required to save both the text and the formatting features.

The use of actions and how to open and save files with a text pane control is illustrated in **Example 9-1** that follows. We have only scratched the surface for using the text pane control. If you are interested in such a control, do some further research. One topic we don't address is how to save, and then reopen a text file (including formatting) created using the text pane control.

Typical use of **text area** control as input device:

> ➤ Declare and create text area, assigning an identifiable **name**. For **myTextPane**, the statement is:

```
JTextPane myTextPane = new JTextPane();
```

> ➤ Place text pane control in properly sized scroll pane control.
> ➤ Initialize **text** property to desired string.
> ➤ Place control within layout manager.
> ➤ In code, give **focus** (use **requestFocus** method) to control when needed. Read **text** property when desired.
> ➤ You may also want to change the **background** property.

Example 9-1

Note Editor (Revisited)

In this project, we will modify the last incarnation of the **Note Editor** project (**Example 6-8**) to allow selective formatting of text (bold, italic, underline, font size). The text area control will be replaced by a text pane control. Follow these steps for modification:

1. Open **Example 6-8** in NetBeans. Open **NoteEditor.java**, highlight the contents of the entire file, select **Edit** from the menu and choose **Copy**. At this point, a copy of the Java code is on your clipboard.

2. Start a new empty project in **NetBeans**. Name the project **NewNoteEditor**. Delete default code in Java file named **NewNoteEditor** – rename the file **NoteEditor**. Go to that empty file, select **Edit** from the menu and choose **Paste**. You now have a copy of the file to modify in your new project.

Try compiling and running the project to make sure it copied successfully. It should look like this:

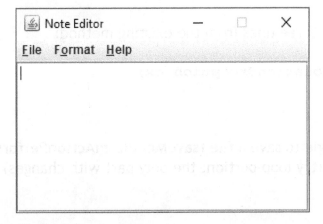

Review how any text formatting affects all text in the text area.

3. Now, we will modify the code. Add this **import** statement:

```
import javax.swing.text.*;
```

4. Change the text area object to a text pane with this declaration:

```
JTextPane editorTextPane = new JTextPane();
```

Correspondingly, change all references to **editorTextArea** to **editorTextPane**. Remove lines setting **lineWrap** and **wrapStyleWord** properties of old text area control (these properties are not used by the text pane).

5. Rewrite the code to open a file (**openMenuItemActionPerformed** method). The new code (**try** loop portion, the only part with changes) is (changes are shaded):

```
try
{
  // Open output file and write
  FileWriter outputFile = new FileWriter(fileName);
  editorTextPane.write(outputFile);
  outputFile.flush();
  outputFile.close();
}
```

Also, delete these three lines from the existing method:

```
catch (BadLocationException ex)
{
}
```

6. Rewrite the code to save a file (**saveMenuItemActionPerformed** method). The new code (**try** loop portion, the only part with changes) is (changes are shaded):

```
try
{
  // Open output file and write
  FileWriter outputFile = new FileWriter(fileName);
  editorTextPane.write(outputFile);
  outputFile.flush();
  outputFile.close();
}
```

7. Delete code associated with reading and writing the configuration file (in constructor and **exitForm** methods). Such a file is no longer needed since we are selectively formatting text. The modified methods will be very short – just one or two lines each.

8. For each of the following menu items objects: **boldMenuItem, italicMenuItem, smallMenuItem, mediumMenuItem, largeMenuItem**, do the following: (1) delete the line creating the menu item, (2) delete the line assigning an accelerator key, (3) delete the line adding the menu item to its respective menu object, and (4) delete the code adding an action listener to each menu item. Also, delete the **sizeGroup** button group object and lines referring to this group. And, delete the **formatMenuItemActionPerformed** method. Next, all of these deletions will be replaced using newly defined **Action** objects.

9. In code constructing the **NoteEditor** object, after the line adding the **formatMenu** to the menu bar, add these lines of code (new code is shaded):

```
editorMenuBar.add(formatMenu);
Action boldAction = new StyledEditorKit.BoldAction();
boldAction.putValue(Action.NAME, "Bold");
boldAction.putValue(Action.ACCELERATOR_KEY,
KeyStroke.getKeyStroke('B', Event.CTRL_MASK));
formatMenu.add(boldAction);
Action italicAction = new StyledEditorKit.ItalicAction();
italicAction.putValue(Action.NAME, "Italic");
italicAction.putValue(Action.ACCELERATOR_KEY,
KeyStroke.getKeyStroke('I', Event.CTRL_MASK));
formatMenu.add(italicAction);
Action underlineAction = new
StyledEditorKit.UnderlineAction();
underlineAction.putValue(Action.NAME, "Underline");
underlineAction.putValue(Action.ACCELERATOR_KEY,
KeyStroke.getKeyStroke('U', Event.CTRL_MASK));
formatMenu.add(underlineAction);
```

Then, after the **sizeMenu** is added to the **formatMenu**, add these lines (new code is shaded):

```
formatMenu.add(sizeMenu);
Action smallAction = new
StyledEditorKit.FontSizeAction("Small", 12);
smallAction.putValue(Action.ACCELERATOR_KEY,
KeyStroke.getKeyStroke('S', Event.CTRL_MASK));
sizeMenu.add(smallAction);
Action mediumAction = new
StyledEditorKit.FontSizeAction("Medium", 18);
mediumAction.putValue(Action.ACCELERATOR_KEY,
KeyStroke.getKeyStroke('M', Event.CTRL_MASK));
sizeMenu.add(mediumAction);
Action largeAction = new
StyledEditorKit.FontSizeAction("Large", 24);
largeAction.putValue(Action.ACCELERATOR_KEY,
KeyStroke.getKeyStroke('L', Event.CTRL_MASK));
sizeMenu.add(largeAction);
```

This code creates each menu item (**Bold**, **Italic**, **Underline**, a new item, **Small**, **Medium**, **Large**), places them in the menu structure and assigns an action and accelerator key.

For reference, the modified **NoteEditor.java** code listing (all new code is shaded – obviously all the deleted code is missing):

```
/*
 * NoteEditor.java
 */
package noteeditor;
import javax.swing.*;
import javax.swing.filechooser.*;
import javax.swing.text.*;
import java.awt.*;
import java.awt.event.*;
import java.io.*;
public class NoteEditor extends JFrame
{
  JMenuBar editorMenuBar = new JMenuBar();
  JMenu fileMenu = new JMenu("File");
  JMenuItem newMenuItem = new JMenuItem("New");
  JMenuItem openMenuItem = new JMenuItem("Open");
  JMenuItem saveMenuItem = new JMenuItem("Save");
  JMenuItem exitMenuItem = new JMenuItem("Exit");
  JMenu formatMenu = new JMenu("Format");
```

```java
    JMenu sizeMenu = new JMenu("Size");
    JMenu helpMenu = new JMenu("Help");
    JMenuItem aboutMenuItem = new JMenuItem("About Note
Editor");
    JScrollPane editorPane = new JScrollPane();
    JTextPane editorTextPane = new JTextPane();
    JFileChooser myChooser = new JFileChooser();
    public static void main(String args[])
    {
      // construct frame
      new NoteEditor().show();
    }
    public NoteEditor()
    {
      // frame constructor
      setTitle("Note Editor");
      setResizable(false);
      addWindowListener(new WindowAdapter()
      {
        public void windowClosing(WindowEvent e)
        {
          exitForm(e);
        }
      });
      // build menu
      setJMenuBar(editorMenuBar);
      fileMenu.setMnemonic('F');
      formatMenu.setMnemonic('O');
      helpMenu.setMnemonic('H');
      newMenuItem.setAccelerator(KeyStroke.getKeyStroke('N',
Event.CTRL_MASK));
      editorMenuBar.add(fileMenu);
      fileMenu.add(newMenuItem);
      fileMenu.add(openMenuItem);
      fileMenu.add(saveMenuItem);
      fileMenu.addSeparator();
      fileMenu.add(exitMenuItem);
      editorMenuBar.add(formatMenu);
      Action boldAction = new StyledEditorKit.BoldAction();
      boldAction.putValue(Action.NAME, "Bold");
      boldAction.putValue(Action.ACCELERATOR_KEY,
KeyStroke.getKeyStroke('B', Event.CTRL_MASK));
      formatMenu.add(boldAction);
      Action italicAction = new StyledEditorKit.ItalicAction();
      italicAction.putValue(Action.NAME, "Italic");
      italicAction.putValue(Action.ACCELERATOR_KEY,
KeyStroke.getKeyStroke('I', Event.CTRL_MASK));
```

```
    formatMenu.add(italicAction);
    Action underlineAction = new
StyledEditorKit.UnderlineAction();
    underlineAction.putValue(Action.NAME, "Underline");
    underlineAction.putValue(Action.ACCELERATOR_KEY,
KeyStroke.getKeyStroke('U', Event.CTRL_MASK));
    formatMenu.add(underlineAction);
    formatMenu.add(sizeMenu);
    Action smallAction = new
StyledEditorKit.FontSizeAction("Small", 12);
    smallAction.putValue(Action.ACCELERATOR_KEY,
KeyStroke.getKeyStroke('S', Event.CTRL_MASK));
    sizeMenu.add(smallAction);
    Action mediumAction = new
StyledEditorKit.FontSizeAction("Medium", 18);
    mediumAction.putValue(Action.ACCELERATOR_KEY,
KeyStroke.getKeyStroke('M', Event.CTRL_MASK));
    sizeMenu.add(mediumAction);
    Action largeAction = new
StyledEditorKit.FontSizeAction("Large", 24);
    largeAction.putValue(Action.ACCELERATOR_KEY,
KeyStroke.getKeyStroke('L', Event.CTRL_MASK));
    sizeMenu.add(largeAction);
    editorMenuBar.add(helpMenu);
    helpMenu.add(aboutMenuItem);
    newMenuItem.addActionListener(new ActionListener()
    {
      public void actionPerformed(ActionEvent e)
      {
        newMenuItemActionPerformed(e);
      }
    });
    openMenuItem.addActionListener(new ActionListener()
    {
      public void actionPerformed(ActionEvent e)
      {
        openMenuItemActionPerformed(e);
      }
    });
    saveMenuItem.addActionListener(new ActionListener()
    {
      public void actionPerformed(ActionEvent e)
      {
        saveMenuItemActionPerformed(e);
      }
    });
    exitMenuItem.addActionListener(new ActionListener()
```

```
    {
      public void actionPerformed(ActionEvent e)
      {
        exitMenuItemActionPerformed(e);
      }
    });
    aboutMenuItem.addActionListener(new ActionListener()
    {
      public void actionPerformed(ActionEvent e)
      {
        aboutMenuItemActionPerformed(e);
      }
    });
    getContentPane().setLayout(new GridBagLayout());
    // position scroll pane and text box
    GridBagConstraints gridConstraints = new
GridBagConstraints();
    editorPane.setPreferredSize(new Dimension(300, 150));
    editorPane.setViewportView(editorTextPane);
    editorTextPane.setFont(new Font("Arial", Font.PLAIN,
12));
    gridConstraints.gridx = 0;
    gridConstraints.gridy = 0;
    getContentPane().add(editorPane, gridConstraints);
    pack();
    Dimension screenSize =
Toolkit.getDefaultToolkit().getScreenSize();
    setBounds((int) (0.5 * (screenSize.width - getWidth())),
(int) (0.5 * (screenSize.height - getHeight())), getWidth(),
getHeight());
  }
  private void newMenuItemActionPerformed(ActionEvent e)
  {
    // if user wants new file, clear out text
    if (JOptionPane.showConfirmDialog(null, "Are you sure you
want to start a new file?", "New File",
JOptionPane.YES_NO_OPTION, JOptionPane.QUESTION_MESSAGE) ==
JOptionPane.YES_OPTION)
    {
      editorTextPane.setText("");
    }
  }
  private void openMenuItemActionPerformed(ActionEvent e)
  {
    String myLine;
    myChooser.setDialogType(JFileChooser.OPEN_DIALOG);
    myChooser.setDialogTitle("Open Text File");
```

```
      myChooser.addChoosableFileFilter(new
FileNameExtensionFilter("Text Files", "txt"));
      if (myChooser.showOpenDialog(this) ==
JFileChooser.APPROVE_OPTION)
      {
        try
        {
          // Open input file
          FileReader inputFile = new
FileReader(myChooser.getSelectedFile().toString());
          editorTextPane.read(inputFile, null);
          inputFile.close();
        }
        catch (IOException ex)
        {
            JOptionPane.showConfirmDialog(null, ex.getMessage(),
"Error Opening File", JOptionPane.DEFAULT_OPTION,
JOptionPane.ERROR_MESSAGE);
        }
      }
   }
  private void saveMenuItemActionPerformed(ActionEvent e)
  {
    myChooser.setDialogType(JFileChooser.SAVE_DIALOG);
    myChooser.setDialogTitle("Save Text File");
    myChooser.addChoosableFileFilter(new
FileNameExtensionFilter("Text Files", "txt"));
    int fp, lp;
    if (myChooser.showSaveDialog(this) ==
JFileChooser.APPROVE_OPTION)
      {
      // see if file already exists
      if (myChooser.getSelectedFile().exists())
      {
        int response;
        response = JOptionPane.showConfirmDialog(null,
myChooser.getSelectedFile().toString() + " exists.
Overwrite?", "Confirm Save", JOptionPane.YES_NO_OPTION,
JOptionPane.QUESTION_MESSAGE);
        if (response == JOptionPane.NO_OPTION)
        {
          return;
        }
      }
      // make sure file has txt extension
      // strip off any extension that might be there
      // then tack on txt
```

```java
    String fileName =
myChooser.getSelectedFile().toString();
    int dotlocation = fileName.indexOf(".");
    if (dotlocation == -1)
    {
      // no extension
      fileName += ".txt";
    }
    else
    {
      // make sure extension is txt
      fileName = fileName.substring(0, dotlocation) +
".txt";
    }
    try
    {
      // Open output file and write
      FileWriter outputFile = new FileWriter(fileName);
      editorTextPane.write(outputFile);
      outputFile.flush();
      outputFile.close();
    }
    catch (IOException ex)
    {
      JOptionPane.showConfirmDialog(null,
ex.getMessage(),"Error Writing File",
JOptionPane.DEFAULT_OPTION, JOptionPane.ERROR_MESSAGE);
    }
  }
}
private void exitMenuItemActionPerformed(ActionEvent e)
{
  exitForm(null);
}
```

```
private void aboutMenuItemActionPerformed(ActionEvent e)
{
   JOptionPane.showConfirmDialog(null, "About Note
Editor\nCopyright 2003", "Note Editor",
JOptionPane.DEFAULT_OPTION, JOptionPane.INFORMATION_MESSAGE);
}
private void exitForm(WindowEvent e)
{
     System.exit(0);
}
}
```

Run the modified **Note Editor**. Type some text in the text pane. Select a section of text and change the style or size. Notice you can format as many text selections as your desire. Try the menu items and the accelerator keys. Notice we never wrote any code to do any formatting – the **Action** objects are automatic, like magic. Try saving and opening files – note, as mentioned, the formatting is not saved. Here's some text I formatted with the different features:

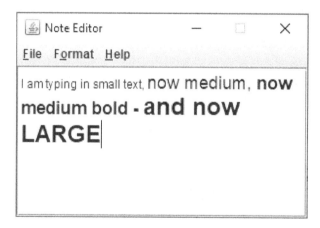

Save your project (saved as **Example9-1** project in the **\LearnJava\LJ Code\Class 9** project group). Run the application.

JToolBar Control

Almost all GUI applications these days use toolbars. A toolbar provides quick access to the most frequently used menu commands in an application. The **JToolBar** control provides everything you need to design and implement a toolbar into your application. Possible uses for this control include: provide a consistent interface between applications with matching toolbars, place commonly used functions in an easily-accessed space and provide an intuitive, graphical interface for your application.

Toolbar Properties:

background	Toolbar background color.
floatable	Indicates whether toolbar is fixed in position or can be repositioned by the user.

Toolbar Methods:

add	Add components to toolbar.
setBackground	Sets the text pane background color.
setFloatable	If set to false, toolbar cannot be moved.

Toolbars are container objects that can hold other controls, usually holding just **button** controls. Clicking a button causes some action to occur. The buttons on a toolbar feature a graphic **icon** depicting the corresponding action and a **tooltip** that describes what the button does. Tooltips are text prompts that appear when the mouse hovers over a control for a couple of seconds. We will look at how to add icons and tooltips to button controls, then how to place the button on a toolbar. We will also look at how to assign some action or code to a corresponding button. Since toolbar buttons provide quick access to already coded menu options, we can just use existing code or **Action** objects. We look at two approaches: (1) add a button with no corresponding **Action** object; (2) add a button with an **Action** object.

If a toolbar button is to represent a menu item with no action object, we first create a button object and set the **Icon** and **ToolTipText** properties. If the button is named **myButton**, the code that does these steps is:

```
JButton myButton = new JButton(new ImageIcon(myImage));
myButton.setToolTipText(myText);
```

In this code, **myImage** is the graphic file containing the image to display on the button and **myText** (**String**) is the corresponding tooltip text. Once created, the button is added to the toolbar (**myToolbar**) in the desired position using the **add** method:

```
myToolbar.add(myButton);
```

Buttons are added to a toolbar in the desired order. Lastly, to connect the button to code with the desired action, a typical listener is needed:

```
myButton.addActionListener(new ActionListener()
{
  public void actionPerformed(ActionEvent e)
  {
        [Java code]
  }
});
```

Again, since toolbar buttons replicate existing menu items, the code in this method would simply be an application of the **doClick** method on the corresponding menu item.

If a toolbar button is to represent a menu item with an already defined action object, our task is a bit easier. The action object may or may not have an icon or tooltip defined. If it does, great. If not, follow these two steps to add an icon and tooltip to an existing action (**myAction**):

```
myAction.putValue(Action.SMALL_ICON, new
ImageIcon(myImage));
myAction.putValue(Action.SHORT_DESCRIPTION, myText);
```

Then, you add the action to the toolbar:

```
myToolbar.add(myAction);
```

This will create a button and assign the corresponding action to that button. No coding is needed! That's the beauty of action objects.

Many times, you like to have some space between groups of toolbar buttons. Such space is obtained using the **addSeparator** method:

```
myToolbar.addSeparator();
```

You may be wondering where the toolbar graphics come from. Each icon should be a 16 x 16 or 24 x 24 **gif** file. You can create such a file in a paintbrush program or borrow someone else's icons. In these notes, we will use a set of icons created by the folks at Java that meet what they call their "look and feel" standards. Such standards were developed to give a common look to GUI applications, no matter what platform they run on. These graphics can be found at:

http://www.oracle.com/technetwork/java/index-138612.html

You can copy and paste the files from this website to your computer. I usually store my toolbar icons in the corresponding project folder - you decide where you want to store them, adjusting your code to point to the proper folder.

Typical use of **Toolbar** control:

> ➢ Declare and create toolbar, assigning an identifiable **name**. For **myToolbar**, the statement is:

```
JToolbar myToolbar = new JToolbar();
```

> ➢ Add buttons using above described procedures (use appropriate icon and tooltips and method code, if needed).
> ➢ Place control within layout manager. It is usually placed just under the menu bar, filling the entire width of the frame.
> ➢ You may also want to change the **background** property.

Example 9-2

Note Editor Toolbar

In this example, we'll add a toolbar to our **Note Editor**, by modifying **Example 9-1**. The toolbar will have six buttons: one to create a **new** file, one to **open** a file, one to **save** a file, one to **bold** text, one to **italicize** text and one to **underline** text. All the graphics files are included in the **\LearnJava\LJ Code\Class 9\Example9-2** folder. Copy these graphic files (from the Java website) into your project's folder:

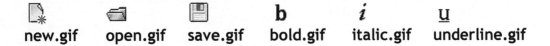

new.gif   open.gif   save.gif   bold.gif   italic.gif   underline.gif

Load Example 9-1. We will list the needed modifications. The finished application will look like this:

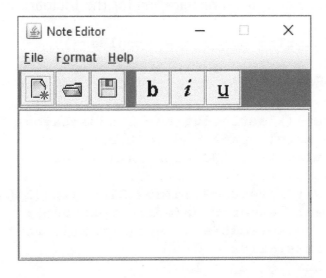

1. Add a toolbar control to the frame. The new **GridBagLayout** is:

	gridx = 0
gridy = 0	editorToolbar
gridy = 1	editorTextPane

Set the following new properties (modified values are shaded):

editorToolbar:

background	BLUE
floatable	false
fill	HORIZONTAL
gridx	0
gridy	0

editorTextPane:

gridy	1

To do this, first add a class level declaration for the toolbar:

```
JToolBar editorToolBar = new JToolBar();
```

Then, in the **NoteEditor** constructor, use this code (new code is shaded):

```
getContentPane().setLayout(new GridBagLayout());
// position scroll pane and text box
GridBagConstraints gridConstraints = new
GridBagConstraints();
editorPane.setPreferredSize(new Dimension(300, 150));
editorPane.setViewportView(editorTextPane);
editorTextPane.setFont(new Font("Arial", Font.PLAIN, 12));
gridConstraints.gridx = 0;
gridConstraints.gridy = 1;
getContentPane().add(editorPane, gridConstraints);

editorToolBar.setFloatable(false);
editorToolBar.setBackground(Color.BLUE);
gridConstraints = new GridBagConstraints();
gridConstraints.fill = GridBagConstraints.HORIZONTAL;
gridConstraints.gridx = 0;
gridConstraints.gridy = 0;
getContentPane().add(editorToolBar, gridConstraints);
```

2. Add six buttons to the toolbar. The first three buttons will be actual controls; the last three will be created from **Action** objects. The two groups will be separated. The first three will have these properties:

newButton:

ImageIcon	new.gif
ToolTipText	New File

openButton:

ImageIcon	open.gif
ToolTipText	Open File

saveButton:

ImageIcon	save.gif
ToolTipText	Save File

To add these to the toolbar, first use these class level declarations:

```
JButton newButton = new JButton(new ImageIcon("new.gif"));
JButton openButton = new JButton(new
ImageIcon("open.gif"));
JButton saveButton = new JButton(new
ImageIcon("save.gif"));
```

Then, for each button, set the tooltip, add the button to the toolbar and add an event listener (clicking the appropriate menu item). This code is placed after the toolbar is positioned in the grid:

```
newButton.setToolTipText("New File");
editorToolBar.add(newButton);
newButton.addActionListener(new ActionListener()
{
  public void actionPerformed(ActionEvent e)
  {
    newMenuItem.doClick();
  }
});
```

```
openButton.setToolTipText("Open File");
editorToolBar.add(openButton);
openButton.addActionListener(new ActionListener()
{
  public void actionPerformed(ActionEvent e)
  {
    openMenuItem.doClick();
  }
});

saveButton.setToolTipText("Save File");
editorToolBar.add(saveButton);
saveButton.addActionListener(new ActionListener()
{
  public void actionPerformed(ActionEvent e)
  {
    saveMenuItem.doClick();
  }
});
```

3. Now, add the 'buttons' represented by existing action objects. The properties are:

boldButton:

ImageIcon	bold.gif
ToolTipText	Bold selected text

italicButton:

ImageIcon	italic.gif
ToolTipText	Italicize selected text

underlineButton:

ImageIcon	underline.gif
ToolTipText	Underline selected text

For each button, establish the action icon and tooltip, and add the action to the toolbar:

```
boldAction.putValue(Action.SMALL_ICON, new
ImageIcon("bold.gif"));
boldAction.putValue(Action.SHORT_DESCRIPTION, "Bold
selected text");
editorToolBar.add(boldAction);
```

```
italicAction.putValue(Action.SMALL_ICON, new
ImageIcon("italic.gif"));
italicAction.putValue(Action.SHORT_DESCRIPTION, "Italicize
selected text");
editorToolBar.add(italicAction);

underlineAction.putValue(Action.SMALL_ICON, new
ImageIcon("underline.gif"));
underlineAction.putValue(Action.SHORT_DESCRIPTION,
"Underline selected text");
editorToolBar.add(underlineAction);
```

Recall the add method will create a button to represent the corresponding action.

The modified, complete **NoteEditor.java** code listing (changes are shaded):

```
/*
 * NoteEditor.java
 */
package noteeditor;
import javax.swing.*;
import javax.swing.filechooser.*;
import javax.swing.text.*;
import java.awt.*;
import java.awt.event.*;
import java.io.*;

public class NoteEditor extends JFrame
{
  JMenuBar editorMenuBar = new JMenuBar();
  JMenu fileMenu = new JMenu("File");
  JMenuItem newMenuItem = new JMenuItem("New");
  JMenuItem openMenuItem = new JMenuItem("Open");
  JMenuItem saveMenuItem = new JMenuItem("Save");
  JMenuItem exitMenuItem = new JMenuItem("Exit");
  JMenu formatMenu = new JMenu("Format");
  JMenu sizeMenu = new JMenu("Size");
  JMenu helpMenu = new JMenu("Help");
  JMenuItem aboutMenuItem = new JMenuItem("About Note
Editor");
  JScrollPane editorPane = new JScrollPane();
  JTextPane editorTextPane = new JTextPane();
  JFileChooser myChooser = new JFileChooser();
  JToolBar editorToolBar = new JToolBar();
  JButton newButton = new JButton(new ImageIcon("new.gif"));
```

```
   JButton openButton = new JButton(new
ImageIcon("open.gif"));
   JButton saveButton = new JButton(new
ImageIcon("save.gif"));

  public static void main(String args[])
  {
    // construct frame
    new NoteEditor().show();
  }

  public NoteEditor()
  {
    // frame constructor
    setTitle("Note Editor");

    setResizable(false);
    addWindowListener(new WindowAdapter()
    {
      public void windowClosing(WindowEvent e)
      {
        exitForm(e);
      }
    });

    // build menu
    setJMenuBar(editorMenuBar);
    fileMenu.setMnemonic('F');
    formatMenu.setMnemonic('O');
    helpMenu.setMnemonic('H');
    newMenuItem.setAccelerator(KeyStroke.getKeyStroke('N',
Event.CTRL_MASK));
    editorMenuBar.add(fileMenu);
    fileMenu.add(newMenuItem);
    fileMenu.add(openMenuItem);
    fileMenu.add(saveMenuItem);
    fileMenu.addSeparator();
    fileMenu.add(exitMenuItem);
    editorMenuBar.add(formatMenu);
    Action boldAction = new StyledEditorKit.BoldAction();
    boldAction.putValue(Action.NAME, "Bold");
    boldAction.putValue(Action.ACCELERATOR_KEY,
KeyStroke.getKeyStroke('B', Event.CTRL_MASK));
    formatMenu.add(boldAction);
    Action italicAction = new StyledEditorKit.ItalicAction();
    italicAction.putValue(Action.NAME, "Italic");
```

```
      italicAction.putValue(Action.ACCELERATOR_KEY,
KeyStroke.getKeyStroke('I', Event.CTRL_MASK));
    formatMenu.add(italicAction);
    Action underlineAction = new
StyledEditorKit.UnderlineAction();
    underlineAction.putValue(Action.NAME, "Underline");
    underlineAction.putValue(Action.ACCELERATOR_KEY,
KeyStroke.getKeyStroke('U', Event.CTRL_MASK));
    formatMenu.add(underlineAction);
    formatMenu.add(sizeMenu);
    Action smallAction = new
StyledEditorKit.FontSizeAction("Small", 12);
    smallAction.putValue(Action.ACCELERATOR_KEY,
KeyStroke.getKeyStroke('S', Event.CTRL_MASK));
    sizeMenu.add(smallAction);
    Action mediumAction = new
StyledEditorKit.FontSizeAction("Medium", 18);
    mediumAction.putValue(Action.ACCELERATOR_KEY,
KeyStroke.getKeyStroke('M', Event.CTRL_MASK));
    sizeMenu.add(mediumAction);
    Action largeAction = new
StyledEditorKit.FontSizeAction("Large", 24);
    largeAction.putValue(Action.ACCELERATOR_KEY,
KeyStroke.getKeyStroke('L', Event.CTRL_MASK));
    sizeMenu.add(largeAction);
    editorMenuBar.add(helpMenu);
    helpMenu.add(aboutMenuItem);
    newMenuItem.addActionListener(new ActionListener()
    {
      public void actionPerformed(ActionEvent e)
      {
        newMenuItemActionPerformed(e);
      }
    });
    openMenuItem.addActionListener(new ActionListener()
    {
      public void actionPerformed(ActionEvent e)
      {
        openMenuItemActionPerformed(e);
      }
    });
    saveMenuItem.addActionListener(new ActionListener()
    {
      public void actionPerformed(ActionEvent e)
      {
        saveMenuItemActionPerformed(e);
      }
```

```
        });
        exitMenuItem.addActionListener(new ActionListener()
        {
          public void actionPerformed(ActionEvent e)
          {
            exitMenuItemActionPerformed(e);
          }
        });
        aboutMenuItem.addActionListener(new ActionListener()
        {
          public void actionPerformed(ActionEvent e)
          {
            aboutMenuItemActionPerformed(e);
          }
        });

        getContentPane().setLayout(new GridBagLayout());
        // position scroll pane and text box
        GridBagConstraints gridConstraints = new
GridBagConstraints();
        editorPane.setPreferredSize(new Dimension(300, 150));
        editorPane.setViewportView(editorTextPane);
        editorTextPane.setFont(new Font("Arial", Font.PLAIN,
12));
        gridConstraints.gridx = 0;
        gridConstraints.gridy = 1;
        getContentPane().add(editorPane, gridConstraints);

        editorToolBar.setFloatable(false);
        editorToolBar.setBackground(Color.BLUE);
        gridConstraints = new GridBagConstraints();
        gridConstraints.fill = GridBagConstraints.HORIZONTAL;
        gridConstraints.gridx = 0;
        gridConstraints.gridy = 0;
        getContentPane().add(editorToolBar, gridConstraints);

        newButton.setToolTipText("New File");
        editorToolBar.add(newButton);
        newButton.addActionListener(new ActionListener()
        {
          public void actionPerformed(ActionEvent e)
          {
            newMenuItem.doClick();
          }
        });

        openButton.setToolTipText("Open File");
```

```
      editorToolBar.add(openButton);
      openButton.addActionListener(new ActionListener()
      {
        public void actionPerformed(ActionEvent e)
        {
          openMenuItem.doClick();
        }
      });

      saveButton.setToolTipText("Save File");
      editorToolBar.add(saveButton);
      saveButton.addActionListener(new ActionListener()
      {
        public void actionPerformed(ActionEvent e)
        {
          saveMenuItem.doClick();
        }
      });

      editorToolBar.addSeparator();

      boldAction.putValue(Action.SMALL_ICON, new
ImageIcon("bold.gif"));
      boldAction.putValue(Action.SHORT_DESCRIPTION, "Bold
selected text");
      editorToolBar.add(boldAction);

      italicAction.putValue(Action.SMALL_ICON, new
ImageIcon("italic.gif"));
      italicAction.putValue(Action.SHORT_DESCRIPTION,
"Italicize selected text");
      editorToolBar.add(italicAction);

      underlineAction.putValue(Action.SMALL_ICON, new
ImageIcon("underline.gif"));
      underlineAction.putValue(Action.SHORT_DESCRIPTION,
"Underline selected text");
      editorToolBar.add(underlineAction);

    pack();
    Dimension screenSize =
Toolkit.getDefaultToolkit().getScreenSize();
      setBounds((int) (0.5 * (screenSize.width - getWidth())),
(int) (0.5 * (screenSize.height - getHeight())), getWidth(),
getHeight());

  }
```

```
  private void newMenuItemActionPerformed(ActionEvent e)
  {
     // if user wants new file, clear out text
     if (JOptionPane.showConfirmDialog(null, "Are you sure you
want to start a new file?", "New File",
JOptionPane.YES_NO_OPTION, JOptionPane.QUESTION_MESSAGE) ==
JOptionPane.YES_OPTION)
     {
        editorTextPane.setText("");
     }
  }
  private void openMenuItemActionPerformed(ActionEvent e)
  {
     String myLine;
     myChooser.setDialogType(JFileChooser.OPEN_DIALOG);
     myChooser.setDialogTitle("Open Text File");
     myChooser.addChoosableFileFilter(new
FileNameExtensionFilter("Text Files", "txt"));
     if (myChooser.showOpenDialog(this) ==
JFileChooser.APPROVE_OPTION)
     {
        try
        {
           // Open input file
           FileReader inputFile = new
FileReader(myChooser.getSelectedFile().toString());
           editorTextPane.read(inputFile, null);
           inputFile.close();
        }
        catch (IOException ex)
        {
           JOptionPane.showConfirmDialog(null, ex.getMessage(),
"Error Opening File", JOptionPane.DEFAULT_OPTION,
JOptionPane.ERROR_MESSAGE);
        }
     }
  }
  private void saveMenuItemActionPerformed(ActionEvent e)
  {
     myChooser.setDialogType(JFileChooser.SAVE_DIALOG);
     myChooser.setDialogTitle("Save Text File");
     myChooser.addChoosableFileFilter(new
FileNameExtensionFilter("Text Files", "txt"));
     int fp, lp;
     if (myChooser.showSaveDialog(this) ==
JFileChooser.APPROVE_OPTION)
     {
```

```java
      // see if file already exists
      if (myChooser.getSelectedFile().exists())
      {
        int response;
        response = JOptionPane.showConfirmDialog(null,
myChooser.getSelectedFile().toString() + " exists.
Overwrite?", "Confirm Save", JOptionPane.YES_NO_OPTION,
JOptionPane.QUESTION_MESSAGE);
        if (response == JOptionPane.NO_OPTION)
        {
          return;
        }
      }
      // make sure file has txt extension
      // strip off any extension that might be there
      // then tack on txt
      String fileName =
myChooser.getSelectedFile().toString();
      int dotlocation = fileName.indexOf(".");
      if (dotlocation == -1)
      {
        // no extension
        fileName += ".txt";
      }
      else
      {
        // make sure extension is txt
        fileName = fileName.substring(0, dotlocation) +
".txt";
      }
      try
      {
        // Open output file and write
        FileWriter outputFile = new FileWriter(fileName);
        editorTextPane.write(outputFile);
        outputFile.flush();
        outputFile.close();
      }
      catch (IOException ex)
      {
        JOptionPane.showConfirmDialog(null,
ex.getMessage(),"Error Writing File",
JOptionPane.DEFAULT_OPTION, JOptionPane.ERROR_MESSAGE);
      }
    }
  }
```

```
private void exitMenuItemActionPerformed(ActionEvent e)
{
  exitForm(null);
}


private void aboutMenuItemActionPerformed(ActionEvent e)
{
   JOptionPane.showConfirmDialog(null, "About Note
Editor\nCopyright 2003", "Note Editor",
JOptionPane.DEFAULT_OPTION, JOptionPane.INFORMATION_MESSAGE);
  }

private void exitForm(WindowEvent e)
{
     System.exit(0);
}
}
```

Run the new project. Make sure all the toolbar buttons work properly. Check out how the tool tips work. Notice you now have three ways to format – menu items, toolbar buttons, and accelerator keys. Here is some formatting I did:

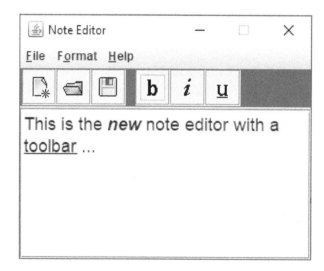

Save the project (saved as **Example9-2** project in the **\LearnJava\LJ Code\Class 9** project group).

More Swing Controls

This completes our look at Swing controls for this particular class. We covered most, but not all, of the controls. Here, we briefly describe some of the other Swing controls available. You decide if you'd like to learn more about how to use such controls. The code for the examples shown is available from the Java website:

http://download.oracle.com/javase/tutorial/uiswing/components/index.html

The **JSplitPane** control displays two components, either side by side or one on top of the other. By dragging the divider that appears between the components, the user can specify how much of the split pane's total area goes to each component. Here's a picture of an application that uses a split pane to display a list and an image side by side:

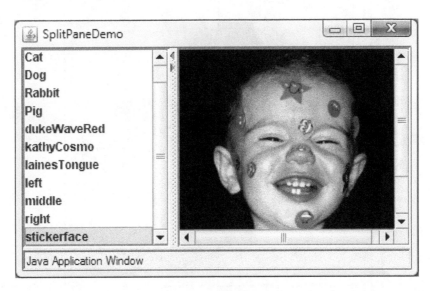

A **layered pane** is a Swing container that provides a third dimension for positioning components: depth, also known as Z order. When adding a component to a layered pane, you specify its depth as an integer. The higher the number, the higher the depth. If components overlap, components at a higher depth are drawn on top of components at a lower depth. The relationship between components at the same depth is determined by their positions within the depth. Here's a picture of an application that creates a layered pane and places overlapping, colored labels at different depths:

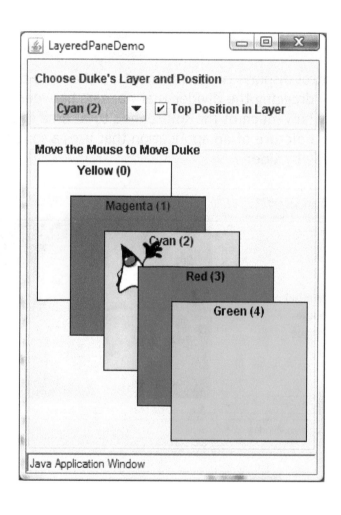

With the **JInternalFrame** control you can display a **JFrame** window within another window. Here is a picture of an application that has two internal frames (one of which is iconified) inside a regular frame:

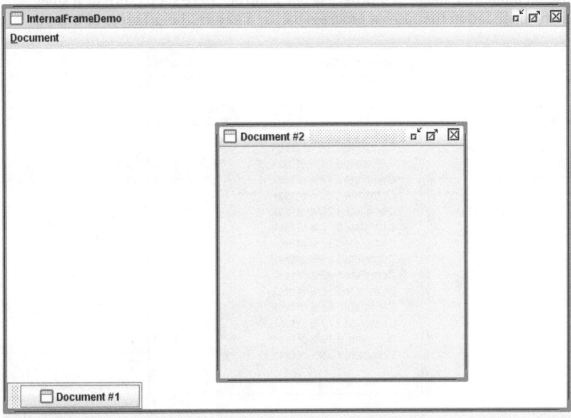

Java Application Window

Sometimes a task running within a program might take a while to complete. A user-friendly program provides some indication to the user that the task is occurring, how long the task might take, and how much work has already been done. One way of indicating work, and perhaps the amount of progress, is to use an animated image in a **progress bar** control. Here's a picture of a small demo application that uses a progress bar to measure the progress of a task:

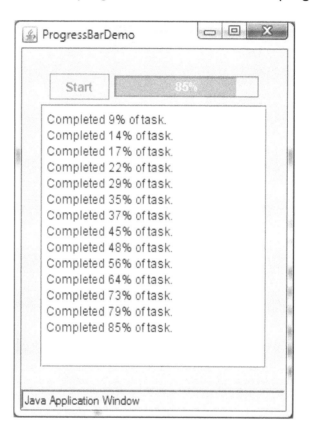

With the **JTree** control, you can display hierarchical data. A **JTree** object doesn't actually contain your data; it simply provides a view of the data. The tree gets data by querying something called a data model. Here is a picture of an application, the top half of which displays a tree in a scroll pane:

With the **JTable** control you can display tables of data, optionally allowing the user to edit the data. **JTable** doesn't contain or cache data; it's simply a view of your data. Here's a picture of a typical table displayed within a scroll pane:

First Name	Last Name	Sport	# of Years	Vegetarian
Kathy	Smith	Snowboarding	5	false
John	Doe	Rowing	3	true
Sue	Black	Knitting	2	false
Jane	White	Speed reading	20	true
Joe	Brown	Pool	10	false

SimpleTableDemo

Java Application Window

Use the **JColorChooser** control to provide users with a palette of colors to choose from. A color chooser is a component that you can place anywhere within your program's GUI. Here's a picture of an application that uses a color chooser to set the text color in a banner:

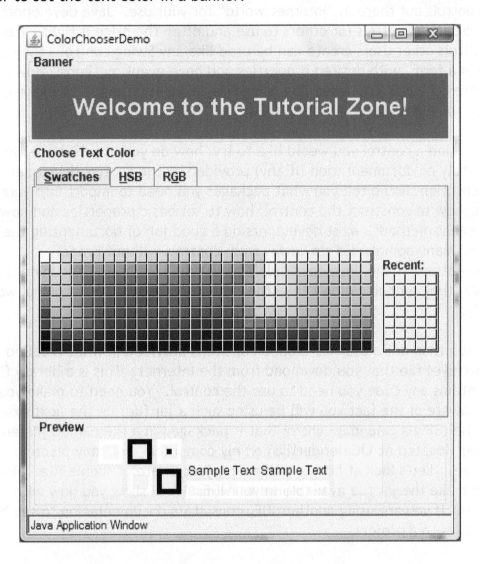

Even More Controls

If you can't find a Swing control that does a task you need, there is a wealth of other controls out there in "Internet world" for your use. Java developers are always creating controls for others to use and often the price is right – free! The controls other users create can be used like any Swing control – they can be placed in a form, with desired properties and have event methods. How do you find these controls? Use a search engine like Google or Yahoo. Use keywords for the task you are trying to accomplish.

Once you find a control you would like to try, how do you use it? Here, you need to rely on documentation (if any) provided by the control developer. The documentation should tell you what packages you need to import into your project, how to construct the control, how to set basic properties and how to access event methods. Most developers do a good job of documenting their controls. Many do not. I'd stay away from controls without proper documentation. If the developer didn't have time to properly document his or her work, they probably didn't take the time to make sure their control works properly.

More often than not a user-developed control is provided in what is called a **jar** (Java archive) file that you download from the Internet. This is a library file that contains any code you need to use the control. You need to make your project aware of the fact you will be using such a jar file. In the next example, we will be using a calendar control that is packaged in a file named **jcalendar-1.3.3.jar** (located at **\JCalendar\lib** on my computer – you may place it elsewhere). Let's look at how to make a project aware of such a file. First, we need to make the jar file available in your IDE. We'll show you how with NetBeans. If you are using another IDE, consult its documentation to see how to add jar files to a project.

In **NetBeans**, the steps to add a **jar** file to its available library are:

In the menu, choose **Tools**, then **Libaries** to see:

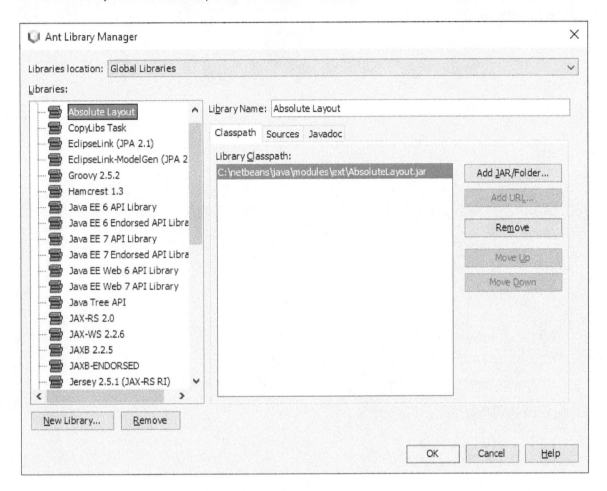

Click **New Library** and name it **Calendar**:

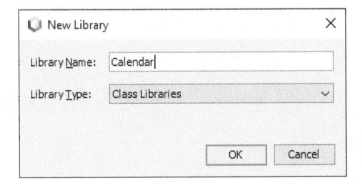

Click **OK** to accept name. In next window, click **Add JAR/Folder**. Navigate to jar location:

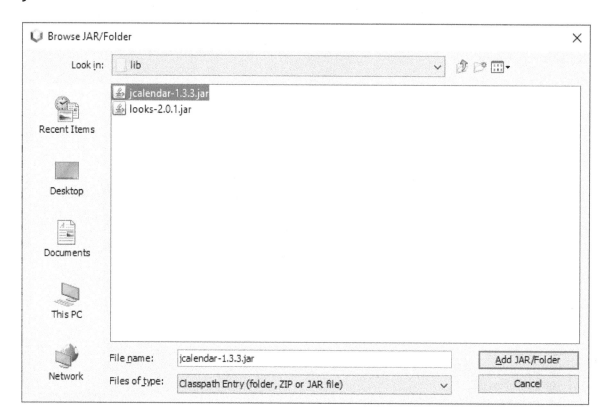

Click **Add JAR/Folder**.

Library is now there:

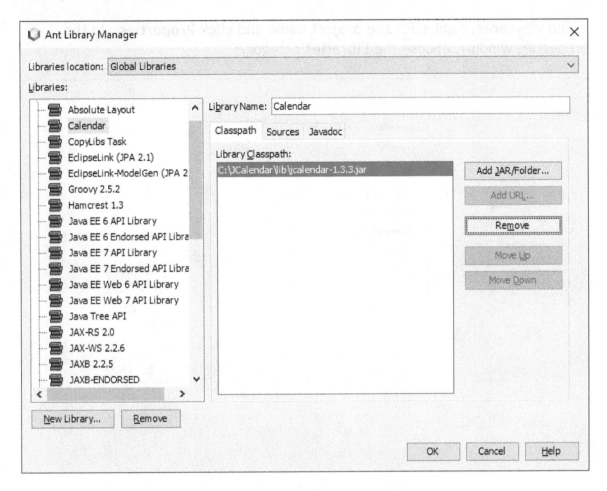

The **Calendar** library can now be added to any project that needs it. Click **OK**.

To add an archived library to a project, follow these steps:

In file view area, right-click the project name and click **Properties**. In the
properties window, choose the **Libraries** category:

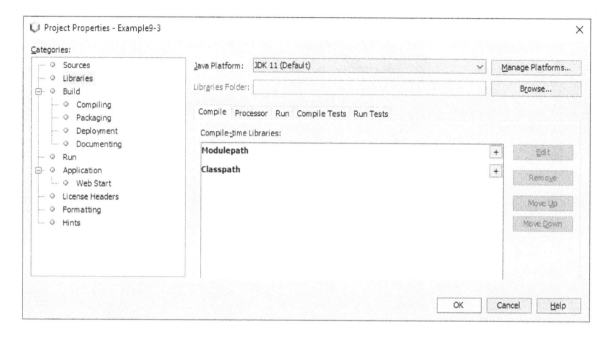

Click the + sign to the right of **Classpath** and select **Add Library** to see

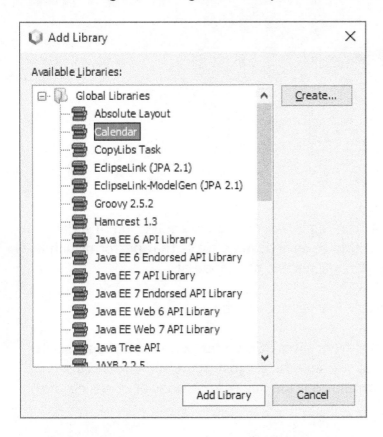

Choose **Calendar**, then click **Add Library**. Click **OK** when returned to the **Properties** window.

Now, the library file(s) and any associated controls or code can be used by your project. You will also need to add an **import** statement to your Java code to use the control – consult the control's documentation for the form of that statement.

When using controls from other programmers, always be aware they may not be complete or even correct. Carefully read the documentation provided by the programmer to insure you are using their control correctly. Most controls work just fine, but be careful. If something is free, many times you get what you pay for. The control we present here seems to work well. There are a few minor annoyances, but again it is a free product.

Calendar Control

The Java Swing library does not have a control that allows selection of a date. A quick search of the Internet will find several Java controls that perform such a task. The calendar control we present here is described at:

http://www.toedter.com/

It is written by Kai Toedter and is free. This **JCalendar** control allows a user to select a date. It is a very easy to use interface – just point and click. This control is useful for ordering information, making reservations or choosing the current date.

To add the control to your computer, go to the above referenced website. On the page, you will find a link to download the zipped control (a file named **jcalendar-1.3.3.zip** – there may be a newer version). The zip file can also be found in the **\LearnJava\LJ Code\Class 9** folder. Download the file and extract (unzip) the files to a directory on your computer (I used **c:\JCalendar**). Many files will be written to your computer, including documentation and source files. The actual jar file (**jcalendar-1.3.3.jar**) will be in the **lib** subfolder. Using the steps in the last section, add this file to the available libraries in NetBeans. It can then be used in any of your Java projects. To use the calendar requires this import statement:

```
import com.toedter.calendar.*;
```

The calendar control is made up of three components a **MonthChooser**, a **DayChooser** and a **YearChooser**:

Operation is simple. A month is selected either from the drop-down box or by clicking the spinner arrows. A day is selected by clicking the desired box. A year is selected using the spinner arrows or by typing a value. By default, a calendar for the current month is displayed initially.

Calendar Properties:

font	Font name, style, size.
background	Calendar background color.

Calendar Methods:

setFont	Sets font name, style, size.
setBackground	Sets the calendar background color.
getDayChooser	Returns calendar DayChooser
getMonthChooser	Returns calendar MonthChooser.
getYearChooser	Returns calendar YearChooser.

Calendar Event:

propertyChange   Event (**PropertyChangeEvent**) triggered when the selected date changes. Added with **PropertyChangeListener** (requires importation of **java.beans.*** files).

To add a listener for such a **propertyChange** event to a calendar control named **myCalendar**, use:

```
myCalendar.addPropertyChangeListener(new
PropertyChangeListener()
{
  public void propertyChange(PropertyChangeEvent e)
  {
    myCalendarPropertyChange(e);
  }
});
```

And, the corresponding event code would be placed in a **myCalendarPropertyChange** method:

```
private void myCalendarPropertyChange(PropertyChangeEvent
e)
{
   [method code]
}
```

Two tasks you usually want to do with a calendar control are to retrieve the displayed date and to set the date. The three components of the date (**month, day, year**) are individually retrieved and set, allowing flexibility in how the values are used. To retrieve the displayed month for a calendar control named **myCalendar**, use:

```
myCalendar.getMonthChooser().getMonth();
```

This method returns an integer value from 0 (January) to 11 (December). This value can be used to establish a month name or a month value for other Java date methods. Java methods usually expect a month value to go from 1 to 12, not 0 to 11 – be aware (this is one of the things I don't like about this control). To retrieve, the day value (an **int** type), use:

```
myCalendar.getDayChooser().getDay();
```

And, the year (**int**) is retrieved using:

```
myCalendar.getYearChooser().getYear();
```

A calendar date is established using the **setMonth, setDay** and **setYear** methods:

```
myCalendar.getMonthChooser().setMonth(myMonth);
myCalendar.getDayChooser().setDay(myDay);
myCalendar.getYearChooser().setYear(myYear);
```

where **myMonth, myDay** and **myYear** are all **int** types. Recall **myMonth** must lie between 0 and 11.

Typical use of **Calendar** control:

➢ Declare and create calendar control, assigning an identifiable **name**. For **myCalendar**, the code is:

```
JCalendar myCalendar = new JCalendar();
```

➢ Place control in layout manager.
➢ Initialize date if desired (default display is today's date).
➢ Add listener for and monitor **propertyChange** event for changes in value.
➢ Use **getMonth, getDay and getYear** methods to determine selected date.
➢ You may also choose to change the **font** and **background** properties of the calendar control.

Example 9-3

Date Selection

Start a new empty project in **NetBeans**. Name the project **DateSelection**.
Delete default code in Java file named **DateSelection**. In this project, we'll
look at date selection using the **JCalendar** controls. The finished project will
look like this:

Make sure you have downloaded and unzipped the **jcalendar-1.3.3.zip** file.
Make sure you have also made the archive (**jcalendar-1.3.3.jar**) available for
use in your Java projects. Follow these steps to make the calendar available in
the **Date Selection** project:

In file view area, right-click the project name and click **Properties**. In the
properties window, choose the **Libraries** category. Click **Add Library**. Choose
Calendar, then click **Add Library**. Click **OK** when returned to the **Properties**
window. Expand the project folder structure to see the added library is there

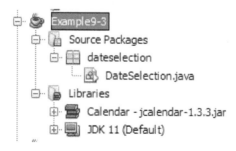

Place a label control and calendar control on the frame. The **GridBagLayout** arrangement is:

	gridx = 0
gridy = 0	**dateLabel**
gridy = 1	**myCalendar**

Properties set in code:

DateSelection Frame:

title	Date Selection
resizable	false

dateLabel:

font	Arial, PLAIN, 18
gridx	0
gridy	0
insets	(10, 10, 10, 10)

myCalendar:

gridx	0
gridy	1
insets	(10, 10, 10, 10)

1. We first build the framework:

```
/*
 * DateSelection.java
 */
package dateselection;
import java.awt.*;
import java.awt.event.*;
import javax.swing.*;
import java.beans.*;
import com.toedter.calendar.*;
public class DateSelection extends JFrame
{
  public static void main(String args[])
  {
    // construct frame
    new DateSelection().show();
  }
  public DateSelection()
  {
    // frame constructor
    setTitle("Date Selection");
    setResizable(false);
    addWindowListener(new WindowAdapter()
    {
      public void windowClosing(WindowEvent e)
      {
        exitForm(e);
      }
    });
    getContentPane().setLayout(new GridBagLayout());

    pack();
    Dimension screenSize =
Toolkit.getDefaultToolkit().getScreenSize();
    setBounds((int) (0.5 * (screenSize.width -
getWidth())), (int) (0.5 * (screenSize.height -
getHeight())), getWidth(), getHeight());
  }
    private void exitForm(WindowEvent e)
  {
      System.exit(0);
  }
}
```

Run to make sure the frame appears.

2. Next, add the controls and the single event method. Declare and create the two controls:

```
JLabel dateLabel = new JLabel();
JCalendar myCalendar = new JCalendar();
```

Position and add the control and change event:

```
GridBagConstraints gridConstraints = new
GridBagConstraints();
dateLabel.setFont(new Font("Arial", Font.PLAIN, 18));
gridConstraints.gridx = 0;
gridConstraints.gridy = 0;
gridConstraints.insets = new Insets(10, 10, 10, 10);
getContentPane().add(dateLabel, gridConstraints);

gridConstraints = new GridBagConstraints();
gridConstraints.gridx = 0;
gridConstraints.gridy = 1;
gridConstraints.insets = new Insets(10, 10, 10, 10);
getContentPane().add(myCalendar, gridConstraints);
myCalendar.addPropertyChangeListener(new
PropertyChangeListener()
{
  public void propertyChange(PropertyChangeEvent e)
  {
    myCalendarPropertyChange(e);
  }
});
```

3. We'll skip checking the project at this point and go right to adding the code - there are only two lines. Use this code in the **propertyChange** event:

```
private void myCalendarPropertyChange(PropertyChangeEvent
e)
{
   String[] monthNames = {"January", "February", "March",
"April", "May", "June", "July", "August", "September",
"October", "November", "December"};

   dateLabel.setText(monthNames[myCalendar.getMonthChooser().
getMonth()] + " " + myCalendar.getDayChooser().getDay() +
", " + myCalendar.getYearChooser().getYear());
}
```

This code simply updates the displayed date when either the selected month, day or year changes. Note the use of the **monthNames** array to convert month **int** value to a name.

The final **DateSelection.java** code listing (code added to basic framework is shaded):

```
/*
 * DateSelection.java
 */
package dateselection;
import java.awt.*;
import java.awt.event.*;
import javax.swing.*;
import java.beans.*;
import com.toedter.calendar.*;


public class DateSelection extends JFrame
{
  JLabel dateLabel = new JLabel();
  JCalendar myCalendar = new JCalendar();

  public static void main(String args[])
  {
    // construct frame
    new DateSelection().show();
  }
  public DateSelection()
  {
    // frame constructor
```

```java
    setTitle("Date Selection");
    setResizable(false);
    addWindowListener(new WindowAdapter()
    {
      public void windowClosing(WindowEvent e)
      {
        exitForm(e);
      }
    });

    getContentPane().setLayout(new GridBagLayout());

    // Position calendar
    GridBagConstraints gridConstraints = new
GridBagConstraints();
    dateLabel.setFont(new Font("Arial", Font.PLAIN, 18));
    gridConstraints.gridx = 0;
    gridConstraints.gridy = 0;
    gridConstraints.insets = new Insets(10, 10, 10, 10);
    getContentPane().add(dateLabel, gridConstraints);

    gridConstraints = new GridBagConstraints();
    gridConstraints.gridx = 0;
    gridConstraints.gridy = 1;
    gridConstraints.insets = new Insets(10, 10, 10, 10);
    getContentPane().add(myCalendar, gridConstraints);
    myCalendar.addPropertyChangeListener(new
PropertyChangeListener()
    {
      public void propertyChange(PropertyChangeEvent e)
      {
        myCalendarPropertyChange(e);
      }
    });

    pack();
    Dimension screenSize =
Toolkit.getDefaultToolkit().getScreenSize();
    setBounds((int) (0.5 * (screenSize.width - getWidth())),
(int) (0.5 * (screenSize.height - getHeight())), getWidth(),
getHeight());

  }

  private void myCalendarPropertyChange(PropertyChangeEvent
e)
  {
```

```
    String[] monthNames = {"January", "February", "March",
"April", "May", "June", "July", "August", "September",
"October", "November", "December"};

dateLabel.setText(monthNames[myCalendar.getMonthChooser().get
Month()] + " " + myCalendar.getDayChooser().getDay() + ", " +
myCalendar.getYearChooser().getYear());
  }

  private void exitForm(WindowEvent e)
  {
      System.exit(0);
  }
}
```

Run the project. Notice how easy it is to select dates for your applications. Here's my birthday (yes, I'm an old guy):

Save your project (saved as **Example9-3** project in the **\LearnJava\LJ Code\Class 9** project group).

Printing with Java

Any serious Java application will use a **printer** to provide the user with a hard copy of any results (text or graphics) they might need. Printing is one of the more tedious programming tasks within Java. But, fortunately, it is straightforward and there are dialog boxes that help with the tasks. We will introduce lots of new topics here. All steps will be reviewed.

To perform printing in Java, we use the **java.awt.print.*** package. The **PrinterJob** class from this package controls the printing process. This class is used to start or cancel a printing job. It can also be used to display dialog boxes when needed. The **Printable** interface from this package is used to represent the item (document) to be printed.

The steps to print a document (which may include text and graphics) using the **PrinterJob** class are:

> ➢ Declare and create a **PrinterJob** object.
> ➢ Point the **PrinterJob** object to a **Printable** class (containing code to print the desired document) using the **setPrintable** method of the **PrinterJob** object.
> ➢ Print the document using the **print** method of the **PrinterJob** object.

These steps are straightforward. To declare and create a **PrinterJob** object named **myPrinterJob**, use:

```
PrinterJob myPrinterJob = PrinterJob.getPrinterJob();
```

If the **Printable** class is named **MyDocument**, the **PrinterJob** is associated with this class using:

```
myPrinterJob.setPrintable(new MyDocument);
```

Once associated, the printing is accomplished using the **print** method:

```
myPrinterJob.print();
```

This **print** method must be enclosed in a **try/catch** (catching a **PrinterException**) block.

The key to printing is the establishment of the **Printable** class, called
MyDocument here. This class describes the document to be printed and is
placed after the main class. The form of this class is:

```
class MyDocument implements Printable
{
  public int print(Graphics g, PageFormat pf, int
pageIndex)
  {
    Graphics2D g2D = (Graphics2D) g;
       .
       .
       .
  }
}
```

This class has a single method, **print**, which is called whenever the **PrinterJob**
object needs information to do its job. In this method, you 'construct' each
page (using Java code) that is to be printed. You'll see the code in this method
is familiar.

Note the **print** method has three arguments. The first argument is a **Graphics**
object **g**. Something familiar! The **Printable** interface provides us with a
graphics object to 'draw' each page we want to print. We cast this to a
Graphics2D object, noting this is the same graphics object we used in Classes 7
and 8 to draw lines, curves, rectangles, ellipses, text and images. And, all the
methods we learned there apply here! We'll look at how to do this in detail
next. The second argument is a **PageFormat** object **pf**, which describes the size
and orientation of the paper being used (we'll see how to modify this later).
Finally, the **pageIndex** argument is the number of the page to print. This
argument is zero-based, meaning the first page has a value of zero.

The **print** method can return one of two constant values:

PAGE_EXISTS	returned if **pageIndex** refers to an existing page
NO_SUCH_PAGE	returned if **pageIndex** refers to a non-existing page

It is <u>very</u> important that **NO_SUCH_PAGE** is returned at some point or your
program will assume there are an infinite number of pages to print!!

Another important thing to remember is that the **print** method may be called more than once per printed page, as the output is buffered to the printer. So, don't build in any assumptions about how often **print** is called for a given page.

Summarizing the printing steps, here is basic Java code (**PrintingExample**) to print a document described by a class **MyDocument**:

```
import javax.swing.*;
import java.awt.*;
import java.awt.print.*;

public class PrintingExample
{
  public static void main(String[] args)
  {
    PrinterJob myPrinterJob = PrinterJob.getPrinterJob();
    myPrinterJob.setPrintable(new MyDocument());
    try
    {
      myPrinterJob.print();
    }
    catch (PrinterException ex)
    {
      JOptionPane.showConfirmDialog(null, ex.getMessage(),
"Print Error", JOptionPane.DEFAULT_OPTION,
JOptionPane.ERROR_MESSAGE);
    }
  }
}

class MyDocument implements Printable
{
  public int print(Graphics g, PageFormat pf, int
pageIndex)
  {
    Graphics2D g2D = (Graphics2D) g;
      .
      .
      .
  }
}
```

Let's see how to develop code for the **Printable** interface **print** method to do some printing.

Printing Pages of a Document

The **Printable** interface provides (in its **print** method) a graphics object (**g**, which we cast to a **Graphics2D** object, **g2D**) for 'drawing' our pages. And, that's just what we do using familiar graphics methods. For each page in our printed document, we draw the desired text information (**drawString** method), any shapes (**draw** method), or graphics (using a **GraphicsPanel** object).

Once a page is completely drawn to the graphics object, we 'tell' the **PrinterJob** object to print it. We repeat this process for each page we want to print. As noted, the **pageIndex** argument (in conjunction with the **return** value) of the **print** method helps with this effort. This does require a little bit of work on your part. You must know how many pages your document has and what goes on each page.

Let's look at the coordinates and dimensions of the graphics object for a single page.

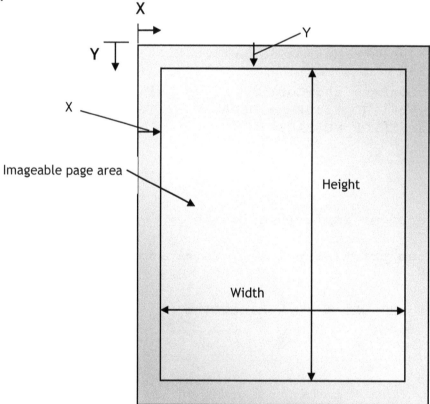

This becomes our palette for positioning items on a page. Horizontal position is governed by X (increases from 0 to the right) and vertical position is governed by Y (increases from 0 to the bottom). All dimensions are type **double**, in units of 1/72 inch. A standard sheet of 8.5 inch by 11-inch paper (with zero margins) would have a width and height of 612 and 792, respectively.

The **imageable area** rectangle is described by the **PageFormat** argument (**pf**) of the **Printable** class **print** method. The origin can be determined using:

```
pf.getImageableX();
pf.getImageableY();
```

These values define the right and top margins, respectively. The width and height of the imageable area, respectively, are found using:

```
pf.getImageableWidth();
pf.getImageableHeight();
```

The returned values are **double** types in units of 1/72 inch.

The process for each page is to decide "what goes where" and then position the desired information using the appropriate graphics method. Any of the graphics methods we have learned can be used to put information on the graphic object. Here, we limit the discussion to printing text, lines, rectangles and Swing components.

Printing Text

To place text on the graphics object (**g2D**), use the **drawString** method introduced in Class 8. To place the string **myString** at position (**x, y**), the syntax is:

```
g2D.drawString(myString, x, y);
```

The string is printed using the current font and paint attributes. With this statement, you can place any text, anywhere you like, with any font and paint. You just need to make the desired specifications. Each line of text on a printed page will require a **drawString** statement. Note **x** and **y** in this method are **int** types, not **double**, hence type casting of page dimensions is usually needed.

Also in Class 8, we saw how to determine the width and height of strings (knowing the font object **myFont**). This is helpful for both vertical and horizontal placement of text on a page. This information is returned in a **Rectangle2D** structure (**stringRect**), using:

```
Rectangle2D stringRect = myFont.getStringBounds(myString,
g2D.getFontRenderContext());
```

The height and width of the returned **stringRect** structure yield the string size (in units of 1/72 inch). These two properties are useful for justifying (left, right, center, vertical) text strings.

Here is a class (**MyDocument**) that will print the text "**Here is a map!!**" in **Bold**, **Arial**, Size **36** font. The text will be centered horizontally and two inches below the top margin.

```
class MyDocument implements Printable
{
  public int print(Graphics g, PageFormat pf, int
pageIndex)
  {
    if (pageIndex > 0)
    {
      return NO_SUCH_PAGE;
    }
    Graphics2D g2D = (Graphics2D) g;
    // Center text string near top of page
    String myString = "Here is a map!!";
    Font myFont = new Font("Arial", Font.BOLD, 36);
```

```
    g2D.setFont(myFont);
    Rectangle2D stringRect =
myFont.getStringBounds(myString,
g2D.getFontRenderContext());
    g2D.drawString(myString, (int) (pf.getImageableX() +
0.5 * (pf.getImageableWidth() - stringRect.getWidth())),
(int) (pf.getImageableY() + 2 * 72));
    return PAGE_EXISTS;
  }
}
```

Notice how the returned value is used with **pageIndex** to specify there is a single page to print (**NO_SUCH_PAGE** is returned if **pageIndex** is greater than zero).

The resulting page will be:

Here is a map!!

Printing Lines and Rectangles

Many times, you use lines in a document to delineate various sections. To draw a line on the graphics object, use the **draw** method and **Line2D** shape (from Class 7):

```
Line2D.Double myLine = new Line2D.Double(x1, y1, x2, y2);
g2D.draw(myLine);
```

This statement will draw a line from (**x1, y1**) to (**x2, y2**) using the current **stroke** and **paint** attributes.

To draw a rectangle (used with tables or graphics regions), use the **Rectangle2D** shape (from Class 7):

```
Rectangle2D.Double myRectangle = new Rectangle2D.Double(x,
y, w, h);
g2D.draw(myRectangle);
```

This statement will draw a rectangle with upper left corner at (**x, y**), width **w**, and height **h**. The rectangle will be drawn using the current **stroke** and **paint** attributes.

We've only looked at printing lines and rectangles. It's just as easy to print rounded rectangles, ellipses and pie segments. Simply define the appropriate shape object and use the draw method.

Here is a modified version of the **MyDocument** class we just saw with a rectangle (2 inches by 6 inches) drawn around the text string and a line in the middle of the page (the changes are shaded):

```
class MyDocument implements Printable
{
  public int print(Graphics g, PageFormat pf, int
pageIndex)
  {
    if (pageIndex > 0)
    {
      return NO_SUCH_PAGE;
    }
    Graphics2D g2D = (Graphics2D) g;
    g2D.setPaint(Color.BLACK);
    // Center text string near top of page
```

```
    String myString = "Here is a map!!";
    Font myFont = new Font("Arial", Font.BOLD, 36);
    g2D.setFont(myFont);
    Rectangle2D stringRect =
myFont.getStringBounds(myString,
g2D.getFontRenderContext());
    g2D.drawString(myString, (int) (pf.getImageableX() +
0.5 * (pf.getImageableWidth() - stringRect.getWidth())),
(int) (pf.getImageableY() + 2 * 72));
    // Draw rectangle around text
    Rectangle2D.Double myRectangle=new
Rectangle2D.Double(pf.getImageableX(), pf.getImageableY()
+ 72, pf.getImageableWidth(), 2 * 72);
    g2D.draw(myRectangle);
    // Draw line at middle of page
    Line2D.Double myLine = new
Line2D.Double(pf.getImageableX(), 5.5 * 72,
pf.getImageableX() + pf.getImageableWidth(), 5.5 *
72);g2D.draw(myLine);
    return PAGE_EXISTS;
  }
}
```

The resulting printed page is:

The code that does this printing is saved as the **PrintingDemo** project in the
\LearnJava\LJ Code\Class 9 project group).

Printing Swing Components

One of the trickier tasks in Java is printing graphics. The approach we take is to assume the graphics to be printed are hosted in a Swing component in your project. To print such a component, we will "borrow" code from open sources.

We will use a modified version of a class named **PrintUtilities** (included in the **\LearnJava\LJ Code\Class 9** folder). The complete code is (also placed in **Appendix I**):

```
import java.awt.*;
import javax.swing.*;
import java.awt.print.*;


public class PrintUtilities implements Printable {
  private Component componentToBePrinted;

  public static void printComponent(Component c) {
    new PrintUtilities(c).print();
  }

  public PrintUtilities(Component componentToBePrinted) {
    this.componentToBePrinted = componentToBePrinted;
  }

  public void print() {
    PrinterJob printJob = PrinterJob.getPrinterJob();
    printJob.setPrintable(this);
    try {
      printJob.print();
    } catch(PrinterException pe) {
      System.out.println("Error printing: " + pe);
    }
  }

  public int print(Graphics g, PageFormat pageFormat, int
pageIndex) {
    if (pageIndex > 0) {
      return(NO_SUCH_PAGE);
    } else {
      Graphics2D g2d = (Graphics2D)g;
      g2d.translate(pageFormat.getImageableX(),
pageFormat.getImageableY());
      disableDoubleBuffering(componentToBePrinted);
```

```
        componentToBePrinted.paint(g2d);
      enableDoubleBuffering(componentToBePrinted);
      return(PAGE_EXISTS);
    }
  }


  /** The speed and quality of printing suffers
dramatically if
   *   any of the containers have double buffering turned
on.
   *   So this turns if off globally.
   *   @see enableDoubleBuffering
   */
  public static void disableDoubleBuffering(Component c) {
     RepaintManager currentManager =
RepaintManager.currentManager(c);
     currentManager.setDoubleBufferingEnabled(false);
  }

  /** Re-enables double buffering globally. */

  public static void enableDoubleBuffering(Component c) {
     RepaintManager currentManager =
RepaintManager.currentManager(c);
     currentManager.setDoubleBufferingEnabled(true);
  }
}
```

We won't go into detail about what goes on in this class. It basically redraws any control on the printer graphics object (and it also toggles something called double-buffering to insure good quality printing).

Use of the **PrintUtilities** class is simple. If the Swing component (control) you want to print is named **myComponent**, it is printed with the single line of code:

```
PrintUtilities.printComponent(myComponent);
```

The component will be printed on its own page in the size defined in your project (scaling and integrating a component within a page is a difficult task we won't discuss). Many times the component to be printed is a **GraphicsPanel** object (recall this was defined in Class 7 to allow persistent graphics). We will see how this is done in **Example 9-4**.

The best way to learn how to print in Java is to do lots of it. You'll develop your own approaches and techniques as you gain familiarity. You might want to see how some of the other graphics methods (ellipses, pie segments) might work with printing. Or, look at different paint and stroke attributes.

Recall when doing persistent graphics back in Class 7 and 8 using the **paintComponent** method, any variable needed by that method needed to be prefaced by the keyword **static**. That is also needed here. Any class level object referred to in the **print** method must also be declared with a **static** preface.

Many print jobs just involve the user clicking a button marked 'Print' and the results appear on the printed page with no further interaction. If more interaction is desired, there are two methods associated with the **PrinterJob** object that help specify desired printing job properties: **pageDialog** and **printDialog**. Using these methods adds more code to your application. You must take any user inputs and implement these values in your program. We'll show what each method can do and let you decide if you want to use them in your work

pageDialog Method

The **pageDialog** method allows the user to set various parameters regarding a printing task. Users can set border and margin adjustments, paper size, and portrait vs. landscape orientation. The Windows version of the page dialog appears as:

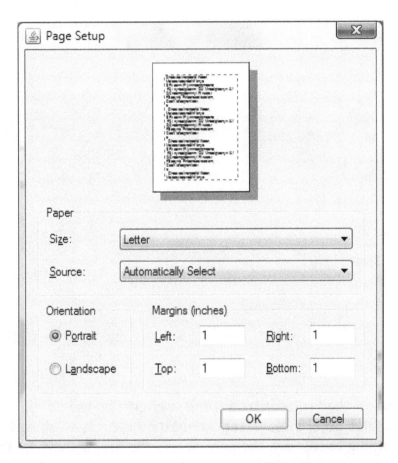

The method returns page format information to be used by the **PrinterJob** object. Here is a code snippet that uses the **pageDialog** method to establish a new page format (it uses a different version of the **setPrintable** method):

```
PrinterJob myPrinterJob = PrinterJob.getPrinterJob();
PageFormat myFormat = myPrinterJob.defaultPage();
myFormat = myPrinterJob.pageDialog(myFormat);
myPrinterJob.setPrintable(new MyDocument(), myFormat);
```

In this code, the **defaultPage** method returns a reference to the default settings. This default settings are passed to the page dialog where they is replaced with any new settings.

printDialog Method

The **printDialog** method displays a dialog box that allows the user to select which printer to use, choose page orientation, printed page range and number of copies. This is the same dialog box that appears in many applications. The Windows version of the print dialog is:

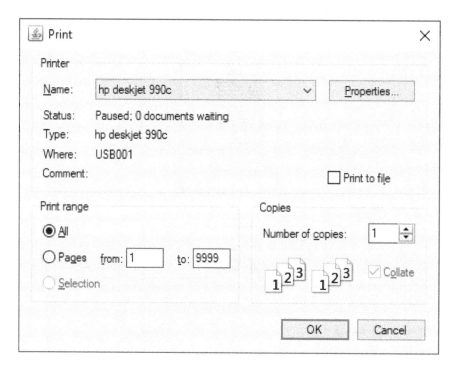

The **printDialog** method returns **true** if the user clicked the **OK** button to leave the dialog and **false** otherwise. After the method returns a value, you don't have to do anything to retrieve the parameters the user selected. The **PrinterJob** object is automatically updated with the selections!

A modified code snippet to incorporate the **printDialog** method is:

```
if (myPrinterJob.printDialog())
{
  try
   {
    myPrinterJob.print();
  }
  catch (PrinterException ex)
  {
    JOptionPane.showConfirmDialog(null, ex.getMessage(),
"Print Error", JOptionPane.DEFAULT_OPTION,
JOptionPane.ERROR_MESSAGE);
  }
}
```

In this modified code, the job is not printed unless the user clicks **OK** in the print dialog.

Example 9-4

Printing

Start a new empty project in **NetBeans**. Name the project **Countries**. Delete default code in Java file named **Countries**. Add the **PrintUtilities.java** file to your project source folder (located in **\LearnJava\LJ Code\Class 9** folder) – add the **package countries;** line at the top of the file. In this project, we'll demonstrate many of the skills just presented by printing out a list of countries and capitals, along with a map of the world. The finished project will look like this:

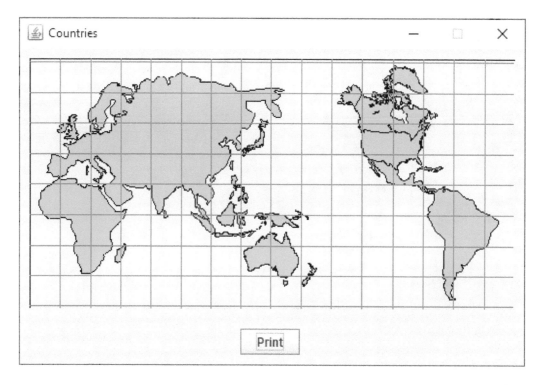

The graphic file used is **world.gif** and is located in the **\Learn Java\LJ Code\Class 9\Example9-4** folder. Copy this graphic file into your project's folder.

1. Add a panel control (will display the graphic) and a button to the frame. The **GridBagLayout** is:

	gridx = 0
gridy = 0	**mapPanel**
gridy = 1	**printButton**

Also include an image object (**myWorld**). Set these properties:

Countries Frame:

resizable	false
title	Countries

mapPanel (a GraphicsPanel class)::

preferredSize	(250, 500)
gridx	0
gridy	0
insets	(10, 10, 10, 10)

printButton:

text	Print
gridx	0
gridy	1
insets	(10, 10, 10, 10)

myWorld:

image	world.gif

2. Build the basic framework:

```java
/*
 * Countries.java
 */
package countries;
import javax.swing.*;
import java.awt.*;
import java.awt.event.*;
import java.awt.geom.*;

public class Countries extends JFrame
{
  public static void main(String args[])
```

```
  {
    // create frame
    new Countries().show();
  }
  public Countries()
  {
    // frame constructor
    setTitle("Countries");
    setResizable(false);
    addWindowListener(new WindowAdapter()
    {
      public void windowClosing(WindowEvent evt)
      {
        exitForm(evt);
      }
    });
    getContentPane().setLayout(new GridBagLayout());

    pack();
    Dimension screenSize =
Toolkit.getDefaultToolkit().getScreenSize();
    setBounds((int) (0.5 * (screenSize.width -
getWidth())), (int) (0.5 * (screenSize.height -
getHeight())), getWidth(), getHeight());
  }
  private void exitForm(WindowEvent evt)
  {
    System.exit(0);
  }
}
```

Run to test.

3. Now, we add controls and methods. Add these class level declarations:

```
GraphicsPanel mapPanel = new GraphicsPanel();
JButton printButton = new JButton();
static Image myWorld = new
ImageIcon("world.gif").getImage();
```

We are printing the image, hence the **static** preface.

Position and add controls and methods:

```
GridBagConstraints gridConstraints = new
GridBagConstraints();
mapPanel.setPreferredSize(new Dimension(500, 250));
gridConstraints.gridx = 0;
gridConstraints.gridy = 0;
gridConstraints.insets = new Insets(10, 10, 10, 10);
getContentPane().add(mapPanel, gridConstraints);

gridConstraints = new GridBagConstraints();
printButton.setText("Print");
gridConstraints.gridx = 0;
gridConstraints.gridy = 1;
gridConstraints.insets = new Insets(10, 10, 10, 10);
getContentPane().add(printButton, gridConstraints);
printButton.addActionListener(new ActionListener()
{
   public void actionPerformed(ActionEvent e)
   {
     printButtonActionPerformed(e);
   }
});
```

And, add an empty event method:

```
private void printButtonActionPerformed(ActionEvent e)
{
}
```

4. Add the **GraphicsPanel** class (from **Appendix I**) after the main class:

```
class GraphicsPanel extends JPanel
{
  public GraphicsPanel()
  {
  }
  public void paintComponent(Graphics g)
  {
  }
}
```

At this point, compile and check for control layout (there will be no map displayed).

5. Use these class level variable declarations (all **static** since used in printing):

```
static final int numCountries = 62;
static final int countriesPerPage = 25;
static String[] country = new String[numCountries];
static String[] capital = new String[numCountries];
static int lastPage = (int) ((numCountries - 1) /
countriesPerPage);
```

6. Use the following code at the end of the constructor (loads **country**/**capital** arrays):

```
country[0] = "Afghanistan" ; capital[0] = "Kabul";
country[1] = "Albania" ; capital[1] = "Tirane";
country[2] = "Australia" ; capital[2] = "Canberra";
country[3] = "Austria" ; capital[3] = "Vienna";
country[4] = "Bangladesh" ; capital[4] = "Dacca";
country[5] = "Barbados" ; capital[5] = "Bridgetown";
country[6] = "Belgium" ; capital[6] = "Brussels";
country[7] = "Bulgaria" ; capital[7] = "Sofia";
country[8] = "Burma" ; capital[8] = "Rangoon";
country[9] = "Cambodia" ; capital[9] = "Phnom Penh";
country[10] = "China" ; capital[10] = "Peking";
country[11] = "Czechoslovakia" ; capital[11] = "Prague";
country[12] = "Denmark" ; capital[12] = "Copenhagen";
country[13] = "Egypt" ; capital[13] = "Cairo";
country[14] = "Finland" ; capital[14] = "Helsinki";
country[15] = "France" ; capital[15] = "Paris";
country[16] = "Germany" ; capital[16] = " Berlin";
country[17] = "Greece" ; capital[17] = "Athens";
country[18] = "Hungary" ; capital[18] = "Budapest";
country[19] = "Iceland" ; capital[19] = "Reykjavik";
country[20] = "India" ; capital[20] = "New Delhi";
country[21] = "Indonesia" ; capital[21] = "Jakarta";
country[22] = "Iran" ; capital[22] = "Tehran";
country[23] = "Iraq" ; capital[23] = "Baghdad";
country[24] = "Ireland" ; capital[24] = "Dublin";
country[25] = "Israel" ; capital[25] = "Jerusalem";
country[26] = "Italy" ; capital[26] = "Rome";
country[27] = "Japan" ; capital[27] = "Tokyo";
country[28] = "Jordan" ; capital[28] = "Amman";
country[29] = "Kuwait" ; capital[29] = "Kuwait";
country[30] = "Laos" ; capital[30] = "Vientiane";
country[31] = "Lebanon" ; capital[31] = "Beirut";
country[32] = "Luxembourg" ; capital[32] = "Luxembourg";
country[33] = "Malaysia" ; capital[33] = "Kuala Lumpur";
```

```
country[34] = "Mongolia" ; capital[34] = "Ulaanbaatar";
country[35] = "Nepal" ; capital[35] = "Katmandu";
country[36] = "Netherlands" ; capital[36] = "Amsterdam";
country[37] = "New Zealand" ; capital[37] = "Wellington";
country[38] = "North Korea" ; capital[38] = "Pyongyang";
country[39] = "Norway" ; capital[39] = "Oslo";
country[40] = "Oman" ; capital[40] = "Muscat";
country[41] = "Pakistan" ; capital[41] = "Islamabad";
country[42] = "Philippines" ; capital[42] = "Manila";
country[43] = "Poland" ; capital[43] = "Warsaw";
country[44] = "Portugal" ; capital[44] = "Lisbon";
country[45] = "Romania" ; capital[45] = "Bucharest";
country[46] = "Russia" ; capital[46] = "Moscow";
country[47] = "Saudi Arabia" ; capital[47] = "Riyadh";
country[48] = "Singapore" ; capital[48] = "Singapore";
country[49] = "South Korea" ; capital[49] = "Seoul";
country[50] = "Spain" ; capital[50] = "Madrid";
country[51] = "Sri Lanka" ; capital[51] = "Colombo";
country[52] = "Sweden" ; capital[52] = "Stockholm";
country[53] = "Switzerland" ; capital[53] = "Bern";
country[54] = "Syria" ; capital[54] = "Damascus";
country[55] = "Taiwan" ; capital[55] = "Taipei";
country[56] = "Thailand" ; capital[56] = "Bangkok";
country[57] = "Turkey" ; capital[57] = "Ankara";
country[58] = "United Kingdom" ; capital[58] = "London";
country[59] = "Vietnam" ; capital[59] = "Hanoi";
country[60] = "Yemen" ; capital[60] = "Sana";
country[61] = "Yugoslavia" ; capital[61] = "Belgrade";
```

7. Add this code to the **paintComponent** method of the **GraphicsPanel** object. This code 'paints' the map in the panel:

```
public void paintComponent(Graphics g)
{
  Graphics2D g2D = (Graphics2D) g;
  super.paintComponent(g2D);
  // draw map
  g2D.drawImage(Countries.myWorld, 0, 0, 500, 250, this);
  g2D.dispose();
}
```

8. Use this code in the **printButtonActionPerformed** method (sets up document for printing, printing countries and capitals first, then the map):

```
private void printButtonActionPerformed(ActionEvent e)
   {
     // print countries and capitals first - defined in
MyDocument
     PrinterJob myPrinterJob = PrinterJob.getPrinterJob();
     myPrinterJob.setPrintable(new MyDocument());
     if (myPrinterJob.printDialog())
     {
       try
        {
        myPrinterJob.print();
       }
       catch (PrinterException ex)
       {
         JOptionPane.showConfirmDialog(null,
ex.getMessage(), "Print Error",
JOptionPane.DEFAULT_OPTION, JOptionPane.ERROR_MESSAGE);
       }
     }
     // print world map
     PrintUtilities.printComponent(mapPanel);
   }
```

9. Lastly, use this **Printable** interface to define **MyDocument**. On pages with countries and capitals, this code prints the headings and then the listings.

```java
class MyDocument implements Printable
{
   public int print(Graphics g, PageFormat pf, int
pageIndex)
   {
     Font printFont;
     Rectangle2D stringRect;
     String myString;
     int y;
     int iEnd;
      Graphics2D g2D = (Graphics2D) g;

     // here you decide what goes on each page and draw it
there
     // print countries/capitals and map on different pages

     if (pageIndex > Countries.lastPage)
     {
       return NO_SUCH_PAGE;
     }

     // put titles and countries/capitals
     printFont = new Font("Arial", Font.BOLD, 20);
     g2D.setFont(printFont);
     myString = "Countries and Capitals - Page " +
String.valueOf(pageIndex + 1);
     stringRect = printFont.getStringBounds(myString,
g2D.getFontRenderContext());
      g2D.drawString(myString, (int) (pf.getImageableX() +
0.5 * (pf.getImageableWidth() - stringRect.getWidth())),
(int) (pf.getImageableY() + stringRect.getHeight()));

     // starting y position
     printFont = new Font("Arial", Font.ITALIC, 14);
     g2D.setFont(printFont);
     myString = "Country";
     stringRect = printFont.getStringBounds(myString,
g2D.getFontRenderContext());
      y = (int) (pf.getImageableX() + 4 *
stringRect.getHeight());
      g2D.drawString(myString, (int) pf.getImageableX(), y);
      myString = "Capital";
      g2D.drawString(myString, (int) (pf.getImageableX() +
0.5 * pf.getImageableWidth()), y);
```

```
      y += (int) (2 * stringRect.getHeight());
      printFont = new Font("Arial", Font.PLAIN, 14);
      stringRect = printFont.getStringBounds("Test String",
   g2D.getFontRenderContext());
      g2D.setFont(printFont);
      iEnd = Countries.countriesPerPage * (pageIndex + 1);
      if (iEnd > Countries.numCountries)
      {
         iEnd = Countries.numCountries;
      }
      for (int i = 0 + Countries.countriesPerPage *
   pageIndex; i < iEnd; i++)
      {
         g2D.drawString(Countries.country[i], (int)
   (pf.getImageableX()), y);
         g2D.drawString(Countries.capital[i], (int)
   (pf.getImageableX() + 0.5 * pf.getImageableWidth()), y);
         y += (int) (stringRect.getHeight());
      }
      return PAGE_EXISTS;
   }
}
```

The complete **Countries.java** code listing (changes to framework are shaded):

```
/*
 * Countries.java
 */
package countries;
import javax.swing.*;
import java.awt.*;
import java.awt.event.*;
import java.awt.geom.*;
import java.awt.print.*;

public class Countries extends JFrame
{
  GraphicsPanel mapPanel = new GraphicsPanel();
  JButton printButton = new JButton();
  static Image myWorld = new
ImageIcon("world.gif").getImage();
  static final int numCountries = 62;
  static final int countriesPerPage = 25;
  static String[] country = new String[numCountries];
  static String[] capital = new String[numCountries];
  static int lastPage = (int) ((numCountries - 1) /
countriesPerPage);
```

```
  public static void main(String args[])
  {
    // create frame
    new Countries().show();
  }
}

  public Countries()
  {
    // frame constructor
    setTitle("Countries");
    setResizable(false);
    addWindowListener(new WindowAdapter()
    {
      public void windowClosing(WindowEvent evt)
      {
        exitForm(evt);
      }
    });
    getContentPane().setLayout(new GridBagLayout());
    // position controls

    GridBagConstraints gridConstraints = new
GridBagConstraints();
    mapPanel.setPreferredSize(new Dimension(500, 250));
    gridConstraints.gridx = 0;
    gridConstraints.gridy = 0;
    gridConstraints.insets = new Insets(10, 10, 10, 10);
    getContentPane().add(mapPanel, gridConstraints);

    gridConstraints = new GridBagConstraints();
    printButton.setText("Print");
    gridConstraints.gridx = 0;
    gridConstraints.gridy = 1;
    gridConstraints.insets = new Insets(10, 10, 10, 10);
    getContentPane().add(printButton, gridConstraints);
    printButton.addActionListener(new ActionListener()
    {
      public void actionPerformed(ActionEvent e)
      {
        printButtonActionPerformed(e);
      }
    });
    pack();
    Dimension screenSize =
Toolkit.getDefaultToolkit().getScreenSize();
```

```
    setBounds((int) (0.5 * (screenSize.width - getWidth())),
(int) (0.5 * (screenSize.height - getHeight())), getWidth(),
getHeight());
```

```
    // Load country/capital arrays
    country[0] = "Afghanistan" ; capital[0] = "Kabul";
    country[1] = "Albania" ; capital[1] = "Tirane";
    country[2] = "Australia" ; capital[2] = "Canberra";
    country[3] = "Austria" ; capital[3] = "Vienna";
    country[4] = "Bangladesh" ; capital[4] = "Dacca";
    country[5] = "Barbados" ; capital[5] = "Bridgetown";
    country[6] = "Belgium" ; capital[6] = "Brussels";
    country[7] = "Bulgaria" ; capital[7] = "Sofia";
    country[8] = "Burma" ; capital[8] = "Rangoon";
    country[9] = "Cambodia" ; capital[9] = "Phnom Penh";
    country[10] = "China" ; capital[10] = "Peking";
    country[11] = "Czechoslovakia" ; capital[11] = "Prague";
    country[12] = "Denmark" ; capital[12] = "Copenhagen";
    country[13] = "Egypt" ; capital[13] = "Cairo";
    country[14] = "Finland" ; capital[14] = "Helsinki";
    country[15] = "France" ; capital[15] = "Paris";
    country[16] = "Germany" ; capital[16] = " Berlin";
    country[17] = "Greece" ; capital[17] = "Athens";
    country[18] = "Hungary" ; capital[18] = "Budapest";
    country[19] = "Iceland" ; capital[19] = "Reykjavik";
    country[20] = "India" ; capital[20] = "New Delhi";
    country[21] = "Indonesia" ; capital[21] = "Jakarta";
    country[22] = "Iran" ; capital[22] = "Tehran";
    country[23] = "Iraq" ; capital[23] = "Baghdad";
    country[24] = "Ireland" ; capital[24] = "Dublin";
    country[25] = "Israel" ; capital[25] = "Jerusalem";
    country[26] = "Italy" ; capital[26] = "Rome";
    country[27] = "Japan" ; capital[27] = "Tokyo";
    country[28] = "Jordan" ; capital[28] = "Amman";
    country[29] = "Kuwait" ; capital[29] = "Kuwait";
    country[30] = "Laos" ; capital[30] = "Vientiane";
    country[31] = "Lebanon" ; capital[31] = "Beirut";
    country[32] = "Luxembourg" ; capital[32] = "Luxembourg";
    country[33] = "Malaysia" ; capital[33] = "Kuala Lumpur";
    country[34] = "Mongolia" ; capital[34] = "Ulaanbaatar";
    country[35] = "Nepal" ; capital[35] = "Katmandu";
    country[36] = "Netherlands" ; capital[36] = "Amsterdam";
    country[37] = "New Zealand" ; capital[37] = "Wellington";
    country[38] = "North Korea" ; capital[38] = "Pyongyang";
    country[39] = "Norway" ; capital[39] = "Oslo";
    country[40] = "Oman" ; capital[40] = "Muscat";
    country[41] = "Pakistan" ; capital[41] = "Islamabad";
```

```
      country[42] = "Philippines" ; capital[42] = "Manila";
      country[43] = "Poland" ; capital[43] = "Warsaw";
      country[44] = "Portugal" ; capital[44] = "Lisbon";
      country[45] = "Romania" ; capital[45] = "Bucharest";
      country[46] = "Russia" ; capital[46] = "Moscow";
      country[47] = "Saudi Arabia" ; capital[47] = "Riyadh";
      country[48] = "Singapore" ; capital[48] = "Singapore";
      country[49] = "South Korea" ; capital[49] = "Seoul";
      country[50] = "Spain" ; capital[50] = "Madrid";
      country[51] = "Sri Lanka" ; capital[51] = "Colombo";
      country[52] = "Sweden" ; capital[52] = "Stockholm";
      country[53] = "Switzerland" ; capital[53] = "Bern";
      country[54] = "Syria" ; capital[54] = "Damascus";
      country[55] = "Taiwan" ; capital[55] = "Taipei";
      country[56] = "Thailand" ; capital[56] = "Bangkok";
      country[57] = "Turkey" ; capital[57] = "Ankara";
      country[58] = "United Kingdom" ; capital[58] = "London";
      country[59] = "Vietnam" ; capital[59] = "Hanoi";
      country[60] = "Yemen" ; capital[60] = "Sana";
      country[61] = "Yugoslavia" ; capital[61] = "Belgrade";
   }

  private void printButtonActionPerformed(ActionEvent e)
  {
     // print countries and capitals first - defined in
MyDocument
     PrinterJob myPrinterJob = PrinterJob.getPrinterJob();
     myPrinterJob.setPrintable(new MyDocument());
     if (myPrinterJob.printDialog())
     {
       try
        {
        myPrinterJob.print();
       }
       catch (PrinterException ex)
       {
          JOptionPane.showConfirmDialog(null, ex.getMessage(),
"Print Error", JOptionPane.DEFAULT_OPTION,
JOptionPane.ERROR_MESSAGE);
       }
     }

     // print world map
     PrintUtilities.printComponent(mapPanel);
  }

  private void exitForm(WindowEvent evt)
  {
```

```
      System.exit(0);
   }
}

class GraphicsPanel extends JPanel
{
   public GraphicsPanel()
   {
   }
   public void paintComponent(Graphics g)
   {
     Graphics2D g2D = (Graphics2D) g;
     super.paintComponent(g2D);
     // draw map
     g2D.drawImage(Countries.myWorld, 0, 0, 500, 250, this);
     g2D.dispose();
   }
}

class MyDocument implements Printable
{
   public int print(Graphics g, PageFormat pf, int pageIndex)
   {
     Font printFont;
     Rectangle2D stringRect;
     String myString;
     int y;
     int iEnd;
      Graphics2D g2D = (Graphics2D) g;

     // here you decide what goes on each page and draw it
there
     // print countries/capitals and map on different pages

     if (pageIndex > Countries.lastPage)
     {
       return NO_SUCH_PAGE;
     }

     // put titles and countries/capitals
     printFont = new Font("Arial", Font.BOLD, 20);
     g2D.setFont(printFont);
     myString = "Countries and Capitals - Page " +
String.valueOf(pageIndex + 1);
     stringRect = printFont.getStringBounds(myString,
g2D.getFontRenderContext());
```

```
    g2D.drawString(myString, (int) (pf.getImageableX() + 0.5
* (pf.getImageableWidth() - stringRect.getWidth())), (int)
(pf.getImageableY() + stringRect.getHeight()));

    // starting y position
    printFont = new Font("Arial", Font.ITALIC, 14);
    g2D.setFont(printFont);
    myString = "Country";
    stringRect = printFont.getStringBounds(myString,
g2D.getFontRenderContext());
    y = (int) (pf.getImageableX() + 4 *
stringRect.getHeight());
    g2D.drawString(myString, (int) pf.getImageableX(), y);
    myString = "Capital";
    g2D.drawString(myString, (int) (pf.getImageableX() + 0.5
* pf.getImageableWidth()), y);
    y += (int) (2 * stringRect.getHeight());
    printFont = new Font("Arial", Font.PLAIN, 14);
    stringRect = printFont.getStringBounds("Test String",
g2D.getFontRenderContext());
    g2D.setFont(printFont);
    iEnd = Countries.countriesPerPage * (pageIndex + 1);
    if (iEnd > Countries.numCountries)
    {
      iEnd = Countries.numCountries;
    }
    for (int i = 0 + Countries.countriesPerPage * pageIndex;
i < iEnd; i++)
    {
      g2D.drawString(Countries.country[i], (int)
(pf.getImageableX()), y);
      g2D.drawString(Countries.capital[i], (int)
(pf.getImageableX() + 0.5 * pf.getImageableWidth()), y);
      y += (int) (stringRect.getHeight());
    }
    return PAGE_EXISTS;
  }
}
```

Run and compile the finished project. You will see:

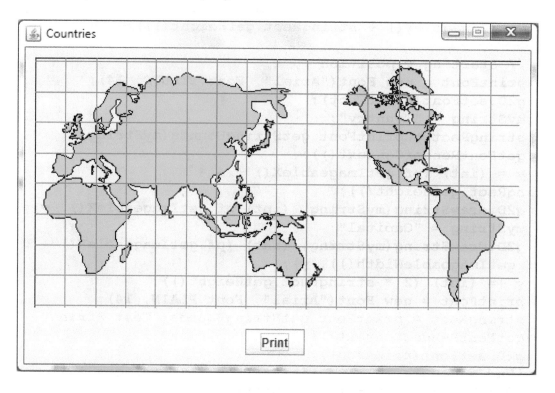

Click **Print** to get the hard-copy output (notice the dialog box controlling the printing). You should get three pages of country/capital listings and a final page with the world map:

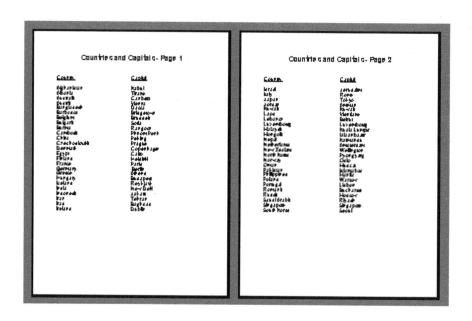

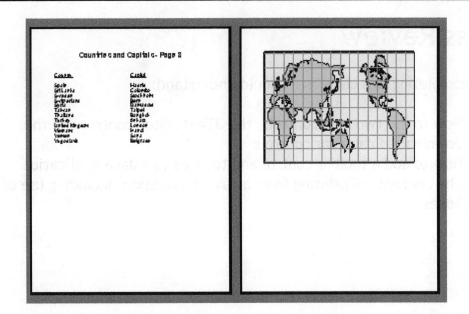

Save the project (saved as **Example9-4** in the **\LearnJava\LJ Code\Class 9** project group).

Class Review

After completing this class, you should understand:

> ➢ How to use two new controls, the **JTextEditor** control and the downloaded calendar controls
> ➢ How to add a toolbar control and tooltips to a Java application
> ➢ The concepts of printing from a Java application, including use of dialog boxes

Course Summary

That's all I know about Java and GUI applications. But I'm still learning, as is every Java programmer out there. The Java environment is vast! You should now have a good breadth of knowledge concerning Java and GUI applications. This breadth should serve as a springboard into learning more as you develop your own applications. Feel free to contact me, if you think I can answer any questions you might have.

Where do you go from here? If the Internet is your world, you should definitely extend your knowledge regarding Web applications and applets. And, if you're into databases, study more on how to build database management systems using Java.

Other suggestions for further study (note that each of these topics could be a complete book by itself):

> ➢ Advanced graphics methods (including game type graphics)
> ➢ Creating and deployment of your own GUI controls
> ➢ Creating and deployment of your own objects
> ➢ Understanding and using object-oriented concepts of overloading, inheritance, multithreading

We have two other GUI tutorials that you can work through. **Kid Games with Java** builds six fun games for kids and adults. **Home Projects with Java** has eight useful projects you can use to manage your life. Check our website for details.

Practice Problems 9

Problem 9-1. Loan Printing Problem. . The two lines of Java code that compute the monthly payment on an installment loan are:

```
double multiplier = Math.pow((1 + interest / 1200), months);
payment = loan * interest * multiplier / (1200 * (multiplier
- 1));
```

where:

interest	Yearly interest percentage
months	Number of months of payments
loan	Loan amount
multiplier	Interest multiplier
payment	Computed monthly payment

(The 1200 value in these equations converts yearly interest to a monthly rate.) Use this code to build a general method that computes **payment**, given the other three variables.

Now, use this method in an application that computes the payment after the user inputs loan amount, yearly interest and number of months. Allow the user to print out a repayment schedule for the loan. The printed report should include the inputs, computed payments, total of payments and total interest paid. Then, a month-by-month accounting of the declining balance, as the loan is paid, should be printed. In this accounting, include how much of each payment goes toward principal and how much toward interest.

Problem 9-2. Plot Printing Problem. In **Problem 8-3**, we built an application that displayed a labeled plot of the win streaks for the Seattle Mariners 1995 season. Build an application that prints this plot and its labeling information.

Exercise 9-1

Phone Directory

Develop an application that tracks people and phone numbers (include home, work and cell phones). Allow sorting, editing, adding, deleting and saving of entries. Add search capabilities. Allow printing of listings. In summary, build a full-featured Java phone directory application.

Exercise 9-2

The Ultimate Application

Design a GUI application using Java that everyone on the planet wants to buy.
Place controls, assign properties, and write code. Thoroughly debug and test
your application. Create a distribution and deployment package. Find a
distributor or distribute it yourself through your newly created company.
Become fabulously wealthy. Remember those who made it all possible by
rewarding them with jobs and stock options.

Appendix I. General Purpose Methods and Classes

Introduction

In this Appendix, we provide code listings for several general purpose methods and classes developed and used in this course. These routines can be used in a variety of applications. Use them as you wish. The programs are listed alphabetically by name:

Method/Class	Page
average	AI-2
BarChartPanel	AI-3
blankLine	AI-6
circleGeometry	AI-7
degFTodegC	AI-8
GraphicsPanel	AI-9
LineChartPanel	AI-10
loanPayment	AI-12
midLine	AI-13
PieChartPanel	AI-14
PrintUtilities	AI-16
randomNormalNumber	AI-18
rectangleInfo	AI-19
sortIntegers	AI-20
soundEx	AI-21
standardDeviation	AI-22
Transparency	AI-23
validateDecimalNumber	AI-24
validateIntegerNumber	AI-26
xPhysicalToxUser	AI-27
yPhysicalToyUser	AI-28

average

This method finds the average value of an array of numbers. The method is named **average**. There are two arguments. The first is **numberValues**, the number of elements in the array, of type **int**. The second argument is the 0-based array **values**. These are the numbers being averaged. Each element of the array is of type **double**. The returned value is the average, type **double**.

```
public double average(int numberValues, double[] values)
{
  if   (numberValues == 0)
  {
    return;
  }  // find average
  double sum = 0.0;
  for (int i = 0; i < numberValues; i++)
  {
    sum += values[i];
  }
  return(sum / numberValues);
}
```

BarChartPanel

This class draws a bar chart in a panel control. The class is named
BarChartPanel. The constructor has five arguments. The first is **border**, the
rectangle (type **Rectangle2D.Double**) within the panel hosting the bar chart.
Other arguments are **nPoints**, the number of points to plot (type **int**), **yValues**
the array of values to chart (type **double**), **base** the base value (type **double**)
and **colorValue** the color of the bars (**Color** type).

```java
import javax.swing.*;
import java.awt.geom.*;
import java.awt.*;
public class BarChartPanel extends JPanel
{
  private Rectangle2D.Double borderRectangle;
  private int n;
  private double[] y;
  private double b;
  private Color c;
  public BarChartPanel()
  {
    // default constructor for initialization
  }
  public BarChartPanel(Rectangle2D.Double border, int
nPoints, double[] yValues, double base, Color colorValue)
  {
    this.borderRectangle = border;
    this.n = nPoints;
    this.y = yValues;
    this.b = base;
    this.c = colorValue;
  }
  public void paintComponent(Graphics g)
  {
    // Draws a  bar chart
    // borderRectangle - rectangle region to draw plot
    // n - number of points to plot
    // y - array of y points (lower index is 0, upper index
is n-1)
    // c - color of bars
    double yMin = y[0]; double yMax = y[0];
    // find minimums and maximums
    for (int i = 1; i < n; i++)
    {
      yMin = Math.min(yMin, y[i]);
```

```
      yMax = Math.max(yMax, y[i]);
    }
    // Extend y values a bit so bars are not right on borders
    yMin = (1 - 0.05 * Double.compare(yMin, 0)) * yMin;
    yMax = (1 + 0.05 * Double.compare(yMax, 0)) * yMax;
    Graphics2D g2D = (Graphics2D) g;
    super.paintComponent(g2D);
    // Find bar width in client coordinates
    // use half bar-width as margins between bars
    double barWidth = 2 * (borderRectangle.width - 1) / (3 *
n + 1);
    double clientBase = yPhysicalToyUser(borderRectangle, b,
yMin, yMax);
    Rectangle2D.Double myRectangle;
    for (int i = 0; i < n; i++)
    {
      // draw bars
      if (y[i] > b)
      {
        myRectangle = new
Rectangle2D.Double(borderRectangle.x + (1.5 * i + 0.5) *
barWidth, yPhysicalToyUser(borderRectangle, y[i], yMin,
yMax), barWidth, clientBase -
yPhysicalToyUser(borderRectangle, y[i], yMin, yMax));
      }
      else
      {
        myRectangle = new
Rectangle2D.Double(borderRectangle.x + (1.5 * i + 0.5) *
barWidth, clientBase, barWidth,
yPhysicalToyUser(borderRectangle, y[i], yMin, yMax) -
clientBase);
      }
      g2D.setPaint(c);
      g2D.fill(myRectangle);
    }
    // draw border
    g2D.setPaint(Color.BLACK);
    g2D.draw(borderRectangle);
    // line at base
    g2D.draw(new Line2D.Double(borderRectangle.x, clientBase,
borderRectangle.x + borderRectangle.width - 1, clientBase));
    g2D.dispose();
  }
  private double xPhysicalToxUser(Rectangle2D.Double r,
double xPhysical, double xMin, double xMax)
  {
```

```
    return(r.x + (xPhysical - xMin) * (r.width - 1) / (xMax -
xMin));
  }
  private double yPhysicalToyUser(Rectangle2D.Double r,
double yPhysical, double yMin, double yMax)
  {
    return(r.y + (yMax - yPhysical) * (r.height - 1) / (yMax
- yMin));
  }
}
```

blankLine

This method blanks out a character array. The method is named **blankLine**. There is one argument **charLine** – the character array to 'blank out.' There is no returned value.

```java
public void blankLine(char[] charLine)
{
  for (int i = 0; i < charLine.length; i++)
  {
    charLine[i] = ' ';
  }
}
```

circleGeometry

This method computes the circumference and area of a circle, given the diameter. The method is named **circleGeometry**. It has one argument, of type **double**, the **diameter**. The method returns the computed values **circumference** and **area** in a **double** array (**geometry**) of dimension 2.

```
public double[] circleGeometry(double diameter)
{
   double [] geometry = new double[2];
   geometry[0] = Math.PI * diameter; // circumference
   geometry[1] = Math.PI * diameter * diameter / 4; // area
   return(geometry);
}
```

degFTodegC

This method converts Fahrenheit temperature to Celsius. The function is named
degFTodegC. It has a single argument (the Fahrenheit temperature), **tempF**, of
type **double**. It returns a **double** data type, the Celsius temperature.

```
public double degFTodegC(double tempF)
{
  double tempC;
  tempC = (tempF - 32) * 5 / 9;
  return(tempC);
}
```

GraphicsPanel

This class allows direct painting of a **JPanel** control (via the **paintComponent** method). You need to add the code to do the painting. The **paintComponent** method passes a graphic object (**g**, which may need to be converted to a **Graphics2D** object).

```
class GraphicsPanel extends JPanel
{
  public GraphicsPanel()
  {
  }
  public void paintComponent(Graphics g)
  {
  }
}
```

LineChartPanel

This class draws a line chart (y vs. x) in a panel control. The class is named **LineChartPanel**. The constructor has five arguments. The first is **border**, the rectangle (type **Rectangle2D.Double**) within the panel hosting the line chart. Other arguments are **nPoints**, the number of points to plot (type **int**), **xValues** the array of x values to plot (type **double**), **yValues** the array of corresponding y values to plot (type **double**), and **colorValue** the color of the line (type **Color**).

```
import javax.swing.*;
import java.awt.geom.*;
import java.awt.*;
public class LineChartPanel extends JPanel
{
  private Rectangle2D.Double borderRectangle;
  private int n;
  private double[] x;
  private double[] y;
  private Color c;
  public LineChartPanel()
  {
    // default constructor for initialization
  }
  public LineChartPanel(Rectangle2D.Double border, int
nPoints, double[] xValues, double[] yValues, Color
colorValue)
  {
    this.borderRectangle = border;
    this.n = nPoints;
    this.x = xValues;
    this.y = yValues;
    this.c = colorValue;
  }
  public void paintComponent(Graphics g)
  {
    // Draws a  line chart - pairs of (x,y) coordinates
    // borderRectangle - rectangle region to draw plot
    // n - number of points to plot
    // x - array of x points (lower index is 0, upper index
is n-1)
    // y - array of y points (lower index is 0, upper index
is n-1)
    // c - color of line
    // Need at least 2 points to plot
    if (n < 2)
    {
      return;
```

```
    }
    double xMin = x[0]; double xMax = x[0];
    double yMin = y[0]; double yMax = y[0];
    // find minimums and maximums
    for (int i = 1; i < n; i++)
    {
      xMin = Math.min(xMin, x[i]);
      xMax = Math.max(xMax, x[i]);
      yMin = Math.min(yMin, y[i]);
      yMax = Math.max(yMax, y[i]);
    }
    // Extend y values a bit so lines are not right on
borders
    yMin = (1 - 0.05 * Double.compare(yMin, 0)) * yMin;
    yMax = (1 + 0.05 * Double.compare(yMax, 0)) * yMax;
    Graphics2D g2D = (Graphics2D) g;
    super.paintComponent(g2D);
    Line2D.Double myLine;
    g2D.setPaint(c);
    for (int i = 0; i < n - 1; i++)
    {
      // plot in user coordinates
      myLine = new
Line2D.Double(xPhysicalToxUser(borderRectangle, x[i], xMin,
xMax), yPhysicalToyUser(borderRectangle, y[i], yMin, yMax),
xPhysicalToxUser(borderRectangle, x[i + 1], xMin, xMax),
yPhysicalToyUser(borderRectangle, y[i + 1], yMin, yMax));
      g2D.draw(myLine);
    }
    // draw border
    g2D.setPaint(Color.BLACK);
    g2D.draw(borderRectangle);
    g2D.dispose();
  }
  private double xPhysicalToxUser(Rectangle2D.Double r,
double xPhysical, double xMin, double xMax)
  {
    return(r.x + (xPhysical - xMin) * (r.width - 1) / (xMax -
xMin));
  }
  private double yPhysicalToyUser(Rectangle2D.Double r,
double yPhysical, double yMin, double yMax)
  {
    return(r.y + (yMax - yPhysical) * (r.height - 1) / (yMax
- yMin));
  }
}
```

loanPayment

This method returns the monthly payment for a revolving loan. The method is named **loanPayment**. Three arguments are needed: **loan** (the loan amount, **double** type), **interest** (yearly interest, **double**), and **months** (the loan term in months, **int** type). It returns a **double** type, the payment.

```
private double loanPayment(double loan, double interest,
double months)
{
  // Compute loan payment method
  double multiplier;
  if (months == 0)
  {
    JOptionPane.showConfirmDialog(null, "Need non-zero value
for Number of Months", "Error", JOptionPane.DEFAULT_OPTION,
JOptionPane.INFORMATION_MESSAGE);
    return(-1); // set negative value for error flag
  }
  if (interest != 0)
  {
    multiplier = Math.pow((1 + interest / 1200), months);
    return (loan * interest * multiplier / (1200 *
(multiplier - 1)));
  }
  else
  {
    return (loan / months);
  }
}
```

midLine

This method places a substring within a character array. The method is named **midLine**. There is are three arguments. The first is the substring **inString** (a **String** type), the second (**charLine**) the character array to place the substring in and the final argument is **pos** (**int** type), the starting position within **charLine** to place **inString**. There is no returned value.

```
public void midLine(String inString, char[] charLine, int
pos)
{
  for (int i = pos; i < pos + inString.length(); i++)
  {
    charLine[i] = inString.charAt(i - pos);
  }
}
```

PieChartPanel

This procedure draws a pie chart in a panel control. The procedure is named
PieChart. The constructor has four arguments. The first is **border**, the
rectangle (type **Rectangle2D.Double**) within the panel hosting the line chart.
Other arguments are **nSegments**, the number of pie segments (type **int**),
yValues the array of data to plot (type **double**), and **colorValues** and array of
pie segment colors (type **Color**).

```java
import javax.swing.*;
import java.awt.geom.*;
import java.awt.*;
public class PieChartPanel extends JPanel
{
  private Rectangle2D.Double borderRectangle;
  private int n;
  private double[] y;
  private Color[] c;

  public PieChartPanel()
  {
    // default constructor for initialization
  }
  public PieChartPanel(Rectangle2D.Double border, int
nSegments, double[] yValues, Color[] colorValues)
  {
    this.borderRectangle = border;
    this.n = nSegments;
    this.y = yValues;
    this.c = colorValues;
  }
  public void paintComponent(Graphics g)
  {
    // Draws a pie chart
    // borderRectangle - rectangle object to draw chart
    // n - number of pie segments to draw
    // y - array of points (Double type) to chart (lower
index is 1, upper index is N)
    // c - color of pie segments
    Graphics2D g2D = (Graphics2D) g;
    super.paintComponent(g2D);
    double sum = 0.0;
    for (int i = 0; i < n; i++)
    {
      sum += y[i];
```

```
      }
      // draw pie
      double startAngle = 0;
      Arc2D.Double myArc;
      // for each slice fill and draw
      for (int i = 0; i < n; i++)
      {
          myArc = new Arc2D.Double(borderRectangle.x,
borderRectangle.y, borderRectangle.width,
borderRectangle.height, startAngle, 360 * y[i] / sum,
Arc2D.PIE);
          g2D.setPaint(c[i]);
          g2D.fill(myArc);
          g2D.setPaint(Color.BLACK);
          g2D.draw(myArc);
          startAngle += 360 * y[i] / sum;
      }
      g2D.dispose();
   }
}
```

PrintUtilities

This class allows printing of any Swing component. The class is named
PrintUtilities. It has a single method with one argument, the component to be
printed.

```java
import java.awt.*;
import javax.swing.*;
import java.awt.print.*;
public class PrintUtilities implements Printable {
  private Component componentToBePrinted;

  public static void printComponent(Component c) {
    new PrintUtilities(c).print();
  }

  public PrintUtilities(Component componentToBePrinted) {
    this.componentToBePrinted = componentToBePrinted;
  }

  public void print() {
    PrinterJob printJob = PrinterJob.getPrinterJob();
    printJob.setPrintable(this);
    try {
      printJob.print();
    } catch(PrinterException pe) {
      System.out.println("Error printing: " + pe);
    }
  }

  public int print(Graphics g, PageFormat pageFormat, int
pageIndex) {
    if (pageIndex > 0) {
      return(NO_SUCH_PAGE);
    } else {
      Graphics2D g2d = (Graphics2D)g;
      g2d.translate(pageFormat.getImageableX(),
pageFormat.getImageableY());
      disableDoubleBuffering(componentToBePrinted);
      componentToBePrinted.paint(g2d);
      enableDoubleBuffering(componentToBePrinted);
      return(PAGE_EXISTS);
    }
  }
```

```
    /** The speed and quality of printing suffers dramatically
if
     *   any of the containers have double buffering turned on.
     *   So this turns if off globally.
     *   @see enableDoubleBuffering
     */
    public static void disableDoubleBuffering(Component c) {
      RepaintManager currentManager =
RepaintManager.currentManager(c);
      currentManager.setDoubleBufferingEnabled(false);
    }


    /** Re-enables double buffering globally. */

    public static void enableDoubleBuffering(Component c) {
      RepaintManager currentManager =
RepaintManager.currentManager(c);
      currentManager.setDoubleBufferingEnabled(true);
    }
}
```

randomNormalNumber

This method returns a number with an approximate normal distribution (mean 0, standard deviation 1). The function is named **randomNormalNumber**. It has no arguments. It returns a **double** data type, the normal number.

```
public double randomNormalNumber()
{
  // Sum 12 random numbers and subtract 6
  double number = 0;
  for (int i = 0; i < 12; i++)
  {
    number += dRand.nextDouble();
  }
  return (number - 6.0);
}
```

To use this method, you need a class level declaration for the **Random** object (**dRand**):

```
static Random dRand = new Random();
```

rectangleInfo

This method computes the perimeter and area of a rectangle, given the length and width. The method is named **rectangleInfo**. It has two arguments, of type **double**. The arguments are the input **length** and **width**. The method returns the computed values **perimeter** and **area** in a **double** array (**info**) of dimension 2.

```
public double[] rectangleInfo(double length, double width)
{
   double[] info = new double[2];
   info[0] = 2 * (length + width); // perimeter
   info[1] = length * width; // area
   return(info);
}
```

sortIntegers

This method randomly sorts n integers. The calling argument for the method are **n** (the number of integers to be sorted). The routine returns an **n** element array **nArray** containing the randomly sorted integers. Note the procedure randomizes the integers from 0 to n - 1, not 1 to n.

```java
public int[] sortIntegers(int n)
{
  /*
  *   Returns n randomly sorted integers 0 -> n - 1
  */
  int nArray[] = new int[n];
  int temp, s;
  Random myRandom = new Random();
  //   initialize array from 0 to n - 1
  for (int i = 0; i < n; i++)
  {
    nArray[i] = i;
  }
  //   i is number of items remaining in list
  for (int i = n; i >= 1; i--)
  {
    s = myRandom.nextInt(i);
    temp = nArray[s];
    nArray[s] = nArray[i - 1];
    nArray[i - 1] = temp;
  }
  return(nArray);
}
```

soundEx

This function computes a 'soundex' code for a string. If two strings have the same soundex code, their spelling is similar. The function is named **soundEx**. It has one **String** type argument, w, which is the input string. The function returns the soundex code as a **string** type.

```
public String soundEx(String w)
{
  // Generates Soundex code for W based on Unicode value
  // Allows answers whose spelling is close, but not exact
  String wTemp, s = "";
  int l;
  int wPrev, wSnd, cIndex;
  // Load soundex function array
  int[] wSound = {0, 1, 2, 3, 0, 1, 2, 0, 0, 2, 2, 4, 5, 5,
0, 1, 2, 6, 2, 3, 0, 1, 0, 2, 0, 2};
  wTemp = w.toUpperCase();
  l = w.length();
  if (l != 0)
  {
    s = String.valueOf(w.charAt(0));
    wPrev = 0;
    if (l > 1)
    {
      for (int i = 1; i < l; i++)
      {
        cIndex = (int) wTemp.charAt(i) - 65;
        if (cIndex >= 0 && cIndex <= 25)
        {
          wSnd = wSound[cIndex] + 48;
          if (wSnd != 48 && wSnd != wPrev)
          {
            s += String.valueOf((char) wSnd);
          }
          wPrev = wSnd;
        }
      }
    }
  }
  else
  s = "";
  }
  return(s);
}
```

standardDeviation

This method finds the standard deviation of an array of numbers. The method is named **standardDeviation**. There are two arguments. The first is **numberValues**, the number of elements in the array, of type **int**. The second argument is the 0-based array **values**. These are the numbers being analyzed. Each element of the array is of type **double**. The returned value is the standard deviation, type **double**.

```
public double standardDeviation(int numberValues, double[]
values)
{
  double sumX = 0;
  double sumX2 = 0;
  // mke sure there are at least two values
  if (numberValues < 2)
  {
    return(0);
  }
  // Compute sums
  for (int i = 0; i < numberValues; i++)
  {
    sumX += values[i];
    sumX2 += values[i] * values[i];
  }
  return(Math.sqrt((numberValues * sumX2 - sumX * sumX) /
(numberValues * (numberValues - 1))));
}
```

Transparency

The **Transparency** class allows the creation of an **Image** object with a transparent color. To use the **Transparency** class, assume you have an image (**myImage**) with a background color (**myColor**) you want changed to transparent. The following line of code will return the same image, with the input background color set to transparent (**myTransparentImage**):

```
myTransparentImage =
Transparency.makeColorTransparent(myImage, myColor);


import java.awt.*;
import java.awt.image.*;

public class Transparency
{
  public static Image makeColorTransparent(Image im, final
Color color)
  {
    ImageFilter filter = new RGBImageFilter()
    {
      // the color we are looking for... Alpha bits are set
to opaque
      public int markerRGB = color.getRGB() | 0xFF000000;
      public final int filterRGB(int x, int y, int rgb)
      {
        if ( ( rgb | 0xFF000000 ) == markerRGB )
        {
          // Mark the alpha bits as zero - transparent
          return 0x00FFFFFF & rgb;
        }
        else
        {
          // nothing to do
          return rgb;
        }
      }
    };
    ImageProducer ip = new
FilteredImageSource(im.getSource(), filter);
    return Toolkit.getDefaultToolkit().createImage(ip);
  }
}
```

validateDecimalNumber

This method insures a value in a text field is a valid decimal number, including only digits, a single decimal point or a negative sign. The method is named **validateDecimalNumber**. There is one argument of type **JTextField**, that being the text field (**tf**) being examined. The method returns a boolean value (**true** if the number is valid, **false** if not).

```
public boolean validateDecimalNumber(JTextField tf)
{
  // checks to see if text field contains
  // valid decimal number with only digits and a single
decimal point
  // or negative sign
  String s = tf.getText().trim();
  boolean hasDecimal = false;
  boolean valid = true;
  if (s.length() == 0)
  {
    valid = false;
  }
  else
  {
    for (int i = 0; i < s.length(); i++)
    {
      char c = s.charAt(i);
      if ((c >= '0' && c <= '9') || (c == '-' && i == 0))
      {
        continue;
      }
      else if (c == '.' && !hasDecimal)
      {
        hasDecimal = true;
      }
      else
      {
        // invalid character found
        valid = false;
      }
    }
  }
  if (valid)
  {
    tf.setText(s);
  }
```

```
  else
  {
    tf.setText("");
    tf.requestFocus();
  }
  return (valid);
}
```

validateIntegerNumber

This method insures a value in a text field is a valid integer number, including only digits and a negative sign. The method is named **validateIntegerNumber**. There is one argument of type **JTextField**, that being the text field (**tf**) being examined. The method returns a boolean value (**true** if the number is valid, **false** if not).

```java
public boolean validateIntegerNumber(JTextField tf)
{
  // checks to see if text field contains
  // valid integer number with only digits or negative sign
  String s = tf.getText().trim();
  boolean valid = true;
  if (s.length() == 0)
  {
    valid = false;
  }
  else
  {
    for (int i = 0; i < s.length(); i++)
    {
      char c = s.charAt(i);
      if ((c >= '0' && c <= '9') || (c == '-' && i == 0))
      {
        continue;
      }
      else
      {
        // invalid character found
        valid = false;
      }
    }
  }
  if (valid)
  {
    tf.setText(s);
  }
  else
  {
    tf.setText("");
    tf.requestFocus();
  }
  return (valid);
}
```

xPhysicalToxUser

This method is used to convert a generic unit to a host control's horizontal axis. The method is named **xPhysicalToxUser**. It has four arguments. **r** the rectangle object (**Rectangle2D** object) that the conversion is based on, the **xPhysical** value, the minimum physical value, **xMin**, and the maximum value, **xMax**. All values are of **double** data type. The method returns the user coordinate (a **double** type).

```
private double xPhysicalToxUser(Rectangle2D.Double r, double
xPhysical, double xMin, double xMax)
{
   return(r.x + (xPhysical - xMin) * (r.width - 1) / (xMax -
xMin));
}
```

yPhysicalToyUser

This method is used to convert a generic unit to a host control's vertical axis. The method is named **yPhysicalToyUser**. It has four arguments. **r** the rectangle object (**Rectangle2D** object) that the conversion is based on, the **yPhysical** value, the minimum physical value, **yMin**, and the maximum value, **yMax**. All values are of **double** data type. The method returns the user coordinate (a **double** type).

```
private double yPhysicalToyUser(Rectangle2D.Double r, double
yPhysical, double yMin, double yMax)
{
   return(r.y + (yMax - yPhysical) * (r.height - 1) / (yMax -
yMin));
}
```

Appendix II. Brief Primer on Classes and Objects

Introduction

We say Java is an **object-oriented** language. In this course, we have used many of the built-in objects included with the Java Swing library. We have used button objects, text field objects, label objects and many other controls. We have used graphics objects, font objects, stroke objects, paint objects, rectangle objects and point objects. Having used these objects, we are familiar with such concepts as **declaring** an object, **constructing** an object and using an object's **properties** and **methods**.

We have seen that objects are just things that have attributes (properties) with possible actions (methods). As you progress in your programming education, you may want to include your own objects in applications you build. But, it's tough to decide when you need (if ever) an object. A general rule is that you might want to consider using an object when you are working with some entity that fits the structure of having properties and methods and has some **re-use potential**.

The big advantage to objects (as seen with the ones we've used already) is that they can be used over and over again. This re-use can be multiple copies (**instances**) of a single object within a particular application or can be the re-use of a particular object in several different applications (like the controls of Java).

The most common object is some entity with several describing features (**properties**). Such objects in other languages are called **structured variables**. One could be a line object using the end points, line thickness and line color as properties. Or, a person could be an object, with name, address, phone number as properties.

You could extend these simple objects (properties only) by adding **methods**. Methods allow an object to do something. With our simple line object example, we could add methods to draw a line, erase a line, color a line, and dot a line. In the person object example, we could have methods to sort, search or print the person objects.

I realize this explanation of when to use your own objects is rather vague. And, it has to be. Only through experience can you decide when you might need an object. Look through other texts and websites to see how objects are employed in Java. And, don't feel bad if you never use a custom object. The great power of Java is that you can do many things just using the built-in objects! In this appendix, we'll look at how to add an object to a Java application, discussing properties, constructors and methods. And we'll look at how to modify an existing object (a Java control) to meet some custom needs.

Objects in Java

Before getting started, you may be asking the question "If Java is an object-oriented language, why have we waited so long to start talking about using our own objects?" And, that's a good question. Many books on Java dive right into building objects. We feel it's best to see objects and use objects before trying to create your own. Java is a great language for doing this. The wealth of existing, built-in objects helps you learn about object-oriented programming (OOP) before needing to build your own.

Now, let's review some of the vocabulary of object-oriented programming. These are terms you've seen before in working with the built-in objects of Java. A **class** provides a general description of an **object**. All objects are created from this class description. The first step in creating an object is adding a class to a Java project. Every application we have built in this course is a class itself. Note the top line of every application has the keyword **class**.

The **class** provides a framework for describing three primary components:

Properties – attributes describing the objects
Constructors – procedures that initialize the object
Methods – procedures describing things an object can do

Once a class is defined, an object can be created or **instantiated** from the class. This simply means we use the class description to create a copy of the object we can work with. Once the instance is created, we **construct** the finished object for our use.

One last important term to define, related to OOP, is **inheritance**. This is a capability that allows one object to 'borrow' properties and methods from another object. This prevents the classic 'reinventing the wheel' situation. Inheritance is one of the most powerful features of OOP. In this chapter, we will see how to use inheritance in a simple example and how we can create our own control that inherits from an existing control.

Adding a Class to a Java Project

The first step in creating our own object is to define the class from which the object will be created. This step (and all following steps) is best illustrated by example. In the example here, we will be creating **Widget** objects that have two properties: a **color** and a **size**. Start a new project in **Netbeans** – name the project **WidgetTest**. Delete default code in file named **WidgetTest.java**. This will be a simple console application for testing any widgets we create. Use this initial code for **WidgetTest.java**:

```
package widgettest;
public class WidgetTest
{
  public static void main(String args[])
  {
    System.out.println("Testing the Widget!!\n");

  }
}
```

Save the project. Run the code to make sure it works. You should see this output window:

```
General Output

--------------------Configuration: WidgetTest - JDK version 1.6
----
Testing the Widget!!


Process completed.
```

We need to add a class to this project to allow the definition of our **Widget** objects. We could add the class in the existing file. However, doing so would defeat a primary advantage of objects, that being re-use. Hence, we will create a separate file to hold our class. To do this, in **Netbeans**, right-click the project name (**WidgetTest**) and add another Java class file to the project (choose **New**, then **Java Class ...**). Name that file **Widget** – and add it to the **widgettest** source package. Delete code that appears in the file. Type these lines:

```
package widgettest;
public class Widget
{

}
```

All code needed to define properties, constructors and methods for this class will be between the curly braces defining this class.

Declaring and Constructing an Object

We now have a class we can use to create **Widget** objects. Yes, it's a very simple class, but it will work. There are two steps in creating an object from a class - **declare** the object, then **construct** the object. Note these are the same steps we've used with the built-in Java objects.

Return to the example project. The **Widget** object will be created in the **WidgetTest.java** file. All the code we write in this example will be in this files **main** method.

To declare a **Widget** object named **myWidget**, type this line of code in this method:

```
Widget myWidget;
```

Now, to construct this object, type this line of code:

```
myWidget = new Widget();
```

This line just says "give me a new widget." Our **Widget** object is now complete, ready for use. The main method should appear as:

```
public static void main(String args[])
{
  System.out.println("Testing the Widget!!\n");
  Widget myWidget;
  myWidget = new Widget();
}
```

There's not much we can do with it obviously - it has no properties or methods, but it does exist! You may wonder how we can construct a **Widget** object if we have not defined a constructor. The line above uses the **default** constructor automatically included with every class. The default constructor simply creates an object with no defined properties.

Adding Properties to a Class

There are two ways to define properties within a class description: creating direct **public variables** or creating **accessor methods.** We look at the first way here. Our **Widget** class will have two properties: **color** (a **String** type) and **size** (an **int** type). Class properties can be any type of variable or object – yes, properties can actually be other objects!

To define these properties in our class, go to the **Widget.java** file and add the shaded lines to the file:

```
public class Widget
{
  public String color;
  public int size;
}
```

The keyword **public** is used so the properties are available outside the class when the object is created.

Now, return to the **WidgetTest.java** file so we can provide some definition to these properties in our instance of the object. In the **main** method, add this shaded code to define and print the properties:

```
public static void main(String args[])
{
  System.out.println("Testing the Widget!!\n");
  Widget myWidget;
  myWidget = new Widget();
  myWidget.color = "red";
  myWidget.size = 15;
  System.out.println("Color is " + myWidget.color);
  System.out.println("Size is " + myWidget.size);
}
```

Note, to refer to an object property, you use this format:

```
objectName.propertyName
```

Run the example project. In the output window you should see the two
properties printed at the end:

```
General Output
    --------------------Configuration: WidgetTest - JDK version 1.6.
    ----
    Testing the Widget!!

    Color is red
    Size is 15

    Process completed.
```

We've created and defined our first object! There's nothing to keep you from
creating as many widgets as you want.

Another Way to Add Properties to a Class

We mentioned there are two ways to add properties to a class. Here, we will look at the second method, creating **accessor methods**. The rationale behind this second method is to allow validation and/or modification of properties, giving you complete control over the property. The Java swing controls use such methods to **get** and **set** properties.

For each property to be established using a method, first determine the property name (**name**) and type (**type**). Declare the property using the **private** keyword (rather than the **public** keyword used now). Then type lines similar to these inside the boundaries of your class:

```
private type name;
public type getName()
{
  return name;
}
public void setName(type n)
{
  name = n;
}
```

There are two methods in this code: a **get** method (called a **getter** method) to determine the current property value and a **set** method (called a **setter** method) to establish a new property value. A local variable (**n**) is used to hold the property value.

With such methods, a **property** for an object (**objectName**)is accessed using:

```
property = objectName.getName();
```

And is set using:

```
objectName.setName(property);
```

Note a user cannot directly access the variable representing the property value.

The use of this technique is best illustrated with example. For our **Widget** class, the **color** property can be established using:

```
private String color;
public String getColor()
{
  return color;
}
public void setColor(String c)
{
  color = c;
}
```

In this snippet, **color** is now a local variable representing the **Widget** color. This variable cannot be accessed directly. The **getColor** method is used to determine the widget color, while the **setColor** method is used to provide a color value.

For the **size** property in our **Widget** class, we can use:

```
private int size;
public int getSize()
{
  return size;
}
public void setSize(int s)
{
  size = s;
}
```

Go to the **Widget.java** file and replace the code with the above accessor methods. The file should appear as:

```java
public class Widget
{
  private String color;
  public String getColor()
  {
    return color;
  }
  public void setColor(String c)
  {
    color = c;
  }

  private int size;
  public int getSize()
  {
    return size;
  }
  public void setSize(int s)
  {
    size = s;
  }
}
```

Now, go to the **WidgetTest.java** file and make the shaded changes to use the set and get methods:

```
public static void main(String args[])
{
  System.out.println("Testing the Widget!!\n");
  Widget myWidget;
  myWidget = new Widget();
  myWidget.setColor("red");
  myWidget.setSize(15);
  System.out.println("Color is " + myWidget.getColor());
  System.out.println("Size is " + myWidget.getSize());
}
```

Run the project. You will see the same results in the console window.

As written, this new code offers no advantage to directly reading and writing the property value. The real advantage to using methods rather than public variables is that property values can be validated and modified. Let see how to do such a validation.

Validating Class Properties

Validation of class properties is done in the **set** method (the **get** method can be used to modify properties before returning values). In this method, we can examine the value provided by the user and see if it meets the validation criteria (in range, positive, non-zero, etc.).

For our **Widget** example, let's assume there are only three color possibilities: **red**, **white**, or **blue** and that the size must be between **5** and **40**. Return to the example and open the code window for **Widget.java**. Modify the **setColor** and **setSize** methods with the shaded changes:

```java
public class Widget
{
  private String color;
  public String getColor()
  {
    return color;
  }
  public void setColor(String c)
  {
    if (c.toUpperCase().equals("RED"))
    {
      color = c;
    }
    else if (c.toUpperCase().equals("WHITE"))
    {
      color = c;
    }
    else if (c.toUpperCase().equals("BLUE"))
    {
      color = c;
    }
    else
    {
        System.out.println("Bad widget color!");
    }
  }
```

```
private int size;
public int getSize()
{
  return size;
}
public void setSize(int s)
{
  if (s >= 5 && s <= 40)
  {
    size = s;
  }
  else
  {
    System.out.println("Bad widget size!");
  }
}
}
```

Notice how the validation works – a message will appear if a bad value is selected.

Return to the **WidgetTest.java** code and make the shaded change (use a bad color):

```
public static void main(String args[])
{
  System.out.println("Testing the Widget!!\n");
  Widget myWidget;
  myWidget = new Widget();
  myWidget.setColor("green");
  myWidget.setSize(15);
  System.out.println("Color is " + myWidget.getColor());
  System.out.println("Size is " + myWidget.getSize());
}
```

Rerun the application and a message announcing a bad color property should appear:

```
General Output
-------------------Configuration: WidgetTest - JDK version 1.6.
----
Testing the Widget!!

Bad widget color!
Color is null
Size is 15

Process completed.
```

Reset the color property to a proper value, change the size property to a bad value and make sure its validation also works.

We suggest that, except in very simple classes, you always use the method approach to setting and reading properties. This approach, though a little more complicated, allows the most flexibility in your application. Using the method approach, you can also make properties read-only and write-only. Consult Java documentation for information on doing this.

Adding Constructors to a Class

Once an object is declared, it must be created using a **constructor**. A constructor is a method with the same name as the class that provides a way to initialize an object. Each class has a default constructor. This is the constructor we have been using with our simple example. The default constructor simply creates the object with no properties at all.

Constructors are usually used to establish some set of default properties. A constructor that does that is:

```
public ClassName()
{
  [Set properties here]
}
```

This code is usually placed near the top of the class description.

One way to establish initial properties for our **Widget** class is:

```
public Widget()
{
  color = "red";
  size = 12;
}
```

This will work, but the properties would not be checked in the validation code just written. To validate initial properties, use this code instead:

```
public Widget()
{
  this.setColor("red");
  this.setSize(12);
}
```

where the keyword **this** refers to the current object. Type the above code in the **Widget** class example. Put the code after the line declaring the **color** variable. Then, return to the **WidgetTest.java** code, delete the two lines setting the color and size properties, and then rerun the application. You should see (in the console window) that the color is now **red** and the size is **12**.

You can also defined **overloaded constructors**. Such constructors still have the class name, but have different argument lists, providing the potential for multiple ways to initialize an object. We have seen overloaded constructors with the built-in Java objects. In our **Widget** example, say we wanted to allow the user to specify the initial color and size at the same time the object is created. A constructor that does this task is:

```
public Widget(String c, int s)
{
  this.setColor(c);
  this.setSize(s);
}
```

Type this code below the default constructor, **Widget()**, in the **Widget.java** code..

Return to the **WidgetTest.java** code and modify the constructor line so it looks like the shaded line:

```
public static void main(String args[])
{
  System.out.println("Testing the Widget!!\n");
  Widget myWidget;
  myWidget = new Widget("blue", 22);
  System.out.println("Color is " + myWidget.getColor());
  System.out.println("Size is " + myWidget.getSize());
}
```

This code now uses the new overloaded constructor, setting the color to **blue** and the size to **22**.

Run the application to make sure it works. You should see:

```
General Output
    --------------------Configuration: WidgetTest - JDK version 1.6.
    ----
    Testing the Widget!!

    Color is blue
    Size is 22

    Process completed.
```

A class can have any number of constructors. The only limitation is that no two constructors can have matching argument lists (same number and type of arguments).

Adding Methods to a Class

Class **methods** allow objects to perform certain tasks. Like constructors, a class can have overloaded methods, similar to the overloaded methods we have seen with the built-in objects of Java.

To add a method to a class description, first select a name and a type of information the method will return (if there is any returned value). The framework for a method named **myMethod** that returns a **type** value is:

```
public type myMethod()
{
}
```

This code is usually placed following the property methods in a class description.

In our **Widget** example, say we want a method that describes the color of the widget. Such a method would look like this:

```
public String describeWidget()
{
   return ("My widget is colored " + color);
}
```

Type the above code before the closing brace for the **Widget.java** file in our example.

To use an object's method in code, use the following syntax:

```
objectName.methodName(Arguments)
```

In this syntax, **objectName** is the name of the object, **methodName** the name of the method and **Arguments** is a comma-delimited list of any arguments needed by the method.

To try the **DescribeWidget** method in our example, return to the
WidgetTest.java code and modify the shaded line as shown:

```
public static void main(String args[])
{
  System.out.println("Testing the Widget!!\n");
  Widget myWidget;
  myWidget = new Widget("blue", 22);
  System.out.println(myWidget.describeWidget());
  System.out.println("Size is " + myWidget.getSize());
}
```

In this code, we now use the method to describe widget color. Run the
application to check that the method works as expected. The output window
should appear as:

```
General Output
-------------------Configuration: WidgetTest - JDK version 1.6.
----
Testing the Widget!!

My widget is colored blue
Size is 22

Process completed.
```

Let's try another method. This method (**compareWidget**) compares a widget's size to a **standard widget** (which has size **20**):

```java
public String compareWidget()
{
  int diff;
  diff = size - 20;
  if (diff > 0)
  {
    return ("My widget is " + String.valueOf(diff) + "
units larger than a standard widget.");
  }
  else
  {
    return ("My widget is " +
String.valueOf(Math.abs(diff)) + " units smaller than a
standard widget.");
  }
}
```

Type the **CompareWidget** method into **Widget.java**, then modify **WidgetTest.java** as (shaded line is new):

```java
public static void main(String args[])
{
  System.out.println("Testing the Widget!!\n");
  Widget myWidget;
  myWidget = new Widget("blue", 22);
  System.out.println(myWidget.describeWidget());
  System.out.println("Size is " + myWidget.getSize());
  System.out.println(myWidget.compareWidget());
}
```

Run the application to see this new output window:

```
General Output
--------------------Configuration: WidgetTest - JDK version 1.6.
----
Testing the Widget!!

My widget is colored blue
Size is 22
My widget is 2 units larger than a standard widget.

Process completed.
```

Methods can also have arguments and overload other methods. Suppose in our example, we want to input the size of a widget (**s**, an **int** type) we would like to compare our widget to. This method does the job:

```
public String compareWidget(int s)
{
  int diff;
  diff = size - s;
  if (diff > 0)
  {
    return ("My widget is " + String.valueOf(diff) + "
units larger than your widget.");
  }
  else
  {
    return ("My widget is " +
String.valueOf(Math.abs(diff)) + " units smaller than your
widget.");
  }
}
```

Note this method has the same name as our previous method (**compareWidget**), but the different argument list differentiates this overloaded version from the previous version.

Type the overloaded version of **CompareWidget** into the **Widget.java** class code. Then, modify the **WidgetTest.java** code to use this method (shaded line is new):

```
public static void main(String args[])
{
   System.out.println("Testing the Widget!!\n");
   Widget myWidget;
   myWidget = new Widget("blue", 22);
   System.out.println(myWidget.describeWidget());
   System.out.println("Size is " + myWidget.getSize());
   System.out.println(myWidget.compareWidget() + "\n" +
myWidget.compareWidget(15));
}
```

Run the modified application and you should see:

```
General Output
-------------------Configuration: WidgetTest - JDK version 1.6.
----
Testing the Widget!!

My widget is colored blue
Size is 22
My widget is 2 units larger than a standard widget.
My widget is 7 units larger than your widget.

Process completed.
```

Inheritance

The people you built the **Widget** class for are so happy with it, they've decided they now want to develop an 'armed' widget. This new widget will be just like the old widget (have a color and size), but will also have arms. This means this new class (**ArmedWidget**) will have one additional property – the number of arms.

To build the **ArmedWidget** class, we could start from scratch – develop a class with three properties, a method that describes the armed widget and a method that compares the armed widget. Or, we could take advantage of a very powerful concept in object-oriented programming, **inheritance**. Inheritance is the idea that you can base one class on another existing class, adding properties and/or methods as needed. This saves lots of work.

Let's see how inheritance works with our widget. Return to the **WidgetTest** project we've been using. Add another class file to the project, naming it **ArmedWidget.java** – and add it to the **widgettest** source package. Delete code that appears in the file.   Use this code for the class:

```
package widgettest;
public class ArmedWidget extends Widget
{
   private int arms;
   public int getArms()
   {
     return arms;
   }
   public void setArms(int a)
   {
     arms = a;
   }
}
```

The key line here is:

```
extends Widget
```

This makes all the properties and methods of the **Widget** class available to our new class (**ArmedWidget**). The remaining code simply adds the unvalidated property **arms**. We could, of course, add validation to this property if desired.

Now, return to the **WidgetTest.java** code file. We will modify the code to create, define, and describe an **ArmedWidget** object. The modifications are shaded:

```java
public static void main(String args[])
{
   System.out.println("Testing the Widget!!\n");
   Widget myWidget;
   myWidget = new Widget("blue", 22);
   System.out.println(myWidget.describeWidget());
   System.out.println("Size is " + myWidget.getSize());
   System.out.println(myWidget.compareWidget() + "\n" +
myWidget.compareWidget(15));
   ArmedWidget myArmedWidget;
   myArmedWidget = new ArmedWidget();
   myArmedWidget.setColor("white");
   myArmedWidget.setSize(33);
   myArmedWidget.setArms(11);
   System.out.println(myArmedWidget.describeWidget());
   System.out.println("My armed widget has " +
String.valueOf(myArmedWidget.getArms()) + " arms.");
   System.out.println("Size is " +
String.valueOf(myArmedWidget.getSize()));
   System.out.println(myArmedWidget.compareWidget() + "\n"
+ myArmedWidget.compareWidget(15));
}
```

Run the application and view the output window to see:

```
General Output
-------------------Configuration: WidgetTest - JDK version 1.6.
----
Testing the Widget!!

My widget is colored blue
Size is 22
My widget is 2 units larger than a standard widget.
My widget is 7 units larger than your widget.
My widget is colored white
My armed widget has 11 arms.
Size is 33
My widget is 13 units larger than a standard widget.
My widget is 18 units larger than your widget.

Process completed.
```

You see the descriptions of both the old 'standard' widget and the new, improved 'armed' widget.

You may have noticed a couple of drawbacks to this inherited class. First, the method used to describe the widget (**describeWidget**) only provides color information. We added an extra line of code to define the number of arms. It would be nice if this information could be part of the **describeWidget** method. That process is called **overriding** methods. Second, we need to know how to use the constructors developed for the **Widget** class in our new **ArmedWidget** class. Let's attack both drawbacks.

When a class extends (or inherits) another class, it can pick and choose what it wants to inherit. If your new class has a method that has the same name (and same argument list) as a method in the base class (the class you inherit from), that new method will **override** (or replace) the base class method. An example will make this clear.

Go to the **ArmedWidget.java** file and add this method to the class definition:

```
public String describeWidget()
{
   return ("My armed widget is colored " + this.getColor()
+ " and has " + String.valueOf(arms) + " arms.");
}
```

Some comments about this method. This adds a method **describeWidget** to the **ArmedWidget** class, allowing the number of arms to be included in the description. It **overrides** the method in the **Widget** class. Since arms is a local variable in the class, it is referred to by its name. The color property is not local to the **ArmedWidget** class. Note, to refer to properties inherited from the base class, you use the syntax:

```
this.getPropertyName()
```

Hence, in this example, we use:

```
this.getColor()
```

to refer to the inherited color property.

Now, rerun the application and the output window should display:

```
General Output
--------------------Configuration: WidgetTest - JDK version 1.6.
----
Testing the Widget!!

My widget is colored blue
Size is 22
My widget is 2 units larger than a standard widget.
My widget is 7 units larger than your widget.
My armed widget is colored white and has 11 arms.
My armed widget has 11 arms.
Size is 33
My widget is 13 units larger than a standard widget.
My widget is 18 units larger than your widget.

Process completed.
```

The armed widget description now includes the number of arms (making the line of code following the **describeWidget** method invocation redundant). Any method in the base class can be overridden using the same approach followed here.

Before leaving this example, let's see how constructors in base classes can be used in the new class. Any base class constructor can be called using this syntax:

```
super();
```

where there may or not be an argument list. Recall the default constructor in the **Widget** class created a **red** widget that was **12** units in size. To use this constructor in the **ArmedWidget** class (while at the same time, setting the number of arms to 4), add this constructor to that class code file:

```
public ArmedWidget()
{
  super();
  this.setArms(4);
}
```

This constructor will first invoke the **Widget** constructor, then add the new property value.

Now, return to the **WidgetTest.java** code and delete the three lines defining properties for the **ArmedWidget** and the line printing out the number of arms (since that information is now in the **describeWidget** method). Run the modified application and note in the output window:

```
General Output
--------------------Configuration: WidgetTest - JDK version 1.6.(
Testing the Widget!!

My widget is colored blue
Size is 22
My widget is 2 units larger than a standard widget.
My widget is 7 units larger than your widget.
My armed widget is colored red and has 4 arms.
Size is 12
My widget is 8 units smaller than a standard widget.
My widget is 3 units smaller than your widget.

Process completed.
```

As expected, the new default armed widget is **red**, size **12**, and has **4 arms**.

We're done playing with our widget example. The information you've learned should help when you want to implement custom objects in your applications. The final version of our **Widget** project is saved as **WidgetTest** in the **\LearnJava\LJ Code\Appendix II** project group.

Let's leave our 'make-believe' widget world and do a real-world OOP example. We'll rebuild the savings account example we did way back in Class 2 using a **Savings** object.

Example II-1

Savings Account

Start a new empty project in **Netbeans**. Name the project **Savings**. Delete default code in Java file named **Savings**. The idea of this project is to determine how much you save by making monthly deposits into a savings account. For those interested, the mathematical formula used is:

$$F = D \left[(1 + I)^M - 1 \right] / I$$

where

F - Final amount
D - Monthly deposit amount
I - Monthly interest rate
M - Number of months

The finished frame will look like this:

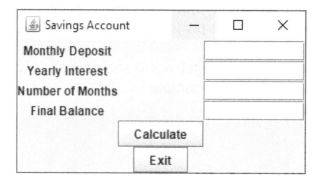

We will do the computation using object-oriented programming (OOP), rather than the 'sequential' process followed in **Example 2-3**. The input values (D, I, M) will be class properties, while the computation of F should be a class method.

1. We will place 4 labels, 4 text fields, and 2 buttons on the frame. The arrangement in the **GridBagLayout** will be.

	gridx = 0	gridx = 1	gridx = 2
gridy = 0	depositLabel		depositTextField
gridy = 1	interestLabel		interestTextField
gridy = 2	monthsLabel		monthsTextField
gridy = 3	finalLabel		finalTextField
gridy = 4		calculateButton	
gridy = 5		exitButton	

Properties set in code:

Savings Frame:
title	Savings Account

depositLabel:
text	Monthly Deposit
gridx	0
gridy	0

interestLabel:
text	Yearly Interest
gridx	0
gridy	1

monthsLabel:
text	Number of Months
gridx	0
gridy	2

finalLabel:
text	Final Balance
gridx	0
gridy	3

depositTextField:

text	[Blank]
columns	10
gridx	2
gridy	0

interestTextField:

text	[Blank]
columns	10
gridx	2
gridy	1

monthsTextField:

text	[Blank]
columns	10
gridx	2
gridy	2

finalTextField:

text	[Blank]
Columns	10
gridx	2
gridy	3

calculateButton:

text	Calculate
gridx	1
gridy	4

exitButton:

text	Exit
gridx	1
gridy	5

2. We will build the project in three stages – frame, controls, code. Type this basic framework code to establish the frame and its **windowClosing** event:

```
/*
 * Savings.java
 */
package savings;
import javax.swing.*;
import java.awt.*;
import java.awt.event.*;

public class Savings extends JFrame
{
  public static void main(String args[])
  {
    //construct frame
    new Savings().setVisible(true);
  }
  public Savings()
  {
    // code to build the form
    setTitle("Savings Account");
    addWindowListener(new WindowAdapter()
    {
      public void windowClosing(WindowEvent e)
      {
        exitForm(e);
      }
    });
    getContentPane().setLayout(new GridBagLayout());
  }
  private void exitForm(WindowEvent e)
  {
    System.exit(0);
  }
}
```

Run the code to insure the frame appears (it will be very small and empty):

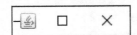

3. Now, we add the controls and empty event methods. Declare and create the
   10 controls as class level objects:

```
JLabel depositLabel = new JLabel();
JLabel interestLabel = new JLabel();
JLabel monthsLabel = new JLabel();
JLabel finalLabel = new JLabel();
JTextField depositTextField = new JTextField();
JTextField interestTextField = new JTextField();
JTextField monthsTextField = new JTextField();
JTextField finalTextField = new JTextField();
JButton calculateButton = new JButton();
JButton exitButton = new JButton();
```

Position and add each control. Add methods for controls we need events for
(**calculateButton** and **exitButton** in this case):

```
// position controls (establish event methods)
GridBagConstraints gridConstraints = new
GridBagConstraints();
depositLabel.setText("Monthly Deposit");
gridConstraints.gridx = 0;
gridConstraints.gridy = 0;
getContentPane().add(depositLabel, gridConstraints);
interestLabel.setText("Yearly Interest");
gridConstraints.gridx = 0;
gridConstraints.gridy = 1;
getContentPane().add(interestLabel, gridConstraints);
monthsLabel.setText("Number of Months");
gridConstraints.gridx = 0;
gridConstraints.gridy = 2;
getContentPane().add(monthsLabel, gridConstraints);
finalLabel.setText("Final Balance");
gridConstraints.gridx = 0;
gridConstraints.gridy = 3;
getContentPane().add(finalLabel, gridConstraints);

depositTextField.setText("");
depositTextField.setColumns(10);
gridConstraints.gridx = 2;
gridConstraints.gridy = 0;
getContentPane().add(depositTextField, gridConstraints);
depositTextField.addActionListener(new ActionListener()
{
  public void actionPerformed(ActionEvent e)
  {
```

```
        depositTextFieldActionPerformed(e);
    }
});

interestTextField.setText("");
interestTextField.setColumns(10);
gridConstraints.gridx = 2;
gridConstraints.gridy = 1;
getContentPane().add(interestTextField, gridConstraints);
interestTextField.addActionListener(new ActionListener()
{
  public void actionPerformed(ActionEvent e)
  {
    interestTextFieldActionPerformed(e);
  }
});

monthsTextField.setText("");
monthsTextField.setColumns(10);
gridConstraints.gridx = 2;
gridConstraints.gridy = 2;
getContentPane().add(monthsTextField, gridConstraints);
monthsTextField.addActionListener(new ActionListener()
{
  public void actionPerformed(ActionEvent e)
  {
    monthsTextFieldActionPerformed(e);
  }
});

finalTextField.setText("");
finalTextField.setFocusable(false);
finalTextField.setColumns(10);
gridConstraints.gridx = 2;
gridConstraints.gridy = 3;
getContentPane().add(finalTextField, gridConstraints);

calculateButton.setText("Calculate");
gridConstraints.gridx = 1;
gridConstraints.gridy = 4;
getContentPane().add(calculateButton, gridConstraints);
calculateButton.addActionListener(new ActionListener()
{
  public void actionPerformed(ActionEvent e)
  {
calculateButtonActionPerformed(e);
  }
```

```
});
exitButton.setText("Exit");
exitButton.setFocusable(false);
gridConstraints.gridx = 1;
gridConstraints.gridy = 5;
getContentPane().add(exitButton, gridConstraints);
exitButton.addActionListener(new ActionListener()
{
  public void actionPerformed(ActionEvent e)
  {
exitButtonActionPerformed(e);
  }
});
pack();
Dimension screenSize =
Toolkit.getDefaultToolkit().getScreenSize();
    setBounds((int) (0.5 * (screenSize.width -
getWidth())), (int) (0.5 * (screenSize.height -
getHeight())), getWidth(), getHeight());
```

Add the methods that transfer focus from one text field to the next:

```
private void depositTextFieldActionPerformed(ActionEvent
e)
{
  depositTextField.transferFocus();
}

private void interestTextFieldActionPerformed(ActionEvent
e)
{
  interestTextField.transferFocus();
}

private void monthsTextFieldActionPerformed(ActionEvent e)
{
  monthsTextField.transferFocus();
}
```

Lastly, add the two methods (empty for now) needed (place after the frame constructor):

```
private void calculateButtonActionPerformed(ActionEvent e)
{
}

private void exitButtonActionPerformed(ActionEvent e)
{
}
```

Run to see the finished control placement:

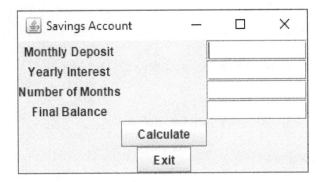

4. Add the **validateDecimalNumber** method for input validation:

```java
public boolean validateDecimalNumber(JTextField tf)
{
  // checks to see if text field contains
  // valid decimal number with only digits and a single
decimal point
  String s = tf.getText().trim();
  boolean hasDecimal = false;
  boolean valid = true;
  if (s.length() == 0)
  {
    valid = false;
  }
  else
  {
    for (int i = 0; i < s.length(); i++)
    {
      char c = s.charAt(i);
      if (c >= '0' && c <= '9')
      {
        continue;
      }
      else if (c == '.' && !hasDecimal)
      {
        hasDecimal = true;
      }
      else
      {
        // invalid character found
        valid = false;
      }
    }
  }
  if (valid)
  {
    tf.setText(s);
  }
  else
  {
    tf.setText("");
    tf.requestFocus();
  }
  return (valid);
}
```

5. Add a **SavingsAccount.java** class file (to the **savings** source package) from
   which to create **SavingsAccount** objects. The class will have three public
   properties: **deposit, interest** and **months,** all **double** types. The class will
   have a single method: **computeFinal,** which will compute the final amount
   (a **double** type).

```
package savings;
public class SavingsAccount
{

   public double deposit;
   public double interest;
   public double months;

   public double computeFinal()
   {
      double intRate;
    if (interest == 0)
    {
      // zero interest case
      return (deposit * months);
    }
    else
    {
      intRate = interest / 1200;
      return (deposit * (Math.pow((1 + intRate), months) -
1) / intRate);
    }
  }
}
```

6. Write code for the **btnCalculate** button **Click** event:

```
private void calculateButtonActionPerformed(ActionEvent e)
{
  // make sure each input is a valid number
  if (!validateDecimalNumber(monthsTextField) ||
!validateDecimalNumber(interestTextField) ||
!validateDecimalNumber(depositTextField))
  {
    // if one or more fields not valid number, then exit
method
    return;
  }
  // create and construct Savings object
  SavingsAccount mySavings;
  mySavings = new SavingsAccount();
  // set properties from text boxes
  mySavings.deposit =
Double.valueOf(depositTextField.getText()).doubleValue();
  mySavings.interest =
Double.valueOf(interestTextField.getText()).doubleValue();
   mySavings.months =
Double.valueOf(monthsTextField.getText()).doubleValue();
  // compute final value and put in text box
  finalTextField.setText(new
DecimalFormat("0.00").format(mySavings.computeFinal()));
}
```

In this code, notice each typed value is checked for proper format. Any text fields with improper values are cleared and given focus to allow the user to try again. Calculations do not proceed until all inputs are valid. Then, the code creates a **mySavings** object from the **SavingsAccount** class. It then reads the three input values (monthly deposit, interest rate, number of months) from the text fields, establishes the object properties, computes the final balance (using the **computeFinal** method) and puts that result in a text field.

Compare this OOP code with the more 'sequential' code used in **Example 2-3**, where we established three variables (deposit, interest, months) and computed a final amount using a formula within the event method. The two approaches are not that different. The advantage to the OOP approach is that the **SavingsAccount** class can be re-used in other applications and it would be very simple to model other savings account objects within this application.

7. Now, write code for the **btnExit** button **Click** event.

```
private void exitButtonActionPerformed(ActionEvent e)
{
   System.exit(0);
}
```

Here is the complete **Savings.java** code listing (code added to basic frame code is shaded):

```
/*
 * Savings.java
*/
package savings;
import javax.swing.*;
import java.awt.*;
import java.awt.event.*;
import java.text.*;

public class Savings extends JFrame
{
   JLabel depositLabel = new JLabel();
   JLabel interestLabel = new JLabel();
   JLabel monthsLabel = new JLabel();
   JLabel finalLabel = new JLabel();
   JTextField depositTextField = new JTextField();
   JTextField interestTextField = new JTextField();
   JTextField monthsTextField = new JTextField();
   JTextField finalTextField = new JTextField();
   JButton calculateButton = new JButton();
   JButton exitButton = new JButton();

   public static void main(String args[])
   {
      //construct frame
      new Savings().setVisible(true);
   }
   public Savings()
   {
      // code to build the form
      setTitle("Savings Account");
      addWindowListener(new WindowAdapter()
      {
         public void windowClosing(WindowEvent e)
         {
```

```
        exitForm(e);
      }
   });

   getContentPane().setLayout(new GridBagLayout());
   // position controls (establish event methods)
   GridBagConstraints gridConstraints = new
GridBagConstraints();
   depositLabel.setText("Monthly Deposit");
   gridConstraints.gridx = 0;
   gridConstraints.gridy = 0;
   getContentPane().add(depositLabel, gridConstraints);
   interestLabel.setText("Yearly Interest");
   gridConstraints.gridx = 0;
   gridConstraints.gridy = 1;
   getContentPane().add(interestLabel, gridConstraints);
   monthsLabel.setText("Number of Months");
   gridConstraints.gridx = 0;
   gridConstraints.gridy = 2;
   getContentPane().add(monthsLabel, gridConstraints);
   finalLabel.setText("Final Balance");
   gridConstraints.gridx = 0;
   gridConstraints.gridy = 3;
   getContentPane().add(finalLabel, gridConstraints);

   depositTextField.setText("");
   depositTextField.setColumns(10);
   gridConstraints.gridx = 2;
   gridConstraints.gridy = 0;
   getContentPane().add(depositTextField, gridConstraints);
   depositTextField.addActionListener(new ActionListener()
   {
     public void actionPerformed(ActionEvent e)
     {
       depositTextFieldActionPerformed(e);
     }
   });

   interestTextField.setText("");
   interestTextField.setColumns(10);
   gridConstraints.gridx = 2;
   gridConstraints.gridy = 1;
   getContentPane().add(interestTextField, gridConstraints);
   interestTextField.addActionListener(new ActionListener()
   {
     public void actionPerformed(ActionEvent e)
     {
```

```
        interestTextFieldActionPerformed(e);
    }
});

monthsTextField.setText("");
monthsTextField.setColumns(10);
gridConstraints.gridx = 2;
gridConstraints.gridy = 2;
getContentPane().add(monthsTextField, gridConstraints);
monthsTextField.addActionListener(new ActionListener()
{
  public void actionPerformed(ActionEvent e)
  {
    monthsTextFieldActionPerformed(e);
  }
});

finalTextField.setText("");
finalTextField.setFocusable(false);
finalTextField.setColumns(10);
gridConstraints.gridx = 2;
gridConstraints.gridy = 3;
getContentPane().add(finalTextField, gridConstraints);

calculateButton.setText("Calculate");
gridConstraints.gridx = 1;
gridConstraints.gridy = 4;
getContentPane().add(calculateButton, gridConstraints);
calculateButton.addActionListener(new ActionListener()
{
  public void actionPerformed(ActionEvent e)
  {
    calculateButtonActionPerformed(e);
  }
});
exitButton.setText("Exit");
exitButton.setFocusable(false);
gridConstraints.gridx = 1;
gridConstraints.gridy = 5;
getContentPane().add(exitButton, gridConstraints);

exitButton.addActionListener(new ActionListener()
{
  public void actionPerformed(ActionEvent e)
  {
    exitButtonActionPerformed(e);
  }
```

```
    });
    pack();
    Dimension screenSize =
Toolkit.getDefaultToolkit().getScreenSize();
    setBounds((int) (0.5 * (screenSize.width - getWidth())),
(int) (0.5 * (screenSize.height - getHeight())), getWidth(),
getHeight());

  }
  private void exitForm(WindowEvent e)
  {
    System.exit(0);
  }


  private void calculateButtonActionPerformed(ActionEvent e)
  {
    // make sure each input is a valid number
    if (!validateDecimalNumber(monthsTextField) ||
!validateDecimalNumber(interestTextField) ||
!validateDecimalNumber(depositTextField))
    {
      // if one or more fields not valid number, then exit
method
      return;
    }

    // create and construct Savings object
    SavingsAccount mySavings;
    mySavings = new SavingsAccount();
    // set properties from text boxes
    mySavings.deposit =
Double.valueOf(depositTextField.getText()).doubleValue();
    mySavings.interest =
Double.valueOf(interestTextField.getText()).doubleValue();
    mySavings.months =
Double.valueOf(monthsTextField.getText()).doubleValue();
    // compute final value and put in text box
    finalTextField.setText(new
DecimalFormat("0.00").format(mySavings.computeFinal()));
  }


  private void exitButtonActionPerformed(ActionEvent e)
  {
    System.exit(0);
  }


  private void depositTextFieldActionPerformed(ActionEvent e)
```

```
  {
    depositTextField.transferFocus();
  }
  private void interestTextFieldActionPerformed(ActionEvent
e)
  {
    interestTextField.transferFocus();
  }
  private void monthsTextFieldActionPerformed(ActionEvent e)
  {
    monthsTextField.transferFocus();
  }

  public boolean validateDecimalNumber(JTextField tf)
  {
    // checks to see if text field contains
    // valid decimal number with only digits and a single
decimal point
    String s = tf.getText().trim();
    boolean hasDecimal = false;
    boolean valid = true;
    if (s.length() == 0)
    {
      valid = false;
    }
    else
    {
      for (int i = 0; i < s.length(); i++)
      {
        char c = s.charAt(i);
        if (c >= '0' && c <= '9')
        {
          continue;
        }
        else if (c == '.' && !hasDecimal)
        {
          hasDecimal = true;
        }
        else
        {
          // invalid character found
          valid = false;
        }
      }
    }
    if (valid)
    {
```

```
      tf.setText(s);
    }
    else
    {
      tf.setText("");
      tf.requestFocus();
    }
    return (valid);
  }
}
```

Run the code. Play with the program. Make sure it works properly. Here's a run I made:

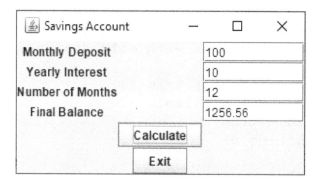

Save the project. This is saved as the **ExampleII-1** project in **\LearnJava\LJ Code\Appendix II** project group.

In **Example 2-4**, we modified this example such that you could enter any three values and have the missing value computed. If you're adventurous, try creating another object that inherits from the **SavingsAccount** class. Have your new object implement methods that compute the missing value. The equations were given in **Example 2-4**.

Inheriting from Java Controls

We saw in the **Widget** example that we could create new, enhanced widgets from an existing widget class. We can do the same with the existing Java Swing controls. That is, we can design our own controls, based on the standard controls, with custom features. (Actually, you can design controls that aren't based on existing controls, but that's beyond the scope of this discussion.)

Inheriting from existing controls allow us to:

Establish new default values for properties.
Introduce new properties.
Establish commonly used methods.

As an example, note whenever a text field is used for numeric input (like the **Savings Account** example), we need to validate the typed values to make sure only numeric input is provided. Wouldn't it be nice to have a text field control with this validation "built-in?" To demonstrate inheritance from Java controls, we will build just this control – a **numeric text field**.

Our numeric text field control will be built in several stages to demonstrate each step. Once done, we will have a control that anyone can add to their "Java toolbox" and use in their applications. The specifications for our numeric text field are:

  - ➤ Blue background color
  - ➤ Yellow foreground color
  - ➤ Size 14, Arial font
  - ➤ Allows numeric digits (0-9)
  - ➤ Allows a backspace
  - ➤ Allows a single decimal point (optional)
  - ➤ Allows a negative sign (optional)
  - ➤ Ignores all other keystrokes

Note some specifications address setting and defining properties while others (entry validation) require establishing a common control event method. Let's start with setting properties.

Building a Custom Control

Let's build a framework to out the new control, start a project named **NumericTextFieldTest**.   Replace the default code with:

```java
/*
 * NumericTextFieldTest.java
*/
package numerictextfieldtest;
import javax.swing.*;
import java.awt.*;
import java.awt.event.*;

public class NumericTextFieldTest extends JFrame
{

  public static void main(String args[])
  {
    //construct frame
    new NumericTextFieldTest().setVisible(true);
  }
  public NumericTextFieldTest()
  {
    // code to build the form
    setTitle("Numeric Text Field Test");
    addWindowListener(new WindowAdapter()
    {
      public void windowClosing(WindowEvent e)
      {
        exitForm(e);
      }
    });

    getContentPane().setLayout(new GridBagLayout());
    // position controls
    GridBagConstraints gridConstraints = new
GridBagConstraints();
    pack();
    Dimension screenSize =
Toolkit.getDefaultToolkit().getScreenSize();
    setBounds((int) (0.5 * (screenSize.width -
getWidth())), (int) (0.5 * (screenSize.height -
getHeight())), getWidth(), getHeight());

  }
```

```
   private void exitForm(WindowEvent e)
   {
     System.exit(0);
   }

}
```

Run to see an empty frame.

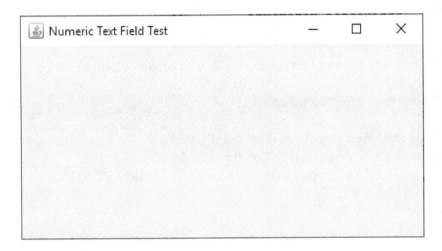

Now, we'll build a text field control with the desired background color (**Blue**), foreground color (**Yellow**), and font (Size **14**, **Arial**). Add a Java class filed named **NumericTextField** to the project's source folder. This file will define our new control. Type these lines in this file:

```
package numerictextfieldtest;
import javax.swing.*;
import javax.swing.event.*;
import java.awt.*;
public class NumericTextField extends JTextField
{
}
```

Here we are creating a new class named **NumericTextField** that inherits from the **JTextField** Swing control. Since there is no other code, this new control will act and behave just like a normal text field. Nothing will change until we add properties and methods of our own.

We want our numeric text field to have a default background color of **blue**, a default foreground color of **yellow** and a default font of size **14, Arial**. These default properties are established in the default constructor for the control. Modify the **NumericTextField** class code with the shaded lines to implement such a constructor:

```java
package numerictextfieldtest;
import javax.swing.*;
import javax.swing.event.*;
import java.awt.*;
import java.awt.event.*;
public class NumericTextField extends JTextField
{
  public NumericTextField()
  {
    this.setBackground(Color.BLUE);
    this.setForeground(Color.YELLOW);
    this.setFont(new Font("Arial", Font.PLAIN, 14));
  }
}
```

To try out the new control, add the shaded code to the
NumericTextFieldTest.java file. The new code simply places a single numeric
text field on a form:

```java
/*
 * NumericTextFieldTest.java
*/
package numerictextfieldtest;
import javax.swing.*;
import java.awt.*;
import java.awt.event.*;

public class NumericTextFieldTest extends JFrame
{
  NumericTextField testTextField = new NumericTextField();

  public static void main(String args[])
  {
    //construct frame
    new NumericTextFieldTest().setVisible(true);
  }
  public NumericTextFieldTest()
  {
    // code to build the form
    setTitle("Numeric Text Field Test");
    addWindowListener(new WindowAdapter()
    {
      public void windowClosing(WindowEvent e)
      {
        exitForm(e);
      }
    });

    getContentPane().setLayout(new GridBagLayout());
    // position controls
    GridBagConstraints gridConstraints = new
GridBagConstraints();
    testTextField.setText("A numeric text field!");
    gridConstraints.gridx = 0;
    gridConstraints.gridy = 0;
    gridConstraints.insets = new Insets(50, 50, 50, 50);
    getContentPane().add(testTextField, gridConstraints);
    pack();
    Dimension screenSize =
Toolkit.getDefaultToolkit().getScreenSize();
```

```
      setBounds((int) (0.5 * (screenSize.width -
  getWidth())), (int) (0.5 * (screenSize.height -
  getHeight())), getWidth(), getHeight());

    }
  private void exitForm(WindowEvent e)
  {
    System.exit(0);
  }

  }
```

Give it a try. Run this example. You should see:

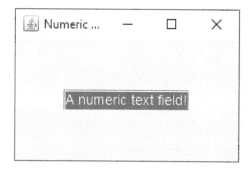

Note the new default colors and font are apparent. Save this project – we will be returning to it.

Adding New Properties to a Control

Many times, when creating new controls, you also want to define new properties for the control. To make the **NumericTextField** control as general as possible, we want the user to be able to determine if they want decimal inputs and/or negative inputs.

We will define two **boolean** properties to allow these selections. If the property **hasDecimal** is **true**, a decimal point is allowed in the input; if **false**, no decimal point is allowed. If the property **hasNegative** is **true**, a minus sign is allowed; if **false**, no minus sign entry is allowed. Let's modify the **NumericTextField** class to allow setting and getting the values of these properties.

Return to the **NumericTextFieldTest** project. Open the **NumericTextField.java** file. Define two private scope **boolean** variables to represent the **hasDecimal** and **hasNegative** properties. And, establish the **Get** and **Set** methods. Add this code to the class to get/set the properties:

```
private boolean hasDecimal;
private boolean hasNegative;
public boolean getHasDecimal()
{
  return hasDecimal;
}
public void setHasDecimal(boolean h)
{
  hasDecimal = h;
}
public boolean getHasNegative()
{
  return hasNegative;
}
public void setHasNegative(boolean h)
{
  hasNegative = h;
}
```

We also need to initialize the two new properties in the constructor code (add the two shaded lines):

```
public NumericTextField()
{
  this.setBackground(Color.BLUE);
  this.setForeground(Color.YELLOW);
  this.setFont(new Font("Arial", Font.PLAIN, 14));
  this.setHasDecimal(true);
  this.setHasNegative(false);
}
```

You could rerun the project with the control at this point and try it, but you won't notice any difference in behavior. Why? Well, for one thing, we aren't doing anything with the two new properties (**hasDecimal** and **hasNegative**). We use them next when writing the code that validates input values.

Adding Control Methods

The major impetus for building this new control is to limit keystrokes to only those that can be used for numeric inputs: numbers, decimal (optional based on **hasDecimal** property), and a negative sign (optional based on **hasNegative** property).

As in previous work with text fields to validate entries, we will write a general method to validate the text field input. We will access this method whenever the control loses focus. Return to the **NumericTextField.java** file and add the shaded code to implement the listener for the lost focus event:

```java
public NumericTextField()
{
  this.setBackground(Color.BLUE);
  this.setForeground(Color.YELLOW);
  this.setFont(new Font("Arial", Font.PLAIN, 14));
  this.setHasDecimal(true);
  this.setHasNegative(false);

  this.addFocusListener(new FocusAdapter()
  {
    public void focusLost(FocusEvent e)
    {
      ValidateText();
    }
  });
}
```

When the text field loses focus, it calls the **ValidateText** method to see if the entries are valid.

The **ValidateText** code is essentially the same code used the **Savings Account** example. The only modification is the use of the **hasDecimal** and **hasNegative** properties. Add this code in the **NumericTextField** class:

```java
public void ValidateText()
{
  // checks to see if text field contains
  // valid number with only digits and a single decimal
point (optional)
  // or negative sign (optional)
  String s = getText().trim();
  boolean decimalThere = false;
```

```
isValid = true;
if (s.length() == 0)
{
  isValid = false;
}
else
{
  for (int i = 0; i < s.length(); i++)
  {
    char c = s.charAt(i);
    if (c >= '0' && c <= '9')
    {
      continue;
    }
    else if  (hasNegative && (c == '-' && i == 0))
    {
      continue;
    }
    else if (hasDecimal && (c == '.' && !decimalThere))
    {
      decimalThere = true;
    }
    else
    {
      // invalid character found
      isValid = false;
    }
  }
}
if (isValid)
{
  setText(s);
}
else
{
  setText("Invalid");
}
}
```

Let's go through this code step-by-step to understand just what's going on. Checking for a number is straightforward. Note in checking for a negative sign, we check two conditions - we make sure **hasNegative** is true and make sure the sign is located at the first character in the text field. Similarly in checking for a decimal point, we make sure **hasDecimal** is true and make sure there is not a decimal point there already.

In the **ValidateText** method, if the input is valid, the variable **isValid** is set to true. If the input is not valid, **isValid** is set to false and the word **Invalid** is placed in the text field. We want the **isValid** variable to be accessible to the user, so it must be declared as a **public boolean** variable in the **NumericTextField** class description. The final version of this class code is (the code added for validation is shaded):

```java
package numerictextfieldtest;
import javax.swing.*;
import javax.swing.event.*;
import java.awt.*;
import java.awt.event.*;
public class NumericTextField extends JTextField
{
  public boolean isValid;

  public NumericTextField()
  {
    this.setBackground(Color.BLUE);
    this.setForeground(Color.YELLOW);
    this.setFont(new Font("Arial", Font.PLAIN, 14));
    this.setHasDecimal(true);
    this.setHasNegative(false);

    this.addFocusListener(new FocusAdapter()
    {
      public void focusLost(FocusEvent e)
      {
        ValidateText();
      }
    });
  }

  public void ValidateText()
  {
    // checks to see if text field contains
    // valid number with only digits and a single decimal
point (optional)
    // or negative sign (optional)
    String s = getText().trim();
    boolean decimalThere = false;
    isValid = true;
    if (s.length() == 0)
    {
      isValid = false;
    }
```

```
    else
    {
      for (int i = 0; i < s.length(); i++)
      {
        char c = s.charAt(i);
        if (c >= '0' && c <= '9')
        {
          continue;
        }
        else if  (hasNegative && (c == '-' && i == 0))
        {
          continue;
        }
        else if (hasDecimal && (c == '.' &&
!decimalThere))
        {
          decimalThere = true;
        }
        else
        {
          // invalid character found
          isValid = false;
        }
      }
    }
    if (isValid)
    {
      setText(s);
    }
    else
    {
      setText("Invalid");
    }
}

private boolean hasDecimal;
private boolean hasNegative;
public boolean getHasDecimal()
{
  return hasDecimal;
}
public void setHasDecimal(boolean h)
{
  hasDecimal = h;
}
public boolean getHasNegative()
{
```

```
      return hasNegative;
   }
   public void setHasNegative(boolean h)
   {
     hasNegative = h;
   }
}
```

Let's try out the validation feature. Return to the **NumericTextFieldTest.java**
file. Modify the code with the shaded changes to add a second text field that
allows negative signs (allows us to shift focus from one control to the next to
initiate the validation).

```
/*
 * NumericTextFieldTest.java
 */
package numerictextfieldtest;
import javax.swing.*;
import java.awt.*;
import java.awt.event.*;

public class NumericTextFieldTest extends JFrame
{
   NumericTextField testTextField = new NumericTextField();
   NumericTextField testTextField2 = new
NumericTextField();

   public static void main(String args[])
   {
     //construct frame
     new NumericTextFieldTest().setVisible(true);
   }
   public NumericTextFieldTest()
   {
     // code to build the form
     setTitle("Numeric Text Field Test");
     addWindowListener(new WindowAdapter()
     {
       public void windowClosing(WindowEvent e)
       {
         exitForm(e);
       }
     });

     getContentPane().setLayout(new GridBagLayout());
     // position controls
```

```
    GridBagConstraints gridConstraints = new
GridBagConstraints();
    testTextField.setText("A numeric text field!");
    gridConstraints.gridx = 0;
    gridConstraints.gridy = 0;
    gridConstraints.insets = new Insets(50, 50, 50, 50);
    getContentPane().add(testTextField, gridConstraints);
    testTextField2.setText("Another numeric text field!");
    testTextField2.setHasNegative(true);
    gridConstraints.gridx = 0;
    gridConstraints.gridy = 1;
    gridConstraints.insets = new Insets(0, 50, 20, 50);
    getContentPane().add(testTextField2, gridConstraints);
    pack();
    Dimension screenSize =
Toolkit.getDefaultToolkit().getScreenSize();
    setBounds((int) (0.5 * (screenSize.width -
getWidth())), (int) (0.5 * (screenSize.height -
getHeight())), getWidth(), getHeight());

  }
  private void exitForm(WindowEvent e)
  {
    System.exit(0);
  }
}
```

Rerun the example. In the first text box, you can only type numbers and a decimal point. Try valid and invalid inputs – notice what happens when you shift the focus to the other text box. Here's what happened when I typed 'A box' in the first text box, then clicked in the second box (changed focus):

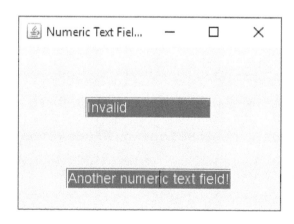

And, here's an example with valid inputs in both text fields:

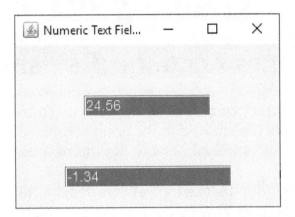

In the second text field, you can type numbers, a negative sign and a decimal point. If you like, stop the application, change **hasDecimal** to **false** in one or both fields and make sure that you then can only type integer values.

This completes our look at inheriting from existing controls. The final result is saved as the **NumericTextFieldTest** in the **\LearnJava\Java Code\Appendix II** project group. With these new found skills, you can probably think of several ways you might modify existing Java controls to fit your needs. Let's rebuild the **Savings Account** using the new numeric text field controls to show how things are simplified.

Example II-2

Savings Account (Revisited)

Reopen the **SavingsProject** created in **Example II-1**. To the project, add the **NumericTextField.java** file created in the notes (change the package line to `package savings;` – this will allow us to use this new control.

Open the **Savings.java** file. Delete the **validateDecimalNumber** method from this file. This validation will now be done in the control.

Make the shaded changes to the **Savings.java** file:

```java
/*
 * Savings.java
 */
package savings;
import javax.swing.*;
import java.awt.*;
import java.awt.event.*;
import java.text.*;

public class Savings extends JFrame
{
  JLabel depositLabel = new JLabel();
  JLabel interestLabel = new JLabel();
  JLabel monthsLabel = new JLabel();
  JLabel finalLabel = new JLabel();
  NumericTextField depositTextField = new NumericTextField();
  NumericTextField interestTextField = new
NumericTextField();
  NumericTextField monthsTextField = new NumericTextField();
  JTextField finalTextField = new JTextField();
  JButton calculateButton = new JButton();
  JButton exitButton = new JButton();

  public static void main(String args[])
  {
    //construct frame
    new Savings().setVisible(true);
  }
  public Savings()
  {
```

```
// code to build the form
setTitle("Savings Account");
addWindowListener(new WindowAdapter()
{
  public void windowClosing(WindowEvent e)
  {
    exitForm(e);
  }
});

getContentPane().setLayout(new GridBagLayout());
// position controls (establish event methods)
GridBagConstraints gridConstraints = new
GridBagConstraints();
depositLabel.setText("Monthly Deposit");
gridConstraints.gridx = 0;
gridConstraints.gridy = 0;
getContentPane().add(depositLabel, gridConstraints);
interestLabel.setText("Yearly Interest");
gridConstraints.gridx = 0;
gridConstraints.gridy = 1;
getContentPane().add(interestLabel, gridConstraints);
monthsLabel.setText("Number of Months");
gridConstraints.gridx = 0;
gridConstraints.gridy = 2;
getContentPane().add(monthsLabel, gridConstraints);
finalLabel.setText("Final Balance");
gridConstraints.gridx = 0;
gridConstraints.gridy = 3;
getContentPane().add(finalLabel, gridConstraints);

depositTextField.setText("");
depositTextField.setColumns(10);
gridConstraints.gridx = 2;
gridConstraints.gridy = 0;
getContentPane().add(depositTextField, gridConstraints);
depositTextField.addActionListener(new ActionListener()
{
  public void actionPerformed(ActionEvent e)
  {
    depositTextFieldActionPerformed(e);
  }
});

interestTextField.setText("");
interestTextField.setColumns(10);
gridConstraints.gridx = 2;
```

```
gridConstraints.gridy = 1;
getContentPane().add(interestTextField, gridConstraints);
interestTextField.addActionListener(new ActionListener()
{
   public void actionPerformed(ActionEvent e)
   {
      interestTextFieldActionPerformed(e);
   }
});

monthsTextField.setText("");
monthsTextField.setColumns(10);
monthsTextField.setHasDecimal(false);
gridConstraints.gridx = 2;
gridConstraints.gridy = 2;
getContentPane().add(monthsTextField, gridConstraints);
monthsTextField.addActionListener(new ActionListener()
{
   public void actionPerformed(ActionEvent e)
   {
      monthsTextFieldActionPerformed(e);
   }
});

finalTextField.setText("");
finalTextField.setFocusable(false);
finalTextField.setColumns(10);
gridConstraints.gridx = 2;
gridConstraints.gridy = 3;
getContentPane().add(finalTextField, gridConstraints);

calculateButton.setText("Calculate");
gridConstraints.gridx = 1;
gridConstraints.gridy = 4;
getContentPane().add(calculateButton, gridConstraints);
calculateButton.addActionListener(new ActionListener()
{
   public void actionPerformed(ActionEvent e)
   {
      calculateButtonActionPerformed(e);
   }
});
exitButton.setText("Exit");
exitButton.setFocusable(false);
gridConstraints.gridx = 1;
gridConstraints.gridy = 5;
getContentPane().add(exitButton, gridConstraints);
```

```
    exitButton.addActionListener(new ActionListener()
    {
      public void actionPerformed(ActionEvent e)
      {
        exitButtonActionPerformed(e);
      }
    });
    pack();
    Dimension screenSize =
Toolkit.getDefaultToolkit().getScreenSize();
    setBounds((int) (0.5 * (screenSize.width - getWidth())),
(int) (0.5 * (screenSize.height - getHeight())), getWidth(),
getHeight());

  }
  private void exitForm(WindowEvent e)
  {
    System.exit(0);
  }


  private void calculateButtonActionPerformed(ActionEvent e)
  {
    // make sure each input is a valid number
    if (!monthsTextField.isValid() ||
!interestTextField.isValid() || !depositTextField.isValid())
    {
      // if one or more fields not valid number, then exit
method
      return;
    }

    // create and construct Savings object
    SavingsAccount mySavings;
    mySavings = new SavingsAccount();
    // set properties from text boxes
    mySavings.deposit =
Double.valueOf(depositTextField.getText()).doubleValue();
    mySavings.interest =
Double.valueOf(interestTextField.getText()).doubleValue();
    mySavings.months =
Double.valueOf(monthsTextField.getText()).doubleValue();
    // compute final value and put in text box
    finalTextField.setText(new
DecimalFormat("0.00").format(mySavings.computeFinal()));
  }
```

```
  private void exitButtonActionPerformed(ActionEvent e)
  {
    System.exit(0);
  }

  private void depositTextFieldActionPerformed(ActionEvent e)
  {
    depositTextField.transferFocus();
  }
  private void interestTextFieldActionPerformed(ActionEvent
e)
  {
    interestTextField.transferFocus();
  }
  private void monthsTextFieldActionPerformed(ActionEvent e)
  {
    monthsTextField.transferFocus();
  }
}
```

In the modified code, we have converted the three input text fields to numeric text fields (adding their validity check in the **calculateButtonActionPerformed** method). We have also disallowed a decimal point in the months entry.

That's all the new coding that's needed. Rerun the program. Make sure it works properly. Here's a run I made:

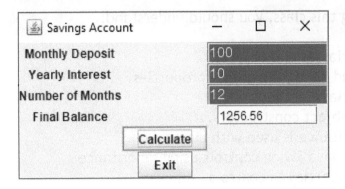

Save the project This is saved as the **ExampleII-2** project in **\LearnJava\LJ Code\Appendix II** project group.

Class Review

After completing this class, you should understand:

> ➢ Creating classes and objects.
> ➢ Setting and validating object properties.
> ➢ Creating class methods.
> ➢ Creating object constructors.
> ➢ How inheritance is used with classes.
> ➢ Extending Java Swing controls using inheritance
> ➢ Adding properties to controls
> ➢ Overriding control methods.

Appendix III - Installing Java and NetBeans

Downloading and Installing Java

To write and run programs using Java, you need the **Java Development Kit** (JDK) and the **NetBeans Integrated Development Environment** (IDE). These are free products that you can download from the Internet. This simply means we will copy a file onto our computer to allow installation of Java. Each product requires a separate download and installation process.

Java Development Kit

1. Start up your web browser (Internet Explorer, Chrome, Firefox, Safari or other browser) and go to Java web site:

https://www.oracle.com/technetwork/java/javase/downloads/jdk11-downloads-5066655.html

This web site has lots of useful Java information. As you become more proficient in your programming skills, you will go to this site often for answers to programming questions, interaction with other Java programmers, and lots of sample programs.

2. The button marked 'Download' downloads the Java JDK (Version 11.0). Click this button. Once on the page with the JDK download links, accept the Licensing Agreement and choose the link corresponding to your computer's operating system.

For Microsoft Windows: select the Windows exe file

Java SE Development Kit 11.0.3

You must accept the Oracle Technology Network License Agreement for Oracle Java SE to download this software.
Thank you for accepting the Oracle Technology Network License Agreement for Oracle Java SE; you may now download this software.

Product / File Description	File Size	Download
Linux	147.31 MB	jdk-11.0.3_linux-x64_bin.deb
Linux	154.04 MB	jdk-11.0.3_linux-x64_bin.rpm
Linux	171.37 MB	jdk-11.0.3_linux-x64_bin.tar.gz
macOS	166.2 MB	jdk-11.0.3_osx-x64_bin.dmg
macOS	166.52 MB	jdk-11.0.3_osx-x64_bin.tar.gz
Solaris SPARC	186.85 MB	jdk-11.0.3_solaris-sparcv9_bin.tar.gz
Windows	150.98 MB	jdk-11.0.3_windows-x64_bin.exe
Windows	171 MB	jdk-11.0.3_windows-x64_bin.zip

Instructions for installing Java on other platforms such as Linux or Solaris can also be found on the website. My screenshots in these notes will be Microsoft Windows.

For Mac OS: click on the macOS dmg file

Java SE Development Kit 11.0.3

You must accept the Oracle Technology Network License Agreement for Oracle Java SE to download this software.
Thank you for accepting the Oracle Technology Network License Agreement for Oracle Java SE; you may now download this software.

Product / File Description	File Size	Download
Linux	147.31 MB	⬇jdk-11.0.3_linux-x64_bin.deb
Linux	154.04 MB	⬇jdk-11.0.3_linux-x64_bin.rpm
Linux	171.37 MB	⬇jdk-11.0.3_linux-x64_bin.tar.gz
macOS	166.2 MB	⬇jdk-11.0.3_osx-x64_bin.dmg
macOS	166.52 MB	⬇jdk-11.0.3_osx-x64_bin.tar.gz
Solaris SPARC	186.85 MB	⬇jdk-11.0.3_solaris-sparcv9_bin.tar.gz
Windows	150.98 MB	⬇jdk-11.0.3_windows-x64_bin.exe
Windows	171 MB	⬇jdk-11.0.3_windows-x64_bin.zip

For Linux OS: click on the Linux deb file

Java SE Development Kit 11.0.3

You must accept the Oracle Technology Network License Agreement for Oracle Java SE to download this software.
Thank you for accepting the Oracle Technology Network License Agreement for Oracle Java SE; you may now download this software.

Product / File Description	File Size	Download
Linux	147.31 MB	⬇jdk-11.0.3_linux-x64_bin.deb
Linux	154.04 MB	⬇jdk-11.0.3_linux-x64_bin.rpm
Linux	171.37 MB	⬇jdk-11.0.3_linux-x64_bin.tar.gz
macOS	166.2 MB	⬇jdk-11.0.3_osx-x64_bin.dmg
macOS	166.52 MB	⬇jdk-11.0.3_osx-x64_bin.tar.gz
Solaris SPARC	186.85 MB	⬇jdk-11.0.3_solaris-sparcv9_bin.tar.gz
Windows	150.98 MB	⬇jdk-11.0.3_windows-x64_bin.exe
Windows	171 MB	⬇jdk-11.0.3_windows-x64_bin.zip

Once you select a file, you may be asked to create an Oracle Account - follow the requested steps.

3. You will be asked what you want to do with the selected download file. Click **Run**. The installation begins.

4. The Java installer will unpack some files and an introductory window will appear:

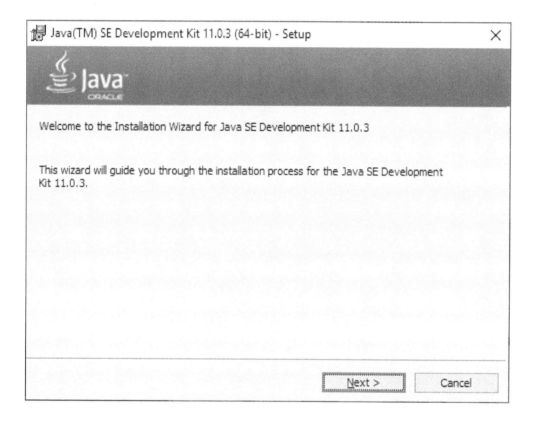

Click **Next** to start the installation. Several windows will appear in sequence. Accept the default choices by clicking **Next** at each window.

When complete (it will take a while), you will see this window:

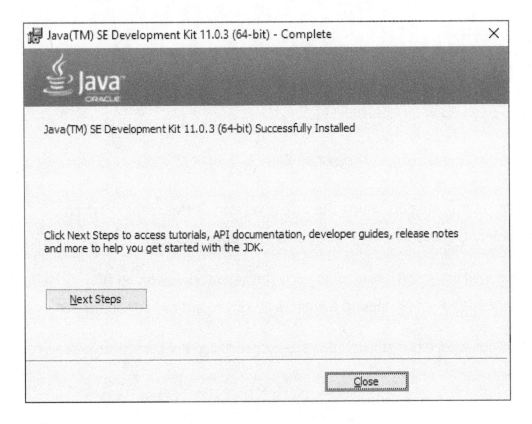

Click **Close** and the installation will complete. Next, let's install NetBeans.

NetBeans Integrated Development Environment

1. Go to this website:

https://netbeans.apache.org/download/nb110/nb110.html

2. On this web page, look for this link

- Binaries: incubating-netbeans-11.0-bin.zip (SHA-512, PGP ASC)

This link downloads a 'zip' file containing the latest version of NetBeans (Version 11.0). Click the link and choose a mirror site to use for downloading.

3. You will be asked what you want to do with the selected download file. Click **Open**. The needed files (in zipped format) will download to your computer.

4. Go to the folder where the zipped files are located. On my computer, I see

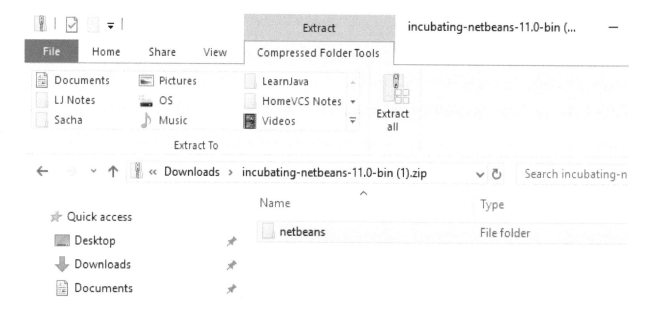

Click the 'Extract all' button.

You will be asked where you want to extract the files. I selected my main hard drive:

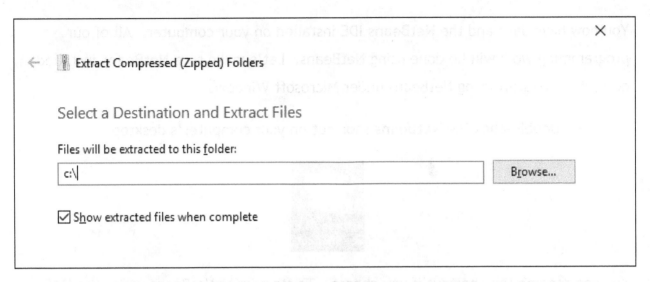

The files (all contained in a folder named 'netbeans') will be extracted to the selected location (it will take a couple of minutes).

5. Open the 'netbeans' folder, then the 'bin' folder. You should see

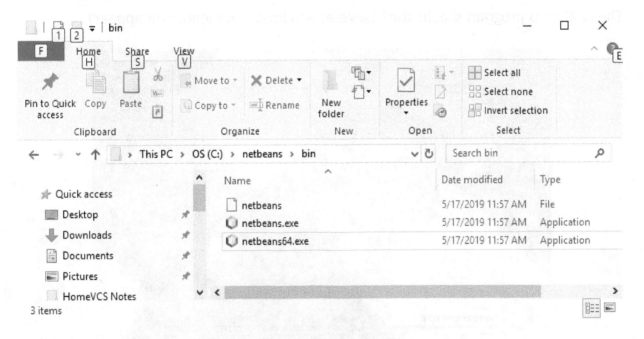

Right-click the **netbeans64.exe** file and choose 'Send to', then 'Desktop'. This will put a shortcut to NetBeans on your computer's desktop.

Running NetBeans

You now have Java and the **NetBeans** IDE installed on your computer. All of our programming work will be done using NetBeans. Let's make sure **NetBeans** installed correctly. To start using NetBeans under Microsoft Windows,

- Double-click the **NetBeans** shortcut on your computer's desktop

You can rename this shortcut if you choose. To start using NetBeans under the MAC OS,

- Click on the **Finder** and go to the **Applications Folder**.

The NetBeans program should start (several windows and menus will appear).

We will learn more about NetBeans in the notes. For now, we want to make some formatting changes. In Java programming, indentations in the code we write are used to delineate common blocks. The NetBeans IDE uses four spaces for indentations as a default. This author (and these notes) uses two spaces. To make this change, choose the **Tools** menu item and click **Options**. In the window that appears, choose the **Editor** option and the **Formatting** tab:

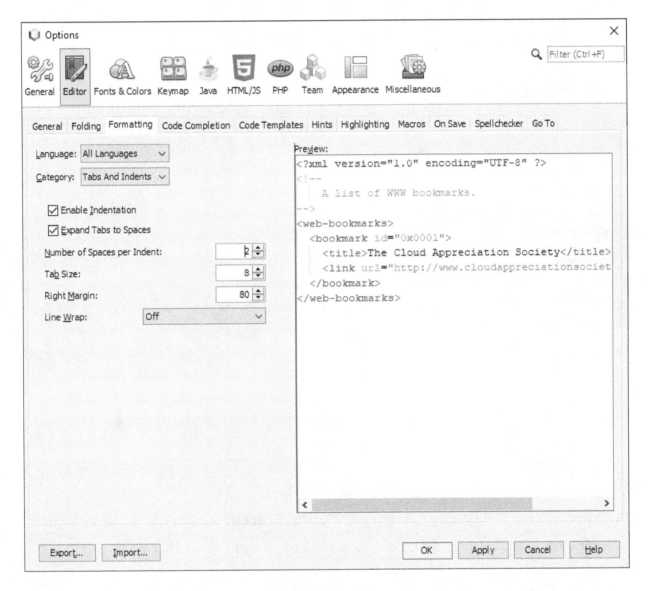

As shown, choose the **Tabs and Indents Category** and set the **Number of Spaces per Indent** to **2**.

Before leaving this window, we make another change. Braces (curly brackets) are used to start and stop blocks of code. We choose to have these brackets always be on a separate line – it makes checking code much easier.

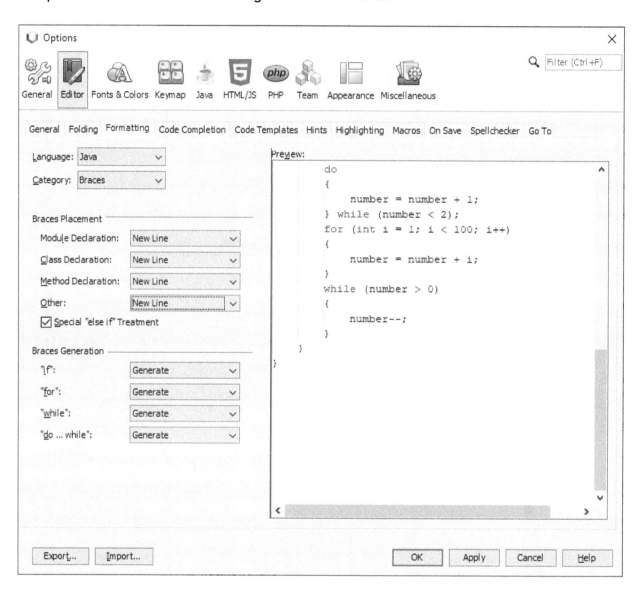

As shown, choose the **Braces Category** and under **Braces Placement**, set all choices to **New Line**. Click **Apply**, then **OK**. Stop **NetBeans** – you're ready to go!

More Self-Study or Instructor-Led Computer Programming Tutorials by Kidware Software

ORACLE JAVA PROGRAMMING TUTORIALS

Java™ For Kids is a beginning programming tutorial consisting of 10 chapters explaining (in simple, easy-to-follow terms) how to build a Java application. Students learn about project design, object-oriented programming, console applications, graphics applications and many elements of the Java language. Numerous examples are used to demonstrate every step in the building process. The projects include a number guessing game, a card game, an allowance calculator, a state capitals game, Tic-Tac-Toe, a simple drawing program, and even a basic video game. Designed for kids ages 12 and up.

Beginning Java™ is a semester long "beginning" programming tutorial consisting of 10 chapters explaining (in simple, easy-to-follow terms) how to build a Java application. The tutorial includes several detailed computer projects for students to build and try. These projects include a number guessing game, card game, allowance calculator, drawing program, state capitals game, and a couple of video games like Pong. We also include several college prep bonus projects including a loan calculator, portfolio manager, and checkbook balancer. Designed for students age 15 and up.

Learn Java™ GUI Applications is a 9 lesson Tutorial covering object-oriented programming concepts, using an integrated development environment to create and test Java projects, building and distributing GUI applications, understanding and using the Swing control library, exception handling, sequential file access, graphics, multimedia, advanced topics such as printing, and help system authoring. Our Beginning Java or Java For Kids tutorial is a pre-requisite for this tutorial

Programming Games with Java™ is a semester long "intermediate" programming tutorial consisting of 10 chapters explaining (in simple, easy-to-follow terms) how to build a Visual C# Video Games. The games built are non-violent, family-friendly and teach logical thinking skills. Students will learn how to program the following Visual C# video games: Safecracker, Tic Tac Toe, Match Game, Pizza Delivery, and Moon Landing. This intermediate level self-paced tutorial can be used at home or school. The tutorial is simple enough for kids yet engaging enough for beginning adults. Our Learn Java GUI Applications tutorial is a required pre-requisite for this tutorial.

Java™ Homework Projects is a Java GUI Swing tutorial covering object-oriented programming concepts. It explains (in simple, easy-to-follow terms) how to build Java GUI project to use around the home. Students learn about project design, the Java Swing controls, many elements of the Java language, and how to distribute finished projects. The projects built include a Dual-Mode Stopwatch, Flash Card Math Quiz, Multiple Choice Exam, Blackjack Card Game, Weight Monitor, Home Inventory Manager and a Snowball Toss Game. Our Learn Java GUI Applications tutorial is a pre-requisite for this tutorial

MICROSOFT SMALL BASIC PROGRAMMING TUTORIALS

Small Basic For Kids is an illustrated introduction to computer programming that provides an interactive, self-paced tutorial to the new Small Basic programming environment. The book consists of 30 short lessons that explain how to create and run a Small Basic program. Elementary students learn about program design and many elements of the Small Basic language. Numerous examples are used to demonstrate every step in the building process. The tutorial also includes two complete games (Hangman and Pizza Zapper) for students to build and try. Designed for kids ages 8+.

The Beginning Microsoft Small Basic Programming Tutorial is a self-study first semester "beginner" programming tutorial consisting of 11 chapters explaining (in simple, easy-to-follow terms) how to write Microsoft Small Basic programs. Numerous examples are used to demonstrate every step in the building process. The last chapter of this tutorial shows you how four different Small Basic games could port to Visual Basic, Visual C# and Java. This beginning level self-paced tutorial can be used at home or at school. The tutorial is simple enough for kids ages 10+ yet engaging enough for adults.

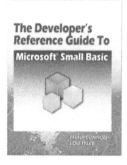

Basic Computer Games - Small Basic Edition is a re-make of the classic BASIC COMPUTER GAMES book originally edited by David H. Ahl. It contains 100 of the original text based BASIC games that inspired a whole generation of programmers. Now these classic BASIC games have been re-written in Microsoft Small Basic for a new generation to enjoy! The new Small Basic games look and act like the original text based games. The book includes all the original spaghetti code and GOTO commands!

Programming Home Projects with Microsoft Small Basic is a self-paced programming tutorial explains (in simple, easy-to-follow terms) how to build Small Basic Windows applications. Students learn about program design, Small Basic objects, many elements of the Small Basic language, and how to debug and distribute finished programs. Sequential file input and output is also introduced. The projects built include a Dual-Mode Stopwatch, Flash Card Math Quiz, Multiple Choice Exam, Blackjack Card Game, Weight Monitor, Home Inventory Manager and a Snowball Toss Game.

The Developer's Reference Guide to Microsoft Small Basic While developing all the different Microsoft Small Basic tutorials we found it necessary to write The Developer's Reference Guide to Microsoft Small Basic. The Developer's Reference Guide to Microsoft Small Basic is over 500 pages long and includes over 100 Small Basic programming examples for you to learn from and include in your own Microsoft Small Basic programs. It is a detailed reference guide for new developers.

David Ahl's Small Basic Computer Adventures is a Microsoft Small Basic re-make of the classic *Basic Computer Games* programming *book* originally written by David H. Ahl. This new book includes the following classic adventure simulations; Marco Polo, Westward Ho!, The Longest Automobile Race, The Orient Express, Amelia Earhart: Around the World Flight, Tour de France, Subway Scavenger, Hong Kong Hustle, and Voyage to Neptune. Learn how to program these classic computer simulations in Microsoft Small Basic.

MICROSOFT VISUAL BASIC PROGRAMMING TUTORIALS

Beginning Visual Basic® is a semester long self-paced "beginner" programming tutorial consisting of 10 chapters explaining (in simple, easy-to-follow terms) how to build a Visual Basic Windows application. The tutorial includes several detailed computer projects for students to build and try. These projects include a number guessing game, card game, allowance calculator, drawing program, state capitals game, and a couple of video games like Pong. We also include several college prep bonus projects including a loan calculator, portfolio manager, and checkbook balancer. Designed for students age 15 and up.

LEARN VISUAL BASIC is a comprehensive college level programming tutorial covering object-oriented programming, the Visual Basic integrated development environment, building and distributing Windows applications using the Windows Installer, exception handling, sequential file access, graphics, multimedia, advanced topics such as web access, printing, and HTML help system authoring. The tutorial also introduces database applications (using ADO .NET) and web applications (using ASP.NET).

VISUAL BASIC AND DATABASES is a tutorial that provides a detailed introduction to using Visual Basic for accessing and maintaining databases for desktop applications. Topics covered include: database structure, database design, Visual Basic project building, ADO .NET data objects (connection, data adapter, command, data table), data bound controls, proper interface design, structured query language (SQL), creating databases using Access, SQL Server and ADOX, and database reports. Actual projects developed include a book tracking system, a sales invoicing program, a home inventory system and a daily weather monitor.

MICROSOFT VISUAL C# PROGRAMMING TUTORIALS

Beginning Visual C#® is a semester long "beginning" programming tutorial consisting of 10 chapters explaining (in simple, easy-to-follow terms) how to build a C# Windows application. The tutorial includes several detailed computer projects for students to build and try. These projects include a number guessing game, card game, allowance calculator, drawing program, state capitals game, and a couple of video games like Pong. We also include several college prep bonus projects including a loan calculator, portfolio manager, and checkbook balancer. Designed for students ages 15+.

LEARN VISUAL C# is a comprehensive college level computer programming tutorial covering object-oriented programming, the Visual C# integrated development environment and toolbox, building and distributing Windows applications (using the Windows Installer), exception handling, sequential file input and output, graphics, multimedia effects (animation and sounds), advanced topics such as web access, printing, and HTML help system authoring. The tutorial also introduces database applications (using ADO .NET) and web applications (using ASP.NET).

VISUAL C# AND DATABASES is a tutorial that provides a detailed introduction to using Visual C# for accessing and maintaining databases for desktop applications. Topics covered include: database structure, database design, Visual C# project building, ADO .NET data objects (connection, data adapter, command, data table), data bound controls, proper interface design, structured query language (SQL), creating databases using Access, SQL Server and ADOX, and database reports. Actual projects developed include a book tracking system, a sales invoicing program, a home inventory system and a daily weather monitor.